D1567478

Joseph Stalin
A Biographical Companion

Joseph Stalin
A Biographical Companion

Helen Rappaport

ABC-CLIO

Santa Barbara, California
Denver, Colorado
Oxford, England

All photographs are courtesy of the David King Collection except the following: frontispiece, Library of Congress; p. 8, Robert Harding Picture Library; p. 24, AP/Wide World Photos; p. 28, AP/Wide World Photos; p. 180, Archive Photos; p. 315, AP/Wide World Photos; and p. 326, Hulton Getty/Liaison Agency.

Library of Congress Cataloging-in-Publication Data

Rappaport, Helen.
    Joseph Stalin : a biographical companion / Helen Rappaport.
        p. cm. — (ABC-CLIO biographical companions)
    Includes bibliographical references.
    ISBN 1-57607-084-0 (alk. paper)   ISBN 1-57607-208-8 (pbk.; UK only)
        1. Stalin, Joseph, 1879–1953—Encyclopedias. 2. Heads of state—Soviet
Union—Biography—Encyclopedias. 3. Soviet
Union—History—1925–1953—Encyclopedias. I. Title. II. ABC-CLIO biographical
companion.

DK268.S8.R337 1999
947.084'2'092—dc21   99-048504

05 04 03 02 01 00 99   10 9 8 7 6 5 4 3 2 1

ABC-CLIO, Inc.
130 Cremona Drive, P.O. Box 1911
Santa Barbara, California 93116-1911

This book is printed on acid-free paper ∞ .

Manufactured in the United States of America

To Michael J. de K. Holman
for encouraging a love of Russia and all things Russian

ABC-CLIO BIOGRAPHICAL COMPANIONS

Benjamin Franklin, Jennifer L. Durham
Thomas Jefferson, David S. Brown
Susan B. Anthony, Judith E. Harper
Napoleon, David Nicholls
Joseph Stalin, Helen Rappaport

ABC-CLIO Biographical Companions are encyclopedic guides to the lives of men and women who have had a significant impact on the social, political, and cultural development of the Western world. Each volume presents complete biographical information in an easily accessible format. An introduction and a chronology provide an overview, while the A-to-Z entries amplify a myriad of topics related to the person. Ample illustrations give the reader an acute sense of the individual's life and times.

CONTENTS

PREFACE

This is not a book for Stalinist historians. The highly selective bibliography that can be found at its conclusion testifies to a vast range of academic study that is at times compelling, at times utterly indigestible. Most of it has been painstakingly gathered, often from obscure and difficult-to-access Russian archival sources, and many of the books cited have been written by highly respected academics who have devoted a lifetime to ground-breaking Stalinist historical research. In so doing, they have, collectively, opened up an endlessly fascinating but also highly contentious debate. Latterly, the field of Stalinist studies has been further complicated by a new and radical revisionist approach, much of which is contained in complex and exhausting arguments over facts, figures, and statistics. While so much serious research is stimulating public awareness about Stalin's rule and constantly throwing up new evidence, it does not necessarily always make for easy or entertaining reading. The collapse of the Soviet Union in 1991 and the economic and political chaos that have since unfolded in Russia have only served further to fuel the Stalinist debate and to bring to the fore a new generation of Stalinists both inside and outside Russia.

It is the intention of this text, therefore, to provide a description of some of the most fundamental aspects of Stalin and of the political system that he instituted, in a form that is accessible not just to the Russianist or Russian student, but also to the lay reader who probably does not speak the language and knows and understands little about the life and times of Joseph Stalin. In so doing, it aims, deliberately, to move away from an emphasis on the complex political aspects of Stalin's rule (and there are plenty of scholarly tomes in print that already do this in exhaustive detail), toward an accent on the personal and an interpretation of some of the ways in which the lives of Russian people—both the population at large as well as some of Stalin's more famous victims—were shaped and affected by thirty-five years of Stalinist rule. The further reading lists that follow most entries are therefore limited to English-language sources that should be reasonably easily available through most good public and university libraries.

Each entry has been written so that it can be read in isolation and is cross-referenced to associated entries that might also be of interest. A particular objective has been to locate entries within the general social and political context and sometimes to relate aspects of Stalin's life and rule by allusion to literature and history outside the Soviet Union. For this reason, and knowing from personal experience how baffling the reader can find books on Soviet history that are littered with unpronounceable and incomprehensible acronyms (of which there are a tedious excess in the Stalin period), a particular effort has been made to spare the reader from the inevitable confusion that these terms create. Brief definitions for those acronyms that are used can be found in the glossary at the end of the book.

Inevitably, the list of entries is very highly selective, and some difficult decisions have had to be made about who and what to leave out. A general rule of thumb has been to exclude those people and events that do not strictly fall within Stalin's years in power, i.e., after about 1928, unless they have a specific bearing on either Stalin the man, his personal experiences, or his policies. By the same token, the biographies of those people who *are* included do not attempt a dry recitation of places, events, and dates in chronological order, but focus on that person's particular relationship with or experience of Stalin and Stalinism. Some of the people and topics missing from the headword list are touched upon within some existing entries; others have a brief definition in the glossary at the end of the book. In the case of political or other issues, the entry is again slanted in terms of Stalin's particular interpretation of or perspective on them. In general, though, it is hoped that the book contains a representative cross-section of Soviet arts, politics, science, and culture during Stalin's lifetime; that it covers some of the key aspects of his policies; and that it also explains the most famous catchphrases and slogans associated with him.

With this objective in mind and in the firm belief that, as Emerson said, "there is properly no history; only biography," what follows has been grounded in an interpretation of the personal experience of events in an attempt to come to grips with the motivations behind individual behavior. The most gratifying end, for any author who tries to explain controversial historical events instinctively and on a more personal level, is that the text will in some small way entertain and inform the lay reader or interested student of Russia who wishes to know more about a hugely complex man and, in so doing, help them make some sense of one of the most impenetrably difficult periods in Soviet political history.

Helen Rappaport
September 1999

Joseph Stalin
A Biographical Companion

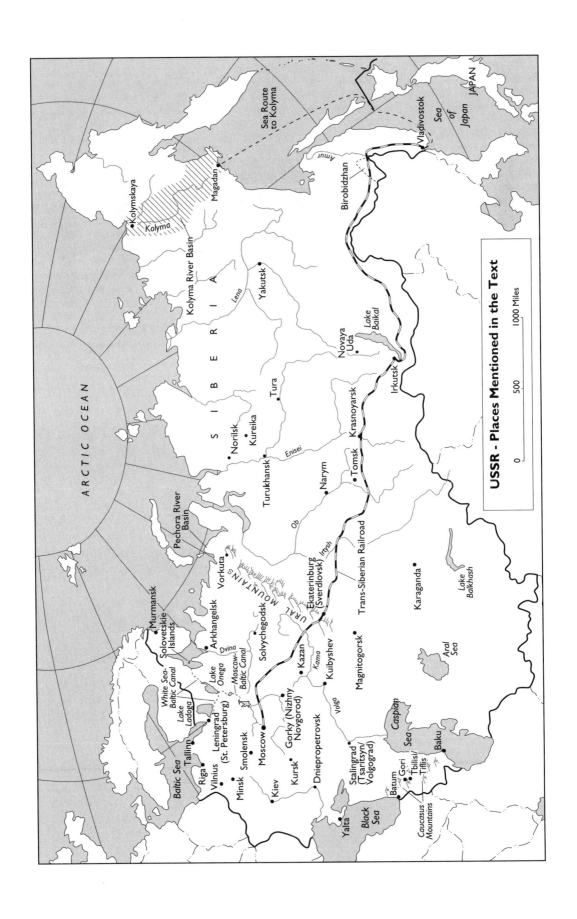

ARCTIC OCEAN

Sea Route to Kolyma

JAPAN

Sea of Japan

Vladivostok

Amur

Birobidzhan

Kolymskaya

Magadan

Kolyma

Kolyma River Basin

Lena

Yakutsk

S I B E R I A

Novaya Uda

Lake Baikal

Irkutsk

Tura

Norilsk

Kureika

Enisei

Krasnoyarsk

Turukhansk

Narym

Tomsk

Ob

Trans-Siberian Railroad

Pechora River Basin

Murmansk

Solovetskie Islands

Vorkuta

Ekaterinburg (Sverdlovsk)

Irtysh

Karaganda

Lake Balkhash

Arkhangelsk

Dvina

Solvychegodsk

U R A L   M O U N T A I N S

Magnitogorsk

Aral Sea

White Sea–Baltic Canal

Lake Onega

Moscow–Baltic Canal

Kazan

Kama

Kuibyshev

Lake Ladoga

Leningrad (St. Petersburg)

Tallinn

Baltic Sea

Riga

Vilnius

Smolensk

Moscow

Gorky (Nizhny Novgorod)

Volga

Dnepropetrovsk

Caspian Sea

Baku

Minsk

Kiev

Kursk

Stalingrad (Tsaritsyn/ Volgograd)

Gori

Tbilisi/ Tiflis

Batum

Caucasus Mountains

Yalta

Black Sea

USSR - Places Mentioned in the Text

0   500   1000 Miles

Agriculture
See Collectivization; Five-Year Plans.

Akhmatova, Anna Andreevna (1889–1966)

One of the great Russian poets and a national heroine, Anna Akhmatova (née Gorenko) is now venerated outside Russia as a major poetic voice of the twentieth century. She seemed born to endure great tragedy in her life and indeed was one of Stalin's most long-suffering literary victims. Her tremendous will to survive, in her self-appointed role as a witness of the Great Terror, testifies to huge inner reserves of moral strength that sustained her through years of extreme poverty and isolation, to ultimately become a latter-day nemesis of the dark days of Stalinism.

As one of the promising young literati in prerevolutionary St. Petersburg, Akhmatova became a leading voice of the Silver Age of Russian poetry, with her collections such as *Evening* (1912) and *Rosary* (1914). She briefly embraced the Acmeist group of poets, led by Nikolay Gumilev (1886–1921), whom she married in 1910 (they divorced in 1918). But her lyrical verses, with their confessional style detailing the pain of love, resisted literary compartmentalization and she went her own way artistically, with the more impressionistic *The White Flock* of 1917. Her individualism survived the early days of foment in Soviet literature, when literary experimentation was for a short while tolerated, but her work was soon looked upon as insufficiently socialist in its concerns and was suppressed as "bourgeois" after the publication of her collection *Anno Domini MCMXXI* in 1922. It was the appearance of this work that prompted the eminent Soviet literary critic Boris Eichenbaum to famously deride Akhmatova as "half nun, half harlot" (an epithet later reprised by Andrey Zhdanov in the campaign against Akhmatova in the 1940s). But greater personal tragedy now began to haunt her, with the arrest and execution of Gumilev in 1921 (on fabricated charges of "counterrevolutionary activity"), and the arrest of their son, Lev, in 1934. Although Akhamatova had ceased publishing by the mid-1920s, condemned, in the words of the *Literary Encyclopedia* of 1929, as "a poetess of the aristocracy who has not found a new function in capitalist society," like many other out-of-favor writers she continued to write and bear witness in private, composing an eloquent cycle of poetry, *Requiem,* on the years of the Great Terror "when only the dead / smiled, happy in their peace. . . . and innocent Russia squirmed / under the bloody boots, / under the wheels of black Marias."

The poet Anna Akhmatova at the height of her beauty in the 1920s. Akhmatova suffered constant persecution under Stalin, but outlived him to commemorate the victims of the Great Terror in her poetry cycle **Requiem.**

During the war (and possibly on the prompting of his daughter Svetlana, who loved Akhmatova's poetry), Stalin allowed Akhmatova to republish a collection of her work *From Six Books,* only to summarily order its withdrawal a few weeks after publication. However, ordinary Russians overcame the virtual impossibility of obtaining Akhmatova's verse in print by circulating it orally among themselves. This had always been a method of preserving the work of proscribed Russian writers, and Akhmatova's (like Boris Pasternak's) poetry was memorized by civilians and soldiers alike. Indeed, Akhmatova received many letters from Soviet soldiers at the front, requesting her autograph, often asking her to confirm the text of poetry that had been circulated only in *samizdat* (the illegal underground press) form. A trickle of Akhmatova's work, mainly as a translator, did begin to appear in

some journals, but the persecution began again in 1946.

This new campaign may have been due in part to a long night she spent, in November 1945, in conversation at her apartment in Leningrad with an English diplomat, Isaiah Berlin (later to become renowned as a historian of ideas), during which she talked about her life and work and discussed with him the state of the arts in Russia. With the Soviet Union now rapidly distancing itself from its wartime Western allies and the Cold War looming, this meeting became the cause of much suspicion and ludicrous accusations of treachery made against Akhmatova for talking to a "British spy." Her apartment was bugged, her every move monitored. It was revealed in 1993 that the authorities had kept detailed files on Akhmatova since 1939, amounting to some 900 pages of "denunciations, reports of phone taps, quotations from writings, confession of those close to her."

Nevertheless, Akhmatova survived this later onslaught with an arrogant pride, and her powerful presence in Russian literature continued to make itself felt despite her virtual incarceration in her Leningrad apartment. In 1946 she was persuaded to venture back into public life and appear at a poetry reading in Moscow with Pasternak. The rapturous welcome given her sealed her fate. Word had already got back to Stalin of the excess of public adulation accorded Akhmatova at a brief public reading she had made in 1944. He is reported to have asked, incredulous at such an outpouring of love for the writer, "Who organized this standing ovation?"

With the end of the war, the relaxation of censorship in the arts that had briefly prevailed began to evaporate, and Akhmatova and the writer Mikhail Zoschenko were singled out as the target of a concerted renewal of literary fascism—initiated by the head of the Leningrad Communist Party, Andrey Zhdanov. On Stalin's behalf,

he launched a virulent vendetta against
Akhmatova and Zoschenko in August
1946, designed to once again tighten the
political screws on wr' ~rs with supposed
"bourgeois" tendenci   ˥ring the
literary establishmen'   ˄
line. But nothing, i'
Akhmatova's dog
transcend the ni
order one day t'
friend Nadezh
her, "she was
abbess of a
were strict t
atoned for.'
   Her p(
wrote be
ally put
the ha'
ror b'
it. T'
onl
he
(

izati(
and the rei(
March 1956, she re
Lydia Chukovskaya: "Each o٫ ˬ
Shakespearean drama raised to the u
sandth degree. Mute separations, mute
black, bloody events in every family. Invisi-
ble mourning worn by mothers and wives.
Now the arrested are returning, and two
Russias stare each other in the eyes: the
ones that put them in prison and the ones
who were put in prison. A new epoch has
begun. You and I will wait for it together."
Two months later, her son Lev was finally
released from the Gulag.

See also The Great Terror; Pasternak, Boris;
Socialist Realism; Zhdanov, Andrey; Zoshchenko,
Mikhail

Further reading: Anna Akhmatova. *The
Complete Poems,* expanded ed. transl. Judith
Hemschmeyer. Edinburgh: Canongate Books,
1997; Gyorgy Dalos. *The Guest from the Future:
Anna Akhmatova and Isaiah Berlin.* London: John
Murray, 1998; Amanda Haight. *Anna Akhmatova:
A Poetic Pilgrimage.* Oxford: Oxford University
Press, 1976; Michael Ignatieff. *Isaiah Berlin: A
˥ ˒fe.* London: Chatto & Windus, 1998; Roberta
         Anna Akhmatova: Poet and Prophet.
            ˀnd Busby, 1995.

dezhda Sergeevna
01–1932)

ith the Bolsheviks now hav-
lished power in Russia, it had
:asingly expedient that Stalin,
.aders, Lenin and Trotsky, should
. With his first, dutiful Georgian
:rina, long dead (she had died of
. 1909), Stalin entertained the idea
.ing to Georgia (his home country)
. for a second suitable bride. But he
.nted this idea as being impractical,
.g that he needed the kind of wife able
.ix socially with the intellectual elite and
, political cadres of the new govern-
ent—someone who could hold her own
vith women such as Lenin's bluestocking
wife, Nadezhda Krupskaya.
   While staying in Petrograd with his friend
Sergey Alliluyev, Stalin found the solution to
his problem in Alliluyev's young daughter
Nadezhda, a meek, compliant girl who
seemed, as yet, untainted. She also had the
right political pedigree, being the daughter
of a fellow revolutionary and the goddaugh-
ter of Stalin's countryman, the prominent
Bolshevik Abel Enukhidze. Stalin soon prevailed on the sixteen-year-old Nadezhda,
who was no doubt star-struck by his reputation as being one of those who had made
the revolution, to travel to Moscow with
him as his personal assistant at the Commissariat of Nationalities. At some stage that
summer Stalin and Nadezhda's relationship
became a sexual one, probably against her

will, and they were married in 1919 at the Tsaritsyn front, where Stalin had been sent to take charge of Bolshevik food supplies during the civil war against the Whites. Five months after the marriage was officially registered in Moscow, Nadezhda gave birth to a son, Vasily, followed by a daughter, Svetlana, in 1926.

Despite the birth of her children, Nadezhda had been keen to assert her independence and escape the stultifying life of a Party wife shut up in the Kremlin. She had joined Lenin's Secretariat as one of his assistants, where she developed a close relationship with both him and his wife. After the birth of Svetlana, Nadezhda spent more and more time with the children and other members of her family at the family dacha at Zubalovo south of Moscow. With Stalin now ensconced for longer and longer hours in his Kremlin office, Nadezhda increasingly came to feel herself the neglected wife, and violent rows—often aggravated by Stalin's heavy drinking and rumors of his womanizing—began regularly to erupt between the couple. In 1926 Nadezhda's attempt to leave Stalin failed and during his turbulent power struggle with Trotsky and the Left opposition in the Communist Party, she became increasingly isolated and depressed. Bored and lonely and desperate to do something useful, Nadezhda enrolled as a chemistry student at Moscow's new Industrial Academy in 1929 in order to train as an engineer.

On 8 November 1932, the day after a party in the Kremlin held to celebrate the fifteenth anniversary of the revolution, during which Stalin had flirted with the wife of a colleague, and he and Nadezhda had had an argument, Nadezhda was found dead from a gunshot wound. Immediately the cover-up of her suicide began; the Party announced her death, but not its circumstances; her children were told she had died of appendicitis. A grand state funeral was mounted with all due solemnity, featuring a Red Army band playing Chopin's "Funeral March" and with the hearse pulled by "four black horses, tasselled and garnished with red, with all the leaders of the government walking five-abreast the half mile to the cemetery." Stalin, who had led the mourners, wearing grey not black, failed to appear at the graveside for Nadezhda's burial. Paranoid about possible assassination attacks, he had left the funeral cortege after covering only a short distance.

After her death, rumors began to circulate that Nadezhda had either been murdered by Stalin in a fit of rage, or by others on his orders, or that she had killed herself as a result of his increasingly intolerable behavior toward her. In terms of a propensity for fits of jealousy and fierce temper, Nadezhda had certainly been Stalin's equal. There had been plenty of talk about her histrionic behavior, that she was a bit "mad" and wildly jealous over Stalin's supposed relations with other women; others more sensibly observed that Nadezhda, a passionate and committed socialist, was in fact profoundly disillusioned with Stalin as a political leader and with his policies, such as the collectivization program.

According to one close friend, Stalin had drunkenly alleged during their row at the party in the Kremlin just before her death that Nadezhda was in fact his own daughter; her mother, a Georgian, had indeed had lovers, including Stalin, around the time she conceived Nadezhda in 1901. This insinuation, whether or not it was true, may well have unhinged Nadezhda in the final desperate hours leading up to her suicide. In any event, with her mental state becoming increasingly unstable, it is likely, had she lived, that Stalin would have inevitably found it expedient to rid himself of her. Stalin himself remained bitter and angry at her death, commenting, on the day of her funeral, that "she went away as an enemy." Although he later went through some ritual breast-beating over his neglect of her, in private he persisted in laying the blame, as he did with all his own shortcomings and failures, at the doors of others. But the person who continued to hold a real corner of his heart was his first wife, Ekaterina. Occasional, flimsy rumors of other women after Nadezhda's death have been circulated since, but Stalin never remarried. He did, however, mete out his revenge on the Alliluyev family during the Great Terror: Nadezhda's sister Anna was sentenced to ten years in prison in 1948; her husband was shot in 1938; her brother's and uncle's wives were both imprisoned, as was her nephew.

See also Alliluyeva, Svetlana; Dzhugashvili, Yakov; Stalin: Dachas of; Stalin: Private Life of; Svanidze, Ekaterina

Further reading: Larissa Vasilievna. *Kremlin Wives.* London: Weidenfeld & Nicolson, 1994; Svetlana Alliluyeva. *20 Letters to a Friend.* London: Hutchinson, 1967.

Allilueva, Svetlana Iosefovna (1926–)

*I*n 1967, the name of Joseph Stalin, for some time excised from the popular consciousness inside and outside the Soviet Union, was suddenly in the newspapers again after the defection to the West of his daughter Svetlana Allilueva and the subsequent publication of her powerful memoir *Twenty Letters to a Friend* (1967). The contents of that memoir and the story of Svetlana's subsequent unsettled life in the West testify to a life dogged by the shadow of her troubled parentage. It was not until she was fifteen years old that Svetlana accidentally found out about the true fate of her mother, Nadezhda, who had died in 1932. The young Svetlana had been told that her mother had died of appendicitis, but, in an English magazine given to her in the winter of 1941, she read that her mother's death had been suicide. Until then she had lived a closed, protected life, first at the Kremlin, and after her mother's death, at the family

dacha at Zubalovo. Svetlana had always been happiest here and on holidays in the Crimea, surrounded by an extended family of Alliluyev relations and visitors such as the Ordzhonikidzes, the Bukharins, and the Voroshilovs. But everything changed after her mother's death, and Allilueva's memoir describes a life of increasing alienation from her father, while at the same time providing the first revealing commentary to reach the West on the working of Stalin's mind and his increasingly obsessive behavior. She also details the sterility of Stalin's private life during his final years, the futile evenings spent at the dacha at Kuntsevo drinking until dawn, his rejection of creature comforts, and the grotesque farce of his final illness and death.

There is no doubt about Stalin's affection for Svetlana, his favorite child. His many touching and affectionate letters to her testify to that, and it was not until she became a woman and fell in love for the first time that she encountered the darker side to his nature, and their relationship began to change. During the war, at a party thrown by her brother Vasily at the family dacha at Zubalovo, Svetlana (then only sixteen years old) met the forty-year-old film director and script writer Alexis Kapler. While not in the least physically attractive, Kapler was a clever man and a great conversationalist, and the impressionable young Svetlana was swept off her feet. Their few encounters—walks, trips to the cinema and art galleries—were closely monitored by Stalin's agents, who also gave him transcripts of all their telephone conversations. A furious Stalin soon found the excuse for getting Kapler out of the way by condemning him as an "English spy" after he was spotted fraternizing with foreign journalists. Kapler was sent into exile for five years and a further term of five years of exile after that was completed.

After the affair with Kapler, Svetlana became estranged from her father. In 1944, while a student at Moscow University, she

Secret police chief Lavrenty Beria clutches an uneasy-looking Svetlana Stalin on his knee at Stalin's Kuntsevo dacha in 1936. Stalin can be seen reading and smoking his pipe in the background.

married Jewish fellow-student Grigory Morozov, but they divorced in 1947, not long after the birth of a son, Josef. She tried to patch up her relationship with Stalin by marrying again in 1949 to Yury Zhdanov, the son of top Party bureaucrat Andrey Zhdanov, a man of whom she thought Stalin would approve. The couple, who had a daughter, Katya, divorced in 1952.

Svetlana's third husband was Indian Communist Brajesh Singh. When he died in 1966 she was allowed an exit visa to travel to India with his ashes. But she did not return to the Soviet Union and defected in Rome, leaving her children behind in the Soviet Union. She settled in Princeton, New Jersey, in April 1967, where she wrote *Only One Year* (1969), about her life in the Soviet Union and the aftereffects of her defection. In the West, as the daughter of a major Soviet political figure, Allilueva was feted by the intellectual glitterati and was frequently interviewed on televi-

sion and in the press. Not long after settling in the United States, Allilueva became a U.S. citizen. She had a fourth, short-lived marriage to American architect William Peters, by whom she had a daughter, Olga, in 1971. In the years that followed, Allilueva underwent a profound religious conversion, and it was for this reason that she moved to England in 1982 in order to send her daughter to a Quaker school.

With the improving political climate in the Soviet Union, Allilueva decided to return in 1984, but her now thoroughly Westernized daughter, who spoke no Russian, hated it there. They had been obliged to settle, with considerable unease but away from public scrutiny, in Stalin's own home country of Georgia. But two years later Allilueva and her daughter left Tbilisi, where they had been living, and returned to the United States. Her stay proved brief, and she moved again to England, determined to keep the press from her door. She became increasingly reclusive, although she has since found spiritual comfort in a new and profound religious faith.

See also Allilueva, Nadezhda; Stalin: Dachas of
Further reading: Svetlana Allilueva. *Twenty Letters to a Friend*. London: Hutchinson, 1967; Svetlana Allilueva. *Only One Year*. London: Hutchinson, 1969.

Anti-Semitism
See Jews.

Art and Architecture

To be a participant in the Russian arts at the time of the revolution was to be at the center of an explosion of talent and creativity across all fields in music, literature, dance, painting, and design. The Russian avant-garde in art was particularly successful in capturing the immediacy of so much tumultuous change, with artists eager to find new ways of depicting the modern world with its emphasis on social change and scientific advances.

Much of Soviet experimental art in its early days was spawned by the antiaesthetic movement known as Constructivism. This was inspired by the Cubist and Futurist movements in art, with their preference for geometric shapes and the Constructivists' use of glass, plastic, metal, particularly aluminum, and other mass-produced materials that reflected the technology of the new Soviet machine age. The Constructivists' Manifesto of 1920 emphasized their objective as being to construct a form of art that was socially directed, an art form that manifested the utopian aspirations of socialism rather than the small-scale preoccupations of the personal and contemplative in other, more traditional art forms. The basic principles of this functionalist approach, which came to be nicknamed "laboratory art," were applied equally and to striking effect in industrial design, in architecture, in utilitarian furniture, textiles, and ceramics, as well as stage, poster, and graphic design, through its major exponents El Lissitzky, Vladimir Tatlin, Varvara Stepanova, Lyubov Popova, and Alexander Rodchenko.

But this flourishing artistic climate of diversity began to change in the 1920s, and the Association of Artists of Revolutionary Russia, established in 1922, began to gain ascendancy with its demands for a Soviet brand of revolutionary realism to which all artists should conform and depict the present day along prescribed lines. Increasing accusations of formalism and decadence began to affect the Constructivists who had embraced the enthusiasm for new forms in their various and idiosyncratic ways. Individualists and experimenters in art were now marginalized in favor of a return to the bland, traditional forms of realist art—as epitomized by the vast canvases of the nineteenth-century school of Russian painters known as the "wanderers" (Ilya Repin, Stalin's favorite, had famously depicted Ivan the Terrible and other notable historical figures). In 1932 Stalin imposed his will across the Soviet arts with the Party decree putting an end to all independent and fringe groups in favor of a single, all-embracing union that would ensure the suppression of all forms of purely subjective art. For under socialist realism, such forms were now superfluous and an indulgent luxury. Art was not a spiritual pursuit; it had one function—to serve the working class and, to do so, it should take its inspiration from real, everyday life.

In the early days after the revolution, several émigré artists, including Marc Chagall, Wassily Kandinsky, and the sculptor Naum Gabo had returned to Russia, eager to find a new role for themselves. But within a few years, this situation was reversed. Throughout the 1920s, the hemorrhage of avant-garde artists leaving the Soviet Union seemed unstoppable. El Lissitsky (who went abroad 1921–1928), Naum Gabo (1922),

Vera Mukhina's famous celebration of the New Soviet Man in her stainless steel sculpture **The Worker** and the **Collective Farm Girl**, *specially created to top the Soviet pavilion at the 1937 Paris World Exhibition.*

Kandinsky (1921), Chagall (1923), sculptor Antoine Pevsner (1923), and painter and designer Aleksandra Exter (1924) were among the many artists who felt they no longer had a place in the new culture.

Many figures from the old avant-garde who stayed spent the rest of their lives languishing in obscurity, unable to exhibit or sell their work. One such figure was the Suprematist painter Kasimir Malevich, best known for his minimalist abstract works of 1918–1919, such as *White Square on White* and *Black Square*. Under Stalin, Malevich was condemned for his ideological alienation and was banned from exhibiting after his last one-man show in 1929 (although by 1922 and under increasing ideological pressure, he had all but abandoned painting, turning to writing and lecturing on art). Now living in a state of increasing penury, Malevich attempted his own interpretation of socialist realism by painting traditional, figurative subjects but in featureless Suprematist shapes and colors, creating an unsettling end product that, in the words of one critic, inspired "a kind of metaphysical terror." On his death in 1935, Malevich was rescued from obscurity and given an official lying in state at the Leningrad Artist's Union, followed by burial in a coffin made from one of his own Suprematist designs.

Those major figures, primarily Tatlin and Rodchenko, who adapted by emphasizing the link between the arts and industry in their work, turned increasingly to design in posters, photo montages, theater sets and costumes. Tatlin had attracted attention in 1919–1920 with his design for the Monument to the Third International. This steel structure, projected to rise like a leaning spire to a greater height than the Eiffel Tower, had been the subject of considerable controversy but never got further than its twenty-two-foot model. From the late 1920s Tatlin spent several years working on a prototype wooden glider, the "Letatlin" (a pun of his name, based on the Russian verb *letat* "to fly"), but when this eccentric project failed, he turned increasingly to theatrical design.

As for Rodchenko, probably the most internationally successful of all the artists of the Stalinist period, he had proclaimed the death of art in 1928, saying that "every modern cultured man must wage war against art as against opium. Photograph and be photographed." It was Rodchenko's choice of the photographic medium, as much as anything, that led to his considerable reputation abroad (a reputation that has now vastly inflated the value of his work). With his camera Rodchenko became the great exponent of Constructivism in photography, developing a style of reportage that celebrated the physical prowess of the new Soviet man and the achievements of industry, which, in so doing, served as the perfect Soviet propaganda vehicle in the West. Rodchenko's imaginative use of perspective, shape, and shadow was also to influence Soviet filmmaking, in particular, the work of Sergey Eisenstein and the documentary filmmaker Dziga Vertov.

In the field of conventional painting, meanwhile, experimentation had been completely stifled for anyone seeking to earn a living as an artist. Painters found themselves rapidly shackled to producing hackwork depicting the same old conventional subjects of happy tractor drivers on the collective farms or steelworkers toiling at blast furnaces. Their only other alternative was to add to the already inflated Stalinist hagiography by producing yet more idealized paintings of the Great Leader in variations on the same heroic pose: Stalin as tousle-haired revolutionary in Baku, Stalin learning revolution at the knee of Lenin, Stalin on the podium, Stalin at the tractor factory or the collective farm, and Stalin at his desk planning the future. Figurative painting suffered more than any other branch of Soviet art during this period and remained stranded in these stultifying doldrums until long after Stalin's death. It is only thanks to the risks taken by numerous private art collectors in the Soviet Union, who bought the paintings of out-of-favor artists and hid them away in their apartments, that the work of some of the most important figures in the Soviet avant-garde during the 1920s and 1930s was saved from destruction.

In 1930, Aleksey Shchusev's striking Constructivist design for the new Lenin mausoleum (inspired, in part, by the recent discovery of the tomb of Tutankhamen in Egypt) became the focal point for a major rebuilding program launched by Stalin in Moscow. Many buildings, including historic churches and old districts, such as the market area of Okhotnyi Ryad (Hunter's Row), were blown up wholesale in order to open up Red Square for the big showpiece parades that would celebrate the achievements of communism. With the introduction of socialist realism in 1932, architects were forced to become part of a single Union of Soviet Architects and forced to abandon small-scale projects in favor of the grandiose Stalinist projects. Ambitious plans for the construction of vast monoliths, such as the Palace of the Soviets, obliged architects to attempt impractical designs that looked wonderful on paper but were financially (and probably structurally) unrealizable.

As the Five-Year Plans placed greater and greater demands on industry throughout the 1930s, architects began to take second place to engineers in the realization of vast industrial complexes, dams, and hydroelectric stations and, increasingly, town planning. In this respect, the work of the Vesenin brothers Aleksandr, Leonid, and Viktor produced architectural landmarks such as the Dnieper Dam and industrial works at Zaporozhe, as well as urban development projects for workers, including that constructed around the Likhachev Car Works. With the acceleration of Soviet industrial output, living spaces for workers became of paramount importance, but homes could no longer be designed to serve individual taste. Housing was envisioned on an increasingly vast scale with whole districts bulldozed and rebuilt as functional and structurally nondescript hangars for the communal necessities of eating and sleeping, all constructed to a precisely prescribed amount of living space per person.

While many of the vast canvases of socialist realist art and, in particular, those depicting Stalin have now been relegated to the forgotten storerooms of Russia's art galleries, the legacy of late Stalinist baroque architecture, popularly dubbed the "wedding-cake" style, is still evident in some of the former Soviet Union's major cities. Perhaps the most familiar landmark is the imposing edifice of the thirty-six-story Moscow University, which began construction in 1945. This return to classical forms in architecture had been endorsed by People's Commissar for Enlightenment Anatoly Lunacharsky, when he asserted in 1932 that "the workers, too, have a right to colonnades." One of the most innovative and individual exponents of the Constructivist style in architecture was Konstantin Melnikov, famous for the design of several workingmen's clubs in Moscow and the Soviet pavilion at the 1924 Paris exhibition. He also built his own extraordinary cylindrical house just off the famous Arbat in Moscow in 1927–1929, as a prototype for an unfulfilled housing development. But in the 1930s he came under increasing attack for his pseudorevolutionary innovationism, partly the result of official sour grapes at his considerable reputation abroad, and in 1936 he was expelled from the Union of Architects.

After the collapse of the Soviet Union in 1991, there was a great rush to remove and destroy much of the monumental art erected to Stalin and other political luminaries of the years of Communist rule. One of the greatest and most enduring pieces of Soviet sculpture to survive this orgy of destruction was Vera Mukhina's *Worker and Collective Farm Girl,* originally executed in stainless steel to grace the Soviet pavilion at the Paris exhibition of 1937. Much admired by Stalin, it was one of the first recipients of the Stalin Prize for art in 1941. Mukhina's work marked the apogee of Soviet triumphalism in sculpture with its powerful symbolic image of the farm girl and the industrial worker raising their hands holding the hammer and sickle aloft in defiant unison. So impressed was Stalin with Mukhina's work that he made overtures for her to sculpt his portrait. Mukhina wisely evaded the honor by insisting on working from life, a request to which Stalin would not accede in his final, reclusive years.

See also Eisenstein, Sergey; Moscow Metro; "New Soviet Man"; Palace of the Soviets; Socialist Realism

Further reading: Matthew Cullerne Bown. *Art under Stalin.* Oxford: Phaidon, 1991; Matthew Cullerne Bown. *Socialist Realist Painting.* New Haven, CT: Yale University Press, 1998; David Elliott. *New Worlds: Russian Art and Society 1900–1937.* London: Thames and Hudson, 1986.

Atheism
See Religion.

Atomic Bomb

In 1949, the Soviets surprised their former wartime allies and, indeed, the rest of the world by exploding their first nuclear device several years before Central Intelligence Agency (CIA) reports had suggested they would have the ability to do so.

Although Soviet scientists had been aware of the principles of nuclear fission, first described by Otto Frisch and Lise Meitner in 1939, no coordinated Soviet research into its potential was begun until 1940, when leading scientists had written to the then head of the Council of the Chemical and Metallurgical Industries Nikolay Bulganin, urging the government to initiate a research project. In July a com-

mission attached to the Academy of Sciences was set up to do this and immediately found itself having to contend with the difficulties of obtaining sufficient uranium for conducting experiments. However, when the Germans invaded the Soviet Union in 1941, the energies of Soviet scientists were hastily redirected to the war effort, and the nuclear project was temporarily sidelined.

While the Americans and British continued to take little account of what information they received on Soviet efforts to achieve nuclear fission, the Soviets themselves were, by the end of 1942, secretly being fed information on the British project by the MI5 double agent John Cairncross and later by Klaus Fuchs (a leading physicist who later worked at the Los Alamos project in the United States), as well as by other Soviet spies in the United States. The Soviet nuclear project was resumed in early 1943, during the defense of Stalingrad, with Stalin ordering the production of at least 100 tons of uranium during 1944–1945. It is unlikely, however, that he had the objective of, or any realistic hope for, its immediate use militarily against Germany. At this particular time he was still naive about the complexities of the bomb's production, as well as its strategic potential, and was simply hedging his political bets in anticipation of the future, postwar balance of power in both military as well as technological terms.

At the Potsdam Conference held at the end of the war in Europe, Stalin appeared to show little interest when President Truman hinted to him that America had a nuclear capability. But after the atomic bomb was dropped on Hiroshima in August 1945, Stalin realized, with a jolt, the enormous power of such weapons, averring that the old political equilibrium had now been destroyed. He immediately ordered the renewal of Soviet research, telling the scientific director of the Soviet nuclear project Igor Kurchatov to spare no expense, "If a child doesn't cry, the mother doesn't know what he needs. Ask for whatever you like. You won't be refused." The task of supervising the crucial intelligence gathering behind this research was given to Lavrenty Beria, head of the NKVD (secret police), while Vyacheslav Molotov, the foreign minister, was put in overall charge of the project. Beria proved to be an outstanding organizer in this respect. It became incumbent upon Igor Kurchatov, however, to warn that the continuing repressive attitude to Soviet scientific research, aimed particularly in the area of genetics, was now turning its attention to physics. If such interference were allowed to spread into the nuclear project, there would be no Soviet bomb. As it was, the scientists warned Stalin that it would take five years to create their own bomb.

Stalin, therefore, demanded that all kinds of risks be taken to speed up research. Scientists were forced to work, often inadequately protected, with untested radioactive materials. Many of those employed at the lower level of nuclear research were prisoners in the Gulag. During the war, Beria had set up special research centers, known as *sharashi,* to utilize the talents of the many scientists and technicians who had been imprisoned during the purges. All those involved were now threatened with the dire consequences of failure. Uranium extraction was made a top priority, with Stalin emphasizing that heavy industry and technology should take precedence over other economic demands and that all the state's resources should be harnessed to the nuclear project. This came at a time when the country was struggling to cope with the terrible depredations of war. Despite this, the Soviet science budget was tripled, and scientists engaged in the nuclear project were given such special privileges as country dachas and various financial incentives.

Soviet nuclear capability would be developed on a major scale at a special, hidden city known as "Arzamas–16," which was built, at Stalin's orders, by convict labor between 1946 and 1954 in a dense birch forest 300 miles east of Moscow. The convicts who built it were subsequently consigned to exile in a remote region on Russia's northeastern Pacific coast, and it was not until after the collapse of communism that the existence of this closed city was actually revealed. The Soviets finally achieved a self-sustaining nuclear chain reaction and built their first production reactor in 1948 at a specially constructed site near Chelyabinsk in the Ural Mountains. The first test explosion of a bomb designed by Yuly Khariton was made in Kazakhstan on 29 August 1949 and witnessed by Beria and Kurchatov. Several of the scientists directly involved in achieving this success within four years instead of the projected five years were decorated as heroes of socialist labor by Stalin.

The Americans and British were taken by surprise by this event (they finally heard of it nearly four weeks later), having been told by the CIA that this event would not take place before mid-1953. Stalin himself later admitted to Kurchatov that "if we had been a year or a year and a half later with the atomic bomb, we would surely have felt it on ourselves." During the Cold War, as both sides accelerated their nuclear programs, several eminent scientists such as Albert Einstein, Robert Oppenheimer (who had run the U.S. project at Los Alamos), and Andrey Sakharov (the father of the Soviet H-bomb) all warned of the terrifying potential of the nuclear monster. Stalin, however, was delighted with his new-found nuclear capability. It opened the doors to a new kind of power-broking—"atomic diplomacy"—that helped him consolidate his control over Eastern Europe and place enormous political pressures on the West, while avoiding actual conflict.

By 1951 the Soviets had created a device equal to that of the United States and Britain. On 12 August 1953, six months after Stalin's death, they tested their first hydrogen bomb. Stalin's successor, Nikita Khrushchev, took no heed of Sakharov's pleading that Soviet nuclear testing should cease, asserting bullishly that the bomb "should hang over the head of capitalists like a sword of Damocles." During the Cuban Crisis in 1962, Khrushchev's combative stance on nuclear weapons was instrumental in bringing the world to the brink of nuclear catastrophe.

See also Cold War; Gulag; Potsdam Conference; Science

Further reading: Taylor Downing and Jeremy Isaacs. *The Cold War: For 45 Years the World Held Its Breath*. New York and London: Bantam, 1998; David Holloway. *Stalin and the Bomb: The Soviet Union and Atomic Energy 1939–1956*. New Haven, CT: Yale University Press, 1994; Alexander Solzhenitsyn. *The First Circle*. London: William Collins Sons, 1968 (a fictional account of Gulag prisoners working on scientific projects in the *sharashi,* during the war years).

Babel, Isaac Emmanuilovich (1894–1940)

The much-admired Jewish short-story writer, who brilliantly evoked the anarchy and violence of the Russian-Polish War of 1919–1920 with his collection *Red Cavalry* (1926), was in reality a warm, gentle, and gregarious personality, who, like the narrator of these stories, "looked on the world as a meadow in May—a meadow traversed by women and horses." No doubt his literary legacy would have been a rich one had he lived longer than his forty-six years, but the stories that he did leave are jewels of observation, with their rich layers of metaphor and allusion, always pervaded by a passionate love of humanity.

Babel grew up in the old Jewish quarter of the cosmopolitan Black Sea port of Odessa. His stories of his childhood capture the atmosphere of a lost time and a lost community. Jewishness colored all his later work, despite the difficulties of being a Jew in Soviet Russia. For the early part of his life, too, Babel struggled with the paradox of being a pacific Jew who welcomed the spirit of the revolution, while rejecting the violence of things done in its name. He was forced to accept, in fact, as his Jewish narrator in *Red Cavalry,* Lyutov, asserts that the International "is eaten with gunpowder—and spiced with best-quality blood."

In the heady days of Petrograd 1915–1917, when he first started out as a writer, Babel wrote vivid naturalistic pieces for Maxim Gorky's journal *New Life,* and Gorky, quick to spot Babel's rare talent, nurtured it, urging him to go out and grasp hold of life and experience in order to become an even better writer. It was an exhortation familiar from his own childhood, when Babel's grandmother, urging him to pay attention to his studies, had insisted, "You must know everything!" Indeed, Babel's innate curiosity about life and people would lead to a lifelong compulsion to ferret out the unusual detail in everything and to turn such observation into brilliant metaphor in his stories.

During World War I, Babel had been exempted from military service (he was shortsighted and suffered from asthma), but he nevertheless volunteered and briefly served on the Romanian front. After the revolution, Babel worked as an interpreter for the Cheka (forerunner of the NKVD) before taking a post as correspondent for the government news agency YugRosta in the spring of 1920. He was assigned (under the alias of Kirill Lyutov, a necessity at a time of anti-Semitic violence among Bolshevik troops) to the already legendary First Cavalry Army, commanded by the swashbuckling Semen Budenny. At that time the First Cavalry, which had been formed to counter Cossack units fighting for the Whites, was

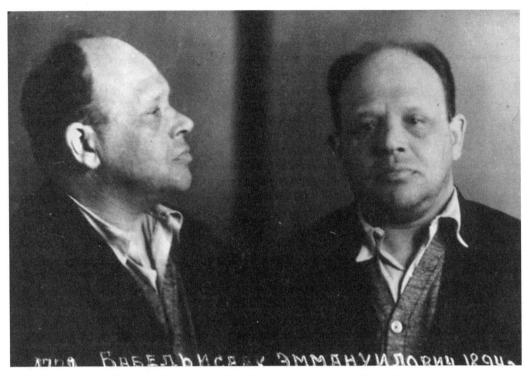

The writer Isaac Babel, from his secret police file after his arrest in May 1939, exhausted by interrogation and without his spectacles. He was shot in the Lubyanka prison in January 1940.

under the overall command of Stalin as political commissar of the southern front. The reputation of Budenny's half-savage and fearless Cossack horsemen preceded them everywhere. Babel, the quiet-spoken, physically weak, intellectual Jew with glasses, could not help admiring their courage and physicality and found himself constantly an impotent and ambivalent witness to the senseless cruelties visited by them on the Jewish population of the shtetl (the Jewish villages of the Ukraine).

By the time he moved to Moscow in 1924, Babel was being feted as one of the best writers of his day for his originality of style and subject matter. The early 1920s was a fertile period for him. He produced most of his best work, including the thirty-four stories later published collectively as *Red Cavalry,* as well as a series of tales about his childhood and the Jewish gangsters of the Moldavanka ghetto of Odessa, later published as *Odessa Tales* (1931). The process

of writing was painfully slow for him. He was a perfectionist who wrote and rewrote, sometimes as many as twenty versions of a single story. He was compelled to earn a greater part of his living writing screenplays and working as a "script doctor," producing several fine scripts, including *Benya Krik the Gangster,* based on his Odessan stories. (He later worked with the director Sergey Eisenstein on the ill-fated *Bezhin Meadow,* suppressed by the authorities in 1937.) But by the early 1930s Babel found it increasingly difficult to adopt the required ideological stance in his work and to write to the demands of socialist realism. He published less and less original work. At the First Congress of Soviet Writers in 1934, he spoke for many other oppressed writers when he jokingly admitted that "my respect for the reader is so great that I keep quiet and do not speak. I have been acknowledged as a great master in the art of silence."

What probably saved Babel for a while from the inevitable arrest, which finally came in 1939, was the continuing friendship and patronage of Maxim Gorky, but after Gorky's death in 1936 Babel became increasingly vulnerable. He retreated to his dacha at Peredelkino, where he refused lucrative inducements to begin publishing again, averring that "creativity does not dwell in palaces." He was arrested there on 15 May 1939. All his manuscripts were confiscated, and as they took him away, a bewildered and shaken Babel was heard to say, "They didn't let me finish."

For fifteen years nothing was known of Babel's fate. On his rehabilitation in late 1954, Babel's family was told that he had died somewhere in the Gulag on 17 March 1941, but the eventual opening of the KGB archives in the 1990s told a different tale. Under relentless interrogation at the Lubyanka from May to September 1939, Babel had made a detailed confession, probably on the promise of a lesser sentence or even of being freed. He admitted to having been a tool of the Trotskyists and to having been recruited as a spy for France on an earlier visit to Paris and duly played the obligatory role as the ideological penitent. Even worse, not only did Babel capitulate to all his interrogators' demands, but in response to the demand that he denounce other "enemies of the people," he also began incriminating his friends—the director Sergey Eisenstein, the Jewish actor Solomon Mikhoels, the writer Yury Olesha, and others. In September, in a last-ditch attempt to save himself, he wrote a letter to Beria from the Lubyanka in which he expressed a burning desire "to work, to repent, and to condemn a life wrongly and criminally wasted." No one knows what physical and mental torments may have led to Babel's betrayal of his friends or his own dignity as a writer, but when he later realized that all was lost, and by now tormented with guilt, he tried several times to recant, asserting that "this slander was prompted by

my own faint-hearted behaviour during the cross-examination."

On 26 January 1940, Babel was finally tried by a military tribunal at Butyrki prison, where he was now being held, when he denied all the charges to which he had previously confessed. He was shot the following morning. One of the great tragedies of his arrest and death is the lost legacy of the twenty-seven folders of Babel's manuscripts confiscated at the time of his arrest, including essays, a book on Gorky, several dozen stories, a play, and a film script . Although the KGB archives have since been opened, there is no sign of these manuscripts. The loss to Russian literature is immeasurable.

See also Budenny, Marshal Semen; Gorky, Maxim; The Great Terror; Socialist Realism; Union of Soviet Writers
Further reading: Isaac Babel. *Red Cavalry.* Harmondsworth, UK: Penguin, 1994; A. N. Pirozhkova. *At His Side: The Last Years of Isaac Babel.* South Royalton, VT: Steerforth Press, 1996; Vitaly Shentalinsky. *The KGB's Literary Archive.* London: Harvill Press, 1995.

Baku

This seaport on the shores of the Caspian Sea in Azerbaijan, which became part of the Russian Empire in 1806, was once the site of the largest oilfields in the world, producing half the world's total supply by the turn of the century. The whole city, "with its chimnies and refineries . . . its grimy naptha-besprinkled streets . . . its shabby conglomeration of peoples, its inky harbour, its canopy of smoke," had become by then "larger, more pungent, and less inviting than ever." It was, however, the ideal recruiting ground for revolutionaries and political activists.

The large-scale exploitation of oil in Baku since the 1870s had attracted a huge influx of workers from all over the Russian Empire, many of them from long-exploited and suppressed ethnic minorities. It was here that Stalin served his revolutionary apprenticeship after being expelled by the Georgian Social Democrats in 1907.

The period 1904–1908 is a particularly shadowy one in Stalin's career and is problematic for historians. He was constantly moving around from one hiding place to another and using several different aliases in order to evade rearrest and the long journey back into Siberian exile. However, Stalinist historiography later claimed a pivotal role for Stalin in agitational activities in Baku from the summer of 1904. Strikes and political unrest here and elsewhere in the Russian Empire contributed significantly to the 1905 Revolution, and it was essential that Stalin was seen to be directly involved in them. In reality, little is clear about his career at this time, and there is nothing to substantiate claims that he did anything more than make the occasional visit to Baku before 1907. Indeed, several members of the Baku underground—in particular Abel Enukhidze—who later wrote their memoirs and failed to mention Stalin's role were forced to rewrite their accounts, minimizing their own contributions at the price of giving greater emphasis to Stalin's.

Stalin was in Baku on a more permanent basis by the autumn of 1907 when he set up a rival Bolshevik branch of the Georgian Social Democrats, publishing a trade union broadsheet, *The Baku Proletarian*. In it he encouraged the 50,000 oil workers to form a single trade union to represent them at the elections to the state Duma. In March 1908, Stalin was arrested again and languished in prison in Baku before being sent back to Solvychegodsk. But he was soon back in Baku, after escaping yet again, and hid out at the Balakhlana oilfield. He began republishing his broadsheet while orchestrating a general strike of the oil workers. Stalin later officially acknowledged his experiences at Baku as formative of his early revolutionary career: "Two years of revolutionary work among the oil workers of Baku hardened me as a practical fighter. . . . I first learned what it meant to lead large masses of workers and received my second revolutionary baptism in combat."

See also Batum; Georgia; Georgian Social Democrats; Historiography; Stalin: Imprisonment and Exile of; Transcaucasia

Further reading: Edward Ellis Smith. *The Young Stalin: The Early Years of an Elusive Revolutionary.* New York, Farrar, Straus and Giroux, 1967; Leon Trotsky. *Stalin, Vol. 1: Rise of a Revolutionary,* London MacGibbon & Kee, 1968; Robert C. Tucker. *Stalin as Revolutionary, 1879–1929: A Study in History and Personality.* New York: W. W. Norton, 1973.

Baltic States

For centuries, the ancient Baltic states of Latvia, Lithuania, and Estonia suffered incursions, wars, and partitions by other invading nations, among them Slavs, Germans, and Scandinavians. In the sixteenth century Lithuania had united with Poland, while most of Estonia and Latvia had come under Swedish control by the seventeenth century. A continuing process of partition and annexation brought the greater part of the region increasingly under the control of the Russian Empire during the nineteenth century, but the Baltic states remained fiercely protective of their national heritage and culture. But at the end of World War I, with all three states seeking to win back their independence, Stalin, as commissar for nationalities, was loudly proclaiming a different scenario.

The Bolsheviks, he announced, would sooner or later liberate the workers of the Baltic from capitalism, and the revolution would sweep away the "petty kinglets" of Estonia, Latvia, and Lithuania. Still, the Baltic peoples resisted Bolshevik attempts to establish Communist regimes there, and the region clung to a degree of independence that, in 1920, the Soviets were obliged to recognize officially. In 1921 all three states became members of the League of Nations and struggled to retain their political neutrality amid the escalating political tensions in Europe in the 1930s.

When Stalin made his secret pact with Hitler in 1939, the two leaders, both of whom were reluctant to let go of their countries' centuries-old control of the Baltic, made a deal on the future state of affairs. Germany would take control of Lithuania; Estonia and Latvia would fall to the Soviet Union. But when the Lithuanians resisted German domination, most of the area was turned over to the Soviets. By the autumn of 1939 Stalin's foreign minister, Vyacheslav Molotov, had persuaded the Baltic states to sign a treaty of "mutual assistance" with the Soviet Union, and Red Army garrisons were rapidly installed in the region. Stalin's annexation of the region under the German-Soviet Pact was followed by the states' formal incorporation as constituent republics into the Soviet Union in August 1940 and by the imposition of one-sided elections to ensure the installation of pro-Soviet governments. The nationalization of Baltic industries was soon begun with the freezing of all business assets. The Sovietization of everyday life saw changes to school and university syllabuses and the removal of potent reminders of national identity. An immediate assessment was made by Stalin's NKVD (secret police) officials of any undesirable elements—such as priests, non-Communists and nationalists, teachers, trade unionists, intellectuals, members of the bourgeoisie, and Jewish leaders in all walks of life. In Estonia in June 1940, 10,000 people were summarily shot or dispatched to the Gulag. This was but the beginning of a policy to deliberately relocate the region's peoples in a drive to water down any resistance to Soviet domination. On a single night—14 June–15 June 1941—132,000 Baltic people were packed into cattle trains and deported to Central Asia and Siberia.

Hopes of a return to their 1918 status as sovereign states faded in the Baltic after the Germans invaded in 1941. Many people had initially celebrated the German invasion as an act of liberation, but it was not long before Hitler's intentions regarding their future became apparent—they were as exploitative as Stalin's. The Nazis designated the region a single territorial unit bearing the characterless name of "Ostland" and made it clear that their objective for it was its wholesale Germanization, the subordination of its population as a source of expendable slave labor, and the plundering of its agricultural land for produce to feed the German war machine. Between July and August 1941 many thousands of the Jews in Latvia and Lithuania were deported to the death camps. Estonian Jews who had not already fled to the Soviet Union were also wiped out in the Holocaust. While resistance to German occupation during the war was limited, a nationalist resistance movement prepared itself underground for concerted resistance to any renewal of Soviet domination in the region after the war, and in 1946 there were numerous armed clashes between nationalist partisans and government troops.

After the war, Stalin sought to continue the process he had begun in 1940. He met considerable resistance to enforced collectivization in Lithuania in the late 1940s, a fact that led to the deportation and deaths of thousands (142,000 were deported from the Baltic during 1945–1949). This forced relocation of the less cooperative peoples of the Soviet Union became a major Stalinist method of ensuring internal security. Many Baltic peasant farmers, who had been labeled "kulaks" (rich, money-making peasants), were deported by 1949. As many as one-quarter of the original people of the Baltic states were eventually forcibly resettled and supplanted by ethnic Russians.

In the postwar years Stalin imposed a rapid industrialization and urbanization program in the region, which raised production levels and the standard of living but also rapidly eroded traditional rural farming economies. The imposition of a Soviet-style bureaucracy was supported by a huge influx of Russian immigrants who took over the homes and jobs of native people, a process that dramatically shifted the ethnic balance of these states (by the 1980s almost half of the populations of Estonia and Latvia were ethnic Russians). A direct consequence of this was the deliberate marginalization of Baltic languages and cultural practices. Yet the strength of national identity persisted among the Baltic peoples, and an increasingly vociferous independence movement gathered ground throughout the 1980s. After the failed coup by Communist hardliners against Mikhail Gorbachev's government in August 1991 threw the Soviet Union into chaos, the Baltic republics wasted no time in declaring their independence from the Soviet Union.

See also Eastern Europe; German-Soviet Non-Aggression Pact; Great Patriotic War; Nationalities
Further reading: G. von Rauch. *The Baltic States: The Years of Independence, 1917–1940.* London: Hurst, 1974.

Batum

The cosmopolitan seaport of Batum (Batumi), on Georgia's Black Sea Coast, was an important center for the Russian oil industry, refining oil from Baku in Azerbaijan. Many workers had settled here from all over the Caucasus, as well as from Russia. In 1901, not long after joining the Georgian Social Democrats in Tiflis, Stalin was sent to Batum to carry out propaganda work among the workers at oil refineries and factories by setting up a secret printing press. In February 1902 he was involved in inciting a strike and later a demonstration at which 300 people were arrested. A violent protest against these arrests led to more arrests and some deaths, and in April Stalin himself was imprisoned, first in Batum and then in Kutaisi, before being exiled to Siberia for three years.

Soviet historiography of the Stalinist period has, of necessity, overemphasized Stalin's role in the demonstration in Batum, as it has his activities in Baku. As one colorful account describes it, "Comrade Soso stood in the midst of the turbulent sea of workers, personally directing the movement." But conflicting testimony and historical opinion make it hard to pinpoint the reality of Stalin's early years as an activist. Growing archival evidence suggests that Stalin's real role here and in his other early activities throughout the Caucasus was much less glamorous and more marginal than Soviet historiography contends. He played a more manipulative role behind the scenes, orchestrating events from a safe and always anonymous distance.

See also Baku; Georgia; Historiography; Transcaucasia
Further reading: Edward Ellis Smith. *The Young Stalin: The Early Years of an Elusive Revolutionary.* London: Cassell, 1968; Leon Trotsky. *Stalin, Vol. 1: Rise of a Revolutionary.* London: MacGibbon & Kee, 1968; Robert C. Tucker. *Stalin as Revolutionary, 1879–1929: A Study in History and Personality.* New York: W. W. Norton, 1973.

Beria, Lavrenty Pavlovich (1899–1953)

The Yugoslav politician Milovan Djilas on meeting Beria in the late 1940s described him as "somewhat plumpish, greenish and pale, and with soft damp hands." Andrey Sakharov, too, noted the "slightly moist and deathly cold hand," an apposite observation since Beria's metaphorical hand of death was felt by thousands. Djilas saw a creepy, lascivious element to Beria's nature. It was a nature that could not be disguised by his love of Rachmaninov (whose music brought him to tears), nor by the prim appearance created by his neat pince-nez, nor belied by pictures taken of him in avuncular mode cuddling Stalin's daughter Svetlana on his knee. In fact, Beria can claim the dubious distinction of being perhaps the most reprehensible of all Stalin's apparatchiks (bureaucrats), not only for his ruthless cruelty, but also for his lewd sexual proclivities and, in particular, his predilection for young girls (whom, as recent studies have revealed, he ordered his bodyguards to abduct from the street for own personal use). This would certainly explain the natural antipathy to Beria described by Svetlana of herself, her mother, and other female members in the Stalin household. Indeed, Stalin's wife tried unsuccessfully to block his frequent invitation.

By this time Stalin had found an important role for him as first secretary of the Georgian Communist Party, from which position Beria ensured the brutal institution of collectivization throughout Transcaucasia. He was also well placed to serve a particular role in singling out and eliminating Stalin's and his own rivals in the region, thus establishing a "proper order" in the country as a virtual minidictator. Svetlana Allilueva asserted that Beria's ascendancy in Transcaucasia was maintained only through Stalin's support and that he had many rivals among the Old Bolsheviks, including Sergey Kirov and Sergo Ordzhonikide (the latter did not mince his words and told Stalin that Beria was a "crook"), who knew the truth of Beria's history there. But as late as 1952 Beria ruthlessly put down a nationalist organization in his native Mingrelia, resulting in the execution of its Communist Party leadership and with them anyone who knew about his nefarious past.

Beria would do anything to ingratiate himself with Stalin and bolster his own political position. In 1935, he wrote a hagiography of Stalin's early years as a revolutionary entitled *On the History of the Bolshevik Organization in Transcaucasia*. In this, one of the seminal examples of the Stalinist falsification of history, Beria asserted that "the whole revolutionary movement of Transcaucasia and Georgia, has, from the first days of its rise, been linked inseparably with the work and name of Comrade Stalin."

Elevation to a senior role in government came with Beria's election in 1934 to the

The much-feared head of the NKVD, Lavrenty Beria was responsible for the deaths of hundreds of thousands.

Central Committee, followed by his candidacy for the Politburo in 1939. In 1938 Stalin had brought Beria to Moscow to replace Nikolay Ezhov as commissar for internal affairs. From here, having set up his own personal fiefdom operated by a mafioso-like gang of mainly Georgian bully boys (which also helped maintain his long-standing foothold on local power in the Caucasus), Beria proceeded to "purge the purgers," including his predecessor, Ezhov. It was, however, a time of deceleration in the rate of arrests; although one can hardly apply the term "liberal" to the regime instituted by Beria, the frenetic terror of Ezhovshchina was at least over, with many who were awaiting trial suddenly and inexplicably finding themselves released. There is, however, a darker side to Beria's hegemony at the NKVD. Accounts testify to the particular pleasure he took on a regular basis in witnessing, if not personally participating in, the torture of suspects. But as the Terror drew to a close, Beria's main task became the administration of the vast network of labor camps of the Gulag.

As deputy prime minister, with responsibility for security from 1941 to 1953, Beria became indispensable as a close aide to Stalin, overseeing arms production during the Great Patriotic War and ensuring that the desperate need for raw materials was addressed by the mass exploitation of slave labor from the Gulag. Some of his most important responsibilities were to oversee the Soviet nuclear project, to organize espionage activities abroad, and to ensure an adequate supply of uranium mined from open casts by unprotected slave laborers in Central Asia. For his efforts Beria was heaped with such awards as the Order of Lenin, the Red Banner, and the Order of Suvorov (for his efficient resettlement of thousands of people from ethnic minorities to Central Asia and Siberia), and, much to the disgust of the officer class, he was made a marshal of the Soviet Union in 1945 (during the entire war he visited the front lines on only two occasions).

It is more than possible that before he died, Stalin was preparing to rid himself of Beria. By then the two men acted in an atmosphere of mutual antipathy and suspicion, but they had become totally dependent on each other. As one Old Bolshevik observed, "The two were lone wolves. And their alliance was lupine." Stalin, who had become increasingly paranoid and reclusive, had no doubt come to rely too heavily on a man whom his daughter Svetlana described as "more treacherous, more practiced in perfidy and cunning, more insolent and single minded" than even Stalin himself. Indeed, she lays much of the blame for Stalin's later excesses at the door of Beria, seeing him in effect as the "evil genius" behind Stalin's throne and asserting that Beria, "a magnificent modern specimen of the artful courtier, the embodiment of Oriental perfidy, flattery and hypocrisy," had succeeded where others had failed in convincing Stalin of his undying loyalty.

In contrast to this view, which sees Stalin succumbing to Beria's manipulative behavior, the historian Adam Ulam points out that Stalin, despite his failing powers, was perfectly well aware that Beria's apparent loyalty was the knee-jerk reaction of the sycophant out to protect his own position. It was nothing but the elaborate concoction of a man who sensed his own vulnerability in the face of the uncompromising hostility of his peers. While Allilueva's desire to find some kind of redeeming feature in her father's behavior is understandable, Stalin had no scruples in exploiting Beria's sadistic tendencies in the ruthless eradication of his enemies, and Beria responded by laying on with a trowel the one thing Stalin craved—flattery. And so the faux joviality of their drinking sessions at the dacha at Kuntsevo, the interchange of coarse jokes, and the sly asides in their native Georgian tongue might have convinced observers that the two men were thick as thieves, but the players themselves knew otherwise. For Beria equaled Stalin in duplicity, and the two men were now locked in their own *danse macabre.*

When Stalin lay immobile and dying at his dacha in March 1953, Beria initially rose to the emotion of the occasion by playing the role of the distraught lackey, only to reveal his true contempt by spitting on the great leader's prostrate body, once he was sure that Stalin had slipped into unconsciousness. On 9 March, at Stalin's funeral, Beria delivered a eulogy to the crowds in Red Square, making clear his own claim to be Stalin's successor.

During the Great Patriotic War, Stalin had divided the responsibilities of Beria's Secret Police into the MGB, responsible for security matters, and the MVD, which dealt with matters of public order, policing, and the administration of the Gulag. After Stalin's death, Beria was quick to reunite these two departments under his sole control, as a power base from which to launch his own bid for the leadership in opposition to Malenkov and Khrushchev. Such a move alarmed his rivals, who were only too aware of Beria's more "liberal" attitudes on matters such as civil rights, the dismantling of the Gulag (though how genuine these attitudes were has been called into question), and his desire for rapprochement with the West, particularly in the case of East Germany, which he was willing to see reabsorbed into a united but neutral Germany. Such a threat to the stability of the old Stalinist system could not be contemplated, and Khrushchev and Malenkov connived at Beria's removal. A careful plan was laid to lure him to a meeting of the Presidium at the Kremlin on 26 June 1953, where he was separated from his bodyguards and surrounded by a phalanx of armed senior Red Army officers (backed up by armored cars hidden outside). Beria was denounced as a traitor and, in the greatest of ironies, as a British spy—a totally fabricated charge that Beria's NKVD officers had used so many times against their innocent victims.

For the next six months, Beria was held in an underground bunker in Moscow. Between 18 and 23 December 1953, he was tried in secret and shot soon after. The precise date is unconfirmed and rumor persists that he may have been already dead by the time of this "trial." Another report claims that he was shot in a scuffle on his way to execution. Immediately after his death was announced, Beria became a nonperson. The long article describing his illustrious career in the third edition of the *Great Soviet Encyclopedia* was replaced in haste with a four-page entry on the Bering Strait. Subscribers to the *Encyclopedia* dutifully followed the instructions issued to them to paste the Bering Strait article over Beria's biography.

See also Ezhov, Nikolay; Georgia; The Great Terror; Gulag; NKVD; Stalin: Death of

Further reading: Lavrentiy Beria. *On the History of Bolshevik Organizations in Transcaucasia.* Moscow: Foreign Languages Publishing House, 1949; Amy Knight. *Beria, Stalin's First Lieutenant.* Princeton, NJ: Princeton University Press. 1993.

"The Big Three"

The widely circulated newspaper photographs of Winston Churchill, Franklin Roosevelt, and Joseph Stalin, seated in a relaxed triumvirate at the conference of Tehran in December 1943 and again in Yalta in February 1945 seemed to uphold the promise made by Churchill in 1941 that a "Grand Alliance" of Britain, the United States, and the Soviet Union would be a lasting achievement. Not only had the three nations succeeded in defeating the common enemy, Hitler, but, more optimistically, Churchill asserted in Parliament in February 1945 that the Soviet Union and its military leaders would "live in honourable friendship and equality with the Western democracies."

Such idealistic talk could not, however, disguise the fact that the coming together of the three powers had been one of overriding expediency in the face of innate mutual mistrust. From Stalin's point of view, the alliance had always been one of brutal necessity, which had become critical once the early successes of Hitler's Operation Barbarossa had brought the Wehrmacht to the outskirts of Moscow. Equally, Churchill and Roosevelt both supported the alliance in the face of their own deep-seated loathing of communism. Indeed, Churchill in earlier times had launched into his characteristic purple prose to condemn the Soviet state and call on the democratic West to "strangle the babe of Bolshevism in its cradle."

When Hitler's army attacked the Soviet Union in June 1941, Churchill's response had been unequivocal: "The Russian danger . . . is our danger." Shortly after, he and Stalin announced an Anglo-Soviet agreement on mutual military assistance, and it took considerable courage on Churchill's part to resist Stalin's constant bullying for a second front to be opened in northern France to take the pressure off the Soviet Union. Churchill adamantly refused, and

Stalin and his wartime allies, Winston Churchill and Franklin D. Roosevelt, relaxing during the conference held in Tehran, November–December 1943, after the tide of the war in Europe had finally turned in their favor.

this would rankle Stalin for the next three years, until the June offensive of 1944 finally got under way. Meanwhile American military aid also began to flow into the Soviet Union, and in October 1941 a Common Law Alliance between the three powers was signed in Moscow. It came at a time when the military fortunes of all three countries were at an ebb and were yet to suffer further catastrophes in the Atlantic, the Western Desert of North Africa, and Southeast Asia. After the Japanese attack on Pearl Harbor in December 1941, Churchill sent his foreign secretary, Anthony Eden, to Moscow to clarify the relationship between the two countries, but progress was stymied by Stalin's entrenched position on Eastern Europe and his insistence, after the war on a return to the "old frontiers" that the Soviet Union had held prior to the Versailles Agreement of 1919.

By March 1942, Roosevelt had joined Stalin in pressing Churchill to agree to a second front and an invasion of Europe. When Stalin issued Churchill an ultimatum on the matter, Churchill traveled to Moscow in August to discuss the situation personally with "the old bear" (as he referred to Stalin in a letter to his wife), taking with him gifts of Dunhill pipes. At their talks, the two men engaged in some heated horse trading over the future balance of power in southeastern Europe. Churchill seemed willing to accede to Stalin's demands for Soviet influence as far as Romania, Bulgaria, and Yugoslavia were concerned, a fact that led to later recrimination from Roosevelt and the Americans. Stalin proved to be an extremely wily negotiator; the British view of him at the end of the Moscow talks was summarized by one of Churchill's entourage, Colonel Ian Jacob: "I don't believe that it is possible to make friends with a man like Stalin, in the sense that we understand friendship. . . . He was absolute master of the situation at all times, and appeared to be cold and calculating. . . . I should say that to make friends with Stalin would be equivalent to making friends with a python."

Between January and October 1943 the balance of the war shifted dramatically in the Allies' favor as the Soviets repulsed the Germans at Stalingrad and Kursk. Italy was invaded and Rommel was routed in North Africa. The time had come for "The Big Three" to meet and plan the final defeat of Hitler and the shape of the postwar world, which they did at Tehran between 28 November and 1 December 1943. Most of the talks were conducted in an atmosphere of amicable agreement, except when the particularly sensitive subject of Poland was brought up—a subject that led to heated interchanges between the two foreign ministers Vyacheslav Molotov and Anthony Eden. But important decisions were made on the opening of the second front, the future of the Baltic states and Eastern Europe, and the setting up of a postwar international peace-keeping organization—the United Nations.

During the course of the conference Roosevelt had three private conversations with Stalin and at Christmas that year publicly stated that he had found him "a man who combines tremendous relentless determination with a stalwart good humor. I believe he is truly representative of the heart and soul of Russia," a Russia that Roosevelt predicted "we are going to get along very well with." From here until the leaders met again at Yalta at the end of the war in 1945, Churchill would be reduced to the status of third fiddle to the political duet played by Roosevelt and Stalin. This development particularly wounded the British leader, who had always valued his special relationship with Roosevelt.

It soon became apparent after the death of Roosevelt (in April 1945) and Churchill's fall from power (in the general election of July 1945) that any romantic notions that might have been nurtured about relations between the Communist East and the democratic West continuing in the spirit of that wartime triumvirate were baseless. Roosevelt's critics felt he had been politically naive for "taking Stalin at his word," but Roosevelt's attitude toward Stalin had been based throughout on the deeply held conviction that cooperation between the "four policemen"—Britain, the United States, China, and the Soviet Union—was the only way of guaranteeing a secure future world. Such a belief had been at the root of his tolerance of the more boorish elements of Stalin's behavior and Soviet negotiating tactics at the wartime summits. Indeed, Roosevelt's understated manner and his skill at handling a man as complex as Stalin ultimately proved more effective than the tactics of other, more volatile negotiators, who were genial and aggressive by turns. As for Stalin, he had proved himself a surprisingly skillful negotiator, as even the American diplomat Averell Harriman, who had been present at all the meetings of "The Big Three," concluded: "I found him better informed than Roosevelt, more realistic than Churchill, in some ways the most effective of the war leaders."

By 1950, however, all the camaraderie of the war years had evaporated, as had the "rainbow of hope" that Roosevelt had talked about at Tehran in 1943. Stalin, in the final and most paranoid years of his rule, reverted to a policy of increasing isolationism bolstered by Soviet hegemony over the new buffer zone of satellite Communist states. The Iron Curtain that had now descended across Europe ensured that a renewal of rapprochement between East and West would be a long time coming.

See also Atomic Bomb; Cold War; Eastern Europe; Great Patriotic War; Potsdam Conference; Yalta Conference

Further reading: Robin Edmonds. *The Big Three.* London: Hamish Hamilton, 1991; Harold

Evans. *The American Century.* London: Jonathan Cape. 1998 (useful summary of bibliographical sources on pp. 681–682); W. Averell Harriman and Elie Abel. *Special Envoy to Churchill and Stalin, 1941–1946.* New York: Random House, 1975; Remi A. Nadeau. *Churchill and Roosevelt Divide Europe.* New York: Praeger, 1990; Richard Overy. *Why the Allies Won.* London: Jonathan Cape, 1995; Richard Overy. *Russia's War.* London: Allen Lane, 1997.

Blyukher, Marshal Vasily Konstantinovich (1890–1938)

Blyukher (a Russian despite his German-sounding name) was a military organizer and leader of the highest caliber and the first Soviet soldier to be awarded the prestigious Order of the Red Banner. But like his contemporary Marshal Mikhail Tukhachevsky, he proved to be too outspoken and independent a force in the military for Stalin to tolerate indefinitely.

Blyukher joined the revolutionary cause as a young factory worker and spent time in prison for organizing a strike. He served in the Russian army during World War I. He joined the Bolsheviks in 1916 and fought with distinction during the civil war, fighting the Whites in the south of Russia and leading his troops in a legendary march across Cossack-held territory in the Ural Mountains. At the end of the war, he was given a post in the Far East to oversee the final expulsion of the Whites and the Japanese from Soviet soil. In 1929, by now commander-in-chief of the Far Eastern Army, he reestablished Soviet control of the Far Eastern Railroad from the Chinese and later led Soviet forces against Japanese incursions into Manchuria, gaining a crucial military victory for the Soviets and laying the foundations of a powerful Soviet fighting force in that region.

In 1937 Blyukher, a man of some political influence who was held in high regard by his peers, was compelled along with other leading military men, as friends and colleagues of an accused (a favorite ploy of Stalin's), to sit on the tribunal that condemned Marshal Tukhachevsky and others to be shot. It is said that Blyukher actually commanded the firing squad at Tukhachevsky's execution. In a grim but typical twist to events at this high point of the Great Terror, even as Blyukher ordered this execution, he was himself being marked by Stalin for the same fate.

Along with most of his staff and commanders, Blyukher was rounded up in a major purge of Stalin's Far Eastern Army in 1938 and allowed a long enough reprieve to travel back to the Far East to command the final military repulsion of the Japanese in July–August at Lake Khasan. On his return in October, Blyukher and his immediate family (including his first wife) were arrested, and he was charged with being a Japanese spy, a favorite accusation at this time. He refused to trade a confession for a ten-year sentence despite long hours of torture in Lefortovo prison. Perhaps this final act of bravery was for him a way of redeeming himself morally for having been a party to the condemnation of his military comrades a year earlier. In any event, it was revealed in the late 1980s that Blyukher had not, in fact, been shot but that he died as a result of the severe beatings he received under torture. His wife was sent to the Gulag for eight years.

See also The Great Terror; Manchuria; Red Army; Tukhachevsky, Marshal Mikhail

Further reading: Robert Conquest. *The Great Terror: A Reassessment.* London: Hutchinson, 1990; Harold Shukman, ed. *Stalin's Generals.* London: Weidenfeld & Nicolson, 1993.

Budenny, Marshal Semen Mikhailovich (1883–1973)

One of the few of Stalin's top military leaders who was not murdered during the purge of the Red Army (in fact he lived to the ripe old age of ninety-eight), Budenny had become a soldier in 1903 and loyally served the tsar. He was much decorated in World War I before joining the Bolsheviks in 1918.

Budenny soon established himself as something of a folk hero, as a result of his exploits against the Polish troops of Marshal Pilsudski during the Russian-Polish war of 1919–1920. He was put in command of the troops of the First Cavalry of the Red Army and was much admired, that is, until the less-than-edifying exploits of his troops, particularly against women and Jews, were vividly described in the stories of Isaac Babel's *Red Cavalry*. Budenny protested loudly at this slander in an open letter to the journal *Red News* in 1928, in which he defended his heroic fighters and dismissed Babel's book as the work of an erotomanic author, who indulged "in old women's gossip" about "some Red Army man taking a loaf of bread and a chicken somewhere."

In the 1930s, Budenny, with his bristling mustache and swashbuckling Cossack air (he was a Don Cossack by birth), became the ideal vehicle for the promotion of Bolshevik Russia's heroic revolutionary past, despite the fact that Budenny himself had never taken comfortably to Marxist dogma. Nevertheless, he slavishly mouthed the appropriate Stalinist slogans and was rewarded by being made one of the first five marshals of the Soviet Union in 1935. He further reinforced Stalin's trust in him by serving as a member of the court that tried and condemned a group of Soviet generals, including Marshal Mikhail Tukhachevsky.

Like many of Stalin's other "yes" men, Budenny was promoted up the ranks and beyond his own capabilities, becoming deputy commissar for defense in 1940. His inability to adapt to modern warfare became apparent during the Great Patriotic War, when in one battle he attempted to lead, saber in hand, from the front—only this time on the top of a tank—as he had done in the old days of cavalry charges. When he was later recalled for his incompetence at the front, he was kept away from active command, although he continued to organize cavalry operations. When he died in 1973 he was accorded, as a recipient of the title Hero of the Soviet Union, the honor of being buried in the Kremlin Wall.

See also Babel, Isaac Emmanuilovich; Blyukher, Marshal Vasily Konstantinovich; Great Patriotic War; Tukhachevsky, Mikhail Nikolaevich

Further reading: Isaac Babel. *Red Cavalry.* Harmondsworth, UK: Penguin Books, 1994; Harold Shukman, ed. *Stalin's Generals.* London: Phoenix, 1997.

Bukharin, Nikolay Ivanovich (1888–1938)

*I*f one were called upon to single out a member of the Bolshevik leadership after the Russian Revolution, possessed of all the attributes of the romantic political hero—charm, good looks, humanity, eloquence, and the ability to be tough when necessary—one would probably settle on Nikolay Bukharin.

He was a charismatic figure of considerable intellect, as well as being preeminent outside the Soviet Union as a leading Bolshevik within the Comintern. Lenin himself had talked of Bukharin as "the darling of the Party." But equally, he also noted Bukharin's vulnerability, observing that he was like "soft wax on which any demagogue can inscribe whatever he likes." Indeed, Bukharin's more moderate economic policies made him a regular object of contempt among the hardline Bolsheviks, one of whom once jealously dubbed him "the Pushkin of NEP." But Bukharin's support for the New Economic Policy, and his particular brand of socialist humanism based on economic policies of cooperation and trust, although never fully developed, offered an alternative to the Stalinist economic system of coercion, for a while at least.

A photograph of Nikolay Bukharin released to the international press on the announcement of his forthcoming trial for treason, held in Moscow in 1938. Bukharin, a leading Soviet economic theoretician, was shot on 13 March.

Bukharin served the statutory revolutionary apprenticeship as an underground activist for the Russian Social Democrats while he was a student of economics at Moscow University. In 1906 he joined the Bolshevik faction. Arrested and sent to Siberia in 1911, he escaped and while traveling in Europe met and worked with Lenin, developing a close relationship with him despite their frequent differences over theory. Later Bukharin made his way to the United States, and in New York, having already worked on *Pravda* for Lenin in Europe, he took over the editorship of *Noviy Mir* (New World). There he worked alongside Trotsky, who was also in exile.

Returning to Russia after the revolution in February 1917, Bukharin soon became a major political player as a member of the Central Committee of the Communist Party. In 1918 Lenin gave him the editorship of *Pravda,* now established as the official organ of the Communist Party. He held this post, which gave him considerable influence over both official Party policy and propaganda, until 1929. By the beginning of the 1920s Bukharin had become a member of the Politburo and chairman of the executive committee of the Comintern. In the early 1920s he set his stamp as the major Bolshevik theoretician, publishing such works as *The Economy of the Transitional Period* (1920), *The ABC of Communism* (1921), and *The Theory of Historical Materialism* (1921).

During the power struggle after Lenin's death in 1924, Bukharin found it expedient to ally himself with Stalin on the right of the Party in opposition to those on the left—Leon Trotsky, Grigory Zinoviev, and Lev Kamenev—who were agitating for a program of rapid industrial change and for enforced agricultural collectivization. At the time, the demonic figure of Trotsky (as he was viewed by the opposition) seemed to pose the greater and more vocal threat as he and his supporters appeared ever more extreme in their campaign to achieve worldwide revolution. Bukharin and Stalin at this time were thus united in criticizing Trotsky's extremism and endorsing a more moderate line on industrialization. The pace of modernization should not be forced, in Bukharin's view, and he advocated a continuation of Lenin's New Economic Policy, which had as its foundation the traditional peasant economy. Bukharin believed that it was crucial to sustain the confidence and support of the peasantry by allowing them a modicum of initiative and free enterprise in keeping their own vegetable plots, in hiring labor, and in leasing land. It was their alliance with the proletariat of the city that had helped overthrow the tsars, and this relationship should not be undermined. Equally, the support of the proletariat in the cities should be maintained by allowing them continued access to peasant produce, as well as some consumer goods. In a moment of ill-judged enthusiasm, however, Bukharin even urged the peasantry to "enrich yourselves, accumulate, develop your economy," words that would later be thrown back at him during the collectivization program as having been tantamount to encouraging the greed of the richer "kulak" peasants.

By 1928 Bukharin was already beginning to see the appalling error of his support for Stalin. He was, as historian Robert Conquest observed, "yet another in the chain of supposedly intelligent men, from Lenin to Roosevelt, who did not understand Stalin's real nature until it was too late." By siding with Stalin against Trotsky, he had made it possible for Stalin to gain the ascendant and destroy inner-Party democracy to the point where there was no longer any balance in the Communist Party leadership. For, just as Lenin had warned before his death, Stalin had by now become firmly entrenched in his power base as secretary of the Communist Party. At last recognizing Stalin's unbridled ambition for what it was, Bukharin began referring in private to his erstwhile ally and colleague as "Genghis Khan."

In an attempt to counter the increasingly dictatorial control of Stalin, Bukharin now allied himself with the moderates in the Party, namely Aleksey Rykov and Mikhail Tomsky. He was still a staunch believer in Lenin's view that the peasants should not be alienated, that they should be allowed to grow into socialism, and that the period of economic transition should continue by allowing the NEP to be extended indefinitely. But Stalin by now had dramatically changed his own position on this issue. He no longer had any patience for such a soft approach to the peasantry (which he called "capitulationism"), and in a reversal of the earlier policies on which he had concurred with Bukharin, Stalin now adopted precisely the policy his old rival Trotsky advo-

cated, convinced that rapid economic growth was the only way to elevate the Soviet Union to its rightful position as a major industrial—and political—power. Such dramatic achievements, as the fulfillment of Stalin's vision of socialism in one country, could only come from cranking up the process of economic and social change to an unprecedented level and introducing the draconian measure of the enforced collectivization of the peasantry.

While Bukharin's was an eloquent voice, his support continued to dwindle throughout 1928 and 1929. He lacked the political muscle to oppose Stalin in any effective way; nor did he possess the subtle skills of Stalin's political maneuvering and intrigue, and in April 1929 he was subjected to a vitriolic attack by Stalin at the Central Committee Plenum, which in turn prompted a tirade of hostile articles in the press. His political marginalization was completed with his removal from the Comintern and his loss of the editorship of *Pravda.* In November Bukharin was expelled from the Politburo. Condemned for his "right deviation," which Stalin claimed sought to divide the Party and deflect its attention from the common purpose of building socialism, Bukharin came under enormous pressure to recant. The crushing of Bukharin's opposition, representing as it did the remaining vestiges of the political legacy of Lenin, marked the end of any notion of political debate and the beginning of the consolidation of Stalin's dictatorship.

By the 1930s, Bukharin, now broken politically, went through the motions of political recantation and reconciliation at the Seventeenth Party Congress in early 1934, where he praised Stalin as the "field marshal of the proletarian forces, the best of the best." Stalin responded to this act of penance by throwing him a few crumbs. He allowed him to work as editor of *Izvestiya* and also to participate in the drafting of the Stalin Constitution of 1936. Despite having an opportunity to become an

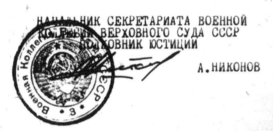

С П Р А В К А   **КОПИЯ**

Военная Коллегия
Верховного Суда
Союза ССР

09 ⟩ ___февраля___ 19 88 г.
№ СП-002/37

(21260). Москва, ул. Воровского, д. 15

Дело по обвинению Бухарина Николая Ивано-
вича, до ареста 27 февраля 1937 г. — Главный
редактор газеты "Известия", пересмотрено Пле-
нумом Верховного Суда СССР 4 февраля 1988 года.

Приговор Военной коллегии Верховного Суда
СССР от 13 марта 1938 года в отношении Бухарина Н.И. отменен и дело прекращено за отсут-
ствием в его действиях состава преступления.

Бухарин Николай Иванович реабилитирован
посмертно.

НАЧАЛЬНИК СЕКРЕТАРИАТА ВОЕННОЙ
КОЛЛЕГИИ ВЕРХОВНОГО СУДА СССР
ПОЛКОВНИК ЮСТИЦИИ

А.НИКОНОВ

The official certificate confirming the posthumous rehabilitation of Nikolay Bukharin, issued by the Soviet Supreme Court in 1988—fifty years after Bukharin was tried and executed on a string of trumped-up charges.

exile while on a trip to Paris in 1936, Bukharin could not stay away from his homeland and returned to the Soviet Union knowing full well that he was a marked man. Before leaving Paris, he perceptively commented to Menshevik émigrés that the driving force behind Stalin's behavior was his consuming jealousy of political rivals—"those who are in any way higher or better than he"—a fact born of his total inability to tolerate the presence of such people as a "perpetual reminder that he, Stalin, is not the first and the best."

After the show trial in August 1936 of Kamenev and Zinoviev, Stalin's other major political rivals, Bukharin was obliged to join the chorus of public outrage that condemned them and even expressed his pleasure at their summary execution. He did not have any compunction about denouncing others of his former supporters who were also rounded up. Like so many at this time, living in fear for their own lives and

the lives of their families, he found himself sucked into the hellish machine of the Great Terror as a collaborator. As historian Walter Laqueur has asserted, his "moral backbone" had been broken.

At a Party Plenum in February 1937 Bukharin's political future was debated, and a vote was taken to put him and his close ally Aleksey Rykov on trial. Meanwhile, living under virtual house arrest in his Kremlin apartment, Bukharin composed a personal testament, which he asked his wife to memorize. In it, he reiterated his loyalty to the state and looked toward the advent of a new and more honest leadership, expressing his hope that some time in the future the Soviet government would "disentangle the ghastly tissue of crimes which in these terrible days is spreading on a grand scale, burning up like a flame and choking the Party." In the letter, which was finally published in the Soviet Union in 1988, Bukharin talked of Stalin's weakness for adulation, commenting that "his revenge-fulness can be appeased only by huge doses of flattery laid on with a trowel."

Bukharin was arrested on 27 February by the NKVD, taken to the Lubyanka prison in Moscow, and charged with espionage and sabotage as a Trotskyist. He had already been dismissed from his job at *Izvestiya* and was now to suffer the political excommunication that he dreaded most—expulsion from the Communist Party and with it the lifeblood of Soviet politics. The NKVD spent the next year in careful preparation of Bukharin's trial, extracting the required confessions from primary witnesses and accomplices. At first Bukharin resisted making a formal confession, writing a deluge of impassioned pleas to Stalin from his cell in which he assured Stalin of his undying devotion and his willingness "to carry out any demand of yours without the least hesitation or reservations." Such was Bukharin's escalating state of nervous hysteria, verging on mental breakdown, that in June he finally capitulated when he realized the lives of his wife and baby son were increasingly in jeopardy. Having duly confessed, he now lived in the naive hope that Stalin would forgive him and that he would be sent into exile and not be subjected to a show trial. "Will Koba really put on a third medieval inquisition in front of the whole world?" he asked. Even now, in a desperate attempt to rekindle something of their former friendship (when Stalin had called him by the pet name Bukharchik), he adddressed Stalin in his letters by his familiar, prerevolutionary nickname of "Koba."

In March 1938 Bukharin was tried along with twenty other members of the Right opposition, including Genrikh Yagoda, Aleksey Rykov, and Nikolay Krestinsky, many of them the last remnants of the Bolshevik Old Guard. The catalog of their collective crimes was exhaustive and included espionage, conspiracy, sabotage, assassination on a grand scale—with Bukharin singled out as the mastermind (and separately

accused of plotting to kill Lenin in 1918). State Prosecutor Andrey Vyshinsky had a field day, reaching new heights of bombast in his description of Bukharin as "a treacherous, two-faced, whimpering, evil, nonentity who has been exposed . . . as a leader of a gang of spies, terrorists, and thieves, as instigator of assassination."

In court Bukharin, in a final, public demonstration of the moral strength he had once had and now had briefly regained, proved himself an eloquent match for the apoplectic Vyshinsky. He had no difficulty in exposing the absurdity of the accusations, and he did it with a mordant sarcasm and wit. He also contrived, in his use of heavily veiled Aesopian language that was often far too subtle for the literally minded prosecution, to take advantage of his cross-examination in court to direct his own accusations at Stalin for setting Russia on the road to ruin. As historian Robert C. Tucker observed, Bukharin did his best to turn the trial into an antitrial directed at Stalin himself, for "he [Bukharin] was . . . in a position to dramatize by his own self-immolation in the show trial what Stalin was doing to the party as earlier constituted."

Bukharin's ten-day trial ended on 12 March with his condemnation to death. Three days later he was shot. His wife was arrested soon after and sent into exile and then to the Gulag for eighteen months. Bukharin himself was not rehabilitated, as expected, in the 1950s with most other prominent victims of the purges because of renewed attacks made on him by prominent Stalinists. It was Mikhail Gorbachev who finally rehabilitated him in 1988.

Historians remain divided over the apparent naiveté of Bukharin's dealings with Stalin and question the almost childlike incredulity that he nursed to the end that Stalin should really wish to destroy him. This can be seen in a pathetic note sent to Stalin at the end of the trial, in which he asked: "Koba, why do you need me to die?" The writer Edvard Radzinsky, who has studied many of the forty-three letters Bukharin wrote to Stalin during his year in prison, argued that in finally settling on his own death as some kind of rationale for the trials, Bukharin was able to accept his fate as being a necessary sacrifice toward achieving "some great and bold political idea." It was a rationale arrived at by the mentally disorienting effects of intimidation, fear, and psychological torture, and some historians, Radzinsky in particular, are harsh in their condemnation of Bukharin's capitulation. Be that as it may, this rationale of accepting his death as the ultimate, romantic sacrifice of the true revolutionary enabled Bukharin to transcend what would otherwise be seen as his abject cowardice.

In her memoirs, Bukharin's widow, Anna Larina, described her husband as seeking his salvation only in Stalin, his accuser, and Stalin as exploiting this gullibility. She also described Bukharin's emotionalism and sensitivity, his impetuousness, and his "great passion and unbridled spirit, whose potential for revolutionary work required dynamics, action." She argued that he was "obsessed with the idea of humanizing society by means of a revolutionary transformation." The émigré writer Ilya Ehrenburg also endorsed the energy of Bukharin's vision, asserting that "he wanted to remake life because he loved it." While much of Bukharin's economic policy may well have been flawed in that it was too embryonic, his desire to develop a form of "communism with a human face" was a passionate attempt at remaking the lives of the Russian people, who had already suffered so much.

See also Collectivization; Five-Year Plans; The Great Terror; Kamenev, Lev; Rykov, Aleksey; "Socialism in One Country"; Trotsky, Leon; Yagoda, Genrikh; Zinoviev, Grigory

Further reading: Stephen F. Cohen. *Bukharin and the Bolshevik Revolution: A Political Biography, 1988–1938.* Oxford: Oxford University Press, 1980; Anna Larina. *This I Cannot Forget.* London: Hutchinson, 1993; Edvard Radzinksy. *Stalin.* London: Sceptre, 1997.

Bulgakov, Mikhail Afanasevich (1891–1940)

Despite having written one of Stalin's favorite plays, *The Days of the Turbins* (1926), which the Great Leader saw several times at the Moscow Arts Theater, the writer and playwright Mikhail Bulgakov fell foul of the authorities in the 1920s and saw most of his works banned under Stalin.

Born into an educated, middle-class family in Kiev, Bulgakov trained as a doctor and worked as a field medic during the civil war. Eventually, like the writer Anton Chekhov, he abandoned medicine for literature. In 1921 Bulgakov considered secretly leaving the Soviet Union from the Black Sea by boat, only to abort his plans and settle in Moscow to pursue a career as a full-time writer. For several years he struggled to scratch a living as a writer and journalist, later turning his hand to writing plays. His first novel, *The White Guard* (1924), was heavily criticized for its sympathetic portrayal of the anti-Bolshevik Whites at the time of the 1917 Revolution. While he successfully reworked this into the play *The Days of the Turbins,* Bulgakov's other published works and those of his plays that were staged (such as *Zoyka's Apartment* [1926] and *The Crimson Island* [1928]) were quickly denounced by the authorities, despite their success with audiences, because of their overt and scathing satire of Communist society. By 1929 Bulgakov, along with many other writers, cultivated the literary genre of silence. In secret he continued work on his masterpiece (begun in 1928), the fantasy satire *The Master and Margarita,* a novel in which many have seen in the central character of the Devil (named Woland) significant allusions to Stalin himself.

By 1930, with one after another of his works being rejected out of hand and unable to earn a living, Bulgakov finally resorted to desperate measures. He wrote a personal letter to the Soviet government in

April of that year, begging to be allowed to leave the country or, failing that, to be given employment. At worst he asked the government "to act towards me as it sees fit" because at present he was "confronted by poverty, homelessness, and imminent death." However, the expected arrest in response to this letter did not come. Three weeks later Bulgakov received a personal telephone call from Stalin, asking him where he would like to work. Bulgakov responded that he would like to be allowed to work again for the Moscow Arts Theater, with which he had had a long association. Not long after, he was taken on as an assistant director there and was commissioned to write a play for them. However, he further endangered his tenuous position by producing *Molière*, a thinly veiled parody of Stalinist Russia based on the life of the French writer, in which he described the anguish of a playwright whose work was constantly banned by the king for failing to conform ideologically. *Molière* was in rehearsal on and off until its premiere in February 1936. Six performances later, it was banned.

In 1939, in a further attempt to rehabilitate himself and get his work published, Bulgakov agreed to write a play about Stalin for the Moscow Arts Theater, to be staged on the occasion of Stalin's sixtieth birthday celebration (it is possible that the suggestion came from Stalin himself). Bulgakov chose a subject that was sure to be approved—Stalin's early revolutionary activities in Batum, at a time when he was using the alias Koba. The play was passed by the censors and accepted for production. Bulgakov set out to research additional material in Batum, only to be told as he was literally boarding the train that the play had been rejected by Stalin and that he must return. This final rejection in the long game of cat and mouse that Stalin had played with him, in addition to the unrelenting moral dilemma he found himself in, aggravated Bulgakov's already poor health, and

he died not long after. His recognition as a major talent of his generation was a long time in coming. *The Master and Margarita* was not published in Russia until the mid-1960s and then only in an expurgated version. The full version finally appeared in 1973.

See also Batum; Pasternak, Boris; Socialist Realism; Zamyatin, Evgeny

Further reading: Mikhail Bulgakov. *Manuscripts Don't Burn: A Life in Diaries and Letters,* compiled by J. A. E. Curtis. London: Bloomsbury, 1991; Mikhail Bulgakov. *The Master and Margarita.* London: Collins and Harvill Press, 1967; A. Colin Wright. *Mikhail Bulgakov: Life and Interpretations.* Toronto: University of Toronto Press, 1978.

Bulganin, Marshal Nikolay Aleksandrovich (1895–1975)

One of the eight-man Presidium that formed Stalin's close entourage during his final years, Nikolay Bulganin rose to international prominence in the postwar years. Like many young revolutionaries, he had come from the ranks of the urban factory workers. On joining the Communist Party after the revolution, he served the Party assiduously, working for the secret police (the Cheka) and on one occasion as head of a detachment at Yaroslavl charged with organizing the first Bolshevik-sanctioned execution of insurgents there, which included the shooting of fifty-seven officers.

After many years in public service as a leading bureaucrat (as mayor of Moscow he helped plan the construction of the Moscow Metro), Bulganin became one of Stalin's political commissars during the Great Patriotic War and rose to prominence, replacing Marshal Klimenty Voroshilov on the Committee for State Defense in 1944. He was made a marshal of the Soviet Union in 1945 and took over from Stalin as minister of defense in 1946. In 1947 he became deputy premier and in 1948 a full member of the Politburo. In the latter days of Stalin's rule Bulganin was one of a handful of top Party officials allowed access to the aging leader, who was now becoming more and more cloistered from public view. Along with Georgy Malenkov, Lavrenty Beria, and Nikita Khrushchev, Bulganin would spend evenings drinking and dining at Stalin's behest at his dacha at Kuntsevo, an uneasy state of affairs of which they were all equally nervous and upon which Bulganin himself remarked, "When you are invited to Stalin's, you can never be sure you will get back home." But survive he did. In fact, Bulganin dined at Kuntsevo the night before Stalin's death and went on to become Khrushchev's right-hand man as premier of the Soviet Union in 1955. He was later peremptorily stripped of his status for aligning himself with a group that tried to oust Khrushchev in 1957. Relegated to a job as a minor bureaucrat in the state bank, Bulganin died in obscurity.

See also Cheka; Khrushchev, Nikita; Politburo; Stalin: Dachas of

C

Cheka

This organization was set up originally in December 1917 under Felix Dzerzhinsky. Its name is an abbreviated version of the acronym Vecheka (All-Russian Extraordinary Commission for Combating Counterrevolution and Sabotage); its objective, as the name suggests, was to combat any opposition to the Bolshevik government and to investigate acts of anarchy, such as looting and black-marketeering, that were rife during the early months after the revolution.

Before long, as the scourge of all enemies of the state, the Cheka became a law unto itself. Its activities escalated unchecked, and in the words of Solzhenitsyn, it evolved into "the only punitive organ in human history that combined in one set of hands investigation, arrest, interrogation, prosecution, trial, and execution of the *verdict*." During its existence, the Cheka adopted and perfected all the sinister techniques of terror and intimidation that would be passed down by the Soviet secret police in its later incarnations, as the GPU (1922), the OGPU (1923) and later Stalin's infamous NKVD (1934). After Stalin's death, the Soviet secret police finally acquired its most familiar acronym, the KGB (1954).

Many of Stalin's later henchmen, such as Nikolay Bulganin and Genrikh Yagoda, as well as Stalin himself, learned the art of political repression with the Cheka. While in Tsaritsyn in southern Russia, Stalin, as director general of food supplies during the civil war, had organized branches of the Cheka to undertake the rounding up and execution of anti-Bolsheviks. When a special department of the Cheka was set up in 1919, responsible for maintaining security in the Red Army and monitoring counterespionage and countersubversion activities, it was ordered to report directly to Stalin. One of the Cheka's most notorious exploits was the brutal suppression of the rebellion at the Kronstadt naval base in 1921; hundreds of the rebels were shot.

The Cheka also pioneered the first corrective labor camps, which were set up in August 1918. By 1922 they housed 85,000 prisoners. Having fulfilled its objectives, the Cheka was replaced in 1922 by the GPU. In the face of the horrors later committed during Stalin's political purges by the OGPU and NKVD, it is easy to forget that in the years of Lenin's leadership the Cheka itself was probably responsible for up to 200,000 executions. For the brief period of its existence, as the writer Ilya Ehrenburg recalls, "the two syllables [Che-ka]" became so "productive of fear and emotion in any citizen who had lived through the years of the revolution" that they were never to be forgotten.

See also Beria, Lavrenty; Civil War; Ezhov, Nikolay; The Great Terror; Lenin, Vladimir; NKVD; Russian Revolution of 1917; Yagoda, Genrikh

Further reading: George Leggett. *The Cheka: Lenin's Political Police.* Oxford: Clarendon Press, 1981.

China

During the years of turmoil in China that followed the nationalist revolt of 1911–1912, the Soviets provided considerable military support to the Nationalists under Chiang Kai-shek, while at the same time committing the growing Chinese Communist movement under the auspices of the Comintern, to maintaining an uneasy united front until reunification of the country had been achieved. Stalin's attitude to Soviet support for the Nationalists was utterly pragmatic, he took the view that "they have to be utilized to the end, squeezed out like a lemon and then thrown away." But tensions grew between Communist and Nationalist forces in China, and, after Chiang Kai-shek's army was victorious in 1927, a bloodbath was unleashed against the Chinese Communists. The country was plunged into a bitter internecine struggle for the next ten years, until this was disrupted by war with Japan.

Stalin continued to take an ambivalent line with the Chinese Communists. He was intent on waiting to see if they would prove themselves as an international power under the leadership of Mao Zedong (who had been elected leader of the Chinese Communist Party in 1935). In many ways a divided China was a more preferable option to Stalin, and he continued to hope for Nationalist dominance, with the Communists forced to take a secondary role. He doubted the ability of Maoist peasant power to defeat Chiang Kai-shek and was even more suspicious of the potential threat from China as a rival Communist power if they did so. Thus, he signed a treaty of friendship with Chiang Kai-shek in August 1945, gaining Chiang's endorsement of the territorial concessions in the Far East that he had demanded of the Allies in return for joining in the war against Japan.

In the end Stalin failed to take into account the ability of Mao's Communist forces to rout the Nationalists under his charismatic leadership, a fact that rapidly became apparent with the brutal revival of civil war in China in 1946. With Mao seizing power in 1949, Stalin was now having to contemplate the possibility of another Communist leader to rival him in the size of his power base, which in China approached half a billion people. And so by the end of 1949, with the proclamation of the People's Republic of China on 1 October, Stalin finally found himself obliged to strike a deal with Mao Zedong.

Mao, in turn, sensed that Stalin was dubious of Chinese loyalty as a mere satellite to Moscow and made the journey to the Soviet Union to disabuse him of the suspicion that "after the victory of the revolution he [Stalin] next suspected China of being a Yugoslavia, and that I would become a second Tito." The Chinese leader arrived in Moscow in December and, after going through the formalities of lauding Stalin on the occasion of his seventieth birthday, set about the serious business of his visit. In an atmosphere of deep-seated antipathy and mistrust, the two leaders spent the next two months haggling over their future relationship and the balance of Communist power in the Far East. In February 1950 they signed a Treaty of Friendship, Alliance and Mutual Assistance,—i.e., military assistance—in the event of any act of aggression from Japan. More important, as far as Mao was concerned, the Soviets promised economic aid, backed up by a loan to China of $300 million, and the cession of Soviet railroad holdings in Manchuria and its base at Port Arthur. Stalin had refused point blank to entrust the Chinese Communists with the atomic bomb. Also, the Chinese were not particularly confident about the lengths to which Stalin's support could be stretched—a fear that was justified when he later failed to make a large-scale commitment of troops to end the stalemate of the war in Korea.

Stalin continued to support the Chinese Communists in the last years of his life through the supply of propaganda material, industrial equipment, and other technical assistance. Military advisers also helped the Chinese reorganize their armed forces along Soviet lines. When Stalin died in 1953, the Chinese themselves were just embarking on an ambitious equivalent of the Soviet Five-Year Plans, during which aid and advice from the Soviet Union would prove to be of considerable value. Within a few years Stalin's successor, Nikita Khrushchev, would find himself having to face in China an equally truculent and confrontational Communist superpower, now itself in the grips of an all-consuming personality cult to rival that of Stalin.

See also Cult of the Personality; Korean War; Manchuria

Further reading: Dmitri Volkogonov. *The Rise and Fall of the Soviet Empire: Political Leaders from Lenin to Gorbachev.* London: HarperCollins, 1998.

Churchill, Winston
See "The Big Three."

Cinema

Of all the powerful and emotive propaganda tools at the disposal of the Bolsheviks for generating enthusiasm for the revolution among the Russian Empire's 160 million largely illiterate people, the cinema was the most potent. Right from the early days of the *agitki*—the special agitprop trains that toured Russia showing crude propaganda films to the rural population—Russian filmmakers grasped hold

of the new medium with enthusiasm and made it their own. But the great irony of the history of Soviet filmmaking is that many of the films of its finest exponents were in their time far greater successes outside Russia—on the art-house circuit of the free-thinking, liberal West—than on their own home territory of the ideologically converted.

Lenin had not been slow to recognize the potential of film, observing that "of all the arts for us the most important is cinema," a view that Leon Trotsky reiterated by describing it as "an instrument which we must secure at all costs." Many of the pioneers of Soviet filmmaking would learn their cinematic skills primarily as propagandists in these early years. During the 1920s, several promising young directors came under the influence of Lev Kuleshov, the father figure of Soviet cinema and a major teacher and theorist. In 1924 Soviet filmmaking was organized under the auspices of a state enterprise, Sovkino, and soon audiences were witnessing the exciting experimental work of such directors as Vsevolod Pudovkin, Dziga Vertov, Aleksandr Dovzhenko, and Sergey Eisenstein. All of them were in various ways influenced by the photomontage techniques of the Constructivist and Futurist movements in avantgarde art, a style pioneered in poster art and collages by Vladimir Mayakovsky, Aleksander Rodchenko, and Vladimir Tatlin.

There was, however, considerable debate among filmmakers during the early 1920s on the true role of film—either primarily as the vehicle for revolutionary propaganda and documentary work or as a popular art form providing entertainment in a fictionalized way. As early as 1924 Stalin himself had no doubts that "cinema is the most important means of mass agitation. We must take it into our hands." The influences of the documentary approach in Soviet filmmaking can be seen in some of the great classics of the silent cinema from the golden age of Soviet filmmaking, such as Eisenstein's *Strike*

(1924) and *Battleship Potemkin* (1925), Pudovkin's *Mother* (1926), Dovzhenko's *Arsenal* (1929), Vertov's *Man with a Movie Camera* (1929). Vertov, in particular, took an extreme position on the role of the new art form: "Only documentary facts! No illusions! Down with the actor and scenery! Long live the film of actuality!" Although these four major directors were all later criticized for elements of formalism in their films and for producing counterrevolutionary work, and their freedom to experiment creatively was cut short in the Soviet Union, their continuing influence on later generations of filmmakers, in terms of composition, use of light and shadow, and editing techniques, remains profound.

As far as the Soviet public was concerned, however, the emphasis on innovative technique rather than convincing story line often resulted in more experimental films being less popular than films such as Dovzhenko's *Earth* (1930), which, with its more conventional storyline depicting the turmoil of collectivization in Ukraine, reached its audience on a more personal level. The traditional fare produced by Hollywood still pulled in large audiences. A typical instance of this is the fact that Eisenstein's succès d'estime, the 1926 classic *Battleship Potemkin,* was actually taken out of circulation in Moscow after a relatively short run in favor of the swashbuckling exploits of *Robin Hood* in Douglas Fairbanks's 1922 Hollywood version. For all the time that the populist product from Hollywood was available, audiences tended to eschew their own indigenous, revolutionary cinema in favor of more escapist fare. This element of choice was soon decisively taken from them by Stalin.

In 1929 Stalin reorganized the Soviet film industry under a new unifying body, Soyuzkino, in order to ensure the dictatorship of socialist realism in filmmaking. As in all the other arts, cinema became subject to rigorous censorship and was soon infected with the disease of unbending political cor-

rectness. Many leading filmmakers, such as Eisenstein, found compromise impossible during the grim 1930s and stopped working altogether. The industry as a whole went into a tragic and inevitable decline in terms of artistic merit. Those directors who struggled to continue were forced to submit detailed scripts for censorship before filming even began. They found themselves increasingly having to produce the same uniform visual fodder required elsewhere of painters and sculptors.

The American film magnate Sam Goldwyn once famously remarked that "pictures are for entertainment; messages should be delivered by Western Union." The analogy could be applied equally to cinema under Stalin, where the element of entertainment was supplied by stilted parodies of Hollywood musicals and melodramas, and where increasingly the medium was overtaken by the stridency of its message. "Talkies" were slow to be adopted in Russian cinema, and it was the mid-1930s before silent films were finally superseded by sound. By this time, the Soviet Union had found its own answer to Hollywood's Fred Astaire and Ginger Rogers movies in a series of all-singing, all-dancing socialist extravaganzas, epitomized by the work of two directors: Ivan Piriev's 1939 *Tractor Drivers* (boy meets girl on the collective farm) and his 1950 *Cossacks of the Kuban,* and Grigory Aleksandrov's 1940 *Bright Path* (a Stakhanovite girl finds that work, not love, is the answer) and *Volga Volga* (see below). Films such as these glorified physical labor on the farm and in industry as the pinnacle of human achievement, and tried to convince the Soviet population that work was the path to both collective and individual happiness.

Stalin loved the cinema and took a personal interest in filmmaking. Despite the fact that there was an official minister for cinema, Ivan Bolshakov to perform this function, Stalin himself vetted all new scenarios and saw the finished films in his private projection room at the Kremlin. Here he was in the habit of watching films late into the night, along with, at his insistence, the members of the Politburo, adding to their feelings of discomfiture by sitting alone, several rows behind them. His tastes were, however, limited and these, in turn, severely circumscribed the kind of films he would pass for public consumption. While secretly nursing a love for American Westerns and Tarzan films, he had a particular predilection for musicals and ordered endless private showings of his handful of favorites, such as Julien Duvivier's *The Great Waltz* (1938) about the Strauss family. He also enjoyed the homegrown version of the Hollywood musical in Grigori Aleksandrov's *The Jolly Fellows* (1934) and *Circus* (1936), both of which, try as they might, were no match for the Hollywood product, the latter featuring a bathetic "Song of the Motherland," which contained the immortal lines "I know of no other country/ Where a man so freely breathes"—this at a time when the country was in the grips of the Great Terror. It was during this period, in particular, that Soviet filmmakers were under particular duress to produce Cinderella stories, depicting the fairy-tale transformation of life under socialism, thus reinforcing Stalin's own slogan that "life has become better, life has become merrier." And what better way to do this than to harness that reliable old standby, the musical comedy? After all, Busby Berkeley was doing the same in the United States, producing "feel-good" musicals that deflected people's misery away from the hardships of the Great Depression. Likewise, in the Soviet Union people needed to occasionally forget the harsh realities of communal living, long working hours, food shortages, and increasing political repression.

The musical was a genre that Stalin found deeply reassuring and comforting in his later years, as he became increasingly isolated and reclusive in his habits. His all-time favorite, of which he never tired and which he saw as many as 100 times, was

A still from the film **Lenin** *in 1918 circulated spuriously as a photograph of Stalin and Felix Dzerzhinsky, head of the Cheka. Directed by Mikhail Romm in 1939, it featured Michael Gelovani (left) as Stalin.*

Grigory Aleksandrov's musical comedy *Volga Volga* (1938). Such was his passion for the film that Stalin even presented a copy of it to President Roosevelt during the Great Patriotic War. Film historian Alexander Birkos related that the film was later used by the U.S. Army language school in its teaching of Russian as an exemplar of current colloquial speech because of its "rich, sparkling dialog"! The story, a humorous tale about the rivalry between groups of amateur folk singers racing down the River Volga to perform at a folk festival in Moscow, featured many nonprofessional performers and was hugely popular with the public. It also featured one of the great heroines of Soviet cinema at this time, actress Lyubov Orlova, who performed the film's theme song, "Song of the Volga." Such was the success of the socialist musical that even the Great Patriotic War was transformed into musical melodrama with Ivan Pyriev's *At 6 P.M. after the War,* in which two soldiers meet up with their sweethearts in Moscow the day peace breaks out. It was a Stalin Prize winner in 1944.

On the eve of the Great Patriotic War, ambitious biopics, such as Eisenstein's *Alexander Nevsky* (1938) and Vladimir Petrov's two-part *Peter the Great* (1937), satisfied Stalin's demand for inspirational films that celebrated the military triumphs of great Russian historical figures. The forerunner of such films had been Georgy and Sergey Vasiliev's *Chapaev* (1934) about a legendary civil war soldier. Now filmmakers also drew upon the military careers of figures such as the great Napoleonic war generals Aleksander Suvorov and Mikhail Kutuzov and the Ukrainian folk hero Bogdan Khmelnitsky, all of whom had routed the enemy from Russian soil. But the one figure promoted above all others was Stalin's personal hero, Ivan the Terrible, the subject of Eisenstein's 1945 film.

By the 1930s, Stalin was basking in the glow of a huge personality cult that promoted him in heroic mode in many films, beginning with Grigory Kozintsev and Leonid Trauberg's *The Vyborg Side* (1938), set at the time of the revolution. In this film Stalin was played by the Georgian actor Mikhail Gelovani, who soon established a monopoly on the role and was to portray the leader in another twenty films.

The trend for portraying both Lenin and Stalin on film was also set in two fine films about Lenin by Mikhail Romm—*Lenin in October* (1937) and *Lenin in 1918* (1939). In the latter Stalin's role as political heir to Lenin had been aggrandized to a degree that set the benchmark for all subsequent cinematic representations. This came at a time when the history books were also rewriting Stalin's role in the days of the revolution and civil war and when even official photographs were being doctored. In *The Defence of Tsaritsyn* (made in 1942 by Georgy and Sergey Vasiliev), Stalin is glorified as a military genius who saves the city (which in 1926 was rechristened Stalingrad) from destruction by the Whites during the civil war.

The war proved to be a particularly fertile period for laudatory films about Stalin as a war leader, producing a crop of blockbusters celebrating his military role. The Georgian director Mikhail Chiaureli (a protégé of the Georgian head of the NKVD, Lavrenty Beria) was to find particular favor with Stalin for his cinematic promotion of the leader to godlike status, first in *The Vow* (a Stalin Prize winner in 1946)—in which he famously depicted Stalin making a solemn vow to carry the torch of the revolution at Lenin's lying-in-state—and in 1950 for his ambitious two-part film *The Fall of Berlin.* In both this and Vladimir Petrov's equally monumental, big-budget film *The Battle of Stalingrad* (1949; in two parts), a considerable effort was made to emphasize Stalin's steely composure in contrast to the neuroses of Hitler and the curmudgeonly behavior of Churchill. It was Chiaureli who again appeared in the last piece of cinematic sycophancy made before Stalin's death, in *Unforgettable 1919* (1952), in which Stalin once more dominated the scene, this time at the defense of Petrograd in 1919.

Soviet cinema waited until the 1980s era of glasnost for the emergence of a film director brave enough to tackle the legacy of Stalin. Georgian director Tenghiz Abuladze's 1984 film *Repentance* (not released until 1986 and made with the backing of Georgian Communist Party leader Edvard Shevardnadze) exposed the grotesque absurdities of the totalitarianism of Stalinist Russia. The film is a surreal parody of Stalin and his regime, written as an allegorical fantasy about a dictatorial town mayor in Georgia, Stalin's home state, where many still revere his name.

See also Eisenstein, Sergey; Ivan the Terrible; Socialist Realism; Stalin: Private Life of

Further reading: Alexander S. Birkos. *Soviet Cinema*. Hamden, CT: Archon Books, 1976; Jay Leyda. *Kino: A History of the Russian and Soviet Film*. London: George Allen and Unwin, 1973; R. Taylor and D. Spring, eds. *Stalinism and Soviet Cinema*. London: Routledge, 1993.

Civil War (1918–1920)

The violence and anarchy of the days after the Russian Revolution, when the Bolsheviks were seeking to assert their political control, resulted in a bitter conflict between them and various political factions between 1918 and 1920 that brought with it tales of appalling atrocities—rape, murder, and looting—on both sides.

It took a while for anti-Bolshevik elements to regroup themselves after the upheavals of 1917, but by the summer of 1918 groups on both the left and the right combined into a volunteer army of opposition of sorts. Their fighting forces were composed of such disparate political elements as supporters of the tsar (including many of the former officer class who wanted to continue the war against Germany), peasant anarchists, socialist revolutionaries, and cadets from the Constituent Assembly of the provisional government, which Lenin had dissolved. They were joined by various national and ethnic groups with their own reasons for rejecting the Bolshevik government, in particular, Cossacks (the traditionally loyal elite tsarist troops), as well as Tatars, Bashkirs, Poles, and Ukrainians.

When the Stalinist reinterpretation of Soviet history went into overdrive in the 1930s, Stalin's role in the civil war was greatly exaggerated, when in reality much of the real credit for Bolshevik military success belonged to Leon Trotsky, who, as commissar for war, had hastily created a new Red Army out of the tattered and demoralized elements of the old tsarist one, swelled by the ranks of eager but untrained Bolshevik supporters. He reorganized the army's structure and its methods of supply.

In the face of Lenin's misgivings and outright opposition from Stalin, he had also argued for the necessity for skilled officers to lead this motley rabble of workers, peasants, and conscripts. After intiating a radical shake-up of the old tsarist officer corps, he introduced up to 40,000 of them into the Red Army as military experts. Many of these former tsarist officers had by now come over to the Bolsheviks, but nevertheless were closely watched by Communist commissars.

In May 1919 Stalin was sent by Lenin to organize the defense of Petrograd against the threat from the northwestern army of the Whites. Here he commandeered the labor of all able-bodied men to build defenses and train for conflict. He was soon asking Lenin for reinforcements, not against the threat from the Whites but from attack launched by rebellious officers at two forts at the Kronstadt naval base who had come out in support of them. The defeat of this relatively minor insurrection gave Stalin the excuse to report back to Lenin that he had "unearthed a big conspiracy in the Kronstadt area" and to justify the launching of a local reign of terror, arrest, and execution, which involved not just the extermination of sixty-seven officers at Kronstadt but many others supposedly in sympathy with them.

Later that summer, Lenin found a more important role for Stalin when White Cossack armies were attempting to capture the strategic city of Tsaritsyn in the south. Stalin was given the post of director general of food supplies and sent to Tsaritsyn with his own personal entourage to deal with a desperate provisioning crisis. He was given unrestricted powers to seize grain and other foodstuffs produced in the Volga and North Caucasus and send them to Red Army troops and the starving populations of Petrograd and Moscow. But Stalin, who performed his assigned task with all the zeal of an already well-trained bureaucrat, was not satisfied in this purely administrative role and sought once more to act the part of secret policeman by involving himself in the local activities of the Cheka in rounding up and executing black marketeers and counterrevolutionaries of all colors.

He also grasped with relish an opportunity to override the authority of Trotsky by refusing to cooperate with his ex-tsarist military experts. Instead, he appointed his old revolutionary crony Klimenty Voroshilov from the North Caucasus military district to a key command at Tsaritsyn and insisted to Lenin that "I must have military powers . . . [and] will remove those army commanders and commissars who are ruining things." Stalin now gave Voroshilov charge of the Third and Fifth Armies on the Tsaritsyn front and even encouraged acts of insubordination against Trotsky's officers.

Trotsky was incensed by Stalin's actions and insisted on his recall to Moscow. Lenin acquiesced and tried to defuse the growing antipathy between Stalin and Trotsky by appointing Stalin to the Revolutionary War Council. The feud between them would continue, with Stalin jealous of Trotsky's continuing ascendancy and seeking to undermine his position at every opportunity. He did so by embarking on a plan to remove the circle of supporters surrounding Trotsky one by one until he became a political pariah.

See also Lenin, Vladimir; Red Army; Russian Revolution of 1917; Trotsky, Leon; Voroshilov, Klimenty

Further reading: W. Bruce Lincoln. *Red Victory: The Russian Civil War.* New York: Simon & Schuster, 1989.

Cold War

*T*he latter years of Stalin's rule, 1946–1953, marked the disintegration of the wartime alliance of "The Big Three" and the onset of the Cold War, an undeclared war of international brinkmanship between Communist Eastern Europe and the Western powers. The seeds of this tension had originated with the Soviet Union's considerable territorial gains at the end of World War II. Winston Churchill, though not the first to allude to an "iron curtain" separating the Communist East from the democratic West, had warned of the threat in March 1946, not long after Stalin had made an election address to the Supreme Soviet in which he endorsed an ambitious industrial and technological program to protect Soviet interests against all eventualities—a clear allusion to the forthcoming race to develop nuclear weapons and to the possibility of Russia's launching another war against Western imperialism and capitalism.

The first warning signs had come with the division of Germany by the Allies at the end of the war. Stalin had sought to keep his troops for as long as possible in occupied Germany in order to enforce his moral and legal right to war reparations in the form of German industrial plants, which were dismantled and transported back to the Soviet Union. German craftsmen and scientists were also coerced into taking their expertise there.

In 1947–1948, with the Americans providing economic aid under the Marshall Plan to the western and southern European countries ravaged by war, the Soviets retaliated by setting up the Cominform to promote the activities of European Communist parties and the Communist regimes of Soviet satellite countries in Eastern Europe. By 1947 there was no doubting the change in the political climate, as the American presidential adviser, Bernard Baruch, famously remarked in April: "Let us not be deceived—we are today in the midst of a cold war." The Americans were now beginning to look upon the Soviet Union as a real menace to world freedom, and the fear of total, nuclear war prompted President Truman to concentrate American postwar efforts on stemming the advance of communism.

The following year, the Soviet blockade of Berlin through which Stalin sought to force the Allies to negotiate total Soviet domination of a weakened Germany resulted in a mass airlift of essential food and other supplies by American B-52 bombers. They flew in 45,000 tons of supplies daily, and in May Stalin was forced to abandon his blockade. Germany was, nevertheless, now formally divided into eastern and western divisions, thus further extending Soviet influence in Europe. In retaliation the Western allies formed the North Atlantic Treaty Organization (NATO), and attention now shifted to the growing Communist influence in China and North Korea.

Much of the atmosphere of confrontation ·in the postwar years was a bluff by Stalin to disguise the fact that the Soviet Union, as yet, had neither the nuclear capacity nor the will to take on the United States militarily but was determined to be seen as though it could and would. Stalin's strategy served its purpose in unnerving the Americans to such a degree that they started their own internal witch-hunt for Communist spies and traitors during the McCarthy era of 1950–1954. By this time Stalin had turned the postwar atmosphere of political nerves into a diplomatic game of "aggravated relations," as his foreign minister Vyacheslav Molotov would describe it, forever pushing the Americans and their allies to a prescribed limit from which he would then retreat, such as in the Korean War. The atmosphere of political tension was relaxed a little after the death of Stalin, only to be resumed with renewed intensity during the period from 1958 to 1962, by which time the Soviet Union had accumulated a considerable and deadly arsenal of nuclear weapons.

See also Atomic Bomb; Korean War; United Nations

Further reading: Taylor Downing and Jeremy Isaacs. *The Cold War: For 45 Years the World Held Its Breath.* New York and London: Bantam, 1998; David Holloway. *Stalin and the Bomb: The Soviet Union and Atomic Energy.* New Haven, CT: Yale University Press, 1994; Vojtech Mastny. *Russia's Road to the Cold War.* New York: Columbia University Press, 1979.

Collectivization

History has taught many politicians and would-be revolutionaries that the key to social control and political power is the control of the food supply. Stalin himself said as much in inaugurating collectivization, when he asserted that "the struggle for bread is the struggle for socialism." The collectivization of the Russian peasantry into efficient, modern-day communes with mechanized machinery originally had been looked upon by the Bolsheviks as something that could be achieved only through gradual change and patient example, as part of the natural progression toward the new socialist society. But under Stalin this policy was overturned. A process of draconian agricultural change began, involving a major social upheaval in the countryside, which developed into not just a struggle but an all-out war on the Russian peasantry, with its major objective being the complete annihilation of the kulaks, a particular class of peasants.

After the Revolution of 1917, the Bolsheviks passed a decree abolishing private ownership of land and redistributing former crown and landed property among the peasantry, mindful of the fact, no doubt, that because it was only fifty-six years since the peasants had been liberated from the yoke of serfdom, they had barely had the time to enjoy the fruits of their own newly acquired plots of land. Indeed, Lenin recognized that without such concessions the Bolsheviks would probably never earn the long-term support of the peasantry for the revolution. Accepting that the creation of agricultural cooperatives of peasants would take time, Lenin, nevertheless, initiated plans for the nationalization of land and the creation of *kolkhozy* (collectively run farms)

Russian peasants stand in line to join one of the collective farms instituted under Stalin in late 1929. This orderly, sanitized image belies the true chaos and violence of this traumatic upheaval in the countryside.

and *sovkhozy* (state-run farms), modeled after the traditional Russian village council, the *mir* (or *obshchina*), a utopian interpretation dating back to the Slavophile movement of the 1830s. It was a concept that had been made much of by the populist movement of the 1860s and 1870s, when idealistic young radicals had seen this body as the prototype for a future socialist society of peace and harmony. The Bolsheviks in turn had developed the concept further, seeking to modify and extend the traditional rural principles of profit sharing and communal labor, but now on a national scale.

Unfortunately, the use of gentle persuasion in matters regarding the Russian peasantry was quickly abandoned by the Bolsheviks during the chaotic and hungry years after the revolution and the subsequent civil war. Food supplies were insufficient to meet the demands of the rapidly growing industrial populations of the big cities and the military, and the Russian peasants now found themselves the target of aggressive requisitioning of grain and livestock by military detachments. This period between 1918 and 1921 became known as the era of war communism. The requisitioning came at a time when the peasants themselves had barely enough food on which to subsist, and it led to unrest, riots, and eventually a famine during 1920–1921 that would have seen a death toll even higher than 5 million had it not been for a concerted international program of famine relief. It is little wonder then that by 1921 many of the peasants looked upon the Bolsheviks as being as bad as, if not worse than, their former masters.

The frequently violent response by the Russian peasantry to grain requisitioning and the appropriation of their property by the state carried on sporadically throughout the early 1920s. The Soviet government's economic policy reinforced many deep-seated hostilities and traditionally held

1933. By June 1929, one million peasant households had joined 57,000 collectives, representing only 3–4 percent of the total population. Still not enough grain was being produced and as much as 250,000 tons of grain had to be imported to satisfy demand, and food rationing was being introduced. In July, a government directive on grain procurement made compulsory quotas legally binding, and, as the process was cranked up, it bore all the hallmarks of a return to the savagery of war communism. By the end of 1929 grain requisitioning had exceeded that of the previous year by 50 percent. Such was the resentment, that peasants felt that even in prison they would get a daily ration of 200 grams of bread, which was more than they often got on the collective farm.

As the pressure increased, the number of peasants joining *kolkhozy* went up from 4 to 21 percent by January 1930. By now Stalin had already grandly announced in his famous 7 November 1929 article in *Pravda* the "Great Turning Point" (written to mark the twelfth anniversary of the revolution), that a mass voluntary revolution was now taking place in the countryside that would result in the transformation of Soviet society. As always, the terminology used was that applied to military offensives, in this case a war against the rural capitalist. The Soviet Union was now "moving full steam ahead along the track of industrialization to socialism, leaving behind our age-old 'Russian' backwardness."

December 1929 marked Stalin's fiftieth birthday celebrations and the inception of the cult of mass adulation that would grow to epic proportions during the thirties. In a speech made at a conference of agrarian Marxists on 27 December 1929 he made his major objective transparently clear—the "liquidation of the kulaks as class." The word would now be used even more indiscriminately to refer to anyone who resisted. The era of NEP was truly over.

During the winter of 1929–1930 an ad-

visory commission worked on an official decree outlining the program of mass collectivization of the poorer and middle peasants in terms of a five-year period nationwide and within two to three years in the most important areas of Soviet grain production, such as Russia's traditional breadbasket, Ukraine. Stalin, however, was dissatisfied with this time scale and in the decree's final version of 5 January 1930 ("On the Tempo of Collectivization and Measures of State Assistance in Collective Farm Construction") he altered the time scale, insisting on the collectivization of Ukraine, the North Caucasus, and the Lower and Middle Volga within a maximum of two years. While eliminating from the draft any right to withdraw from the collective and any concessions to peasants retaining any smaller livestock or private property, Stalin also put an end to any debate about whether or not the kulaks should be allowed to join the collectives. After the wholesale seizure of their property, kulaks were to be excluded from collectives, since their presence would be nothing but a pernicious influence that would work against the natural socializing objectives of the *kolkhoz*.

At the end of January 1930 the Politburo endorsed the official Central Committee policy on "measures for the liquidation of kulak holdings." The kulaks were categorized into three major groups and a policy for each group was outlined accordingly. Already collectively condemned as incorrigibly hostile and "the biggest class enemy of them all," the most productive element in the agricultural sector was now to be punished with deportation and exile. The first and most militant group of kulaks, labeled as counterrevolutionaries, were to be arrested and either shot or sent to the Gulag and their families deported. The second group of less violent resistants were also to be deported to remote and often hostile regions, where the land was unproductive. The final group of poorer kulaks were simply to be dumped, after confiscation of their property, in the less productive areas of land outside the collective farms in their home districts.

But by the time the Politburo approved this decree, resistance to collectivization on an increasingly violent and extreme scale was already sweeping the countryside. For now the peasantry were being incited into a war among themselves, culminating in the confiscation and vandalization of kulak property. Committees of poor peasants, roused by envy and resentment, were formed to help identify and denounce kulak hoarders in their midst and were duly rewarded for their militancy. Children betrayed their parents as kulaks, simply for trying to save something against leaner times. Many kulaks, having already seen the warning signs, had deliberately planted less grain rather than continue being forced to accept lower prices. Others had sold and hidden their valuables during 1927–1928. But any secret stores of grain kulaks might have saved were quickly unearthed by search parties organized by Communist Party members, supported by Red Army units and police. Soon the kulaks began retaliating with their own savage variation of the "scorched earth" policy, later practiced so effectively against the Germans during World War II.

Kulaks now destroyed everything they had rather than hand it over to the state. Farmsteads were burned down, machinery wrecked in Luddite fashion, rail and truck transports taking peasant grain away were sabotaged, home brewed vodka was consumed to the point of stupor, and livestock was slaughtered en masse. Rather than surrender their solitary cow, or their few pigs, or sheep, many peasants slaughtered them and ate all they could themselves. The government retaliated by limiting the sale of salt to try to prevent meat from being preserved for future consumption. In this way, Soviet agriculture lost a staggering 14 million of a total 70.5 million head of cattle, a

rural disaster that would create a general deficit in livestock (cows, pigs, and sheep) by 1933, when their numbers equaled less than half of the 1928 figures. The Soviet Union would not recover from this loss until the 1950s.

Sometimes whole villages resisted collectivization. American journalists reported that in Ukraine an entire town of 30,000 people was deported to Siberia for its act of collective resistance. In other cases, the Red Army and air force attacked villages with bombs and artillery. Kulaks were frequently seen to surrender their property only after being surrounded by machine guns. And many middle-range peasants who were reluctant to join the collective also found themselves coerced into joining at the end of the barrel of a gun. Deportations of kulaks by train to resettlement areas in Siberia and the Urals began to take place. When they arrived, after long and exhausting journeys by cattle train, the peasants often found that no provision had been made for them, and they were forced to live in holes in the ground or makeshift shelters until proper living accommodation could be constructed. In some cases whole families committed suicide rather than face deportation. Others went into hiding. As many as 100,000 peasants left their villages during 1930–1932 and fled to the cities seeking work. Thousands more were absorbed into the Soviet Union's vast industrial construction sites. It is estimated that as many as 1,900,000 kulaks were deported during 1931–1932 to special settlements.

Meanwhile, Stalin quickly discovered the value of the kulaks sent to the Gulag as a vast untapped labor force, kept alive on subsistence rations. Many of them were worked to death as slave laborers on such projects as the industrial complex at Magnitogorsk (which 18,000 kulaks helped construct) and the White Sea–Baltic Canal. Few survived the appalling conditions in the gold fields of Magadan, Siberia. Exactly how many families suffered as a result of the dekulakization process is, as with so many of the acts of mass social repression of the Stalin years, impossible to quantify due to an absence of reliable, documented figures. But the generally held view is that in excess of 1.1 million peasant households comprising some 7 million people were affected during the process of dispossession.

In the early stages of collectivization a concerted attack on the traditional focus of peasant life, the Orthodox Church (which at the time was the object of a fierce campaign against religious practice generally) had aimed at further undermining peasant morale to enforce their acceptance of the changing social order. With their priests hounded out, their churches destroyed, and icons destroyed in front of their eyes, for many of the older generation of peasants, still locked into their traditional Orthodox beliefs, the chaos of collectivization seemed like the end of the world and forewarned of the coming of the anti-Christ. All kinds of rumors circulated about what collectivization entailed, the most widespread being that all peasants would be expected to sleep together in one communal bed under one "common blanket," and that children and even husbands and wives would be shared. There was also a rumor that the women would be made to have their hair cut short so it could be sold.

In official circles, such was the frenzy to collectivize, that the process had turned into a race to see who could achieve the best and fastest results. A Stakhanovite mentality prevailed in certain areas, predating the movement of 1935 that would give its name to an excess of zeal in the overfulfillment of Stalinist economic objectives. Much of this zeal was the product of a group known as the "Twenty-Five Thousanders," brigades of mainly urban workers with no knowledge of agricultural practices, who were sent into the countryside to propagandize among the peasantry and help wrest their grain from them. They were so called because they numbered some 25,000 (on average one for every five collective farms). These eager volunteers, who have been dubbed "the final working-class vanguard," were in some respects like the many naive and inexperienced radicals who went "to the people" in the 1870s. They were given only a rudimentary training and even fewer guidelines on *kolkhoz* administration, all of which was guaranteed to further antagonize the peasants.

Such massive dislocations in the lives of the Russian peasant provided Stalin with the kind of economic successes on paper that were his lifeblood; but it became apparent, even to him, by March of 1930 (by which time over half the peasantry had been hastily collectivized) that the whole process had acquired a momentum that was now spiraling out of control. Levels of resistance to collectivization, often provoked by the oppressive behavior of local officials and twenty-five thousanders who had in many places become a law unto themselves, were compounded by the worrying mass slaughter of livestock. In his article in *Pravda* of 2 March 1930 entitled "Dizzy with Success," Stalin called a temporary halt to the process and reverted to the original Bolshevik line on the voluntary nature of collectivization. Eight million peasant families promptly took him at his word and left the *kolkhozy*, although they were not allowed to take any of their animals or implements with them.

But this conciliatory move came too late to stave off the cumulative effect of the previous months of unrest, deportations, bad management of the *kolkhozy*, and the increasing depopulation of the Russian countryside, as increasing numbers of peasants made destitute by collectivization continued to invade the cities looking for work. By the autumn the respite was over, and Stalin renewed the collectivization process. By the following August it was virtually complete in the important grain-producing areas of Ukraine, the North Caucasus, and the Volga. But the reality of grain production rates did not match the success story of on-paper statistics. A bumper harvest in 1930 had led officials to estimate 1931 quotas at unrealistic levels, partly due to the erroneous method of projecting yields by the size of the planted field and not by the amount of actual, harvested grain. Stalin chose to ignore the warning signs of a projected 20 percent drop in grain yields and fueled the impending famine by continuing to sell high levels of grain abroad in order to fund the industrialization programs of the first Five-Year Plan. In 1933, at the height of the famine, 1.7 million tons of desperately needed grain were exported.

In order to fulfill the high quotas for 1931, peasants were now deprived not only of their own subsistence supplies but also of their stocks of seed grain for the planting of the next harvest. By the spring of 1932 famine had hit Ukraine, and the following year had spread to the North Caucasus, the Volga, and Kazakhstan. The magnitude of the ensuing famine was, for fifty years or more, subject to repeated official and public denial by the Soviet government. Stalin actively refused to allow relief handouts to be made from existing grain stocks, or to appeal to the West for food aid, as the Bolsheviks had done during the famine of 1921–1922. He could not afford to let the West know that his great social experiment in the countryside had turned into a disaster.

Lenin had been equally callous about the welfare of the peasantry. In 1892, during a terrible famine in the Volga region, he had dismissed talk of peasant suffering as the "saccharine-sweet sentimentality so characteristic of our intelligentsia." But Stalin, the master of understatement, went one step further in 1933, when in one of his characteristically bald statements, he tastefully referred to the famine as certain "difficulties and shortages" in the countryside. On the occasion of official visits by foreign dignitaries or Communist fellow travelers from the West, the Soviets artfully revived the old trick of creating "Potemkin villages" (a practice pioneered during Catherine the Great's time by her court favorite Grigoriy Potemkin) by creating phony shop windows full of consumer goods, or feeding up a few hand-picked peasants for display at showcase collective farms.

The existence of famine was actively denied and people spreading rumors about hunger in the villages were arrested for anti-Soviet propaganda and counterrevolutionary agitation. In order to contain the spread of news about the famine inside the Soviet Union, roadblocks were set up around the worst affected areas of Ukraine and the North Caucasus, preventing peasants from leaving for the city. Such was Stalin's ability to perpetuate what writer Boris Pasternak called "the inhuman power of the lie," that visiting luminaries such as Bernard Shaw were totally hoodwinked as to the true situation prevailing in Russia. Indeed, Shaw's friend Sir John Maynard reacted with indignation at talk of famine in his classic 1943 study *The Russian Peasant,* feeling compelled to "expunge an error from current history." Since he had had some personal experience with the phenomena of actual famine in Russia in the early 1920s and had seen the evidence of the bumper harvest in 1933, Maynard had thought it "right to place on record" that he saw no signs of the emaciation and hunger he had seen in 1921–1922 and that the reported scarcity of 1932–1933 was "in no way comparable to the great famines!"

Fortunately, enough accurate accounts of the horrific levels of starvation have filtered through to testify to the suffering of a peasantry totally abandoned to its fate by the Soviet authorities. In the worst hit areas, "corpses [were] piled up like bales of straw" or "piles of logs," leading Robert Conquest to draw the analogy that the scenes resembled "one vast Belsen." People would eat anything to try and stay alive. Having consumed all their livestock and even their domestic cats and dogs, the hungry were forced to kill and eat field mice, wild birds, earth worms, and forage for anything edible

An extremely rare photograph of the 1932–1933 famine that killed approximately 7 million people. Stalin refused to acknowledge that it had taken place.

such as bark, grass, leaves, weeds. People even fought over horse manure for the few grains of seed it might contain. Numerous incidences of cannibalism were recorded, with some peasants even killing and eating their own children. By far the most pitiable sight were the starving children with their dead eyes, blue-tinged skin, and bloated bellies. Hordes of starving peasants besieged the railway stations in an attempt to escape the famine areas. Here they would sit for days or even weeks on end "staring fixedly ahead like victims of dementia praecox," waiting for a train to come and take them somewhere, anywhere, out of the misery in which they were living.

Driven to desperation, peasants would do anything to scavenge a few ears of corn. At night, women would creep into the wheat-fields of the *kolkhozy* and cut off a few stalks of grain to feed their children. Collectives retaliated by constructing watchtowers over their fields and enlisting members of the Komsomol youth movement to keep an eagle eye open for people trying to steal. In August 1932, an official decree "On the Safeguarding of State Property" designated all collective farm property as state property and anyone found making use of it without authority would be liable to the death penalty or ten years of forced labor. Known as the "law of seven-eighths" (because it was promulgated on the seventh day of the eighth month) or more popularly as the "five stalks law" (the minimum amount of grain designated a prosecutable offense), this legislation saw the conviction by January 1933 of 55,000 and the execution of some 2,110 people in all.

The death toll in the famine reached its highest point between March and May 1933. It is now suggested that as many as 5 million died in Ukraine alone that year. And in the aftermath of famine came disease, typhoid and typhus, rural depopulation, deserted farms, land left uncultivated, and, in the biggest irony of all, fields of grain left to rot. The famine also created a generation of *beprizorniki*—homeless orphans left to wander and beg an existence wherever they could.

In 1988 the Gorbachev government finally admitted that the 1932 famine had been part artificial, the direct result of Stalin's deliberate use of starvation as a means of coercion and social control. By allowing the famine to proceed in Ukraine, in particular, he had effectively put an end to nationalist aspirations in what for him had always been a troublesome region. The total number of deaths as a result of this act of genocide is generally given as 7 million, although the recent revisionist debate in Stalinist historiography has offered a figure of "upwards of 4 million" of which 2.9 million were deaths in Ukraine. Other Soviet historians in the liberalizing era of glasnost under Mikhail Gorbachev have suggested much higher figures. Most commentators still respect the detailed study made by Robert Conquest and concur with his figures of 5 million in Ukraine, 1 million in the North Caucasus, and 1 million elsewhere. Most damningly, the estimated number of child deaths is put at 3 million.

The fate of the peasantry was finally sealed in 1932–1933 when the old tsarist system of internal passports was reintroduced as a means of controlling the mobility of labor and preventing peasants, in particular, from deserting the collectives to seek work in the city. Many of the *kolkhozy* were now seriously undermanned. This was a situation Stalin could not allow to prevail. While the internal passports circumscribed the areas in which an urban worker could seek employment, the peasants were deprived of even that choice. Since, by the nature of their work they were deemed to be tied to the land and the *kolkhozy*, they were not issued with passports at all. Thus, within seventy years of emancipation, the Russian peasantry had effectively been reenserfed. Meanwhile, at the celebratory Seventeenth Party Congress "of the Victors" of 1934, Stalin proudly announced that "the foundation of a socialist economy has been laid." And indeed it had, at the expense of the subjugation of the majority of the rural population. By 1936, 90 percent of the peasantry had been collectivized and, while the statistics seemed a validation of the economic triumphs of socialism, a centuries-old rural way of life had been destroyed forever.

In 1933, as yields continued to drop, ominous warnings had begun to circulate about "wrecking in agriculture." With the kulaks no longer there to take the blame, Stalin found yet another means for shifting blame away from government mismanagement and onto the shoulders of a collective bogeyman. In this case it was the technical personnel and supervisors of collective farms, who were now accused of "putting machines out of order, sowing badly, squandering *kolkhoz* property, undermining labour discipline, organizing the theft of seeds, secret granaries, and the sabotage of the grain harvest." Thus began the new popular Soviet preoccupation with hunting down "wreckers," the trials of whom would presage the mass political purges of the second half of the 1930s.

By 1935, after the country had finally begun to recover from the catastrophe of the famine, Stalin was forced to allow certain concessions on free enterprise for peasants on the collective farms. The Model Kolkhoz Statute now allowed them to cultivate their own produce on small plots of land within the collective and to keep one cow plus a few sheep and pigs. They were also permitted to sell their surplus at special state markets. And in this way the peasants managed to survive economically and once more regained an incentive for enterprise. But to sustain their own plots for private use was not easy when the collective demanded the bulk of their labor time. If production targets for the collective were not met, the peasants would go short. Peasants continued to complain about the government's maintenance of artificially low grain prices and now, in 1936, they were being driven by the Stakhanovite obsession with overfulfilling already exacting quotas, all of which did nothing to raise incentives. Continuing shortages in 1935–1936, due to yet more crop failures, resulted in city people being forced once again to queue for hours and hours for their bread. The peasant response to the situation was, as ever, to revert to what they knew best—private enterprise. Despite the demands for their work on the collective, peasants devoted more and more time to their own little plots and their own livestock. By 1938 private plots had grown to such a level that their produce provided one-fifth of total production on a twenty-fifth of the total cultivated land.

The pattern of rural decline continued after the war. The rural population had dropped from 80 percent of the population in 1926 to only 52 percent by 1959. Meanwhile, Stalin continued to announce increases in the production of marketable grain, with foreign sales reaching 30 million tons during 1938–1940, compared to 10 million in 1926–1928. In 1946–1947 another famine occurred after a year-long drought in Ukraine. Once again, the government requisitioned all grain stocks. Meanwhile, men returning from military service were reluctant to work the land because the rates of remuneration were so poor, thus leading to a preponderance of women working in Soviet agriculture. By 1952 the grain harvest still had not recovered to its 1940 levels, and there were still fewer head of cattle to feed a bigger population. And private plots, which comprised only 1–2 percent of arable land, were providing an increasingly disproportionate amount of foodstuffs, including two-thirds of the nation's meat, potatoes, and milk.

Much tortuous political and economic debate has continued since Stalin's death over the necessity for collectivization and whether or not the same levels of growth could have been achieved through a continuation of the policies of NEP. It is a debate too complex and contentious to take up here. What continues to fascinate, however, is the ambitious dimensions of Stalin's blueprint for the social engineering of the peasantry. The level of his obsessive "statistical transformation" of society and the sheer size of all his modernizing operations, both in agriculture and in industry, have been described as "gigantomania." As Stalin told U.S. photographer James E. Abbe in 1932 when asked if he had any message for the outside world: "I have no time for political interviews, I have a hundred million hectares of land to sow." Yet while Stalin was always precise about industrial statistics and figures and would later produce detailed lists of livestock losses during collectivization, he was careful never to admit to the precise number of human casualties (their numbers, in any event, were never officially recorded). When asked by Churchill at the Potsdam Conference in 1945 how many deaths and deportations had resulted from the collectivization process, all Stalin could do was give a shrug and estimate the numbers on the fingers of his hands—at some 10 million.

See also Bukharin, Nikolay; "Dizzy with Success"; The Great Turn; Lysenko, Trofim; Magnitogorsk

Further reading: Alan Bullock. *Hitler and Stalin: Parallel Lives.* London: Fontana Press, 1993; Robert Conquest. *The Harvest of Sorrow: Soviet Collectivization and the Terror Famine.* London: Hutchinson, 1986; Moshe Lewin. *The Making of the Soviet System: Essays in the Social History of Inter-War Russia.* London: Methuen, 1985; Alec Nove. *Economic History of the USSR.* London: Penguin, 1989; Mikhail Sholokhov. *Virgin Soil Upturned* (for a literary view of the tragedy). London: Putnam, 1935; Robert C. Tucker. *Stalin in Power: The Revolution from Above, 1928–1941.* London: Chatto and Windus, 1990. For Western eyewitness accounts see Abbe, Hindus, Scott in bibliography.

Cominform (1947–1956)

The Communist Information Bureau, which was known by its abbreviation Cominform, was set up at a conference in Poland in 1947 at Stalin's behest. It came into being as a direct response to the U.S. Marshall Aid Program of Relief, which had been set up at the end of the war to aid western and southern European nations recovering from the depredations of war. Stalin, however, interpreted the Marshall Plan as a blatant challenge to his control of the Eastern bloc. He was determined that Cominform should "take the lead in resisting the plans of American imperialist expansion and aggression in all spheres." Another of its major roles was to coordinate the propaganda activities of the nine major postwar national Communist Parties of the Soviet Union, Bulgaria, Czechoslovakia, Hungary, Poland, Romania, and briefly Yugoslavia, as well as the parties in France and Italy.

After Yugoslavia was expelled in 1948, Cominform moved its headquarters from Belgrade to Bucharest, Romania. Its attempts to attack the implementation of the Marshall Plan were in vain, and it turned its activities to stemming the rise of European social democracy in France, Germany, and Britain. Cominform's official message, disseminated through a journal named by Stalin himself, with inspired cynicism, *For a Lasting Peace, for a People's Democracy,* failed to make much of an impression. The organization was disbanded by Khrushchev in 1956 during the thaw years as part of his campaign to seek reconciliation with Yugoslavia and the West.

See also Comintern; Eastern Europe
Further reading: Fernando Claudín. *The Communist Movement: from Comintern to Cominform.* New York: Monthly Review Press, 1996.

Comintern (1919–1943)

Otherwise known as the Third International and in many respects a predecessor of the Cominform, this association of national communist parties had as its original objective the promotion of world revolution. It was set up by Lenin and Leon Trotsky in 1919 in direct opposition to the conciliatory stance taken by the Second International, which had been founded in 1889 in Paris and had endorsed the cause of world peace. The Bolsheviks had become impatient with the Second International, however, stating in the manifesto for the Third that "the international proletariat will not sheathe its sword until we have created a world Federation of Soviet Republics." Lenin's rallying cry, at the helm of this body, became one of "civil war, not civil peace" and the organization became increasingly dictatorial with Lenin insisting that members toe the Soviet Communist line.

After Stalin became general secretary of the Central Committee of the Communist Party in 1922, he began angling for control of the Comintern and, by association, the Communist Party abroad. He was not able to do so freely until he had rid himself of the continuing influence of the left wing led by Trotsky (whom he consigned to exile in 1927) and Comintern's President Grigory Zinoviev (who was expelled in 1926). As for his only other rival to absolute control within the Comintern, the right-wing Communist Nikolay Bukharin who had succeeded Grigory Zinoviev, Stalin dismissed him from office in 1929.

Stalin now set about ensuring that the Comintern evolved into the controlling force behind the international Communist movement by orchestrating its subversive activities on an international scale. By 1928, at its Sixth Congress, he adopted an extreme line that squeezed out the more moderate elements in the organization and began manipulating the Comintern as a vehicle for his own ideas, particularly on matters of foreign policy. During the 1930s Stalin refused to be drawn by calls to ally with the social democrats in Germany against the rise of Hitler's national socialism. He had privately concluded that the rise of Hitler might provide a useful diversion by perhaps precipitating a war in the West, thus leaving the Soviet Union free to continue consolidating its own position. But Stalin was later forced to make an about-face on his policy toward Hitler's Germany when he realized that the unchecked rise of Nazism was providing a greater threat than he had anticipated. In 1935 he issued instructions through the Comintern that national Communist Parties should set up a united front to campaign against fascism. Many dedicated young Communists supported this united front by taking up the fight in the Civil War in Spain. Their commitment and sacrifice received a body blow with yet another reversal of policy when Stalin, to the dismay of many of the members of the Comintern, formally allied himself with Hitler when he signed the German-Soviet Non-Aggression Pact of 1939.

Finally, in 1943, to demonstrate the degree to which the Comintern had become a pliant tool in Stalin's hands, the organization was quietly dissolved as a placatory act toward Stalin's American and British allies, who were mistrustful of aligning themselves with the Communists against Hitler and were apprehensive about dealing with them in the postwar carve-up of Europe.

During the Great Terror, the Comintern's foreign members based in the Soviet Union were caught up in the wave of arrests and executions going on around them. Many Old Guard Communists from the parties of Western Ukraine, Latvia, Estonia, and Lithuania were the first to suffer in the prelude to a campaign against foreign Communists in general from 1937. Prominent members of the German Communist Party living in the Soviet Union were the

first to disappear, many to be murdered in secret and others to eventually turn up in the Gulag. One of several well-known leaders of the CommunistCommunist Revolution in Hungary of 1919 who were murdered was Béla Kun, a member of the Comintern's international executive, who was shot in Butyrki prison in August 1938. And so the killings went on—200 Italian Communists, 100 or more Yugoslav Communists, including the whole of the Yugoslav Central Committee, and many members of the Finnish and Romanian Communist Parties. Over 1,000 Bulgarian Communists were sent to the Gulag, of whom only about 100 returned. The only Communist Party to remain unaffected by all this was that of the Chinese. The greatest losses came in the Polish Communist Party, which lost its entire leadership. One estimate suggests that as many as 5,000 Polish Communists in the Soviet Union perished. Outside the Soviet Union, the NKVD organized mobile groups of agents to seek out those on Stalin's "hit list" and dispatch them. In Spain, in particular, a campaign was mounted to track down the Trotskyists in the international brigades and thousands of Spanish Communists who fled to the Soviet Union after defeat in the Spanish Civil War, were either shot or deported to Central Asia.

See also Baltic States; Bukharin, Nikolay; Cominform; Eastern Europe; NKVD; Spanish Civil War; Zinoviev, Grigory

Further reading: E. H. Carr. *The Twilight of Comintern, 1930–1935*. London: Macmillan, 1982.

Congress of the Victors (1934)

Congresses of the Communist Party of the Soviet Union, inaugurated in 1925, were the showpiece political event of the year. On such occasions, the leading members of the Party would elect a new Central Committee (which in turn elected the Politburo and the Secretariat)

and rubber-stamp policy for the coming year. The attendant speech-making would focus on the previous year's achievements and failures (under Stalin the only failures recognized were those of other Party members to toe the political line). Although the intention had been to hold congresses annually, they became increasingly infrequent and after those held in 1925 and 1927 there was a three-year gap before the Sixteenth Congress in 1930 (the numbering of the congresses was taken from the First Congress held on the establishment of the Bolshevik Party in 1903).

Much was to be made of the Seventeenth Congress of 1934. It took place in the historic setting of the Great Kremlin Palace at the height of the cult of Stalin-worship. Stalin, now elevated as the Great Leader or *vozhd,* took center stage to celebrate the triumphant successes of collectivization and industrialization under the First and Second Five-Year Plans (hence the title "Congress of the Victors").

The Congress of 1,225 elected delegates and some candidates was timed to open on 26 January, not long after the tenth anniversary of Lenin's death, as a reminder to all that the new leader was following in the great Leninist tradition. Stalin also intended it to be a public act of reconciliation and solidarity within the Party after what he hoped was the final taming of all factional elements on the left and right (the conferences of the 1920s had been used to ostracize Leon Trotsky and bring Lev Kamenev, Grigory Zinoviev, and Nikolay Bukharin and other ideological waverers into line). In his keynote speech, part of what would be a 700-page transcript of the proceedings, Stalin confidently announced that there was now "nothing to prove, and, it seems, nothing to fight." His complacency was, however, premature. Despite the obligatory prolonged, standing ovations accorded him, his position was, in fact, by no means secure.

At first all seemed well. The delegates who took the podium one after another endorsed the belief that the Soviet Union was now smoothly on course for the achievement of a "classless, socialist society" under Stalin's undisputed leadership. Those former oppositionist or deviationist delegates who had now recognized the error of their ways—prominent figures such as Kamenev, Zinoviev, and Bukharin—seemed to be changed men and publicly recanted their political sins while upholding Stalin's transcendent wisdom and genius. The pathetic spectacle of Bukharin's humiliating abandonment of his moral and political integrity can be seen in his hollow words of submission, that "Stalin was entirely correct when he smashed a whole series of theoretical premises of the right deviation which had been formulated above all by myself," and in his exhortation that "it is the duty of every party member to rally round Comrade Stalin as the personal embodiment of the mind and will of the party, as . . . its theoretical and practical leader."

And so the encomiums poured forth, most notably from Sergey Kirov, leader of the Leningrad Communist Party and candidate member of the Politburo who, in a lively and popular speech punctuated by laughter and enthusiastic applause, found occasion to mention Stalin's name twenty-two times, lauding him as "the greatest strategist of the emancipation of the toilers of our country and the whole world." Some, however, noticed that the standing ovation Kirov received went on longer and was more enthusiastic than that accorded Stalin. Such things would not be forgotten by the Great Leader.

By the last day of the congress, when people had exhausted their stock of superlatives, there merely remained the formality of the secret vote for the new Central Committee (for the posts of key ministers, including the general secretary), using ballot papers issued only for the precise number of candidates to be elected by a simple majority. And suddenly the atmosphere backstage changed. The tellers who sat counting the votes through the night of 9 February announced with temerity that there was something worrisomely wrong with the ballot.

Extraordinarily, approximately 166 of the delegates had voted *against* Stalin (the figure is still disputed and estimates vary between 150 and 300). Delegates had also expressed their disapprobation of Vyacheslav Molotov and Lazar Kaganovich by voting against them, while only three had rejected Kirov. There is considerable controversy and unsubstantiated rumor about what happened after this, but the vote was most certainly tampered with and ballot papers destroyed. It is alleged that Politburo member Lazar Kaganovich, who was the organizer of the congress, destroyed enough ballot papers to make it appear that a handful had voted equally against Stalin (3) and Kirov (4). Some Soviet historians have alleged the number of votes against Stalin was 297, others put the figure at 270, still others at 292. Archival evidence from Russia has since indicated that of the 1,225 elected delegates only 1,059 had actually handed in a ballot paper, suggesting that those papers of 166 members with the right to vote must have been destroyed, presumably because they had cast their votes against Stalin. It is, however, still not known (as revisionist historians are anxious to point out in support of their own argument over the level of Kirov's popularity and Stalin's unpopularity) exactly how many ballot papers were handed out in total.

The fact that somewhere around 166 delegates had been sufficiently and privately disgruntled with Stalin's leadership not to vote for his return as general secretary of the Communist Party, while not in itself being sufficient to affect his formal re-election, must have rattled Stalin who, forever alert to betrayal and treachery, saw this as a clear demonstration of "double-dealing" among Communist Party members. And while people might have lived in terror of openly defying Stalin and had be-

come inured to, if not cynical about, the process of public recantation for acts of political heresy, it is clear that matters of personal conviction still counted for something in a secret ballot. Some of the remaining Old Guard Bolsheviks (including Anastas Mikoyan and Grigory Ordzhonikidze allegedly), as well as lesser Party delegates from the regions, had by now become sickened by the Stalin cult. Many had also heard rumors about Lenin's dying "testament," a letter that was addressed to the Twelfth Party Congress instructing that Stalin be removed from the post as general secretary and that Stalin had managed to suppress. They saw the congress as an opportune moment to finally oust Stalin from his power base at Party headquarters and transfer him to a lesser post, chairing either the Council of People's Comissars or the Central Executive Committee. Several delegates are said to have approached Kirov behind the scenes, asking him to stand for general secretary, although not necessarily viewing him as a replacement as premier. Kirov, however, had declined the suggestion, seeing it as undermining Party authority. In a fatal misjudgment of Stalin's psychology, Kirov reportedly told him about this and of his refusal of the offer, confirming his undying loyalty to Stalin. But the damage had already been done. The seeds of hostility and mistrust had been sown in Stalin's mind, and in the months that followed there was a distinct cooling off in his relationship with Kirov.

The traditional interpretation of the onrush of arrests and purges in the Communist Party that took place as the central phase of the Great Terror from 1934 to 1938 sees this congress and the assassination of Kirov in December of the same year as their main catalysts. Stalin was badly shaken in his belief that he had by now achieved unanimity of support as Party secretary. He determined to consolidate his position once and for all by launching a radical and ruthless attack on what he saw as double dealers and oppositionists. Early in 1935

Stalin instituted a purge of thousands of Party members both at senior level and throughout regional Party cadres through verification of their Party cards and checks on their allegiance to the Party (appointing to the task an up-and-coming apparatchik Nikolai Ezhov, who would later succeed Genrikh Yagoda as head of the NKVD).

As the machinery of political cleansing gathered pace, most of the delegates to this 1934 Congress of Victors (including Kirov, who named it so) would ultimately become its victims, as historian Robert Tucker has pointed out. It has also been described as the "Congress of the Victor," with Stalin singled out as the only person who, retrospectively, gained anything from it. But, perhaps, in memory of those 1,108 delegates out of the 1,966 (and the 110 out of 139 Central Committee members) who had been arrested and/or shot before the next congress was held in 1939, and who can be seen applauding Stalin with such compulsive ferocity in newsreel footage of the event, one might retrospectively rename it the Congress of the Vanquished.

See also: General Secretary of the Communist Party; The Great Terror; Kirov, Sergey Mironovich

Further reading: J. Arch Getty. "The Politics of Repression Revisited," in Chris Ward, ed., *The Stalinist Dictatorship*. London: Arnold, 1998; Roy Medvedev. *Let History Judge: The Origins and Consequences of Stalinism*. New York: Columbia University Press, 1989; Dmitri Volkogonov. *Stalin: Triumph and Tragedy*. London: Weidenfeld & Nicolson, 1991.

governed the Soviet Union from 1917 until 1946. Lenin as the chairman of this Council purported to preside over a new workers' and peasants' government that, in fact, proved to be only a disguised version of the previous ministerial bureaucracy of the tsars with many of its civil servants still in place. Originally intended to report back to the All-Russian Central Executive Committee of the Congress of Soviets, Sovnarkom soon began passing legislation without recourse to this body in a breach of the executive committee's sovereignty. Thus, this supposedly federal set-up with the member republics of the Soviet Union each having their own council's subordinate to Sovnarkom in Moscow became, in reality, a centralized system of government with its subsidiaries serving only to rubber-stamp policy decisions made at Sovnarkom's daily meetings.

Stalin himself headed two People's Commissariats within Sovnarkom—the Commissariat for Nationalities and the Commissariat of the Workers and Peasants' Inspectorate. After Lenin's death Stalin favored using the bureaucracy of the Central Committee of the Communist Party itself as the means of consolidating his power base, and with it the Party gained ascendancy over the administrative bureaucracy of Sovnarkom. In 1946 Stalin renamed it the Council of Ministers.

See also General Secretary of the Communist Party; People's Commissariat of the Workers and Peasants' Inspectorate

Council of People's Commissars

*K*nown in Russian under the abbreviation of Sovnarkom, the council was the cabinet of the first solely Bolshevik government set up by Lenin at the Second All-Russian Congress of Soviets held in October 1917.

Based in Moscow, the group of ministries that comprised the People's Commissariats

Cult of the Personality

*T*hroughout the years of Khrushchev's political thaw, all public mention of Stalin's name was proscribed. Despite Stalin's being obliquely referred to as the unnamed object of the cult of the personality, which in his 1956 secret speech Khrushchev had urged should be abolished

КАПИТАН СТРАНЫ СОВЕТОІ
ВЕДЕТ НАС ОТ ПОБЕДЫ
К ПОБЕДЕ!

A 1930s poster, typical of the imagery of the period of the cult of the personality, depicting Stalin as the trusty helmsman and "captain of the country" steering the Soviet state "from victory to victory."

"decisively, once and for all," Stalin's enduring presence would pervade Soviet life for many years to come.

The term "cult of the personality" had first been used by Georgy Malenkov in 1953 at a Plenum of the Central Committee not long after Stalin's death, but the concept of a Soviet political "cult" was not new with Stalin. His veneration had been a natural progression from the cult of Lenin which Stalin himself had so meticulously stage-managed from the moment of Lenin's death.

The term in itself has a sinister resonance, conveying the idea of mass indoctrination that characterized Stalin's rule. It was also, no doubt, applied as a deliberate act of depersonalization, as an inversion of all the many and grandiloquent epithets that had been attributed to Stalin during his lifetime, including such ludicrous assertions as Sergey Kirov's (1934) that Stalin was "the greatest man of all times, of all epochs, and peoples." Such language marked the apogee of an era when Stalin, the man, was accorded superhuman powers—when he was "taller than the Himalayas, / wider than the ocean, / brighter than the sun" (in the words of Kazakh poet Dzhambul Dzhubaev). Indeed writers and speech makers invested a great deal of energy in trying to outdo each other with ever more hyperbolic expressions of Stalin's infallibility as a man whose wisdom transcended everything that had gone before in human history, including even the ministry of Jesus Christ, if not perhaps the deity himself.

This religious analogy of god-building was repeatedly drawn on, with Stalin becoming a modern-day *batyushka* or "little father" for the great mass of the Russian peasantry—a term of veneration traditionally applied to the Russian tsars as father protectors of their people and by association marking a resurgence of the old Russian mindset of total subservience to an all-powerful, all-seeing ruler. It was thus a case of "*plus ça change, plus c'est la même chose,*"

One of the glut of monolithic statues of Stalin produced in the 1930s. He is shown here with Lenin in order to emphasize his position as the Bolshevik leader's disciple and as continuer of Lenin's socialist vision.

and the Russian people, while no longer having a tsar and officially denied the right to practice Orthodoxy or any other religion, seemed able to adapt their former religious practice to a new god, namely Stalin. After all, as Stalin himself had once remarked to his brother-in-law, "the Russian people is really a tsaristic people. It needs a tsar."

The comprehensive Stalinization of the

Soviet Union began in the mid-1920s with the naming of towns, factories, and public institutions after him—in particular, Stalingrad in 1925. The manipulation by Stalin and his acolytes of historical fact to suit Stalin's scenario of Russian and Soviet history, combined with the growth of a Stalinist hagiography that emphasized Stalin's own role in the revolution, put him and his contribution as a political thinker on a par with Lenin. It also served to inculcate in the public mind the idea of Stalin as Lenin's natural successor through the use of such slogans as "Stalin Is the Lenin of Today," and, to underline his God-given role as a latter-day Saint Peter to Lenin's Jesus Christ, a role that, therefore, could not be challenged.

It was the official Party newspaper *Pravda* that opened the floodgates when it published a lead article on 21 December 1929 on the occasion of Stalin's fiftieth birthday in which his name was emblazoned across the front page of the paper as the "true continuer of the cause of Marx and Lenin." For the first time in its history *Pravda* also published a full-sized portrait of Stalin on its front page and then spent the next five days listing the birthday greetings sent to him from various Communist organizations throughout the Soviet Union. The sycophantic tone of all of these messages set a trend that would escalate during the 1930s, to be repeated on his sixtieth birthday in 1939. During the war years, Stalin crowned his already legendary political achievements by proving himself to be a true, military "Generalissimo" (a title he awarded himself in 1945). The final mass public celebration of Stalin as a cult figure came on the occasion of his seventieth birthday in 1949 when a huge parade was staged in Red Square and groups of beribboned children, clutching bouquets of flowers, chanted in unison in front of the assembled crowds and with Stalin standing on top of the Lenin mausoleum: "We are the children of Lenin and Stalin. We strive to the summit of learning. Teacher, leader, beloved friend. Father Stalin welcome."

Back in 1929, Stalin had demonstrated all the consummate skill of the arch manipulator in his response to the tide of good wishes heaped upon him in *Pravda*. He was one of the great masters of faux humility, and played his own line in gruff modesty to perfection. His thank-you note to *Pravda* was a typical response when he humbly accepted these congratulations "on behalf of the great party of the working class which gave birth to me and which raised me in its own image and likeness" (didn't God do the same with his own son?). No one in Soviet politics has ever come close to Stalin in exploiting the gullibility of the public to such a degree.

While Stalin was surrounded on all sides by toadies and sycophants, most visibly Lavrenty Beria, with their obsequiousness poorly disguised (mainly because it was driven by fear and inadequacy), Stalin's false modesty (based on the conviction that he was a genius and therefore had nothing to prove) was always subtly underplayed. Such was Stalin's self-effacing "niceness," that, as one U.S. ambassador put it, "a child would like to sit in his lap and a dog would sidle up to him." It was also precisely this aspect of his cult persona that convinced most of the Soviet people that Stalin couldn't possibly know all that was going on during the Great Terror. And such was the atmosphere of fear generated at that time that people became convinced that acts of slavish adoration, no matter how grotesquely excessive, could hold some kind of currency in their favor if their political loyalty should later be called into question. Loyalty was stretched to absurd lengths and can be typified with just one example—it became a dangerous thing to be seen as the first person to stop applauding during the obligatory and ferocious standing ovations that were given Stalin at every public appearance he made. These would go on for ten minutes or more, and people's hands became so sore

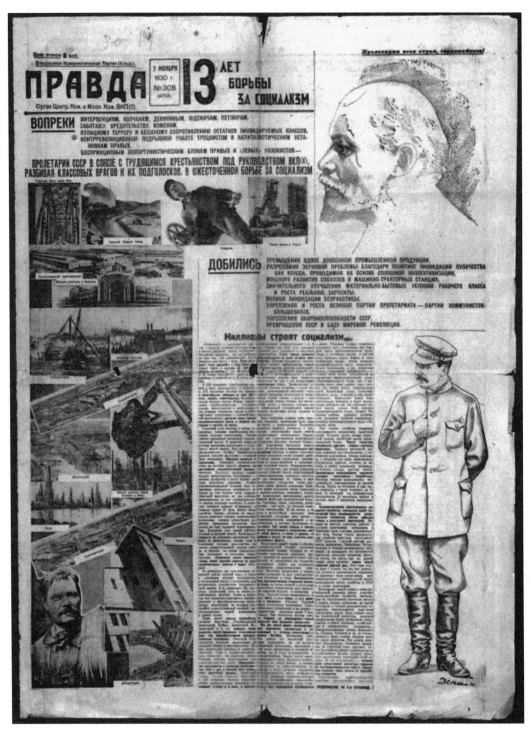

The front page of the Soviet newspaper **Pravda** *for 7 November 1930, featuring a full–length drawing of Stalin alongside an article celebrating the industrial achievements of the proletariat during the First Five–Year Plan.*

from the clapping that they would be provided with buckets of salt water in which to soothe them.

While contemporary accounts make it clear that Stalin had a contemptuous attitude to sycophancy and grew to hate many of the toadies surrounding him, he seemed at times to have gained a perverse pleasure from witnessing the efforts of those squirming to invent new ways in which to affirm his life-giving genius and wisdom. Leon Trotsky perceptively argued in his unfinished study of Stalin, published after Trotsky's assassination in 1941, that Stalin had become trapped within the machinery of his own cult and that "it was not he who created that machine, but the machine that created him." By the end of his life it had become impossible to separate the real personality from the public persona, or to put a stop to the industry that compulsively spewed out panegyrics to him. Ultimately, Stalin became the prisoner of his own cult and was completely isolated by it. His last days were not spent in the bosom of a loving family, as any ordinary father's should have been, but as a bitter, solitary figure who had cut himself off from the real world and who would die a frightening and lonely death.

See also Art and Architecture; Cinema; Historiography; Lenin, Vladimir; Lenin Mausoleum; Socialist Realism, Stalin: Nicknames, Aliases, and Official Titles; Stalin: Personality of; Stalin: Private Life of

Further reading: H. Günther, ed. *The Culture of the Stalin Period.* London: Macmillan, 1990; Nikita Khrushchev. "The Cult of Personality." In Robert V. Daniels, ed. *The Stalin Revolution.* Boston: Houghton Mifflin, 1997; Rosalind Marsh. *Images of Dictatorship: Portraits of Stalin in Literature.* London: Routledge, 1989; Roy Medvedev. *Let History Judge: The Origins and Consequences of Stalinism.* New York: Columbia University Press, 1989; Robert C. Tucker. *Stalin in Power: The Revolution from Above, 1928–1941.* London: Chatto and Windus, 1990.

De-Stalinization

*I*n her powerful memoir of her father, published in 1967, Svetlana Allilueva spoke eloquently of Stalin's enduring influence over Soviet life fifteen years after his death. "He is gone, but his shadow still stands over all of us. It still dictates to us and we, very often, obey," she wrote. Twenty-four years later with the breakup of the Soviet Union in 1991, the Stalinist specter was still lingering. At the turn of the century the Old Guard Stalinists were still bemoaning the chaos of the post-Communist years and the loss of that constrained but ordered existence—economic, social, political—that had prevailed under the Great Leader.

The immediate reaction to Stalin's death in 1953 was one of complete bewilderment among ordinary people, who felt "as if they had lost their religion" and whose main preoccupation now was how they could possibly manage without him. As the journalist Hedrick Smith observed, "[Stalin] was the linchpin of their universe, their compass, their czar, the ruler who held life together and gave it meaning. His death shattered their national self-confidence, leaving them feeling bereaved and abandoned, vulnerable to external enemies and uncertain of a future without him."

In the jostling for the Soviet leadership after Stalin's death, Vyacheslav Molotov, Georgy Malenkov, and briefly Lavrenty Beria appeared to be the major candidates. Together they began to take steps to suppress the cult of the individual that had been perpetuated under Stalin. They now favored a return to the traditional view of history, as propagated by Karl Marx and also by Leo Tolstoy, that history is made by the collective will of the masses and not by single totalitarian leaders. However, none of them condemned the pernicious Stalin cult outright, although in private they began discussing the problems of its legacy. When Beria's ambition to stage his own political takeover was quashed, Nikita Khrushchev gained the ascendant and in 1953 he became first secretary of the Central Committee.

Khrushchev now seemed eager to debunk the career of his predecessor, Stalin, and in so doing obfuscate his own complicity in the purges (he ordered the quiet removal from the archives of any condemned lists bearing his own signature). At the Twentieth Congress of the Communist Party on 25 February 1956 Khrushchev delivered a four-hour speech in closed session on "the cult of the individual and its consequences." During the course of the speech he cataloged Stalin's crimes, taking as his starting point the "unjustified repression and other violations of Soviet legality" (i.e., the purges of the 1930s). But he ignored the earlier political trials, the repressions, and all the abuses of enforced collectivization under the First Five-Year Plan. In the process Khrushchev effectively washed his own and his contemporaries' hands of responsibility for crimes that they had themselves committed in imposing Stalin's draconian policies. His objective was clear—to preserve the monolith of the Stalinist state and bureaucracy while destroying its figurehead, Stalin, and the iconography associated with him. But the reputation of Lenin had to be protected at all costs.

Despite Khrushchev's 1956 denunciation of Stalin to the Soviet Union's political elite, the onset of a political and cultural thaw as reflected in the publication of such works as Solzhenitsyn's *One Day in the Life of Ivan Denisovich* in 1962, and the rehabilitation of many prominent figures murdered during the Great Terror, Stalin's official public dethronement did not come until 1961, when his corpse was removed from Lenin's Mausoleum. This brief period of discussion of the Stalinist years, albeit in veiled terms, ended with the fall of Khrushchev in 1964, and for another twenty years the subject was once more taboo with Soviet historians. But the process of demystification had at least begun, with the removal of portraits, statues, and other visual ephemera and the changing of place names (Stalingrad reverted to its former name of Volgograd in 1961). However, many of the Stalinist historical and political texts, such as the *History of the All-Union Communist Party,* which had been written under Stalin's aegis, remained as standard textbooks, although in newly published editions. Any mention of Stalin was now reduced to brief summaries, which merely hinted at the "negative repercussions" of his personality traits without initiating any sustained condemnation of him.

For years to come the "errors and excesses" of the grim years of Stalin's rule would remain a euphemism, the true significance of which younger generations failed to grasp until most of Stalin's die-hard supporters in government and the bureaucracy were dead or out of power. It was, therefore, not until Mikhail Gorbachev's bold experiment with glasnost (the Soviet policy permitting open discussion of political and social issues) and the growth of the organization Memorial (set up to discover the true fate of those murdered and imprisoned during the Great Terror) during the second half of the 1980s that information began to filter out slowly and Russians began to come to terms with the truth of their history. This process gave birth to a new wave of rehabilitations and the publication of long-suppressed literature about the Stalinist years, with powerful memoirs by those who had survived the Gulag—Nataliya Ginzburg's, for instance—appearing as a painful testimony to the full horrors of the Great Terror.

As early as 1962, the poet Yevgeny Yevtushenko spoke publicly about the problem that faced Soviet society: "We removed / him / from the Mausoleum. / But how do we remove Stalin / from Stalin's heirs?" Despite more recent and penetrating accounts of Stalin's rule published in Russia, nothing, it seems, can dent the devotion of some to the memory of Stalin. Many of the older generation have continued to nurse an innate superstition that "speaking ill of the czar [i.e., Stalin] is bad business," a superstition that goes back to peasants' reverence for the tsar as the *batyushka* or "little father." In his home country of Georgia Stalin's portraits and his statue (at his birthplace in Gori) are still in evidence, his memory is still toasted, and his humble birthplace is revered. One of many typical responses to such continuing affection in Georgia is, "We love Stalin here. He was a strong boss. With Stalin, people knew where they stood." This attitude resurfaced during the dislocations of the economic crisis of the late 1990s when, more than ever, people found themselves let down by their new "democratic" style of government, a government increasingly incapable of exerting a unifying hold on its disgruntled masses.

In a poll taken on the 1998 anniversary of Stalin's death, one in six people affirmed that Stalin was the best leader the country had ever had. It seemed that his image was gaining a new foothold, with more and more of the older generation wishing for a return to the economic security and order and the authoritarian style of leadership that had prevailed during the days of Stalinism.

Hedrick Smith has pointed out that the Russians have a propensity for "historical amnesia"—an ability to forget the worst excesses of the Stalinist years and remember only the good times. Equally, it would seem that many people feared having to come to terms with the huge sacrifices made by the nation in the name of a man whom Leon Trotsky would have wished to see consigned "to the dustbin of history" (along with the Mensheviks, to whom he was originally referring). To admit to the sham of the cult of the personality would be to admit complicity in the collective national guilt for allowing Stalin's ascendance in the first place. And this sense of responsibility and guilt has continued to plague the survivors of his generation, who can only remember that under Stalin they built a new socialist state, industrialized the country, achieved high levels of mass literacy, and fought and won a long and bitter war.

See also Cult of the Personality; The Great Terror; Khrushchev, Nikita

Further reading: *Russia: The Wild East. Granta* no. 64 (winter 1998); Robert Harris. "The West Prefers Its Dictators Red." *Sunday Times,* 11 October 1998; Adam Hochschild. *The Unquiet Ghost: Russians Remember Stalin.* London: Serpent's Tail, 1995; Nikita Khrushchev. *The Secret Speech.* Nottingham, UK: Spokesman Books, 1976; Hedrick Smith. *The Russians.* London: Sphere Books, 1976; Hedrick Smith . *The New Russians.* London: Hutchinson, 1990; Robert Service. *A History of Twentieth-Century Russia.* London: Allen Lane, 1997.

"Dizzy with Success"

In March 1930, Stalin realized that the frenzy to collectivize the peasantry at record speed was snowballing out of control, with insufficient attention to proper planning and organization. He decided to call a temporary halt to the process, before it resulted in total chaos in the countryside and threatened the country as a whole with serious economic collapse.

On 2 March 1930 Stalin's article "Dizzy with Success" chastised local Communist Party officials for losing sight of the fact that the move to collectivize the peasants was a voluntary one. "They become dizzy with success, lose all sense of proportion, lose the faculty of understanding realities, reveal a tendency to overestimate their own strength and to underestimate the struggle of the enemy; reckless attempts are made to settle all the problems of socialist construction in 'two ticks,'" he wrote. Barely fifteen months into the program, approximately 55 percent of peasant households had been absorbed into the collective system. Stalin now insisted that those peasants who had been coerced into joining collectives should be allowed to leave. The peasantry were more than ready to take advantage of this unexpected turnaround in policy. Of the 14 million who had joined collective farms by the time of Stalin's article, only 5 million remained two months later.

The logic behind this surprising act of what seemed like altruisim on Stalin's part in his defense of the peasantry left local officials totally bewildered, having privately congratulated themselves on their recent successes. But Stalin was by now seriously worried that the chaotic situation in the countryside would severely affect the spring planting and the autumn harvest at a time when grain was one of the Soviet Union's most precious commodities. In reality Stalin had been betrayed by his own lack of economic skills and his miscalculation of the degree of bitter resistance to collectivization by the peasants, who were increasingly resorting to acts of violence rather than submit to collectivization.

It was, of course, a simple matter for Stalin to assume the role of benign leader and shift the blame for such excesses conveniently onto the shoulders of overzealous local officials, while simultaneously making a magnanimous gesture toward the hard-pressed peasantry. This, however, was only a short-term measure. By the time the cereal crops had been harvested, the collectivization program was once again reinvigorated, and by July 1931, with the help of various fines and inducements, it was almost back to its March 1930 levels.

See also Collectivization; Five-Year Plans

Doctors' Plot

In the winter of 1952, not long before his death, Stalin was preparing a renewed attack on the Soviet Union's Jews. He had already made clear his new anti-Semitic campaign in eastern Europe that November with the arrest, trial, and execution of ten prominent Jews, including General Secretary Rudolph Slansky, all of the Czechoslovakian Communist Party.

Stalin had become obsessed with the rise of Zionism since the establishment of Israel in 1948 and was now bent on rooting out Zionists and cosmopolitans (as Jewish intellectuals were called) from Soviet society. In 1953 Lavrenty Beria was given the task of launching a hysterical campaign against a supposed cabal of nine, mostly Jewish, Kremlin doctors that would become the last manifestation of Stalin's medieval-style witch-hunt. The announcement was made in *Pravda* that nine doctors who had infiltrated the Kremlin as physicians to the leading members of the government had conspired to murder several eminent politicians, including Andrey Zhdanov (a member of the Politburo who had died

suddenly in 1948) and his brother-in-law Alexander Shcherbakov (secretary of the Central Committee), by either poisoning them or deliberately mismanaging medical care to cause their deaths.

Those arrested included Stalin's own personal doctor, V. N. Vinogradov, and six others who were Jewish, including M. S. Vovsi (the surgeon general of the Red Army and a cousin of the Jewish actor Solomon Mikhoels, who had died under suspicious circumstances in 1948), M. B. Kogan, A. Feldman, and Professor Y. Etinger. On Stalin's explicit instructions, confessions were beaten out of all but one of the accused. According to Khrushchev, Stalin had ordered that the interrogators "beat, beat, and beat [them] again" until the accused confessed. These confessions amounted to admitting to the charge, in the case of the Jewish doctors, of being Zionists and agents of "Jewish bourgeois-nationalist" organizations in the United States. Etinger died under interrogation; the others were all crippled, both mentally and physically, by the torture they suffered.

Anti-Semitism was further whipped up among the population at large, with rumors being spread that drugs in the chemists' shops had been contaminated by the Jews. The rumors became so potent that people stopped going to see their (often Jewish) medical practitioners. Solzhenitsyn alleged in *Gulag Archipelago* that rumor had it at the time that Stalin planned to stage a public hanging of the Kremlin doctors in Red Square. This would have had the desired effect of inciting anti-Jewish pogroms, upon which Stalin would have "come to the rescue" of the oppressed Jews by magnanimously agreeing to arrange their resettlement far away from European Russia to the "safety" of Kazakhstan and Siberia. He had already done as much with Volga Germans, Crimean Tartars, and other ethnic minorities who had been deported en masse during the war, and it seems probable that the trial of the Kremlin doctors was but the

A rare portrait of a smiling Stalin with his mother, Ekaterina Dzhugashvili, in 1935. Seen here wearing traditional Georgian dress, Keke, as she was known in the family, never left Georgia and lived extremely modestly.

prelude to a much larger act of systematic ethnic cleansing of the Jews.

It was only Stalin's death in March 1953 that saved the doctors from the gruesome fate planned for them. The charges against them were immediately dropped, and those who had been responsible for beating them into submission were punished. M. D. Ryumin, the chief investigator who had fabricated the case, was shot. Dr. Lydia Timashuk, the dutiful junior radiologist at the Kremlin hospital who had written to Stalin describing what she had considered to be mismanagement in the treatment of Zhdanov, was obliged to give back the Order of Lenin awarded her for her watchfulness.

See also The Great Terror; Jews

Further reading: Louis Rapoport. *Stalin's War against the Jews: The Doctors' Plot and the Soviet Solution.* New York: Free Press, 1990; Yakov Rapoport. *The Doctors' Plot: Stalin's Last Crime.* London: Fourth Estate, 1991.

Dzhugashvili, Ekaterina Georgievna (ca. 1858–1937)

Born Ekaterina Georgievna Geladze, Stalin's mother, known to the family as Keke, was the daughter of serfs (who were not emancipated in Russia until Alexander II's reign in 1861). She nevertheless received a rudimentary education as a child in Gori, Georgia, before being married at age sixteen. When Stalin, her third son but the first to survive, was born, the devout Ekaterina, grateful to God for sparing him, resolved that he would become a priest.

Effectively deserted by her husband, who spent most of the time working as a shoemaker in Tiflis, Keke worked hard as a laundress and seamstress to support Stalin. Although she was devoted to her Soso (Georgian for "little Joe"), as she called him, her rigorous sense of discipline resulted in severe beatings for acts of disobedience. She was rewarded after Stalin rose to power, when he uprooted her from her humble home to the splendid isolation of the former palace of the tsar's viceroy in Tiflis. A simple God-fearing peasant with modest needs, Keke never adapted to such a large living space and confined herself to one little room, lived abstemiously, and made no material demands on her son.

Although he saw her only a couple of times after the revolution (she refused his invitations to go to Moscow, and Stalin rarely left the capital), Stalin made sure Keke was provided for and wrote tender, albeit brief, letters to her in Georgian. It was not until she was seriously ill in 1935 that he finally went to see her in Tiflis. Even then Keke remained stubbornly unimpressed by his rise to political glory, telling him that he "would have done better to remain a priest." Despite his sentimental devotion to her, however, Stalin did not attend his mother's funeral. While his dislike for traveling and fear of assassination were probably the main reasons for his nonattendance, this was considered by many of his fellow Georgians as a callous rejection of deeply held Georgian traditions regarding the proper veneration of the dead. The funeral arrangements were made for Stalin by his loyal Georgian plenipotentiary (and later head of the NKVD) Lavrenty Beria.

See also Dzhugashvili, Iosif; Dzhugashvili, Vissarion
Further reading Edvard Radzinsky. *Stalin.* London: Hodder and Stoughton, 1996.

Dzhugashvili, Evgeny (1936–)

Stalin's grandson Evgeny Dzuhugashvili (the son of Stalin's eldest son Yakov Dzhugashvili) is an ardent supporter of his grandfather. He accentuates the similarities in his appearance to the Great Leader and venerates his memory by campaigning obsessively to restore Stalin's reputation. "I

adore Stalin," he declares, "He was a genius. He was a great man and a great leader."

Based in Georgia, Stalin's homeland, Dzhugashvili was previously a colonel in the Soviet army. He now spends his time tending his own shrine to Stalin's memory and compiling a blacklist of Stalin's critics, whom he dubs in characteristically Stalinist style "enemies of the people." He claims (in similar fashion to apologists for the Holocaust) that the statistics gathered on the Great Terror are lies. "No more than 37,000 people died in the camps under him." After the collapse of the Soviet Union, Dzhugashvili set up his own organization—the Patriotic Movement for the Study of Stalin's Heritage—which he claims has 100,000 supporters in Georgia alone. His present objective is to open more offices and recruit more members in other pro-Stalinist parts of the former Soviet Union—Russia, Belarus, and Ukraine. In 1999 he announced his intention to run as a presidential candidate in the 2000 elections, representing an extreme left coalition, the Patriotic Union, that seeks to restore Communist rule.

See also De-Stalinization; Dzhugashvili, Yakov; Svanidze, Ekaterina

Dzhugashvili, Iosif Vissarionovich

Stalin ceased to use his birth name Iosif Dzhugashvili after first engaging in underground revolutionary activities and leaving the Tiflis Seminary in May 1899. Like all true Russian revolutionaries, he adopted a code name, "Koba." By 1912 he had found it necessary to divest himself of his very identifiable Georgian name (the ending "vili" is a typical Georgian patronymic suffix), if only because his Russian colleagues in the Bolshevik Party found it difficult to remember. Lenin himself had been hard-pressed to recall it and in 1915 was still asking a colleague to "find out for me

Koba's name (Josef Dzh . . . ? We've forgotten)." Stalin effaced the obvious public reminders of his Georgian background and even came to reject his Georgian alias, Koba, settling instead for a name with similar euphonic characteristics as that of Lenin. He took the name Stalin—"man of steel."

Throughout his life, rumors persisted that Stalin's ethnicity was actually Ossetian (a fact alluded to in Osip Mandelstam's famous poem about him) through his paternal grandfather, and some alleged that his father's name had been Dzhugaev rather than Dzhugashvili. Such a shift in ethnic attribution (Ossetians were Iranian by ethnic origin), convincing or not, may well have been contrived in order to relieve the proud Georgian republic of a possible sense of shame for having produced him. Since the border between the South Ossetian Republic and Georgia was not far from Stalin's home village of Gori, such a suggestion is not an impossibility. Like so much else in Stalin's early life, Stalin's true ancestry is riddled with unsubstantiated rumor and conjecture.

Various apocryphal stories about Stalin's possible illegitimacy have accumulated over the years, ranging from the ridiculous—that he was the son of the famous nineteenth-century Russian explorer Nikolay Przhevalsky—to the more plausible—that he was the result of a liaison between his mother and her one-time employer, a merchant called Egnatashvili. Stalin himself is supposed to have once remarked that he was "the son of a priest." This may well have been an ironic joke, referring to his studies in the Tiflis Seminary, or simply a better alternative to the drunken shoemaker, Beso Dzhugashvili, who was supposed to have fathered him. The rumors over Stalin's illegitimacy seem to have been inspired by Beso's frequent absences from home while working in Tiflis or while on drunken benders. Whatever his true paternity, Stalin ensured, as much as possible, that this aspect of his past remained buried or at least obscured. There were, however, aspects of his appearance and his private life that would always betray his roots—his swarthy features, his Georgian accent, his favorite tipple (Georgian wine), and his love of Georgian poetry.

See also Georgia; Stalin: Nicknames, Aliases, and Official Titles; Stalin: Physical Appearance of; Stalin: Private Life of
Further reading: Edvard Radzinsky. Stalin. London: Hodder & Stoughton, 1996.

Dzhugashvili, Vissarion Ivanovich (ca. 1850–?)

Stalin's father, Vissarion Dzhugashvil, or Beso, as he was known in the family, came from the small village Didi-Lilo in the mountains of Georgia, which he left to learn a trade as a shoemaker in Tiflis. He met Ekaterina Georgievna Geladze, Stalin's mother, known as Keke, on a visit to friends in Gori and married her in 1874. Even on their wedding day, Beso's propensity for drunken aggression manifested itself, and his mean and moody character would lead to violent outbursts that would haunt Stalin's childhood. Beso spent most of his time after his marriage working in Tiflis at a factory that made boots for the tsarist army in the Caucasus, returning home sporadically, only to beat both his wife and his son, known then as Soso. He does not appear to have stayed long to comfort Keke after the death in infancy of three of their other children and derided her for having ambitions in the church for their fourth child, Soso. Some time around 1888 Beso disappeared altogether, and according to rumors, he later died in a drunken brawl in the 1890s. While Stalin described his father as being dead in 1912, Beso was reportedly seen alive as late as 1931 in Sukhumi. No one knows what finally happened to him. Undoubtedly such vicious treatment by his father inspired feelings of deep and bitter resentment in the young Stalin, a bitterness that remained with him for the rest of his life and that led him to destroy all links with such an unappealing father.

See also Dzhugashvili, Ekaterina; Dzhugashvili, Iosif

Dzhugashvili, Yakov Iosifovich (1907–1943)

Stalin's son, Yakov Dzhugashvili, by his first wife, Ekaterina Svanidze, is officially given the birthdate of 1908 in Soviet records, but he must have been born in 1907, as his mother died later that year. He grew up with his aunt's family in Tiflis, not joining his father until Stalin summoned him to Moscow in 1922.

After studying engineering, Yakov trained for the military at the Red Army artillery academy. There was no love lost between father and son, and Stalin was uneasy at his son's presence as a reminder of his Georgian past—Yakov spoke with a strong Georgian accent. They disagreed violently on everything. On occasion Stalin, contemptuous of what he considered a rather lackluster son, meted out the same kind of violence to him as had been inflicted on him by his own father. Yakov tried to do his duty but proved an undistinguished scholar, failing particularly badly and unforgivably in the sacred subject of Marxism-Leninism. After volunteering at the outbreak of World War II, Yakov was promoted to lieutenant in the 14th Armored Division, but in 1941 was taken prisoner by the Germans at Vitebsk, Belarus.

The Germans immediately took advantage of this political gift horse, claiming in the propaganda leaflets that they rained on Soviet troops that Yakov had defected. Whether or not Stalin believed this and whether he considered it a deliberate act of revenge on Yakov's part, Stalin disowned him for what he considered to be an act of cowardice in surrendering. During his imprisonment Yakov behaved with dignity and loyalty and even tried to escape. Later in the war the Germans offered to trade him for a German officer held prisoner—some say Field Marshal Friedrich von Paulus, who had recently surrendered at Stalingrad—but Stalin adamantly refused such a deal, denying that he had a son who had been taken prisoner. (A story later circulated that Stalin had alleged that he would not trade a field marshal for an ordinary soldier.) Depressed and anxious about the possible fate that might await him on repatriation to the Soviet Union at the end of the war, one day in April 1943 Yakov deliberately approached the perimeter fence of Sachsenhausen, where he was being held, and was fatally shot while attempting to escape.

In 1935, Yakov had infuriated his father by marrying a Jew, Yulia Meltzer. She was arrested after Yakov's capture and imprisoned for two years during the war (she was released in 1943). Their son, Evgeny, is currently a leading keeper of the Stalinist flame in Georgia.

See also Dzhugashvili, Evgeny
Further reading: Svetlana Alliluyeva. *Twenty Letters to a Friend*. London: Hutchinson, 1967. Dmitri Volkogonov. *Stalin: Triumph and Tragedy*. London: Weidenfeld and Nicolson, 1991.

Eastern Europe

As long ago as 1920, a Western traveler in the Soviet Union, Ethel Snowden, made mention of an "iron curtain" dividing Bolshevik Russia from the West, but it was Winston Churchill who openly and famously expressed collective Western apprehension on the subject, when in a speech made at Fulton, Missouri, in 1946 he solemnly intoned that "from Stettin in the Baltic to Trieste in the Adriatic, an iron curtain has descended across the Continent."

When Stalin first made clear his ambitions for the pursuit of Soviet interests in Eastern Europe after World War II, he was, in part, perpetuating an age-old Russian obsession with territorial expansion. It was a tradition that went back to the late fifteenth century when Russia had first begun acquiring stretches of territory from other ailing empires on its borderlands in Poland, Lithuania, and the Ottoman Empire. By the end of World War II, in gratitude for the heroic levels of sacrifice made by both the Soviet military and the civilian population in helping defeat Hitler, there was little that the grateful Allies could do but condone the military reality of the occupation of great stretches of Eastern Europe by Soviet troops. In Stalin's view the subsequent Sovietization of Eastern Europe would be his legitimate spoils of war.

Poland had for long been a regular casualty of Russian territorial ambition and was also the easiest prey. It had been partitioned three times between Russia, Austria, and Prussia, in 1772, 1793, and 1795. It had enjoyed only a brief period as an independent republic after World War I (albeit under the dictatorial rule of Marshal Josef Pilsudski), only to be carved up again by the Soviet Union and Germany as a result of the German-Soviet Non-Aggression Pact of 1939.

During the summer of 1944, as the Soviets drove the Germans out of Poland, Stalin's immediate priority was to renew his claim to the Polish territories he had annexed under the German-Soviet Pact that had subsequently fallen under German occupation. A Communist Polish Committee of National Liberation was quickly established in July in Lublin, purportedly as the core of a future democratic government. Any Polish nationalist groups and resistance fighters who dissented from this were rounded up by the Soviet secret police. On 17 September Stalin's intentions were made clearer when 1 million Red Army troops invaded Poland as the Wehrmacht retreated. Stalin's pretext was that instability in Poland threatened its nearby neighbors and left it open to renewed German incursions. In an attempt to reclaim Warsaw before the Soviets arrived to drive the Germans out, the Polish government in exile initiated an ill-judged and badly timed uprising there. It was thought that the city could be taken in a week, in advance of the arrival of the Red Army. But the uprising lasted two months, during which 15,000 Polish fighters and 200,000 civilians were killed and Warsaw was almost flattened while the Red Army watched the conflagration from the other side of the Vistula River. Thus, the destruction of precisely those dissident national and anti-Soviet elements that might well have proved obstructionist to Soviet ambitions was achieved before Stalin made his own move on Polish territory.

In 1945 the Polish frontier with the Soviet Union in the east had been settled on the Curzon line and with Germany to the west on the Oder-Neisse line. Thus, geographically sandwiched as it was between these two demarcation lines, Poland once again found itself a buffer state—in the front line against any future revival of German territorial ambition. As a result it was here, more than in any other Eastern European state, that Stalin exercised the closest control. The Western Allies, anxious to placate Stalin, did not oppose this, betraying the legitimate Polish government in exile, which on its return to Poland was forced into a coalition with the Communists. Supposedly democratic elections were set up by the Soviets but were orchestrated to block the selection of candidates for the opposition Polish People's Party. A Moscow-trained Communist and loyal Stalinist, Boleslaw Bierut, was eventually installed as Poland's first president in 1945. An all-too-familiar pattern of mass arrests of anti-Communists, of collectivization imposed on the Polish peasantry, and of nationalization of the country's industries followed. A Soviet-style constitution was also adopted.

The Soviets found it hard to extinguish the flame of Polish nationalism, for a time briefly rekindled under the leadership of Wladyslaw Gomulka (who was dismissed in 1948). Political opposition was suppressed until sporadic acts of resistance to Soviet domination returned with a series of strikes and riots in 1956 as a result of Khrushchev's program of de-Stalinization throughout the Eastern bloc.

Elsewhere in Eastern Europe the transition to the Soviet and thus Communist sphere of influence in the late 1940s was achieved with less resistance. In the first years after the war, Stalin had aimed to exert enough influence on Eastern European states to ensure their political loyalty, rather than impose a rigorous Communist system on them. All thought of initiating a European Communist revolution had long since evaporated. The priorities were now those of security, achieved through some strategic territorial acquisitions (in particular in eastern Prussia and eastern Poland), and economics, achieved by building interdependence in Eastern Europe and through Comecon (the Council for Mutual Economic Assistance established for Eastern Europe in 1949) while simultaneously exerting independence from the West and thumbing the nose at the U.S.-backed Marshall Plan for European recovery.

For a while, therefore, a modicum of mutal cooperation between various socialist, Communist, and nationalist groups in coalition governments was condoned (in Hungary, for example, Communists held only two ministerial posts). Finland, which had a long history of fierce resistance to Russian domination and which had held the Soviet Union at bay during the Winter War of 1939–1940, managed to retain its independence. No doubt Stalin realized that any renewed attack on the Finns would not be condoned in the West, nor could he risk a repetition of the previous military debacle.

At a 1944 conference in Moscow, Stalin and Churchill had privately struck their own deal over Greece, which the Soviets left alone in return for a controlling influence in Romania and Bulgaria. Romania (which had fought with the Germans) and Bulgaria were quickly occupied and lost their monarchies. Bulgaria, by far the most acquiescent convert to Communist government, became a staunch supporter of Stalinism under the leadership of Georgy Dimitrov, but only after his aspirations for a socialist federation of states in southeastern Europe, to include Yugoslavia and Romania, had been swiftly and firmly quashed by Stalin.

The only countries in Eastern Europe initially sustaining single-party Communist states were Yugoslavia and Albania. Partisan resistance based in the mountains of Albania had helped secure the country's liberation from the Germans in 1944 with little Allied help. A provisional government under hard-liner Enver Hoxha secured a Communist People's Republic (based on Albania's own Communist Party, founded in 1941) that would later break with the Soviet Union and become the most entrenched and isolated dictatorship of all the Eastern European Communist regimes until the death of Hoxha in 1985.

In the case of Romania, a country whose fascist government had allied itself with Germany during the war, the transition to communism began after the Soviets invaded in 1944. The monarchy was pushed out in 1947, and the following year the Romanian Workers' Party gained control and instituted a changeover to Soviet-style government. Although Romania paid lip service to the Soviet Union through its membership of Comecon and Cominform, it managed to maintain a degree of independence from Moscow after President Nicolae Ceauşescu instituted his own particular brand of totalitarian control in the 1960s.

In 1944 Romanian troops had numbered among those Soviet forces sent into Hungary to take part in a bloody campaign to liberate the country from German occupation. Soon after, the Hungarian Social Democrats were compelled to cooperate with the Communists in the setting up of a "Republic of Workers and Working Peasants" under a coalition government led by the ruthless head of the Hungarian Communist Party, Matyas Rakosi. Rakosi's gov-

ernment became increasingly Stalinist in character and persisted until a brief period under the liberalizing Prime Minister Imre Nagy ended in the tragedy of the Hungarian uprising of 1956.

In Czechoslovakia, the leader of its government in exile, Eduard Beneš, returned optimistically from wartime exile to lead what was advertised as a showcase coalition government made up of Communists and Czech resistance leaders. For a brief period the new government enjoyed popular support, but by 1948 it had been fragmented by dissent between Communists and non-Communists. A Communist coup swept it all away, instituting a government that quickly adopted a Soviet-style constitution and toed the line with Moscow.

In 1949 the German Democratic Republic became the last Eastern European state to join the other Soviet satellites. Created from the Soviet-occupied territories of Germany and the Soviet sector of Berlin, under the dictatorial rule of the Socialist Unity Party and its Stalinist leader Walter Ulbricht, East Germany was for forty years one of the most hard-line Communist states, with a notorious secret police, the Stasi, closely modeled on the Soviet NKVD and KGB.

The thorn in Stalin's side proved to be Yugoslavia, which had proclaimed itself a Socialist Federal Republic under Marshal Tito in 1945. After a turbulent relationship with the Soviet Union in Cominform, during which Tito repeatedly resisted Soviet attempts at domination, Yugoslavia was expelled in 1948. Tito had no regrets about no longer being a member of "the family of fraternal Communist Parties" and successfully steered Yugoslavia along a nonaligned path until his death in 1980.

It was probably the break with Yugoslavia that, more than anything else, made clear to Stalin the difficulties of sustaining a merely benign, guiding interest in Eastern Europe through the offices of Cominform and its economic counterpart

Comecon, in the hope that these bodies would sufficiently ensure Eastern Europe's loyalty to the Soviet Union. Stalin, forever watchful of signs of treachery and dissent and now entering a new phase of strained relations with Western Europe as the Cold War gathered pace, determined that the only safe course was to establish governments that were uniformly Communist and unquestioningly loyal to Moscow. After a series of purges throughout opposition groups in Eastern Europe that included the execution of senior politicians in Hungary, Bulgaria, Albania, and Czechoslovakia, Stalin had by 1952 instituted from above the only form of political control with which he felt safe. With a string of satellite states controlled by leaders, most of whom had been drilled into allegiance under training in Moscow, their peasantry and industries now nationalized along Soviet lines and often to Soviet advantage, Stalin ensured the isolation of the greater part of Eastern Europe, both politically and economically, on the other side of his impenetrable Iron Curtain.

Ironically, it was the sudden and dramatic collapse of the Communist regime of one of Stalin's most loyal allies, East Germany, in November 1989 that initiated the domino effect of change throughout the rest of the Eastern European Communist monolith. It was an event quickly followed by the joyful and much-televised destruction of the most tangible and evocative symbol of the Cold War years—the Berlin Wall. Alexander Solzhenitsyn was quick to warn, however, that though "the clock of communism has stopped striking" and the demolition of the Communist monolith had begun, the Eastern European nations should protect themselves "from being crushed by the rubble."

See also "The Big Three"; Cold War; Comintern; Great Patriotic War; Tito, Marshal

Further reading: Milovan Djilas. *Conversations with Stalin.* Harmondsworth, UK: Penguin, 1962; Hélène Carrère d'Encausse. *Big Brother: The Soviet Union and Soviet Europe.* New York: Holmes and Meier, 1987.

Economic Policy
See Collectivization; Five-Year Plans.

Education

At the time of the 1917 Revolution about 60 percent of the Russian population was illiterate. Under the Bolsheviks, beginning in 1922, education became a fundamental part of state planning with the ambitious objective of providing education for all. By 1939 the illiteracy level had dropped to about 20 percent, but education was now dominated by a rigid Stalinist system that strictly controlled the intake of proscribed knowledge, according to Communist Party doctrine and in texts vetted by Stalin.

The primary motive behind the Bolshevik campaign to educate had been the emancipation of women and the opening of higher education to them at the universities, which under the tsars had been extremely circumscribed. A system of kindergartens and preschool education was set up not only to allow mothers to resume work or their studies after childbirth but also as part of the psychology of cradle-to-grave control of the lives of the masses. Basic education would become the cornerstone of mass edification and ultimately of mass indoctrination colored by Stalin's particularly xenophobic and nationalistic attitudes. Thus in 1934 nursery school teachers were instructed that their role was "to instill love for the Soviet Motherland, for their own people, its leaders, the Soviet Army, making use of the richness of their native land, national creativity and striking events in the life of the country, accessible to a child's mind."

In 1931 Stalin passed a decree making the compulsory minimum number of years of schooling for children in rural areas four and for children in cities, seven. Education was organized into a system of grades from one to ten, taking children from infant to secondary education. During the early years of the New Economic Policy (NEP) there had been a flirtation with progressive methods in teaching, but under Stalin new trends in education being pioneered in the West were rejected in favor of traditional, authoritarian methods that emphasized regimentation of thought (achieved through constant recitation and learning by rote) and, above all, loyalty to the state. The crucial element of self-monitoring was encouraged through the auspices of the youth organizations the Young Pioneers and the Komsomol, the junior thought-police who, drilled in the arts of administering discipline and monitoring ideological and moral correctness among their peers, often took delight in taking their own parents to task for their shortcomings.

In higher education, the primary objective was to move away from the old elitist concept of academia as a world where abstract thought could be indulged toward a restructuring of universities as a training ground for new generations of such key workers as agriculturalists, engineers, scientists, and economists who could contribute to the modernization and industrialization programs. At a lower level, technical schools (*tekhnikumy*) taught vocational skills useful for the factory floor and for the semiskilled professions. In general the system had originally aimed to give preferential treatment to children from working-class and peasant backgrounds (by 1933 these amounted to 58 percent of students) and to squeeze out prerevolutionary bourgeois elements in the teaching profession. Life became increasingly difficult for teachers and professors of the older generation who had yet to embrace communism. Those who were not members of the Party were rapidly forced out.

Part and parcel of the educational program was the emphasis on social responsibility and usefulness. Pupils were increasingly involved in communal projects outside their schools, in factories and on collective farms. In some areas of the Soviet Union this involvement would result in schoolchildren being used as cheap labor, for example, in the Donbass coal mines and the cotton fields of Central Asia.

In 1935 the policy regarding university admissions changed again, shifting away from the socialist emphasis on social (i.e., working-class) background to a reemphasis on ability. This led to a degree of suspicion leveled at those considered class enemies (i.e., those not from working-class backgrounds), but during the period of the First Five-Year Plan their numbers, nevertheless, continued to rise. By early 1938, 42.2 percent of students came from the more privileged background of the professional classes, while peasants, who made up the vast proportion of the population, were still underrepresented in higher education. Policy continued to favor those from more privileged backgrounds with the introduction of tuition fees in 1948 for further education and the setting up of State Labor Reserves. The latter were designed to bolster industry by calling up as many as 1 million young men a year between the ages of fourteen and seventeen for training in industrial schools.

Such measures seemed to many a retrograde step, forcing many poorer working-class students to abandon their studies. Meanwhile, the children of Party officials and apparatchiks were being given precedence in educational opportunities, thus guaranteeing the perpetuation of the Soviet *nomenklatura* within its own closed ranks.

See also Family Life; Historiography; Komsomol; *Nomenklatura; History of the All-Union Communist Party;* Women

Further reading: Sheila Fitzpatrick. *Education and Social Mobility in the Soviet Union, 1921–1934.* Cambridge: Cambridge University Press, 1979; J. Muckle. *Education in Russia Past and Present: an Introductory Study Guide and Select Bibliography.* Nottingham, UK: Bramcote Press, 1993.

Eisenstein, Sergey Mikhailovich (1898–1948)

One of the most influential figures in twentieth-century cinema, Sergey Eisenstein built his reputation on the development of powerful, ground-breaking cinematographic techniques. His consummate skill in juxtaposing striking and even disturbing images, which he named the "montage of film attractions," has enshrined him as the abiding inspiration for many later generations of sometimes unduly reverential filmmakers. Eisenstein's opus was small (he completed only seven films), and much of it was produced under conditions of political uncertainty and personal duress. He also wrote some notable works on film theory, including *The Film Sense* (1942) and *Film Form* (1949).

Of Jewish descent, Eisenstein left his birthplace in Riga, Latvia, in 1910 to settle in St. Petersburg. An imaginative and sensitive boy who loved literature and art, the young Eisenstein nevertheless acceded to his architect father's demand that he should follow in his footsteps by studying civil engineering. At this time Eisenstein began to develop an interest in the theater and soon fell under the spell of the innovative director Vsevolod Meyerhold, whose experimental work at the Alexandrinsky Theater combined techniques derived from personal favorites of Eisenstein's—the circus and the commedia dell'arte.

After the 1917 Revolution and during the ensuing civil war, Eisenstein was attached to a Red Army construction unit as a civil engineer. In 1920, having decided to abandon his engineering career, he settled in Moscow and soon became drawn back into the theater. He took a job at the Proletkult Theater as a scene painter and set designer, and his early work there displayed his natural talent for inventiveness and flamboyant design. In 1921 he developed his techniques further, again under Meyer-

hold, at the State School for Stage Direction. Meyerhold would later assert that "all Eisenstein's work has its origins in the laboratory where we once worked together as teacher and pupil," a debt that Eisenstein would always acknowledge. Returning to Proletkult as artistic director of its touring theater in 1922, Eisenstein made his first major impact with a production of Nikolay Ostrovsky's play *Enough Simplicity for Every Wise Man*. Having already begun experimenting with the medium of film, in 1924 Eisenstein was finally given the opportunity of directing a film documentary to coincide with the twentieth anniversary of the 1905 Revolution.

The end product *Strike* (1924) introduced Eisenstein's idiosyncratic cinematic style of montage and the use of often violent visual metaphors to arouse emotional responses in his audiences. These techniques proved somewhat baffling to the film-going public, although those on the cutting edge of filmmaking acknowledged the cinematic challenges of the director's innovative style. Eisenstein's next film, *Battleship Potemkin* (1925), took these techniques a step further, but such gritty realism in the depiction of violent revolution, which was a far cry from the anodyne product of the Hollywood nickelodeons, didn't necessarily go down well with audiences hankering after Douglas Fairbanks and Mary Pickford films. Equally, public officials abroad worried about the films' potential for inciting political unrest. Film censors in the United States, Britain, and France all hesitated over the release of *Battleship Potemkin*, which was banned from general release in Britain until as late as 1954. No doubt they were particularly disturbed by the scenes epitomizing what the film critic David Thomson has described as Eisenstein's "demonic, baroque visual theatricality."

Eisenstein's ground-breaking cinematic techniques were manifested in particular in *Battleship Potemkin* in the famous montage sequence of the massacre on the Odessa

Steps during the 1905 Revolution (a massacre that, in fact, never took place). This included the shot of a baby's pram careering out of control to the bottom of the steps—probably one of the most famous, emotive images in cinematic history. It also proved to be one of the many compelling propagandist images to come out of early Soviet cinema that would have a political impact on the world at large.

Eisenstein's next films, *October* (1927, based on U.S. journalist John Reed's classic account of the revolution, *Ten Days That Shook the World*) and *The Old and the New* (1929, later retitled *The General Line*), continued to deal with the changeover to the new Soviet order, but neither satisfied Stalin. He ordered Eisenstein to cut out all scenes involving Leon Trotsky from *October* and demanded considerable revisions to *The Old and the New,* making it more didactic in its depiction of Soviet agriculture and collectivization. Now feeling increasingly hamstrung by the tightening political climate in the Soviet Union, Eisenstein obtained permission to travel abroad to study new sound techniques and also to explore filmmaking possibilities in Hollywood. Having spent six months in Europe lecturing and meeting with other filmmakers, Eisenstein traveled to the United States in May 1930 to take up a contract with Paramount Pictures to make a series of films. He also took with him his favorite cameraman Edouard Tisse and actor Grigory Aleksandrov.

But Eisenstein's time in the United States was unhappy and artistically frustrating. A certain degree of hostility in the press and elsewhere from right-wingers, who abhorred the fact that a Communist filmmaker—a "Jewish Bolshevik"—should be invited to the United States, was exacerbated by the inability of mainstream Hollywood to understand the true nature of his talents. A typical response came from the producer Sam Goldwyn, who, having seen *Potemkin,* expressed his admiration, and passed on a message that Eisenstein should "do something of the same kind, but rather cheaper, for Ronald Colman."

In any event, it proved extremely difficult for Eisenstein to find the right screenplay material. In his desire to get across a social message in the three scripts that he completed, he failed to conform to the demands of the Hollywood "feel-good" factor. The three scripts were all rejected. They included an adaptation of Theodore Dreiser's *An American Tragedy,* which Paramount producer David O. Selznick, having praised it as "the most moving script I have ever read," rejected on the grounds that the screenplay was far too depressing and "cannot possibly offer anything but a most miserable two hours to millions of happy-minded young Americans."

His contract with Paramount terminated, Eisenstein decided to use the remaining months of his visa traveling to Mexico to fulfill a personal ambition to make a film about Mexican history and culture. The resulting project—*Qué Viva México!*—also had a history fraught with political, artistic, and financial difficulties involving his backer, left-wing U.S. author Upton Sinclair and his wealthy wife, Mary, who provided the finance. After the film went wildly over its shooting schedule and budget, the Sinclairs pulled out of their investment and took possession of all the footage, promising that eventually they would send the film for editing to Eisenstein in Moscow. This never happened, and the rushes were later crudely reedited for American and European release in several different versions, including *Time in the Sun* (1939)—none of them satisfactory, and all of them disowned by Eisenstein, who described them as "cinematographic discordances cobbled together by the filthy hands of moneymakers."

After returning to the Soviet Union in 1932, Eisenstein found that his former avant-garde style of montage was no longer acceptable in the rigorous new artistic climate of socialist realism, which demanded a more conventional genre of filmmaking. He found it difficult to adjust and for a while confined imself to teaching and writing. It was four years before he began working again on another film, *Bezhin Meadow.* His first sound project (production of sound films was very slow to take off in the Soviet Union), Eisenstein worked on the film between 1936 and 1937 with the eminent short-story writer and scenarist Isaak Babel, who wrote the second version of the script. Even though it took as its inspiration the more-than-politically-correct real-life story of the young pioneer hero Pavlik Morozov, who was murdered by relatives after denouncing his father as a grain speculator (see entry on the Komsomol), the authorities did not approve of the lyrical and mystical elements in the film's depiction of life in the countryside (blossoms in the apple orchards of Kolomenskoe, for example) or of the portrayal of peasants on the collective farm as victims of coercion. Eisenstein and Babel were criticized for not following a sufficiently socialist-realist line. Babel in his later prison confession of 1939 talked of the film's "Catholic extravagance," an allusion to what the authorities saw as the film's excessively religiose elements.

Not long after filming was completed in 1937, after a two-year shoot (interrupted by Eisenstein's bouts of illness) that had cost the huge sum (by Soviet standards) of 2 million rubles, the head of Soyuzkino (the All-Union Soviet Film Trust) Boris Shumyatsky closed the project down as politically unsatisfactory. All prints of *Bezhin Meadow* were confiscated and burned on official orders. A few fragments and out-takes survived in the archives to testify to the tragedy of the loss of Eisenstein's most lyrical piece of work and a new artistic departure.

By the late 1930s, his health failing, Eisenstein seemed in danger of going the way of so many of his artistic friends—Babel and Meyerhold were both arrested in 1939 and later shot. Increasingly accused of "formalism" and of making the political message subsidiary to his own preoccupation with film theory and artistic values, Eisenstein was also particularly vulnerable to denunciation and arrest as a Europhile, Jew, and latent homosexual open to blackmail/political pressure, as well as the general homophobia of the times. And yet Stalin left him alone. Eisenstein's most recent biographer, Ronald Bergan, suggested that this was partly due to Stalin's "respect for Lenin's view about the importance of the cinema as an art form in a socialist society." It is more probable, however, that Stalin placed greater value on having Eisenstein, as a leading Soviet artist, make a forced and groveling act of ritual public confession, in which he recanted his artistic errors as being "rooted in a deeply intellectual, individualist illusion."

Eisenstein found himself on safer political ground with his next project, a sweeping visual narrative of the heroic career of a thirteenth-century Russian historical figure. *Alexander Nevsky,* made in 1938, was enhanced by a powerful musical score by Sergey Prokofiev—a triumph of Soviet film music—and its unforgettable battle on the ice between the Russians and the invading Teutonic knights (which was in fact shot at the height of a sweltering summer with glass and sand substituting for the ice and snow). The film's sense of spectacle, achieved with the help of thousands of Red Army troops, had a tremendous impact on audiences and met with Stalin's approval. This march of the Teutonic knights into Russia seemed an apposite metaphor for Hitler's invasion of the Sudetenland. However, a year later, with the signing of the German-Soviet Non-Aggression Pact, it became politically expedient to withdraw the film from general release. But the political climate changed again when Hitler's Wehrmacht invaded the Soviet Union in June 1941.

Alexander Nevsky was now rereleased and exploited as a powerful piece of anti-Nazi propaganda, which did much to rouse a collective feeling of Russian national pride and defiance. Stalin now shrewdly invoked the names of Nevsky and other great Russian historical figures as guiding lights in Mother Russia's struggle against Hitler's Germany. For a while, Eisenstein—awarded an Order of Lenin in 1939, the Stalin Prize in 1941, and in 1940 the directorship of Mosfilm (the state film company)—was back in favor again and received the additional kudos of a commission to make an ambitious film trilogy about Stalin's alter ego, Ivan the Terrible.

At about this time it had become necessary once again for Eisenstein to reaffirm his political loyalty and salute Stalin's Russia as "the only place in the world where the artist can create in peace." The story of his work on *Ivan the Terrible* belied this statement, however. Although Part I (premiered in 1944) was a considerable critical success, Part II ran into trouble with Stalin in 1947. Eisenstein and Nikolay Cherkassov (who had portrayed Ivan) were summoned to a personal meeting with Stalin at the Kremlin, at which the Great Leader, discomfited that the film failed to point up the obvious positive parallels between his own and Ivan's firm, wise, and purposeful rule, expressed his dislike of the depiction of the tsar as being "indecisive, like Hamlet." In Stalin's view, Eisenstein had not sufficiently explained the necessity for Ivan's many acts of cruelty. After being given a collective dressing down by Stalin, Vyacheslav Molotov, and Andrey Zhdanov on the film's shortcomings, Eisenstein was given permission to rework Part II and begin planning the final part of the trilogy. But the stresses and strains of dealing with continual political and artistic opprobrium had taken their toll on Eisenstein's weak heart, and he died of a heart attack while reediting Part II (it was finally shown in the Soviet Union in 1958).

See also Babel, Isaac; Cinema; Great Patriotic War; Ivan the Terrible; Meyerhold, Vsevolod
Further reading: Ronald Bergan. *Eisenstein.*

London: Little, Brown, 1997; Alexander S. Birkos. *Soviet Cinema.* Hamden, CT: Archon Books, 1976; Jay Leyda. *Kino.* London: Allen & Unwin, 1973.

"Engineers of Human Souls"

*T*his suitably utilitarian tag, coined by Stalin in the 1930s, became the popular synonym for Soviet writers in their new role as literary shock workers in the construction of the Soviet state. It also underscored Stalin's attitude to the Soviet population as raw material, "cogs" in the machinery of the state, who in the hands of such literary engineers could be honed into Stalin's ideal of the "New Soviet Man."

The phrase has often been attributed to Maxim Gorky, who used it on several occasions in his speech to the First Congress of the Union of Soviet Writers in 1934. The congress was the occasion for the promulgation of the basic tenets of the new art form of socialist realism, at which Gorky stated that "the proletarian state must bring up thousands of excellent 'mechanics of culture,' 'engineers of the soul.'" But, in fact, the phrase had been coined by Stalin himself two years earlier in a remark (not necessarily an impromptu one) that he had made at a meeting of writers at Gorky's house on 26 October 1932. After dinner and the exchanging of toasts, Stalin talked about the role Soviet writers would play in the new socialist society. He made it quite clear that they were no longer to be considered an elite class, who wrote as and when it suited them, but were now to fulfill quotas like other workers. Soviet literature was now no more and no less than any other sector of industry. It would produce literary goods in much the same way as the great industrial centers were now turning out trucks and combine harvesters. Its new and challenging role was to mold the very minds and souls of the population at large in the drive for socialism and one happy, homogeneous society. From now on the creative method was to be subservient to the state.

See also Gorky, Maxim; "New Soviet Man"; Socialist Realism

Further reading: Katerina Clark. *The Soviet Novel: History as Ritual.* Chicago: University of Chicago Press, 1985; B. Groys. *The Total Art of Stalinism.* Princeton, NJ: Princeton University Press, 1992; A. Kemp-Welch. *Stalin and the Literary Intelligentsia, 1928–39,* London: Macmillan 1991.

Ezhov, Nikolay Ivanovich (1895–1939)

The diminutive figure of Nikolay Ezhov, known as the "iron hedgehog" (his name is derived from the Russian *ezh,* "hedgehog") and, more chillingly, as the "bloodthirsty dwarf," would seem an unlikely candidate for the role of mass murderer. But like his predecessor at the head of the Soviet secret police, the NKVD, Genrikh Yagoda, Ezhov, who masterminded the hellish final years of mass terror, undertook his task with considerable aplomb; in true Stalinist style he "overfulfilled the plan" and exceeded his execution quotas.

A bureaucrat of limited intelligence, who had joined the Bolsheviks in 1917 and served as a political commissar during the civil war, Ezhov had a narrow political understanding. He was no expert in the more subtle techniques of political subterfuge, and like others of his kind who lacked Machiavellian skills and needed to stay one jump ahead of Stalin, he resorted to a particular style of terrified, obsessive loyalty. He stuck like a limpet to Stalin, as though some measure of protection could be gained from close proximity with the very person who could, at a whim, destroy him. Like other instigators of mass murder throughout history, Ezhov compensated for his lack of physical stature with a pathological cruelty and the use of brute terror. As a bred-in-the-bone Party man, he soon became one of Stalin's creatures and rose through the ranks to be elected to full membership of the Central Committee in 1934 (without going through the generally obligatory candidate stage) and became a member of the Orgburo the same year. In January 1935 he took over the post left vacant by the assassinated Sergey Kirov as secretary of the Leningrad Communist Party. Stalin now had Ezhov in position, ready to undertake an important new role.

In 1936, when head of the NKVD Genrikh Yagoda fell from favor for failing to identify and arrest sufficient numbers of the "Trotskyist-Zinovievite bloc," Stalin, much in the spirit of his earlier exhortations to raise the rate of industrialization, made it known that the rate of arrests was lagging behind by four years. Ezhov was now appointed to Yagoda's post at the NKVD and given the newly created title of general commissar for state security, as well as becoming a candidate member of the Politburo. He soon set about escalating the rate of arrests and had no difficulty in finding enemies of the state everywhere, initiating the phase of mass purges named after him as the *Ezhovshchina* of 1936–1938.

During this time, Ezhov reported daily to Stalin, and together they would go through the lists of who in the Soviet political elite was to be purged and what the sentence should be. In this manner Ezhov, with his passion for quotas, contrived to rid the Soviet Union of the cream of its *nomenklatura,* in particular, its Red Army officer class and most of the regional leadership of the Communist Party, as he passed the lists of thousands of death sentences for Stalin's signature. During 1937–1938 alone, Ezhov submitted 383 such lists with the names of 44,000 people. Recently, revisionist historians have demurred on just how many death sentences Stalin personally endorsed. They also question the actual extent to which he was aware of the number of death sentences being carried out, arguing that it was Ezhov (who was known to have a sadistic streak) who turned the *Ezhovshchina* into his own personal crusade and who was thus the true agent of many of its excesses. There may be some truth in the suggestion that in the last period of frenzied purging, 1937–1938, the repressions were on too vast a scale for Stalin to have control over all of them, but there is obviously an inherent danger in any attempt at minimizing Stalin's fundamental culpability by shifting responsibility to Ezhov.

Eventually Ezhov's excess of zeal in killing so many people led to his rapid moral degeneration and a physical decline into chronic alcoholism. Stalin himself now stepped in and called a halt to the rate of repression, which had so depleted the ranks of certain professions that the country was threatened with economic collapse. Ezhov, of course, had already set himself up as the ideal scapegoat. By the autumn of 1938 his role in the NKVD had already been taken over by Lavrenty Beria. In December Ezhov was dismissed. He was subsequently relegated to the post of commissar for water, and it was at this commissariat that he was arrested on 10 April 1939 on charges of espionage and conspiracy. Ezhov's fate was not made known to the public; he simply disappeared, since Stalin did not wish to advertise the fact that his second successive head of the NKVD (Yagoda had been shot in March 1938) had turned out to be an "enemy of the state." Ezhov was shot on 4 February 1940 after supposedly requesting that Stalin be told "that I shall die with his name on my lips." Soon afterward, his figure was carefully airbrushed from all the official photographs of him and Stalin together.

In 1999, Ezhov's adopted daughter, Nataliya Khayutina (whose own parents were shot, probably on Ezhov's orders), launched a campaign to clear his name, insisting that he had been "blinded by his love for Stalin," who had turned him into a "beast." The father *she* had known had taught her to skate, ride a bicycle, play tennis, and had brought her gifts of furry toys. "Why did he commit those crimes? He adopted me and loved me. How could he be so brutal?" she asked in bewilderment.

See also Beria, Lavrenty; The Great Terror; Gulag; NKVD; Prisons; Torture; Yagoda, Genrikh

Further reading: Robert Conquest. *The Great Terror: A Reassessment*. London: Pimlico, 1992; Boris Levytsky. *The Uses of Terror: The Soviet Secret Police, 1917–1990*. New York: Coward, McGann & Geoghegan, 1972.

Ezhovshchina
See The Great Terror.

Family Life

After overturning the tsarist regime in 1917, the Bolsheviks sought to introduce numerous reforms in family life in order to provide women with the equal status that had long been promised and to release more and more of them into the workplace as builders of the new Communist utopia. One of the first decrees of the new Bolshevik government in December 1917 was the automatic granting of divorce in cases of mutual consent, and it was with such legislation that Russia led the way. Religious marriage ceremonies were also abolished and replaced with civil weddings, and illegitimate children were given equal rights with legitimate children. In 1920, in a wave of sexual liberation, abortion was legalized on an unrestricted basis. The Family Code of 1926 made divorce even easier for either partner on written application.

However, the pleasures of family life became increasingly curtailed, with both mothers and fathers working long hours in the factories and elsewhere. Living conditions, too, became desperate. After the years of disruption from both revolution and civil war and with the rigors of the New Economic Policy introduced in 1923, living space became a precious commodity. Each person was allotted a statutory nine square meters in which to live. Daily life became increasingly difficult as families of several generations were crowded into inadequate communal apartment blocks, where they had to share even more inadequate bathroom and cooking facilities. Whether or not families liked these arrangements, they could not move because of the strict laws of residence, which prevented a Soviet citizen from moving without a residence permit. Not surprisingly, all these factors led to a reluctance to have children. As the birth rate plummeted, the abortion rate rose. In 1926 it was calculated that 102,709 abortions took place, predominantly of women in urban areas. Babies were often abandoned by their parents, leading to large numbers of homeless and destitute children, and although men, even in common-law marriages, were obliged by law to provide for their families if they deserted them, such a law proved impossible to implement. While divorce remained easily obtainable, the shortage of housing often compelled couples to continue sharing the same space after their relationships had broken down.

By the late 1920s a moral backlash began to take hold in the Soviet Union against the increase in sexual promiscuity. Individual preoccupations with sex and love had no place in socialist society, and freedom of sexual activity was curtailed, with prostitution condemned and homosexuality outlawed in 1934. In order to achieve his vision of the socialist future, Stalin had to ensure that there were enough people to build it. The entrenchment of the nuclear family—with women fulfilling the triple role of wife, mother, and worker—was to be the cornerstone of social policy. The family, as the focus for social and political stability, now became of paramount importance to Stalin, who, alarmed by the plummeting birth rates, made abortion (except in life-threatening circumstances) illegal in June 1936. The availability of contraceptives was also curtailed. Divorce was made more difficult, and absent fathers found it more difficult to evade alimony payments. While the divorce rate dropped by as much as 61.3 percent in a year and abortions rapidly declined, there was little change in the birth rate. Nothing, it seemed, could induce women to have children in surroundings in which they were ill-equipped to rear them. Inevitably many women resorted to back street abortions; other more desperate women committed suicide rather than face another pregnancy. As one typical reaction in the press argued, "[h]ow can you say no to an abortion when your family consists of five people and you have fourteen meters' living space?"

Huge strains were placed on family ties and loyalties during the years of collectivization and the Great Terror, when families were broken up by arrest, denunciations, transportation, and execution. In 1934 a new category was added to the criminal code—the "Ch.S" (*chlen sem'i;* "member of a family"), which justified the arrest and punishment of people simply because they were related to someone who had been branded an enemy of the state. The interests of the state—represented by Stalin as the true "father" of the people—were paramount and came before the interests of the family. Children were strongly targeted, often through their membership in and indoctrination by the Komsomol ("Young Pioneers"), to denounce their parents. The process began in 1928 with one of the first political show trials of the Shakhty

mining engineers, when the son of one of the accused wrote a letter to *Pravda* in which he berated his father as "a confirmed enemy and hater of the working people" and demanded that he be severely punished. Furthermore, the son announced that he was changing his name.

While the freedom of choice over having children was curtailed for women by Stalin in the mid-1930s, the sexual infidelities of married men were actually protected. The Family Edict of 1944 prevented women from claiming maintenance for their children if their husbands left them; illegitimate children were similarly denied legal and financial rights. There were as many as 4 million of these children by the end of the Great Patriotic War. After the war, couples were offered numerous inducements to start reproducing again to make up the huge demographic deficit. Divorce was made extremely difficult; those who were unmarried or childless were penalized by higher tax rates; and the status of unmarried mothers and their children eroded. After Stalin's death, government spending on social welfare was increased in 1956 and abortion was once again legalized.

See also Collectivization; The Great Terror; Gulag; Komsomol; "New Soviet Man"; Shakty Trial; Women

Further reading: H. Kent Geiger. *The Family in Soviet Russia.* Cambridge, MA: Harvard University Press, 1968; W. Goldman. *Women, the State and Revolution: Soviet Family Policy and Social Life, 1917–1936.* Cambridge: Cambridge University Press, 1993; Mikhail Heller. *Cogs in the Soviet Wheel: The Formation of Soviet Man.* London: Collins Harvill, 1988.

Famine
See Collectivization.

Fellow Travelers

Western sympathizers and supporters of the new Bolshevik

regime in Russia had begun visiting Russia at the time of the revolution, eager to witness for themselves the great new socialist experiment. The first to make the pilgrimage were such romantic figures as American journalist John Reed (author of the classic *Ten Days That Shook the World* [1919]), who was later accorded the honor of being buried in the Kremlin Wall after dying in Moscow of typhus.

Reed was followed by several other prominent people from the domains of literature and politics, all of whom had been "waiting for Russia to prove its case," according to English Fabian Sidney Webb, and who wanted to be able to go home and proclaim to communism's detractors that the new Russia was establishing a viable alternative to the Western capitalist system. After the disillusion of World War I, which had exposed the abuses of autocracy and the despotic rule of empires, many sincerely looked to Russia as offering hope for the future.

While the basic impulse of natural curiosity that prompted many eminent figures to visit the Soviet Union seemed understandable, several writers mystified their admirers at home by returning from visits to Stalinist Russia completely taken in by the very carefully packaged view of the Communist system that had been laid out for their benefit. Stalin, with his relaxed, pipe-smoking manner seemed to beguile even the most skeptical, and several eminent writers appeared to have fallen completely under his spell, sometimes to the point of embarrassing adulation and sometimes, and more worrisomely, to the point of openly speaking out in support of the show trials during the Great Terror. Visitors included such personalities as French writers Henri Barbusse and Romain Rolland, German writers Lion Feuchtwanger and Thomas Mann, and British writers George Bernard Shaw and H. G. Wells. The latter averred that he had "never met a man more candid, fair, and honest" than Stalin.

French socialist and pacifist Romain Rolland, a writer who had won the Nobel Prize for literature in 1915 and who had become the conscience of the French nation with his campaign against anti-Semitism in the wake of the Dreyfus affair of 1898, became an unlikely apologist for the Stalinist regime during the 1920s. Having spent the war years urging intellectuals in France and Germany to seek a better way of peace and harmony, Rolland, like many others on the left, had become interested in communism after witnessing with anxiety the growth of fascism in Europe. He visited the Soviet Union in 1935, met Stalin, and commended him for his modesty and "panhumanism." Yet his private writings (upon which Rolland placed a publishing embargo until 1985) reflected a different impression from the uncritical public pronouncements. Rolland showed an awareness of the reality of Stalinist Russia, the truth of which he had felt compelled to suppress in order to protect the Communist cause at large from its many enemies.

Rolland's compatriot Henri Barbusse, who had produced a compelling account of life in the trenches during World War I with his *Under Fire* (1917), was another French writer to travel to Russia and, in fact, became one of Stalin's first non-Russian biographers. Barbusse's experiences in the war had led him to become a pacifist and to join the Communist Party in 1921. But his early promise was sadly dissipated as he became ever more subservient to Communist ideology in his writing, which reached its apogee with *Stalin: A New World Seen through One Man,* the biography he had researched and written on a trip to the Soviet Union in 1934. Published in 1935, the year of Barbusse's death in Moscow, the book destroyed much of Barbusse's remaining literary credibility in the West. Such a cringing eulogy of Stalin added to the growing Stalinist cult of the personality, demonstrating how even a writer of Barbusse's integrity could stoop to the worst kind of sycophancy by averring in the closing lines of his book, that "the finest part of your destiny is in the hands of that . . . man [Stalin] who also watches over you and who works for you—the man with a scholar's head, a workman's face, and the dress of a private soldier."

The behavior of Lion Feuchtwanger, the German Jewish playwright, novelist, and founder of the eminent newspaper *Der Spiegel,* remains hard to fathom. As author of the classic and much-admired novel *Jew Süss* (1926), a powerful psychological analysis of anti-Semitism in eighteenth-century Germany, he had good reason to be wary of Stalin, an unrepentant anti-Semite. Yet, in 1937 Feuchtwanger (now an exile from Germany) accepted an invitation from the Soviet journalist and editor of *Pravda* Mikhail Koltsov, for whom he had in the past written articles, to visit the Soviet Union. According to Feuchtwanger, the Soviet people seemed happy with their lot. The show trial of Radek and Pyatakov, which he had witnessed, seemed to him justified and a necessary part of the democratizing process. What is baffling, however, is that a writer and humanist of Feuchtwanger's integrity could have produced the book *Moscow 1937,* which was memorable, in the words of historian Robert Conquest, "for the pathos of its idiocy." It has been argued that Feuchtwanger's stance was partly a tactical one (like Rolland's) of defending the Soviet regime in preference to what he saw as the far worse menace of fascism in the late 1930s. In any event, Stalin, flattered by this gift horse from an eminent Western writer, had the book translated and published in an edition of 200,000 copies.

But the reputation to suffer the most embarrassment, although it did little to undermine his long-established literary preeminence, was undoubtedly that of George Bernard Shaw, a committed socialist who for years had been pointing out the moral and social dilemmas of his times in his plays and essays. After he became a professed Communist, a visit to the Soviet Union was essential for him. His 1932 nine-day visit, on the invitation of Stalin, came at the height of the famine in Ukraine, brought on by the intensification of the collectivization program. Shaw was accorded all the trappings of welcome due to a head of state and was taken on visits to an assortment of carefully selected venues and toasted at endless receptions. Like all Stalin's other famous visitors, Shaw went to the Soviet Union wishing to be convinced of the conclusion he had already come to—that the Communist system was a "triumph of common sense." He particularly wished to meet Stalin, which he did on 29 July. "I expected to see a Russian working man and I found a Georgian gentleman," he noted. Stalin faultlessly played his part as romantic political hero ("I scented the soldier and the ecclesiastic, certainly not the cobbler" said Shaw of him) and remained calm and dignified in the face of accusatory onslaughts about human rights in the Soviet Union and the murder of the tsar from Shaw's traveling companion, Lady Astor. Stalin waited quietly and patiently "before modestly venturing to speak himself."

Shaw came away convinced of Stalin's iconic, almost godlike, status. The experience had certainly moved him, and he seemed sincerely convinced, as he had told an audience in Moscow, "that the new Communist system is capable of leading mankind out of its present crisis." He returned to England insisting that all talk of famine and political repressions was deliberate anti-Soviet propaganda ("Hunger in Russia? Nonsense. I've never been fed as well anywhere as in Moscow"). Shaw seemed prepared to face his critics in his conviction that, although there was an obvious high price to pay, the Soviet Union had achieved the longed-for socialist utopia that had eluded the West. He had concluded, much as had the American journalist Lincoln Steffens on a visit in 1919, that he had "seen the future" and proceeded to spread the message among his friends—

stubbornly refusing to see things otherwise. Shaw continued to encourage a conciliatory policy toward the Soviet Union, even suggesting Stalin for the Nobel Peace Prize! While later conceding that Stalin was "unscrupulous in trying to reach his goal" and "entirely opportunist as to *means*," Shaw concluded that he was an "openhearted, just, and honorable man . . . who owes his outstanding elevation to those very qualities, and not to anything dark and sinister."

Five years after his visit, and after his friends Beatrice and Sidney Webb had come back from the Soviet Union telling the same story, Shaw was still sticking to his assessment of Stalin. Despite the onset of the political purges of the Great Terror, all three dismissed such negative reports as anti-Soviet propaganda, with Shaw averring that: "I find it just as hard to believe that he [Stalin] is a vulgar gangster as that Trotsky is an assassin."

See also Cult of the Personality; Stalin: Personality of

Further reading: David Caute. *The Fellow Travelers: Intellectual Friends of Communism.* New Haven, CT: Yale University Press, 1988; Paul Hollander. *Political Pilgrims: Travels of Western Intellectuals to the Soviet Union, China and Cuba, 1928–1978.* New York: Oxford University Press, 1981; Michael Holroyd. *Bernard Shaw, Vol. 3: The Lure of Fantasy, 1918–1950.* London: Chatto & Windus, 1991; Malcolm Muggeridge. *Chronicles of Wasted Time.* London: Collins, 1972–1973.

Finland

For more than two centuries the Russians had coveted the strategically important territory of Finland, which shared control of the easternmost corner of the gulf of water dividing itself from Russia, whose overland border was only eighteen miles from the capital, St. Petersburg. Since the Middle Ages, the Swedes had had control of the country, and as soon as they relinquished their rule, tsarist Russian troops invaded and took control in 1809.

Finland became a semi-autonomous grand duchy of the Russian Empire, until it was able to reclaim its independence during the turbulent days of the revolution, in December 1917.

During the period of political unease leading up to the German invasion of Russia in 1941, Stalin, aware that the independent-minded Finns might provide a bridgehead for attack from the west, sought to increase the Soviet military presence around the Gulf of Finland. In 1939 he approached the Finns about changes to the frontier with Finland in Karelia, near their defensive Mannerheim line, which would remove the border another twenty-five miles further away from the Soviet Union. He also asked for a naval base at Hangö on the gulf. When the Finns failed to come to a decision after considerable negotiation, Stalin ordered Soviet troops to invade, expecting a decisive outcome within twelve days. It was a military operation designed to take a leaf out of Hitler's book in overrunning Poland. International outcry at this invasion was soon followed by the Soviet Union's expulsion from the League of Nations on 14 December. Soviet forces became embroiled in a bitter Winter War with Finland, lasting from November 1939 to March 1940, during which the Finns defied the odds by bravely holding them off for five months. During this struggle, the Finns lost one-fifth of their army and were finally forced to capitulate and relinquish 16,000 square miles of their eastern territory in the Karelian isthmus and the northeastern shore of Lake Ladoga to the Soviets.

Soviet military prestige received a considerable jolt as a result of what was effectively a pyrrhic victory over the Finns. Soviet losses of 126,875 men, as confirmed in 1993, testify to the weaknesses of a Soviet army hampered by poor equipment (soldiers often did not have adequate maps), shortages of food, and inappropriate clothing (the Finns were well provided with white winter camouflage and skis, while many Soviet troops suffered from cold and frostbite), and the poor, if not confused, military strategy of Marshal Klimenty Voroshilov's high command (which had predicted Soviet tanks in Helsinki in six days). There was no denying that this military debacle was a direct result of the loss of the cream of the Red Army officer class during the purges of 1937–1938; the German general staff, too, made a point of analyzing events and reported back to Hitler that "The Soviet 'mass' is no match for an army and superior leadership." A month after the end of the war, Voroshilov was replaced as defense commissar by Marshal Timoshenko.

A strong sense of national resentment at the outcome of the Winter War led to the Finns supporting Hitler's attack on the Soviet Union in June 1941 and reoccupying their ceded territories. They continued to fight the Soviets for another three years, until forced to agree to another punitive peace settlement in 1944, which gave the Soviets access to the Norwegian border in the north and a military base at Porkkala on the Gulf of Finland and which cost the Finns a considerable amount in war reparations as well. But despite these strategic Soviet gains, Finland remained politically neutral after the war, and Stalin never had another chance at making a Soviet satellite out of Finland, as he had done with the other Baltic states of Latvia, Estonia, and Lithuania.

See also Eastern Europe; Great Patriotic War; Voroshilov, Klimenty Yefremovich
Further reading: C. van Dyke. *The Soviet Invasion of Finland 1939–1940*. London: Frank Cass, 1997; Anthony F. Upton. *Finland 1939–40*. London: Davis Poynter, 1974.

Five-Year Plans

Stalin's ambitious objective of uniting Soviet agriculture and some fifty major Soviet industries in a drive to achieve "socialism in one country" was encapsulated in a succession of five yearly economic cycles of intensive production. By mobilizing the entire Soviet nation in a military-style operation and bringing millions more people—particularly women—into the workforce, he set out to create a command economy in which those who labored became "shockworkers" in an economic war on Russia's backwardness. This emphasis on production, no matter at what sacrifice, also marked a transition in Soviet economic policy. Henceforth it would be closely locked into the political life of the country, thus strengthening Stalin's dictatorial control. This was a direct contradiction of original Marxist thinking, which had condemned the capitalist obsession with production and the accumulation of profit.

The most draconian changes came with the First Five-Year Plan for Economic Construction, laid down in a 1,700-page document and introduced on 1 October 1928 (and completed four and a quarter years later, on 31 December 1932). Its objective was to raise the Soviet Union to an equal footing with the highly industrialized nations of the capitalist West. Russia's outmoded and inefficient industrial infrastructure was to be supplanted by major new concentrations of heavy and manufacturing industries in specially constructed industrial complexes, many of them in the mineral-rich Urals and the undeveloped wastelands of Siberia. The First Five-Year Plan also involved a complete overturning of the traditional rural way of life of the peasantry and brought an end to the period of modest private enterprise that they had enjoyed during the New Economic Policy (NEP). Their enforced collectivization in collective farms (the *kolkhozy*) or huge state-run farms (the *sovkhozy*) would destroy the little autonomy they had enjoyed since being emancipated in 1861 by Alexander II and bring them once again under the centralized control of the government, where, as Stalin saw it, they could be molded into a more politically conscious unit that would subordinate itself to the will of the Party.

Nearly 1,500 major industrial concerns were constructed during this period. As a result, the Soviet Union at last acquired its own motor, aircraft, tank and tractor, machine tools, electrical, and chemical industries. Amid all this the workforce, already laboring to the limits of their physical capabilities, were exhorted to make great sacrifices in order to achieve the now statutory production norms. Soviet shops offered them nothing on which to spend their hard-earned money, and they frequently ran out of even the most essential commodities such as soap. As a result, the standard of living declined during this period and wage levels were severely eroded, so that by 1932 wages for workers were at about 49 percent of their 1928 level.

To raise the surplus capital needed for such an ambitious industrialization program and to acquire foreign equipment and expertise (Stalin wasn't averse to buying capitalist skills and technology to achieve his goals), controls were constantly tightened on wages. Stalin also set about brutally restricting the food consumption of a nation that was already living on rations (a situation that persisted until 1935). In the Soviet Union's underdeveloped economy, foodstuffs were the only realistic commodity available for trade, and so much-needed Soviet stocks of grain were exported abroad. As a result, the peasantry, left to starve in the villages, suffered an appalling famine between 1932 and 1933.

The projected outputs laid down by Stalin for the First Five-Year Plan—during which he aimed to increase overall production by 20 percent—included the doubling of coal and iron output and the tripling of steel and pig iron production. His objective was to transform the Soviet Union into a "second America." In every respect Stalin thought big, and his obsessive gigantomania would be reflected in such vast industrial projects as the Dnieperstroy dam and hydroelectric station on the River Dnieper, the tractor factory at Chelyabinsk, and the iron and steel works at Magnitogorsk (modeled on the iron and steel works of Gary, Indiana). Indeed, U.S., British, and German expertise was sought in many areas of Soviet industry. Henry Ford sent technicians and engineers to help in the construction of a major automobile works at Nizhni Novgorod (later Gorky). American engineer Hugh Cooper oversaw the construction of the hydroelectric plant on the River Dnieper, and other Americans played an important part in the construction of the blast furnaces at Magnitogorsk. But, as one American observer later commented, Russian planning tended to be characterized by a tendency "to leap before looking." In the case of the Dnieperstroy Dam, intended to provide electricity for factories within a 300-mile radius, the hydroelectric plant was up and running when only half a dozen or so factories had actually been constructed to make use of it, while the rest were still languishing at the blueprint stage. And, in a further example of the absurdities of bureaucratic bungling, the first major building to go up on the site of an aluminum plant that would take its power from Dnieperstroy was not the factory itself, but a repair shop to service it.

The implementation of the Five-Year Plans was overseen by Gosplan (the State Planning Commission), which under Stalin "acquired a mystique that conveyed power, authority, gospel." It was the organ of central planning at the heart of that vast new hydra—the Stalinist bureaucracy—that worked out the formulas for maximum growth, decided on prices and wages, allocated manpower and resources, and laid down the quotas to be filled by various industries. Gosplan also produced the statistics that everyone wanted to hear: industrial production increased annually by 12–18 percent, so that by 1933 it was proclaimed that Soviet industry had reached 281 percent of the 1913 levels under the tsar, and by 1938 this figure had shot up to 658 percent. Western historians have long been skeptical about these figures, and in the late 1980s, in the climate of glasnost under President Gorbachev, even Soviet economists revealed that these figures had been an exaggeration and that, in fact, the Soviet rate of industrial growth during the period of the first two plans was more realistically 3.5 percent, on a par with that of Germany. Be that as it may, burgeoning Soviet industry, transport systems, and building programs provided full-time employment for 22.8 million people and had doubled the Soviet workforce.

But all the grand statistics, graphs, and complex data about production levels laid out on paper could not hide the reality behind the rush to industrialize—the sacrifice of quality for quantity and the widespread shortages of basic commodities. These were placed second to less essential products (as factory workers once commented sardonically "the speeches are good but there's no bread"). The primary importance of quantity laid down in production quotas led to inevitable abuses, as hard-pressed factory directors struggled to meet their targets. Those targets quantified by weight led to excess weight being deliberately added to industrial products. Similarly, targets quantified by expenditure in rubles led to profligacy and waste and the use of unnecessarily costly materials. In addition, there was, as at Dnieperstroy, a persistent absence of proper planning behind the plethora of hastily constructed industrial enterprises. Many factories remained empty shells because the machines to equip them had not been constructed. Mountains of useless spare parts lay in rusting stockpiles because they did not fit the machines that needed them. Equally, when essential machinery broke down in factories, there were frequently no parts available to repair them (this often being the result of the counterproductive hoarding of spare parts by managers anticipating inevitable supply shortages). Even grandiose projects such as the White Sea–Baltic Canal, built by forced labor from the Gulag and completed at breakneck speed by 1933, turned out to be disastrously ill conceived. The canal had been constructed without proper surveying and with inadequate materials and proved too shallow to take most of the boats for which it was designed.

Despite all these problems, Stalin continued to galvanize support for the plan by appealing (as he later did during the Great Patriotic War) to his trusted ally—Russian national pride. In an uncharacteristically passionate speech made in Moscow on 4 February 1931, he exhorted the Soviet people to finally leave behind the bitter memory of the old defeats and incursions of the past. He argued that over the centuries Russia had suffered because of its weakness and backwardness. It had been invaded and exploited, first by the "Mongol khans" then by "Turkish beys . . . Swedish feudal lords . . . Polish and Lithuanian gentry . . . British and French capitalists . . . Japanese barons." His solution was emphatic: "We are fifty or a hundred years behind the advanced countries. We must make good this distance in ten years. Either we do it, or they crush us. . . . There are no fortresses that Bolsheviks cannot capture." Soviet citizens, equating this new economic struggle with a call to arms, once more did their patriotic duty.

During the 1930s, with levels of pay (and food bonuses) increasingly dependent on productivity, the Stakhanovite mentality for "overfulfilling the plan"—the mantra for every conscientious worker—became ever more pervasive. Stalin's exhortation "to catch up and overcome" encouraged Soviet workers to fulfill impossible production targets and even to fulfill the objectives of the five-year term within a shorter space of time. Various national incantations such as "The Five-Year Plan in Four" (first used in 1930) now became the rallying cry throughout industry. Overfulfillment of the plan became equivalent to military glory and the lists of economic achievements displaced real news more and more in Soviet newspapers. These were now taken up with photographs of heroic workers who had achieved undreamed-of targets and with row upon row of statistics illustrating production figures.

An inevitable backlash to such unrelenting pressure developed. Many workers began shying away from exceeding production targets, since doing so would only result in higher expectations set the next time. Others actively spurned the Stakhanovites in their midst, occasionally resorting to violence against them. Already having to pay the price of sickness, physical exhaustion, and injury, the workforce now had its freedom of movement curtailed. In 1930 a law was introduced preventing factories from employing people who had left their previous jobs without permission. In 1932, the introduction of internal passports meant that workers no longer had the autonomy to choose where they lived and worked, a measure directed partly at preventing peasants in depressed rural areas from moving to the city to seek work in industry. Strikes, too, were banned. Unauthorized absenteeism was punished with instant dismissal, and the traditional bastions of the proletariat—the trade unions—were increasingly used to discipline workers. At every turn workers were let down by shortages and faulty equipment and machinery (safety precautions in factories were almost nonexistent), all of which compounded to cause frequent breakdowns on the assembly line. And while acts of sabotage were not uncommon from workers who could no longer maintain the tempo of output, the powers that be were all too ready to lay charges of sabotage and "wrecking" at the doors of the beleaguered Soviet workforce. As *Pravda* sternly proclaimed in 1937: "Assembly lines do not stop by themselves, machines do not break down by themselves, boilers do not burst by themselves. Somebody's hand is behind every such action. Is it the hand of an enemy? This is the first question we should ask."

With the Second Five-Year Plan of 1933–1937, Stalin had as his final objective "the uprooting of the vestiges of capitalism from people's consciousness." The plan made some attempt to provide a breathing space for workers and peasants and tried to redress some of the failures of the First Five-Year Plan by concentrating on improving levels of technical expertise and controlling production levels so that there was no excessive overproduction of particular commodities. It also, at long last, raised wages and with it followed a modest improvement in living standards and the provision of a limited quantity of consumer goods. Workers, many of them poorly housed in barracks or overcrowded communal apartments and still grumbling about the continuing squeeze on food and wages (the latter, in 1933 being only about one-tenth of what they had received in 1926–1927), were exhorted to keep going with slogans that tried to convince them that "life has become better, life has become more joyful."

With the inception of the Third Five-Year Plan, the screws were turned on the workers once again. It brought a return of the all-too-familiar lines in shops and shortages of virtually everything. And then, halfway through, the plan was interrupted by Hitler's invasion of the Soviet Union in June 1941. The bureaucrats at Gosplan immediately changed tack to convert industry to the production of military supplies. Stringent demands for armaments and military vehicles were now imposed. These were supported by tight controls on money to prevent inflation levels spiraling out of control. In a feat of logistical planning, the bulk of essential Soviet heavy industry was dismantled and moved eastward to the Urals, thus enabling output levels to be sustained at two-thirds of the 1940 figure, an astonishing achievement considering the appalling depredations the war brought with it.

Despite the disruption of war, by 1940 Stalin had achieved his own economic miracle and basked in the satisfaction of having overseen an industrial revolution that was all of his own making. For him this revolution was an important psychological achievement that at last put his reputation on a par with that of Lenin, who had achieved the political Revolution of 1917. The Soviet Union was now a major industrial power. It had acquired a vast range of new and essential industries, a network of major new industrial centers and towns, and had begun to harness its previously underexploited vast natural resources. Stalin allowed his people no time to recover from the dislocations of war. In March 1946 the Fourth Five-Year Plan for postwar recovery was inaugurated, calling for even greater improvement in electrification and communications. Stalin's objective was clear—complete the process of modernization that would make the Soviet Union totally self-sufficient and secure, a fact that would also presage its increasing political and economic isolation during the Cold War.

See also "Dizzy with Success"; Family Life; Kataev, Valentin; "Life Has Become Better, Life Has Become Merrier"; Magnitogorsk; Stakhanovites; White Sea–Baltic Canal

Further reading: R. W. Davies. *The Industrialization of Soviet Russia,* 3 vols. Cambridge: Cambridge University Press, 1980–1991; T. Dunmore. *The Stalinist Command Economy: The Soviet State Apparatus and Economic Policy, 1945–1953.* London: Macmillan, 1980.

General Secretary of the Communist Party

Stalin assumed the role of "Gensek" (abbreviation for General Secretary; as he was popularly called) in April 1922 and held the post until 1952; during that time he made shrewd use of the position to turn the Secretariat of the Communist Party into his personal fiefdom at the apex of a vast Party bureaucracy that would keep him in power for thirty-five years.

The move to promote Stalin to this new role came at the end of the Communist Party's Eleventh Congress in 1922. In 1918, when the Bolsheviks had established their first government, their party—the Russian Social Democratic Workers' Party—had assumed the title of All-Russian Communist Party. The post of secretary of the Communist Party had originally been created in 1919, at which time it carried little significant political weight. The original Soviet Constitution of 1918 had identified the Party as a separate body from the Soviet government, but in practice the Communist Party, as it mushroomed from a small political elite composed of the Bolshevik leadership to a major bureaucratic organization, became the ruling force, with membership becoming mandatory for anyone in high office. And as the Party's power in-

creased so did the stranglehold that it had over all aspects of Soviet life.

By 1922 the Party apparatus had developed to an unmanageable sprawl of different bodies, each with its own leading lights and often its own particular agenda, a fact that became all too apparent when infighting regularly flared up at their congresses. The decision to ban these various political factions and to create the post of one single executive general secretary to take control over them, all within the Communist Party, was Lenin's. His wisdom in according that role to Stalin has been called into question ever since. Leon Trotsky at the time reported that Lenin had expressed his own reservations on Stalin's suitability (Stalin was known for his abrasive manner), observing of Stalin's new role that "this cook can only serve peppery dishes."

Stalin was, of course, only too aware of the potential such control gave to his own campaign for power. He had proved adept, since the revolution, at taking on the mundane administrative roles that appealed to no one else, and by 1922, Lenin, his health already in decline, was more than happy to be relieved of the political infighting of Party business. He was supported by his close colleague Lev Kamenev in his decision to appoint Stalin. Stalin had already had experience in administering the Workers' and Peasants' Inspectorate (Rabkrin) that monitored the running of various government departments and had become a member of the Organization Bureau (Orgburo) in 1919, which liaised with regional Party organizations.

While there were even more onerous tasks involved in running the Secretariat of the Communist Party and monitoring its hive of apparatchiks, as well as coordinating the Party membership of 585,000 (by 1921), many of his managerial roles now consolidated to give Stalin ample opportunity to manipulate both the Party leadership and the apparatus that served it. Not least of these was the opportunity of feeding the Politburo with the agenda and paperwork for its meetings and then, in turn, administering and recruiting for the regional Party apparatus (which he ensured was closely monitored for him by the Cheka [the secret police]). In this way Stalin was able to advance the careers of his own chosen officials in the army, in industry, on the collective farms, and in trade unions—all of whom were directly involved in implementing Politburo decisions.

It was not long before Stalin's contemporaries saw the danger in investing so much power in a single person. Stalin had control over the three key organs of the Soviet government—the Politburo, Orgburo, and the Secretariat, with some 600 staff at his beck and call. Lenin himself had realized his mistake within nine months of Stalin's appointment. Alarmed at Stalin's growing abuse of power and, in particular, his coarseness and ill manners, Lenin composed his famous letter to Congress, the "Testament" of 1924, in which he left instructions to the Soviet leadership that Stalin should be removed from his post. Lenin's observations on Stalin's unsuitability were damning: "Stalin is too rude, and this failing, which is entirely acceptable in relations among us Communists, is not acceptable in a General Secretary. I, therefore, suggest that the comrades find a means of moving Stalin from this post and giving the job to someone else who is

superior to Comrade Stalin in every way, that is, more patient, more loyal, more respectful and attentive to the comrades, less capricious and so on."

Some historians contend that several members of the Central Committee of the Communist Party were gathering support to remove Stalin from his post as Gensek in 1934 and began discussing this among themselves at the Seventeenth Party Congress. It was only the assassination of Sergey Kirov, one of Stalin's major potential rivals, a few months later that deflected attention away from Stalin and to the more worrisome and immediate enemies of the state.

See also Congress of the Victors; Kirov, Sergey; Lenin, Vladimir

Further reading: C. Merridale. *Moscow Politics and the Rise of Stalin: The Communist Party in the Capital 1925–1932*. Basingstoke, UK: Macmillan, 1990; Leonard Schapiro. *The Communist Party of the Soviet Union*. London: Methuen, 1970.

Genetics
See Lysenko, Trofim; Vavilov, Nikolay.

Georgia

Georgia is the country of Stalin's birth, officially given as 1879 (he was in fact born a year earlier). While he never held its people or the country itself in any high regard and spent much of his later life disassociating himself from his Georgian roots, Stalin did have an enduring love of Georgian poetry and literature and a soft spot for the legendary heroes of this ancient, mountainous Transcaucasian kingdom, taking his first alias, "Koba," from the name of a fictitious Georgian freedom fighter.

Georgia has a legendary history dating back to classical times. It is said that ancient Colchis (the plain of Kolkhida on Georgia's eastern Black Sea coast) was the location for the Argonauts' search for the golden fleece of Greek legend. Its fiercely proud

A sober portrait of the young Iosif Dzhugashvili (Stalin) taken in 1894 when he was a student at the Theological Seminary in Tiflis and before he acquired the familiar bushy mustache.

people have hung on tenaciously to their ancient language and traditions through centuries of incursion from Turks, Persians, and finally Russians, who annexed it piece by piece during the nineteenth century. By the time of Stalin's birth, the Georgian nation had become deeply disaffected by the years of Russian domination, by the forced assimilation of its ethnic minorities, and by the suppression of its distinctive culture under rigid tsarist rule. Unrest among workers and intelligentsia alike had led to the blossoming of a strong nationalist movement, which Stalin joined in the 1890s. In its early years the Georgian revolutionary movement produced the majority of those Mensheviks elected to the Duma before 1917, and several Georgians were to take a prominent role in the revolutionary events in Petrograd in February–March 1917.

A short-lived independent Georgian state was set up after the 1917 Revolution, but despite its support from the British and French, it could not resist the onslaught of attack by the Red Army in 1921. Stalin, as commissar for nationalities, and his compatriot Grigory Ordzhonikidze, head of the Transcaucasian Regional Committee, took matters into their own hands to install a Soviet regime, uniting the three republics of Transcaucasia—Georgia, Armenia, and Azerbaijan—into a politically homogeneous and more controllable unit. This was a direct breach of Lenin's more conciliatory policy on the nationalities question, but it came at a time when he was sidelined through illness.

Georgia was subsequently incorporated into the Soviet Union as a member of the Transcaucasian Soviet Federated Socialist Republic. Continuing resistance to Soviet rule by Georgian nationalists was ruthlessly suppressed by Stalin in 1924, and during the Great Terror the pattern of arrest and execution spread from Russia to all the Soviet republics, including Georgia. Here the purging was carried out with ruthless and brutal efficiency by the Georgian NKVD (secret police) under direct instructions from, ironically, another Georgian, Lavrenty Beria (who was then head of the Communist Party in Transcaucasia). The percentage of Georgian victims was particularly high (425 out of 644 members of a congress of the Georgian Communist Party in 1937 were arrested and shot later that year). Many Georgian Mensheviks perished, as well as some of Stalin's comrades from his early days as a revolutionary, most notably Grigory Ordzhonikidze and Abel Enukidze.

In 1936 Georgia became the Georgian Soviet Socialist Republic and came under tight control from the Kremlin. The reluctance with which it had remained part of the Soviet Union was finally made manifest in April 1991, when Georgia was the first of the former Soviet republics to declare its independence after the collapse of communism.

See also Beria, Lavrenty; Ordzhonikidze, Grigory; Stalin: Nicknames, Aliases, and Official Titles; Stalin: Private Life of

Further reading: Ronald Grigor Suny. *The Making of the Georgian Nation.* Stanford, CA: Hoover Institution Press, 1988.

Further reading: Edward Ellis Smith. *The Young Stalin: The Early Years of an Elusive Revolutionary.* New York: Farrar, Straus, and Giroux, 1967; Ronald Grigor Suny. *The Making of the Georgian Nation.* Stanford, CA: Hoover Institution Press, 1988; Robert C. Tucker. *Stalin as Revolutionary 1879–1929.* New York: Chatto and Windus, 1974.

Georgian Social Democrats

The Mesame Dasi (literally "Third Group"), as the Georgian Social Democrats were known in their homeland, were an illegal group of activists whom Stalin surreptitiously joined in 1898 while still studying at the Tiflis Seminary.

The Social Democrats, founded in 1893, had named themselves Mesame Dasi, in order not to be confused with the Pirveli Dasi (First Group) and Meori Dasi (Second Group), two earlier groups of Georgian liberal intellectuals who had established themselves in the 1870s–1880s. The Mesame Dasi concentrated its efforts in spreading Marxist propaganda among the workers on the oil fields of Baku and the refineries at Batum, as well as in looking for support among railway workers on the rapidly expanding Transcaucasian railway with its large workshops based in Tiflis. The group's objectives were mainly moderate and obtained through legal channels by legal methods. It published its ideas in the newspaper *Kvali*. Stalin's role in the group was to take charge of study circles of workers, but he soon became discontented with the majority, Menshevik view under Noe Zhordania and took sides with other radicals on the left wing of the party. Stalin's pro-Bolshevik sympathies and confrontational manner became an irritation to the group's leadership in Tiflis, and in December 1901 they expelled him. By this time, in any event, Stalin had decided that more productive direct action was needed, and he transferred his activities to Batum and Baku.

See also Baku; Batum; Historiography; Tiflis State Bank Robbery; Tiflis Theological Seminary

German-Soviet Non-Aggression Pact (23 August 1939)

Despite negotiating this treaty, which helped spark World War II, the German and Soviet leaders, Hitler and Stalin, never actually met. The talks were conducted by their respective foreign ministers, Joachim von Ribbentrop and Vyacheslav Molotov, at a number of meetings held in rapid succession in Moscow.

At the end of the successful negotiations, Stalin toasted the Führer's health and the German delegation left, impressed with the Soviet leader's charm. Stalin, confident that he had outsmarted Hitler, reassured his Politburo colleagues that the Soviet Union had bought an extended period of neutrality. For Stalin it was a political triumph and a slap in the face to his would-be allies, Britain and France, who earlier had been slow to commit themselves to an alliance with the Soviet Union.

Many Soviet people, still remembering the war with Germany of 1914–1918, were horrified by this pact, as they had been bewildered by Stalin's earlier encouragement of the rise of fascism, which he had considered a necessary counter to the far greater threat of social democracy in Germany. Stalin had also been angered that the Western powers had not considered the Soviet Union a useful ally at the Munich talks on collective national security in 1938 and had decided to make his own tactical move to stall German military expansion in Eastern Europe. He was now no longer prepared to "allow our country to be drawn into conflicts by warmongers who are accustomed to have others [i.e., the Soviet Union] pull the chestnuts out of the fire for them."

Under the pact, both countries renounced the waging of war between them and promised to adopt a neutral stance if either was attacked. Secretly, in protocols of 23 August and 28 September, the Soviet Union and Germany also agreed to divide Poland between them. In return for being allowed a free hand in Latvia, Estonia, Finland, and Bessarabia, the Soviets would turn a blind eye to any German moves on Lithuania. As an immediate act of goodwill, Stalin ordered the return to Germany of hundreds of German Communists who had sought political asylum in the Soviet Union. He also ordered the cessation of antifascist propaganda.

There is no doubt that Stalin was as deeply mistrustful of Germany as he was of Britain and France and that the pact was in some way an act of damage limitation to compensate for his miscalculation over the military threat from Nazism. It also bought him crucial months in which to prepare for a possible later attack by Germany. This was at a time when the leadership of the Red Army and Navy had been bled dry by the purges in the officer corps and when the Soviet Union's military capabilities, stretched by the threat of war with Japan in Manchuria, were far inferior to those of Germany. The pact also offered the possibility for the Soviet Union to reap other territorial advances unchallenged, while the European powers were otherwise occupied in their own war.

The pact also served Hitler's purposes perfectly, since it preempted having to fight a war on two fronts. He later made it clear to prominent Nazis that his intention was to crush the Soviet Union. But he did, however, have a sanguine view of Stalin, later remarking that he "must command our unconditional respect. In his own way, he is a hell of a fellow." By the end of September, the Soviet Union and Germany had both invaded Poland to meet at the agreed demarcation line and divide the territory between them. Stalin further shored up his defenses against German attack by annexing the Baltic republics in August 1940.

When the pact was broken by the German invasion of the Soviet Union on 22 June 1941, Stalin quickly saw to it that the Soviet Union's neutrality toward Germany underwent radical ideological reshaping into a "people's war against fascism." Before long Hitler would discover that the subjugation of the Soviet Union would be a long and hard task and that Stalin was "a beast, but he's a beast on the grand scale."

See also Comintern; Great Patriotic War

Further reading: Alan Bullock. *Hitler and Stalin: Parallel Lives.* London: Fontana Press, 1993; Joachim von Ribbentrop. *The Ribbentrop Memoirs.* London: Weidenfeld and Nicolson, 1953; Robert C. Tucker. *Stalin in Power: The Revolution from Above, 1928–1941.* London: Chatto and Windus, 1990.

Germany

See German-Soviet Non-Aggression Pact.

Gori

*T*his small market town on the River Kura in central Georgia, where Stalin grew up and studied at the church school (1888–1894), has an ancient history, dating back to the seventh century. The surrounding wild landscape of ancient ruins, fast-flowing rivers, and the imposing sight of the Caucasus Mountains in the background would provide a suitably romantic setting for the early life of a future revolutionary in the heroic mold of the heroes of Georgian legend and the stories of Mikhail Lermontov and Leo Tolstoy. Yet this humble background, reflected in the details of Stalin's internal passport, which described him as a "peasant from the Gori District of Tiflis Province," was one that he assiduously sought to underplay throughout his later life.

Stalin's mother, Keke, worked hard to send him to the church school in Gori in 1888, having rescued him from his father, who had abducted him to Tiflis to learn shoemaking. Keke was convinced that his good singing voice and his exceptionally good memory (a characteristic others would note throughout Stalin's career) would set him up well for the priesthood. Stalin didn't let her down. Forced to now study in Russian rather than his native language of Georgian, it took him six instead of four years to get through his course of study. Despite the harsh regime—corporal punishment was an integral part of daily life—he studied hard at school, doing well in theology, geography, and history. He completed his studies in 1894 with top marks and a certificate of honor. From here he entered the Church Seminary at Tiflis.

In 1935, Lavrenty Beria (another Georgian, who would later become head of the secret police, the NKVD) in his capacity as head of the Georgian Communist Party ordered the construction of a grandiose marble pavilion over the modest wooden house in which Stalin had grown up in Gori. Stalin's daughter, Svetlana, was horrified when she saw it years later, remarking that it resembled "one of the minor subway stations in Moscow."

It still stands today, lovingly preserved by loyal Georgian Stalinists, although many suggest that the authenticity of the little hovel that it shelters is dubious. Despite the dismantling of Stalinist iconography in the years of the thaw after Stalin's death in 1953 and even since the collapse of the Soviet Union, a large statue of Stalin still holds pride of place in modern-day Gori. The authorities have also recently reopened the Stalin Museum, a sign of a revived nostalgia for the good old days of Stalinism during a time of post-Communist economic and political instability.

See also Dzhugashvili, Ekaterina; Dzhugashvili, Vissarion; Georgia; Tiflis Theological Seminary

Gorky, Maxim (1868–1936)

Maxim Gorky (pseudonym of Aleksey Maksimovich Peshkov) was undoubtedly the most influential of the new breed of proletarian Soviet writers—both at home and in the West—during the period of Stalin's rule. Gorky's relationship with the state was an ambivalent one, accentuated by his long absences abroad. Despite his prolific, if somewhat ponderous output, the bulk of which is now unread in Russia, he is remembered as much, if not more, as a mentor and father figure to many other writers.

Born in Nizhny Novgorod, the young Maksim Peshkov was brought up by his maternal grandparents and sent to earn his living at the age of eight. His early life mirrored the tough and bitter struggle to survive that he later so vividly depicted in his writings. The choice of his pseudonym—from the adjective *gor'kii,* meaning "bitter"—was a reflection of those early hardships of hand-to-mouth existence as an itinerant worker—errand boy, dishwasher, stevedore, baker, and hobo. Gorky's literary skills were entirely self-taught, and in 1898 he published his first collection, *Sketches and Stories,* in two volumes. Here, he described in romantic vein (much like U.S. writer Jack London) the seamy side of life as a down-and-outer. Gorky's gritty view of life on the skids was further graphically depicted in his play *The Lower Depths* (1902), written with the encouragement of Anton Chekhov and a work with which Gorky seemed poised to follow in the great playwright's tradition.

By this time Gorky had become a committed Marxist and was openly involved in revolutionary propaganda. In the years leading up to the revolution, he published a series of popular novels and committed

Maxim Gorky on the podium, under the all-seeing eye of Stalin, delivering the keynote speech at the First All-Union Congress of Soviet Writers, held in August 1934, at which socialist realism was formally adopted.

much of his now-substantial literary earnings from works such as *Foma Gordeev* (1899—Stalin's favorite) to the Bolshevik cause. After being briefly imprisoned in 1905 for his activities, Gorky went abroad, first on a Bolshevik fundraising tour to the United States and later to Capri, where he remained until 1914.

Gorky opposed what he considered to be the antidemocratic Bolshevik seizure of power in the 1917 Revolution and took an independent position, affiliating with a non-Bolshevik left-wing group. He highlighted his disquiet at escalating Bolshevik violence and repression in his journal *New Life,* which he published in Petrograd in 1917–1918, one of the first to describe the unraveling tragedy of Lenin's compulsion to achieve socialism at any price. Despite his close friendship with Lenin, the journal was eventually closed down because of its critical stance—but not before publishing some of the early writings of Isaac Babel, a talented protégé of Gorky's. During this difficult period of shortages and hardship, when writers were struggling to survive, Gorky did much to help keep cultural life going by keeping starving writers in work, setting up a major translation project of the world's classics, and establishing the All-Russian Commission for Improving Living Conditions of Scholars and Scientists.

In 1913 Gorky began publishing his classic three-volume autobiography, *My Childhood* (1915), *In the World* (1916—known in English as *My Apprenticeship*), and *My Universities* (1922). His *Reminiscences* (1923), a series of portraits of Russian writers, including Tolstoy and Chekhov, were hugely popular in the Soviet Union. By 1924, still in moral conflict with the Soviet regime, he went live in Italy again, this time in Sorrento. His departure had come under pressure from Lenin, supposedly for the sake of his health (Gorky had tuberculosis), but in reality because he had become a political embarrassment by taking too independent and too vocal a position against the Bolsheviks' growing abuses of political power. Gorky was by now an established inheritor of the great realist tradition in Russian writing and consolidated his reputation abroad as an eminence grise of the Revolution and Russian letters. Over the years many of the great and the good beat a path to his door in Italy. In 1928 Gorky was lured back to the Soviet Union to be feted on the occasion of his sixtieth birthday, in a deliberately staged foretaste of what was to come should he be prevailed upon to return permanently.

For Stalin now needed a unifying figure of Gorky's preeminence to help bring Soviet writers into line ideologically. In 1931 he instructed his secret police chief, Genrikh Yagoda, to put pressure on Gorky to return. Yagoda organized a deluge of letters to be sent to the exiled Gorky, begging him to come home. A barrage of flattery, gifts, money, and honors was heaped at Gorky's feet when he did finally agree to return. His home city was renamed Gorky, as were a street in Moscow, and the Moscow Arts Theater—pioneer of the work of Chekhov and Stanislavsky. Eventually schools, factories, collective farms, and even camps in the Gulag would bear his name. Gorky was also allocated an entourage of servants and minders (several in the pay of the secret police) to look after him in a fine, art nouveau house in Moscow that had been confiscated from a Russian newspaper baron after the revolution. He was also allocated dachas in Gorky and the Crimea. Stalin, meanwhile, inveigled his way into the kind of close friendship with Gorky that Lenin had enjoyed and from which Gorky would later be unable to withdraw. There was even talk of Gorky's writing Stalin's official biography. At every turn the writer was monitored, manipulated, and pushed in the appropriate directions in order to maximize his usefulness and "bind him with cables to the Party," as Stalin saw it.

Part of the attractive package offered to Gorky was the promise of a prominent role, to equal the cult status of Stalin himself, in the vanguard of Soviet literature as the spokesman of the new, official genre of socialist realism. Promulgated in 1932, socialist realism set down Gorky's own 1906 novel *Mother* as the archetype to which all writers should aspire. In Europe he had been a small fish in a much wider and more eminent literary pool. In the Soviet Union Gorky was once again preeminent in his old guise as the "Stormy Petrel of the Revolution," as he had been known from the title of one of his own much-loved poems.

In 1934 Gorky became chairman of the newly established Union of Soviet Writers and a regular and forceful figure on the podium, from which he propagated Stalin's pet catchphrase for writers as "engineers of human souls." Honors continued to be heaped on him as Gorky became increasingly the captive of his own vanity. His subservience to Stalin reached its nadir when he headed a group of writers who compiled a collective paean to Soviet achievement in their study of the construction of the White Sea–Baltic Canal. The sense of moral outrage that had led Gorky to condemn Bolshevik violence after the revolution had now completely evaporated. He was able to turn a blind eye to the abuses inflicted on the forced laborers and convicts constructing the canal and allowed himself to be persuaded that this, like the collectivization of the peasants, was all part of a well-intentioned program designed to rehabilitate the more recalcitrant elements in Soviet society. Gorky's total moral capitulation seemed complete with his own pronouncement in 1930, at the height of the deportations of the kulaks, that "if an enemy does not surrender, he must be exterminated."

Gorky spent his last years trapped in a permanent and shaming paradox. He found himself, once the grand old man of Russian letters, the former literary scourge of tsarist Russia's rotten bourgeoisie, the moral guardian of the new socialist state, now transformed by that state into "the old bear with a ring in his nose," as the French writer Romain Rolland described him. He was now a virtual prisoner in his own home, who remained mute about the excesses of Stalinist rule and who, in the words of Vitaly Shentalinsky, had become "not only a victim of Stalin and the NKVD but also one of their weapons in the country's spiritual enslavement." Gorky was now sick and exhausted and admitted that it was "as if they've put a fence around me—I can't step over."

Debate continues about the true circumstances of Gorky's death in 1936. Rumors have persisted that Stalin, seeking to rid himself, as he always did, of someone who had outlived his usefulness, had ordered him to be poisoned. It is also possible that Gorky's by now inevitable physical end was hastened because he was on the point of coming to the defense of his old friend Lev Kamenev, who was about to go on trial in Moscow. When Gorky died, he was accorded a grand funeral befitting his status, and his ashes were buried in the Kremlin Wall. One clue suggesting his true and privately held feelings about Stalin surfaced briefly after he died in a diary found among his literary papers, but it was quickly confiscated by the NKVD. In it, Gorky likened Stalin to a massive, bloated flea that had been fed to monstrous proportions by the lifeblood of propaganda and self-promotion. Perhaps at the end of his life Gorky finally awakened to his own role in sustaining the life of that parasite. Perhaps in mitigation, his not speaking out against Stalin had been part of a conscious decision to use his position of preeminence to try to protect the lives of others under greater threat. This is certainly true in the case of Isaac Babel, who after Gorky's death prophesied, "Now they are not going to let me live."

See also Babel, Isaac; "Engineers of Human Souls"; Socialist Realism; Union of Soviet Writers; White Sea–Baltic Canal

Further reading: F. B. Borras. *Maxim Gorky the Writer: An Interpretation.* Oxford: Clarendon Press,

1967; Dan Levin. *Stormy Petrel: The Life and Work of Maxim Gorky.* London: Frederick Muller, 1965; Vitaly Shentalinsky. *The KGB's Literary Archive,* ch. 12. London: Harvill Press, 1995.

Great Patriotic War

The Russian people have been described as the world's "most passionate patriots." It is certainly hard to think of any other people who, within the short space of twenty-four years (1917–1941), suffered the misery of revolution, civil war, enforced collectivization, famine, and the Great Terror and then found the strength and the resolve to combat yet another onslaught—this time from Hitler's Wehrmacht, the most powerful modern military machine. But just as Napoleon had misjudged the will of the Russian people to defend their motherland in 1812, so Hitler had no expectation of the staggering levels of physical and material sacrifices that the Russian people would make in order to finally win.

The Soviet name for World War II—the Great Patriotic War—adds an emotional and personal element to the nature of the war, projecting it as a poetic defense of national freedom. It is a perfect example of Stalin's shrewd manipulation of the Soviet psyche. His tried and trusted formula of appealing to national pride through the use of the most bombastic propaganda had never failed to galvanize the population at large, in particular during the First Five-Year Plan. The Russian name for the war also appears in the form "Great Fatherland War" (and "Second Great Fatherland War" as Stalin called it after July 1943, the first being that against Napoleon). The epithet, while linguistically correct (*otechestvennaya* means "of the native land/home country"), seems a misnomer in terms of the very feminine resonances of Russia throughout its cultural history as a "motherland" (*rodina*).

On 22 June 1941 Hitler unleashed some 3 million troops, arranged in 153 divisions and supported by Romanian, Hungarian, and Finnish contingents, on the Soviet Union in a campaign with the code name "Operation Barbarossa." Hitler's intention was that "Russia will be finished in three weeks." The first phase of the war in the east was indeed over in weeks. Supported by 3,350 tanks, 7,000 field guns, and 2,000 aircraft, the Wehrmacht had soon established a front line stretching along 1,800 miles of the Soviet Union. The Soviet losses in the first three weeks of fighting were catastrophic. Two million Red Army soldiers were already in captivity.

Many civilians in western Russia, particularly ethnic minorities in Ukraine and the recently annexed Baltic states, welcomed what seemed at the time an army of liberation. Church bells pealed out a welcome, and girls in national dress offered flowers. But the celebrations were premature. These "liberated" people were soon to learn that Hitler was no more humanitarian than Stalin. All their hopes of a return to national autonomy were crushed in the wake of brutal reprisals against partisan activity, razing of villages, confiscation of property, and the subjugation of their people as slave laborers for the Reich.

Stalin's response to the invasion baffled the Politburo. It has also proved to be one of the most controversial issues of the whole war, and historians have found it difficult to adequately explain the reasons behind his inaction. For thirteen days Stalin remained slumped in a state of deep depression and locked himself away, mostly at his villa at Kuntsevo, paralyzed by shock and indecision. That he had had countless intelligence warnings from his own spies and also from his allies that Hitler was amassing a vast army of invasion is without doubt. But the invasion seemed to knock him off balance. Meanwhile, his military leaders, still suffering the aftereffects of the terrible purges among the ranks of the Red

Army during the late 1930s, were also gripped by the terror of taking any kind of military initiative. Dogmatic and stubborn by nature, Stalin was convinced that the intelligence reports were deliberate "English provocation" (*angliiskaya provokatsiya*), a ploy by Churchill to gain his military support for Britain's war against Hitler.

A situation of black farce quickly developed. Army commanders on the Ukrainian border were forbidden by Stalin to take defensive action against what he was convinced was unauthorized attack by German troops, for fear of "provoking Hitler." Stalin had for a long time been convinced that sooner or later there would be another war in Europe (he had already ordered increases in armaments production and raised conscription levels in anticipation of this). He had also believed that Hitler would not dream of invading the Soviet Union (and thereby open up an eastern front) before he had dispatched Britain. Equally, he did not feel inhibited by the terms of the German-Soviet Non-Aggression Pact of 1939 in taking preemptive action against Germany himself if he should choose to do so. He was far too ruthless to consider such an agreement morally binding. It was simply that in 1941, in terms of military hardware, he did not consider that the Soviet Union was ready to undertake an offensive, although he did not doubt the Red Army's ability to repulse any attack, should it come. But it is precisely on this point that Stalin miscalculated badly, by wildly overestimating the Red Army's ability to counter the might of the Wehrmacht. Soviet historiography after the war would go to considerable lengths to quietly sidestep the debacle of the German invasion and the first catastrophic Soviet losses of the war in favor of glorifying the later heroic period of the defense of Stalingrad and the Soviet offensive from 1943.

It was not until 3 July that Stalin finally made a radio broadcast to an anxious nation. Having acceded to the Politburo's suggestion that he set up a State Defense Committee with himself as chairman, he now called upon the Soviet people, not as comrades but as "brothers and sisters" and "my friends," and proceeded to describe the dark days of sacrifice that lay ahead. The Soviet people did not disappoint him and quickly mobilized. The old and young, women, and even children formed themselves into workers' brigades to dig antitank trenches and fortifications. Despite their efforts, however, the Wehrmacht's advance across the Soviet Union was rapid, and the unprepared and disorganized Red Army forces were overwhelmed by a series of catastrophic defeats in the southwest at Kiev and Kharkov. The bulk of the Soviet air force, as many as 900 planes, had already been destroyed on the ground in the first days of the war. In the confusion of the first six months, as many as 3 million Soviet troops (65 percent of the total) were captured or surrendered as the Wehrmacht swept through the Ukraine and threatened Moscow and Leningrad. Stalin's attitude to the surrender of Soviet troops was unequivocal. Order No. 270 of August 1941 announced that those taken prisoner would be deemed traitors to the motherland. Any Soviet prisoners returning from Germany at the end of the war would pay a terrible price for their act of surrender.

One of the major contributing factors to the ultimate success of the Soviets in routing the Wehrmacht was the fact that Soviet industry managed to maintain a high level of supplies and arms to the frontline troops. Under the advice of his minister of industry, Lazar Kaganovich, Stalin ordered the dismantling and relocation of important industries, factories, and their workforces beyond the Urals. In the first five months of the war over 1,500 strategically important factories, such as the Zaporozhie steel mills and Kharkov tractor plant, were loaded piecemeal onto endless convoys of freight trains and shipped east. Eventually, as many as 25 million people would also be sent east to man these industries. Those in the vanguard arrived to a bleak and desolate landscape in the first days of winter, only to face the grueling task of digging the bare, frozen earth with inadequate tools and living on frugal rations in primitive dugouts with little protection against the cold. Yet during the four years of war against Germany, Soviet industry miraculously managed to produce 100,000 tanks, 130,000 planes, and 800,000 field guns—production levels achieved through the imposition of martial law in the factories and a compulsory sixty-six-hour week. Factory employees had no muscle to resist such demands, since to do so would result in the withdrawal of their precious ration cards.

Back in Leningrad and Moscow, a considerable effort was also expended by the devoted staff of the nation's great museums, such as the Hermitage, to pack up and evacuate en masse their most important and irreplaceable art treasures. The nation's most sacred religious relic of all—Lenin's mummified corpse—was also carefully packed and transported by special train to faraway Tyumen in western Siberia.

Although a State Committee of Defense, including Stalin, Vyacheslav Molotov, Klimenty Voroshilov, Georgy Malenkov, and Lavrenty Beria, had been set up on 30 June, Stalin had been reluctant to delegate either its political or military management in the early days of the war. Nothing, it seemed, could stem the tide of early Soviet losses. Smolensk was in German hands by mid-July, and in September the long siege of Leningrad's civilian population of 3 million had begun in the north. By October, Moscow was also under serious threat, with the Wehrmacht only sixty miles away, and Stalin was forced to consider transferring the capital to Kuibyshev in southeast Russia. Instead, he decided not to leave the city, thus signifying the refusal of the Soviet nation as a whole to capitulate. It was an important propaganda move. Stalin's belligerent response to the German assault on

Moscow was to insist that the traditional march past of Soviet troops in Red Square on the anniversary of the October Revolution should take place as usual. He himself appeared, on top of the Lenin Mausoleum, to inspect the troops, many of whom were immediately dispatched to the front lines.

At last, Hitler miscalculated. Against the advice of many of his senior officers to break off the advance and wait for the spring of 1942, Hitler ordered the push to Moscow to continue. Unfortunately, the Wehrmacht could not break through the defenses hastily built around Moscow by battalions of Soviet soldiers and civilians. And then, suddenly, the Russian winter descended, and the soldiers of the Wehrmacht, who had not been provided with adequate clothing to see them through a Russian winter, began to succumb to frostbite and exposure and suffered their first heavy losses as a result. In contrast, the Soviet military wisely ensured that Red Army soldiers had proper winter clothing and that each received a regular ration of vodka. Soviet troops under Marshal Georgy Zhukov now began to turn the tide, and by March 1942 the German threat to Moscow had receded.

However, during the following summer of 1942 the Wehrmacht continued its advance across Ukraine and into southeastern Russia and the Crimea. Hitler's objective was clear—to seize the rich oilfields of the Caucasus and cripple the Soviet war effort. The strategically crucial city of Stalingrad on the Volga, a major center of industry and grain production, was now the prime target. Refusing to contemplate any more catastrophic losses, Stalin issued his notorious directive—Order No. 227 of 29 July—in which he called a halt to any further retreat by the armed forces because "to retreat further would mean to destroy ourselves and with us our motherland. Not one more step backwards! That has to be our main slogan from now on."

The second winter of 1942–1943 proved to be a sobering time for the Wehrmacht's ambitions. They had not managed to crush the resistance of the civilian population of Leningrad, and, while they had succeeded in pushing hard into the suburbs of Stalingrad, 330,000 Wehrmacht troops had become encircled in the city. Cold, exhaustion, equipment that would not work in the freezing temperatures, the difficulty of supplying such a vast front, low morale among the hungry and now lice-infested German troops—all contributed to a slowing of momentum. With Wehrmacht food and ammunition supplies beginning to run out, there was a clear shift in the military advantage to the Soviet side. Above all, the Russians were used to fighting in bitter winter conditions. With the specter of 1812 and the rout of Napoleon's Grande Armée once more appearing, Soviet troops began to counterattack in December. In January 1943 Field Marshal Friedrich von Paulus and 91,000 men surrendered to the Soviets.

To celebrate the triumph of Stalingrad in March 1943, Stalin was made a Marshal of the Soviet Union. By now the Russians had taken an eighty-mile stretch of territory into the German lines, creating a "bulge" known as the Kursk salient. The largest tank battle in history (until the Arab-Israeli war of 1967) took place here in July 1943 and at last turned the tide of the war for the Soviet Union and, indeed, for the Allies in general. By August 1944 the Wehrmacht had retreated all the way to Poland, and Zhukov's troops eventually pushed them the entire 400 miles back to Berlin, to take the city on 12 January 1945.

The eventual Soviet success in repulsing the Wehrmacht was in no small measure aided by a massive injection of Allied lend-lease aid. Vast supplies of every conceivable commodity, including technical equipment, jeeps, uniforms, and that good old wartime standby, American Spam, were shipped by Allied convoys, often taking the perilous sea route to Murmansk. About one-fifth of the Soviet Union's gross domestic product (GDP) was provided by the Allies, allowing precious time for Soviet industry to relocate and recoup. In return for this essential support Stalin had offered a token sacrifice—the disbanding of the Comintern in May 1943.

In Soviet society at large the war had created, ironically, a most welcome respite—a loosening of political and religious controls, including the relaxation of censorship. Indeed, the war had allowed the reemergence of that most dangerous of all human activities—independent thought. Many Russian people, despite the terrible hardships, reveled in the unexpected atmosphere of intellectual liberation. Such was the resurgence of the Russian Orthodox Church that Stalin even allowed priests to be released from the Gulag in order to cater to the needs of a nation that had rediscovered its spiritual identity and was once more allowed to publicly parade its sacred icons in open appeals to divine, rather than Communist, intervention in their great struggle. And Stalin shrewdly bolstered this old-world rebirth by reintroducing officers' epaulettes and uniforms reminiscent of the days of tsarism. Many witnesses of this period have written about the sense of spiritual relief experienced by ordinary Russians, of how "the war was the one time when poets were writing poetry sincerely." The war brought a brief revival in the fortunes of poets such as Anna Akhmatova and Boris Pasternak. It also marked an artistic return of composers, such as Dmitry Shostakovich, who produced his magnificent Seventh Symphony in besieged Leningrad, and filmmakers, such as Sergey Eisenstein, with his *Ivan the Terrible,* both of which probably did more to fuel propaganda than any other creative works in the history of Stalinist Russia.

Stalin himself laid on all the essential set dressing appropriate to a war scenario on the grand scale. He ceased to refer to the country as the "Soviet Union" but as the more emotive "Russia." He made appeals to the spirit of the 1812 defeat of Napoleon, revived the trappings of military glory, not just in the form of fancy uniforms, but also in honors and medals named after past heroes—the Kutuzov and Suvorov medals and the Order of Alexander Nevsky, for example, were introduced. And he provided the equally important element of rhetoric with such speeches as the one made to troops on 7 November in Red Square, in which he exhorted them to "let the manly images of our great ancestors—Alexander Nevsky, Dmitri Donskoi, Kuzma Minin, Dmitri Pozharsky, Alexander Suvorov and Mikhail Kutuzov—inspire you in the war!" Ultimately, all this would have counted for very little had it not been for the national will. People, at last, saw this as a chance to exert their individuality and no longer be dictated to by the state. They began to look upon the conflict in personal and not just political terms as "our war." As one Russian pertinently described it to the American journalist Hedrick Smith: "It was not *their* country then, but *our* country. It was not *they* who wanted this or that to be done, but *we* who wanted to do it. It was not *their* war, but *our* war. It was *our* country we were defending, *our* war effort."

In the desperate urgency to feed the Soviet army, a fact that was reflected in the exhortation on every billboard in every factory urging "everything for the front!" the civilian population had been left pretty much to fend for itself, apart from receiving its meager bread rations. A concerted effort was made by ordinary people to plant and grow food anywhere and everywhere; every scrap of open ground in Leningrad, for example, was dug up and planted with vegetables during the siege. The countryside was decimated by starvation, by the relocation of much of its population to work in industry, and by the conscription of young men from collective farms into the army. When all the livestock had been killed and eaten, or taken by the Germans, women and children worked the land and pulled the ploughs.

In addition, the civilian population in Ukraine, Belarus, and elsewhere in the western Soviet Union suffered exploitation and ethnic cleansing at the hands of the Germans, who classified the Slavic peoples as subhumans (*Untermenschen*). Hitler's consuming racialist policies would serve as a potent reminder to the Soviet people that failure to support Stalin in the war could lead to his being supplanted by an even more terrible regime. From the first days of the Wehrmacht invasion, Hitler's specialist Einsatzgruppen (the Nazi military police) had rounded up and murdered Jews, gypsies, and Bolshevik bosses and commissars, as well as other "undesirable elements," and transported them to the extermination camps. Those fit and strong enough to work fared little better as slave laborers, doomed to die of exhaustion and malnutrition.

In the face of the German invasion, the Soviet people did not hesitate to retaliate with a scorched earth policy, slaughtering their animals and destroying their homes, as well as committing acts of sabotage by blowing up bridges, railroad lines, and rolling stock. Partisan resistance was fierce and was encouraged by Stalin, who in mid-1942 set up a central partisan headquarters staff to coordinate activities. As many as 100,000 Soviet people would become active as partisans during the war, but their acts of sabotage led to terrible reprisals by the Germans.

Hitler's advisers had originally estimated that once the Wehrmacht had overcome the Soviet Union's 150 army divisions in the West there would be little left to contend with. In the event, the Germans had soon found themselves confronted by another 200 freshly formed divisions. And these troops offered the same levels of stubborn, self-sacrificing resistance that the Germans had encountered among the civilian population. Although many thousands of Soviet troops did capitulate and cross over to the Wehrmacht, particularly at Stalingrad, many German servicemen were deeply impressed by the courage of their Russian opponents. It was popularly recognized that Soviet troops would hold out long after others would have surrendered. The Russians in particular seemed able to endure any kind of privation and had a particular talent for night fighting. German soldiers frequently commented on the Russian indifference to death and suffering: "Everywhere they 'will fight till the last man,'" a posture born of the simple phlegmatic attitude, expressed by so many Russians, that "there are so many of us."

Soviet casualties were enormous, but always, somehow, as fast as one attacking line was shot down more would keep coming. While later Stalinist hagiography would have us believe that many soldiers hurled themselves at the enemy with the words "For the motherland! For Stalin!" on their lips, a more sobering revelation, recently made by Anthony Beevor in his superb study of the battle of Stalingrad is that here alone the Soviet security police executed 13,500 of their own troops for various acts of "cowardice." Stalin himself had no qualms about using Soviet troops as cannon fodder. Indeed, what better supply could there be than the Gulag, overflowing with prisoners whom the state had long since abandoned to their fate? (During the war years 622,000 prisoners starved to death in the Gulag as a result of a 30 percent reduction in rations.) In the early days of the war, many former Red Army soldiers, rounded up during the purge of the army, had been released from the Gulag to be drafted into penal regiments and sent into the most dangerous front lines. Their function was to clear German minefields ahead of Soviet tanks, often with the knowledge that, in their rear, special troops of the NKVD (secret police) would ensure that any who turned back would be shot.

By the end of the twentieth century, estimates of the total Russian war dead were still being revised upward. Most historians had agreed on a figure in the region of around 20 million civilian war dead (including 1 million in Leningrad alone), but recent Russian estimates vary between nearly 17 million and 24 million. The figures for military losses (including as many as 4 million Soviet prisoners of war, who either died in captivity or were murdered on their return to the Soviet Union) tend to be more consistent, at just over 8.5 million. The figures for material losses are equally staggering: 1,710 towns and 70,000 villages almost totally destroyed, 65,000 kilometers of railroads wrecked, as well as countless millions of livestock killed or confiscated and hospitals, libraries, and museums wrecked and looted. The great eighteenth-century palaces at Pavlovsk and Pushkin were reduced to blackened shells, and many of ancient Russia's glorious churches were burned and bombed.

At the end of the war, Stalin was proclaimed "generalissimo" of the Soviet Union. And while during the course of the war he had learned the skills of an able technician and military leader, his popular support had been achieved with very little personal effort. Unlike Winston Churchill, and even the ailing Franklin Roosevelt, Stalin had made few public broadcasts to the nation and had never visited his frontline troops. Yet despite this, Stalin, the arch manipulator and self-publicist, had managed to transform this terrible war into his greatest propaganda campaign, and the Great Patriotic War became Stalin's finest hour as a political leader.

At the end, however, there was one thing that still rankled Stalin. At the Potsdam Conference in the summer of 1945, he was asked by a U.S. diplomat if he felt gratified that Red Army troops had been the first to enter Berlin. Stalin's response was a wry shrug and the comment "Tsar Alexander got to Paris"—an allusion to the 1812 rout of Napoleon from Russia. In 1999, British documents revealed that Churchill had been wary of precisely these political and territorial ambitions nurtured by Stalin and had drafted a plan for "Operation Unthinkable" on 1 July 1945, in which he outlined a combined U.S.-British campaign, enlisting 100,000 conquered German troops in the "elimination of Russia," should this become necessary.

See also German-Soviet Non-Aggression Pact; Leningrad; NKVD; Red Army; Rokossovsky, Marshal Konstantin; Stalingrad; Voroshilov, Klimenty; Zhukov, Georgy

Further reading: J. D. Barber and M. Harrison. *The Soviet Home Front: A Social and Economic History of the USSR in World War II.* London: Longman, 1991; Anthony Beevor. *Stalingrad.* London: Viking, 1998; Walter Laqueur. *Stalin: The Glasnost Revelations.* London: Unwin Hyman, 1990; Brian Moynahan. *The Russian Century.* London: Chatto and Windus, 1994; Richard Overy. *Russia's War.* London: Allen Lane, 1998; Harold Shukman, ed. *Stalin's Generals.* London: Pimlico, 1997. (Most of the standard studies of Stalin cited in the bibliography have useful discussions of the Great Patriotic War, but see, in particular, Alan Bullock. *Hitler and Stalin: Parallel Lives.* London: HarperCollins, 1991.)

The Great Terror

*I*n a decree of 5 September 1793, the revolutionary government of France announced the implementation of harsh measures against those considered to be "enemies of the revolution," under the slogan "terror is the order of the day." For the next nine months this reign of terror throughout France, inaugurated and orchestrated by Maximilien Robespierre's Committee of Public Safety, resulted in the deaths of 17,000 mainly innocent people.

One hundred and sixty-one years later Stalin announced his own decree of terror. On 1 December 1934, after the murder of Leningrad Party Secretary Sergey Kirov, Stalin urgently gave out instructions on the special procedure to be followed "in dealing with terrorist acts against officials of the Soviet regime." But unlike Robespierre, Stalin was extremely careful to ensure that he himself was never publicly associated with what Nikolay Bukharin called the "hellish machine" that acquired gigantic power in the Soviet Union over the next four years. This machine, which would mete out retribution and punishment to enemies of the Soviet state, was the People's Commissariat for Internal Affairs, better known as the NKVD.

Historian Robert Conquest's choice of the title *The Great Terror,* with its allusion to the horrors of the French Revolution, for his groundbreaking 1968 study of the Stalinist years, while proving a powerful analogy, was not intended as a direct comparison. For the scale and duration of the Russian experience bear no comparison with the French Terror. In fact Stalin's concerted policy of coercion and terror spanned three decades, and since Conquest first coined the phrase "Great Terror" there has been a considerable variation in the term's application by others. In their search for an appropriate way of encapsulating both the prevailing atmosphere of coercion and fear of Stalin's rule and its concomitant arrests, purges, deportations, and executions, historians have referred variously, in English, to the Purge(s), the Great Purge(s), the (Stalinist) Terror, the Great Terror, the (Moscow) Show Trials (emphasizing merely the public prosecution of major political figures during 1936–1938), and so on.

In Russia, the term *"Ezhovshchina"* is applied to the worst period, 1936–1938, when Nikolay Ezhov was head of the NKVD, thus emphasizing the underlying assumption (particularly among ordinary Soviet people at the time) that the responsibility was *his* and not Stalin's. More general, euphemistic catch-alls are also applied, such as the Russian terms "repressions" (*repressii*), "purges" (*chistki*—literally "cleansing," often used with specific reference to card-carrying members of the Communist Party), and the more sinister Bolshevik expression "liquidations" (*likvidatsii*). This latter term, much loved by Leon Trotsky, gained currency, particularly among the Bolshevik military and officers of the secret police, during the 1920s.

There is also a certain confusion, if not disagreement, over the dating of the worst period of the Great Terror, which some say began just before the first secret trial of Lev Kamenev and Grigory Zinoviev in July 1936, and others pinpoint to their official second show trial in August. But most people generally agree that the major escalation of terror began with Ezhov's appointment in September 1936, was officially sanctioned by Stalin at the February–March Plenum of 1937, and was abruptly brought to a halt after Lavrenty Beria replaced Ezhov in November 1938. It is not surprising, therefore, that the general reader is confused when confronted with this contradiction in dates and terms, used interchangeably in different texts, and varying from author to author according to preference. Such confusion lends support to a recent revisionist contention that the use of one single word "terror, with its implication of unitariness, tends to obfuscate the overlapping patterns and cross-currents of repression."

The use of terror as a means of social and political control had first been advocated by Lenin and the Bolsheviks soon after they took power in 1917. Lenin had had no doubt that intimidation and reprisals were legitimate tools in the fight to establish socialism and rid the country of parasites, malingerers, hooligans, and counterrevolutionaries. In an essay written in January 1918 he had urged the people to unite in "purging the Russian land of all kinds of harmful insects," in other words "enemies of the state," and on his orders the Cheka (the first Soviet secret police) had set up a network of special revolutionary tribunals to deal with any acts of counterrevolution. By an order of January 1921, an intensification of repression after the savagery of the civil war was instituted. In 1923 the OGPU (as the Cheka had been renamed) was given even broader investigative and judicial powers. The Cheka had even established the first prototype concentration camp for the incarceration of enemies of the state—the

Solovetsky Special Purpose Camp, a converted monastery complex in northern Russia, on an island in the White Sea.

Stalin, in his turn, shared Lenin's obsession with the ruthless eradication of perceived enemies of the state and the maintenance of internal security at any price. It is important to distinguish between the different elements and phases of the years of terror that characterized his rule, as well as the people who promoted it, and those against whom it was directed. While the term "Great Terror" was originally used by Conquest with specific reference to the Ezhov years, he and other historians have demonstrated that it can also be used comprehensively to describe the prevailing atmosphere of fear that colored all of Stalin's years in power. Thus, the pattern of terror under Stalin had its roots in events reaching back into the mid-1920s, when shortly after Lenin's death Stalin had begun eliminating his political rivals among the Mensheviks (particularly those in Georgia), the Old Bolsheviks (contemporaries of Lenin), and those on the extreme left, beginning with the hounding of Trotsky and the arrest of other "political deviationists" associated with him.

Stalin first tested the water in terms of public show trials in the late 1920s, when a new category of "enemies" was found in the supposed "wreckers" in heavy industry and the railroads. Several—most notably the engineers accused at the Shakhty trial in 1928—were put on trial, accused of subverting the tempo of industrialization through their inefficiency, corruption, and premeditated sabotage.

Some historians also extend the period of the Great Terror to encompass Stalin's personally initiated revolution—his war against the peasantry, the mass collectivization drive of 1929–1930. This involved the enforced collectivization of 14 million peasant families and the dispossession and deportation to Central Asia and Siberia of thousands more, who had been classified as capitalist and uncooperative kulaks. And then there was the famine of 1932–1933, brought on by bad harvests and excessively high government grain requisitioning. After Stalin refused to provide relief supplies or appeal for international aid, it is said to have killed as many as 7 million people.

The terrorization of the Soviet peasantry during collectivization was a reflection of the traditional Bolshevik attitude toward its people as one "amorphous, anonymous crowd" who only understood one thing—coercion. But during the early months of 1930, a rampant excess of bureaucratic zeal in instituting collectivization in the countryside forced Stalin to call a temporary halt to the process. Local Party officials, in their anxiety to implement far-reaching changes to traditional agricultural practice, had overstepped the mark in their levels of efficiency. It was the same compulsion to overachieve that later gave a Stakhanovite-like impetus to the unbridled years of the Ezhovshchina of 1936–1938, at the end of which Stalin was again forced to take similar action in reestablishing control over the killing machine that the NKVD had become by the end of 1938.

In 1932–1933 Stalin had been forced to come to terms with the fact that he still had some political dissenters in his midst. He had to deal with a call for his removal led by Martimyan Ryutin and others, who sought a "return to Lenin." And again in early 1934, Stalin had been painfully reminded, at the end of the Seventeenth Communist Party Congress, that there were those who sought his removal as general secretary—even though most of his more prominent opponents, such as Grigori Zinoviev, Lev Kamenev, and Nikolay Bukharin, had by now been fatally weakened and politically isolated.

One of the most significant events of the years of Stalinist terror was the murder of Sergey Kirov in December 1934. This murder has also become one of the most contentious issues in Soviet history, with many

seeing it as the major catalyst for the mass arrests and purge of the Communist Party that followed and that culminated in the later show trials. But bearing past history in mind—both Stalin's and the longer Bolshevik tradition—it is hard to see how Kirov's death alone could suddenly have acted as the sole catalyst. Stalin was by now convinced of widespread treachery in the Party rank and file and decided to strike against any potentially disloyal elements, particularly in the bureaucracy and the military; in particular he had a pathological fear that the Red Army might form a fifth column against him in the event of war.

Within hours of Kirov's murder, Stalin issued a decree to speed up the investigation process into political treachery, which also limited the investigation of other crimes against the state to a mere ten days. He also introduced trial by military courts, from which there was no right to legal defense or appeal and which could immediately implement the death sentence. Within two weeks of Kirov's murder the government announced the uncovering of a vast Zinovievite plot and, as the NKVD gathered to itself an ever-growing network of spies and informers, treachery was exposed in every possible area of Soviet society and the professions. A clean-up of the Party through a mass verification of party cards led to thousands of arrests in 1935 and a 20 percent drop in membership. In May Stalin further accelerated the process by instituting three-man NKVD *troikas* to travel the regions and Soviet republics meting out summary justice.

The first public victims of the main phase of terror were leading political figures. In January 1935, Zinoviev, Kamenev, and seventeen others had been tried and sentenced in closed court, leading to mass arrests of Party members in Leningrad. In August, Zinoviev and Kamenev, along with fourteen others, were tried again in the grand Tsarist Nobles Club in Moscow. There would be two more major show trials. The first was of

Georgy Pyatakov, Karl Radek, and other Old Bolsheviks in January 1937, after which public fury against these traitors was whipped up and thousands of "oppositionists" under arrest were shot. In March 1938, after a year's detailed preparation and careful rehearsal by the Soviet Ministry of Justice, Bukharin, Aleksey Rykov, Yagoda, and eighteen others were prosecuted. All the major trials were witnessed by specially invited foreign diplomats and pressmen, one of whom, Fitzroy Maclean, has left a penetrating eyewitness account of the Bukharin trial, noting the carefully handpicked Soviet citizens who were allowed to witness the trial, "sitting there like schoolchildren out for a treat, in their neat blue suits and tidy dresses . . . men and women who could be counted on to place the correct interpretation on what they saw and heard, to benefit from the lessons and, for that matter, the warnings which it might contain."

In September 1936 Stalin, with his usual impatience, had confided in a secret telegram to members of the Politburo that his head of secret police, Genrikh Yagoda, was inefficient and had "definitely proved himself to be incapable of unmasking the Trotskyite-Zinovievite bloc." The NKVD investigation was "four years behind," and Stalin wanted results. No matter what the situation, he always thought like a bureaucrat. There were timetables to be observed, quotas of arrests and executions to be met—what did it signify if human lives were the commodity involved? Having castigated Yagoda for his failures (he was eventually shot after being tried with Bukharin and Rykov in 1938), on 26 September Stalin appointed Nikolay Ezhov in his stead as head of the NKVD.

Ezhov threw all his energies into the mass arrests and, describing the task in hand to his officers, resorted to the words of a Russian proverb: "Better that ten innocent people should suffer than one spy get away. When you cut down the forest, woodchips fly." Stalin, meanwhile, was keeping a very low profile and ensured, during the worst excesses from March 1937 to early 1939, that he made no public appearances or speeches, thus allowing rumor to ferment among ordinary citizens that Ezhov had embarked on a one-man vendetta against society and that Stalin didn't know what was going on.

The three major show trials of 1936–1938 are the only trials that are well documented. In fact, only seventy major political figures were to enjoy the privilege of seeing the inside of a court of law during the Great Terror. For the Soviet people as a whole, the four years between 1934 and 1938 were lived in an atmosphere of paralyzing fear of arrest, denunciation, deportation, and execution. Such a protracted period of psychological strain did irreparable damage to the national psyche.

What happened to all the thousands of Ezhov's "woodchips" that disappeared during this final onslaught? Their fate might well have been similar to that of Lara in Boris Pasternak's *Dr. Zhivago:* "One day Lara went out and did not come back. She must have been arrested in the street, as so often happened in those days, and she died or vanished somewhere, forgotten as a nameless number on a list that was afterwards mislaid, in one of the innumerable mixed or women's concentration camps in the north." This was most certainly the fate of many Soviet citizens. Arrest, when it came, was not necessarily in the dead of night, although the NKVD favored the hours between 11 P.M. and 3 A.M. It has been observed that during the 1930s "Russia was full of insomniacs." Writer Alexander Solzhenitsyn described the element of surprise often used in the timing and manner of arrest, which did not necessarily take place at home, but could occur, as in Lara's case, on the way to work, at the theater, in the factory corridor, in the hospital, even straight off the hospital operating table, in the grocery store, on a bus or train, preventing the arrested person any opportunity to destroy papers, however innocuous, that might in any way be considered incriminating.

A handful of people, mainly more vulnerable political figures such as Mikhail Tomsky, who anticipated the horror of what might befall them, preempted arrest by killing themselves, but a haunting characteristic of the mass terror that began unraveling in 1937 is that few *did* commit suicide. Such was the swiftness and arbitrariness of the NKVD's way of operating that many people, rather than be taken completely unawares, would keep a small suitcase packed and ready, just in case the midnight knock should be heard at their door. But there was also something else common to most of those arrested—a lack of resistance—a weary capitulation "without any spirit, helplessly, [and] with a sense of doom," as Solzhenitsyn described it.

It has taken a poet of the stature of Anna Akhmatova to crystalize the agony of those years in a deeply moving poetic form. Her poetry cycle *Requiem* is an evocative lament for the Soviet dead, in which she describes her own experiences of standing in line for days outside a prison, waiting for news of her arrested son. She made a promise to herself and others to one day describe it all, and she is one of the few who was lucky enough to survive to do so. Her testimony is endorsed by others. Nataliya Ginzburg's moving account of her own arrest, torture, and incarceration in the Gulag in her *Into the Whirlwind;* Varlam Shalamov's extraordinary, visceral *Kolyma Tales;* and Vasily Grossman's epic novel *Children of the Arbat* are but a few representative works that transcend the dry, analytical fact of purely historical accounts. Solzhenitsyn's monolithic *Gulag Archipelago* remains an extraordinary hybrid, an exhaustive collection of eyewitness testimony that describes the many incomprehensible aberrations and absurdities of the Great Terror; but in its urgent need to set the record straight it is too often hostage to excessive hyperbole and religiosity, with a pontificating tone that has alienated some historians and wearied many readers.

The period of Ezhov's hegemony has been likened by many to the atmosphere of the fifteenth-century Spanish Inquisition. It was a time when, as the writer Isaac Babel wryly remarked to a friend only two years before his own arrest, "a man talks frankly only with his wife, at night, with the blanket over his head." Much of the fabric of ordinary, civilized society was inexorably undermined, as all the basic human instincts of respect, trust, honor, and decency were relentlessly worn away in the mania for rooting out treachery. Even the closest of relatives and the most intimate of friends became mutually suspicious, and the unity of the family was shattered. Children were given awards for denouncing their own parents, wives were forced to divorce their convicted husbands in the faint hope of protecting themselves and their children, and the relatives of those who had been arrested and shot were treated like pariahs.

The list of treasonous charges in Article 58 of the Criminal Code, under which people could be arrested and which in the majority of cases were utterly unfounded, is extensive, but the most-used charges were Trotskyism (there are even cases of teachers being arrested simply for using out-of-date textbooks with his picture in them), political deviationism, sabotage, industrial "wrecking," spying (particularly for the United Kingdom, Germany, or Japan), conspiring to overthrow the state, and conspiring to murder Stalin himself. But the reasons for arrest became more absurd, once the obvious candidates in the Party and bureaucracy had been rounded up and the net was thrown wider. Any pretext, however ridiculous, would be found in order to make up the arrest quotas demanded. People with the remotest link with a foreign country could be hauled in as traitors (on this count, stamp collectors, international athletes and devotees of the international language Esperanto proved ready victims). The writer Adam

Hochschild related the case of one old man being held in prison who, when asked why he had been arrested, said it was because "he was the brother of the woman who supplied the German consul's milk."

One of the greatest crimes inevitably became any act of irreverence, however innocent or unintentional, toward the image or words of Stalin, the Great Leader. Such acts of treachery included one unfortunate decorator, who was arrested for removing Stalin's portrait to paint a wall and insulted his image by stacking it under a painting of the Volga boatmen. And even in the Gulag, "if a newspaper with Stalin's portrait was found discarded somewhere on the ground, somebody had to be found and punished."

People were frequently taken away under arrest in black vans marked "meat" or "milk," which became known as Black Ravens. Their distraught relatives would then wait for days on end outside prisons for news, only to be told that the accused had been sent to the Gulag "with no right to correspond." It soon became apparent that this was an NKVD euphemism for the death sentence.

But the ordeal for those arrested had only just begun. In addition to suffering the humiliation of trumped-up charges and fabricated denunciations, often made against them by friends and colleagues, those arrested would then be required to satisfy Stalin's great abiding obsession—a "total moral capitulation" in the form of a full, written confession of their guilt. Isaac Babel, who had been on close terms with Yagoda and his wife, once asked the former NKVD head what he should do if he should ever be arrested. Yagoda replied that the essential was to deny everything "whatever the charges, just say *no* and keep on saying *no*. If one denies everything, we are powerless." And to a certain extent this was true in the case of those indicted in the Moscow Show Trials, since the official script to which the whole corrupt process ran demanded a public act of breast-beating by the accused, who would have to be seen to have cooperated voluntarily.

For the ordinary person who resisted confession, however, the end result was savage beating and often torture resulting in death. Once inside major prisons, such as the Lubyanka, Butyrki, or Lefortovo, very few, once subjected to the conveyor-belt system of interrogation, were able to resist the pressure to confess. They would often do so on the promise of a prison sentence rather than the death penalty, or out of fear for the safety of their loved ones. After confessing, the person arrested and condemned was expected to provide lists of accomplices, for which the NKVD set quotas for the numbers of people to be denounced. These were usually in the range of five to ten, but, sometimes, in the case of people higher up in the Soviet bureaucracy or the military, the number could run into the hundreds. Searching for a suitable pretext on which to denounce someone else frequently stretched the imagination of those doing the denouncing. The most preposterous crimes were concocted. The historian Roy Medvedev described how one military commander was denounced because he "deliberately chose spotted horses for the army in order to spoil the camouflage of the cavalry in any future encounter with the enemy," and a naval mechanic, having wracked his brains, denounced the entire crew of his steamship. The NKVD, under pressure to keep the quotas up, were happy to accept any charge, however risible. And if this failed, they would simply swoop on local collective farms and round up everyone they could find.

The prisons of the Soviet Union soon became filled to overflowing with victims from all walks of life and, in particular, from the professions. Medvedev, in his classic account *Let History Judge,* was with Solzhenitsyn, the first Soviet Russian to extensively catalog the roll call of the victims of Stalinism. His text rapidly became the basis of a reinterpretation of the Stalinist Terror, both in Russia and the West. It revealed the frightening extent to which so many of the essential institutions of the Soviet administration had been critically weakened by arrests by 1938. Those professions hardest hit included administrators in factories and industrial plants; regional Communist Party cadres of officials (the regional Communist Parties in Turkmenistan and Kazakhstan were left entirely without officials); candidate members of the Central Committee (of 139 who attended the Seventeenth Party Congress in 1934, 98 were executed during 1937–1938); scientists and economists, especially those who did not support the spurious theories of Trofim Lysenko; academics in universities, especially those survivors of the prerevolutionary intelligentsia; ambassadors; and Comintern members living and working in the Soviet Union. Soviet literature and letters suffered the loss of 1,000 writers, but few painters and musicians were targeted—which no doubt testifies to the age-old fear of the pen on the part of dictatorships and tyrannies of every persuasion. Books might be proscribed and burned, but nothing could stop people from memorizing and passing on to others the work of great writers. The work of poets, in particular, was kept alive in this way.

The most eminent recipients of the prescribed "eight grams of lead," traditionally administered by an automatic pistol in the back of the head, included ten of Lenin's leading Old Bolsheviks; the elite of the Red Army (three marshals of the Soviet Union, including Chief of Staff Mikhail Tukhachevsky; half its generals and 15,000 officers and political army personnel; eight admirals, including Commander-in-Chief of the Navy Admiral Aleksandr Orlov); fifty-five full and sixty candidate members of the 1934 Central Committee of the Communist Party; 1 million Party members; five first secretaries of the Komsomol; and six members of the Politburo. Historian Alan Bullock, in his study of Hitler and Stalin, cited the prophecy of a moderate Girondin

guillotined during the French Revolution in 1793, that Saturn (the revolution) had ended up devouring its own children. This was certainly the case in the Soviet Union. It is estimated that one in every eight citizens of the country perished or was consigned to the Gulag. In a final twist to the story, the purgers themselves would be purged, with eventually all three heads of the NKVD—Yagoda, Ezhov, and Beria—as well as all twenty top commissars listed in 1935 and 20,000 officers, all suffering the fate of their own victims.

By early 1938, even Stalin realized that the country's infrastructure was in a precarious state. He called a halt to the purges and, castigating Ezhov for the excesses of the NKVD meat grinder, removed him from his post. Stalin was not, however, quite finished. While the assassination of Trotsky in Mexico in 1940, which eliminated his greatest political enemy, proved to be an important psychological milestone for Stalin, there were still certain recalcitrant national and ethnic elements in the Soviet Union with which he had yet to deal. In one huge exercise in ethnic cleansing, Stalin deported many of the country's ethnic minorities—the Volga Germans, the Chechens and Ingush, the Crimean Tatars—during the war years. At the end of the war, under the terms of the Yalta Agreement and after their compulsory repatriation from Europe by the Allies, thousands of Soviet nationals, including Cossacks who had fought with the Germans, prisoners of war, slave laborers, and even Russian émigrés, were murdered on their return to the Soviet Union.

From the late 1940s and prior to his death in 1953, Stalin appears to have been preparing his own "final solution" for the Soviet Union's Jews. The Great Terror had done much to reawaken traditional Russian animosity toward the Jews and to associate them in the popular consciousness with the bureaucratic excesses of bigwigs in the *nomenklatura* and with the intellectual elite (many prominent writers, scientists, and so on were Jews). In the late 1940s many Yiddish-speaking writers and intellectuals were purged, and the fabrication of the Doctors' Plot early in 1953 (a plan by mainly Jewish doctors in the Kremlin to murder top officials) was possibly designed by Stalin as a prelude to the mass deportation of the Jewish population to the deserts of Central Asia and beyond.

The peculiar mentality of the Soviet population during the Great Terror has been much commented on; many voice disbelief at the degree of incredulity displayed by a great many Soviet people in their dogged acceptance that many of the arrests were justified and that the accused *must* be guilty. Soviet people, for so long indoctrinated by the cult of the personality, simply could not associate their god Stalin with such evil. Even those sent to the Gulag refused to blame him. Nataliya Ginzburg confirmed this, recalling that "at the camp, I was to come across many people who managed strangely to combine a sane judgment of what was going on in the country with a truly mystical personal cult of Stalin." There is even eyewitness testimony of people being executed still expressing their undying loyalty to him and of prisoners in the Gulag weeping when he died.

Indeed, there was even a degree of popular support for the purges. While the Terror was decimating the intelligentsia and Party bureaucracy, many ordinary workers and peasants remained generally indifferent and even voiced their support for some of the arrests of local Party officials who had made their lives a misery. They also sometimes expressed their satisfaction at the condemnation of the more prominent political "enemies of the state," although some decried the execution of such popular figures as Zinoviev ("Lenin's pupil") and Tukhachevsky ("the best commander"). In many cases, workers saw the Terror in the simplistic terms of a traditional battle between good and evil that did not impinge on their everyday lives. As one group of factory cleaners commented on a trial of Trotskyists, "We clean the floor; *that* doesn't concern us." In any case, people everywhere became weary of searching for a rational explanation for it all. The words *zachem/za chto?* (why?/ for what reason?) were often found scratched on the walls of prison cells, constantly reiterating the general public bewilderment at the whole process. Most difficult to explain, though, was the moral cowardice that induced people to behave as they did and made accomplices of them. The weight of that complicity still troubles many Russians today. Nadezhda Mandelstam is of the opinion that "we were all the same: either sheep who went willingly to the slaughter, or respectful assistants to the executioners. Whichever role we played, we were uncannily submissive, stifling all our human instincts. . . . Crushed by the system each one of us had in some way or other helped to build, we were not even capable of passive resistance. Our submissiveness only spurred on those who actively served the system."

While a lack of control allowed the level of purging to run to extreme levels in some regions of the Soviet Union, it is clear that Stalin kept a very careful, personal check on what was going on in the higher political echelons. With Vyacheslav Molotov, he personally vetted the lists of those to be purged, which were presented to him on a daily basis by Ezhov. Archival evidence that has survived confirms that Stalin certainly reviewed 383 lists of 44,000 names of leading Communists. By the time most of the older, and in Stalin's eyes, inefficient and poorly trained generation of apparatchiks in the bureaucracy and professions had fallen victim to the purges, he had replaced them with new blood. Half a million new members of the Communist Party, indoctrinated and drilled in his version of Party history, as epitomized by the *History of the All-Union Communist Party,* would secure him politically once and for all.

The ultimate and most contentious issue

of the Great Terror is, of course, the question of how many people were arrested, condemned to death, or died in the Gulag. Stalin is reported to have once remarked that "one death is a tragedy—a million deaths is a statistic." Such a remark has a perverse logic. It is hard to relate individual human suffering in real terms to the bald lists of figures quoted by various authorities, even though there is something reprehensible in reducing the whole story of the Great Terror to an argument over statistics. In general, though, since the original publication of Conquest's book in 1968, the consensus among Western historians had for some time settled at around 20 million, which would appear to be in line with a drop in the Soviet population of about the same figure for the period 1929–1953 (excluding war casualties). But the revisionist debate that developed in the second half of the 1980s, based on an analysis of newly available Soviet archival sources, has opened the whole issue up to fierce and often bitter controversy.

The few figures released since Nikita Khrushchev's political thaw and under the glasnost policies of Mikhail Gorbachev have been deduced from limited archival sources and serve only to further confuse the issue, because they are incomplete and because one cannot be certain to what extent these official figures might have been doctored. Khrushchev declared a figure for those shot between 1930 and 1953 at approximately 800,000. A KGB figure, released in the 1990s on the basis of their own archives, talks very precisely of "686,480" executions for the years 1936–1939 alone and a figure of 1.3 million being held in the Gulag in 1939. Other Russian analyses of such archives that have been made available have suggested between 3.5 and 7 million casualties. But the problem, of course, is that the figures offered by different bodies and different historians cover different periods and have variable terms of reference. Some figures are only for known executions and some

include subsequent deaths in the Gulag. Some include arrests and deportations to the Gulag, others include those held under arrest in prisons, and so on.

The recent lower estimates have become the cornerstone of a revisionist argument in Stalinist studies. It seeks to dramatically reevaluate the traditional Western interpretation of Stalin and argues not only that there were far fewer deaths during the Great Terror, but also that there was more popular support for many of Stalin's repressive policies than had previously been thought. Although not necessarily intended as an apologia for Stalinism, the revisionist argument might easily be misinterpreted as such. In truth, the whole argument over precisely how many died has now become a dry and futile statistical exercise, for (to paraphrase the poet John Donne) *any man's death diminishes us*. The only historian to try to quantify the figures for the worst period of 1937–1938 with any clarity and consistency remains Robert Conquest. In a 1990 reassessment of his 1968 study, he suggested that between 7 and 8 million people were arrested during 1937–1938 alone, 1 million of whom were executed. Two million people died in the Gulag during the same period, and by the end of 1938, a further 7 million were still in the Gulag, resulting in a total of 17–18 million victims. But if one were to add those who also died as a result of the wider ramifications of the Great Terror—collectivization, the famine, and the postwar revival of terror under Beria until Stalin's death in 1953—the figure rockets to around 40 million.

See also Beria, Lavrenty; Bukharin, Nikolay; Cheka; Ezhov, Nikolay; Gulag, Kamenev, Lev; NKVD; Prisons; Pyatakov, Georgy; Red Army; Rykov, Aleksey; Ryutin Manifesto; Tomsky, Mikhail; *History of the All-Union Communist Party: Short Course;* Torture; Tukhachevsky, Mikhail; Vyshinsky, Andrey; Yagoda, Genrikh; Zinoviev, Grigory

Further reading: Robert Conquest. *The Great Terror: A Reassessment*. London: Pimlico, 1992 ("traditional" view of Great Terror); Gregory

Freeze, ed. *Russia: A History*. Oxford: Oxford University Press, 1997 (useful brief summaries of the revisionist statistics); J. Arch Getty. *Origins of Great Purges: The Soviet Communist Party Reconsidered, 1933–1938*. Cambridge: Cambridge University Press, 1985 (revisionist view and revised statistics); J. Arch Getty and R. T. Manning, eds. *Stalinist Terror: New Perspectives*. Cambridge: Cambridge University Press, 1993; Adam Hochschild. *The Unquiet Ghost: Russians Remember Stalin*. London: Serpent's Tail, 1995 (a recent retrospective Russian account based on eyewitness testimony); Fitzroy Maclean. *Eastern Approaches*. London: Jonathan Cape, 1949 (eyewitness description of the Moscow Show Trials); Evan Mawdsley. *The Stalin Years: The Soviet Union, 1929–1953*. Manchester: Manchester University Press, 1998; Roy Medvedev. *Let History Judge: The Origins and Consequences of Stalinism*. New York: Columbia University Press, 1989; Chris Ward. *Stalin's Russia*. London: Arnold, 1993. (See also the works of Alexander Solzhenitsyn, Nataliya Ginzburg, Anna Akhmatova, and Vasily Grossman.)

The Great Turn

Also often referred to as the "Great Turning Point" or the "Great Breakthrough (in Socialist Production)" (*veliki perelom*), this catchphrase was coined by Stalin to describe the period of accelerated and revolutionary economic change that he inaugurated at the end of 1929. The marked upsurge in the rate of industrialization would in turn be funded by the centralized control of grain production and achieved through the mass collectivization of the peasantry. The Great Turn would, once and for all, lay the ghost of the confused years of Lenin's New Economic Policy (NEP).

The collectivization program had been initiated two years earlier at the Fifteenth Party Congress, but Stalin was now anxious to achieve economic revolution as quickly as possible and at any price. His change to an all-out offensive on the peasantry was marked by an article—"The Year of the Great Breakthrough"—which he published in *Pravda* on 7 November 1929 to commemorate the thirteenth anniversary of the 1917 Revolution. The subject of this "breakthrough" was the mass, allegedly voluntary collectivization of the peasants, that, taken with the rapid rate of industrial growth, was transforming the Soviet Union "into a country of metal, a country of automobiles, a country of tractors," and one that would catch up rapidly and outstrip the countries of the capitalist West.

As history would show, this "Great Turn" in the economic order of the Russian countryside would, in social terms at least, be less a breakthrough than a great upheaval. It would completely revolutionize the traditional rural life of Russia, but only through the use of widespread methods of intimidation and coercion. The stringent imposition of Stalin's "revolution from above" would cost millions of lives, and the social effects of the draconian Five-Year Plans would be to create an increasingly homogenized Soviet society, tied to quotas, plans, and deadlines.

In 1946, Stalin returned to his words of 1929 in a postwar election speech (though he, of course, was the only candidate), confirming his predictions. He announced that it had taken only thirteen years to transform the Soviet Union from a predominantly agricultural country into a highly industrialized one. He produced an extremely impressive set of statistics and described the military-style precision with which economic objectives had been achieved. At last, it would seem, the Soviet workforce had stormed all the fortresses that were left to storm (to reiterate Stalin's own words to a group of industrial managers in 1931). Stalin was never satisfied, however. At the end of his speech, he announced to a nation still recovering from the sacrifices of war even higher objectives for the future, including his goal of seeing industrial output increase threefold compared with its prewar levels.

See also: Collectivization; Five-Year Plans; "Revolution from Above."

Gulag

The epigraph to part III of Alexander Solzhenitsyn's epic study of the Stalinist Gulag system sums up with painful simplicity the impossibility of conveying the true extent of what its inmates endured: "Only those can understand us who ate from the same bowl with us." Few writers, other than those who actually lived it, suffered it, and somehow managed to survive it, have found ways to adequately convey such a brutalizing experience. Only Solzhenitsyn has provided any sustained synthesis of the system. Indeed, by the end of its existence in the 1950s the Gulag had become synonymous not just with the system, but also a whole way of life, conjuring up the particular world and mentality of the *zek* (the Soviet camp inmate) created and sustained by it.

The word "Gulag" is itself an acronym for Glavnoe upravlenie ispravitelno-trudovykh lagerey (Chief Administration of Corrective Labor Camps), applied somewhat inaccurately to describe the vast network of the Stalinist labor camps as a whole, a network that eventually stretched some 6,000 miles across the Soviet Union, from the Russian heartland around Moscow to the desolate wastes of Kolyma in the Far East. Strictly speaking, the Gulag constituted the chief administrative body that oversaw the running of this system of so-called corrective labor camps, detention centers, and prisons. With time, the system of incarceration that the Gulag spawned, and that ruthlessly exploited the unpaid labor of political and other prisoners, evolved into an economic entity that became the linchpin of the whole Stalinist system. Without the laborers of the Gulag, Stalin could never have industrialized the Soviet Union on such a monumental scale and within such a short time.

The Stalinist camps were not new inventions: Lenin had first empowered the Cheka to set up camps in July 1918, when the Bolsheviks needed a place of internment for political and military opponents during the civil war. The Soviets were not alone in this. The British had employed a concentration camp system in South Africa during the Boer War of 1899–1902. In Russia too, the tsars had for centuries made use of Siberia as a place of imprisonment and exile. But the prison regime suffered by political prisoners, such as Lenin and Stalin, in the years before the revolution, had been positively benign compared to what later prevailed under Stalin—an "Auschwitz without the crematoria," as one inmate described it.

Under Stalin, the Gulag became a place of oblivion for millions of ordinary men and women. By a law of 7 August 1932, children as young as twelve could also be convicted for capital offenses and sent there. Most of the political prisoners were innocent Soviet citizens, condemned by Stalin's inquisition for crimes against the state, and branded as "spies, saboteurs, terrorists, Trotskyites, Rightists, Mensheviks, SRs [Socialist Revolutionaries], Anarchists, nationalists, White émigrés." In the Gulag, political prisoners were forced to cohabit with the most hardened common criminals, who, as experts in camp survival, banded together into their own tight clans, monopolized the "cushy" indoor jobs, and preyed constantly on the more vulnerable political prisoners.

In the early 1920s the camps held only about 100,000 prisoners and many of those held for political reasons were not subjected to forced labor. For a while a naive belief prevailed in the positive benefits to be gained from reeducating inmates into better socialists. But by the end of the 1920s, as Stalin pushed forward his ambitious plans for the industrialization of the Soviet Union and was faced with the lack of financial capital to do so, the opportunity to utilize convict labor, gratis and on an unprecedented scale, was irresistible. In March 1928 a decree gave the official stamp of

Gulag prisoners breaking stones. The prisoners had only the most primitive tools and did much of their work with their bare hands in the most arduous extremes of heat and cold.

approval to various economic projects that would make "great savings in expenditure . . . by means of widespread use of the labor of individuals sentenced to measures of social protection." The prototype of the Gulag camp was set up at the ancient monastery on Solovetsky Island in the White Sea. It had for some time been used as a prison (Ivan the Terrible had incarcerated people here), and by 1926 its 3,000 convicts were already generating a valuable income in gold rubles from logging. In 1929, the efficacy of Stalin's new economic program for this camp saw income rise to 3.5 million rubles; by 1930 the convicts of Solovetsky had increased their productivity tenfold to an annual turnover of 10 million rubles.

In 1930 Stalin's mass deportations of kulak peasants, as part of his collectivization program, provided a major influx of new slave labor, and the camps rapidly filled to overflowing. The new network of corrective labor camps that Stalin now rubber-stamped was controlled by the secret police—the OGPU, under Genrikh Yagoda. Its draconian regime, as Alexander Solzhenitsyn observed, rapidly lost all sight of its supposed "corrective" purpose, becoming mercilessly destructive in its exploitation of prisoners as a source of expendable labor. During the period 1933–1935, peasants made up 70 percent of the Gulag population and their numbers were further inflated by a huge intake of the victims of the mass arrests of the worst years of the Great Terror (1936–1938). Estimates vary greatly on the number of prisoners held in the Gulag by 1939 from as high as circa 15 million to a low of 1.3 million. A great proportion of the Gulag's newer inmates by this time were members of the intelligentsia and professional classes, from the highest government official, to ardent, card-carrying Communists, to people of all walks of life and religious persuasions—and, in particular, to banned religious groups such as the Baptists. During the years of the Great Patriotic War, figures were further bolstered by an intake of ethnic minorities deported from their homelands—Chechens, Crimean Tartars, Volga Germans, as well as thousands of Japanese and German prisoners of war.

The average camp, constructed by the prisoners themselves, held around 2,000 people. There were 35 major clusters of camps and within each cluster 200 or more individual, satellite camps, most of them linked by their own railway system. Although there were camps in the northern, European part of Russia, some were located in Central Asia and the vast majority in Siberia. Together, these camps or islands in the "Gulag Archipelago" (as Solzhenitsyn named them) formed a metaphorical subcontinent of its own within the Soviet Union.

Kolyma, the largest, and probably the most notorious area of camps, was located in far-eastern Siberia. It is one of the best-documented Gulag camps and seems to have enjoyed a higher concentration of intellectuals and writers. Solzhenitsyn called it "the pole of ferocity." It was a place from which escape was futile and where the mortality rate was the highest. Virtually inaccessible by land, since it was surrounded by trackless forests and mountains, Kolyma was cut off for most of the year by the extreme climate. In winter temperatures would plummet, as the writer and former inmate Varlam Shalamov described: "if you exhaled easily but in a rasping fashion, it was fifty degrees below zero; if there was a rasping and it was difficult to breathe, it was sixty degrees below; after sixty degrees below zero, spit froze in mid-air." As many as 2 million people in total were abandoned to their fate in Kolyma, and the estimated death toll for this region alone is between 250,000 and 1 million.

Convicts died in their hundreds just getting to their place of imprisonment. They often died on the sea journey from Vladivostok to Magadan in Kolyma, and many did not survive the rail journey to the east, crammed into boxcars on the Trans-Siberian route (sometimes on trains fifty cars long, carrying a total of as many as 7,000 prisoners). The journey could take over a month and conditions were as terrible as they were for those crammed into the Nazi death trains that took Jews to the concentration camps during World War II. Unable to lie down and sleep, with little water and food, and nothing more than a single bucket in which to relieve themselves, many of the old and weak died before they even arrived. In winter prisoners froze to death; in summer they suffocated.

Prisoners arriving in Vladivostok on the Pacific coast often waited for months in transit camps before being sent on to their final destination, a destination that would provide virtually no protection against the elements. They were often housed in tents, or even primitive holes dug in the ground. Prisoners frequently had to construct their own prison camps, using little more than pickaxes, spades, and shovels. Some were fortunate enough to live in very basic barracks, where they were squeezed into bunks on a strict sleeping rotation, but such accommodations were for the luckier ones. Perpetually cold and hungry, prisoners had to endure an arduous twelve-hour day of labor that began at 5 A.M. The predominant industries of the Gulag also took their physical toll. Construction work (such as that described in Solzhenitsyn's *One Day in the Life of Ivan Denisovich*) was the most common form of labor. Most of this labor was done by brute force and without mechanization in sub-zero temperatures that lasted for eight months of the year, and where prisoners developed the art of laying bricks quicker than the mortar froze solid. One woman recalled having to dig foundations for buildings at the new settlement at Norilsk with her bare hands, sometimes as far down as forty feet: "When you had finished you would get into the bucket for the earth, like in a well, and they would pull you out. More than once the rope broke. And that was that. The bodies were left at the bottom. Norilsk is built on bones."

Other industries included gold mining in Kolyma, which is said to have taken the lives of 1,000 convicts for every ton of gold mined; tree felling in the upper reaches of the Ob in western Siberia; and coal-mining in Vorkuta and Karaganda in Central Asia. During the Great Patriotic War prisoners with particular technical or scientific skills were put to work in special prisons, known as *sharashi,* where they worked on armaments projects. Aircraft designer Andrey Tupolev, who had been arrested and sent to the Gulag in 1937, had his own team of prisoners working with him on the design of the TU-2 bomber. In Butuguchag in Kolyma, convicts were put to work, unprotected, on dangerous projects such as the mining of uranium for the Soviet atomic bomb project, which also began during the war. Solzhenitsyn estimated that no prisoner could survive for longer than ten years in the camps. At Butuguchag the life expectancy for prisoners mining uranium was a mere three months.

Gangs of laborers from the Gulag were also used to build the Moscow Metro and major industrial complexes, such as the steel mills at Magnitogorsk, where a quarter of the workforce was convict and forced laborers, many of them women, some even priests. The notorious White Sea–Baltic Canal, which was dug at a furious pace in just twenty months by men and women often using their bare hands, cost the lives of over 60,000 Gulag prisoners. An official book celebrating the construction of the canal, and edited by the eminent writer, Maxim Gorky, commented (much to the dismay of his many admirers) on this laudable exercise as "a uniquely successful effort at the mass transformation of former enemies of the proletariat . . . and Soviet society into qualified representatives of the working class and even into enthusiasts of nationally significant labor."

At Vorkuta, a mining town in the Arctic, second in importance to Kolyma, the gates bore the slogan "Labor is a matter of honor, courage, and heroism." Its words have a familiar ring. They echo the slogan that can still be seen above the gates at Auschwitz: "Arbeit macht Frei" (work liberates) And yet, strange to say, the camps of the Gulag often cultivated a perverse kind of pride in their work in some prisoners, as Solzhenitsyn described in *One Day in the Life of Ivan Denisovich,* when his hero Shukhov, at the end of his working day goes to bed content that "they hadn't put him in the cells; . . . he'd pinched a bowl of kasha at dinner . . . he'd built a wall and enjoyed doing it; he'd bought that tobacco, And he hadn't fallen ill." The stories of Varlam Shalamov also vividly describe the ingenuity and resourcefulness acquired by prisoners in their struggle to stay alive and underline the great bartering value of the three most important camp commodities—tea, bread, and tobacco.

Food rations varied from camp to camp but were never enough, and prisoners were plagued by constant, gnawing hunger. The daily ration of bread averaged 800 grams and was supplemented by thin soup and kasha, morning and evening, and occasional pieces of salt fish. Food became the daily, waking obsession of every prisoner, as it did for Solzhenitsyn's Shukhov: "That bowl of soup—it was dearer than freedom, dearer than life itself, past, present, and future. . . . There it comes, that brief moment for which a zek lives." In the all-too-brief summers, those sent on work gangs into the forests were able to forage a few wild blueberries or mushrooms to provide some much needed vitamins. In Kolyma, a considerable amount of convict labor was expended in boiling vast quantities of needles from dwarf cedar trees to produce a noxious brew that was supposed to guard against scurvy.

The worst punishment that could be meted out to any prisoner was to reduce his bread ration to 500 grams (or 300 for punitive reasons). Such a meager diet could not fuel a fully grown adult through a twelve-hour working day, and so productivity levels were low, with prisoners falling sick and collapsing from exhaustion. Life expectancy for Gulag prisoners was short. An average camp would lose half of its workforce in two to three years, and by 1938 the death rate was running at 20 percent. Prisoners succumbed on a large scale to cold, hunger, and such diseases as meningitis, tuberculosis, pneumonia, frostbite, scurvy, ulcers, and gangrene, as well as summary execution (special camps, such as Serpentinnaya, were used for culling the Gulag population by mass execution—28,000 were killed here in 1938 alone).

Although the average sentence was between five and eight years, many inmates were reimprisoned when their sentences expired. In 1956 it was found that 25 percent of inmates had already been imprisoned once before. But by the time of Stalin's death, the head of the NKVD (secret police) Lavrenty Beria was already recommending that the Gulag system be wound down. It had become too vast to administer efficiently. Prisoners had also become increasingly difficult to contain, and had started staging rebellions—in Vorkuta and Norilsk in 1953, at Steplag in 1954, Kolyma in 1955, and Ozerlag in 1956. The Gulag was disbanded in 1956 after Nikita Khrushchev's secret speech at the Twentieth Party Congress initiated de-Stalinization and announced an amnesty for some Gulag prisoners. The main labor camps were then reorganized under a Chief Administration of Corrective Labor Colonies.

It has proved impossible to calculate the numbers who were incarcerated and died in the camps. Soviet figures, released in the glasnost years of the 1980s, estimate that by the time of Stalin's death in 1953, there were as many as 12 million in the camps. Soviet historian Dmitri Volkogonov estimated, however, that no more than 4 or 5 million prisoners could have been contained within the system in any one year. Solzhenitsyn, considered by many to be the authority, claims 40–50 million were sent to the Gulag between 1928 and 1953, but estimates of the numbers of deaths vary so dramatically that there is no consensus and, as Solzhenitsyn himself wearily concluded, "We divide, we multiply, we sigh, we curse. But still and all, these are just numbers. They overwhelm the mind and then are easily forgotten." They are not forgotten, however. The Russian organization Memorial (much like those organizations seeking to discover the fate of "the disappeared" of Argentina and Chile) is working to preserve the memory of those who vanished into the Gulag. While their numbers may never be known, the collective suffering of so many has found a lasting memorial in the testimony of such writers as Alexander Solzhenitsyn, Nataliya Ginzburg, and Varlam Shalamov.

See also The Great Terror; Memorial; Prison; Solzhenitsyn, Alexander; Torture

Further reading: Edward Buca. *Vorkuta.* London: Constable, 1976; Robert Conquest. *Kolyma: The Arctic Death Camps.* Basingstoke: Macmillan, 1978; Robert Conquest. *The Great Terror: A Reassessment.* London: Pimlico, 1992; Evgenia Ginzburg. *Into the Whirlwind.* Harmondsworth, UK: Penguin, 1968; Adam Hochschild. *The Unquiet Ghost, Russians Remember Stalin.* London: Serpent's Tail, 1995; Varlam Shalamov. *Kolyma Tales.* Harmondsworth, UK: Penguin, 1994; Michael Solomon. *Magadan.* Princeton, NJ: Princeton University Press, 1971; Alexander Solzhenitsyn. *The Gulag Archipelago, 1918–1956: An Experiment in Literary Investigation,* 3 vols. London: Collins: 1974–1978.

Historiography

Stalin's attitude to the manipulation of historical fact was a simple one, characterized by his famous remark that "paper will put up with anything that is written on it." With the growth of the cult of the personality from late 1929, he set about methodically doctoring the historical record of his own early career and that of his political opponents.

Stalin was determined that his own underground activities during the 1900s in Transcaucasia and later in Petrograd at the time of the 1917 Revolution should appear as illustrious and as crucial to the Bolshevik struggle as those of Lenin. Validation of his contribution would confirm his rightful accession to the leadership as Lenin's political heir, while denigrating the real, central role in events played by others, most especially Leon Trotsky. Stalin's mendacious version of Soviet history (written for him by others under his close supervision) would remain the only official teaching version available in schools and universities until long after his death. It is sobering that several generations of Soviet children since the 1930s were reared on this bogus version of history and that it was not until revelations about the Stalin years became public knowledge under Mikhail Gorbachev's policy of glasnost during the mid–1980s that the history books at last began to be rewritten.

The mainspring for the "Stalin School of Falsification," as Trotsky described Soviet historiography, came in October 1931, when Stalin wrote an angry letter to the journal *Proletarian Revolution*. In it he criticized an article the journal had published, in which its author had dared to challenge the infallibility of Lenin's assessment of the German Social Democrats at the time of World War I. Stalin insinuated that political deeds and not archival records should be the basis of serious historical analysis from now on (no matter that the deeds in question were frequently bound up in the apocrypha of the revolution and were not substantiated). Nevertheless, historians thereafter felt obliged to reject the traditional approach to scholarship and make the historical fact fit Stalin's Marxist-Leninist view of history. Soviet historiography immediately turned its efforts to correcting the "facts" of Stalin's early career, while Stalin himself in 1933 began issuing directives on how history should be taught in schools. From that point on every history textbook was to be vetted by the Commissariat of Education, and all discussion should limit itself to the prescribed facts and not indulge in abstract historical theorizing.

In Georgia, Communist Party head Lavrenty Beria, an ambitious apparatchik anxious to ingratiate himself with Stalin, set about rewriting Stalin's role in the Bolshevik movement in Transcaucasia. He drew attention to Stalin's prescient denunciation of the Georgian Mensheviks, made in an obscure article he had written in 1909; Beria had it republished and widely circulated. In 1934 Beria began writing the "real" history of events in Transcaucasia, dominated, of course, by Stalin's one-man struggle against the Menshevik faction.

Stalin's pronouncements had also prompted Beria to launch an attack on a leading Georgian Communist, Abel Enukhidze, who had committed the heresy in the memoirs he wrote about his time as a revolutionary in Baku (published in 1922) of failing to mention Stalin's role between 1901 and 1905 in setting up and running the illegal printing press there. This press was one of the legendary artifacts of the revolution, since it had been responsible for publishing many important early Marxist pamphlets, including Lenin's seminal work *What Is to Be Done?* (Stalin, in fact, had hardly visited Baku much before 1907, having spent the years in question either underground in Batum and Tiflis or in Siberian exile).

Enukhidze was induced to apologize for his factual "mistakes" in *Pravda* in January 1935 and to concoct a leading role for Stalin. "Literally on his own shoulders he [Stalin] bore the brunt of the entire struggle with the Mensheviks in the Caucasus, beginning in 1904 and ending with 1908," he wrote. In so doing, Enukhidze, an honorable man, was forced to denigrate the crucial role played in Baku by the group's true leader, Lado Ketskhoveli. Soon after, Beria published his own account, *On the History of Bolshevik Organizations in Transcaucasia,* in an edition of 100,000. In it, he berated Enukhidze and others, who had turned their hand to writing Stalinist history, for "deliberate distortion and falsification of the history of the Transcaucasian organization."

Beria's *History* was much praised for enlightening the nation on a little-known period in Bolshevik history, and he naturally basked in the accolades. At the time of Beria's arrest in 1953, however, it would be revealed that the book had in fact been written by several people, including the rector of Tiflis University. And, as Amy Knight has pointed out in her biography of Beria, in later reprints of *History* Beria further altered the record by eliminating altogether any mention of Stalin's colleagues who had since fallen from grace. Meanwhile, Stalin's role as the father of Transcaucasian Bolshevism was extended even further back to youthful activities leading workers' circles and organizing strikes, at a time when in reality he had been shut away in the Tiflis Theological Seminary.

The Soviet archives opened since the late 1980s have revealed the truth about many events in the history of Bolshevism in Transcaucasia. In fact, the movement as such never took root there. It was the Mensheviks who remained predominant, not just in this region but even in Petrograd, up until the Revolution of 1917. But by the early 1930s the image of Stalin as a Caucasian hero in the mold of nineteenth-century freedom fighters had been permanently established in the public's mind by socialist realist hagiography, which depicted him as a romantically dark, shock-headed agitator among the workers of Baku and Batum.

Stalin's own version of Soviet history had always placed the emphasis on the central role of the Communist Party and his own guiding role as general secretary, and he was determined that a standard textbook should now be written with this in mind. He commissioned the collective writing of an official *History of the All-Union Communist Party* in 1935, which would on its publication in 1938 become the bible of Stalinism, popularly known as the *Short Course.* This, like all other historical accounts now being propagated at his behest, portrayed Lenin and Stalin as brothers in arms from as early as 1912 (when they had, in fact, only worked together briefly in Cracow, Poland). The year 1912 became the defining moment in the development of the Bolshevik Party, with Lenin and Stalin depicted on an equal political and ideological footing, singing the same harmonious tune. The *Short Course* became prescribed reading for anyone who sought to rise through the ranks of the *nomenklatura,* and the authorities made it clear that this was the definitive guide to Party history, "permitting no willful interpretations."

It was not just recent events, however, that became subject to dramatic reinterpretation along strictly Marxist-Leninist lines. Stalin even demanded the rewriting of early Russian history in order to obscure what are now known to be important external influences on the growth and economic development of the ancient state of Rus by such nearby states as Khazariya. To an anti-Semite such as Stalin, Khazariya, with its Turkic and Jewish peoples, was not viewed as a desirable source of inspiration for the ancient Slavic state. Similarly, Stalin's great historical heroes, such as Ivan the Terrible and Peter the Great, had their reputations readjusted. Ivan, known for his tempestuous moods, his cruelty, and his ruthless purge of the old aristocracy, the boyars, became transformed in the *Short Course* into a great and wise statesman who rid the Russian state of its enemies. Peter, who had built his new capital, St. Petersburg, with ruthless efficiency on the backs of serf labor, was admired for his military successes and empire-building.

Latent Russian nationalism and sentimentality about Mother Russia's past glories enjoyed a considerable revival during the war years in the cause of fueling Soviet patriotism, and many books, films, and plays resurrected the exploits of old popular military heroes and likened Stalin's heroic leadership to them. There remained, however, one particular sacred cow of Stalinist historiography during the Great Patriotic War, and that was the issue of Stalin's role as a military leader—in particular, in terms of his unpreparedness for the German invasion in 1941. In the 1950s a vast six-volume *History of the Great Patriotic War of the Soviet Union* was set in motion, which went some way toward telling the truth by admitting Stalin's mismanagement of the early days of the war, but which also succumbed to the continuing Soviet compulsion to pander to the egos of leadership, this time by allotting the new premier, Nikita Khrushchev, with an exaggerated role in events!

During Stalin's rule, political and economic science also atrophied or became distorted by his crude and dictatorial theoretical monopoly, which even extended into the areas of linguistics and genetics. Every single field of serious academic study felt the dead hand of Stalinist political orthodoxy upon it, and archival research, which was controlled by the NKVD (secret police) after 1938, became severely restricted. The choice of reading matter became dominated by either socialist realist literature or by books covering every aspect of the life and thoughts of the Great Leader. Soviet historian Roy Medvedev observed that "between 1946 and 1952 alone, no less than six hundred books and pamphlets, in a total printing of twenty million copies" were preoccupied with Stalin's every waking prognostication on every conceivable subject.

One of the main reasons that Khrushchev's government, while initiating the process of de-Stalinization, failed to set the historical record straight is that, by deconstructing the Stalinist version of events, it would also by association "delegitimize the revolution and its own claims to power" (as historian Gregory Freeze has pointed out). Thus, a new history of the Communist Party, published in 1959, while critical of the excesses of the cult of the personality and Stalin's political purges, still emphasized the country's positive economic and industrial achievements under his rule. Even school history books published as late as 1986 attached great importance to the collectivization of the peasantry, while totally ignoring the horrors of the famine that followed, which left approximately 7 million people dead. And even when the history books were further revised in 1989, there was still no challenge, either moral or theoretical, to the reputation of Lenin, which remained sacrosanct.

The falsification of official photographs also became closely interwoven with the official histories of the Stalin years, as David King's extraordinary study *The Commissar Vanishes* has shown in disturbing detail. Official photographs of Leon Trotsky, in particular, were subjected to rigorous doctoring. Even in some of the most famous images from the year of the revolution, Stalin saw to it that Trotsky's figure was entirely eliminated. And, as Stalin's old revolutionary colleagues and friends one by one were perceived by him, first as rivals, then as bitter opponents, and finally disappeared into the Lubyanka or the Gulag, so, too, their faces disappeared from books, encyclopaedias, official histories, and even family photograph albums. Such was the atmosphere of fear that families of those arrested and condemned were compelled to destroy even the image of their loved ones in their own personal records. The diligence with which the historical record was manipulated was so far-reaching under Stalin that, as the hero of Arthur Koestler's novel *Darkness at Noon* (which was based directly on the Great Terror) observed, "the only thing left to be done was to publish a new and revised edition of the back numbers of all newspapers."

See also Beria, Lavrenty; Lysenko, Trofim; Marr, Nikolay; *Short Course of the History of the Communist Party;* Trotsky, Leon

Further reading: David King. *The Commissar Vanishes: The Falsification of Photographs and Art in Stalin's Russia.* Edinburgh: Canongate Books, 1997; Amy Knight. *Beria: Stalin's First Lieutenant.* Princeton, NJ: Princeton University Press, 1993; Bertram D. Wolfe. *Three Who Made a Revolution.* Harmondsworth, UK: Penguin, 1964.

History of the All-Union Communist Party: Short Course

Popularly known as the *Short Course,* this is probably the defining document of Stalin's rule and political mentality. Published in 1938, it sold nearly 43 million copies in 300 printings and remained, years after Stalin's death, the only official book on the subject available. Even during the years of the thaw under Nikita Khrushchev, it took a long time for the mendacious version of history that the *Short Course* had disseminated to be gradually modified and replaced by Soviet scholarship. It was a process that continued into the 1980s.

The Soviet historian Dmitri Volkogonov described it as "the true encyclopedia of dogmatism, the miscellany of mummies, half truths and anti-truths." The collective of historians who prepared the *Short Course,* under Stalin's editorship, were obliged to describe Soviet history in accordance with Stalin's own simplistic view of it as a chain of cause and effect, viewed primarily from the perspective of the Communist Party's struggle to gain ascendancy over other political factions and anti-Bolshevik elements. Originally described as being "edited by a commission of the Central Committee," the book was begun in 1935 on Stalin's detailed instructions and submitted to him two years later.

Unhappy with the insufficient emphasis on his own role, Stalin modified and rewrote parts of it, including a chapter on "Dialectical and Historical Materialism," and the book's eventual authorship was credited as being "written by Comrade Stalin and approved by a Commission of the Central Committee." Throughout, Stalin overemphasized his own role alongside Lenin's, consigning Leon Trotsky to a minor and disruptive role. In his mind only two figures held center stage, Stalin and Lenin, and in that order. As historian Bertram D. Wolfe pointed out, Stalin had no qualms about putting his own name in front of Lenin's in statements in the book such as "only the Bolsheviks had a Marxist program on the national question, as set forth in Comrade Stalin's article, *Marxism and the National Question,* and in Lenin's articles, *The Rights of Nations to Self-Determination* and *Critical Notes on the National Question*."

In other areas of the book Stalin deflected attention from his own shortcomings as a true theoretical successor to Lenin and obscured his lack of sophisticated political insight and grasp of polemic by concentrating his argument around his own personal obsession—the elimination of the enemies of the revolution. The *Short Course* was for years the standard textbook available in schools and universities for teaching the political history of the Soviet Union, which pivoted on the achievement of "socialism in one country" by its chief architect, Stalin. Like Chairman Mao's *Little Red Book* (which far outstripped Stalin's, selling 700 million copies) the *Short Course* was prescribed reading for all loyal Communists and Party members. Many people learned whole sections of it by heart. It became venerated as the cornerstone of the Stalinist political canon, helping to impose the uniformity of public thought characteristic of Stalinist Russia. What people believed or thought in private, was, of course, another matter.

See also Education; Historiography
Further reading: Robert C. Tucker. *Stalin in Power: The Revolution from Above, 1928–1941.* New York: Chatto and Windus, 1990.

Ivan the Terrible (1530–1584)

Stalin's worst excesses have often been compared to those of the infamous Russian ruler, Ivan IV (known as "the Terrible"), the first self-appointed "tsar" (an abbreviation of "Caesar") of Russia. For this act of self-promotion alone, Stalin admired him greatly. It was also, certainly, an analogy applied to Stalin in private by his political opponents, as he proceeded to build his own empire with the same ruthless determination that Ivan the Terrible had exercised centuries earlier.

Stalin had always admired the statesmanship of Ivan the Terrible and looked upon him as a historical mentor. In 1922 he had read and made a mental note of a biography of the tsar by Moscow professor R. Iu. Wipper, and later he took a particular interest in Aleksey Tolstoy's 1942 play *Ivan the Terrible*. Stalin personally vetted the text and made corrections, writing the word "teacher" several times over his own copy.

As the Great Terror gathered momentum during the 1930s, Stalin's elimination of supposed enemies of the state through the offices of his secret police, the NKVD, seemed to resemble more and more the ruthless suppression of Ivan's dissident, hereditary nobility—the boyars—by the *oprichniki,* his elite military guard, an allusion that did not go unnoticed when

Sergey Eisenstein played on the similarity in his film *Ivan the Terrible*. And even ordinary workers picked up on the historical analogy in Stalin's methods of repression, complaining in the 1930s that "the time for respect for the Bolsheviks has passed for they are traitors and oppressors of everyone except their *oprichniki.*" Others commented on the rivalry between Stalin and Trotsky as being a historical parallel with Ivan's own conflict with Prince Andrey Kurbsky. In both cases, the opponents in question were driven into political exile. Stalin's irrational acts seemed more the result of megalomania, if not sheer madness, and in this respect his mental instability was further likened to that of Ivan the Terrible, who also suffered from periodic bouts of mental breakdown and who had, in a fit of rage in 1581, mortally wounded his eldest son. And yet, just as many Russian people grieved bitterly at the loss of Stalin even after thirty years of despotic rule, so too did Ivan's subjects, including his victims, mourn his loss. As the French traveler the Marquis de Custine observed of Ivan's rule: "An endless source of astonishment and awesome contemplation, is the effect that this unequalled tyranny produced on the nation decimated by it. Not only did the people not revolt, its loyalty was actually increased."

During World War II, or rather the Great Patriotic War as Stalin astutely renamed it,

Ivan the Terrible, as Stalin's favorite historical character, was harnessed to the war effort as a symbol of Russian invincibility. Stalin was fulsome in his praise of Part I of Eisenstein's ambitious film trilogy *Ivan the Terrible*, released in 1944, with its depiction of a determined autocrat bent on unifying his country at any price, and duly awarded it a Stalin Prize. Part II ran into trouble in 1947 when Eisenstein was called before Stalin at the Kremlin and told that the tsar had not been depicted in a sufficiently heroic fashion, that he had not been "terrible" enough, and that his only failing had been not to exterminate the powerful boyar families that were the greatest threat to his rule. Stalin had made absolutely sure that all potential opponents had been ruthlessly suppressed.

As it stood, the allusions to Stalin and his rule within Eisenstein's film were many and pointed. Stalin cannily observed that Eisenstein had made the *oprichnina* look like the Ku Klux Klan. Despite Stalin's admiration for what he deemed Ivan the Terrible's progressive suppression of his opponents, Ivan's rule was followed by the turbulent "Time of Troubles," which, in another historical parallel, in many ways mirrored the atmosphere of the Great Terror.

See also Eisenstein, Sergey; The Great Terror; Historiography

Further reading: S. F. Platonov. *Ivan the Terrible*, ed. and transl. Joseph L. Wieczynski. Gulf Breeze, FL: Academic International Press, 1986; R. G. Skrynnikov. *Ivan the Terrible*, ed. and transl. Hugh F. Graham. Gulf Breeze, FL: Academic International Press, 1981; Robert C. Tucker. *Stalin in Power: The Revolution from Above.* London: Chatto and Windus, 1990.

J

Japan
See Manchuria.

Jews

In one of his earliest efforts at demonstrating his grasp of Russian social democratic political theory, Stalin had published an essay in 1901 on the many tasks facing the party on the road to power. One of these was to bring justice to the Russian Empire's many oppressed peoples, including the Jews. He wrote, "Groaning are the unceasingly persecuted and humiliated Jews, deprived even of those miserable rights that other Russian subjects enjoy—the right to live where they choose, the right to go to school, etc." During his later years in power, when he had done his best to suppress national and ethnic aspirations of every shade within the Soviet Union, Stalin had a radically different view of these "groaning" people. "I can't swallow them, I can't spit them out. They are the only group that is completely unassimilable," he wrote. Such an admission would lead, in the final year of his rule, to draconian plans to finally solve Stalin's own "Jewish question."

Such had been the oppression of the Jews under the Russian tsars that many had been attracted into the Russian revolutionary movement during the late nineteenth century. By 1897, with Russia's Jewish population of 5 million forced to live within the confines of the Pale of Settlement, Jewish socialists had set up their own organization known as the Bund, which actively tackled anti-Semitism and sought national autonomy for the Jews. The vicious anti-Jewish pogroms of the early 1900s only served to strengthen support for the Bund among Jewish intellectuals. Other Jewish activists, such as Leon Trotsky, Grigory Zinoviev, Lev Kamenev, Yakov Sverdlov, and Karl Radek, all of whom later worked alongside Stalin, joined the Russian Social Democrats.

After the Bolshevik-Menshevik split in the Social Democratic Party in 1903, many Bundists gave their support to the Menshevik faction, which led to an image later perpetuated by the Bolsheviks that the Menshevik opposition constituted a hotbed of Jewish sedition, a fact that would lead to general support for Stalin's later purge of the Mensheviks in the Communist Party. By 1920, most committed Jewish Marxists had joined the leading Jewish revolutionary, Leon Trotsky, in the Communist Party, but Stalin was to remain suspicious of their loyalty, looking at them as a cosmopolitan and renegade element who harbored their own national interests, interests that would always be a potential danger to his own political hegemony. With the rare exception of

Lazar Kaganovich, who became a member of the Politburo and eventually outlived Stalin, very few Jews gained long-term positions of political prominence during the years of Stalin's rule.

That Stalin disliked and distrusted Jews is without doubt, but in the early years this ingrained dislike was born not so much of anti-Semitism as of an innate peasant distrust of all ethnic groups and national minorities, including his own people, the Georgians. This policy was underpinned by Stalin's harsh treatment of several ethnic minorities in 1941, who were deported for supposed collaboration with the German invaders. As historian Walter Laqueur has asserted, Stalin's anti-Semitism was basically "political-psychological and instinctive" and differed from that of Hitler, whose anti-Semitism sprang from a "biological-scientific" view and racial theories that had been propagated earlier by such nineteenth-century writers as Joseph-Arthur Gobineau.

The number of Jews in official jobs and positions of power in the Soviet Union declined rapidly between 1924 and 1941, with a high proportion suffering during the years of the Great Terror. While the White opposition during the civil war had stirred up long-held Russian resentment against Jews by misleading ordinary people into thinking that the Bolsheviks were predominantly Jewish and that, by association, the overthrow of the tsars was all part of some vast international Jewish conspiracy, there was, in fact, a considerable degree of hostility toward the Jews among the Bolshevik membership. Old primordial prejudices die hard, and many still looked upon the Jews in their ranks as a race apart and as a people not to be trusted.

Although synagogues were widely suppressed during the 1930s as part of Stalin's campaign to promote atheism throughout the Soviet Union, in many respects he was merely continuing policies begun under Lenin. Over 800 synagogues were closed between 1921 and 1925, their property

confiscated, and Jewish emigration severely curtailed. While the 1917 Revolution had initially brought Jews the civil liberties so long denied them, such as freedom of movement and profession, many Jews had remained ghettoized in the Pale of Settlement on Russia's western borders, where much of the old tradition persisted. Stalin tried hard to Russianize the Jews, as he did all the other Soviet ethnic minorities, and the process of their secularization and assimilation was accelerated by further repressive measures to eliminate the use of the Yiddish language and the teaching of Jewish children in separate Jewish schools. Jews were also discriminated against in many of the professions and deliberately excluded from jobs that were deemed politically sensitive. The introduction of internal passports in 1932 had also reintroduced a system, formerly used by the tsars, which identified people by their racial origins (under entry no. 5 in their passports).

Stalin made a token offer to the Jews of their own autonomous region of Birobidzhan in 1934. But this "national Jewish unit," as it was labeled, was located as far away as possible, in the Soviet far east near the border with Manchuria. Naturally enough, few Jews wished to uproot themselves and settle in this unfamiliar and inhospitable environment so far away from their traditional Ashkenazi Jewish roots in White Russia and Poland. The drive to resettle Jews in Birobidzhan never took off (unlike the mass immigration to the traditional homeland of Palestine by Jews at the end of the war). As a result, only 7,000 Jews originally agreed to settle there, and by 1936 their numbers had only risen to 19,000.

A disproportionate number of Jews perished during the Great Terror of the 1930s, since many of them figured strongly in those intellectual and cultural circles that were heavily targeted. Many leading Jews also perished in the purge of the last remnants of the Old Guard Bolsheviks. Similarly, many of the major figures accused in the great Moscow show trials of 1936–1938 were Jews, among them Grigory Zinoviev, Lev Kamenev, and Karl Radek. The atmosphere of fear at this time accentuated the deep-rooted anti-Semitism among the population at large as resentment grew against the Jews as an intellectual and political elite, few of whom toiled on the collective farms or worked in the factories. Stalin exploited the propaganda image of the Jews as power-hungry capitalists out for world domination.

In 1939–1940, under the German-Soviet Non-Aggression Pact, Stalin's annexation of territories in eastern Poland, Bessarabia, and the Bukovina absorbed many more Jews into the Soviet population. As a result of the later German occupation, as many as 2.5 million Soviet Jews were rounded up and perished in the Holocaust. Many Soviet Jews found renewed hope with the establishment of the new state of Israel in 1948, and hundreds of thousands sought permission to be allowed to emigrate. But the emergence of the state of Israel served only to accentuate Stalin's increasing paranoia about the global threat of Zionism. A witch-hunt against "rootless cosmopolitans" (the favorite catchphrase for Jews) and "Zionists" was initiated, and the Jewish Anti-Fascist Committee, which had done important work during the war fundraising and campaigning for U.S. support, became a major object of suspicion and was dissolved for its supposedly subversive activities.

In the late 1940s, Stalin's henchman Andrey Zhdanov launched a comprehensive attack against "decadent" Jewish influences, and all Jewish cultural institutions, including the famous Moscow Jewish Theater as well as Yiddish-language publications, were closed down. Jews were also excluded more and more from certain professions—the law, the diplomatic service, and academic posts—due to the imposition of strict quotas on their admission. This made life extremely difficult for the large Jewish intelligentsia of Moscow and Leningrad, the latter containing the greatest density of Jews in the whole of the Russian Soviet Federated Socialist Republic. In 1948 even Foreign Minister Vyacheslav Molotov's wife, who was Jewish, was arrested and accused of having connections with Jewish nationalists. She was exiled to Central Asia until after Stalin's death.

But Stalin was not content to stop here. On 12 August 1952, he once again ordered Lavrenty Beria to purge Jews in the arts on the pretext that a move was afoot among leading Jewish intellectuals to set up a Jewish secessionist homeland in the Crimea. Twenty-four leading Jewish cultural figures were rounded up, among them many Yiddish writers, including David Bergelson and the poets Peter Markish and Itzhik Feffer, who were shot in the Lubyanka after being held for three years. In addition, some 217 Yiddish writers and poets, 108 actors, including the great Solomon Mikhoels, 87 painters and sculptors, and 19 musicians disappeared to the Gulag.

Just before his death Stalin had been preparing a major show trial of Kremlin doctors, most of them Jews, as a prelude to the mass deportation of Soviet Jews to special reservations in Siberia and Central Asia. By the end of 1952, the next in line for purging would no doubt have been the party's higher-ranking members with Jewish connections, such as Lazar Kaganovich. Only Stalin's death in March 1953 prevented the onslaught of a new wave of persecution of the Soviet Union's beleaguered and much-maligned Jewish population.

See also Babel, Isaac; Doctors' Plot; Eisenstein, Sergey; Mandelstam, Osip; Meyerhold, Vsevolod; Mikhoels, Solomon; Nationalities; Religion
Further reading: Lionel Kochan. *Jews in Soviet Russia.* Oxford: Oxford University Press, 1978.

Kaganovich, Lazar Moiseevich (1893–1991)

Known as the "Iron Commissar," Lazar Kaganovich, one of Stalin's closest confidants, has the distinction of being the one to outlive him the longest. A member of the Politburo, he was the only Jew to rise to high office under Stalin and to survive.

Kaganovich grew up in Ukraine, in the Jewish Pale of Settlement, the son of a tailor. As a young boy he worked in a shoe factory. After hearing Leon Trotsky speak in Kiev in 1911, he joined the Bolsheviks and became an itinerant revolutionary, using a succession of aliases. After the revolution he fought in the civil war in Voronezh against General Anton Denikin's forces. He proved himself an efficient administrator of the new regime as head of the Soviet government of Tashkent, and under Stalin's watchful eye he worked his way up through the ranks, becoming head of the organizational department of the Central Committee in 1922, first secretary in Ukraine (1926–1928), and a member of the Politburo by 1930. As first secretary in the Moscow Party organization he also undertook the important role of overseeing the building of the Moscow Metro in the early 1930s.

During the collectivization of the peasantry Kaganovich was given the task of organizing transport and heavy industry, a role he maintained to the end of Stalin's rule. In this capacity, he became a ruthless implementer of Stalinist policy, as he toured the country on troubleshooting missions, always on the lookout for industrial "wreckers" and inciting managers and workers to greater efforts, his ethos being that "the ground should shake when the director goes around the factory." Kaganovich was unshakable in his view that anything and everything might be sacrificed for the sake of the Party, and he unhesitatingly supported the worst excesses of the Great Terror, instituting purges of local provincial committees of the Communist Party in Ivanovo and Smolensk. From his position in many of the key posts in the power structure of the Party, Kaganovich initiated the purge of as many as half a million people. When during the Great Patriotic War his elder brother Mikhail, who was People's Commissar for the Defense Industry, was arrested on charges of being a German collaborator, Kaganovich made no attempt to save him. Indeed, he is said to have assisted him in committing suicide.

By the late 1930s Kaganovich had become one of the ever-shrinking select inner circle surrounding Stalin—the cronies who drank with him at night at his dacha at Kuntsevo. His support appeared never to waver. He became one of the first to be awarded the Soviet Union's highest honor in 1935, the Order of Lenin. Kaganovich finally fell from favor in 1957 when his former protégé Nikita Khrushchev (who had worked with him on the construction of the subway system) gained power. Now at last he cracked at the prospect of his own possible demise, which reduced him to a groveling wreck. He telephoned Khrushchev, begging him "not to allow them to deal with me as they dealt with people under Stalin." Instead, Kaganovich was humiliated by being sent to languish in obscurity, managing a cement factory in the Ural Mountains, and was eventually expelled from the Communist Party.

See also The Great Terror; Khrushchev, Nikita; Moscow Metro

Further reading: Stuart Kahan. *The Wolf of the Kremlin.* London: Robert Hale, 1989.

Kamenev, Lev Borisovich (1883–1936)

An eminent Bolshevik, intellectual, literary editor, and talented journalist, Lev Kamenev (originally Rosenfeld) was a man after Lenin's own heart. No doubt if he had not become caught up in revolutionary politics, this erudite man, who, with his spectacles and neat goatee, had the mien of an Anton Chekhov, would have lived a quiet, untroubled life as a leading academic. Indeed, Kamenev's fatal lack of political ambition and ruthlessness later led Stalin to exploit his vulnerability as a pawn in the drive to rid himself of the Old Guard.

Kamenev was born in Moscow into a working-class family of committed radicals. His father was a railway engineer who was sent to work for the Transcaucasian railroad, as the result of which Kamenev grew up in Stalin's home country of Georgia, where he was educated at the Tiflis gymnasium (sec-

ondary school). Later arrested for such illegal activities as leading strikes and demonstrations when he was studying law at Moscow University, Kamenev was deported back to Tiflis. Not long after, he went to Paris, where he developed a close relationship with Lenin and met and married Olga Davidova Bronstein, a fellow revolutionary and sister of Leon Trotsky. Like his fellow Bolsheviks Lenin, Stalin, Vyacheslav Molotov, and Trotsky, Kamenev had also opted for a pseudonym, based on the Russian word *kamen'* ("stone"). In 1903 Lenin sent Kamenev back to Tiflis to continue propaganda work in the Georgian revolutionary underground, where he was joined later that year by Stalin. For the next few years he traveled in and around Europe; he saw the inside of several prisons, in Russia, England, and Finland.

In 1914 Lenin, by now an admirer of Kamenev's journalistic work in numerous Social Democratic publications, sent him back to St. Petersburg to run the Communist Party newspaper, *Pravda,* and to lead the Bolshevik members of the tsarist Duma. But Kamenev was soon arrested for treason, after instructing his fellow Bolshevik deputies to oppose Russia's entry into World War I, and in November 1914 he was exiled to Turukhansk in Siberia. Here, he associated again with Stalin and other exiled revolutionaries until news came of the February Revolution in 1917. Kamenev and Stalin made their way back together from exile in Achinsk, in southern Russia, to Petrograd, where, as members of a small coterie of revolutionaries, they assumed effective control of the Bolsheviks while awaiting Lenin's return from exile.

Kamenev was, from the start, one of the leading moderates among the Bolsheviks and urged cooperation with Kerensky's provisional government and other political factions, including the Mensheviks. His views, however, were overruled by Lenin and Stalin, and Kamenev together with Grigory Zinoviev stood firm in opposition to the idea of the Bolshevik coup in October 1917. In articles in *Pravda* Kamenev warned of the dangers inherent in one-party control and called for a broader base of power sharing. Despite his disagreements with Lenin over revolutionary methods, Kamenev retained Lenin's respect for his political skills and his even-handedness, and after the October Revolution he was the official spokesman who announced the new Bolshevik government. He was elected to the chair of the Central Committee of the Congress of Soviets—effectively becoming the first Bolshevik head of state—only to resign a few months later over Lenin's continuing unwillingness to share power. Despite this, Kamenev had by now garnered considerable political respect and was elected to the Politburo in March 1919.

For the next few years Kamenev ran the Party organization in Moscow and did valuable work as head of the Council of People's Commissars (Sovnarkom), earning Lenin's further approval as "a superb work horse" for the Party. He also applied his literary skills as chief editor of the first collection of Lenin's writings. As a natural moderator and conciliator, Kamenev became apprehensive at Stalin's rapid accumulation of power after his appointment as general secretary of the Communist Party in 1922, but after Lenin's death in 1924, he made the fatal mistake (as did several others) of aligning himself, along with his close colleague Zinoviev, in a triumvirate with Stalin against the party's big bogeyman—Leon Trotsky. By nature a "timid intellectual" and lacking any real political muscle, Kamenev nevertheless openly criticized Stalin for building a power base as general secretary and sole political leader, which he saw as "harmful to the party," and more presciently, condemned him for engendering what would later develop into the 1930s cult of the personality. But Kamenev's warning, given in a speech to the Fourteenth Party Congress in December 1925, was shouted down, and shortly after, he was demoted to a candidate member of the Politburo and forced out of the leadership of the Moscow Party.

Now realizing that Stalin was by far the greater political threat, Kamenev had no option but to transfer his support to an unlikely but tactically necessary alliance with Trotsky and others in the United Left Opposition, in hopes of restoring some kind of political balance. But the alignment failed, and Trotsky was exiled and later deported from the Soviet Union. In January 1927, as punishment for his alignment with Trotsky, Kamenev was packed off to Rome for a year as ambassador to Mussolini's government, a particularly distasteful role for a man of Kamenev's democratic sensibilities. In December of the same year, Kamenev was expelled from the Communist Party. In 1928, after the deportation of Trotsky, Kamenev was exiled to Kaluga in Siberia. A few months later, now duly repentant and having finally denounced Trotsky, he was allowed to return.

Over the next few years Kamenev would be driven into a typical pattern of craven behavior. He was expelled from the Communist Party on two more occasions, each time begging to be taken back into the fold. But his support within the Central Committee was now rapidly declining, and he never reestablished himself politically. In 1932, after being dismissed from office again, Kamenev was exiled to Siberia for a year before being allowed back in May 1934, averring that he now wanted to "lead a quiet untroubled life." It seemed a genuine desire, for he turned down Bukharin's suggestion of renewing his journalistic career on *Pravda* in preference for a post in academic publishing. Once again he was able to exercise his great intellectual skills, as he had done before and after the revolution—this time editing the works of the great nineteenth-century Russian radical Alexander Herzen—and to continue with his direction at the Lenin Institute, which housed Lenin's archives.

By the time of the 1934 Party Congress of the Victors—a triumphal celebration of the ascendancy of Stalin over his political rivals—Kamenev looked prematurely aged; his hair had turned white. At the congress he was called on to make a public confession of his sins, during which he disassociated himself from his former political being: "I want to state from this rostrum that the Kamenev, who from 1925 to 1933 struggled with the Party and its leadership, I regard as a political corpse." Thus, Kamenev consigned his own political and historical contribution to oblivion. These were the words of a tired and defeated man who realized that such capitulation was necessary in order to avert his total exclusion from public life. Unfortunately for Kamenev, he had one more important political role to play as a central figure in Stalin's public exorcism of the Bolshevik Old Guard.

On 16 December 1934, not long after the assassination of Leningrad Party boss Sergey Kirov, Kamenev and his friend Zinoviev were arrested and tried in secret in January 1935 for moral complicity in the murder. They were not executed but were sentenced to five years in prison, only to be rearrested eighteen months later and arraigned in the first big Moscow show trial of 1936, which took place on 19–24 August. Once again, Kamenev was accused of conspiring with others to murder Kirov and other members of the Soviet leadership, as well as collaborating in a Trotskyist-Zinovievite center that had plotted to overthrow the Soviet state. Kamenev was by now completely broken and had, like many others who would follow him, capitulated under duress in prison (in this case, heat torture in his cell at the height of summer). It would become a favorite Stalinist ploy to extract cooperation from the accused on the promise of mercy. In this instance, Stalin offered Kamenev and Zinoviev their lives in exchange for a full confession. No doubt both hoped that whether or not this would affect their own particular fates, their admission of guilt might at least save their families. Thus, in his final words in court Kamenev accepted that his sentence was "just" and urged his children to "follow where Stalin leads."

But Kamenev was not spared. After the sentence he was immediately shot in the Lubyanka on the night of 24–25 August. While eyewitnesses testify that Kamenev accepted his fate in shocked silence and with dignity, the executioner failed to do the job properly with a single bullet and Kamenev had to be given a coup de grâce. During the Great Terror others in his family suffered. His wife, Olga, was arrested and died or was shot in 1941. His elder son was shot in 1939, and his younger son spent years in orphanages in Siberia before being exiled for seven years; he was released under Nikita Khrushchev's 1956 amnesty. Even a grandson of Kamenev's was arrested as late as 1951 and spent most of his youth in the camps.

One of the most famous pictures ever taken of Lenin is that of him leaning over a wooden podium haranguing a crowd of troops in 1920. In the original photograph Kamenev and Trotsky can clearly be seen standing to the lower right of the podium. Both men were later airbrushed out of the picture by Stalin, and their extensive written works removed from libraries. Since Kamenev's rehabilitation in 1988, his image has been restored here and in many other photographs in which Stalin sought to deny his outstanding talent and important political role during the early years of the Soviet state.

See also Congress of Victors; The Great Terror; Kirov, Sergey; Trotsky, Leon; Zinoviev, Grigory
Further reading: Isaac Deutscher. *The Great Purges.* Oxford and New York: Blackwell, 1984. David King. *The Commissar Vanishes.* Edinburgh: Canongate Books, 1997. Tucker, Robert C. *Stalin in Power: The Revolution from Above, 1928–1941.* New York: Chatto and Windus, 1990.

Kataev, Valentin Petrovich (1897–1986)

A writer of undeniable talent, Valentin Kataev shrewdly adapted to the Stalinist regime and produced the archetypal socialist realist classic in his novel *Time, Forward!* (1932), in which he immortalized the superhuman achievements of shock workers building a metallurgical plant at the industrial complex at Magnitogorsk.

Kataev was born in Odessa and worked as a journalist in Moscow, while publishing short stories that captured the mood of the civil war and Lenin's New Economic Policy. He achieved his first notable success with the picaresque novel *The Embezzlers* (1927). His early grotesque and at times whimsical style did not, however, conform to the demands of socialist realism, which was inaugurated in the 1930s, and he was obliged to tailor his craft, in what the writer Nadezhda Mandelstam has described as a "special blend of talent and cynicism," to the demands of the new medium. As Mandelstam explained, Kataev, like many other writers, had suffered too much in the turbulent years of revolution and civil war to desire anything now but "peace and stability, money and women," even if it meant being obliged to "write like Walter Scott." With poets of the caliber of Vladimir Mayakovsky enthusiastically writing poems such as "March of the Shock-Brigades," it is perhaps less difficult to comprehend the appeal of a novel about workers breaking the world record in pouring concrete, which is the subject of Kataev's novel.

The exploits of the Stakhanovite workers at Magnitogorsk during the period of the First Five-Year Plan had become legendary and provided the ideal inspiration for Kataev, who traveled to the Urals to research material for the novel. As the title suggests, the main drive of Kataev's often humorous and surprisingly exciting narrative is a race against time, described on two levels. On one level, it is the twenty-four hours during which the concrete mixing team at Magnitogorsk must beat the record set by a Ukrainian team in Kharkov and, on a broader level, it is the Soviet people's metaphorical race against time to catch up with the West in industrial terms. The subsequent accolades heaped on Kataev for such a canny piece of writing, which delivered all the right political ingredients, brought a comfortable life and privileges—a new apartment, an American car—to a man who had judged rightly that the best thing a writer could do was "not to upset the powers-that-be."

While *Time, Forward!* brought him the desired public and official acclaim, it was Kataev's later autobiographical novel, the warm and humorous *Lonely White Sail* (1936), set in Odessa at the time of the 1905 Revolution, that is the more artistically satisfying work; it also became hugely popular with all age groups. He continued to dominate Soviet literature throughout the Stalinist period. Finally released from literary constraints in the thaw years, he produced some interesting and more experimental work, notably *The Grass of Oblivion* (1967).

See also Magnitogorsk; Socialist Realism; Stakhanovites; Union of Soviet Writers

Further reading: Edward J. Brown. *Russian Literature since the Revolution*. London: Collier Books, 1969; Katerina Clark. *The Soviet Novel: History as Ritual*. Chicago: University of Chicago Press, 1985; Valentin Kataev. *Time Forward!* Bloomington: Indiana University Press, 1976.

Katyn Massacre

On 13 April 1943, German occupying forces made a grim discovery in the Katyn Forest outside the city of Smolensk in Russia. In a vast burial pit the bodies of 4,443 Polish army reserve officers—civilians recruited from the leading professions—were discovered, all with neat bullet holes in the backs of their heads and their hands bound behind their backs with wire. Hitler's Ministry of Propaganda immediately capitalized on the discovery of this atrocity by launching anti-Soviet propaganda in newsreel footage of the gruesome scene alleging that the massacre was the work of the Soviets, a charge that was vigorously repudiated by them.

The International Red Cross was called in to ascertain the true circumstances of this massacre. They were informed by General Wladyslaw Sikorski, head of the Polish government in exile, that these might well be the bodies of some of a group of approximately 15,000 Polish nationals, most of them officers, deported in 1940 to camps at Kozelsk, Starobelsk, and Ostashkov, of whom the Polish government had heard nothing since. When Sikorski had agreed to raise a Polish force to support the Soviets against the German invasion of 1941 and had requested the reinstatement of these 15,000 men to the Polish fighting forces, the Soviet government had informed him that the majority of these prisoners had miraculously "escaped to Manchuria" or had dispersed elsewhere and that the dislocations of war made it impossible for them to now be located.

The murdered Polish officers found at Katyn had, no doubt, been seen by Stalin as a threat to Soviet authority, since they could have been the potential leaders of a Polish national revival. They had fallen into Soviet hands and had been deported to the Soviet Union from Poland at a time when Stalin's nonaggression pact with Hitler had condoned the Soviet occupation and partition of eastern Poland. The archives of the Soviet secret police, the KGB, opened since the demise of the Soviet Union, have since revealed that in September 1939, the head of the NKVD (the KGB's predecessor), Lavrenty Beria, had issued the order to remove some 15,131 Polish officers being held in three different camps in Russia near the frontier with Poland. But the Germans did not capture any camps containing these prisoners after they invaded the Soviet Union, nor did these prisoners reemerge from anywhere in the Soviet Union at the end of the war.

Stalin, furious at the accusations, accused the Poles of deliberate provocation and collusion with the Nazis and broke off relations with Sikorski and his government. A year later, when the Wehrmacht was repulsed on the eastern front and the Soviets reoccupied the Katyn area, they exhumed the corpses and reiterated their accusations. For the next forty-seven years the Soviets stuck to their version of events—that this was a Nazi atrocity and that the officers had been murdered by German troops after they invaded in the summer of 1941. The Communist government of postwar Poland was forced to live with this explanation until, in the atmosphere of glasnost promoted by Mikhail Gorbachev in the mid-1980s, a non-Communist coalition government in Poland decided that the time had come to get to the truth of the matter. It was subsequently revealed that Stalin's wartime allies, Britain and the United States, had been only too well aware of the truth, having been presented with intelligence reports giving incontrovertible evidence pinpointing the massacre to early 1940, at a time when the Soviets had been occupying the Katyn area. However, for obvious reasons of political and military expediency, the British and American authorities remained silent on the matter and quietly suppressed official documents alluding to the truth.

It was not until April 1990 that Mikhail Gorbachev's government finally and officially admitted that the murders had been carried out by the NKVD between March and May 1940, on the direct orders of Stalin and the Politburo. Gorbachev also revealed the location of two other, similar sites. Later discoveries supported long-held rumors that since the mid-1930s the Katyn Forest had been one of several killing fields used on a regular basis by the NKVD. The hands of the Germans were not untainted either, for mass graves of Soviet prisoners of war who had been murdered by the Nazis were also found here. In the event, the catalog of war crimes under which the Nazi leaders had been prosecuted at Nuremberg had included responsibility for the massacres at Katyn, but this particular case against the Germans was never pursued.

In 1995 a memorial service was held at the Katyn site, and there are movements to erect a permanent monument to the dead, although doubts persist as to whether the bodies are still there. They may well have been removed and dumped elsewhere by the Soviets after the second exhumation. The head of the Russian Security Service revealed in 1995 that the NKVD had reported back to Nikita Khrushchev in the 1950s that a total of 21,857 Polish nationals had been liquidated under Stalin's orders in the various wartime camps, including 4,421 at Katyn (a figure that conflicts with the one given in 1943), 6,311 at Ostashkov, and 3,820 at Starobelsk.

See also Beria, Lavrenty; Eastern Europe; Memorial; NKVD

Further reading: Norman Davies. *Europe: A History.* London: Pimlico, 1997, pp. 1004–1005; Allen Paul. *Katyn: The Untold Story of Stalin's Polish Massacre.* New York: Charles Scribner's, 1991.

KGB
See NKVD; Cheka.

Khrushchev, Nikita Sergeevich (1894–1971)

Western perceptions of the wily, boisterous, and argumentative Russian statesman, most graphically remembered for pounding the table with his shoe at the United Nations, have at times unfairly characterized Nikita Khrushchev

as the buffoon of Soviet politics. Indeed, he was a larger-than-life personality made up of many contradictions. As a successor to the reclusive, suspicious, and watchful Stalin, the extrovert and down-to-earth Khrushchev initiated the "thaw," breaking the deadlock of the Cold War. He gave promises of a warming in East-West relations through his policy of "peaceful coexistence" and as a result can rightly claim to be "the unwitting father of glasnost."

Like Stalin, Khrushchev was possessed of a native intelligence that compensated for his lowly social background, about which he had no pretensions. He was born of peasant stock in Kalinovka in Ukraine. His grandfather had been a serf and his father a miner. Khrushchev himself had a rudimentary education and took up an apprenticeship as a metalworker, fitting pipes in a factory, where he became involved in the revolutionary movement. Yet despite the disadvantages of his background and his lack of the veneer of sophisticated political and intellectual skills, Khrushchev, the boorish proletarian, became the epitome of the self-made apparatchik, working his way diligently through the apparatus of the Communist Party, first in Ukraine and then in Moscow, to eventually become the Soviet premier.

A member of the Bolsheviks since 1918, Khrushchev joined the Red Army in 1919 and fought during the civil war. He resumed his work for the Communist Party in Kiev and in Moscow in the second half of the 1920s. In 1929 he took up further education, although he was already in his thirties, studying metallurgy at Moscow's prestigious Industrial Academy. But by this time his organizational talents had already been spotted by Lazar Kaganovich, head of the Moscow region of the Communist Party. From 1931 Khrushchev, having resumed full-time work for the Communist Party, worked closely with Kaganovich on overseeing the construction of Stalin's great showpiece—the Moscow Metro (subway),

A surprisingly sophisticated portrait of the young Nikita Khrushchev. A wily and temperamental personality of peasant stock, Khrushchev became Soviet premier after a power struggle, 1954–1957, and in 1956 he initiated the process of de-Stalinization.

major political role in the affairs of Ukraine. In between, he served during the Great Patriotic War as a political officer on the southwest front (where he organized the evacuation of important industrial plants to the Urals, as well as civilian resistance to the German occupation) and later at Stalingrad. After the war Khrushchev devoted considerable energies to the reconstruction of the shattered Ukrainian economy and, in particular, the restoration of its agriculture, the destruction of which had led to widespread famine.

Stalin transferred Khrushchev to Moscow in 1949 and put him in charge of what was to become a disastrous reorganization of Soviet agriculture. Stalin had embraced the bogus theories of the agrobiologist Trofim Lysenko on ways of dramatically increasing crop yields, and Khrushchev, who had little or no comprehension of science or agriculture but who recognized the pressing need to increase Soviet grain production (which, by 1952 had fallen below prerevolutionary levels), enthusiastically adopted Lysenko's promises of good harvests. Not long after Stalin's death in 1953, Khrushchev took up a pet agricultural project of his own when he decided to cultivate vast tracts of virgin land in Kazakhstan, the southern Urals, and Siberia. As much as 70 million acres was ploughed for the production of wheat, in order to create what Khrushchev hoped would become a new Soviet breadbasket to relieve the pressure on Ukraine, which would now grow the corn to feed livestock instead. Between 1954 and 1958 the results were spectacular, with a 35.3 percent improvement in output, but ultimately the terrain proved unsuitable (it suffered from high levels of soil erosion), and the project ended in catastrophe. By 1963 the Soviet Union needed to import large amounts of grain from the United States.

for which Khrushchev was awarded the Order of Lenin in 1935. He also directed the remodeling of central Moscow, taking a ruthlessly philistine attitude toward historic architecture and later joking that "we've demolished the Triumphal Arch. The street is wonderful without the arch. We tore down the Sukharev Tower and the Kitaigorod Wall, even though the architects told us it was a historic monument."

By the mid-1930s Khrushchev had taken over Kaganovich's role as first secretary of the Communist Party of the Moscow region, and in 1938 he became a candidate member of the Politburo. At this point in his career, Khrushchev was moved back to his home territory in Ukraine as first secretary of the region, where Stalin put him in charge of a purge of the military in Kiev in 1938. For the next ten years he took a

After Stalin's death, Georgy Malenkov seemed the man most likely to take political control. Meanwhile Khrushchev was elected first secretary of the Central Committee of the Communist Party and, combining this with his membership in the Politburo six months later, was given a perfect opportunity to consolidate his position over Malenkov by appointing his own men to key posts within the Party apparatus. Malenkov was ousted as premier in 1955, although he and some of Khrushchev's other rivals remained in the Politburo. After an attempt to remove him failed in 1957, Khrushchev dismissed his protégé Nikolay Bulganin from the premiership and in March 1958 took over the office himself.

Khrushchev's decision in 1956 to denounce Stalin would appear to have been prompted as much by his desire to distance himself personally from the era of Stalin as it was to initiate a new phase of government freed from the shackles of one-man dictatorship. Historian Dmitri Volkogonov reported that Khrushchev ensured that any incriminating lists of those to be sentenced to prison or execution bearing Khrushchev's signature were quietly removed from the archives. Like all of the members of Stalin's Politburo, Khrushchev too had played his part in the political purges of the 1930s. And now Khrushchev's colleagues in the Presidium (as the Politburo was now called), Klimenty Voroshilov, Lazar Kaganovich, Georgy Malenkov, and Vyacheslav Molotov, began dreading the possibility of being called to account for their involvement.

After more than thirty years of Stalinism, which few had had the temerity to challenge, Khrushchev's "secret speech," given in closed session at the end of the February 1956 Party Congress, despite its limitations was undoubtedly brave and groundbreaking. During the four-hour speech Khrushchev attacked the lawlessness of Stalin's rule, particularly in the years following the 1934 assassination of Sergey Kirov. Yet, while he openly alluded to the execution of leading Communist figures during the years of the Great Terror, Khrushchev made no attempt to relate this to the suffering of the country as a whole and deliberately avoided being critical of such issues as collectivization, which were a fundamental part of the Soviet system in which he and members of the current leadership had taken part. While calling for the abolition of "the cult of the personality decisively, once and for all," he skirted any direct analysis of the murderous personality at work in all this, preferring to couch his accusations against Stalin in the euphemistic terminology of Partyspeak about "violations of Leninist norms," "grave perversions of party principles," and "mass acts of abuse against socialist legality."

The contents of the "secret speech" soon became widely known both within the Soviet Union and abroad. Thousands of prisoners began returning from the Gulag, and the cases of others murdered in the purges were reviewed and many were rehabilitated. Khrushchev's denunciation of Stalin did much to confuse nations abroad about his real intentions as a leader. While Western politicians saw hope in the introduction of a new brand of liberal-reformist communism, the satellite states in the Soviet bloc found their aspirations rekindled by Khrushchev's prognostications on a policy of "different roads to Socialism." Many became restive, a situation that led to demonstrations in Poznan in Poland and to the Hungarian uprising in late 1956.

During the period of thaw in East-West relations, Khrushchev's relationship with the West proved to be extremely volatile, characterized by his boorish manner at high-level summits and his unpredictable fits of behavior. Whether people liked him or not, Khrushchev never ceased to entertain with his idiosyncratic manner; his bumbling, garrulous, ebullient personality became familiar, sometimes causing him to be seen, mistakenly, as a figure of fun. Khrushchev was the first Soviet leader to travel widely abroad (something that Stalin had deliberately avoided). He was also the first Soviet president to visit the United

States, where he toured in tandem with his dapper and urbane prime minister, Nikolay Bulganin, and was wined and dined by both Eisenhower and the Kennedys. He was even taken on a tour of the Hollywood film studios, where he famously berated his hosts for the decadence of the dancing in the film *CanCan* (1959). He went on to cast decorum and diplomacy to the winds by throwing a famous tantrum, just before a Los Angeles banquet in his honor, because he had been refused permission to visit Disneyland for security reasons.

In the late 1950s Khrushchev began allowing foreign tourists access to the Soviet Union, initiating some cultural exchanges, and loosening the ties of censorship by allowing a modicum of debate between liberal and conservative elements in the press. But even here he proved erratic and inconsistent in his political decisions. During 1957–1958 he led a witch-hunt against the writer Boris Pasternak for permitting his novel *Dr. Zhivago* to be published abroad. Khrushchev refused to allow Pasternak to leave the Soviet Union to accept the Nobel Prize for literature. And yet in 1962 Khrushchev personally sanctioned the publication of Alexander Solzhenitsyn's far more outspoken novel about the Gulag, *One Day in the Life of Ivan Denisovich,* which was published in the liberal Soviet literary journal *New World (Novy Mir).*

Not surprisingly, the old-school Soviet leadership had become increasingly alarmed at Khrushchev's policies and his tendency to act impulsively and frequently alone without proper consultation, all of which seemed a threat to the stability of the old Soviet order. The Soviet Union's scientific achievements had given Khrushchev good reason to boast on his many trips abroad. The launching of the first Sputnik in 1957 and the first man in space, Yuri Gagarin, in 1961 bolstered his confidence in Soviet preeminence. Yet much of Khrushchev's economic policy had by now begun to come apart. The concentration of resources on defense and space exploration had led to stagnation in industry and shortages of consumer goods. But more alarming for the Old Guard was the rapidly deteriorating relationship with Mao Zedong, whom Khrushchev rashly denounced as "another Stalin," leading to a serious threat of Sino-Soviet conflict.

Khrushchev was ousted by Leonid Brezhnev and Aleksey Kosygin in October 1964 while he was vacationing on the Black Sea. The official pretext for his removal from power was his "advancing age and deterioration." Given a state pension and the continued use of his dacha, Khrushchev lived out the rest of his life in an increasingly reclusive manner and was not even accorded the honor of burial in the Kremlin Wall. The deadening Brezhnev regime that supplanted Khrushchev's did all it could to turn back the clock and allow a tacit revival of the Stalin cult that Khrushchev had so assiduously tried to dismantle.

With the gray-faced bureaucrats returning to a Kremlin that was once more retreating to Stalinist Cold War policies, Khrushchev in retrospect seemed a much more attractive figure. At times benign, warm-hearted, and approachable, the epitome of the jovial peasant when wearing his embroidered Ukrainian shirt, Khrushchev was well known for such homespun pronouncements as "if you cannot catch the bird of paradise, better take a wet hen" (1958) and "if you start throwing hedgehogs under me, I shall throw a couple of porcupines under you" (1963). And yet, this same jovial figure also suffered from dangerous bouts of impetuosity and once brought the world close to the brink of the nuclear abyss when he gravely miscalculated by basing Soviet atomic missiles in Cuba, thus precipitating the Missile Crisis of 1962.

See also China; Cold War; De-Stalinization; Kaganovich, Lazar; Malenkov, Georgy; Moscow Metro

Further reading: Nikita Khrushchev. *Khrushchev Remembers,* vol. 1. Boston: Little,

Brown, 1970; Nikita Khrushchev. *The Last Testament,* vol. 2. Boston: Little, Brown, 1974; Nikita Khrushchev. *Khrushchev Remembers: The Glasnost Tapes,* ed. and transl. Jerrold Schecter and Vyacheslav V. Luchkov. Boston: Little, Brown, 1990; Roy Medvedev. *All Stalin's Men.* Oxford: Oxford University Press, 1983; William J. Thompson. *Khrushchev: A Political Life.* Basingstoke, UK: Macmillan, 1995; Dmitri Volkogonov. *The Rise and Fall of the Soviet Empire.* London: HarperCollins, 1998.

Kirov, Sergey Mironovich (1886–1934)

Few figures in world history have, by their deaths and the events those deaths precipitated, become more famous dead than alive. But Sergey Kirov (born Sergey Mironovich Kostrikov) must rank alongside Archduke Franz Ferdinand, murdered in Sarajevo in 1914, for just such unsolicited notoriety. His murder in 1934 helped set in motion the political purges that marked the final sequence of the years of Stalin's Great Terror.

Kirov's revolutionary pedigree was exemplary—membership of the Bolsheviks in 1904, clandestine terrorist activities in the 1900s that resulted in arrest and imprisonment, and an active role in the Revolution of 1917 and the ensuing civil war, during which he became friends with Stalin. A career in provincial Communist politics in Transcaucasia saw him work his way up through the ranks of the Communist Party bureaucracy to membership in the Central Committee by 1923. In 1926 Stalin brought Kirov to Leningrad to take charge of the Party's regional branch.

For most of his career Kirov remained self-effacing, modest, and efficient in fulfilling his duties in Transcaucasia and moderate in his political standpoint. He could, however, be tough when needed, particularly in regard to his control of the Leningrad Party. Stalin had solicited and won his friendship and loyalty; by the year of his death, Kirov had been taken into Stalin's inner sanctum and seemed poised for a major role in government, as both secretary of the Central Committee and a member of the Politburo. He had also established himself as a popular local figure among the workers of Leningrad by allocating them extra food rations during hard times and as an innovator of technical and industrial projects in the city. Kirov now had a strong power base in Leningrad, and many saw him as the most popular choice for a successor to Stalin, a fact that was confirmed by his appearance at the Seventeenth Party Congress in 1934, when he was given a standing ovation.

Stalin, increasingly envious and suspicious of Kirov's popularity, pressed hard for his relocation to Moscow, where he could keep a closer eye on him. Stalin was also apprehensive that his enemies, such as Nikolay Bukharin, aware of Kirov's approachability, would attempt to maneuver him to their side of the political fence. This apprehension had been heightened by Kirov's conciliatory stance toward those charged with treason over the Ryutin affair of 1932, when he had opposed Stalin's call for Martimyan Ryutin's execution and the mass suppression of his supporters.

On 1 December 1934, Kirov was shot dead at his Party headquarters at the Smolny Institute in Leningrad by disgruntled Party member Leonid Nikolaev. Although it appears that Nikolaev acted alone, historians have expressed doubt about how he could have gained such easy access to the building or why Kirov's bodyguards were absent at the time. Rumors proliferated that Stalin had connived in some way at Kirov's death. The NKVD (secret police) were well aware of Nikolaev's instability, having arrested him carrying a gun near Kirov's headquarters on two previous occasions. Nikolaev and thirteen "accomplices" were arrested and quickly shot for Kirov's murder. Stalin revealed that Kirov's assassination had been the first manifestation of a vast plot uncovered by the NKVD to annihilate the entire Soviet leadership. A government document entitled "Lessons of the Events Connected with the Evil Murder of Comrade Kirov" appeared soon after, laying down stringent procedures for limiting the process of trying and executing those accused of acts of terror to a maximum of ten days. There would be no room for investigations and lawyers, for appeals and pardons. A vast and efficient machinery for the "judicial" elimination of enemies of the state was now put into motion, and complicity in Kirov's murder was used repeatedly against all the major defendants—Grigory Zinoviev, Nikolay Bukharin, Lev Kamenev, Aleksey Rykov, Genrikh Yagoda—in the three big Moscow show trials that followed between 1936 and 1938.

Debate continues as to whether the murder of Kirov was orchestrated by Genrikh Yagoda on direct instructions from Stalin. New evidence discovered in the KGB archives by Russian historian Yury Zhukov has thrown the debate open again by suggesting that the conspiracy theories, while logical, were in fact erroneous. According to Zhukov, Nikolaev's act was nothing more than a *crime passionel*. Kirov, a well-known womanizer, had been having an affair with Nikolaev's wife, Milda Draule. The affair was common knowledge among people in the Leningrad Party headquarters, where she also worked, and Kirov had been killed by Nikolaev at one of his assignations with Draule in the Smolny Institute. Perhaps the truth lies somewhere in the middle. All the signs point to Stalin's becoming increasingly worried by Kirov's independence and popularity. His inevitable removal of a powerful political rival was probably preempted by a jealous husband, but it is equally possible that, knowing of Nikolaev's wife's infidelity with Kirov, the NKVD deliberately incited him to murder.

See also Congress of the Victors; General Secretary of the Communist Party; The Great Terror; Ryutin Manifesto

Further reading: Robert Conquest. *The Great Terror: A Reassessment*. London: Pimlico, 1992; Edvard Radzinsky. *Stalin*. London: Sceptre, 1997;

Robert C. Tucker. *Stalin in Power: The Revolution from Above, 1928–1941*. New York: Chatto and Windus, 1990; Chris Ward, ed. *The Stalinist Dictatorship*. Arnold Readers in History Series. London: Arnold, 1998.

Koltsov, Mikhail Yefimovich (1898–1940)

A gifted and popular journalist who covered the Spanish Civil War for *Pravda*, Mikhail Koltsov was an ardent Stalinist. Despite his high public profile in both Soviet and international newspapers and newsreels, he was arrested in 1938.

Koltsov first started writing articles for *Pravda* in 1922, eventually becoming a member of its editorial board. He was sent to Madrid as a correspondent during the Spanish Civil War, and his dispatches from the front became a popular column in *Pravda*. He also made himself known to other famous figures involved in the war. In particular, Ernest Hemingway remarked on his intelligence, his wit, and his bravery, calling him "one of the most important figures in Spain." Hemingway later based the character of Karpov in his novel *For Whom the Bell Tolls* on Koltsov and in 1952 remarked on Koltsov's commitment to putting across the Communist case: "He knew I was not a Communist and never would be one. But because he believed in me as a writer he tried to show me how everything was run so that I could give a true account of it."

Koltsov returned from Spain at the height of the Great Terror and was called to the Kremlin to see Stalin in 1937; the Great Leader congratulated him for his bravery. Koltsov, in return, produced some of his purplest prose to condemn the accused in the Bukharin-Zinoviev trial, stooping to the strident, jingoistic language that had become de rigueur in describing enemies of the state: "When [the accused] stand up and start describing their monstrous crimes in detail . . . you feel like jumping up and shouting, thumping your fist down on the table and seizing these filthy, blood-smeared blackguards by the throats. . . ."

Stalin is said to have initially dismissed a verbal denunciation of Koltsov when it was made to him, but he changed his mind when he saw it written down. He had a propensity for being convinced of any act of treason if sufficient documentary evidence was produced (no matter how it was acquired) and seemed quite ready to accept that the heretofore loyal demagogue Koltsov was in fact a traitor. Koltsov's interrogators succeeded in manufacturing two thick dossiers of evidence, in which Koltsov confessed to a string of typically preposterous charges—such as being an agent of the British newspaper magnate Lord Beaverbrook; spying for the Germans, the Americans, and the French; and being a covert Trotskyist. In prison, like many others, Koltsov had been tortured to the point of full confession of these crimes, only to recant later.

After Koltsov's arrest in 1938, his brother was told that he had been sent to a remote camp in the Gulag, where he was denied the right to send or receive letters. For years the family nurtured the false hope that Koltsov might one day be released, when all along he had been shot the day after he was sentenced—the same day as Vsevolod Meyerhold, 2 February 1940.

Whatever the reasons for Koltsov's arrest, which almost certainly was part of the general round-up of Russian Communists returning from taking part in the Spanish Civil War, the writer Ilya Ehrenburg in his memoirs summed up the senseless arbitrariness of Koltsov's death and that of many others: "When I think of the fate of my friends and acquaintances, I can see no logic at all in it. Why did Stalin not touch Pasternak, who maintained his independence, while he destroyed Koltsov, who dutifully did everything he was asked to do?"

Koltsov was rehabilitated in 1955.

See also Pasternak, Boris; Spanish Civil War

Komsomol

The Kommunistchesiky Soyuz Molodezhi or Communist League of Youth, popularly referred to by its acronym Komsomol, was established in 1918 as an adjunct to the Communist Party. Its youthful members took an active part in the vanguard of political activity after the revolution and in the civil war.

During the early days of postrevolutionary economic uncertainty, good use was made of the unpaid labor of eager Komsomol volunteers, who were organized into "shock brigades" to help on many industrial and building projects. In 1932–1933 several thousand of them labored on the construction of a new industrial center in the Far East that would bear their organization's name—Komsomolsk. Members of the Komsomol also contributed considerably to the speeding up of the collectivization process in the countryside. The Komsomol's role was, however, primarily one of ideological control and the indoctrination of Soviet youth between the ages of fourteen and twenty-eight with the dogma of Marxism-Leninism. The process, of course, did not start here but in childhood, with junior offshoots of Komsomol—the Young Pioneers (ages nine to fifteen) and the Little Octobrists (introduced in 1923–1924 for seven-to-nine year olds).

Much of Komsomol initiation and practice was a modified form of the rituals of the old scouting movement, with its uniform and badges, its oath of allegiance, and its adherence to the moral values of truth, courtesy, and national duty. Whereas scouts and guides in the West did not get much beyond learning a few homilies by rote and sewing on badges awarded for making cakes and building campfires, young Komsomol members were faced with a daunting curriculum that included "Komsomol history, fundamentals of Marxism-Leninism and current Party policy."

From the early 1920s, children were

attracted into the Komsomol and Young Pioneers through their various sporting and recreational activities, but in reality recreation had little to do with the movement. Its primary objective was to raise a class of suitably indoctrinated candidates for the important jobs in the Soviet bureaucracy and Communist Party. As an official recruiting ground, therefore, Komsomol provided future candidates for the *nomenklatura,* and its members would be given preference over nonmembers for important government jobs in later life.

In a chilling parallel with the activities of the Hitler youth movement in Germany, such became the devotion to duty on the part of Komsomol's members that they would berate their own parents for their political lapses and, during the days of the Great Terror in the Soviet Union, would even denounce them to the authorities. Throughout its existence, Komsomol was predominantly an urban movement, and peasants in the countryside did not always take kindly to its evangelizing methods. A notorious case in point was that of fourteen-year-old Pavlik Morozov, who was the sole local representative of the Komsomol in his village in the Sverdlovsk district. In 1932 young Pavlik took it upon himself to report his father, Trofim, to the authorities for withholding a proportion of the grain produced on the local collective farm (of which Trofim was chairman) and of taking part in supposed black-marketeering. The father was duly tried and given the standard draconian sentence of consignment to the Gulag. In retaliation Pavlik's relatives murdered both him and his younger brother.

Soon after, the Stalinist propaganda machine took up Pavlik's story and the mythologizing process went into overdrive, elevating Pavlik to the status of Communist sainthood. During the 1930s, Morozov, like the industrial hero Aleksey Stakhanov, became a cult figure, commemorated in paintings and statues—there was even discussion in 1938 of erecting a statue to him in Red Square. His example spawned a whole generation of dutiful Komsomol informers. The story even became the basis of a film by Sergey Eisenstein, *Bezhin Meadow* (1935), which was later banned by authorities.

Despite the relative youth of the bulk of its membership, the Komsomol was not immune from the depredations of the purges, nor were all of its members committed Stalinists. Some Komsomol members, particularly in rural areas, voiced their open dissent on political matters or their discontent about food shortages. The Central Committee of Komsomol came under attack by Stalin in 1937; he complained about its failure to effectively fulfill its role as "a youth auxiliary of the NKVD" (secret police), to use the words of historian Robert Conquest, by seeking out and denouncing enemies of the state. A purge of the leadership of the central and several regional committees of Komsomol followed. Seventy-two of its ninety-three full members, including its leader, Alexander Kosarev, were arrested; many of them perished or were sent to the Gulag. Meanwhile, the organization's more obedient members took part in the weeding out of "undesirables" in their midst in the universities and technical colleges by hounding the children of families of the old intelligentsia and those academics whom they considered bourgeois. Others actively joined in the campaign against religious practice by disseminating propaganda and joining shock brigades engaged in wrecking churches and burning icons.

During the years of the Great Patriotic War, Komsomol members rallied to the nationwide call "Do you want to defend your Motherland?" by collecting scrap metal for the war effort and helping to dig antitank trenches and defense systems. At Stalingrad many female Komsomol members helped to man the antiaircraft batteries. By now thoroughly indoctrinated by the call to fulfill quotas, Komsomol members were exhorted to kill as many of the enemy as possible, and those in the front lines of the 57th Army at Stalingrad were reprimanded when their political officer reported that "out of 1,697 Komsomol members, 678 have not yet killed any Germans."

So strong was the pressure on Soviet youth to join Komsomol, as it was on their parents to belong to the Communist Party if they wanted to improve their lives, that by the end of the 1970s the movement boasted over 40 million members. Not surprisingly, this vast membership rapidly disintegrated after the demise of the Soviet Union, and the Komsomol was disbanded in 1991.

See also Collectivization; Education; Eisenstein, Sergey; Family Life; The Great Terror; *Nomenklatura*

Further reading: Allen Kassof. *The Soviet Youth Program: Regimentation and Rebellion.* Cambridge, MA: Harvard University Press, 1965.

Korean War

The seeds of the Korean War were sown with the Sino-Soviet alliance of January 1950, under which the two Communist powers guaranteed to provide military support and assistance should either party be attacked by Japan. After the withdrawal of Soviet and U.S. troops from occupied Korea at the end of World War II, the Soviets had supported the Communist regime of Kim Il Sung in the north.

Trained in the Soviet Union, Kim had quickly established a powerful fighting army with which he aimed to unite the two countries of North and South Korea under his sole rule (Korea had been divided along the 38th parallel after Japan surrendered it at the end of World War II). Stalin and Chinese leader Mao Zedong were convinced that the South would quickly crumble when faced with the military might of the Communist North, and they gave Kim their covert backing for the invasion, believing that this would not be an

issue the United States would go to war over. The reasoning behind Stalin's decision to support the unification of Korea (without sending in his own troops) was probably related to maintaining political and military pressure against Japan, by supporting the increased Communist presence in Asia that a unified Korea would provide. Others have argued that it was a tactical move, aimed at keeping China firmly in the Soviet camp. By supporting the Communist regime in North Korea, Stalin might provoke the Americans into taking a retaliatory position in support of Nationalist Taiwan, an act that in turn would ensure China's siding with the Soviet Union against the United States. In any event, the potential was there for the foundation of an intimidating new global alliance between China and the Soviet Union.

Convinced of his strategy, Stalin attempted to accentuate the advisory nature of his support for the North, when, in fact, he was also sending considerable amounts of military hardware—tanks, artillery, rifles, mortars, and shells, as well as millions of rounds of bullets and aircraft spares and providing technical and military advisers and medical supplies. This influx of armaments continued throughout 1949 and early 1950, including a special corps of Soviet fighter planes and antiaircraft batteries, which during the war were ultimately responsible for downing 1,309 U.S. planes. In return Kim supplied the Soviet Union with much-valued consignments of lead, silver, and gold. On 25 June 1950, North Korea attacked the South and within days occupied Seoul. When the hoped-for Communist uprising in the South in support of this attack failed to materialize, Stalin suddenly found his policy backfiring—for the Americans took the North Korean invasion seriously and began mobilizing forces rapidly in eastern Asia. The UN supported this act and backed a mainly U.S. expeditionary force to be sent to Korea under the command of General Douglas MacArthur.

Stalin now hastily backpedaled by stating that the Korean War was a civilian war in which he would not intervene, a cover for the fact that he had no desire to be drawn into a war with the United States that he could not win.

After UN forces under MacArthur succeeded in stemming the North Korean invasion at Inchon in September 1950 and joined the South Koreans in capturing Seoul, South Korean forces entered the North, followed by the Americans. Kim Il Sung now looked to Stalin to save the situation but to no avail. Stalin realized that he had little to gain from the war and promptly shifted the onus onto China. Mao, apprehensive about potential American nuclear attacks of retaliation on China, wavered but, nevertheless, launched an invasion of the North, convinced that to allow a continuing American presence in Korea would threaten stability in China itself. He did so on the basis of considerable military aid, especially gasoline from the Soviet Union, in return for a valuable consignment of 50,000 tons of natural rubber.

The success of the Soviet-supported Chinese counteroffensive in late 1950 changed the nature of the war. Many of America's allies were becoming nervous that it would be extended into China, an event that would likely force the Soviet Union into the war as well. Stalin now dug in his heels, convinced that the Americans would be routed by the Chinese. He was also counting on the fact that the escalation of the war in Korea would weaken defenses in Western Europe by diverting American military strength. While Stalin was resolute in not being drawn into a war with the United States, he had no qualms about using the war as an occasion for the economic exploitation of his allies and for whipping up the current international war of nerves. His handling of the war also served as an important propaganda tool, by depicting the Soviet nation as peace-loving conciliators in the face of Western, capitalist aggression.

After an armistice was called in Korea in July 1951, Stalin backed down from supporting a negotiated settlement, happy to leave the Americans and Chinese bogged down in a military stalemate and protracted peace negotiations that went on until several months after Stalin's death and which further prolonged the Cold War.

See also China; Cold War; United Nations
Further reading: S. Goncharov and J. Lewis. *Uncertain Partners: Stalin, Mao and the Korean War.* Stanford, CA: Stanford University Press, 1993; David Holloway. *Stalin and the Bomb: The Soviet Union and Atomic Energy, 1939–1956.* New Haven, CT: Yale University Press, 1994; Dmitri Volkogonov. *The Rise and Fall of the Soviet Empire,* chapter 2. London: HarperCollins, 1998.

Kremlin

Originally a wooden medieval fortress, built in the center of Moscow in the fourteenth century, the Kremlin was replaced by a group of stone buildings constructed under the orders of Ivan III between 1475 and 1500. It remained the seat of power, with numerous later structures added and undergoing an extensive later remodeling by the Romanovs, until Peter the Great switched the Russian capital to his new northern city of St. Petersburg in 1712.

After the Bolsheviks seized power in October 1917, Lenin made the Kremlin the headquarters of the provisional government. When the Bolsheviks later negotiated with Germany to take Russia out of World War I they decided to forestall any possible German about-face and renewed attack by moving the capital back to the safety of Moscow and the government to the relative security of the Senate building within the Kremlin walls. This relocation also removed the seat of government away from the numerous and querulous political factions that made Petrograd such a volatile place for the establishment of a new order.

Within its perimeter walls, the Kremlin

is an ensemble of exquisitely beautiful cathedrals, churches, and palaces—an absurdly incongruous setting for the atheistic government of the new Bolshevik leaders, who found themselves dining off plates bearing the imperial twin-headed eagle. All the Kremlin's churches ceased functioning as places of worship after the revolution, and the chimes of the clock on the Spassky (Savior's) Tower were changed from playing "God Save the Tsar" to the tune of the Marxist "Internationale." In the 1930s the Kremlin was closed to visitors. In 1935 the splendid imperial eagles that topped its towers were taken down and replaced with glowing red stars.

Under Stalin, the name Kremlin became synonymous with the machinery of the Soviet state and, in the darker days of the Great Terror and Cold War, a symbol of the terrifying and impenetrable mystique of his rule. Stalin's own private apartments within the Kremlin during the 1920s and early 1930s were located at the Poteshny Dvorets (Amusement Palace), so called because it was originally used for theatrical productions during the seventeenth century. After his wife Nadezhda's death in 1932, Stalin moved to a smaller apartment, converted from offices located on the first floor of the Senate building. It was not an environment conducive to happy family life and his daughter Svetlana found it an uncomfortable place to live. It also provided the deadening ambience that presaged Stalin's withdrawal into a nocturnal, closed-off existence as "the recluse of the Kremlin." Literary hacks, eager to please during the years of the cult of the personality, were quick to pick up on the emotive image of the light in Stalin's study burning into the late hours of the night, describing it in characteristically religiose tones as "the light shining in darkness"—a symbol of Stalin's paternal, even godlike, devotion to his people. When he did leave the stronghold of the Kremlin, it was late at night in one of a fleet of armored cars that swept

through the Borovitsky gates to his dacha at Kuntsevo eight miles away. Here Stalin stayed overnight, before returning for another sixteen-hour working day.

In 1999 a major restoration and refurbishment of the Kremlin was completed at a cost to the impoverished Russian taxpayer of more than 1 billion. The work, carried out over a two-year period at the behest of President Boris Yeltsin, involved the removal of all interior features redolent of the old Communist past—right down to the door handles and the hammer and sickle insignia. In their place Yeltsin ordered the restoration of the prerevolutionary Russian crest of the double-headed eagle. Many of the fixtures and fittings removed from the former offices of Stalin and his secret police chief, Lavrenty Beria, were sold off to private buyers at a fraction of their true market value.

See also Stalin: Dachas of; Stalin: Private Life of
Further reading: G. Markova, ed. *The Great Palace of the Moscow Kremlin.* Leningrad: Aurora Art Publishers, 1990.

Krupskaya, Nadezhda Konstantinova (1869–1939)

The wife of Lenin and grand old lady of the Bolshevik Party, Nadezhda Krupskaya initially took a combative stance against Stalin in the days after Lenin's death. But she never seemed able to penetrate the darker complexities of his political intrigue and eventually her own resistance evaporated in the escalating climate of terror, to leave her in her last days an isolated and frightened remnant of the Old Guard.

Krupskaya was one of many women from the Russian intelligentsia in the late nineteenth century who, as dedicated feminists and socialists, joined in the groundswell of political discontent by embracing the revolutionary movement. She came from a family of impoverished gentry and proved an exceptionally gifted student. But soon, under the influence of Marxist literature, she went to St. Petersburg to act as a propagandist for the Russian Social Democrats among factory workers. In 1894 she met Lenin at a Marxist study group. When they were both arrested and sentenced to exile in Siberia for their revolutionary activities, they married in 1898, in order to spend their exile together and at Nadezhda's mother's insistence (she went everywhere with them hereafter).

Krupskaya remained Lenin's loyal helpmate and secretary, following him doggedly around Europe during his years of exile and even condoning his later love affair with the beautiful French activist Inessa Armand. Krupskaya was no physical match for Armand. Indeed, such was her unprepossessing, matronly appearance that her Zurich landlord during her years of exile had even remarked that "Frau Lenin would have made a good *Hausfrau,* but she always had her mind on other work." Indeed such was her devotion to the work—Lenin's work—that she not only tolerated Inessa Armand's covert installation in the Kremlin as Lenin's close companion after the revolution, but also proposed, on Lenin's death, that he be buried alongside her in the Kremlin Wall rather than be subjected to the indignity of being put on display in the Lenin Mausoleum. Perhaps some of this excessive unselfishness was due in part to her own inability to have children, for whom both she and Lenin showed genuine affection.

After Lenin was disabled and politically sidelined by several strokes in 1922–1923, Krupskaya attempted to keep him abreast of political events, while he was recuperating outside Moscow, at a time when he had become increasingly mistrustful of Stalin's ambitions. Stalin, on finding out about what he deemed to be Krupskaya's interference, became rude and abusive during the course of a telephone conversation with her. On Lenin's insistence Stalin later grudgingly wrote her a brief apology. By now, however, Lenin had already dictated his famous "Testament" (January 1923) in which he recommended, in a postscript, Stalin's removal from power. After Lenin's death, in May 1924, Krupskaya further incurred Stalin's wrath when she passed a copy of the testament to Lev Kamenev, in advance of the imminent Thirteenth Party Congress, at which Lenin had intended it be read out. Stalin, however, was saved from the dismissal called for by Lenin, by the intervention of Zinoviev and Kamenev, both of whom saw Stalin's removal as only laying the way open for the ascendancy of Trotsky and the left wing.

For a while longer, Krupskaya remained a thorn in Stalin's side, and a constant reminder of the Old Guard of the Party that he was now seeking to eliminate. In the past, he had been heard by Molotov to grumble about her interfering manner, saying that "she may use the same lavatory as Lenin, but that doesn't mean she knows anything about Leninism." In 1935 the last straw came for Stalin when Krupskaya joined with other Bolsheviks of the Old Guard to attempt to defend Kamenev who had now come under attack by Stalin. It was then that he was said to have made his classic remark that if Krupskaya continued to meddle in political affairs the party would nominate someone else as Lenin's widow. In other words, Stalin would deliberately fabricate an undisclosed divorce and Lenin's "remarriage" to someone more appropriate. Stalin even had a likely candidate lined up in the Old Guard Bolshevik Elena Stasova. At this point Krupskaya's resistance to Stalin finally crumbled, her political influence declined (she was hived off to a job as assistant people's commissar for education), and she spent her last few years in fear for her life.

In 1938, after being formally denounced by Stalin's henchman Nikolay Ezhov at the Central Control Commission, Krupskaya collapsed. By now sick and plagued with thyroid problems that had caused her eyes to bulge, she died not long afterward of "a sudden attack of appendicitis." However, some of the symptoms described on her death certificate (vomiting and cyanosis) suggest a different scenario.

See also General Secretary of the Communist Party; Kamenev, Lev; Lenin, Vladimir Ilyich; Russian Revolution of 1917

Further reading: Nadezhda Krupskaya. *Memories of Lenin.* London: Lawrence & Wishart, 1970; Larissa Vasilieva. *Kremlin Wives.* London: Weidenfeld and Nicolson, 1994.

Krylenko, Nikolay Vasilievich (1885–1938)

At the time of the revolution Nikolay Krylenko seemed to have all the right credentials for a top military role. He later abandoned these ambitions in favor of holding sway, along with Andrey Vyshinsky, over the show trials of the Great Terror, where one of his several famous prognostications was that "we must execute not only the guilty. Execution of the innocent will impress the masses even more."

A talented theoretician, Krylenko studied history and philosophy, later moving on to law at St. Petersburg University. He had joined the Social Democrats in 1904 and became a political activist and member of the editorial board of *Pravda,* but during World War I he resumed the military career he had pursued between 1911 and 1913, serving as an officer. He continued his military role after the revolution as a member of the Military Revolutionary Committee. Recognizing his abilities, Lenin promoted him to commander-in-chief of the army in 1917 and people's commissar for military affairs. But Krylenko was unable at this time to reconcile his differences with a dictatorial Trotsky, who had overall control of the army as commissar for war, and he decided to exploit his legal talents instead.

In 1918 Krylenko took a post in the Commissariat of Justice, becoming chief state prosecutor from 1918 to 1931. His legal skills were employed in helping to draft the Soviet constitutions of 1918, 1924, and 1936. Promoted to procurator general of the Russian Soviet Federated Socialist Republic (a post he held from 1922 to 1931) and People's Commissar for Justice for Russia in 1931, and the whole of the U.S.S.R. in 1936, Krylenko first publicly demonstrated his legal skills at the trial of the Shakhty in 1928 and of a group of Mensheviks in 1931. He set the tone for political trials with his full-throated invective against the accused, a style that was also promoted by its presiding judge, Andrey Vyshinsky, who was to succeed Krylenko as chief state prosecutor.

As a member of the Soviet judiciary and a leading writer on Soviet jurisprudence, Krylenko was an eager participant in the tearing down of the old legal mechanisms and supported the creation of "a new law and new ethical norms." In his view, political trials were not obliged to clarify whether or not a defendant was guilty, but should be evaluated "from the point of view of class expediency," thus ensuring that the outcome was in the interests of "the masses of workers and peasants." In line with this expediency Krylenko exacted the harshest sentences of the courts and had no qualms about supporting the methods of torture by which confessions were extracted. He noted that "for us . . . the concept of torture inheres in the very fact of holding political prisoners in prison."

At the first major show trial of its kind, that of the Shakhty in 1928, Krylenko failed to get the clear-cut result expected of him (some of the accused refused to confess), a fact that writer Alexander Solzhenitsyn suggested may in part account for Krylenko's own later arrest by a disgruntled Stalin. As with so many others who eagerly lent their hands to cranking the machinery of the purges, the machinery eventually caught Krylenko in its maws. After an absurd attack made on him in the Supreme Soviet, in which he was criticized for spending too much time away from the job playing chess (he was chairman of the All-Union Chess Section of the Council for Physical Culture), he was removed from his post.

On 31 January 1938 Krylenko was arrested. He was executed in July after a closed trial lasting a mere twenty minutes. The day before his arrest he had received the traditional kiss of death from Stalin in the form of a friendly telephone call assuring him that all was well.

See also The Great Terror; Shakhty Trial; Vyshinsky, Andrey

Further reading: Vaksberg, Arkady. *The Prosecutor and the Prey: Vyshinsky and the 1930s Moscow Show Trials.* London: Weidenfeld and Nicolson, 1990.

L

Labor Camps
See Gulag.

Lenin, Vladimir Ilyich (1870–1924)

*I*n the polite drawing rooms of Petrograd society in April 1917 the series of strikes and demonstrations unfolding on the streets outside seemed little more than the usual irritating and sporadic political disturbances to which people had become accustomed since 1905. At an afternoon tea party held at the home of a certain Madame Rodzyanko, the hostess was asked if she had heard about the arrival of Vladimir Lenin in the capital. *"Lenin? Qui est Lenin? Est-ce qu'il est gentil?"* she had queried (in the French that most of the upper classes had adopted as a social affectation since the eighteenth century), only to be told that he was *"un de ces affreux révolutionnaires!"* By November of that year the whole world would have come to hear about this shabbily dressed little man, with his bald head, high forehead, and screwed-up Tatar-looking eyes, a man of such unprepossessing appearance that a British diplomat described him as looking like a "provincial grocer." Yet this was the dedicated revolutionary who had waited and plotted for seventeen long, penurious years in exile for the opportunity to "give history a push" into the new age of socialism.

For the seventy years or more of Communist rule that followed the Russian Revolution of 1917, the image and reputation of Lenin remained inviolable. As leader of the Bolsheviks, guiding light of the revolution, and the first head of the new socialist state, Lenin had set his stamp on the Bolshevik interpretation of Karl Marx, Friedrich Engels, and other radical socialist thinkers. It had been his iron will, his breadth of vision and incontrovertible wisdom, and his determination in stamping out political divisiveness that had laid the foundations for the monolithic state that Stalin later extended and reinforced. Lenin's voluminous writings—the fifth edition (1958–1965) comprised fifty-five volumes—remained set in stone throughout the Soviet era. They were much discussed, annotated, and quoted, first by Stalin in order to support his own policies (based on his own résumé of Lenin made in *The Foundations of Leninism*) and subsequently throughout the Communist states of the world. An industry in Leninist studies proliferated under the auspices of the noble institutions of the Lenin Institute and the Marx-Engels Institute. And as soon as Lenin's corpse had been preserved for all time and installed in its own mausoleum—but not before his brain had been sectioned into 30,963 slices for detailed scientific study—Moscow became a Mecca for the secular faithful of the new orthodoxy of Leninism.

At Stalin's instigation a reverential cult grew up around Lenin's life and works that treated his every utterance as gospel and projected a Christlike image of the dead leader, perpetuated in such slogans as "Lenin Lived. Lenin Lives. Lenin Will Live." Lenin's image appeared everywhere as a benign figure of inspiration and guidance. He was, for all Soviet citizens, a humane man who genuinely cared about the well-being of the Soviet people.

The Lenin cult created by Stalin was, however, something Lenin himself would have detested. As the English author Arthur Ransome, in Russia at the time of the revolution, had observed of Lenin, "he is the first great leader who discounts the value of personality." Indeed, Lenin had once complained how he hated reading about himself in the papers: "Wherever you look they write about me. I consider this un-Marxist emphasis on an individual extremely harmful. It is bad, entirely inadmissible and unnecessary. And these portraits? Everywhere! What is the purpose of all this?"

There was of course a very good purpose in it all. Stalin's methodical mythologizing of Lenin's life and works was the bedrock on which he constructed his own image, as Lenin's acolyte, or in a religious analogy noted by many historians, as the faithful disciple—St. Peter to Lenin's Christ. The Stalinist school of historiography was for many years busily employed in cosmetically reworking Stalin's early political career, up to the point of Lenin's death, in order to link his every action and political decision with the perceived legitimacy of Leninism. Thus in Stalinist Russia to question the regime would be to deny the legacy of Lenin and, in turn, Stalin's legitimacy as "the best Leninist" and "the most outstanding continuer of Lenin's cause." Even after the collapse of communism in 1991, while

Stalin's legacy continued to unsettle and haunt, Lenin's image remained in the eyes of many untarnished. By the end of the 1990s, however, the vast echoing halls of the Lenin Museum with its 10,000 exhibits was rarely visited, and young Russians born since 1991 respond blankly when asked the significance of his name. But while the statues of many other Communist leaders have been torn down or desecrated, Lenin's remains standing in most Russian cities, pointing imperiously toward the "Socialist Future"—although the popular Soviet joke long prevailed that he was actually pointing to the local jail.

The demystification of Lenin began toward the end of the twentieth century in historiographical terms with the release of previously unseen material from the Soviet archives. It is material that challenges the long-held "myth of a humane Lenin" and testifies to a very different person—a man as hard and ruthlessly determined as Stalin, who was implacable toward enemies of the state and who was opportunistic and calculating in seizing the political moment at any cost. Indeed, his whole being was driven by his intellect and his commitment to theory, so much so that there was no room left for humane concerns, even though he had a genuine sentimental fondness for little children and animals. He was in fact a man eaten up by social hatred; in particular he despised the Russian intelligentsia for their ineffectualness. Having once espoused the cause of revolution, he trained himself with the most exacting self-discipline, which at times reached monastic levels, to eschew all human pleasures. Even music, including his much-loved Beethoven, was rejected, because such emotional pursuits distracted him from his fanatical devotion to the political cause. It was a cause Lenin had espoused in 1887, when his elder brother Alexander (who had been studying zoology at St. Petersburg University) had been hanged for his involvement in a plot to assassinate Tsar Alexander III.

Lenin (his original surname was Ulyanov) was born in Simbirsk, one of six children of an educated, middle-class family, whose father was director of schools in the province. While his background was not luxurious, it was a far cry from Stalin's own poverty-stricken, intellectually narrow, and brutish childhood. As a young man, Lenin had had no particular interest in politics until the execution of his brother and had seemed destined for a brilliant career in law when he went to study at Kazan University. But the year of his brother's execution, Lenin was arrested and expelled for taking a fairly minor part in a demonstration. He spent the next four years in limbo, filling his time with reading and mixing with exiled revolutionaries in Kazan. Having seen from his brother's experience the shortcomings in the theories and methods of the Russian Socialist Revolutionaries, in 1889 Lenin began studying the works of Marx. His sharp, analytical mind was attracted by Marx's "scientific" approach to socialism, and he saw the Marxist path as a more natural process, "embedded in the objective evolution of society." But he also felt that the revolutionary movement needed a push in order to achieve its objectives, leading to the development of one of Lenin's most distinguishing political theories—the idea of a revolutionary elite.

After petitioning the tsar, Lenin was allowed to sit for his law finals in 1891 as an external candidate at St. Petersburg University, graduating first out of 124 with a gold medal. He began practicing law in Samara, but was taken up more and more with his political writings under the pseudonym "Tulin," which Stalin himself first came across and read in 1893. That autumn, Lenin came to St. Petersburg to meet other Marxists, and he became involved in revolutionary activities in St. Petersburg.

There Lenin met his future wife, Nadezhda Krupskaya, a young teacher, in the spring of 1894 when he was working with other socialists for the illegal Union for the Struggle for the Liberation of the Working Class. It was during this brief period that Lenin had his only real experience of the Russian proletariat at first hand. The greater part of his theorizing, writing, and debating on the liberation of the Russian masses and their transformation under socialism would be written in the vacuum of exile, first in Siberia and then in Europe. And while Lenin's theories would be constantly fueled by the heady atmosphere of émigré politics, he would, for many crucial years in Russia's history, be cut off from the reality of the Russian experience. And equally, his followers in Russia would be preparing the Russian proletariat for the acceptance of a revolutionary leader they had never seen, a "veiled oracle," as the historian E. H. Carr has described him.

Arrested in December 1895 for his political activities, Lenin spent fifteen months in prison before being sent to Siberia. Here in 1898 he married Krupskaya, who had also been sent into exile. The relationship was from the outset a marriage of minds and a coming together of revolutionaries dedicated to the same cause. To Lenin, Krupskaya was a comrade; to Krupskaya, Lenin was simply "Ilyich." Krupskaya suffered from numerous physical ailments and was never able to have children, and it is likely that their sexual life may not have lasted for long—they slept in separate beds. Indeed, Lenin was renowned for an extremely puritanical attitude toward sex, insisting that "dissoluteness in sexual life is bourgeois" and a distraction from politics. (Recently released archival material relating to his relationship with French activist Inessa Armand suggests that like all mere mortals, he did in fact feel the need for some kind of emotional and sexual life, although it is unclear exactly how long his physical relationship with Armand lasted.)

Life in exile for the couple, while spartan, was not as arduous as it might sound. They lived in a reasonably comfortable wooden house in Shushenskoye, "quite a

Lenin rousing Soviet troops during the Russian–Polish war of 1920. To his left can be seen Leon Trotsky and behind him Lev Kamenev, both subsequently murdered at Stalin's behest and painted out in later versions of the photograph.

nice village," as Lenin described it in a letter to his mother; "the Shushensk flows past the village and about a mile and a half off there is a broad tributary of the Yenisei where one can swim." Such a location sounds like a veritable paradise compared to the abject misery in which the prisoners of Stalin's Gulags in Siberia were later forced to exist. Lenin and Krupskaya took their mutual pleasures from the intellectual side of life, such as together translating a history of trade unionism written by the British Fabians Beatrice and Sidney Webb, thus fulfilling Lenin's own later dictum that "it is necessary to prepare men who devote to the revolution, not only their free evenings, but their entire lives." Lenin also read, studied, and wrote voraciously, producing his first major work on Russian economics, *The Development of Capitalism in Russia.* It would be typical of his future polemical writings, which while groundbreaking in their interpretation of political and eco-

nomic theory, had a shrill and hectoring tone that was so preoccupied with instilling their message that they never aspired to literary eloquence.

In 1900 Lenin and Krupskaya went into exile in Western Europe, moving between such cities as Munich, Brussels, Paris, London, Cracow, and Geneva and living in penury in cheap lodgings. They were frequently without contact with family and friends in Russia. It was in 1901 that Vladimir Ulyanov finally assumed the alias of Lenin, taking his new name from that of the River Lena in Siberia. It would be one of many pseudonyms he would use during his revolutionary career, including Richter, Fedor, Tulin, and Ilyin. In Munich Lenin met and worked closely with fellow Russian Social Democrats (the RSDWP—an organization of Russian Marxists that had been formed in 1898 in Minsk), in particular his close friend Yuli Martov and the eminent Marxist theorist Georgy

Plekhanov. Together in December 1900 they founded a Marxist journal, *Iskra* (The Spark), which would become the rallying point for the Russian Social Democrats in exile.

Stalin at this time was living undercover in Georgia, running his own illegal newspaper *Brdzola* (The Struggle) and became deeply impressed by Lenin's polemical articles. Under their influence, in December 1901 Stalin published in his own paper his inferior derivative offering, "The Russian Social Democratic Party and Its Immediate Tasks"—laced with his characteristic hyperbole. In this and in other subsequent articles by him, written in similar pro-Leninist vein, he seemed, to those political exiles far removed from the situation, to be taking a lone stand against the Menshevik-dominated Georgian revolutionary movement. This filtered back to Lenin in exile and impressed him. Stalin seemed diligent, eager to please, and a person who could be relied on.

In 1902 Lenin published his seminal work *What Is to Be Done?* in which he addressed the fundamental problem of the application of Marxism to the Russian situation and put forward a new, non-Marxist principle—that of the revolutionary elite. He argued that since there was no urban proletariat to guide the revolution in Russia, and the Russian bourgeoisie was inherently too weak to initiate revolution either, then a "vanguard of the proletariat" should be established by a close inner circle of professional, educated party activists, who would initiate revolution on behalf of the masses. While it seemed a logical and pragmatic attitude, born of a careful assessment of the realities of the particular Russian situation, it betrayed for the first time the inherently cynical and condescending attitude to the proletariat that Lenin would always have. He looked upon them as fundamentally guided by self-interest and their own immediate economic needs and remained contemptuous of their inability to embrace the grander vision of the socialist revolution. In his relations with the proletariat, he always felt the need to "give concrete answers to all questions"—in other words, spell things out for them.

It soon became apparent to several in the RSDWP that Lenin was exerting an excessive influence over party decisions in the *Iskra* group. At the Second Party Congress held in July–August 1903 in Brussels and London, he demonstrated a legendary display of willpower when he harangued the delegates to the point of physical collapse, staying on his feet well into the early hours of the morning. It was a tactic he would use time and again, wearing down his opponent with the sheer force of argument and then tenaciously refusing to budge. As the Marxist theoretician Georgy Plekhanov presciently observed: "Of such stuff are Robespierres made." At the end of the congress Lenin finally won a small majority to lead a new Bolshevik group in opposition to the Mensheviks, who, led by his friend Yuli Martov, continued to resist his political elitism as being undemocratic. The break with Martov was something Lenin always lamented, showing that no matter how profound his political quarrels with others were, unlike Stalin, he never harbored grudges. From now on Lenin would live on his political instincts, constantly revising and adapting his interpretation of Marx as the revolutionary movement in Russia developed. During the 1905 Revolution, he briefly returned in secret to organize the St. Petersburg Soviet of Workers and Peasants, but after the revolution's failure he escaped back to Finland.

In December 1905 at Tammerfors in Finland, Stalin finally met Lenin on his first trip out of Russia as a delegate to a Bolshevik conference. After years of reading and writing about his hero, Stalin was bitterly disappointed. For Lenin turned out to be utterly unprepossessing: "I was expecting to see the mountain eagle of our party, a great man, not politically, but if you will, physically, for

I had formed for myself an image of Lenin as a giant, stately and imposing. What was my disappointment when I saw the most ordinary-looking man, below middle height, distinguished from ordinary mortals by nothing, literally nothing."

Despite his initial disappointment, Stalin spent his time at the conference in awe of Lenin's charisma as a speaker and took mental notes on his strength of will. The next time Stalin saw Lenin again was in 1906 at the Stockholm Unity Congress; the official Stalinist histories would later retrospectively assign him a role here at Lenin's right hand. In reality, the surviving records of the conference do not mention Stalin's name. Nevertheless, Stalin did occasionally make his political mark, for instance, by taking a moderate position against Lenin's radical one of total nationalization of land in Russia and by supporting the alternative of its division between the peasants. This political initiative of Stalin's, despite demonstrating that he had a few ideas of his own, was later left out of the official histories, because to emphasize his disagreement would suggest that he doubted Lenin's superior wisdom. Such an act did not fit the "disciple" image. Later, of course, Stalin would overturn his original moderate view and achieve what Lenin had hardly even begun—the enforced collectivization of the entire Soviet peasantry.

For the ten years of 1907–1917 the Bolsheviks were in the doldrums, as official reaction to the political unrest in Russia of 1905 set in. Undaunted, Lenin continued vigorously studying, writing, and debating endlessly at Bolshevik and RSDWP congresses around Europe, while also trying to keep tabs on subversive activities in Russia. In January 1912 after the Prague conference of Bolsheviks (at which the Menshevik group finally split to form their own separate faction), Lenin co-opted Stalin as a member of the Central Committee. The other delegates had failed to elect Stalin voluntarily and considered Lenin's act a

premature elevation of Stalin to a position of unjustified seniority. But Lenin's choice was a rational one made as a result of his weariness with factional disputes and his desire for committed party workers with no axe of their own to grind. He also seems to have acquired a particular respect for the work of the Baku committee, of which Stalin had been a member. This committee, in Lenin's view, had done much to raise worker consciousness in the Caucasus, as well as expropriate funds for the cause. Lenin had no problem condoning armed robbery undertaken to raise money in Georgia; other means of fund raising, such as the later melting down or selling off of priceless church treasures, were in his eyes also totally justifiable. At last, too, Lenin had found the ideal role for the Georgian Stalin, a member of one of the Russian Empire's many national groups.

At the end of 1912 Lenin summoned Stalin to Cracow, where he commended his journalistic efforts and assigned him to prepare a discussion of the nationalities problem in Russia in order to help garner support for the Bolsheviks from minority groups. Stalin traveled to Vienna in January 1913 to gather material for the article, later published as "Marxism and the National Question." When Stalin was on his way back to Russia, Lenin, well pleased with his diligence, wrote to Maxim Gorky telling him of the "wonderful Georgian" he had working for him on the project—praise, indeed, from a man who set no store by personal accolades.

At the outbreak of the social disturbances in February 1917, Lenin, desperate to get back to Russia to be in the vanguard of revolutionary activities, now contemplated trying to have himself flown in or crossing the frontier disguised as a Swede. Despite protests from many Bolsheviks inside Russia, including Stalin himself, that the time was not yet ripe for revolution, Lenin was impatient and throughout March sent a deluge of cables, telegraph messages, and letters urging that the Bolsheviks take up arms. When the German General Staff, still at war with Russia and anxious to undermine the tsarist regime, offered to provide a special train, Lenin jumped at the chance. He and an entourage of thirty dedicated followers (including Inessa Armand) left Berne, Switzerland. On the journey, the party stopped at Stockholm where Karl Radek, anxious about the leader's public persona, "took Lenin to a shop and bought him a new pair of shoes, insisting that he was now a public man and must give some thought to the decency of his appearance."

On the night of 3 April (Easter Monday) Lenin arrived at the Finland Station in Petrograd and was taken to the tsar's restroom before being whisked off by armored car to the opulent Kseshinskaya Mansion (former home of the famous ballerina and ex-mistress of the tsar), where those assembled heard for the first time his "thin squeaky voice" call for the seizure of power. On 4 April Lenin outlined his blueprint for immediate, revolutionary action, known as the "April Theses," which were published in *Pravda* on 7 April as "The Tasks of the Proletariat in the Present Revolution." Throughout the summer he relentlessly hammered his argument home at rallies and conferences, but the time was still not ripe, despite his insistence, and in July Lenin was forced back into hiding in Finland. He remained there until September, working on his latest book, *State and Revolution,* but on 10 October he once again returned to Russia in disguise to again call for armed insurrection. The Bolshevik Central Committee (which included Stalin) finally agreed by a majority vote, and on the night of 24–25 October Lenin moved into revolutionary headquarters at the Smolny Institute, the following day declaring the fall of the Provisional Government. The new Bolshevik regime, administered by a Council of People's Commissars under Lenin's chairmanship, immediately introduced a series of decrees, based on their slogan of "Peace, Bread and Land."

The transition to the new socialist state was by no means a smooth one, and the year 1918 saw a hardening in Lenin's attitude as he instituted an increasingly ruthless regime in his efforts to hold together a country suffering the dislocations of hunger and civil war. Lenin was now becoming more and more dependent on methods of intimidation and terror carried out by the Cheka, the secret police, which had been set up in December 1917 to deal with counterrevolutionaries. During the first two years of its existence, a period known as the "Red Terror," the Cheka would execute 9,677 people. Terror had originally been initiated as official retaliation for an attempt on Lenin's life made on 30 August by anarchist Fanya Kaplan. The shots she fired at Lenin were not fatal, but two of the bullets remained lodged in his body. His health never really recovered, and an ill-advised operation to remove one of the bullets in his neck weakened and aged him.

In March of 1921, after a disastrous famine and increasing unrest in the countryside, Lenin was forced to bring Russia back from the brink of total collapse with the introduction of a modified form of state capitalism—the New Economic Policy, which allowed the peasantry a degree of private enterprise. Throughout this turbulent period, he had grown to rely heavily on the good offices of Stalin. In April 1922, Lenin did the one thing Stalin had been working quietly and patiently toward but which for Lenin would be a great error of judgment—he appointed Stalin General Secretary of the Communist Party. Many in the leadership voiced their serious concern at Stalin's being given yet another senior post; he was already a member of the Politburo and the Workers' and Peasants' Inspectorate (Rabkrin), which monitored the Soviet civil service. Stalin had been appointed to this latter post during the civil war, at a time when a beleaguered Lenin deemed it essential to have people he

Stalin and Lenin in 1922, the year Lenin elevated him to general secretary of the Communist Party.

There seemed to be no obvious candidate. All his colleagues had their own, different imperfections and limitations. Leon Trotsky, for example, was too arrogant and intolerant of others, his policies too divisive. And Trotsky's and Stalin's mutual antipathy was potentially disastrous and could have a dangerously destabilizing influence on the Communist Party. The other main rivals for the leadership—Lev Kamenev and Grigory Zinoviev—had both strongly opposed the Bolshevik coup of 1917, and their loyalty could not be relied on. Nikolay Bukharin was a brilliant theoretician but lacked political muscle. Stalin, however, although virtually unknown to the public at large and neither an orator like Trotsky nor a skillful theoretician like Lenin himself, had demonstrated a talent in one of the most fundamental areas of efficient government, particularly in a country as vast as the Soviet Union. It was a talent that others in the Bolshevik leadership had grossly undervalued—the gift of an able bureaucrat and administrator.

Lenin now realized that he had placed too much emphasis on these skills. He had undoubtedly allowed himself to be beguiled by Stalin's efficiency and lulled into a false sense of security by them. He had also come to depend too much on Stalin's always discreet advice and support over major issues of policy. Lenin had also failed to take into account the unattractive side to Stalin's character—his physical coarseness and abrasive manner toward his colleagues. It was clear to Lenin that Stalin's moral shortcomings made him unsuitable for a top Party position such as that of general secretary. Having promoted Stalin's career through the Party bureaucracy, Lenin was now faced with the worrying consequences of that political ascendancy. Despite his final secret "Testament's" importance in revealing something of Lenin's growing apprehensions about Stalin in the last months of his life, it fell short, however, of being a categorical warning that Stalin would turn

could trust in positions of authority. He had insisted that Stalin was the only man of sufficient rigor and authority capable of coping with such a demanding role. Unfortunately, Lenin soon realized that the Inspectorate was rapidly mutating into a Bolshevik form of the old and corrupt tsarist administrative system and that "we are being sucked into a foul, bureaucratic swamp." He also now began to harbor concerns about Stalin's policies toward the nationalities, in particular, his very personal obsession with a vendetta against his own rebellious homeland of Georgia.

But before Lenin could take any practical steps to strip Stalin of his political power, he suffered a stroke on 25 May 1922. His health improved in June, and he was back at his desk in October, only to be felled by a second stroke in November. Between 23 December 1922 and 4 January 1923, realizing that he would now never recover, Lenin became deeply depressed about the failure of the revolution to live up to his expectations. There was also the problem of who would take over from him.

Lenin's draped coffin at his funeral service held on a bitterly cold 27 January 1924 in Red Square. A temporary wooden mausoleum, designed by Alexander Shchusev, was erected soon after to house his embalmed corpse.

into some kind of monster. And whether, by 1923, having finally recognized the magnitude of his own misjudgment Lenin would have been able to remove Stalin from office easily is by no means certain.

On 21 January 1924 Lenin died after a final, massive stroke. One of the many unanswered questions about him is whether, had he lived longer, Lenin would have allowed the degeneration of the Soviet state into a regime as dehumanizing and repressive as Stalin's. As some now argue, had not that process already been initiated under Lenin, and was not Stalin the true son of the father? It is easy retrospectively to apply qualities of democracy and humanitarianism to Lenin in order to counter the abuses of civil and human rights that followed under his successor. But in their absolute dedication to the cause of revolution and the fulfillment of a social vision, Lenin and Stalin were both equally ruthless. Evidence of the darker

side to Lenin's policies of coercion during the Red Terror continues to trickle from the archives, including a much-quoted order he issued in August 1918—to hang hundreds of kulaks who had been hoarding grain "without fail, so the people will see." Such an obsession with imposing his extraordinary, implacable will had first been noted on the occasion of Lenin's fiftieth birthday in 1920 by writer Maxim Gorky, who presciently observed that there was "something frightening about the sight of this great man, who pulls the levers of history on our planet as he wishes."

See also Bukharin, Nikolay; General Secretary of the Communist Party; Kamenev, Lev; Lenin Mausoleum; Russian Revolution of 1917; Trotsky, Leon; Zinoviev, Grigory

Further reading: Orlando Figes. *A People's Tragedy: The Russian Revolution 1891–1924.* London: Jonathan Cape, 1996; Nadezhda Krupskaya. *Memories of Lenin.* London: Panther, 1970; Moshe Lewin. *Lenin's Last Struggle.* London: Faber and Faber, 1969; Richard Pipes, ed. *The Unknown Lenin*. New Haven, CT: Yale University Press, 1996; Robert Service. *Lenin: A Political Life,* 3 vols. Basingstoke, UK: Macmillan, 1985–1995; Dmitri Volkogonov. *Lenin: Life and Legacy.* London: HarperCollins, 1994; Edmund Wilson. *To the Finland Station.* London: Fontana, 1967; Bertram D. Wolfe. *Three Who Made a Revolution.* Harmondsworth, UK: Penguin, 1966.

Lenin Mausoleum

This showcase for the embalmed corpse of Lenin was built alongside the Kremlin Wall between the ancient Spassky and Nikolsky Towers. There had been a tradition for burying victims of revolutionary clashes in communal graves here since the first days of the October Revolution in 1917. Under Stalin, the location became a secular place of pilgrimage—a pilgrimage that was to become a duty for all loyal Communists.

When Lenin died on 21 January 1924, his widow Nadezhda Krupskaya had wished him to be interred in the Kremlin Wall alongside other Bolshevik luminaries, or even alongside his former lover, Inessa Armand, but she was overruled by Stalin. During the days of mass public grieving, when Lenin was lying in state in the Hall of Columns (the former Nobles Club in Moscow), half a million people had lined up for hours in subzero temperatures to file past his body. Witnessing the palpable grief, Stalin realized that this emotive power could be exploited to perpetually endorse the infallibility of Lenin and the legitimacy of his heir—Stalin. Stalin decided that Lenin's corpse must be immortalized by keeping the deceased leader on permanent display as a venerated relic, as the focal point of a new "religion," Leninism—a realization born in part, no doubt, of Stalin's early training as a priest.

After Lenin's official funeral, his body remained in Red Square, encased inside a temporary wooden structure. For a while the cold winter weather maintained the body in a frozen state, but in spring the corpse would begin to decompose, and with many thousands still filing into Red Square to pay their last respects, it was decided to enlist the aid of science. Defying those who said it could not be done on a long-term basis, Lenin's body was embalmed by chemist Vladimir Vorobev, who was made an honorary professor for his efforts. He was later assisted by biochemist Boris Zbarsky in keeping the body in optimum condition by reembalming it every eighteen months. For the benefit of posterity, Lenin's brain was removed, pickled, and sectioned into slices for scientific analysis. By 1939 the preservation of this illustrious corpse had spawned a whole "Preservation Institute" of its own with a team of experts, including thirteen doctors, employed to make regular checks on the body and retouch it whenever necessary. Zbarsky later recalled his thirty-year custodianship of Lenin's corpse: "I was connected with the Mausoleum by phone twenty-four hours a day. I instructed my collaborators to call me even if a fly settled on him, and strictly forbade any attempt to move it in my absence."

The original Lenin Mausoleum was a temporary structure, designed by the Constructivist architect Aleksey Shchusev, which was hastily put together in oak and painted red. The design for the mausoleum and the idea of having Lenin embalmed were inspired in part by the recent discovery in Egypt of the tomb of Tutankhamen. The original building was later replaced in 1929 with another design by Shchusev—the present more grandiose red granite edifice, which took four years to build. It was completed by November 1934 to become the focal point of the newly restructured Red Square. From the balcony of the Lenin Mausoleum, Stalin and other Communist leaders could view the meticulously staged parades on May Day, the anniversary of the revolution and other official occasions. After the German invasion of the Soviet Union in 1941, Lenin's mummified body was carefully packed up and sent off to the safety of Tyumen in western Siberia.

After his death, Stalin was embalmed and displayed alongside Lenin. But even after Khrushchev's secret speech at the Twenty-second Party Congress in 1956 initiated the dismantling of the cult of Stalin, his body was not immediately removed from the Lenin Mausoleum. It was not until after dark on 31 October 1961 that Stalin's embalmed corpse was put into a coffin and buried by the Kremlin Wall. The desirability of continuing to display Lenin's corpse in a post-Communist era that has seen the destruction of most of the other statuary and icons of Communist rule is now the subject of some debate in Russia. Many would like to see Lenin's corpse quietly removed and buried alongside his mother in the Volkovo Cemetery in St. Petersburg.

See also Cult of the Personality; Krupskaya, Nadezhda; Lenin, Vladimir Ilyich; Science

Further reading: Nina Tumarkin. *Lenin Lives! The Lenin Cult in Soviet Russia.* Cambridge, MA: Harvard University Press, 1983; Dimitri Volkogonov. *Lenin: Life and Legacy.* London: HarperCollins, 1994; Ilya Zbarsky and Samuel Hutchinson. *Lenin's Embalmers.* London: Harvill Press, 1998.

Leningrad, Siege of

The 900-day siege (8 September 1941–27 January 1944) of the Soviet Union's great northern city and former capital was the scene of immense suffering, courage, and endurance, an experience that earned the city collectively the highest Soviet accolade, the Order of Lenin, awarded by Stalin on 26 January 1945.

It took Hitler's Wehrmacht only two months to sweep across Russia to the outskirts of Leningrad in the early days of the German invasion of 1941 known as "Operation Barbarossa." Aided by Finnish troops from the north, who cut off routes through Karelia, the Germans encircled the city, despite a heroic effort by the population of Leningrad, including women, children, and the elderly, to stem their advance by joining the Red Army in building antitank fortifications around the city.

German plans for the city were ruthless. A secret directive of 22 September 1941 made clear that "[t]he Führer has decided to wipe the city of Petersburg [*sic*] from the face of the earth." For the next sixteen months they made every effort to do just that by starving the population into submission and subjecting them to a constant bombardment by heavy artillery. So heavy was the shelling that signs went up all over Leningrad—"Citizens: In case of shelling this side of the street is the most dangerous." Those signs can still be seen today. But the threat to Leningrad had initiated an immediate and inflammatory propaganda drive within the city, masterminded by Leningrad Communist Party leader Andrey Zhdanov, which galvanized the inhabitants into a fierce determination to save "the city that first made revolution."

Opinions still differ as to how many of Leningrad's population of 3 million died in the siege, but the figure certainly approaches 900,000. Most of the victims died of starvation, as rations were pared back time and time again, eventually to a meager 125 grams (a slice and a half) of bread a day for civilians (workers got 250 grams and soldiers in the front line 500). When flour became short the bread was adulterated with sawdust and wood cellulose. Eventually the city ate all its birds, both pets and those that could be caught in the street, its horses, cats, dogs, and even its rats and mice. When these ran out, people ate tooth powder and medicines and bookbinder's glue. They also tried boiling up leather boots and belts and scraping the flour paste from the back of wallpaper. Some even resorted to cannibalism. The signs of butchering of corpses left on the streets and in the cemeteries were clear to see. After the war, 300 people were arrested and executed for acts of cannibalism during the siege. With the failure of the water pumping and sewerage systems, many people died in epidemics of typhoid and other diseases, often as a result of drinking water drawn straight from the River Neva. Those who didn't succumb to hunger were often finished off by the freezing winter temperatures, which plummeted as low as minus 40 degrees centigrade. The city could do little to resist this after its electricity and heating systems ran out of coal and could no longer function.

The dead were quickly denied any of the dignity of a proper funeral. Their corpses were often left on the streets in frozen mounds during the bitter winter. Their relatives were too sick and weak to drag them to the cemetery for burial. And burial, when it did finally happen, was in mass common graves. When someone dropped dead on the street from hunger, others passed by, leaving the corpse where it fell. Some were murdered for their ration cards. People would hold off reporting deaths for as long as possible, in order to continue collecting the deceased's meager bread ration. Whole families died within days of each other and parts of the city became a ghost town. And through all this, for the most part the Soviet population at large were kept in the dark about the terrible suffering in Leningrad in order to avoid further lowering Soviet morale.

In the early days of the siege of Leningrad, Stalin had been prepared to quite ruthlessly sacrifice this beautiful city in order to save the capital, Moscow, which was also threatened with capture. He did not wish to further accentuate Leningrad's reputation by advertising its heroic resistance. He had never liked the city and had always been jealous of its independent spirit as a potential rival power base to Moscow. While he continued to nurse his own secret agenda for dealing with the growing power of its Party elite (unleashed in the purge of the Communist Party there known as the Leningrad Affair of 1949–1950), the city's agony and sacrifice provided an opportu-

nity for a major propaganda exercise to impress his British and American allies.

One of the great artistic works born of Leningrad's struggle, which came forever after to symbolize the heroism of Soviet resistance to the Nazi invasion, was Shostakovich's extraordinary Seventh Symphony, composed in the besieged city and broadcast across the nation by radio on 5 March 1942. Five months later, the symphony was performed in the city itself by an orchestra of dedicated but half-starved musicians, in a high-profile act of defiance, on the occasion of which the Soviet artillery was deliberately deployed to draw away the German fire. In another famous manifestation of the selfless dedication of Leningraders, the staff of the Hermitage Museum had worked day and night for the first sixty days after the German invasion in 1941, packing over 1 million art treasures and paintings for safe evacuation to Sverdlovsk, thus preventing the expropriation and destruction of the cream of one of the world's greatest art collections.

It was probably the ice road across Lake Ladoga that saved Leningrad from total annihilation, for during the winters of 1942 and 1943 this road enabled some supplies to get through by sleighs (and even trucks, when the ice became thick enough). It also facilitated the evacuation of 550,000 of the sick and elderly, as well as many children.

Soviet counterattacks against the Germans in early 1943 began to ease the situation in Leningrad, but it was not until January 1944, after a strategic railroad junction was recaptured, that the Red Army eventually managed to break through the German lines and liberate the city. Much of it was now a battered ruin, populated by fewer than 600,000 emaciated and exhausted people. Yet their spirit remained undimmed. As one seventeen-year-old expressed it, "All of us Leningraders are one family, baptised by the monstrous blockade—one family, one in our grief, one in our experience, one in our hopes and expectations." Such courage more than merited the title given to Leningrad in

1965, when it was made a "Hero City of the Soviet Union." Yet Stalin had never bothered to visit Leningrad, not once in its hour of need, nor in its hour of glory after the siege was over. In fact, he never went there again after the murder of Sergey Kirov, the Leningrad Party boss, in 1934.

See also Great Patriotic War; Red Army; Shostakovich, Dmitry

Further reading: Geraldine Norman. *The Hermitage: The Biography of a Great Museum,* chapter 13. London: Cape, 1997; Harrison E. Salisbury. *The Siege of Leningrad.* London: Secker and Warburg, 1969; Solomon Volkov. *St. Petersburg.* London: Sinclair Stevenson, 1996.

"Life Has Become Better, Life Has Become Merrier"

At a conference of 300 Stakhanovite workers held on 17 November 1935 at the Kremlin, Stalin elaborated on the many advances in the Soviet economy as a result of the Five-Year Plans, all of which were now combining to make the life of the average Soviet citizen a much happier one. The famous phrase in which he assured his audience that "life has become better, comrades, life has become merrier" was a message to the peasantry and the workforce at large that an end had finally come to food shortages, rationing, and queues.

This propagandist slogan was uttered by Stalin at a time when the Soviet professional classes were enduring the first phase of the political purges that followed the murder of Sergey Kirov in December 1934. At that time, the peasantry and industrial workforce were, in the main, unaffected if not unmoved by the purges of Party bureaucrats and were more concerned to hear that at long last the country was enjoying the fruits of the years of their personal and material sacrifices. They had grown restless at the continuing low standard of living and the absence of consumer goods in the shops and were now enjoying the respite of an

end to rationing and what would later be called the "three good years" of 1934–1936, between the end of one rigorous Five-Year Plan and the onslaught of the next.

The Soviet propaganda machine, which regularly scoured Stalin's public and published utterances for words of wisdom to impart to the masses, was quick to promote this catchphrase as a popular morale-raising slogan. It was soon seen everywhere—on factory walls, in schools and institutes, and in newspapers. It was even set to music as a popular song. The words were, of course, hollow, and the slogan was but one more manifestation of extreme bureaucratic cynicism in the face of continuing widespread hardship. For in material terms, the period of 1936–1937 proved to be neither better nor merrier. In fact economic conditions declined once again with a drop in wages, numerous price increases, and a shortage of essential commodities such as shoes. All of this prompted workers to complain bitterly that they now had less to eat than during the economic crisis of 1932–1933. Far from being merrier, life in Stalin's Russia had now become a whole lot worse.

See also Five-Year Plans; The Great Terror; Stakhanovites

Linguistics
See Marr, Nikolay.

Lubyanka
See Prisons.

Lysenko, Trofim Denisovich (1898–1976)

The founder of the Soviet "science" of agrobiology, Trofim Lysenko single-handedly obliterated the study of genetics within the Soviet Union for the best part of twenty-five years, replacing it with his own phony scientific theories on the inheritance of acquired characteristics in the plant world. Much of Lysenko's bogus research was only exposed after his scientific dictatorship had done a great deal of long-term damage to Soviet agriculture.

Born in Ukraine of peasant stock, Lysenko studied at the Poltava Horticultural School and the Kiev Agricultural Institute. He eventually became director of the All-Union Selection and Genetics Institute of Odessa. Having rejected the chromosome-based theory of the genetics of Gregor Mendel as "bourgeois pseudo-science," he espoused the spurious thinking on the hybridization of plants devised by the Russian plant breeder Ivan Michurin, adding to it his own environmentally based thesis that plants could inherit and genetically transmit characteristics developed as a result of climatic conditions. Lysenko further asserted that his method of "vernalizing" grain seed by moistening and then chilling it before planting would produce far better crop yields. With the intensification of agricultural methods introduced under the Five-Year Plans such spectacular promises were just what Stalin wanted to hear. Seduced by Lysenko's ideas on plant breeding and seemingly convinced that they would wave a magic wand over Soviet agriculture, Stalin gave him his full backing, despite the absence of detailed scientific substantiation of these claims. After all, in Stalinist thinking, why should not the natural world also be harnessed to the building of the new socialist society?

Lysenko's election to the Lenin Academy of Agricultural Sciences in 1938 and his appointment in 1940 as director of the academy's Institute of Genetics opened the way for him to build his own scientific empire, to the extent that many scientific voices raised in protest at his methodology, including the eminent geneticist Nikolay Vavilov, were quickly silenced. Now entrenched as the official voice of Soviet biology, Lysenko's ideas became even more fanciful as he proceeded to categorize scientific disciplines into those he condemned as "bourgeois" and those he deemed "socialist."

By 1948, Stalin was so convinced of the infallibility of Lysenko's theories that he personally ordered the Central Committee of the Communist Party to issue a decree condemning genetics and reinforcing Lysenkoism. The campaign against scientific dissidents was cranked up even more—twelve members of the Academy of Agricultural Sciences alone were expelled, many laboratories closed down, and 3,000 biologists thrown out of their jobs. The apogee of Stalin and Lysenko's grandiose attempts at playing God was reached with the 1948 adoption of the Stalin Plan for the Transformation of Nature, Lysenko's ambitious plan for planting vast belts of trees across the Soviet Union to moderate extremes of climate and minimize soil erosion.

The rehabilitation of orthodox genetics in the Soviet Union was a long time coming after Stalin's death. It was not until Nikita Khrushchev's fall from power in 1965 that Lysenko was finally discredited and the study of orthodox genetics was reintroduced.

See also Five-Year Plans; Science; Vavilov, Nikolay

Further reading: David Joravsky. *The Lysenko Affair.* Cambridge, MA: Harvard University Press, 1970; Zhores Medvedev. *The Rise and Fall of Trofim Lysenko.* New York: Columbia University Press, 1991.

Magnitogorsk

The industrial town of Magnitogorsk, 850 miles east of Moscow, mushroomed in the wastelands of the Urals between 1929 and 1931 and marked the apogee of Stalin's rapid industrialization of the Soviet Union under the First Five-Year Plan. Its name means "magnetic mountain," an appropriate epithet for a town built around the mining industry of the Urals, in particular the local magnetite iron. The contract to supervise the construction of Magnitogorsk had gone to an American company from Cleveland, Ohio—the ambition was to construct an industrial complex to rival that of the steelworks at Gary, Indiana.

For those fired with the messianic zeal to construct this and other new industrial complexes in the Soviet Union, working conditions were harsh and living conditions often primitive. But such was the energy with which the First Five-Year Plan was embraced that the thousands of ordinary working people who traveled to Magnitogorsk to construct the blast furnaces and ironworks made enormous sacrifices in order to build the new utopia. In the words of American volunteer John Scott, "tens of thousands of people were enduring the most intense hardships to build blast furnaces. . . . I would wager that Russia's battle of ferrous metallurgy alone involved more casualties than the battle of the Marne." Indeed, accidents were frequent, particularly falls from unsafe scaffolding; many of the workers were untrained and unfit for their strenuous tasks. As Scott observed, "At thirty-five below without any breakfast in you, you didn't pay as much attention as you should."

Not all of those working on the construction of Magnitogorsk, who numbered women and children in their ranks, were there voluntarily. Some of the workers were forced laborers, others criminals from corrective labor camps. There was even a gang of priests and bishops—political prisoners—forced to labor in their long, cumbersome priests' robes. By far the greatest number of workers were some 20,000 kulaks, forcibly rounded up and exiled from their homes as part of the collectivization program.

The workers lived in the most rudimentary shelters—in tents and self-made mud huts (for example, the Bashkirs and Tatars from Central Asia). The lucky workers, who lived indoors in spartan barracks, often had to sleep in shifts on the same bunk, all of them existing on rationed bread and cereals. The wages were good enough, but most of the time there was nothing in Magnitogorsk to buy, not even the most basic foodstuffs of meat, butter, and sugar. Everyone but the privileged managerial elite, who inhabited their own separate enclave, known as "American city," went hungry. And for those who worked themselves to the point of physical exhaustion and still failed to meet their required targets, or those whose machinery failed them through lack of adequate maintenance, there was the further ignominy of being accused of deliberate sabotage and being labeled "wreckers."

No amount of sacrifice was enough: "Men froze, hungered and suffered, but the construction work went on with a disregard for individuals and a mass heroism seldom paralleled in history." Within a few years, Magnitogorsk had a population of a quarter of a million. By 1930 the capacity of its steelworks had quadrupled, from 650,000 to 2,500,000 tons. By 1975 Magnitogorsk had become one of the world's largest iron and steel complexes. And by the end of the twentieth century, along with many of the other industrial monoliths created under Stalin, it had become one of the most heavily polluted cities in Russia.

See also Collectivization; Five-Year Plans; Gulag; Kataev, Valentin; Women

Further reading: Valentin Kataev. *Time Forward.* New York: Farrar and Rinehart, 1932 (for a classic work of socialist-realist literature that captures the enthusiasm of the construction of a huge industrial plant at Magnitogorsk); Brian Moynahan. *The Russian Century.* London: Chatto and Windus, 1994; John Scott. *Behind the Urals: An American Worker in Russia's City of Steel.* Bloomington: Indiana University Press, 1973 (a vivid contemporary account by a non-Russian). See also the photographs at Syracuse University, Syracuse, N.Y., of U.S. photographer Margaret Bourke-White, who went there on a special assignment, 1930–1931.

Malenkov, Georgy Maksimilianovich (1901–1979)

The Soviet elder statesman who became Stalin's heir apparent in the late 1940s was one of the youngest members of the Politburo. For the most part Georgy

Malenkov submissively did his job, so much so that historian Roy Medvedev described him as "a man without a biography" whose life was so tied to bureaucratic duty that he "had no image of his own, not even his own style." Malenkov fell from grace under Nikita Khrushchev, who looked upon him as "a typical office clerk and paper-pusher," to end his career in obscurity. The occasion of his death was ignored in the Soviet press.

Malenkov had an oddly clownish moon-face that made him the butt of cruel remarks by his colleagues. Andrey Zhdanov referred to him derisively by the peasant name "Malanya"; another colleague, equally spitefully, described him as a "fat, flabby, cruel toad." Malenkov was, however, probably more educated and intelligent than either of them. As a qualified engineer, he had directed an advanced technical school before becoming an astute politician. During his career, as one of the more intellectually minded and unpretentious members of the Politburo, Malenkov made it clear that ideology and dogma were not his concern. He lived modestly and concerned himself only with acting his part as a loyal "servant of the State," as he said in 1941.

As a young man, Malenkov gave up his university studies to fight with the Red Army in Turkestan during the civil war. He joined the Communist Party at the end of the war, in 1920, and having resumed his education, graduated as an engineer in 1925. His rise through the *nomenklatura* as a Party official followed the conventional pattern, beginning with his recruitment in 1925 to work on the Party's Central Committee, where he soon became a protégé of Stalin's on the Secretariat (1925–1930). Malenkov's proven organizational and administrative skills led to a succession of posts in Party administration, as a result of which during the 1930s he was deeply involved in the "criminal violations of socialist legality" of which he was later accused by Khrushchev in 1958. This charge related to his appointment in July 1935 as deputy under Nikolay Ezhov of the Central Committee's Department of Cadres and Assignments, in which capacity Malenkov supervised regional purges of the Communist Party in Kazan, Belorussia, and Armenia in 1937. In 1939 Malenkov became a member of the Central Committee and in 1941 a candidate member of the Politburo. During the Great Patriotic War he served on the five-man State Defense Committee in charge of armaments and technical supplies and organized the crucial relocation of Soviet industry beyond the Urals.

During the war years, Malenkov had often acted as Stalin's spokesman, and in 1946 he was made deputy prime minister and put in charge of the Committee for the Rehabilitation of the Economy of Liberated Areas. This "rehabilitation" was in fact a euphemism for the wholesale plundering of the industry of occupied East Germany by the Soviets, who proceeded to dismantle entire factories and industrial plants and transport them piece by piece back to the Soviet Union.

In the postwar period, a bitter rivalry developed between Malenkov, as Stalin's right-hand man, and Stalin's rising protégé Andrey Zhdanov, whose prime interest as Stalin's spokesman on culture and issues of ideology was a crackdown on the few civil freedoms that had been salvaged during the war years. Initially, Malenkov and Zhdanov clashed over economic policy; in particular Zhdanov thought German industry should be left intact so that the country could better pay its war reparations. It has also been suggested that Zhdanov's crackdown on the writer Anna Akhmatova was partly a result of his intense rivalry with Malenkov, who had sanctioned the publication of Akhmatova's verses after a long silence. The resulting rivalry between the two men culminated in Zhdanov's gaining the ascendant and Malenkov's being dropped from the Secretariat and sidelined for a year in a job in Central Asia, until secret police chief Lavrenty Beria talked Stalin into reinstating him.

After his promotion to full membership of the Politburo in 1946, Malenkov had begun to develop a close relationship with Beria. Stalin's daughter, Svetlana Allilueva, noted that they became something of a double act during Stalin's final years and were often seen "walking arm in arm . . . as a couple." On his reentry into Stalin's inner sanctum in 1948, with Zhdanov now dead and Vyacheslav Molotov's career in decline, Malenkov began to be looked upon as Stalin's successor. This was resented by others in the Politburo who considered him an upstart with no regional Party base to merit such a position. Malenkov's supremacy was later endorsed when, at the 1952 Party Congress, he was delegated by an ailing Stalin to read the five-hour keynote address—the Political Report of the Central Committee.

When Stalin's fatal collapse came in 1953, Malenkov and Beria were the first members of the Politburo on the scene. Their dilatoriness in calling for immediate medical help no doubt hastened Stalin's inevitable demise. Like Beria, Malenkov manifested no outward public grief at the death of Stalin and seemed eager to take over the leadership. His relationship with Beria had deepened (they were both later closely implicated in the 1952 purge of the Leningrad Communist Party, and Malenkov seemed happy to be steered into political position as de facto prime minister and general secretary of the Communist Party by his wilier and more ambitious associate. However, Malenkov's lack of a track record in Party leadership continued to underline his unsuitability for the role, and he was soon pressured into relinquishing the Party leadership.

In 1955 Malenkov was forced to resign as prime minister after a battle with Khrushchev over industrialization and agricultural policy. Malenkov had belittled Khrushchev's pet agricultural policies and had argued for a reduction in arms production for a greater concentration on light industry and consumer goods. He was now relegated to the Ministry of Electric Power

Stations, and in 1957, after being accused with Molotov and Lazar Kaganovich of setting up an anti-Party group to plot Khrushchev's overthrow, he was finally dismissed from all his government posts. There then followed the usual penalty meted out to Soviet bureaucrats who fell from grace in the post-Stalin years—consignment to political oblivion. Malenkov was sent to the Ust-Kamenogorsk hydroelectric plant in Kazakhstan, and in 1961 he suffered the final ignominy of expulsion from the Communist Party.

See also Beria, Lavrenty; The Great Terror; Molotov, Vyacheslav; Politburo; Stalin; Private Life of; Voznesensky, Nikolay; Zhdanov, Andrey
Further reading: Roy Medvedev. *All Stalin's Men*. Oxford: Oxford University Press, 1983; Dmitri Volkogonov. *The Rise and Fall of the Soviet Empire*. London: HarperCollins, 1998.

Manchuria

The Russians had long had their sights set on gaining influence over Manchuria, a frontier area between the southeastern corner of the tsarist empire and northeastern China. They had fought the Japanese over each country's imperialist territorial claims on Manchuria in a disastrous war (1904–1905), which left the defeated Russians being forced to cede all their interests in southern Manchuria, including the strategically important naval base of Port Arthur, to the Japanese.

In 1932 the Japanese turned Manchuria into the puppet state of Manchukuo and built it into a powerful industrial and military base. When the Japanese later formed an alliance with Germany, Stalin sought rapprochement with the Chinese Kuomintang (nationalist Chinese forces of Chiang Kai-shek) and sent his troops to fight Manchukuo forces in 1939. For years the Soviets remained nervous about this far-eastern front. Stalin's move, when it came in 1939, was as much aimed at settling old scores as preempting the opening of a second far-eastern war against Japan.

At the Yalta Conference, held after the fall of Berlin in the summer of 1945, Stalin finally seized his moment, using Manchuria as a bargaining counter to underwrite the Soviet commitment to entering the war in the Pacific against Japan. On the promise by the Allies that all former Russian rights in Manchuria would be restored, in August 1945 Stalin ordered the Soviet invasion of Manchuria. Despite the difficulties of invading across a 5,000-kilometer (3,100-mile) frontier and advancing over difficult desert and mountainous terrain, the Soviet army quickly defeated the Japanese army and brought the territory under its control.

Having concluded a treaty with the Nationalist government of Chiang Kai-Shek, the Soviets proceeded to systematically plunder the country's food stockpiles, its industrial machinery, and its gold reserves, as well as taking control of the Chinese Eastern Railroad. By this time the United States had secured the Japanese surrender in World War II with the dropping of atomic bombs on Hiroshima and Nagasaki, thus preempting any further expansionist claims by Stalin on Japanese territory.

Soviet forces were withdrawn from Manchuria in 1946, leaving the Kuomintang to fight it out with the Chinese Communists led by Mao Zedong, as the Chinese sought to establish their hegemony in the region. It was not until the defeat of the Nationalist forces in 1949 that Stalin finally recognized the Communist Chinese regime of Mao Zedong and relinquished Port Arthur and the Manchurian railroad to China.

See also Blyukher, Marshal Vasily; China; Korean War
Further reading: Harold Shukman, ed. *Stalin's Generals*. London: Phoenix, 1997.

Mandelstam, Osip Emilievich (1891–1938)

Osip Mandelstam, a man of fragile constitution but of ferocious moral scruples and dedication to his art, shared with his friend the poet Anna Akhmatova an inability to remain silent in the face of Stalinist oppression. He courted inevitable disaster by writing a derogatory poem about Stalin in 1933; although it was not published, it circulated rapidly by word of mouth. His eventual death in the Gulag proved the truth of his own remark that writers were, for Stalin, a particular and unsettling threat: "Poetry is respected only in this country—people are killed for it."

Mandelstam came from a cultured Jewish family. He grew up in St. Petersburg, where in the 1900s he became closely involved with the leading school of Russian poetry, the Acmeists, and published his first collection of poetry, *Apollon,* in 1910. Forced to support himself with bread-and-butter work as a translator and journalist, he nevertheless managed to publish poetry, such as *Tristiya* (1922), as well as prose and literary criticism. By the late 1920s, however, his uncompromising attitude to the government and his highly literary, arcane poetry had attracted official disapproval, and his account of his years working in the provinces as a journalist in *Journey to Armenia* (1933, translated 1973) resulted in his being banned from publishing. By now appalled at Stalin's savage treatment of the peasants under collectivization, which he had witnessed in Ukraine and the Kuban, Mandelstam was no longer able to remain silent on Stalin's abuse of power. In the winter of 1933–1934 he wrote a poem in which he expressed what many people felt but dared not express in public, describing Stalin, surrounded by sycophants, as "the Kremlin's mountaineer" who forged laws "to be flung / Like horseshoes at the head, the eye, or the groin."

Mandelstam's friends were horrified when he read the poem to them, and they begged him to destroy it. The poet Boris Pasternak (himself a lapsed Jew and mindful of Stalin's anti-Semitism) was incredulous, asking how Mandelstam could write such a poem "when he's a *Jew?*" Inevitably word filtered back to Stalin. His head of secret police, Genrikh Yagoda, took particular delight in it and learned it by heart. In May 1934 Mandelstam was arrested and later that month was sentenced to three years in exile. Stalin, it appeared, had decided that it would be a bad political move to have such a respected poet shot in what would be perceived as an act of petulant retaliation for a mere poem. Instead, Mandelstam was exiled to Voronezh with his wife. Here he wrote three major collections of poetry, *Voronezh Notebooks,* but privately he was convinced that he was doomed. The second of the *Notebooks* includes an "Ode to Stalin," written in an attempt perhaps not so much to save himself as to protect his wife, Nadezhda. Returning to Moscow in 1937, the Mandelstams struggled to survive with the help of friends such as Anna Akhmatova, but in May 1938 Osip was again arrested for anti-Soviet activities and sent to a labor camp in Kolyma for five years. Already in poor mental and physical health, he did not last long in the environment of one of the harshest camps of the Gulag. He died on 27 December 1938, only a couple of months after arriving there.

During the political thaw of the 1950s Mandelstam's widow attempted without success to gain his official rehabilitation. An emasculated edition of his poetry came out in 1973, but the print run was so small that few Soviet people could obtain a copy, and most of these were sold abroad. It was not until 1987, in the era of Mikhail Gorbachev's policy of glasnost that Mandelstam's poetry was at long last widely circulated and published in the Soviet Union; his name was also finally cleared.

See also Akhmatova, Anna

Further reading: Clarence Brown. *Mandelstam.* Cambridge: Cambridge University Press, 1973; Nadezhda Mandelstam. *Hope against Hope.* Harmondsworth, UK: Penguin, 1975; Osip Mandelstam. *Selected Poems.* Cambridge: Cambridge University Press, 1973; Vitaly Shentalinsky. *The KGB's Literary Archive.* London: Harvill Press, 1995.

Mao Zedong
See China.

Marr, Nikolay Yakovlevich (1865–1934)

Academician Nikolay Marr's spurious theories in the field of linguistics attempted to mold the discipline to a Marxist interpretation of human development along social and class lines. In many ways Marrism (as it became known) equaled the phony scholarship of Trofim Lysenko, who redefined Soviet genetics, in marking the nadir of the degradation of Soviet scholarship during the Stalinist period.

As a professor at St. Petersburg University in the 1900s, Marr had become a specialist in Caucasian languages and had initiated research into languages in the non-Indo-European group. In the 1920s he published the eccentric theory that all languages derive from four basic sound elements—*rosh, sale, ber,* and *yon*—and developed this theory further to suggest that since all languages had this common root, they were capable of evolving into one multipurpose, proletarian language. Unfortunately, such thinking was based on a logic that defied the influence of national and cultural characteristics on the established language families. But it fitted the ideological bill and was soon adopted by philologists eager to conform to accepted Marxist thinking.

Although Marr died in 1934, his theories continued to dominate linguistics. In 1949, in a move to equal Lysenko's dictatorship in the field of genetics, it was announced that Marrism was "the *only* materialist Marxist theory of language." But a year later Stalin had realizied that things had gotten out of hand; he confounded this academic toadying by stepping into the debate on linguistics and making one of his characteristic reversals of policy. In an article in *Pravda* in May 1950 entitled "Marxism and the Question of Linguistics," Stalin now opined that Russian alone and not Marr's prototype hybrid was the language of the proletariat. His dismissal of Marrism as being vulgar, dictatorial nonsense caused consternation among the ranks of those who had so assiduously promoted the doctrine for the previous twenty years, and who now found themselves accused by Stalin of having "acted in a willful, high-handed manner." Duly chastised, the Marrists now acknowledged the greater wisdom of Stalin, and his article was promoted as a major contribution to the field of Soviet linguistics.

See also Lysenko, Trofim

"Marxism and the National Question"

In January 1913, during a brief period of freedom between arrests, Stalin was encouraged on a clandestine visit to Lenin in Cracow to write the first and only major political article he would produce prior to the revolution in 1917.

From Cracow, Lenin dispatched Stalin to Vienna to gather material from Austrian socialists on their policy on the national question within the Austro-Hungarian Empire. Like Russia, this empire also had a rich ethnic mix, of Magyars, Germans, Czechs, Slavs, and a large population of Jews. Even though Stalin wrote much of the article under Lenin's guidance, it remained one of the few original works he could lay claim to in his later *History of the All-Union Communist Party.* The article had been inspired by Lenin's increasing concern about the Jewish Bundist elements within the Bolshevik Party, who were asserting their right to national-cultural autonomy within any future Communist state. He also needed to move against nationalist tendencies within the powerful, Menshevik-dominated Georgian Social Democrats, which is why he chose Stalin, a Georgian and a member of one of Russia's national minorities, to write this article. Lenin did not feel that the Jews were a special case for autonomy, having no distinct national territory of their own, unlike the Ukrainians, Poles, and so on. Their only option, in his view, was one of assimilation. In his article, Stalin came to the same conclusion, emphasizing the importance of integrating *all* nationalities into one cosy, homogeneous proletariat.

The article, Stalin's first stab at serious Marxist theory, was published in three consecutive issues of the Party's sociological journal *Prosveshchenie* (Enlightenment). Stalin signed it "K.[oba] Stalin." After this the underground alias Koba was replaced with Stalin in all his published articles. It was largely on the strength of his supposed specialist knowledge of the subject that Stalin, as a member of cabinet of the new government, was offered the job of People's Commissar for Nationalities in October 1917.

See also Georgia; Historiography; Nationalities; Russian Revolution of 1917; Transcaucasia

Further reading: Robert Conquest, ed. *Soviet Nationalities Policy in Practice.* London: Bodley Head, 1967; Graham Smith, ed. *The Nationalities Question in the Soviet Union.* London: Longman, 1990; Robert C. Tucker. *Stalin as Revolutionary: A Study in History and Personality, 1879–1929.* New York: Norton, 1974.

Mayakovsky, Vladimir Vladimirovich (1893–1930)

One of the most vociferous poets and physically dynamic personalities of the Russian Revolution, the bold and confrontational Vladimir Mayakovsky always demanded to be heard. He probably preempted his own arrest by committing suicide in April 1930. His death in many ways marks a symbolic end to the brief period of intellectual freedom and creativity of the 1920s.

A talent as idiosyncratic and uncompromising as Mayakovsky's seemed to be made for the upheavals of revolution. He was a natural nihilist who was exhilarated by the heady atmosphere of artistic experimentation in the early postrevolutionary days. He had learned the art of subversion early, both as an activist for the Russian Social Democrats and as a student at the Moscow School of Art, where he was a member of the controversial Futurist movement. The title of this avant-garde group's manifesto, published in 1912, could itself describe Mayakovsky's own approach to the arts as "A Slap in the Face of Public Taste." In everything he did, Mayakovsky was loud, brash, larger than life. For him, the poet's duty was to "blare like brazen-throated horns in the fog of philistinism and in seething storms" (lines from a poem bizarrely entitled "Conversation with an Inspector of Taxes about Poetry," 1926).

Boris Pasternak recalled Mayakovsky vividly: "He frowned, he loomed, he drove about and made public appearances; and in the wake of all this, as behind a skater dashing straight forward at full speed, there always seemed to be some day he had made particularly his own—the day which had preceded all other days, the one in which he had acquired that astounding momentum, giving him the appearance of being wholly direct and utterly free."

Mayakovsky's gift for subverting conventional poetics through his strident use of the vernacular, Soviet jargon, and disjointed rhythms combined with his determination to *épater le bourgeois,* seemed a gift to the authorities who turned it to good use. As Pasternak observed, "Mayakovsky began to be introduced forcibly, like potatoes under

The penetrating gaze of the poet Vladimir Mayakovsky testifies to his magnetism as the most compelling of Soviet poets. A passionate individualist who could not adjust to the Stalinist regime, Mayakovsky shot himself in 1930.

Catherine the Great." He became a popular figure on the podium. His declamatory style and ability to infect his audience with the urgency and immediacy of the drive to build the socialist utopia made his poetry a powerful propagandizing tool, and he seemed only too willing to harness his talent to it. He also proved to be equally talented in designing posters and cartoons and writing propagandist tracts. His foray into drama produced two of the most innovative plays of the early Soviet period—*The Bedbug* and *The Bathhouse* (first staged in 1929 and 1930 in dazzling Constructivist style by Vsevolod Meyerhold); both of these reflected his growing apprehension at the tightening straitjacket of Soviet life.

Mayakovsky was a man tormented by his passions, and he frequently sank into bouts of melancholy. His powerful love poetry (such as "I Love," 1922 and "About This," 1923) testified to a life lived on the brink, much of it spent in a turbulent relationship with the artist Lili Brik and her husband, the literary critic Osip Brik. Eventually Mayakovsky's fanatical faith in the revolution faltered and failed. With the period of the New Economic Policy losing momentum and being replaced by the rigid bureaucratization of the first Stalinist Five-Year Plan, Mayakovsky suffered a crisis in his work. The revolution was stagnating. He was pressured into joining the authoritarian Russian Association of Proletarian Writers (RAPP) and would now be expected to conform artistically. In one of his last poems, "At the Top of My Voice" (1931), he bitterly recognized that he had subordinated his true poetic gifts to the production of worthless propaganda: "I subdued myself, / Setting my heel on the throat / Of my own song."

On the morning of 14 April 1930, Mayakovsky shot himself through the heart. In a postscript to his last letter he apologized to RAPP: "Comrades of the Proletarian Literary Organization, don't think me a coward. Really, it couldn't be helped." His death was officially condemned as a "bourgeois act," but in all other respects Mayakovsky served as the perfect icon of the early, unsullied days of the revolution. Stalin himself canonized Mayakovsky in 1936, giving him the official seal of approval as "the best and most talented poet of our Soviet epoch." With Mayakovsky conveniently dead and his work immutable, it was now safe to deify him as the State Poet, but had he lived, it is hard to imagine how Mayakovsky would have survived the ideological oppression of socialist realism during the 1930s.

See also Meyerhold, Vsevolod; Pasternak, Boris; Socialist Realism

Further reading: A. D. P. Briggs. *Vladimir Mayakovsky: A Tragedy.* Oxford: William A. Meeuws, 1979; Edward J. Brown. *Mayakovsky: A Poet in Revolution.* Princeton, NJ: Princeton

University Press, 1973; Ann Charters and Samuel Charters. *I Love: The Story of Vladimir Mayakovsky and Lili Brik*. London: André Deutsch, 1979.

Memorial

The Memorial organization was set up in 1986 in Moscow and elsewhere in the Soviet Union by a group of people who were anxious to uncover the truth about the victims of the Stalinist era, to campaign for their rehabilitation, and to set up lasting memorials to them.

Memorial initially had to fight to be given government recognition as a bona fide organization in order to be able to set up an official office. Even in the atmosphere of glasnost during the late 1980s, there were neo-Stalinists in high places who opposed the idea of such a society, and the anniversary of Stalin's death each year was often the focal point for rival demonstrations between pro-Stalinists from the extreme nationalist group Pamyat' ("Memory") and supporters of Memorial. Thanks to the support of such leading intellectuals as the scientist Andrey Sakharov, the poet Evgeny Evtushenko, and the historian Roy Medvedev and the coverage of its activities in the press, Memorial was eventually able to establish itself with a set of statutes and 100 branches across Russia. There are additional branches in the Baltic states, in Belarus, and Ukraine—areas where the organization is particularly strong. Fundraising grew apace for the major objectives of setting up permanent memorials at eight major mass graves where victims of the Great Terror are buried, such as at Kuropaty in Belarus and Chelyabinsk in the Urals, with the ultimate goal of placing a monument in Red Square itself. At this time, too, Memorial began publishing its own newsletter, *Vedomosti Memoriala* (Memorial News), in which it laid out its plans to campaign for the opening of official archives so that it could set up a proper library and re-search facilities. The organization also set itself the ultimate goal of opening a museum; possibly in one of the notorious Moscow prisons Lefortovo and Butyrki, where so many of those arrested during the Great Terror were taken.

Two of Memorial's most important revelations were the location of mass graves at Chelyabinsk and Kuropaty in 1988–1989. The grave uncovered at Chelyabinsk was found to contain 80,000 skeletons. The victims had all been shot in the back of the head. At Kuropaty, near Minsk in Belarus, 50,000 were found in the grave. Many more sites are known to exist in Belarus in particular, and Memorial is in the process of documenting them. It has also now begun compiling computerized data on victims of the purges and people sent to the Gulag, in order to aid those still trying to trace the whereabouts or fate of lost family members. For those survivors who need help, Memorial also provides welfare assistance where it can.

As Memorial's work continues, its roll call of the dead grows ever larger. Memorial groups across the former Soviet Union are now compiling a vast dossier of names and photographs, which—in an act reminiscent of wartime casualty lists—are appearing in a regular daily news column in the paper, *Evening Moscow*.

See also Eastern Europe; The Great Terror; Gulag; Katyn Massacre; Prisons; Solzhenitsyn, Alexander

Meyerhold, Vsevolod Emilevich (1874–1940)

The Jewish theater producer, actor, and director Vsevolod Meyerhold staged some of the most dazzlingly innovative productions during the early postrevolutionary years, including the plays of Mayakovsky.

Born into a German-Jewish family in Penza, western Russia, Meyerhold studied music and law before joining the Moscow Art Theater under the great actor and director Constantin Stanislavsky. But his predilection for the symbolist drama of Maurice Maeterlinck, Alexander Blok, and Leonid Andreev led him into conflict with Stanislavsky over his controversial staging of their plays, and Meyerhold left to pursue his own experimental style, which drew on the mechanistic conventions of commedia dell'arte and the stylized theater of the Orient. As a leader of the theatrical avant-garde in the 1920s, Meyerhold had enthusiastically embraced the revolution, with a call to "put the October Revolution into the Theater." He attracted many enthusiastic pupils as director of the State School for Stage Direction (opened in 1921), among them Sergey Eisenstein, who owed his later techniques of improvisation as a film director to Meyerhold's inspiration.

Although some of Meyerhold's productions brought him considerable artistic success during the 1920s, his increasingly idiosyncratic, expressionistic work remained incomprehensible to the masses and rapidly began to be seen as artistic indulgence by the authorities. The bizarre acting mannerisms and stage sets of Meyerhold's Constructivist productions of Mayakovsky's *The Bedbug* (1929) and *The Bathhouse* (1930), although extraordinarily innovative, were accused of "formalism" (a term attached by Stalin to anything nonconformist), and his later productions were suppressed. Meyerhold continued to bravely flout the strictures of the official artistic method—socialist realism—which he considered utterly sterile, until eventually his theater was closed as being "alien to Soviet art."

Meyerhold was one of several eminent figures in the Soviet arts who disappeared in the last wave of the Great Terror. It has been suggested that he, together with the writer Isaac Babel and Nikolay Ezhov, the architect of the last years of the purges, had been singled out by Stalin as the targets for one last, great show trial. Meyerhold's own account

of the brutalities he suffered under interrogation in the Lubyanka have recently come to light in a letter he wrote to Foreign Minister Vyacheslav Molotov in which he describes being beaten on the soles of his feet and on his spine until he was a physical wreck: "I began to incriminate myself in the hope that this, at least, would lead quickly to the scaffold." Not long after Meyerhold's arrest in June 1939, his wife, the actress Zinaida Raikh, was found savagely stabbed to death, murdered by officers of the NKVD. Meyerhold himself was shot on 2 February 1940. He was eventually rehabilitated in 1955.

See also Art and Architecture; Eisenstein, Sergey; Mayakovsky, Vladimir; Socialist Realism
Further reading: Vsevolod Meyerhold. *Meyerhold on Theatre*, ed. and transl. Edward Braun. London: Methuen, 1969.

Mikhoels, Solomon (1890–1948)

The gifted Jewish actor and director Solomon Mikhoels was one of the most famous victims of Stalin's postwar drive against the Jews in the Soviet Union, although his death was faked to look like an accident.

Mikhoels, doyen of the Moscow State Jewish Theater, had been a popular stage actor, particularly with Yiddish-speaking audiences for his performances in plays by Yiddish writers. His films, such as *Wandering Stars* (1927), *Jewish Luck* (1925), and *The Return of Nathan Becker* (1932; also dubbed in a Yiddish version), all reached a wider Jewish audience outside the Soviet Union, where he was much admired. On the latter film he had collaborated with the Jewish writer and scenarist Isaac Babel, a friend who, when arrested and taken to the Lubyanka in 1939, was forced under interrogation to denounce Mikhoels as a spy.

Mikhoels had achieved considerable acclaim for his portrayal of Shakespearean

characters and was given the ultimate accolade of being invited to give private recitals
to Stalin, including excerpts from his most
famous role, as Shakespeare's *King Lear.* As a
prominent Soviet Jew, Mikhoels had become a member of the Jewish Anti-Fascist
Committee, which had been set up during
the war to influence Western opinion on
the opening up of a second front and to
drum up financial support, particularly in
the United States, a country Mikhoels visited on the invitation of Albert Einstein.

By the end of the war, the committee
had outlived its usefulness to Stalin, and
Mikhoels had become too influential and
popular internationally for Stalin's liking.
Now also influenced by Babel's denunciation of Mikhoels, Stalin ordered Minister of
State Security Viktor Abakumov to organize his "removal." Mikhoels died in a faked
accident while in Minsk playing *King Lear.*
Apparently he had been invited to an evening social gathering at a dacha outside the
city belonging to the chief of the secret police in Belorussia. A car was sent for Mikhoels and his traveling companion, a Jewish
theater critic. Both men were murdered at
the dacha and their bodies taken back to the
city, where they were dumped in the street
and run over with a truck to make it look
like an accident. *Pravda* duly accorded
Mikhoels a fulsome obituary, but a year later
his theater was closed. In 1953 Mikhoels's
brother was one of the Jewish doctors arrested in the Doctors' Plot.

See also Babel, Isaac; Doctors' Plot; The Great
Terror; Jews

Further reading: Lionel Kochan, ed. *The Jews
in Soviet Russia since 1917.* Oxford: Oxford
University Press, 1978; S. Redlich. *Propaganda
and Nationalism in Wartime Russia: The Jewish
Antifascist Committee in the U.S.S.R., 1941–1948.*
East European Monographs no. 108. Boulder,
CO: East European Quarterly, 1982; Nahma
Sandrow. *Vagabond Star: A World History of Yiddish
Theater.* New York: Limelight, 1986.

Mikoyan, Anastas Ivanovich (1895–1978)

From a poor Armenian family, Anastas
Mikoyan, like Stalin, studied to become a priest, only to exchange the discipline of the church seminary for the life of
a revolutionary in 1915, when he joined
the Bolsheviks. Later, he was to take a
prominent role as minister for internal and
external trade under Stalin and was to acquire an international reputation as one of
the more accessible members of the Politburo. Mikoyan's career was unique in Soviet
politics, surviving as he did from Stalin
through to Brezhnev ("from Ilyich [Lenin]
to Ilyich [Brezhnev]" as Soviet people described their Communist dynasty), and no
doubt this Old Bolshevik owed much to his
own astuteness and natural abilities as an in-
veterate survivor.

Mikoyan's career as a revolutionary
began, again like Stalin's, in the oilfields of
the Caucasus, where he took part in revolutionary activities among the workers in
Baku and narrowly escaped death there
during the later civil war. Having established himself as an expert on the region, he
progressed into the Communist Party bureaucracy as head of the Party for the north
Caucasus in 1922. A year later he became a
member of the Central Committee.

Now a trusted aide of Stalin, Mikoyan
supported him in his power struggle with
Leon Trotsky and helped him eliminate
Trotsky's supporters on the left. In 1926
Mikoyan was promoted to a major post in
the Soviet government, as minister for internal and external trade, where he would
be responsible for the supply of consumer
goods. His role led to the tag "Mikoyan
prosperity" being applied to the years
1936–1937, when for a brief period after
years of austerity under the Five-Year Plans,
there were at long last such goods as toilet
soap in the shops.

One of Mikoyan's lesser-known tasks

during the period of the First Five-Year Plan (when one of his other unsavory roles was the ruthless acquisition of grain supplies from reluctant peasants) was to organize the export and sale abroad of numerous paintings and other works of art as a means of raising funds for Stalin's program of industrialization. Stalin, who professed no interest in art except in terms of its propaganda or financial value, had no qualms about "selling off the family silver"—in this case priceless Old Masters by Rembrandt, Titian, and Rubens and modern works by van Gogh, as well as sculpture, silver, and items from Catherine the Great's superb dinner services. These were all removed from the Hermitage Museum in Leningrad; the price for which they were sold (mainly to millionaire collectors in the West such as Armand Hammer and Calouste Gulbenkian) never approached their real value.

Elected to the Politburo in 1935, Mikoyan became a full member in 1937 and also deputy prime minister. Although his realm was trade, he played his part in the purges of the 1930s. He was known to have been sent on a mission to Erevan with Transcaucasian Party boss Lavrenty Beria in 1937 in order to oversee the purge of the Party leadership in Armenia that resulted in the deaths of thousands of his own countrymen. Earlier that same year he also headed the subcommission that had voted to arrest Nikolay Bukharin and put him on trial.

During the war years, Mikoyan performed a crucial role in charge of transport and food supplies to the armed forces, and in 1946 he was appointed deputy premier with a continuing responsibility for trade. But along with Vyacheslav Molotov and Klimenty Voroshilov, two of Stalin's other longest-serving bureaucrats, Mikoyan was removed from power by Stalin in 1949. He lost his job as minister of foreign trade and although he remained in the Presidium, he now found himself excluded from Stalin's inner circle. Evidence suggests that at the time of his death Stalin was planning a purge of the top men in the Presidium, which would have included Mikoyan. Like Molotov (whose wife was arrested), Mikoyan had had his loyalty to Stalin tested to the limit by the arrest of one of his sons. He prepared himself for the possibility of suicide. In later life he would even admit to having discussed the possibility of Stalin's assassination, a thought that had been in the minds of many when Stalin, in the decline toward senility, became increasingly irascible and unpredictable.

Nevertheless, Mikoyan remained in the Presidium after Stalin's death and regained his influential position in Soviet trade. He supported Nikita Khrushchev during his struggle for power and became his deputy from 1955 until Khrushchev's fall in 1964. During the political thaw of the 1950s Mikoyan had been made responsible for establishing the rehabilitation commissions that would reappraise the charges made against victims of the purges. When asked whether the process might not be accelerated by simply granting a mass pardon to all concerned, Mikoyan had replied that to do so would be to effectively admit the large-scale abuse of human rights under Stalin and acknowledge that the government had been run "by a group of gangsters," to which he added with surprising candor, "Which, in point of fact, we were."

Mikoyan's career enjoyed something of a revival in the post-Stalin years. His skills as a politician attracted some attention in the West, especially after he visited the United States in 1958. The visit made a deep impression on both him and his wife, and they learned to like the creature comforts of the Western capitalist world. Later, Mikoyan would play an important role in the Cuban Missile Crisis of 1962, when he was sent on a face-saving mission to Cuba by Khrushchev to persuade Castro to allow the withdrawal of Soviet missiles. He later ruefully reported that the mission had rekindled something of his glory days as a revolutionary at the turn of the century.

After Khrushchev's removal in 1964, which Mikoyan approved while arguing for him to be treated honorably, Mikoyan stayed on as a token elder statesman under a third Soviet leader, Leonid Brezhnev, in his position as president of the Presidium of the Supreme Soviet, 1964–1965. He was allowed to enjoy a peaceful old age at his luxurious dacha outside Moscow with its greenhouses and stables and manicured lawns (all maintained, along with his retinue of four sons and assorted relatives, by the Soviet government). He devoted his time to writing the dull and uncontroversial memoirs of a man whose conscience appeared not to trouble him. He died a comfortable death as the proud recipient of Five Orders of Lenin.

See also Art and Architecture; Five-Year Plans; The Great Terror; Molotov, Vyacheslav

Further reading: Svetlana Alliluyeva. *Only One Year.* London: Hutchinson, 1969 (for an interesting account of Mikoyan and other aging members of Stalin's Politburo in the 1960s); Roy Medvedev. *All Stalin's Men.* Oxford: Oxford University Press, 1983; Geraldine Norman. *The Hermitage: The Biography of a Great Museum.* London: Jonathan Cape, 1997 (for Mikoyan's role in the sale abroad of Russian art treasures).

Molotov, Vyacheslav Mikhailovich (1890–1986)

One of Stalin's secretaries once summed up his foreign minister, Vyacheslav Molotov, as "a very conscientious, not at all brilliant but extremely capable bureaucrat." Lenin in more forthright fashion dubbed him "stone arse," in recognition of his mulelike ability for hard work (the pseudonym Molotov was derived from the Russian *molot,* "hammer," which traditionally has a stone head). Molotov's public image, particularly with Western statesmen and diplomats, was that of a neutral personality—a "complete modern robot" as Winston Churchill described him—who while able to turn on the charm, gave away little emotion.

The Yugoslav politician Milovan Djilas, who spent time in Moscow in the late 1940s, also endorsed the impression of Molotov as the archetypal apparatchik: "With [him] it was impossible to tell what he was thinking or how he had arrived at his thoughts. His mind remained sealed and inscrutable. . . . [he] seemed to look upon everything—even upon Communism and its final aims—as relative, as something to which he had to, rather than ought to, subordinate his own fate." It was precisely these qualities that ensured Molotov's political longevity, along with Georgy Malenkov, as one of Stalin's right-hand men. His intractability in his endorsement of Stalinism persisted until the day he died. As foreign minister during the war years and then in the early 1950s he was on many occasions the official obdurate face of the Soviet Union—particularly during the postwar partition of Germany into East and West and the growing Soviet hegemony over Eastern Europe. His enduring reputation on a more prosaic level lies, perhaps, in the association of his name with the Molotov Cocktail—an improvised antitank incendiary bomb first used by the Finns against the Soviets during the Winter War of 1939–1940—so named as a mark of Finnish contempt for Soviet foreign policy, which sought to dominate their country, and of Molotov's role as minister of foreign affairs.

Born Vyacheslav Skriyabin (he was related to the Russian composer Scriabin), he joined the Bolsheviks in 1906 and, like Stalin and Lenin, assumed an alias, "Molotov." After a period in exile he returned to Russia to help edit the Bolshevik newspaper *Pravda.* Molotov's career as a Communist Party apparatchik began in the 1920s. He was the youngest candidate member of the Politburo in 1921 and achieved full membership in 1926. Stalin, who had an eye for those with good organizational skills, placed Molotov in a controlling position in his own inner circle, appointing him as second secretary of the Central Committee in

1922. From then on Molotov's loyalty was unshakable. He proved it by acting with ruthless efficiency during the 1929–1930 collectivization program, when he headed a commission that planned the brutal "solution" to the problem of the kulak peasants by arranging either their imprisonment in the Gulag or their deportation to Central Asia, Siberia, and elsewhere. Such loyalty won him appointment as Soviet prime minister in 1930 and established him clearly as Stalin's number two.

Molotov became well known in the West in the following decade as Soviet minister for foreign affairs, taking over from Maxim Litvinov in 1939. He held the position until 1949 and again from 1953 to 1956. In 1939 he had been delegated by Stalin to sign the German-Soviet Non-Aggression Pact with his German counterpart Joachim von Ribbentrop and was a close adviser to Stalin as a member of the war cabinet from 1941, accompanying him to the Allied conferences at Tehran, Yalta, and Potsdam. Here Molotov impressed the Allies, first with his air of intellectual charm—conveyed by his preference for pince-nez—and second with his inscrutable way of keeping his audience or interlocutor waiting on tenterhooks for a carefully deliberated answer. He was nicknamed "Mr. No" (a sobriquet that persisted during his appearances at the United Nations). In a shrewdly stage-managed double act with Stalin, Molotov would continually push negotiations to the limit—a part of Stalin's practiced art of stalling. Stalin, having allowed Molotov to bring everyone to the edge of their seats, would step in at the last moment to play the calm and reassuring conciliator.

Toward the end of the 1940s the close relationship between Stalin and Molotov began to falter. Stalin, now showing signs of senility, was growing irritable and suspicious of all his old entourage. In 1949 Molotov was replaced as minister of foreign affairs by his deputy, Andrey Vishinsky (the chief prosecutor of the purge trials), and

disaster struck when Molotov's wife, Polina, a Jew, became one of the victims of Stalin's witch-hunt against the Jews and was imprisoned. This did nothing, however, to shake Molotov's loyalty, and he remained at his post. By 1952 he had realized that he too was living on borrowed time when Stalin reorganized the Politburo into the Presidium and omitted him from its membership. It is possible that the head of the secret police, Lavrenty Beria, had a hand in provoking Stalin's suspicions by insinuating that British Foreign Minister Anthony Eden had recruited Molotov as a spy when he had been on a diplomatic mission in England during the war. At this stage of his life, Stalin would believe almost any accusation of betrayal made against his old colleagues.

It was only Stalin's death a few months later that saved both Molotov and his wife from death. Despite this, Molotov refused ever to openly condemn Stalin. In interviews he gave at the age of ninety-two, he was still justifying the necessity of the purges in the cause of political stability and blandly accepting the inevitability of "innocent heads" rolling: "Of course there would have been fewer victims had things been done more cautiously, but Stalin insisted on being doubly sure—spare no one, but guarantee a reliable situation during the war and after the war, for a long period—and that in my opinion was achieved." Such blind belief in mass execution as a political necessity is confirmed by Molotov's signature alongside Stalin's on many of the death lists during the Great Terror. On 12 December 1937 alone, they both upheld the death sentence on a list of 3,167 people.

Molotov returned to the Politburo (now called the Presidium) and resumed the role of foreign minister not long after Stalin's death. But he was stripped of power in 1957 for his opposition to Khrushchev and was consigned to the backwater of an ambassadorship to the Mongolian People's Republic 1957–1960. He later served as a Soviet delegate to the International Atomic

Energy Agency in Vienna. Although Khrushchev expelled Molotov from the Communist Party in 1962, he was at least allowed to die in his bed at the age of ninety-six, leaving writers like Alexander Solzhenitsyn to rail against the fact that Molotov and other senior bureaucrats of his kind had been allowed to go unpunished for their complicity in the deaths of thousands.

See also German-Soviet Non-Aggression Pact; The Great Terror; Politburo; Potsdam Conference; Yalta Conference

Further reading: Roy Medvedev. *All Stalin's Men*. Oxford: Oxford University Press, 1983; Vyacheslav Molotov. *Molotov Remembers, Inside Kremlin Politics: Conversations with Felix Chuev*, ed. Albert Resis. Chicago: University of Chicago Press, 1993; Lars T. Lih, Oleg V. Naumov, and Oleg V. Khlevniuk, eds. *Stalin's Letters to Molotov, 1925–1936*. New Haven, CT: Yale University Press, 1995.

Morozov, Pavel

See Komsomol.

Moscow Metro

The Moscow subway system, which began construction in 1932, remains one of the great showpieces of Stalinist architecture and transport and is famous for the elaborate, palatial style of its stations, embellished with marble, stained glass, wall paintings, mosaics, bronze statues, and chandeliers.

Under the First Five-Year Plan, Stalin was anxious to see the Soviet Union leading the way in terms of not only industrial development but also the efficient mechanization of its city transport systems. The construction of the Moscow Metro was

One of the artistic glories of High Stalinism, the Moscow Metro was constructed at record speed and opened in 1935. It featured frescos, sculptures, metalwork, and mosaics by leading exponents of socialist realist art.

undertaken at the beginning of the 1930s as part of Stalin's grandiose plan to rebuild central Moscow. A major propaganda exercise, it necessitated the wholesale blowing up of several ancient Russian monuments as part of the construction work. What mattered to Stalin, however, was that it would be built in record time and would serve as a permanent memorial to the heroic achievements of socialism. Only the finest materials were used—marble from the Caucasus and granite from Ukraine. The gilding and stucco at stations such as the Komsomolskaya were on a par with the great Russian palaces.

The Metro was designed by Aleksey Shchusev, the architect of Lenin's Mausoleum and was to feature some of the best of socialist realist art, such as the fluorescent mosaics at Mayakovskaya station designed by Aleksander Deineka and the beautiful sculptures of Matvei Manizer to be found at Ismailovskaya. Two of the stations on the Metro later won grand prizes at international expositions for the quality of their designs—the Mayakovskaya in 1938 and the Komsomolskaya in 1948.

Lazar Kaganovich (as first secretary of the Moscow Party committee) and his deputy, Nikita Khrushchev, were delegated the role of on-site supervisors of construction. Workers were commandeered from all over the Soviet Union, including the Gulag. Seventy thousand of them were organized into three round-the-clock shifts on what the workers themselves nicknamed "a time schedule that grabbed us by the throat." Some, such as members of the Komsomol, were children as young as eleven; others, such as soldiers of the Red Army, labored for nothing but the kudos of having made a lasting contribution. No expense was spared in constructing the most efficient and largest underground system in the world, named after its overseer, Kaganovich. The opening of its first station in time for the May Day celebrations of 1935 was much trumpeted across the Soviet Union. In line with Stalin's obsession about his own personal security, the Metro also had secret links to the Kremlin and to Stalin's dacha at Kuntsevo.

After the war, to celebrate the Soviet victory, a new line, Komsomolskaya-Koltsevaya, was constructed in the style of Russian baroque church architecture. All of these extravagantly decorated stations are now suffering the depredations of time and lack of resources. The current Moscow authorities are having to struggle with the legacy of Stalin's many grandiose architectural projects, including finding the money to maintain and restore the Metro's spectacular interiors.

See also Art and Architecture; Kaganovich, Lazar; Khrushchev, Nikita; Palace of the Soviets

Nationalities

The old tsarist empire that came under the control of the Bolsheviks after 1917 included many races, creeds, and colors. Quite apart from the dominant Slavs— a mixture of Russians, Ukrainians, and Belarussians, known collectively as the Great Russians, who formed about two-thirds of the population—the newly created Russian Socialist Federated Soviet Republic (RSFSR) contained a huge diversity of peoples.

The nationality "Russian" as a collective term, therefore, embraced peoples as diverse as Eskimo-like nomadic tribes of Siberia, Ashkenazi Jews from the Pale of Settlement, and Turkic-speaking peoples of Central Asia and the Far East. Many of the latter group were Muslim and included the Tatars and the many mountain people of the Caucasus, such as the Chechens and Ingush. The Russian Empire also included Mongolian people of southeast Siberia, many of whom, like the Buryats, were Buddhists, as well as ethnic Germans, descended from the many Germans who had immigrated into Russia from the Baltic region from the eighteenth century onward.

In October 1917, when Lenin appointed his first government after the revolution, he gave Stalin, as commissar for nationalities, responsibility for the lives of some 65 million of these non-Russian peoples. As a member of a minority group himself— Stalin was a Georgian—he seemed well equipped to deal with what historian Isaac Deutscher has described as "Russia's vast, inert, oriental fringe." Indeed, many of these peoples were still largely illiterate and often living in remote settlements where the message of communism had yet to filter through and where lives were dominated by age-old customs, religious practices, and local ethnic rivalries.

One of the major principles of Lenin's policy regarding these minorities was the upholding of national self-determination and the preservation of cultural autonomy. In 1913 he had delegated Stalin to produce an article, "Marxism and the National Question," outlining Bolshevik thinking on the subject. Lenin had argued that the incorporation of Russia's many national groups into a federalist structure of government, composed of an assortment of smaller republics, was the only way to hedge against an upsurge of nationalist movements that had been long suppressed by the tsars. Between March 1919 and December 1936, fourteen autonomous republics were set up within the Soviet Union. While being allowed their own regional administrations, they had little effective autonomy and were increasingly called upon to rubber-stamp centralized policy from Moscow, which retained control over foreign and military affairs, trade, and security.

One of the first stages on the road to the creation of a homogeneous socialist state had been the subjugation of the dissident Polish, Belarussian, and Ukrainian elements in Russia's western borderlands, whose inhabitants had seen the revolution as an opportunity to finally break free from Russian domination. During the Russian–Polish War of 1919–1920 that followed the Russian civil war, these nationalist aspirations were extinguished, resulting in final subordination to the government in Moscow in 1922, when Ukraine and Belarus were incorporated into the Soviet Socialist Republic. In December 1922 the Union of Soviet Socialist Republics (U.S.S.R.) was born of the amalgamation of Ukraine, Belarus, and the Transcaucasian republic with the RSFSR—all now under the political domination of the Russian government in Moscow. For a while during the 1920s, Ukrainian and Belarussian culture continued to flourish, aided by growing literacy rates. Their later suppression under Stalin served only to strengthen national identity, which would continue to fuel national Russian-Ukrainian antipathies throughout the lifetime of the Communist state.

In 1918 Stalin had tried to resolve the situation regarding the RSFSR's relationship with the union republics of the Caucasus—Georgia, Azerbaijan, and Armenia—by merging them into a single Transcaucasian Federal Republic. The three republics, which had for centuries nursed their own local rivalries and territorial claims on each other, made uneasy bedfellows, and the Federal Republic collapsed within two months. In 1922, despite fierce Georgian resistance, which was put down with considerable brutality by Stalin, the three republics were once again united, this time as the Transcaucasian Soviet Federated Socialist Republic.

After the death of Lenin in 1924, Stalin, incapable of countenancing ethnic independence in any form, set out to create a multinational, Russian-speaking Soviet monolith that gradually eroded the Bolshevik promises of 1917. Any opportunities ethnic minorities might have had of consolidating themselves through regional Communist parties were removed by the imposition of a "divide and rule" policy, whereby the Soviet Union's many Muslims, in particular, were separated into smaller and often incompatible regional units along totally artificial borders. Such a policy was designed to forestall the rise of a pan-Islamic movement but in reality fomented unrest by deliberately ignoring linguistic or religious divisions. It lumped disparate peoples together; in places such as Kabardino-Balkaria, Checheno-Ingushetiya, and Nagorno-Karabakh this would result in bitter conflict during the late 1980s and after the break-up of the Soviet Union.

Throughout the 1930s, the Soviet Union's Turkic peoples had to adjust to the rapid Sovietization of their homelands through the immigration of Russian bureaucrats and security police to administer local government. Such was the influx of Russian nationals, combined with a high level of losses of ethnic political cadres during the purges, that the local sense of national identity was severely eroded. The mass enforcement of collectivization during the 1930s did irreparable damage to many local farming traditions and economies, as Party officials sought to impose large-scale agricultural methods on pastoral regions where the nomadic people and the land itself were ill suited for such draconian changes. The republics of Central Asia—Tajikistan, Turkmenistan, Kazakhstan, Uzbekistan, Azerbaijan, and Kirghiziya, in particular—resented control of their economies being absorbed by Moscow. In time their role would devolve into that of old-style Asiatic colonies, obliged to grow, produce, and supply those commodities demanded of them by a monopolistic client—the Soviet state.

Stalinist educational policy at this time also sought to underline loyalty to the state in a revived form of Russian nationalism, which directed its attention at the young in particular. Non-Russian-speaking people soon found their native tongues under attack, as Russian became increasingly the compulsory second language in schools and the primary language at university level. With the phasing out of Arabic script in favor of a Latinized version (in 1929) and later (1939) Cyrillic script and the suppression of Muslim and other ethnic literatures, it became increasingly difficult for regional nationalities to hold on to their traditional identities. The cornerstone of such identity was, for many, their indigenous religious practice.

The mass propaganda program launched against religion by Stalin in the early 1930s affected many Muslim communities, as well as the ethnic Christian churches of Armenia and Georgia, the Catholics of Ukraine, and the Buddhists of the Far East. Equally, the Russian Orthodox Church came under concerted attack, so that even traditional identities, such as those unifying Russians themselves as an ethnic group, were lost. Attempts to clamp down on the rituals of Islam practiced among the Chechen peoples of Central Asia resulted in calls for resistance and the declaration by local imams of a *jihad* against the Soviet regime with such slogans as "Death to all Bolsheviks, students, engineers, indeed all those who write from left to right." Despite the inherent incompatibilities of Bolshevism and Islam, however, some of the Soviet Union's Muslim communities assimilated Communist doctrines faster than Christian doctrines, in particular, the Tatars, who remained as a pocket of dogged Communist resistance even after the collapse of Communism.

With the Stalin Constitution of 1936, the larger nationalities were given their own union republics, and fifty-one nationalities were granted varying forms of limited statehood, including the three Trans-

caucasian republics of Armenia, Azerbaijan, and Georgia, who now ended their uneasy partnership. In 1940, as a result of the signing of the German-Soviet Non-Aggression Pact, Stalin was able to annex the Baltic states unchallenged, and the Soviet Union absorbed three major new nationalities—Latvians, Lithuanians, and Estonians. But these people fiercely resisted Soviet domination, and fifty years of Soviet rule failed to suppress their powerful sense of national identity and tradition.

By the time the Soviet Union was at war with Germany, Stalin had decided to take action against any revival of nationalistic aspirations fostered by the German invasion and to punish those ethnic groups, who were perceived to have collaborated with them, by deporting them to remote and unproductive regions of Central Asia and Siberia. The first group to be deported were the 4 million Volga Germans, who in 1941 were sent to Kazakhstan for having, supposedly, harbored German agents. In 1943, 93,000 Kalmyks, an ancient Mongol and Buddhist people from the steppe, and 75,000 Turkic Karachai of the Caucasus were deported east en masse.

Other groups were also accused of collaboration with the Germans in 1944 and shared the same fate—7,000 Turkic Balkars, 200,000 Meshketians, and 225,000 Crimean people—Tatars, Bulgars, Greeks, and Armenians who disappeared in the space of two months. On 18 May the Crimean Tatars were given fifteen minutes in which to gather their belongings before being crowded into cattle trucks and taken east on a long and grueling journey by train that took up to five weeks. By the time the trains arrived, many had already died and half of those left died of disease and malnutrition in the first few years. Many of the Crimean Tatars who had fought in the Red Army returned from the front at the end of the war to find their villages deserted or taken over by Russian immigrants.

After the Germans retreated from Russia

in 1944, the Chechens and Ingush of the north Caucasus came under attack. Their traditional hatred for Russians and the fact that the Germans had promised them independence after the war had made their persecution by Stalin inevitable, and he ordered the head of the NKVD (secret police), Lavrenty Beria, to organize their deportation to Kazakhstan. On 25 February 1944, Beria was pleased to report to Stalin that "the eviction of the Chechens and Ingush is proceeding normally" and that there were "no serious instances of resistance, or other incidents." Within days, 91,250 Ingush and 387,229 Chechens had been packed into cattle trucks for the long train ride east. As writer Alexander Solzhenitsyn notes in his *Gulag Archipelago,* the Chechens were the one group who "never cracked," who resisted what he called "the psychology of submission." Their suffering only reinforced their long-nurtured hatred of Russian domination. Some 200,000 Chechens are said to have died as a result of the mass deportations. The survivors were eventually allowed back to their homelands in 1957. But Chechen resentment would erupt again in violent civil war with Russia in 1994–1995, resulting in 24,000 civilian casualties.

See also Baltic States; Education; Jews; "Marxism and the National Question"; Religion; Transcaucasia

Further reading: Robert Conquest. *The Nation Killers: The Soviet Deportation of Nationalities.* London: Sphere Books, 1972; Geoffrey Hosking. *A History of the Soviet Union 1917–1991.* London: Fontana Press, 1992; Graham Smith, ed. *The Nationalities Question in the Soviet Union.* London: Longman, 1990.

NEP
See Collectivization.

"New Soviet Man"

One of the fundamentals of Stalinist ideology was not simply the building of a monolithic socialist state but also the creation of a population of compliant, ideologically conformist citizens to populate it. In order to achieve this objective, Stalin embarked on a vast program of Communist indoctrination and a radical overhaul of teaching practices during the 1930s. This set out to bring forth a race of "New Soviet Men" who would not only embody the morality, values, and characteristics deemed essential in the good Soviet citizen but also demonstrate the efficient working of the Communist state to its Western detractors.

The idea, however, was not originally Stalin's. It had been very much in Lenin's mind as an important component of his own vision of the socialist future. It was also one of the first aspects of the new Bolshevik government in Russia that worried some Western observers and intellectuals. Some had been horrified by what they had seen in the Soviet Union in the 1920s and 1930s and, like the philosopher Bertrand Russell, warned that the Soviet state had come to the conclusion that "human nature can be completely transformed by force." Some writers, including George Orwell and Aldous Huxley, as well as Russian writer Evgeny Zamyatin, warned of the dangers of Soviet totalitarianism in novels that featured a mutated form of "New Soviet Man."

Stalin's belief that people could be programmed in this way was partly inspired by his support for the Soviet pseudoscience of Lysenkoism, which had convinced him that the principle of the genetic transmission of acquired characteristics from one plant generation to the next could be applied equally to humans. Lysenko himself had loudly proclaimed this possibility: "In our Soviet Union people are not born. What are born are organisms. We turn them into people—tractor drivers, engine drivers, academicians, scholars and so forth." Stalin's policies toward Soviet society also contained elements of Hitler's *Lebensborn* program, in which women's primary function was to serve as brood mares for the next generation of archetypal Soviet citizens (a major reason why Stalin banned abortion in 1936).

Stalin's campaign to remold Soviet society was also closely bound up with his will to transform Russia from a backward to a modern industrial society. If old, tsarist Russia could be remolded to take its rightful place as a reborn socialist state in the international arena, then Russian man could also be transformed from his traditional and still persisting image as an illiterate peasant into a paragon of social responsibility and moral virtue and a willing servant of the state. But the terminology with which Stalin and policymakers referred to human beings, whose lives they were so busy remolding, betrayed the hollowness of their phony altruism. Stalin and his bureaucrats saw the vast mass of the population as a commodity, a raw material. They were now "valuable forms of capital," the cogs who, as Stalin averred, "keep our great state machine in motion."

The transformation of the Soviet people was targeted mainly at the young, through the education system and through youth organizations such as the Komsomol. Soviet writers were also enlisted to depict the "New Soviet Man" in suitably heroic and edifying narratives, where he is seen overcoming physical hardship (rather than indulging in the more subjective preoccupations of love and inner, spiritual turmoil; there was no room for such introspection in the new society). Nikolay Ostrovsky's novel *How the Steel Was Tempered* (1932–1934) would become the template for the genre. In it he presented the archetypal "New Soviet Man" in the guise of his exemplary hero Pavel Korchagin who resisted the pleasures of the flesh ("First of all I will belong to the Party and then to you") in favor of self-sacrifice in the name of Bolshevism and the revolution. This, the work of an undistinguished and now obscure writer, sold in excess of 5 million copies.

See also Education; "Engineers of Human Souls"; Family Life; Komsomol; Science; Socialist Realism; Women

Further reading: Mikhail Heller. *Cogs in the Soviet Wheel: The Formation of Soviet Man.* London: Collins Harvill, 1988.

NKVD

The Narodniy Kommissariat Vnutrenikh Del (NKVD) or People's Commissariat for Internal Affairs, as it was euphemistically called, was but one of several incarnations of the Soviet secret police, most familiar as the KGB. Under Stalin it became synonymous with the worst years of the Great Terror, as the official machinery that implemented political repression and hunted down that vast army of plotters, spies, and counterrevolutionaries that Stalin had insisted was seeking to undermine Soviet society.

The Soviet secret police began life as the Cheka in 1917, set up to deal with acts of sabotage and counterrevolution. It mutated through several name changes over the next twenty-seven years, each time extending its jurisdiction, until it arrived at its most familiar acronym—the KGB—in 1954. Between these dates, it was variously known as the OGPU (1923–34), the NKVD (1934–1943, when it acquired far-reaching investigative powers and staged the major Moscow Show Trials), the NKGB (1943–1946), the MGB (1946–1953), and the MVD (1953). Three successive heads of the organization were themselves devoured by their own monster (Genrikh Yagoda in 1936, Nikolay Ezhov in 1938, and Lavrenty Beria in 1953).

The location for many of the most gruesome acts of torture (the use of which was officially endorsed by the Central Committee in 1937), which were carried out in the course of extracting the required confessions that Stalin rigorously insisted upon, was the NKVD headquarters in Moscow—the Lubyanka on Dzerzhinsky Square. In time, mention of the name alone would be enough to instill fear into people. Only a few people taken there under arrest would ever come out again. The building itself had once been the rather grand premises of the Rossiya Insurance Company (on Lyubyanskaya Square as it was then called—and the name to which it has now reverted). While the square itself was renamed by the Bolsheviks after the founder of the Cheka, Felix Dzerzhinsky (whose imposing statue, which stood in the center of the square, was one of the first casualties of the collapse of the Soviet Union in 1991), the Lubyanka building itself always retained its name. Under the Soviets, new monolithic wings were added to its original structure, turning the NKVD building into one great impenetrable fortress.

When Stalin rose to power after the death of Lenin in 1924, the OGPU was carefully cultivated by him as a major organ of political and social control. When its head Dzerzhinsky died in 1926, the "epoch of romantic terror," as it has been called, died with him and a new and far-reaching epoch was inaugurated. The OGPU was given a budget of 4 million rubles per year, and the loyalty of its officers was bought with access to their own officers club (Yagoda later even introduced expensive dress uniforms for senior officers in 1936), special goods, and privileges. As members of the chosen few, the officers of the OGPU, under Stalin's watchful eye, built up a state within the state, administered by hundreds of thousands of lesser servants, that was answerable only to Stalin. NKVD officers now watched and controlled every aspect of Soviet life through a vast network of informers, as well as vetting the appointment of all Communist Party officials. Even the NKVD rank and file were themselves not above suspicion, and a secret inner section monitored their activities.

At the height of its power the NKVD also controlled the Soviet spy network and agents provocateurs abroad. But a greater part of its work was taken up with the administration of the Gulag system and the exploitation of its slave labor, which had become a major contributor to the Soviet economy. One of the NKVD's first, great showpiece projects to exploit this labor was the construction of the White Sea–Baltic Canal in 1931.

During the years of the Great Terror, the NKVD reverted to history by organizing terror on the grand scale. Terror, condoned by Lenin and Leon Trotsky, had been a natural element of the revolution and had been exercised with great brutality by the Bolsheviks during the period known as the "Red Terror," which was unleashed in September 1918 after an attempt on the life of Lenin.

Toward the end of the Great Terror, such had been the level of diligence in the betrayal and denunciation of friends and families of each other, that in 1937 senior minister Anastas Mikoyan could confidently announce that "every citizen in the U.S.S.R. is an employee of the NKVD." For his services in the suppression of counter-revolution and espionage, NKVD head Nikolay Ezhov was awarded the Lenin Prize. It was also by this date that prisoners were denied the last vestiges of legal process. From July 1937, three-man boards of NKVD and Party officials were empowered to pass sentence of death after a mere 10 minutes of ritual paper shuffling, after which the accused would be taken away and summarily shot.

On the eve of World War II, the NKVD arranged the mass deportation and murder of thousands of Ukrainians, Poles, and people from the Baltic states. During the war the NKVD efficiently deported many more thousands of ethnic minorities from their homelands, including the Chechens, the Crimean Tatars, and ethnic Germans from the Volga region. The NKVD was also responsible for the massacre in 1940 of 4,000 Polish officers, whose bodies were found at Katyn, and the systematic murder between

1937 and 1941 of over 250,000 Belarussians, who were taken to the Kuropaty Forest near Minsk in truckloads (as many as sixteen trucks a day), where they were shot and their bodies dumped into mass graves.

The NKVD/NKGB (the roles of the two became difficult to separate) fulfilled an important role during the war years, enforcing political control in the army, censoring mail, and ensuring that Stalin's orders forbidding retreat and surrender were adhered to. They formed special units that followed frontline troops into battle and saw to it that anyone who turned back was shot. An NKVD Special Department dealt with cases of desertion, anti-Soviet activity (such as being caught reading German propaganda leaflets), and counterrevolutionary propaganda, usually off-the-cuff remarks made by Red Army soldiers that were critical of the Stalinist regime. Such a momentary lapse of caution sent writer Alexander Solzhenitsyn to the Gulag in 1945.

In 1945 the NKVD had a major hand in one of the most contentious events in the history of World War II—the repatriation of prisoners of war (POWs), slave laborers, and other Russian émigrés and Soviet nationals from German-occupied Europe. Under Stalin's instructions, the NKVD set up at least 100 holding camps where these people were investigated and interrogated. More than 5 million people were to be dealt with in this way, and they were not given the option of remaining in Western Europe, even if they had valid claims for political asylum. As a result, only about 20 percent ever made it back to their homes and villages in the Soviet Union. Many of the Cossacks and other Russians who had fought for the Nazis in General Andrey Vlasov's Russian Liberation Army (made up of Russian POWs and slave laborers who had been taken to Germany) were summarily shot by the NKVD on their arrival, by sea, at either Odessa or Murmansk. Others were dispatched directly to the Gulag in Siberia on sealed trains to suffer and die as slave laborers long before their ten- and even twenty-five-year sentences were up. In this way, the NKVD oversaw the "repatriation" straight to the Gulag of as many as 2.5 million people.

And then, of course, there were the individual deaths and assassinations of more prominent Soviet figures. Historians are divided on the level of NKVD involvement, and there is no tangible evidence to prove it, but Stalin's controlling influence can be discerned in the circumstances of the suspicious deaths of Sergey Kirov, Maxim Gorky, Sergo Ordzhonikidze, and others.

The NKVD itself was by no means immune from purges within its own ranks. Each time its leadership changed, the previous executioners were themselves eliminated. When Yagoda fell from power in 1936, the remaining Leninists from the original Cheka were purged from the NKVD's ranks by Yagoda's successor Ezhov. Inevitably, when Ezhov was purged in 1938, as a result of his excessive zeal in overfulfilling arrest and execution quotas between 1936 and 1938, many of his equally diligent lieutenants also found themselves taken away to receive a bullet in the back of the head, administered, in many cases, in their own former workplace in the basement of the Lubyanka.

One of the final, major acts of political repression by Stalin's secret police was its purge and executions of members of the Leningrad Communist Party in 1948 and the stage-managing of the so-called Doctors' Plot of 1953. By now the Soviet secret police had extended its surveillance over the Communist satellites of Europe, instituting its own purge trials among the various national Communist Parties, in particular, that in Czechoslovakia, which resulted in the trial and execution of Vice-President Rudolf Slansky in 1952. By the time of Stalin's death in March 1953, current head of the MGB Lavrenty Beria had built himself a considerable power base as a latter-day mafioso, from which he launched his own bid for the leadership, only to be arrested as an imperialist agent, taken to the Lubyanka, and shot in December 1953.

See also Beria, Lavrenty; Ezhov, Nikolay; Great Patriotic War; The Great Terror; Gulag; Nationalities; Prisons; Torture; White Sea–Baltic Canal; Yagoda, Genrikh; Yalta Conference

Further reading: Robert Conquest. *Inside Stalin's Secret Police: NKVD Politics, 1936–1939.* Stanford, CA: Hoover Institution Press, 1985; Amy Knight, *Beria: Stalin's First Lieutenant.* Princeton, NJ: Princeton University Press, 1993; Boris Levytsky. *The Uses of Terror: The Soviet Secret Police, 1917–1970.* New York: Coward, McGann & Geoghegan, 1972.

Nomenklatura

This vast network of Soviet patronage, involving those holding sensitive posts in the Communist Party and Soviet bureaucracy, was in many ways the child of the old tsarist system of bureaucracy—a system built on privilege and status where the chosen few, through dint of loyal and unquestioning service, could work their way through the system to positions of considerable power.

The *nomenklatura* grew out of recommendations made at the Ninth Party Congress, held in 1919, that local committees of the Communist Party should compile lists of people suitable for particular jobs who were politically trustworthy. Those chosen were then appointed to a special list of posts—ministerial, diplomatic, military, management in factories and industry, and headships in schools—all of which were crucial in sustaining the political orthodoxy of the Soviet state. In return for their loyalty, members of the *nomenklatura,* of which there were 60,000 by September 1922, had access to better health care and housing and were able to buy luxury goods, which they could obtain in special government stores. Some of them also enjoyed the privileges of chauffeur-driven cars, dachas, foreign travel, and holidays at sanatoria on the Black Sea.

This system of official appointments inevitably eroded individual autonomy over the choice of job and career. In addition, the *nomenklatura* was dominated by Slavs over other ethnic groups. They inhabited their own inner world, as members of a protected and powerful, self-perpetuating elite or "clan." It was an elite that percolated right down through Soviet society, like one vast masonic fraternity, with members across the whole social spectrum from the Politburo to the local collective farm. It was also entirely subservient to the Stalinist state. Individual members, for example, officials running local Communist Party branches or state farms (the *sovkhozi*), often wielded considerable local power and influence, a fact about which workers who looked upon such officials as Party "fat cats" frequently complained. It was not unknown, therefore, that pressure for administrative change in certain regions was initiated from below by disgruntled workers who took part and endorsed the denunciation of domineering officials to whom they had taken a particular dislike.

During the 1930s many local Party officials (some of them members of the old Leninist guard), who had become too powerful or independent in this way, were removed from their jobs by Stalin and supplanted with a new generation of young and untested workers from the rank and file. Many of the Old Guard of the *nomenklatura* were also arrested during Stalin's purge of the Communist Party from 1935 on. But once these apparatchiks had been shot or sent to the Gulag (by the thousands), Stalin found himself faced with the urgent need to replace them. He was therefore obliged to promote great numbers of inexperienced replacements through the ranks, many of whom, taking a far more cynical view of their administrative tasks than the old school Leninists, were open to corruption.

Promotion in this way, however, did offer an opportunity of advancement to many who later became leading Soviet ministers, such as Nikita Khrushchev, a Ukrainian peasant who eventually became Soviet president. But the abuses also became rife. The system created what many historians consider to be a Soviet "high society" or even unofficial "aristocracy," whose children enjoyed special schooling and trips abroad, as well as plum jobs. Blatant careerism and the complacency nurtured by a life of privilege would ultimately irretrievably weaken the Soviet government and would be seen as a subversion of everything for which the revolution had originally stood.

See also Education; The Great Terror

Further reading: T. H. Rigby. *Political Elites in the U.S.S.R.: Central Leaders and Local Cadres from Lenin to Gorbachev.* Aldershot, UK: Edward Elgar, 1990.

Nuclear Weapons
See Atomic Bomb.

Ordzhonikidze, Grigory Konstantinovich (1886–1937)

Grigory Konstantinovich (Sergo) Ordzhonikidze, a Georgian revolutionary and long-standing comrade in arms, brought the important news to Stalin, in exile in Vologda in 1911, that he had been elected to the Central Committee of the Communist Party.

Ordzhonikidze had joined the Russian Social Democrats in 1903 and, like Stalin, was imprisoned and exiled several times for his revolutionary activities. After the revolution he became a member of the Central Committee of the Communist Party. As chairman of its Caucasian Bureau, at Stalin's behest (and contrary to Lenin's wishes) he organized the Red Army's ruthless suppression of the Mensheviks in the Georgian Communist Party and the country's incorporation into the Transcaucasian Federal Republic in 1921. Lenin, mistrustful of Ordzhonikidze's reliability and incensed by his hot-headedness in purging the Georgian Communists, had been planning at the time of his last illness in 1923–1924 to reprimand him for this and other acts of insubordination.

After Lenin's death, as a loyal supporter of Stalin, Ordzhonikidze worked his way through the Party ranks, joining the inner sanctum of the Politburo as a candidate member in 1926 and a full member in 1930, where he was poised to become second in the Party to Stalin. But in the early 1930s, by now promoted to commissar for heavy industry (1932), he fell out with Stalin over the harshness of the industrialization program. Ordzhonikidze had also by now become increasingly alarmed at the summary arrest and execution of many old friends and comrades and had tried to save some of them, including his deputy Georgy Pyatakov. In the latter case, he boldly telephoned Stalin in January 1937, and trading on his long-standing relationship with him as a fellow Georgian, demanded that "this authoritarianism cease." Ordzhonikidze was also foolhardy enough (since Stalin never forgave an insult) to promise his old comrade (using Stalin's Georgian alias) that he was "going to raise hell, Koba, if it's the last thing I do before I die."

The words proved prophetic. By now Stalin sensed that Ordzhonikidze was the only figure around whom others might rally to remove him from power. Ordzhonikidze was, in any case, by now so deeply disillusioned that he was even contemplating suicide. He died in suspicious circumstances the following month on 18 February. The official story was given out that Ordzhonikidze, the "ardent, fearless Bolshevik-Leninist," had suffered a heart attack, but reports in the Russian press in the late 1980s confirmed that he died of a gunshot wound, the result of either a forced suicide or murder.

Recent evidence also suggests that Ordzhonikidze may have been preparing to take a public stand against Stalin at the impending Central Committee Plenum (to be held in June 1937). As historian Robert C. Tucker pointed out, he was by this time "the one prominent leader left who was capable of openly resisting Stalin." A few days before Ordzhonikidze's death in February 1937, his brother Papuliya, who had been held under arrest since November 1936, was shot on the instructions of Lavrenty Beria. Other members of the family, who dared to voice their suspicions over the circumstances of Ordzhonikidze's death, were also imprisoned or shot. In 1944 the towns bearing Ordzhonikidze's name in the Soviet Union were given new names.

See also Georgia; The Great Terror; Transcaucasia
Further reading: O. Klevniuk. *In Stalin's Shadow: The Career of "Sergo" Ordzhonikidze.* New York: M. E. Sharpe, 1995; Amy Knight. *Beria: Stalin's First Lieutenant.* Princeton, NJ: Princeton University Press, 1993.

Orgburo

*T*he Organizational Bureau (Orgburo) was established in tandem with the Politburo (which dealt with policy) at the Eighth Party Congress, held in 1919, to take charge of the organization and personnel of the Communist Party. As the head of its five elected members, Stalin was responsible for appointing the bureau's provincial bosses and keeping control of the regional cadres of Communist Party staff.

It was in the course of assembling his exhaustive card index of members of the various Orgburo cadres that Stalin acquired the nickname "Comrade Card Index" (*tovarishch kartotekov*). While the name seemed harmless enough at the time, Stalin's ability for methodically gathering and storing facts during these early years of service, in what was effectively the bureaucratic backwaters of the Party, was put to good use by him later. His phenomenal powers of recall would enable him to never forget a face or a fact. He was also quietly and carefully working toward his own game plan. As a member of both the Politburo and the Orgburo, Stalin had a foot in both bureaucratic camps, and by 1922 he would further extend his aegis over Party administration and policy, as general secretary of the Party.

The Orgburo and the Politburo were abolished at the 19th Party Congress in 1952 and replaced by Stalin with the Presidium.

See also General Secretary of the Communist Party; Politburo

Palace of the Soviets

One of the worst acts of vandalism perpetrated in the course of creating Stalin's architectural vision of a new Moscow was the destruction of one of its historic churches—the Cathedral of Christ the Savior—to make way for a mighty new Palace of the Soviets, projected to dominate the Moscow skyline and rival the world's tallest buildings.

The Cathedral of Christ the Savior had begun construction in 1837 during the reign of Alexander I to celebrate the Russian victory of 1812 over Napoleon. It was not consecrated until 1883, during the reign of his grandson Alexander III. While not of great significance architecturally, the cathedral had a powerful symbolic and historical significance, and its interior boasted some splendid icons and religious paintings, as well as extensive gilding. These were stripped from the cathedral, as was the bronze from its cupola, before it was dynamited in 1931. The construction of the new palace had also necessitated the demolition of several blocks of workers' flats in the center of Moscow's densest residential district—a totally counterproductive act considering the drastic shortage of housing at the time. It meant that 5,000 dislocated people had to be transported to the suburbs of Moscow, where they were left huddled into temporary wooden barracks.

A competition was launched in 1931 to find the best design for the new Palace of the Soviets that would supplant the cathedral. This building would be the apotheosis of Stalinist "wedding-cake" architecture, a monolith that would "show how Lenin and Stalin led the people of the [Soviet] Union to freedom and happiness." The design finally accepted in 1937, and chosen from 160 entries (there was no outright winner), was based on an entry by Boris Iofan. The palace was to be crowned with an enormous 75-meter-high statue of Lenin that would be three times taller than New York's Statue of Liberty; and the palace would also contain conference halls large enough to seat 20,000 people. But construction got no further than the foundations when money had to be diverted into munitions production with the onset of war. The building's unfinished steel framework was taken down for valuable scrap metal and the site itself was later turned into a large open-air swimming pool.

In the 1990s, an exact replica of the original cathedral was rebuilt on the site, at an estimated cost of £200 million (the funding for which included donations from the Coca-Cola and McDonald's corporations). It was officially opened in 1997 (although construction was still incomplete) in time

A version of the neoclassical design (1933) by Boris Iofan for a Palace of the Soviets, to be built in Moscow, featuring an enormous, 100–meter (110-foot) statue of Lenin. Construction never got beyond the foundations.

to celebrate the 850th anniversary of the founding of Moscow.

See also Art and Architecture; Family Life; Moscow Metro

Further reading: David Elliott. *New Worlds: Russian Art and Society 1900–1937.* London: Thames and Hudson, 1986; Selim O. Khan-Magomedov. *Pioneers of Soviet Architecture: The Search for New Solutions in the 1920s and 1930s.* London: Thames and Hudson, 1987.

Pasternak, Boris Leonidovich (1890–1960)

A preeminent Soviet writer and Nobel Prize winner, Boris Pasternak was one of a handful of extraordinary artistic talents, along with Anna Akhmatova, Dmitry Shostakovich, and Mikhail Bulgakov, whom Stalin chose not to consign to the terrible fate shared by so many during the years of the Great Terror. Bulgakov's biographer, J. A. E. Curtis, suggests that this choice was born of a "curious kind of respect" for the uniqueness of their irreplaceable talent. One might also consider that together they shared what has been defined as the *yurodivy* trait in the Russian character—that quality, verging on the mystical, that imbued all of these creative artists with the gift to see and understand beyond conventional wisdom as prophets of their times, "with license to allude to awful truths while enjoying protection from reprisal."

Pasternak came from a cultured and artistic Moscow family of assimilated Jews. His father was a well-known artist who had illustrated the novels of Tolstoy, and his mother was a talented concert pianist. He had a happy childhood in a comfortable home. Like his mother, Pasternak seemed poised for a musical career (although he had been writing poetry since an early age). But after studying music for six years he changed over to philosophy, traveling abroad for a while to study at the University of Marburg in Germany.

In 1913, Pasternak published his first collection of poems—*Twin in the Stormclouds,* which showed influences of the work of Vladimir Mayakovsky and the Futurists. *My Sister—Life,* his third collection of poetry in 1917, became the defining moment in his career as a poet and demonstrated the power of his personal vision and his empathy with nature. It established Pasternak's reputation as a leading lyrical poet and master of rhyme and metaphor alongside Anna Akhamatova, to whom he would later admit his lifelong debt.

In 1917, Pasternak initially welcomed the revolution, but he soon grew to abhor the political excesses of Bolshevism, which he saw as crushing the spirit of the individual. Criticized as "bourgeois" for writing poetry about his personal preoccupations with nature, love, and the human condition, and also for failing to openly support the Communist Party, Pasternak turned increasingly from poetry to prose with *The Childhood of Lyuvers* in 1922 and his autobiography *Safe Conduct* (1929).

As time went on Pasternak's increasing spiritual alienation from the Soviet regime deepened and despite his popularity as a living legend of Russian poetry—a legend built on very modest print runs of his work—he continued to resist the increasing pressure to become an "official" poet after the introduction of socialist realism during the 1930s. He made it clear that for him "art is unthinkable without risk and spiritual self-sacrifice; freedom and boldness of imagination have to be gained in practice," but for Pasternak, as for other dissident writers, that practice would have to be maintained in private. Unable to compromise his artistic beliefs and kowtow to what he himself called "the diabolical power of the dead letter," Pasternak was forced to abandon original writing in order to earn a living.

Between 1933 and 1943 he published no new works, turning instead to translation of the plays of Shakespeare (including *Hamlet* and *King Lear*), and the poetry of Keats, Shelley, Goethe, Verlaine, and Rilke. He also had a particular love of Georgia and the Georgian poetry of Paolo Yashvili and Titsian Tabidze, and his translations of their work found favor with Stalin, himself a Georgian, who had a soft spot for his national literature. Sadly, both Yashvili and Tabidze, who were also close friends of Pasternak's, perished during the Great Terror. It has been argued by some that Pasternak's Georgian translations may well have saved him from arrest. Historian Robert C. Tucker related the unconfirmed story that when offered Pasternak's name on a list of those to be arrested, Stalin wrote alongside it, "Don't touch this cloud-dweller"—a statement which further confirms Stalin's perception of Pasternak as a "saintly fool."

Pasternak had undoubtedly become extremely disturbed by the arrest and disappearance of so many literary friends, and his mind particularly dwelled on the fact that in 1933 he had not done enough to save the poet Osip Mandelstam from persecution. This had been after Stalin became aware of the satirical poem Mandelstam had written about him and circulated among his friends. Pasternak saw this as "an act of suicide" on Mandelstam's part and had been taken aback when he received a personal phone call from Stalin, during which he questioned Pasternak about Mandelstam and his poetry. Pasternak, uncertain how best to respond to Stalin's loaded questions, had been evasive in his reply. This had irritated Stalin, who retorted, "If I were a poet and a poet friend of mine were in trouble, I would do anything to help him," and put the phone down.

Like many other writers, Pasternak answered the call of patriotism and produced some pedestrian verse during the war years, but in the postwar climate of Zhdanovism when writers once again found themselves hemmed in by political and ideological constraints, he once more retreated into silence. He now continued work on his semiautobiographical epic masterpiece *Dr. Zhivago*, a tragic and lyrical account of the spiritual despair suffered by a Russian doctor-poet in his experience of the Russian Revolution and its chaotic aftermath. The Christian and symbolic overtones of the book's narrative, as well as its central character's name, which was derived from the Russian for "living," confirmed it as a poet's novel, which in several aspects paralleled Pasternak's own spiritual journey. As he once said: "I always dreamt of a novel in which, as in an explosion, I would erupt with all the wonderful things I saw and understood in this world."

In 1946, at the age of fifty-six, Pasternak met the writer Olga Ivinskaya, who became his mistress, although he never divorced his wife, Zinaida. Ivinskaya, who would become the inspiration for Zhivago's lover, Lara, was arrested in 1949 and sent to the Gulag for five years. The couple were reunited after Stalin's death in 1953, when Ivinskaya took a dacha not far from Pasternak's in Peredelkino, so that she could work with him as his literary assistant. For the rest of his life Pasternak divided his time between his wife and her. With the lifting of the oppressive political climate after the death of Stalin in 1953, Pasternak decided to offer *Dr. Zhivago* for publication. But after it was turned down by the literary journal *New World (Novyi Mir)* in 1957, he gave permission for the Milanese Communist publisher Feltrinelli to go ahead with publication of the novel in Italian; translations into French, German, and English followed soon after. The publication brought the wrath of Soviet premier Nikita Khrushchev down on Pasternak and the whipping up of a widespread hate campaign among the masses of the Soviet nation, none of whom, of course, had even read the novel.

In October 1958 Pasternak was awarded the Nobel Prize for literature but reluctantly refused it. His position in Russia had become extremely difficult, and he feared that by leaving the country to collect the prize he would be forced into exile, not only from his native land but also from Ivinskaya. Despite his refusal and a letter to Khrushchev in which he asserted, "I am tied to Russia by birth, by life, and by work. I cannot imagine my fate separated from and outside Russia," the persecution continued and Pasternak was expelled from the Union of Soviet Writers as "a literary Judas who has betrayed his people for thirty pieces of silver." The stress aggravated his failing health (he had cancer and heart disease), and he died in May 1960, having spent the last two years of his life as a political and literary pariah under constant surveillance at Peredelkino. Pasternak's last collection of verse, *When the Weather Clears,* had been published in 1957; its tone of meditative melancholy and resignation clearly anticipated his own imminent death.

Some 2,000 people attended Pasternak's funeral at Peredelkino. His dacha became the Pasternak Museum in 1990, and his grave is still a place of pilgrimage. The huge international success of David Lean's 1965 film of *Dr. Zhivago* (despite being an emasculation of the original novel) and the esteem in which Pasternak was held internationally served only to make the Soviet authorities dig their heels in over the book's continuing suppression in the Soviet Union, although *samizdat* (underground) copies had been in circulation for years. The book was not published in Russia until 1987. Pasternak had made it clear before his death that he would "never lift a finger to bring back from oblivion three-fourths of what I have written" and that *Zhivago* was his "chief and most important work, the only one I am not ashamed of and for which I can answer with the utmost confidence."

See also Akhmatova, Anna; Mandelstam, Osip; Socialist Realism; Zhdanov, Andrey

Further reading: Christopher Barnes. *Boris Pasternak: A Literary Biography, Vol. I: 1890–1928, Vol. II, 1928–1960.* Cambridge: Cambridge University Press, 1989, 1999.

People's Commissariat of the Workers' and Peasants' Inspectorate

Known by its Russian acronym of Rabkrin, the commissariat was set up by Lenin in April 1919. With Stalin at its head, it was the official organ of state control of the Soviet bureaucracy until he had it abolished at the Seventeenth Party Congress in 1934 and assigned its functions to the Commission of State Control. It was Stalin himself who suggested the idea of the commissariat to Lenin after seeing at first hand, on a visit to the Urals, how the provincial civil service was still a stronghold of former tsarist bureaucrats and a prey to corruption and mismanagement.

The commissariat's primary function at its inception was, therefore, to monitor the everyday workings of the various departments of the central government and to eradicate inefficiency. This latter function was carried out by a "control-auditing commission" of inspection teams of peasants and workers, aided by the Special Department of the secret police, the Cheka (which dealt specifically with counterespionage and with security within the Red Army). As such, a job as mundane as running the commissariat seemed to have little appeal and Stalin had no competitors for the post. In any event, it was envisaged that the commissariat's role would evaporate with the spread of international revolution and the recognition of the voluntary accountability of every Soviet citizen to the democratic socialist state. But as this prospect receded, the commissariat grew in importance. With the Special Department reporting back to Stalin on a weekly basis, he was able to remove potential troublemakers and opponents from the government apparatus and to begin to consolidate his control, building a power base of his own apparatchiks; by 1920 Stalin already headed a bureaucratic machine numbering 100,000 officials.

Stalin relinquished his post at the commissariat when he achieved his goal of becoming general secretary of the Communist Party in 1922. In 1940 the function of the commissariat was incorporated into the People's Commissariat of State Security—the official euphemism for the Soviet secret police—which in 1946 became the Ministry of State Control.

See also Cheka; General Secretary of the Communist Party; *Nomenklatura*

Petrograd Soviet
See Russian Revolution of 1917.

Pilnyak, Boris Andreevich (1894–1938)

A Volga-German by ethnic descent, Boris Pilnyak (born Boris Andreevich Vogau) was one of the foremost writers of experimental fiction during the 1920s. His first major novel, *The Naked Year* (1922), was a stylistically vivid re-creation of the turbulent years of the revolution and civil war.

Pilnyak's literary acceptability and popularity on the strength of this novel and his early short stories was short-lived. His ideological loyalty was frequently called into question, and in 1926 he miscalculated badly and unnecessarily endangered his position by submitting the short story "The Tale of the Unextinguished Moon," which was suppressed before publication. Pilnyak based this story on rumors about the death on the operating table (with Stalin's supposed connivance) of Deputy Commissar for War Mikhail Frunze, in which he alluded to Stalin as "the unbending man of steel."

After being forced to publicly admit the "gross error" of "The Tale of the Unextinguished Moon," Pilnyak attempted to stay out of trouble by avoiding contemporary themes, but he further enraged authorities by allowing a Berlin publishing house to print his novel *Mahogany* in 1929 before its publication in the Soviet Union. The work was immediately denounced as anti-Soviet, and Pilnyak's position was protected from a hysterical campaign of vilification in the Soviet press only by the intercession of the eminent writer Maxim Gorky, who managed to defuse the situation. Pilnyak recanted again and then dutifully set about writing a conformist novel, *The Volga Falls to the Caspian Sea* (1931). In it he reworked material he had used for *Mahogany* about the construction of a dam in which, in an allegory of the successes of communism, he described the conquering of the forces of nature as but one of the triumphs of the Five-Year Plan. But by now Pilnyak's position was untenable. He was spiritually broken and sensed the machinery of the purges closing in on him.

In October 1937 Pilnyak was arrested at his dacha in the writer's colony at Peredelkino on charges of being a Japanese spy and a Trotskyist. Seven months later, after being held and interrogated in the Lubyanka, he was accorded the token formality of a fifteen-minute trial before being shot the following day, 21 April 1938. Immediately on his arrest, Pilnyak's works disappeared from the bookshelves, and his name was expunged from books on Soviet literature. Pilnyak was rehabilitated in 1956, but his works were not published again in the Soviet Union until 1976.

See also Gorky, Maxim
Further reading: Vitaly Shentalinsky. *The KGB's Literary Archive.* London: Harvill Press, 1995.

Place Names

U nder Communist rule, many towns, cities, and even mountain peaks of the Soviet Union were renamed to underline the rejection of names linked to the tsarist past. During Stalin's rule, what had seemed a legitimate (if costly, considering the disruption and expense incurred in doing so) recognition of Communist triumphs became part of the machinery of the cult of personality. Stalin's name was given to countless industrial plants, institutes, schools, factories, and even kindergartens, and his name would be incorporated into the names of towns and cities across the farthest reaches of the Soviet Union.

Barely a year after Lenin's death the southern city of Tsaritsyn, where Stalin had fought during the civil war, became Stalingrad, soon to be joined—in the Russian Republic—by Stalinogorsk and Stalinsk. Other republics dutifully followed suit, with Georgia creating a Staliniri, Tajikistan creating a Stalinabad, and Ukraine a Stalino. The two highest mountains in the Soviet Union, on the borders of Kyrgyzstan and Tajikistan, were also named Lenin and Stalin Peaks, and even Communist Bulgaria created its own Stalin Peak and Stalin Reservoir. In 1938, however, Stalin turned down suggestions that Moscow be renamed Stalinodar (literally "Stalin's Gift").

Despite Nikita Khrushchev's denunciation of Stalin in 1956, it was not until 1962, when Stalin's body was finally removed from the Lenin Mausoleum, that many of these places began to be given new Soviet names in yet another costly exercise. But the process slowed down after Khrushchev was removed from power in late 1964, when there was a distinct revival of Stalinism among the Soviet leadership, including annual attempts to rehabilitate him on his birthday. Some of these cities (which have gone through *three* changes of name in the course of the century) have since changed their names again since the collapse of the Soviet Union in 1991, reverting to their former, tsarist names.

A particular controversy is raging over the renaming of Volgograd, which was formerly Stalingrad (and before that Tsaritsyn). In the late 1990s, several Communist deputies in the Russian Duma proposed that the city should once again be called Stalingrad. One deputy insisted that "there were two Stalins. There was the one who killed and repressed and there was Stalin the supreme commander who won the war against fascism." This deputy, together with some of the 6,000 veterans still living in the city, venerate Stalin's wartime leadership, seeing the battle at Stalingrad as a symbol of Russian patriotism and heroic sacrifice. They feel strongly that Stalingrad was the city they fought for and that to call it Volgograd "makes no sense." But the younger generation, who have no nostalgia for the Stalinist past, see no point in reverting to the name Stalingrad, asking why they should name their city after someone who was, after all, not even a Russian, but a Georgian.

See also Cult of the Personality; Stalingrad

Politburo

The Politburo (in full, "political bureau") was for seventy-one years the supreme policymaking body of the Soviet Union, elected by members of the Central Committee of the Communist Party.

The precursor to the Politburo was the Bureau of the Central Committee, composed of Lenin, Lev Kamenev, Grigory Zinoviev, and Stalin. It was set up by the Bolsheviks in May 1917. After the revolution in October, the functions of the bureau were split between a seven-man Politburo, which included Lenin, Stalin, and Leon Trotsky and which dealt with matters of policy, and the Orgburo (organizational bureau), which supervised the organization and staffing of the Communist Party. The Politburo was reformed again in 1919 at the behest of the Eighth Party Congress, this time with a number of candidate members (varying from five to eight) who were subordinate to the five full members.

When Stalin became general secretary of the Communist Party in 1922, he achieved a major controlling influence in the Soviet government. The person who was Gensek (as the post was popularly known) was also automatically chairman of the Politburo. Stalin's dual roles involved considerable liaison between the two bodies and gave him a position of unrivaled authority after Lenin's death in 1924. And, as historian Robert Conquest has pointed out, of those members of the new Politburo elected in June 1924—Grigori Zinoviev, Lev Kamenev, Leon Trotsky, Nikolay Bukharin, Aleksey Rykov, Mikhail Tomsky, and Stalin—the latter would be responsible for the deaths of the other six.

By the early 1930s Stalin had an impressive range of support—across the Central Committee, the Politburo, and the Orgburo—that would rubber-stamp his every decision, including the initiation of the purges after the murder of Politburo luminary Sergey Kirov in 1934. The Politburo thus became the real nerve center of political authority in the Soviet Union and, together with the Communist Party, was effectively the seat of Soviet government, despite the existence of the official body, the Congress of Soviets (which after 1936 became the bicameral Supreme Soviet).

Although members of the Politburo were formally elected to their posts by the Central Committee of the Communist Party, the inner circle, who operated as Stalin's cabinet of ministers, always had the last word on who would or would not be admitted into their ranks. The Politburo also included some of the most powerful men in the country, such as the minister of defense and the head of the NKVD (later the KGB—the secret police). But as Stalin's rule became increasingly dictatorial, even the inner circle saw their influence eroded. In the final years of Stalin's life, the members of the Politburo found themselves increasingly relegated to the role of Stalin's drinking companions, their primary purpose being to keep him company through his long nights of insomnia at his dacha at Kuntsevo. Although the members of the Politburo were supposedly Stalin's most trusted friends and advisers, when he had his last, fatal collapse at his dacha, to a man they were far too terrified to take any decisive action in time to save his life.

By 1952 most of these men, Stalin's leading apparatchiks, had seen the writing on the wall. Stalin had, in fact, been preparing the ground to liquidate the last remnants of his former revolutionary colleagues in the Old Guard in one final spectacular show trial. In order to prepare for this purge he renamed the Politburo the Presidium, increasing its membership considerably. The old, tight-knit Politburo, made up of such political heavyweights as Georgy Malenkov and Anastas Mikoyan, now had to contend with an injection of new and younger political rivals, who, as Khrushchev later commented, seemed only too eager to supplant them. When both Malenkov and Mikoyan were excluded by Stalin from the new Bureau of the Presidium (the inner circle) it seemed clear to all that their arrest was inevitable. It was only Stalin's death soon after that saved them.

In 1966 President Leonid Brezhnev restored the name Politburo in a covert attempt at reviving the political legacy of Stalin.

See also General Secretary of the Communist Party; Orgburo

Further reading: John N. Hazard. *The Soviet System of Government*. Chicago: University of Chicago Press, 1980; Roy Medvedev. *All Stalin's Men*. Oxford: Basil Blackwell, 1983.

Poskrebyshev, Alexander N. (1891–1965)

When Stalin died in 1953 his loyal and long-suffering private secretary, Alexander Poskrebyshev, was awaiting what seemed his own imminent demise,

An elusive but key figure in Stalin's life was his personal secretary, Alexander Poskrebyshev. A dullard, capable of enduring the long working hours demanded of him, Poskrebyshev was rewarded for his devotion with dismissal in 1953.

having finally fallen from Stalin's favor the previous year. He had served Stalin unflinchingly for twenty-five years. Of the many compliant, self-effacing bureaucrats who surrounded Stalin, Poskrebyshev was the only person to whom Stalin became attached, nicknaming him with ironic affection "the chief." Toward the end of Stalin's life, theirs became a relationship of increasing dependency. This, however, did not prevent the sick and suspicious leader from finally turning on his private secretary. Everyone was expendable, and when rumors of Poskrebyshev's treachery were whispered in Stalin's ear by secret police chief Lavrenty Beria, he chose to believe that they were true.

Poskrebyshev was one of a considerable entourage that accompanied Stalin everywhere and was thus expected to work the same sixteen-hour days and to be there to waken Stalin after his brief periods of sleep. An uneducated, coarse man of boorish

habits, he was possessed of one great talent—a tremendous memory—which facilitated his ability to be at Stalin's beck and call, advise him on issues, and produce all the appropriate documents. He also had the ability to endure the abuse and practical jokes meted out to him by Stalin and members of the Politburo on their late-night binges at Stalin's dacha at Kuntsevo. Stalin could be physically cruel to his timid secretary. On one occasion he attached rolls of paper to his fingers and set light to them as "candles" during a New Year's party.

Poskrebyshev was the son of a humble boot maker and had originally started his working life as a medical orderly. His career in the Party, which he joined in 1917, began in 1922, when he was taken on as one of the Central Committee secretaries. By 1928 he was working closely with Stalin. His right-hand role as "Stalin's personal arms bearer" (as Nikita Khrushchev sarcastically referred to him) was confirmed when in 1933 he was given the highly sensitive post of head of the Special Sector of the Central Committee. This was the inner sanctum of the Communist Party, which operated as Stalin's own private secretariat or chancellery. It held sway over a network of subordinate Special Sectors in the Party and throughout the regional committees, which, among other things, was responsible for tapping the telephone lines of all senior Party figures. From this position Poskrebyshev was probably privy to those more contentious political acts of Stalin's for which documentary evidence has so far eluded historians—the assassinations of Sergey Kirov and Leon Trotsky and the "suicide" of Grigory Ordzhonikidze, for example. Poskrebyshev would also, by necessity, have played an important role in setting up the major show trials of the 1930s. On a more mundane, but to the suspicious Stalin, crucial level, it was the trusty Poskrebyshev who prepared Stalin's various medicines and made his tea and who often tasted his food for him in the leader's latter days

In 1934 Poskrebyshev was made a candidate member of the Central Committee; he became a full member in 1939. During the war Stalin also made him a major general. It was at this point that Poskrebyshev's loyalty was tested to the extreme. His wife, Bronislava, was arrested by Beria's men and accused of espionage; she was shot three years later. Stalin refused to intercede despite Poskrebyshev's desperate pleading on her behalf, telling Poskrebyshev that it was purely a matter for the NKVD (secret police) and that he (for some unfathomable reason) could not influence things.

In 1952 Beria, anxious to clear the ground for his own bid for Stalin's mantle, implicated Poskrebyshev in the Doctors' Plot and finally persuaded Stalin to get rid of him on the unsubstantiated grounds that he had "passed secret documents." By this time Stalin was intent anyway on destroying the last of his most loyal servants who knew too much about him. Poskrebyshev

was dismissed, no doubt counting himself lucky not to have been sent to the Gulag.

Poskrebyshev, the regular butt of Stalin's impatience and irascibility, had remained a nonentity in the background of whom few people took note. After Stalin's death he was rehabilitated and given a post in the Presidium of the Central Committee until his retirement. He kept no diary of his long service with Stalin. It was probably a wise decision, considering how dangerous and incriminating such a document could be in Stalinist Russia; he also did not write any valuable memoirs, the mark, no doubt, of an extraordinary and perversely loyal servant of Stalinism.

See also Doctors' Plot; Molotov, Vyacheslav; Stalin: Private Life of

Potsdam Conference

Two months after the Allies had taken Berlin and the war in Europe was over, Stalin made a triumphant progression by special, armored train to Potsdam, a suburb of Berlin, along a route closely monitored by thousands of secret police agents. The purpose of his journey was to attend the conference, held between 17 July and 2 August, that decided the treatment of postwar Germany and the terms of war reparations, as well as to discuss strategy for the continuing war with Japan.

The major players had changed since the Yalta Conference in February 1945. Stalin now met with the new U.S. president, Harry S. Truman, and the newly elected British prime minister, Clement Attlee (who had replaced Churchill midway through the conference). Stalin also found himself having to share the limelight with his charismatic minister for foreign affairs, Vyacheslav Molotov, who had proved himself as intractable as Stalin around the negotiating table. While the majority of the Soviet contingent, including Molotov, antagonized some of the British and Americans (in particular British Foreign Secretary Ernest Bevin, who could not get along with Molotov at all) with their bad behavior, Stalin continued to have the grudging respect of Churchill and now the guarded admiration of Truman, who commented in his diary of 17 July, "I can deal with Stalin. He is honest—but smart as hell." Later on, when he recognized his naive political idealism at Potsdam, Truman still admitted that he "liked the little son of a bitch."

Between 17 July and 2 August, a series of talks were held with a view to ensuring that Germany would never again threaten its neighbors or the peace of the world. By now there was also a subtext. With the former warm relations between the Allies at Yalta now rapidly becoming decidedly chilly, the Americans and British were anxious to contain Stalin's expansionist ambitions. However, the settlement of the new boundary between Poland and Germany along the Oder-Neisse line (which made a gift to Soviet influence of, among other things, the German industrial heartland of Silesia), served only to underline the Allies' tacit accession to the Soviet domination of Eastern Europe and to provide Stalin with the scope to establish another loyal Communist satellite—East Germany. The Baltic city of Königsberg, formerly part of East Prussia, was now ceded to the Soviet Union, and Poland was compensated for land taken by the Soviets in its eastern territories with German territory in the west, a deal that involved the resettlement in Germany of several million Germans from those areas. The four previously agreed occupation zones of Germany, including Berlin itself, were now ratified, with each of the Allies given the go-ahead to carry out a policy of de-Nazification and take its war reparations from the zone it occupied.

The final act of the talks in Potsdam was to issue an ultimatum for the unconditional surrender of Japan. At the talks, President Truman had hinted to Stalin about American capabilities for ending the war with Japan by the use of a nuclear device. Stalin had appeared to show little interest, a fact that led Allied observers to conclude that he did not have a clear understanding of the true import of the atomic bomb. At the end of the conference, a farewell banquet was held by the British for the delegates, at which a contingent of resplendently uniformed Soviet diplomats, with Stalin center stage in "the most fetching white cloth mess jacket blazing with insignia" according to Churchill's daughter Mary, stole the show from their drably suited Allies. As the party progressed, Stalin even went around collecting the autographs of his fellow negotiators, like the head boy at an end-of-term party. It was to be the final act of conviviality in his relationship with his wartime comrades. A few days later, after the Americans dropped the atomic bomb on Hiroshima, Stalin suddenly woke up to the full potential of nuclear weapons and ordered the immediate escalation of the Soviet nuclear research program. This decision set the scene for the ensuing Cold War.

See also Atomic Bomb; "The Big Three"; Cold War; Yalta Conference

Further reading: David McCullough. *Truman.* New York: Simon & Schuster, 1993; Richard Overy. *Russia's War: A History of the Soviet War Effort, 1941–45.* London: Allen Lane, 1998.

Pravda

This daily Soviet newspaper served between 1918 and 1991 as the official mouthpiece of the Communist Party. Its name, ironically, means "the truth," but this is something it rapidly lost sight of as a vehicle of Communist conformity. The truth it presented was a carefully manipulated version of the Party's indigestible version of facts; as a government worker sardonically remarked to the U.S. journalist Hedrick Smith, "Reading our press is like eating dry noodles—no flavor."

Pravda first began publishing in St. Petersburg on 22 April 1912 as an underground Bolshevik newspaper, and it featured an editorial statement by Stalin (alias Koba during a brief period on the run from exile). Surprisingly, it was funded by wealthy shipping magnate Viktor Tikhomirov, who like several other members of the old Russian intelligentsia had flirted with Marxism in its early incarnation. Even more bizarre is the fact that two members of *Pravda*'s editorial staff were also police agents—Miron Chernomazov and Roman Malinovsky; the latter, a close ally of Lenin, later became a member of the Central Committee of the Communist Party.

Pravda was regularly closed down by the tsarist authorities as an illegal publication, only to quickly reappear somewhere else under a slightly different title. Its circulation fluctuated between 20,000 and 40,000 until, on the eve of World War I, the government closed it down for the eighth time. The paper reappeared yet again in March 1917 and eventually established itself after the revolution with Stalin, Lev Kamenev, and M. K. Muranov taking over its editorship. With all other independent newspapers quickly swept away—only the government newspaper *Izvestiya* remained—*Pravda* became the supreme exponent of the art of presenting news that was devoid of facts. In 1929, in response to a public demand to know something about their leader on the occasion of his fiftieth birthday, *Pravda,* in a break with precedent, published a full-length portrait of Stalin as part of an article entitled "Stalin the Enigma." This leading article marked the inception of what would become known as the cult of the personality.

During the purges of the 1930s *Pravda* became the showpiece for hysterical denunciations of enemies of the state. It exhorted its readership that it was the "sacred duty of every Bolshevik" to defend the motherland against the enemy within. One of the paper's own erstwhile editors, Nikolay Bukharin, joined the ranks of the condemned in 1937. As the voice of the Communist Party, *Pravda* became a powerful propaganda tool, and during the Great Patriotic War it was used by Stalin to whip up national feeling, particularly after the German invasion of 1941. Now, for once, it actually became expedient to tell the truth, and the paper began carrying gruesome reports about German atrocities in order to galvanize the Soviet people into action.

Pravda's role came full circle when, in an editorial of 10 June 1953, it became the first official Soviet publication to associate Stalin, posthumously, with the term "cult of the personality," a cult that the paper itself had spent the previous twenty-four years promoting. By 1985 the circulation of *Pravda* had reached 10.5 million, but, in the growing atmosphere of glasnost and plummeting popular support for the Communist Party, its circulation dropped to an all-time low of 2 million by 1991. It had to reinvent itself in order to stay in existence by changing its overtly Communist logo and dropping the affiliation to the Communist Party on its masthead.

See also Cult of the Personality; Historiography
Further reading: Angus Roxburgh. *Pravda: Inside the Soviet News Machine.* London: Victor Gollancz, 1987.

Presidium
See Politburo.

Prisons

*T*he main prisons of Moscow and Leningrad where people were held, interrogated, and tortured during the Great Terror were the Shpalerny, Nizhnegorodsky, and Kresti prisons in Leningrad and the Butyrki, Lefortovo, and Lubyanka prisons in Moscow. The latter three took the bulk of the so-called political prisoners during the widespread purge of the Communist Party. Here, in one of the many bizarre anomalies of this barbaric period in Soviet history, great pains were taken to prevent acts of suicide, even by those who were daily being beaten and tortured close to death.

Overcrowding, appalling sanitation, and subsistence-level food rationing ensured that the life of prisoners was one of total misery. Prison life during the Great Terror was, in fact, no life at all. Ironically, it was much worse than that experienced by many political prisoners in tsarist times, when many of these prisons were built. Eyewitness accounts suggest, however, that conditions in the big-city prisons were still better than those found in some of the provincial prisons—those in Minsk, Vyatka, and Vologda, for example—and certainly better than in the Gulag itself. It was not uncommon for cells originally designed to hold around 25 people to have over 100 people crowded in them, literally like sardines, virtually unable to move. They were forced to impose their own rosters of whose turn it was to lie down and sleep.

A staple diet of black bread, thin cabbage soup, and occasional rations of barley or groats, combined with a lack of sunlight, fresh air, and basic personal hygiene ensured that prisoners quickly succumbed to such perennial diseases of malnutrition as scurvy, dysentery, and scabies. The regimen for those kept under interrogation in solitary confinement was far worse, since they lacked even the filthy conviviality of the noisy communal cells. While they had more space, prisoners were further tormented by silence and isolation and the constant watch through spy holes by the guards.

By far the most notorious prison, which has become synonymous with the brutalities of the Great Terror, by virtue probably of its more distinguished unwilling guests, was the Lubyanka, headquarters of the NKVD (secret police) in Moscow. In 1918 the Bolshevik secret police, known then as the Cheka, had moved its headquarters from St. Petersburg (at that time Petrograd) to Moscow, taking over the former premises of the Rossiya Insurance Company on Dzerzhinsky (now Lubyanskaya) Square, to which they added additional wings in the 1930s and after the war. The cells were actually former hotel rooms for employees of the insurance company and were, therefore, cleaner and more spacious than those in most other prisons.

During the Great Terror, it was to the 110 cells of the Lubyanka that the more important political and intellectual prisoners were taken to be interrogated and often shot in its grim cellars. The writer Nadezhda Mandelstam described how, at the height of the the Great Terror, the Lubyanka had the "atmosphere of a front-line hospital—screams, groans, broken bodies, stretchers." Some of its more famous inmates were writers Isaac Babel, Osip Mandelstam, Boris Pilnyak, and theater director Vsevolod Meyerhold. The Soviet historian Roy Medvedev estimated that between 1937 and 1938 it was not uncommon for 200 people to be executed every day at the Lubyanka. But it was apparently Lefortovo that people dreaded even more. It was here that those who "refused to sign" the obligatory confession were sent to be finally broken.

See also The Great Terror; Gulag; Torture
Further reading: Robert Conquest. *The Great Terror: A Reassessment.* London: Hutchinson, 1990; Nadezhda Mandelstam. *Hope Abandoned.* London: Harvill Press, 1974; Vitaly Shentalinsky. *The KGB's Literary Archive.* London: Harvill Press, 1995 (an account of the experiences of some prisoners sent to the Lubyanka); Alexander Solzhenitsyn. *The Gulag Archipelago,* 3 vols. London: Collins/Fontana, 1974, 1978.

Prokofiev, Sergey Sergeevich (1891–1953)

One of the Soviet Union's most gifted and innovative composers, Sergey Prokofiev, after having lived in exile since the 1917 Revolution, made the decision to return to his homeland in the early 1930s at a time many would have considered inopportune.

Prokofiev's musical talent had manifested itself at an early age. In 1904 he left his home in Ukraine at age thirteen to study at the St. Petersburg Conservatoire under Rimsky-Korsakov. In the capital he came under the influence of the Modernist movement in Russian art, poetry, and theater that dominated the arts before the revolution, and he became a leading composer of the Russian avant-garde. In 1918, Prokofiev left Russia to pursue his musical career with a tour abroad. He made the decision to stay in Europe, resolving to return to the Soviet Union only when the political climate had stabilized and would accommodate the artistic experimentation of his kind of music. In the United States he attracted considerable attention as the "Bolshevik pianist" and was a popular performer. He also continued to compose, premiering his opera *The Love of Three Oranges* in Chicago in 1921. In Paris, where he settled in 1923, he wrote music for Diaghilev's Ballets Russes, as well as several of his major symphonies and piano concertos.

During his years abroad, Prokofiev made occasional return tours to the Soviet Union, where his performances were enthusiastically received, a fact that always rekindled his desire to return to his Russian artistic and cultural roots. In his memoirs, composer Dmitry Shostakovich suggested that Prokofiev's decision to return in 1933 was more a pragmatic than an artistic one. He was in debt, and with the current vogue in Europe for new music from the Soviet Union, he hoped to recoup his finances. Prokofiev's return to the Soviet Union was something of a shock to the now thoroughly Westernized composer. In fact, he could not have chosen a worse time to go home, for Soviet arts were now being shackled to the rigid conventions of socialist realism. He later insisted that he had re-turned in order to rediscover his musical self, but this proved extremely difficult. While he produced some of his finest work back in the Soviet Union—the ballet *Romeo and Juliet* and *Peter and the Wolf* in 1936—by 1937 Prokofiev was also obliged to attempt more orthodox pieces of Soviet music, composing, for example, the *Cantata for the 20th Anniversary of the October Revolution* with its libretto based on unlikely texts from Marx, Lenin, and Stalin. During the war years, with his health in serious decline, Prokofiev nevertheless composed a suitably heroic piece to satisfy the authorities and raise morale during the national effort to drive the Germans out of Russia—an opera based on Tolstoy's *War and Peace* (1941–1947), which depicted the rout of Napoleon in 1812.

During the Great Patriotic War, Prokofiev also collaborated again with the director Sergey Eisenstein, for whom he had written a symphonic cantata to accompany Eisenstein's film *Alexander Nevsky* (1938), on the two-part film of *Ivan the Terrible* (1944, 1948). But like his musical contemporary Shostakovich, Prokofiev fell victim to the renewed climate of artistic oppression under Andrey Zhdanov in 1947, when both he and Shostakovich were accused of writing bourgeois music. Prokofiev had to go through the humiliating ritual of confessing his artistic errors in an open letter to the Union of Composers, after which he waited for the worst to happen. Instead, it was his former wife who was to become the sacrificial lamb. She was taken off to the Gulag, where she managed to outlive her former husband.

By the strangest of ironies, Prokofiev died only three hours before Stalin, on 5 March 1953, with a pile of musical scores still unfinished. His funeral had to be postponed because so many were killed in the stampede at Stalin's lying in state that a coffin was not available in all Moscow. In 1957 Prokofiev's Seventh Symphony was given a posthumous Lenin Prize.

See also Eisenstein, Sergey; The Great Patriotic War; Shostakovich, Dmitry; Socialist Realism

Further reading: David H. Aple, ed. *Prokofiev by Prokofiev: A Composer's Memoir.* New York: Doubleday, 1979; Harlow Robinson. *Sergei Prokofiev: A Biography.* London: Robert Hale, 1987.

Purges
See The Great Terror.

Pyatakov, Georgy Leonidovich (1890–1937)

A left-wing Communist, Georgy Pyatakov, despite distinguished and invaluable service as an economic expert during the Five-Year Plans, became one of the major defendants in the second great show trial of the purges in 1937.

Pyatakov joined the Russian Social Democrats as a student in St. Petersburg in 1910. After being expelled for his subversive activities, he went into exile until the revolution, aligning himself closely with Nikolay Bukharin on the left of the Communist Party. Lenin took note of Pyatakov's political skills, remarking that he was "undoubtedly a person of outstanding strength of purpose and abilities" and earmarking him as one of the six key figures in the Party. During the civil war, Pyatakov was sent to his home territory in Ukraine to take charge of the Kiev Soviet. By 1923 he had become a key administrator of economic policy and a full member of the Central Committee of the Communist Party. However, his continued support of the left of the Party led to his expulsion in 1927 for aligning himself with Leon Trotsky in opposition to Stalin.

Stalin allowed Pyatakov back into the political fold in 1929 after Trotsky's expulsion from the Soviet Union and after Pyatakov had formally recanted. It was an act of expediency rather than one of conciliation.

Stalin needed Pyatakov's expertise in economic affairs during the implementation of his industrialization program and put him in control of the State Bank and the Soviet Union's chemical industry until such time as he had served his purpose. Pyatakov took an equally pragmatic attitude to his situation, fulfilling the duties required of him by Stalin while admitting privately to the hollowness of his loyalty: "For the Party's sake you can and must at 24 hours' notice change all your convictions and force yourself to believe that white is black."

In September 1936 Pyatakov (despite Sergo Ordzhonikidze's attempt as people's commissar for heavy industry to protect him as a much-valued deputy) was arrested along with Karl Radek. He finally capitulated after thirty-three days of interrogation, during which he confessed to being a Trotskyist and to having plotted against the Soviet Union with Germany and agreed to deliver a carefully scripted and rehearsed denunciation of Trotsky at his trial in January 1937. He also confessed to involvement in deliberate acts of industrial wrecking and sabotage, as well as fueling the growing number of denunciations against his former friend and colleague, Nikolay Bukharin. Such total capitulation was won on the promise that his life would be spared. In his own final defense at the end of the trial, Pyatakov described his abject humiliation: "Here I stand before you in filth, crushed by my own crimes, bereft of everything through my own fault, a man who has lost his Party, who has no friends, who has lost his family, who has lost his very self." Pyatakov was shot soon after his trial. It was not until 1988 that he was finally rehabilitated.

See also Bukharin, Nikolay; Ordzhonikidze, Sergo; Radek, Karl

Further reading: Robert Conquest. *The Great Terror: A Reassessment.* London: Pimlico, 1992; Robert C. Tucker. *Stalin in Power: The Revolution from Above, 1928–41.* London: Chatto and Windus, 1990.

Radek, Karl Berngardovich (1885–1939)

Born in the Austro-Hungarian Empire at Lodz, Galicia, Karl Radek (originally Sobelsohn) was a Polish Jew and old-school romantic revolutionary. He pursued a colorful early career as a professional agitator and political gadfly around Europe, seeking to promote worldwide revolution before returning to Russia as a supporter of Leon Trotsky. Together with Trotsky and Lev Kamenev he was one of several prominent Jews in the early days of Soviet government, where his talents were primarily utilized as a brilliant political writer and polemicist. In a savage twist of fate he would later find himself forced to use these talents in the scripting of his own trial for treason during the Great Terror.

Radek took an antimilitarist position during World War I, when he leafleted German troops urging them to stop fighting the Russians and join the cause of world revolution. He joined the Bolsheviks in 1917 and traveled to Russia from Germany on the famous sealed train that brought Lenin and his entourage to Petrograd's Finland Station after the revolution. He tried to get Bolshevik support for a revolutionary war against the German state and was against the negotiation of a peace settle-

ment with Germany to end World War I, convinced that the revolutionary impetus should be maintained and that most of Europe would soon be Communist—by spring of 1919, or so he hoped.

Lacking the charisma of either Lenin or Trotsky as a major political personality, Radek, "a little light-haired spectacled revolutionary goblin of incredible intelligence and vivacity" (as writer Arthur Ransome described him) had operated primarily as an activist for the German Social Democrats before World War I. By 1919, convinced that Germany too was now ripe for revolution, Radek returned there, where he took up undercover work as a Bolshevik secret agent based in Berlin. Here, he harangued the German left relentlessly for the next four years to take up the cause of socialist revolution, taking part in the Spartakist rising of German Communists led by Rosa Luxemburg in 1919, as well as other revolutionary activities.

Returning to Russia in 1922, Radek assumed the secretaryship of the Comintern, to which he had been elected while in prison in Germany, and pursued a successful journalistic career. But with the ascendancy of Stalin, he soon came to grief due to his continuing support for Trotsky and his theory of worldwide revolution. He was expelled from the Communist Party in 1927 and a year later exiled to Tomsk in

Siberia. At this point Radek began a concerted campaign of ingratiation with Stalin that would lose him the respect of his political colleagues, if not earn him their outright hatred. For he proved to be a cynical and astute master of Stalinist intrigue and turned political recantation into an art form. Giving Stalin what he wanted would become second nature to Radek, no matter how reprehensible his behavior might seem in the light of his past political idealism.

Having recanted his Trotskyist connections, Radek was allowed to return from exile in 1929. Now that he was politically sidelined, Radek adapted his considerable journalistic skills to the vast industry of Stalinist eulogy, where before he had praised Trotsky. In 1934 he wrote a tongue-in-cheek paean to Stalin entitled "The Architect of Soviet Society," which appeared across a two-page spread in the 1934 New Year's Day issue of *Pravda*. The article, written to serve the purposes of the cult of the personality, spoke of how "the waves of love, and of our people's trust lap against the serene, rocklike figure of our leader." There was such a demand for copies of the issue that it was brought out as a pamphlet and sold 225,000 copies. Meantime, Radek was privately developing a reputation as "the best fabricator of anti-Soviet jokes," according to the composer Dmitry Shostakovich. A typical example of his talents was the quip that "Moses led the Jews out of Egypt. Stalin led them out of the Politburo," a reference to Stalin's expulsion from power of Jewish Bolsheviks, condemned as members of the Trotskyist opposition.

By the time Stalin called upon Radek to work with Nikolay Bukharin on the drafting of the new Soviet Constitution in 1935–1936, Radek hoped that he had finally succeeded in winning Stalin's favor. But the allegations of continuing support for Trotsky in exile revived in 1936, and he was expelled from the Communist Party. A moral and physical coward, he now had no compunction about damning Trotsky in a trenchant attack in *Izvestiya* at the time of the first show trial in August of that year, but it did not save him. Radek was arrested in September, accused of organizing a Trotskyist center, and put on trial in January 1937.

It was now that Radek turned in the performance of his life with his courtroom "confession" and in the process of its public recitation betrayed many of his old friends and colleagues, including Bukharin. It was a piece of theatrical bravado in which he totally dominated his prosecutor, Andrey Vyshinsky. But the performance, while probably saving him from the death penalty, did not spare Radek from being sentenced to ten years' hard labor. It was originally thought that he had been released from the Gulag in 1941, only to disappear into obscurity, but it is now known that Radek died in a labor camp in 1938. He was, by all accounts, murdered by another inmate, who had been given the specific mission (by persons unknown) of exacting revenge on Radek for his acts of betrayal.

See also Bukharin, Nikolay; The Great Terror; Zinoviev, Grigory

Further reading: David J. Dallin. "The Piatakov-Radek Trial." In *From Purge to Coexistence: Essays on Stalin's and Khrushchev's Russia.* Chicago: University of Chicago Press, 1964; Warren Lerner. *Karl Radek: The Last Internationalist.* Stanford, CA: Stanford University Press, 1970.

Red Army

*I*n the post–World War II euphoria after the defeat of the Wehrmacht, its expulsion from Soviet soil by the Red Army, and its subsequent rout across Eastern Europe all the way back to Berlin, much praise was heaped on the Soviet Union's indomitable fighting forces. Yet only three years before the onslaught of war the Soviet armed forces had suffered a terrible purge of their officer class, as a result of which 43,000 Red Army and Navy officers had been shot

A group of leading Red Army officers circa 1935, featuring (center) Klimenty Voroshilov and the swashbuckling figure to his right (outdoing him with handlebar mustache) of Semen Budenny, leader of the legendary Red Cavalry.

or sent to the Gulag. Thus, at a time when the country could least afford it, the Red Army's leadership had lost the cream of its experienced general staff. This fact, coupled with a shortage of modern military hardware and a lack of sophistication in military strategy, made the achievements of the Soviet fighting machine during the Great Patriotic War seem all the more extraordinary. For it was a machine that had been converted by the Bolsheviks from a mismatched rabble of fighters barely twenty-five years earlier.

After the collapse of the Russian imperial army during World War I, closely followed by the Revolution of 1917, the Russian army was in disarray. Many of its conscripted soldiers, exhausted and disillusioned by the debacle of the war, had deserted in droves or taken themselves back home to their villages during the process of demobilization. The original intention of the Bolsheviks, in any event, had been to abolish the old tsarist standing army and

raise an entirely voluntary force of people's militias, devoid of the trappings of rank, insignia, and precedence and true to Marxist ideology as "military detachments of the world revolution." As a result, workers' battalions had been set up soon after the Revolution of 1917, many of their troops recruited from the factories of Petrograd and Moscow.

The Red Army came into existence by a decree proclaimed on 23 February 1918, during the course of the civil war of 1918–1920. At that time the Bolsheviks had set up a defense council under the leadership of Leon Trotsky to coordinate the mobilization of the worker and peasant battalions into a fighting force able to deal with the many factions opposing the Bolsheviks, in particular the Whites. Subsequent Stalinist historiography would do its utmost to remove all mention of Trotsky's name in connection with the founding of the Red Army, but his contribution during these early days was vital.

The ideal of a volunteer proletarian army led by elected commanders soon proved ineffective. In the two months following the February decree, the Bolsheviks had managed to enlist only 106,000 men. They were soon compelled to introduce the compulsory conscription of peasants and workers, as well as to institute a system of general military training to deal with the additional 350,000 that this new intake provided. By the spring of 1919 the Red Army had 3 million troops (although during a period of demobilization during the 1920s its numbers dropped to 562,000). By 1934 the social composition of the remnants of the former tsarist army had changed quite dramatically. The Red Army had now become fairly evenly balanced between 42.5 percent peasants and 45.8 percent workers.

Despite their general lack of support for the new Bolshevik regime, Trotsky had had no qualms about making use of the tsarist officer class in the new Red Army, redefining their role as that of "military specialists." Others in the Bolshevik leadership, Lenin and Stalin among them, had questioned the loyalty of such officers, whom they looked upon as class enemies. But without them— they numbered as many as 40,000—Trotsky argued that the Red Army would be rudderless and inoperative. As a counter to this, the newly formed divisions would have loyal Communist commissars attached to them, who would monitor the conduct of both troops and officers, always on the watch for acts of counterrevolution, and who would ensure that the intensive political indoctrination of the troops was sustained. In addition, no command issued by an officer could be enforced without the endorsement of a political commissar. Nevertheless, Trotsky, bent on achieving what seemed the impossible task of uniting so many disparate elements into an efficient army under centralized command, had a hard struggle imposing his will over many revolutionaries in the ranks of the Red Army who refused to subordinate themselves to former tsarist officers.

The Bolshevik dream of an egalitarian military force finally evaporated during the social upheavals that took place in Stalinist Russia in the wake of the First Five-Year Plan of 1928–1932. Stalin introduced a major reform of the Red Army in 1936. He was anxious that the Soviet Union should demonstrate its military muscle in tandem with its new ascendancy as a major industrial power, and to do so he reorganized the army as a standing force possessed of all the normal paraphernalia of rank, precedence, and discipline. In every respect these changes were a reversal of the original Bolshevik ideals of a fighting army guided by the spirit of internationalism and proletarian class consciousness. The emphasis was now on a return to the familiar old tsarist standbys of nationalism and patriotism. The public was exhorted by the newspaper *Izvestiya* in 1941 that "the strength of the Red Army lies not only in its numbers, or in its mighty technique, but in the fact that [it] is flesh from the people's flesh, blood from the people's blood."

The rank of marshal was introduced into the Soviet military, and the first five marshals of the Soviet Union were appointed in 1936—Vasily Blyucher, Semen Budenny, Andrey Egorov, Mikhail Tukhachevsky, and Klimenty Voroshilov (of these five, two would later be demoted for their hopeless incompetence during the war; the other three would be shot during the purges). By the outbreak of war sixteen military academies had also been established across the Soviet Union, including the prestigious Frunze Military Academy and the Dzerzhinsky Artillery Academy, specifically to train a new military elite.

The heroic, monolithic image of the new Red Army was also further promoted through its depiction in Soviet art as the latter-day incarnation of the Russian fighting spirit. Vast canvases, such as *The Storming of Perekop,* illustrating the defining military moments in Soviet history were embarked upon, often by teams of several artists. *The*

Storming of Perekop depicted an engagement during the civil war for which the Red Army itself was called upon to restage tableaux from the battle in order to serve as a model for the collective of artists who created the painting between 1934 and 1938. On the occasion of its twentieth jubilee in 1938 a major exhibition about the Red Army was staged (at which Stalin made a rare public appearance).

In 1937–1938, just when the army was establishing its reputation at home and abroad, the cream of its officer class was systematically decimated by Stalin who, fearing the nebulous possibility of a potential Red Army "fifth column" led by officers in time of war, ordered their mass arrest, execution, or deportation. Of its 142,000 commanders, the army lost at least 28,000. While the psychological motives for such a devastating bloodletting of the armed forces remain baffling, particularly in light of the onslaught of war four years later, there is now considerable revisionist debate over its ultimate impact on events during the early days of the war, at a time when combat losses were far higher and when the Red Army was still not an effective fighting force. Be that as it may, the purge was yet another tragic manifestation of Stalin's compulsion to rid himself of any potential enemies and to preempt any possible challenge to his control, not only of society at large, but of all facets of the machinery of state.

The nine major accused from the Soviet high command who were summarily tried and executed in June 1937 were all generals in their physical prime and experienced campaigners, including the recently promoted Marshal Tukhachevsky, one of the great modernizing forces in the Soviet army and, by general consensus, one of its finest military minds. They were charged with taking part in an alleged German plot to oust Stalin from power. All the accused were broken under torture to admit their complicity in the alleged plot, were tried in closed session—in Tukhachevsky's case by two of his fellow marshals, Blyucher and Budenny—and were shot the following day. This trial was followed by a further roundup of 980 lower-ranking officers and political commissars, who in turn incriminated others in nonexistent conspiracies, again under the duress of torture. According to historian Robert Conquest, the Red Army was to eventually lose 3 of 5 marshals, 15 of 16 commanders, 60 of 67 corps commanders, 136 of 169 divisional commanders, and 221 of 397 brigade commanders, contributing to a total loss of 36,761 army officers prior to the outbreak of war. In this manner the higher echelons of the Red Army were seriously depleted, and with the German invasion in 1941, their replacements had to be quickly found from a pool of (in the main) intellectually inferior and militarily inexperienced juniors who were abruptly raised through the ranks. As Conquest pointed out, in October 1941 battalions fighting the Germans in the front lines were under the command of lieutenants, while 300 experienced officers languished in the Lubyanka jail in Moscow.

A second purge of the Red Army was the inevitable response by Stalin to the debacle of the German invasion in June 1941. Several generals were dismissed for incompetence, to be replaced by such men as Ivan Konev, Georgy Zhukov, Semen Timoshenko (who had replaced the hopeless Voroshilov after the debacle of the Winter War against Finland of 1939–1940), and Konstantin Rokossovsky. The latter was released from the Gulag and rehabilitated for this purpose and proved to be one of the most gritty and charismatic commanders of the war years. But several officers, twelve of them from the western front, where resistance to the German invasion had collapsed in the face of the Wehrmacht onslaught, were made to pay the price of the German invasion and were shot. (The officer corps of the Red Air Force, the bulk of whose planes had been destroyed on the ground by Luftwaffe bombers, also bore the brunt of reprisals. The Red Navy, too, had been purged of all but one of its admirals in 1937.) Tragically, such was the fear of retribution engendered at this time that a further twenty generals committed suicide rather than face trial.

A desperate scramble to reorganize and regroup took place in the Red Army in the months following the German invasion. The army had already learned some bitter lessons from the Winter War with Finland and instituted new codes of discipline, as well as specialized training regimens, to take account of the particular difficulties of fighting in winter conditions. Georgy Zhukov referred to this process as "the year of the great transformation." In 1940 the ranks of major-general, lieutenant-general, and army general were introduced into the army (and corresponding ranks into the navy). Three hundred sixty Soviet officers, many of whom had yet to acquire any real military track record, were elevated to the rank of general. For days on end *Pravda* published great lists of the newly promoted officers.

Gaudy new military orders and decorations, named after historical military heroes, were also introduced. Stalin reviewed the military achievements of Peter the Great and readopted his army regulations and introduced guards regiments and divisions. In 1940 epaulettes and gold braid (imported from England in huge quantities—the British saw this as "absurdly frivolous" in time of war) could once again be worn by officers. In a particularly undemocratic move that echoed the old days of Russian imperialist privilege, officers' messes were established. The Red Army that now emerged was most definitely no longer a revolutionary army of proletarians. A network of nine elite Suvorov Schools for military cadets further ensured that the Red Army's future officers were taught English, fine manners, and old-time ballroom dances (the waltz, the mazurka, the pas de quatre, to name some). And there, leading the vanguard of this legendary fighting force, resplendent in his uniform and military decorations, was the figure of Joseph Stalin—Red Army Marshal, Commander-in-Chief of the Soviet military, Minister of Defense, Chairman of the Supreme War Council (the Stavka), and, in 1945, as his own answer to Germany's Führer, Generalissimo of the Soviet Union.

The Great Patriotic War also witnessed the rapid and necessary modernization of the Red Army's hardware and its acquisition of modern tanks, fighters, and weapons. Much of the modernization in military strategy was in accordance with the theories on combined operations warfare and deep battle that had been vigorously promoted in the 1930s by the murdered marshal, Mikhail Tukhachevsky. By the spring of 1942 a complete overhaul of the organization and technical hardware of the Red Army was in progress, with the emphasis on improving communications and deploying heavy artillery, antiaircraft guns, and, most important, the establishment of motorized divisions of tanks to rival the Panzers of the Wehrmacht. By the time the tide of war had been turned at Stalingrad in the winter of 1942–1943, Stalin had learned to decentralize command, to listen to his senior commanding officers, and to take their advice on matters of strategy and tactics, even to the point of allowing open argument.

The Soviet officer corps was on the ascendant by the end of the war. Many of its leading officers had received awards, honors, even honorary titles and knighthoods from the Allies. Stalin himself was presented with the sword of Stalingrad by Churchill at the Potsdam Conference in December 1943. Hero worship of Zhukov, who had joined the Red Army as a volunteer in 1918 and had led the defense of Stalingrad and Moscow, reached unprecedented heights, and he became the object of his own minicult. But once the celebrations were over, Stalin reversed his wartime policy and began to deflect public attention away from the Red Army as the focal point of national striving back to the tight, centralized leadership of the Communist Party.

When the Wehrmacht invaded the Soviet Union in 1941, Hitler had based his Operation Barbarossa on an assumption that the Red Army would capitulate within six weeks. But as early as July of that year, the German press had reported on the "animal obduracy" and "primordial persistence" of the Red Army, stating that its soldiers were "fighting like madmen, to the point of absolute exhaustion." The Germans were soon forced to concede that this would be a long and difficult campaign. "They do not surrender," reported the German newspaper *Voelkischer Beobachter* (National Observer), "Any effort to weaken the spirit of this adversary by methods previously employed in the West would be in vain." Such a reputation served after the war to underpin the growing awareness throughout the world that the Red Army was a force to be taken on at one's peril.

See also Blyukher, Marshal Vasily; Budenny, Marshal Semen; Great Patriotic War; Rokossovsky, Marshal Konstantin; Voroshilov, Klimenty; Zhukov, Georgy

Further reading: Anthony Beevor. *Stalingrad.* London: Viking, 1998; Robert Conquest. *The Great Terror: A Reassessment.* London: Pimlico, 1992; Brian Moynahan. *The Claws of the Bear: A History of the Soviet Armed Forces from 1917 to the Present.* London: Hutchinson, 1989; Richard Overy. *Russia's War: A History of the Soviet War Effort 1941–45.* London: Allen Lane, 1998; Harold Shukman, ed. *Stalin's Generals.* London: Phoenix, 1997; Alexander Werth. *Russia at War 1941–1945.* London: Pan Books, 1964.

Religion

In 1843, Karl Marx made his classic pronouncement that "religion . . . is the opium of the people." The narcotic power of religion was recognized by the Bolsheviks after the revolution, when they sought to supplant religious faith with a new religion—atheistic nationalism—making this, and not the Russian Orthodox Church, the focal point for collective aspirations.

One of the first acts of the new government was to officially separate church and state by a decree of 23 January 1918. After the civil war came to an end, the Bolsheviks inaugurated a vigorous propaganda campaign intended to eradicate religious practice of every kind. Religious persecution based on such racial hatred as the anti-Semitism that had been endemic under the tsars was also encouraged. The primary target for suppression, however, was Russian Orthodoxy, the traditional spiritual crutch of the Russian peasantry and the symbol of the old and despised tsarist past.

The Russian Orthodox Church came under concerted attack from 1928 with the large-scale confiscation of its priceless icons and church ornaments, as well as anything else of value. Church bells had their clappers removed or were melted down for use in heavy industry. Icons were stripped of their precious gold and silver cladding. The silencing of the bells in Russia, a place once known as "the country of churches," and of great historical religious centers such as Rostov suggested to many simple peasants that the end of the world had come. Many ancient and historic churches and monasteries were vandalized; they were either blown up or appropriated as warehouses or cinemas or, in a cruel insult to believers, turned into museums of atheism. The policy of repression reached its zenith under Stalin. The churches of St. Paraskevi and Christ the Savior in Moscow and the Trinity Cathedral in St. Petersburg were among many that were demolished on his orders to make way for new Soviet building developments.

As early as 1918, monasteries, nunneries, and other religious establishments, with their often isolated locations and well-fortified buildings—refuges such as the Andronnikov, Novospassky, Ivanovsky, and Torzhok monasteries—were singled out as the ideal premises for the concentration camps being

A familiar scene during the late 1920s with the wholesale rejection of the old Russian Orthodox way of life. Thousands of ancient Russian churches were looted, vandalized, converted to museums and warehouses, or simply blown up.

set up by the secret police, the Cheka, for the incarceration of political, social, and religious undesirables. Perhaps the most infamous was the fifteenth-century monastery on the Solovets Islands, part of which had been used as a prison by the tsars. When it was looted by the Cheka and turned into a prison camp in 1923, many of the Solovets camp's first inmates were the very same monks and priests who had previously inhabited it. In this way, many Russian religious establishments were assimilated into the vast network of the Gulag.

In 1925 elections of patriarchs of the Russian Orthodox Church were banned, and in 1927 the nominated head of the church, Metropolitan Sergius, was forced to compromise himself and the church by endorsing its allegiance to the Soviet government. It was a last, desperate act to save the church from further repressions, an act that precipitated a rift with its émigré branches in the United States and Europe. Unfortunately, this had little effect in stopping continuing restrictions. In 1929 new legislation outlawed religious worship except in certain registered congregations, and public religious activities (such as preaching, proselytizing, and religious funeral processions) were banned.

The mass destruction and closure of churches gathered pace during the 1930s, as did the bombardment of the Soviet people with antireligious propaganda through the offices of thought police such as the League of the Godless (the *bezbozhniki*). By 1939 as few as 100 churches remained open, and by the end of the Great Terror only 12 out of 163 bishops were still alive. Yet despite the official suppression of places of worship, nothing, it seemed, could dim the strong, almost superstitious regard for the religion of the tsars among the nation at large. An official census taken in 1937 (which was later aborted and its records long hidden in the archives) revealed that 57 percent of the population still admitted to religious beliefs of one kind or another. Those who wished to continue practicing their faith did so in private or went underground, only to overcrowd the few churches that were allowed to hold services at Christmas and Easter. In the countryside, in particular, religious faith was never completely suppressed, with many religious festivals and saints' days still covertly observed and the elderly passing on their religious beliefs orally to the younger generation. Many of the Soviet youth who inherited this oral tradition adopted a pragmatic attitude, one of religious belief tailored to expediency. Locally held religious holidays, after all, provided a brief respite from work on the collective farm.

Stalin—himself a former seminarist who had long understood the emotive power of religion—shrewdly tapped into the deep-seated Orthodoxy of the Russian people (a fact recently highlighted by the huge resurgence in the church since the collapse of communism) and used it as a focus for galvanizing nationalistic fervor in defense of Mother Russia during the Great Patriotic War (as World War II became known to Russians). He allowed some relaxation of rules on religious observance, several seminaries and churches were allowed to reopen, and Metropolitan Sergius was officially elected patriarch in 1943. In an unprecedented step, Stalin received Sergius at the Kremlin, on which occasion Sergius begged Stalin for more seminaries to be opened to train priests. When Stalin asked him why, the old man wryly replied, in a direct allusion to Stalin's past: "We lack personnel for several reasons, one of which is that we train a man to be a priest, but he becomes a Marshal of the Soviet Union." For a while Russian Orthodoxy appeared to be recovering. Sergius was succeeded by Alexis in 1945, and by the end of the war as many as 25,000 churches were once again holding services. Men were being allowed back into seminaries to study for the priesthood, and there were as many as 33,000 priests to officiate at religious services.

Elsewhere in the republics of the Soviet

Two young Soviets avidly read a copy of the publication "The Godless One," which from 1929 onward promoted the activities of vigorous young atheists recruited to drive out the last vestiges of religious practice among the Russian population.

Union similar patterns emerged. Both the Georgian Orthodox Church and the Armenian Orthodox Church endured repressions and the widespread destruction and closure of their churches during the 1930s, to enjoy a brief respite during the war. Of the non-Christian religions, the numbers of practicing Buddhists in the Soviet Far East declined dramatically under Stalin. Many Buddhist priests (as well as Muslim imams) in the Far East fell victim to absurd charges of sedition and espionage as agents of the Japanese during the hysteria of the Great Terror. Unlike Christian groups, however, the large Muslim populations of central Asia proved more difficult to suppress, a fact that had originally prompted a tolerant approach under Lenin. Islam had come under antireligious propaganda attack from the late 1920s. Its mosques, schools, and hospitals were closed down and its sharia law courts suppressed, while a propaganda campaign was launched against Islamic customs, such as ritual fasting at Ramadan and the veiling of women. However, diplomatic expediencies later made it important for Stalin to relax the oppression of Muslims in order not to endanger Soviet relations with its Islamic neighbors and potential allies.

In the early days after the revolution, other sectarian groups such as the Baptists (one of the most vigorous groups, of whom there were 500,000 by 1927) and Evangelical Christians (who numbered as many as 4 million by the same date), who had been persecuted under the tsars, were viewed as victims of social repression and were therefore briefly tolerated. For them, at least, conditions actually improved. Baptists in particular seemed more flexible and able to adapt to changing restrictions on practice. But the legislation of 1929 severely curtailed the proselytizing activities of all these groups. Many religious sectarians, such as Jehovah's Witnesses, were sent to the Gulag during the Great Terror. Other fringe sects, such as the Old Believers, went underground or hid in the forests of remote regions. During the

war years, like the Orthodox Church, the Baptist and Evangelical groups also enjoyed a revival, particularly in the new industrial cities in Ukraine and Siberia. In 1944 the Baptists and Evangelical Christians were merged as an All-Union Council of Evangelical Christians–Baptists, after which they suffered a decline in numbers. After the war, what was left of the small community of Mennonites in the Soviet Union was dissolved and its members scattered.

Religious groups elsewhere in the Soviet Union were also targeted for repression and persecution in the Stalinist drive against religion. The Roman Catholics in Lithuania, the Lutherans of Estonia and Latvia, and the Lutheran ethnic German community within the Soviet Union all suffered. In Ukraine, where Stalin was determined to bring recalcitrant nationalist elements into line after the war, the Uniate or Eastern Catholics (who recognize the supremacy of the pope) were forced to unite with the Russian Orthodox Church in 1946.

See also Baltic States; Gulag; Jews; Nationalities; Palace of the Soviets
Further reading: Geoffrey Hosking. *A History of the Soviet Union 1917–1991.* London: Fontana Press, 1992; W. Kolarz. *Religion in the Soviet Union.* London: Macmillan, 1961; Dmitry Pospielovsky. *The Russian Church under the Soviet Regime 1917–1982.* Crestwood, NY: St. Vladimir's Seminary Press, 1984.

Repatriations
See NKVD; Yalta Conference.

"Revolution from Above"

*I*n Leninist politics the concept of proletarian revolution, far from relying on an initial spontaneous overthrow of government by the people from below, was grounded in the essential role to be played by a professional elite of revolutionaries who would mastermind revolt from above.

But the degree of that control from above, while originally limited in Lenin's mind to the elimination of those opponents of the revolutionary process, gradually and inexorably evolved, once he was in power, into the wholesale imposition of Bolshevik policies, if necessary by force.

This, the concept of "revolution from above" was developed further by Stalin in 1928, after he had rid himself of his major political opponents on the left—Leon Trotsky, Lev Kamenev, and Grigory Zinoviev. The term was now applied to Stalin's institution of the far-reaching and potentially unpopular processes of industrialization and collectivization on a population that was not yet ready, either socially or economically, for such draconian change. The manifestation of this policy was the introduction of the first of the Five-Year Plans. Enforced collectivization began the following year in 1929. Stalin's opponents on the right, such as Nikolay Bukharin, had argued that the peasantry should be broken in gradually to the idea. The will to collectivize should therefore come primarily from below, but Stalin went ahead with the process in the face of bitter resistance from most of the peasantry.

The definitive work of Soviet historiography, *The History of the All-Union Communist Party: Short Course,* written on Stalin's instructions and published in 1938, set the formula in stone when it singled out the distinguishing feature of collectivization as being "accomplished from above, on the initiative of the state, and directly supported from below, by the millions of peasants, who were fighting to throw off kulak bondage and to live in freedom in the collective farms." Thus, Stalin's historiographers underlined that the economic "revolution from above" was also effectively a class war against the kulaks, those marginally richer peasants who had the most to lose, and in doing so they found a way of motivating many of the poorer peasants to support the policy.

Once initiated by Stalin, the notion of imposed change from above allowed no recourse to popular opinion, although this is not to say that workers did not complain. They did complain bitterly in numerous factory and works meetings and in often anonymous letters to their local branch of the Party. And as the 1930s wore on, workers became more and more convinced that the authorities were riding roughshod over their interests, as the physical demands made on them by Stalin's command economy began to bite. Revolution from above became the lynchpin for state control over all walks of life, including even the arts, with the imposition of socialist realism. In the postwar years it permeated across the satellite states in Eastern Europe, which succumbed one by one to Soviet-style government and methods of social control—if need be, enforced by the presence of Soviet troops.

As historian Robert C. Tucker has argued, the revival under Stalin of a traditional style of tsarist state-building, as imposed in the seventeenth century by Peter the Great (who also happened to be one of Stalin's favorite historical figures), also brought with it the revival of the old familiar practices of repression and subjugation and the development of a state supported by a vast bureaucracy. The end result of Stalin's "revolution from above" was his own self-promotion as a latter-day autocratic Communist "tsar" and the indoctrination of the nation under his cult of the personality. For a people conditioned by centuries of subservience to the tsars—and who had believed in some kind of mystical union between them and their ruler—it is not difficult to comprehend how Stalin came to rule over the Soviet Union as though it was his own personal patrimony. But in order to sustain this position he was obliged to create a means of efficiently ridding himself of opponents and "enemies of the state" and to find the quiescent servants to undertake this through a series of social and political purges during the second half of the 1930s.

See also Bukharin, Nikolay; Collectivization; Five-Year Plans; The Great Terror; Historiography; *History of the All-Union Communist Party: Short Course;* Lenin, Vladimir

Further reading: Geoffrey Hosking. *A History of the Soviet Union, 1917–1991,* chapter 6. London: Fontana Press, 1992; Robert C. Tucker. *Stalin in Power: The Revolution from Above, 1928–1941.* London: Chatto and Windus, 1990.

Rokossovsky, Marshal Konstantin Konstantinovich (1896–1968)

Marshal Konstantin Rokossovsky was one of the few leading Red Army officers rounded up in the military purge of 1937 who were later released and reinstated and went on to serve with distinction at important battles during the Great Patriotic War (World War II).

Rokossovsky's military career had begun with service in the tsarist army as a noncommissioned officer during World War I. He joined the Red Army after the revolution and later the Bolshevik Party (1919), serving during the civil war in the Far East, where he established a reputation for bravery. Further tours of duty in command of cavalry troops in the Far East followed, but in August 1937 Rokossovsky was arrested on charges of being a Polish spy and various other "crimes against the people," as part of the purge of the Red Army in the Far East that had come in the wake of the arrest of Marshal Blyukher.

A shrewd and dignified man, Rokossovsky outfaced his accusers in court by revealing that Adolf Yushkevich, who had supposedly denounced him for his counter-revolutionary activities and on whose "testimony" the case against him had been based, had in fact been killed during the civil war in 1920. The case against him collapsed; Rokossovsky was lucky enough to be sent to prison near Leningrad, rather than being shot or imprisoned in the Gulag.

In 1939, after the fall of Nikolay Ezhov, the chief architect of the major show trials of the Great Terror, some Red Army officers who were still languishing in prison were rehabilitated. By 1940, with the growing threat from Nazi Germany, Stalin had realized to what degree the Red Army was lacking in competent officers should war with Germany break out, and Rokossovsky, along with several other much-needed generals, was released. He had been in prison for three years and bore the scars of his beatings. All of his teeth had been knocked out during interrogations. The writer Alexander Solzhenitsyn related that on two occasions during his imprisonment, Rokossovsky had been subjected to the mental ordeal of being taken out into the forest at night for execution by firing squad, only to be returned to his prison cell (a favorite practice of the tsarist authorities and an experience that the writer Dostoevsky had endured in 1849).

Rokossovsky's dedicated military professionalism and charismatic leadership soon brought a string of military successes; he was known among the German high command as "the Red Army's best general." In 1941 Rokossovsky's troops successfully prevented the encirclement of Soviet armies near Smolensk, and he went on to help organize the defense of Moscow later that year. In 1942 he was sent to the Stalingrad front, where he played a crucial role in the command of the six Soviet armies that succeeded in trapping General von Paulus's 6th Army in the city. At the huge tank battle at Kursk in July 1943, Rokossovsky organized the Soviet lines of defense and held off the German attack.

After further military successes in Belarus, at Lublin, and at Brest-Litovsk, Rokossovsky was sent into Poland and crushed the Warsaw Rising, moving on to take command of the Soviet troops sweeping through East Prussia in the last days of the war in Europe. In Berlin in July 1945 Rokossovsky was one of several Soviet commanders to receive the British Order of Knight Commander of the Bath from Field Marshal Bernard Montgomery. For his considerable military achievements, Rokossovsky was made a marshal and given the honor of leading the march past of Soviet troops at the victory parade held in front of Stalin in Red Square on 24 June 1945. After the war, because he was Polish by origin, Rokossovsky was made minister of defense and deputy prime minister in Poland. But the Poles, convinced that he was a Soviet spy, insisted on his removal by Khrushchev in 1956.

See also Blyukher, Marshal Vasily Konstantinovich; Civil War; Great Patriotic War; Stalingrad

Further reading: Anthony Beevor. *Stalingrad.* London: Viking, 1998; Overy, Richard. *Russia's War: A History of the Soviet War Effort 1941–45.* London: Allen Lane, 1998; Harold Shukman, ed. *Stalin's Generals.* London: Phoenix, 1997.

Roosevelt, Franklin D.
See "The Big Three."

Russian Orthodox Church
See Religion.

Russian Revolution of 1917

A cursory glance through any general account of the revolutionary upheaval of the year 1917 in Russia, which culminated in a virtually bloodless coup d'état by a disciplined, revolutionary elite, quickly reveals the surprising fact that Joseph Stalin was conspicuous by his absence. Indeed, Leon Trotsky went so far as to dub him "The Man Who Missed the Revolution." Even in more detailed historical studies of the period, references to

Stalin's contribution to events are few and rather uninspiring. The political scene is dominated by the more romantic figures of Lenin and Trotsky, even though they were periodically absent from the revolutionary scene through exile or arrest.

While there is no doubting Stalin's own unique brand of political charisma, this was not something he had yet acquired, let alone exercised, in 1917. It would, however, be erroneous to assume that his seemingly self-effacing behavior during those months indicated a lack of political intent or a valid contribution to events. The will and ambition were certainly there, but Stalin chose his own more subtle route into the political spotlight, not as a charismatic speaker like Trotsky or a brilliant theoretician like Lenin. The energies of both men made Stalin, in comparison, look strangely lethargic in his own pursuit of revolution. Instead, Stalin, who was well aware of his own shortcomings as an intellectual and speaker, chose to do what he knew he did best—to work as an efficient party functionary and indispensable servant of Lenin. Thus, as the master of self-effacement, by means of which he would prepare the ground for his own later rise to power and outmaneuver his rivals, Stalin would be commended by Lenin in April 1917 as "a good worker in all responsible jobs."

It was thus that Stalin's contribution would be grossly undervalued if not ignored by leading revolutionaries at the time who, like the Menshevik Nikolay Sukhanov, dismissed him as a nonentity, "a gray blur, now dimly visible, now fading from trace." It was no doubt deeply embarrassing to Stalin that even Lenin's writings of the period July–October 1917 made virtually no mention of his name. To counter this and manufacture a political contribution to equal Lenin's and eclipse Trotsky's, Stalin would later reinvent himself, setting up a vast industry in historiography and the distortion of the photographic record. These joined forces to aggrandize the humble and socially inept Georgian revolutionary's role to epic proportions (particularly through the medium of socialist realist art, which depicted "an oddly handsome daredevil Stalin," as the historian Isaac Deutscher observed, in the forefront of events in which, in reality, he had only a minimal role).

The immediate impact of the Revolution of 1917, and an emphasis in accounts of it on the role of individuals in molding those events, would for many years give the impression that it was the great Bolshevik leaders Lenin and Trotsky who had made history by seizing the moment while the masses looked on. In fact, their opportunistic seizure of power came after months of mounting popular and often violent unrest in Petrograd, in which they had played no part. Beginning in February, the unrest had lacked only one thing—authoritative and coordinated political direction. The revolution, when it came, therefore, was much more the culmination of a long and mounting disaffection with the old, moribund tsarist regime; it was also a manifestation of the more immediate, accelerated period of political and social unrest following Russian military setbacks in World War I in 1915. In addition, the Bolsheviks managed to seize power despite being in the political minority at the time, and for the next two or three years the success of the revolution was by no means a foregone conclusion. Indeed, Lenin himself later remarked that his initial hope had been that the revolution would at least last longer than the eleven weeks of the Paris Commune of 1871.

Russian history of the turbulent period from 1905 to 1917 is full of a succession of "what ifs," dating particularly from the failure of the tsarist regime's first attempt at constitutional government—the Duma. This had been inaugurated by a reluctant Nicholas II in 1905 and was constantly blocked and subverted by him and weakened by the persistent failure of its many disparate political groups to find common ground. The failure of the autocracy to offer genuine encouragement to any form of parliamentarism in the period up to World War I, except under duress and despite the efforts of some of the more enlightened liberal elements in the Duma, was exacerbated by popular opposition to Russian involvement in the war. The tsar's foolhardy abandonment of his capital in order to command Russia's troops at the front in the heroic style of days long past, and which necessitated his leaving the state in the caretakership of the unpopular tsarina Alexandra, marked his total lack of a sense of reality in regard to the desperate state of the nation.

The revolution that unraveled in fits and starts between February and October, as the two 1917 revolutions are referred to in Russia (they actually took place in March and November, according to the European [Gregorian] calendar; dates here are given in old-style Russian [Julian]), was to be, not a sudden and apocalyptic event but, in the words of historian Norman Davies, the result of "several interwoven chains of collapse." Unrest in Russia, simmering since the Bloody Sunday Massacre of 1905, escalated during the harsh winter of 1916–1917. The diversion of food supplies from the hungry workers in the cities to the soldiers at the front had led to serious bread shortages. The peasants in the countryside also fiercely resented the mobilization of conscripts, which was disrupting farming and thus further fueling an already incipient grain crisis. In addition, a growing voice of nationalist dissent was being heard in various parts of the empire, including Latvia, Lithuania, Finland, and Ukraine. At the front, poorly supplied troops, often without ammunition or even proper boots and uniforms, became restive and frustrated by a lack of solid leadership. Lack of morale showed itself in an extremely high rate of capture and desertion.

In the capital Petrograd (renamed by the tsar in 1914 in an attempt to make St. Petersburg's name less Germanic-sounding), demonstrations and strikes broke out after an International Women's Day rally on 23 February had turned into a demonstration. By the twenty-fifth the mood had become increasingly violent, when 200,000 workers came out on strike in sympathy. On the twenty-sixth, troops of the Imperial Guard were instructed to fire upon demonstrators in Znamensky Square. Before long many soldiers—in particular, troops of the prestigious Pavlovsky and Preobrazhensky Regiments—were actively refusing to coerce demonstrators. Many mutinied to join the ranks of workers' city and regional soviets (a loose and uncoordinated network of councils in existence since 1905 to organize agitational activities). As historian Orlando Figes has pointed out, the violence and anarchy of the February days was far darker in nature and would claim more lives than the relatively peaceful coup by the Bolsheviks in October, which would later be commemorated as the official date of the revolution.

On 1 March the crisis deepened for the autocracy when the executive committee of the Petrograd Soviet issued Order No. 1, which attempted to deal with some of the many grievances of the soldiers against the government. It instructed them henceforth to take their orders, not from their tsarist officers, but directly from the soviet. With the soviet soon calling for an end to the war, it was virtually impossible for tsarist officers to exercise authority over their men. Soon a whole network of lesser workers' soviets began to orchestrate widespread strikes in the factories of major towns and cities, proving themselves a potent, albeit anarchic force for civil disobedience and taking control of the infrastructure of railways and telegraphs. Despite all this, the leaders of the Petrograd Soviet failed to display either the will or the political maturity to seize power at such an opportune moment of political dislocation. Figes suggested that their inability was born of their inherent fear of the volatile masses at large and demonstrated an "abdication of statesmanship." In any event, at the time of the February Revolution of 1917, the Bolsheviks were not a sufficient force to single-handedly take power; they numbered only about 20,000. They were in the minority in the Petrograd Soviet, which was dominated by the Socialist Revolutionaries and Mensheviks. By September, however, this situation had dramatically changed after a period of massive recruitment to the Bolshevik side.

Meanwhile a hastily elected Provisional Government of liberals, Mensheviks, and members of the bourgeois intelligentsia from the fourth Duma, under the leadership of Prince Georgy Lvov, had come into being. It attempted to fill the power vacuum and give equilibrium to an increasingly volatile situation. Soon it was riven with disagreements and could make no political headway. The tsar, having long struggled against a tide of antipathy toward the German-born tsarina, which had made it increasingly difficult to prosecute the war against Germany, was finally forced to face the reality of his untenable position. In the face of the breakdown of government at home and mutiny in the ranks of the army, he abdicated on 2 March "for the good of Russia." He was later exiled to Tobolsk and then to Ekaterinburg, Siberia, where in July 1918 he and his family were murdered.

The Bolsheviks, now receiving from Lenin in Zurich a stream of exhortations to organize, began recalling to the capital their dispersed ranks from exile both abroad and in Siberia. Stalin at the time was serving out his exile in Achinsk in southern Russia and made his way back with Lev Kamenev, arriving on 12 March 1917 and staying with old friends, the Alliluyevs (the parents of his future wife, Nadezhda). Stalin soon became a delegate to the Petrograd Soviet, which began to challenge the Provisional Government through its inner executive of twenty-four members. In the absence of Lenin, still in exile, Stalin enjoyed three weeks as effective leader of the Bolshevik Party as its most senior member. But the Executive Committee had declined to elect him into its ranks, deciding to give him only a consulting vote "in view of certain personal characteristics." One can only surmise what precisely this meant, but Stalin had certainly alarmed some with his uncouthness and his use of unscrupulous methods. Certainly, to many of the more intellectual Bolsheviks in Petrograd, particularly Trotsky, he seemed a rude provincial whose lack of political and social sophistication barred him from a prominent role.

With the official Bolshevik newspaper *Pravda* now declared legal, Stalin and Kamenev took over its editorship. During the months between the revolutions of February and October Stalin would be in close correspondence with Lenin, but he produced few published articles. In the columns of *Pravda* he initially held a conciliatory line, advocating cooperation with the Provisional Government. At this time, he held to the dogmatic Marxist line on the achievement of the first stage of conventional revolution—the hegemony of the bourgeoisie. In the ensuing months Stalin would undertake tasks assigned him with diligence, trying to find a middle way through the minefield of Petrograd revolutionary politics. Unlike Lenin, who lived on instinct and lived from revolutionary moment to moment, Stalin, who was by nature cautious and calculating, found it difficult to jump through the intellectual hoops created by Lenin's constant and unpredictable ideological revisions.

At the All-Russian Conference of Bolsheviks held between 27 March and 4 April, Stalin continued to avoid being controversial, adopting a patient and even-handed approach to the querulous elements at the conference and supporting tentative hopes of uniting all the various political factions in Petrograd in the cause of revolution. He was convinced that chaos in their ranks would ill equip them for a later concerted stand against the Provisional Government, when the time became right to do so. Stalin was also shrewdly aware that

extremist views and behavior drew attention to themselves and diluted the possibility of success.

On 3 April Lenin arrived at the Finland Station in Petrograd by sealed train from Berne in Switzerland, courtesy of the German High Command, who had ensured his safe passage. He had been taken unaware by the rapidly escalating events in Petrograd as much as everyone else, having averred only in January of that year that "we of the older generation may not live to see the decisive battle of this coming revolution." With Lenin now in the capital, Stalin once again blended into the background. Lenin, burning with impatience, without allowing himself time to take stock of a country and a people from whom he had long been absent, now took control of the situation. On 4 April he presented his famous "April Theses" to the Bolshevik Party conference, setting out the Bolsheviks' main objectives: an end to the war, nationalization of the land, and an end to hunger and food shortages. He also stressed the immediate and, to some, precipitate transfer of political power to the workers through the network of soviets—in other words, the long-awaited establishment of the dictatorship of the proletariat.

Stalin's first major political challenge after Lenin's return was dealing with his dramatic revision of traditional ideology in the April theses, which Stalin found too radical, if not downright reckless. Lenin had already been quick to give Stalin a dressing-down for his conciliatory articles in *Pravda*. Stalin later had to recant his opposition to Lenin's calls for what he considered a premature seizure of power as having been "profoundly mistaken" because it had given rise to "pacifist illusions" and had "brought grist to the mill of defencism, and hindered the revolutionary education of the masses." It was one of the few occasions on which Stalin would admit to an error of political judgment, the motive in this instance being his determination to appear always unquestioning in his loyalty to Lenin.

At the end of April Stalin's efforts were rewarded when, at a national Bolshevik Party conference (by which time the Bolsheviks numbered 76,000), Lenin recommended him for election to the Central Committee, confirming his years of good work for the cause in the Caucasus. Between then and October, Stalin would be happy to take a back seat in events, setting up negotiations between the various political groups, soldiers, and sailors, as well as helping to organize demonstrations, including a huge march of 500,000 through the capital on 18 June.

By early May the beleaguered Prince Lvov, a well-meaning social reformer and liberal, had found it impossible to keep his Provisional Government together and agreed to a coalition with the members of the increasingly powerful Petrograd Soviet. A heady period of discussion of reform and experimental democracy followed, with a date set for elections to a genuinely democratic Constituent Assembly in the autumn. But the Provisional Government's authority was hollow, and the coalition only heightened conflict. It soon became patently obvious that Lvov's government increasingly depended for its continuing existence on the will of the Petrograd Soviet, which now constituted the real source of military and political power.

On 3 June the First All-Russian Congress of Soviets, another of the plethora of congresses and conferences that came and went that year, was held. Stalin was a delegate and served as a party whip. Here the Bolsheviks were still in the minority, with only 16 percent of the delegates. When crowds of striking workers and soldiers gathered outside in the streets, demanding that the soviet should take over power from the Provisional Government, the Bolsheviks prevaricated, again uncertain that they had sufficient power to achieve a decisive victory. Rather than provoke an armed insurrection that would only end in their defeat, they allowed the civil unrest to dissipate. Public support for the Bolsheviks began to fall away as a result of their failure to seize the initiative, amid rumors of treachery and betrayal.

In mid-June the Provisional Government's minister of defense, Alexander Kerensky, launched a major military offensive—optimistically billed as leading "to the victorious end"—in its continuing, inept prosecution of the war against Germany. The offensive, launched in the southwest, did nothing to inspire a renewal of hoped-for popular patriotism and support for the government; in fact, it did the opposite. The country was war weary and peasant conscripts were now deserting in their thousands. In July Prince Lvov, unable to hold the government together, resigned and was succeeded by Kerensky. Throughout the summer, as the Provisional Government dragged its heels over the process of redistributing the land among the peasantry, as it had promised, Russia's peasants had become increasingly restive and belligerent. Many of them were now starving and desperate for more land in order to grow more food. Many, too, were nursing a smoldering resentment against their old masters and began taking matters into their own hands. In an orgy of violence and anarchy, fueled by a desire for retribution after centuries of enslavement by the gentry, peasants began attacking and looting estates, destroying valuable artwork, murdering their former masters, and raping their wives and daughters.

Back in Petrograd, increasing radicalization among trade union groups in the factories and newly formed committees of soldiers was also once more leading to an escalation of chaos, and between 3 and 7 July a disparate grouping of Bolshevik workers and soldiers staged armed demonstrations (later to be known as the "July Days"). The Bolsheviks began to prepare for a coup only to be discredited when the Provisional Government revealed details of Lenin's secret dealings with the Germans over his return to Russia and his receipt of funds from the German treasury to promote the Bolshevik cause. The public mood now suddenly turned against the Bolsheviks. On Stalin's advice, and with his personal help, Lenin fled into hiding in Finland on 11 July, where he would make the time count by writing "The State and Revolution," further expanding on his concept of the "dictatorship of the proletariat." Leon Trotsky and Lev Kamenev were arrested not long after, but Stalin, having carefully underplayed his role all this time, was left alone by the Provisional Government and now again found himself virtually in charge of the Bolsheviks. He appealed for calm and began rebuilding confidence among the rank and file, throwing down the gauntlet to Russia's oppressors on the pages of *Pravda:* "The Revolution is alive, and will yet let you feel it, Messieurs the grave-diggers."

The Bolsheviks, having missed their opportunity in early July, hotly debated the issue of armed insurrection again at the 26 July–3 August Sixth Bolshevik Party Congress. Stalin, having taken time to methodically digest the arguments of both Lenin and Trotsky (the latter was now throwing the weight of his faction behind the Bolsheviks), spoke out openly in favor of Lenin's demand for an end to prevarication. He also now sided with Lenin (who had been rapidly revising his original position on Trotsky's revolutionary theories) in arguing that there was no reason any longer for Russia to be dependent on the domino effect of revolutions throughout Europe for its own revolution to be self-sustaining. At long last Stalin had begun to see the advantages to be gained from mastering the Leninist art of "creative Marxism."

The political situation in Russia failed to settle and in August General Lavr Kornilov, frustrated by the ineptitude of the Provisional Government in putting down unrest in the capital, sent troops from the front to Petrograd in an attempt to impose civil order. His failure finally underlined how in-effective all other opposition groups were in comparison to the Bolsheviks. Lenin was now convinced that they had sufficient control within the Petrograd Soviet, supported by the increasing muscle of the growing factory committees and soviets not just in Petrograd but in other major cities and towns, to initiate revolution. By 25 September the Bolsheviks had at last gained the majority under Trotsky's dynamic leadership of the Petrograd Soviet, and from mid-September Lenin had once again begun exhorting them to seize power. The demand once again greatly alarmed such moderates in the party as Grigory Zinoviev and Kamenev, and even for a while Stalin, who still advocated a "wait-and-see" policy in anticipation of the November elections to a Constituent Assembly. Feeling more confident in his indispensability to Lenin, Stalin now tested the water by actually criticizing Lenin's angry lambasting of Zinoviev and Kamenev for their opposition and even attempted to resign his editorship of the *Worker's Path* (as *Pravda* had been renamed). Not surprisingly, in Stalinist Russia much of the conflict between Lenin and the Bolshevik leadership in Petrograd during this period, and this incident in particular, would be quietly buried in order to preserve the myth of unquestioning consensus on all Lenin's political decisions.

By now Lenin was incandescent with impatience. He returned to Russia in secret, to preside over a secret meeting of the Bolshevik Central Committee on the night of 10 October, during which a majority of ten to two, including Stalin, finally voted for armed insurrection. This was to be overseen by an inner circle of Bolsheviks, who had based themselves at a former girls' school, the Smolny Institute. Prime Minister Kerensky finally took belated action in an attempt to preempt the Bolshevik seizure of power. He closed down Bolshevik publications, including Stalin's *Worker's Path,* and made a series of arrests. Meanwhile, the Military Revolutionary Committee of the

Petrograd Soviet ordered the mobilization of its Red Guards. On 24 October, contingents of armed workers from the soviets seized strategic government buildings, including the post office, telegraph stations, and national banks.

On the night of 24–25 October Lenin (who had been holed up in the working-class Vyborg quarter of Petrograd) made his way to the Smolny in disguise to witness the occupation of the city by the Red Guards. On the night of 25–26 October the final revolution took place. On the firing of a signal from the battleship *Aurora,* a group of 300 or so Red Guards moved into the Winter Palace, meeting little resistance (only 6 were killed in the entire operation). They arrested the members of the Provisional Government, who had assembled in the Malachite Chamber. Kerensky managed to flee into exile.

On 26 October Lenin announced that political power was now in the hands of the Military Revolutionary Committee of the Petrograd Soviet and issued a decree offering "democratic peace, the abolition of the landed property of the landlords, worker control over production, and the creation of a Soviet Government." On the same day the Second All-Russian Congress of the Soviets was convened and voted in a new Provisional Government.

And where was Stalin in these last momentous days? While strategic buildings were being seized across Petrograd, he remained quietly beavering away in a back room on his Bolshevik newspaper, *Workers' Path.* At the Second All-Russian Congress of the Soviets an executive body—the Council of People's Commissars—was appointed, in which Stalin was given the position of people's commissar for nationalities. It was a role he did not want, having by now discovered that real political ambition was better pursued through the bureaucratic machinery of the Party. But to Lenin he was, as a non-Russian, the obvious choice, and one who had already supposedly stamped his "authority" on the subject with his 1913 article on the nationalities.

The setting up of Sovnarkom (as the Council of People's Commissars was known in its abbreviated form) quickly put an end to hopes of a democratic coalition of socialist groups, and five members of the Bolshevik Central Committee, including the moderates Zinoviev and Kamenev, resigned in protest. The Bolsheviks also found themselves left with one uncomfortable legacy of the Provisional Government—the elections to the Constituent Assembly, scheduled for November. These were allowed to go forward, despite obvious Bolshevik misgivings, which were confirmed when the liberal socialist revolutionaries won a clear majority and the Bolsheviks polled only 24 percent of the vote. On 5 January 1918 the first and only sitting of the Constituent Assembly was held. It was quickly dissolved by Lenin, who realized that the body gave no mandate to the Bolsheviks and would be a constant threat to their authority. The Russian people, therefore, enjoyed true democracy on just this one brief occasion, and it would be more than seventy years before they would be able to once again exercise their democratic rights.

And what of the revolution itself—that supposedly great, dramatic opening set-piece of Soviet history? Such early products of Soviet cinema as Sergey Eisenstein's 1927 film *October* would later propagate a romantic, unforgettable popular myth of the revolution as a spontaneous mass upheaval. With its documentarylike re-creation of hordes of revolutionaries attacking the gates of the Winter Palace, the film seemed so convincing that people thought it was the real thing. But in truth, the actual day of the revolution, driven by Lenin's close elite of professional revolutionaries, was ultimately something of an anticlimax. It was the previous long, dark months of brutish destructiveness and anarchy that had demonstrated the true visceral nature of popular revolt, with the Russian population at large demonstrating with an at times chilling ferocity the real human tragedy of revolution.

The Soviet version of events, soon relegated to endless impenetrable tomes of indigestible historiography, only testifies to the futility of the factional infighting and debate over theory and tactics that went on among the revolutionary elite while the population at large was suffering and hungry for change. And while there is no doubt about the strength of feeling in that vast, inchoate movement of popular protest, the unanswered question is whether it could ever have been unified into a disciplined and concerted attack on the seat of authority without the leadership of the Bolsheviks. It is also hard to conceive how revolutionary change, if it had come, could have been sustained during the establishment of the new political order without the dynamic, iron will of one man—Vladimir Ilyich Lenin. Having made the revolution happen, he drove himself to exhaustion to sustain its momentum.

Historians have debated the psychological effect on Stalin of his failure to play a commanding role in the crucial events of October 1917. It certainly fueled his jealousy of Trotsky and led to his later vindictiveness against others such as Zinoviev and Kamenev who had taken a stand against Lenin. It also triggered deeper personal impulses, such as what historian Alan Bullock described as Stalin's desperate "psychological need" to ultimately create a revolution of his own that would be wider-reaching and more successful even than Lenin's. Much, no doubt, stemmed from Stalin's own painful self-consciousness about his humble roots in Georgia, whereas both Trotsky and Lenin had come from intellectual families and had been better educated. He certainly resented being relegated to the small print as a nonentity. In fact, he later banned John Reed's classic account of the revolution, *Ten Days That Shook the World*, precisely because it makes not a single mention of him. Interestingly, though, Reed himself was perceptive enough to observe shortly before his death in 1920 that Stalin knew exactly what he wanted and to predict that "he's going to be on top of the pile some day." Whatever may have been Stalin's inner feelings of resentment or frustration, his experience of revolution was a steep learning curve for him, during which time he stored away in his photographic memory a close observation of the Bolshevik leaders. But it was his first-hand experience of the ruthless single-mindedness and powers of concentration of Lenin that proved conclusively to Stalin precisely which were the essentials for successful and undisputed leadership.

See also Cinema; Eisenstein, Sergey; General Secretary of the Communist Party; Kamenev, Lev; Lenin, Vladimir; Stalin: Personality of; Stalin: Private Life of; Trotsky, Leon; Zinoviev, Grigory

Further reading: E. H. Carr. *The Russian Revolution from Lenin to Stalin 1917–23.* London: Macmillan, 1950; Isaac Deutscher. *Stalin: A Political Biography.* London: Oxford University Press, 1967; Orlando Figes. *A People's Tragedy: The Russian Revolution 1891–1924.* London: Jonathan Cape, 1996; Roy Medvedev. *The October Revolution.* London: Constable, 1979; Richard Pipes. *The Russian Revolution, 1899–1919.* London: Collins Harvill, 1990; Richard Pipes. *Three Whys of the Russian Revolution.* London: Pimlico, 1998; Robert Service. *The Russian Revolution 1900–27.* London: Macmillan, 1986; Robert M. Slusser. *Stalin in October: The Man Who Missed the Revolution.* Baltimore: Johns Hopkins University Press, 1987; Robert Tucker. *Stalin as Revolutionary 1879–1929: A Study in History and Personality.* London: Chatto and Windus, 1974. (For memoirs and eyewitness accounts, see bibliography: Maxim Gorky, Nadezhda Krupskaya, R. H. Bruce Lockhart, Arthur Ransome, John Reed, N. N. Sukhanov; many of these are quoted in Harvey Pitcher, *Witnesses of the Russian Revolution.* London: John Murray, 1997.)

Russian-Polish War, 1919–1920
See Civil War.

Rykov, Aleksey Ivanovich (1881–1938)

From a peasant family, Aleksey Rykov was a forceful and uncompromising personality who became an important industrial administrator under Lenin. Together with Mikhail Tomsky, he was a leading supporter of Nikolay Bukharin as a member of the "Right Opposition."

Rykov joined the Bolsheviks in 1903 but broke with them in 1910 after several years as an underground activist in order to lead his own, more moderate faction, which sought rapprochement between the various socialist groups. From 1911 until the 1917 Revolution he was in exile in Siberia, returning to reiterate his belief in a coalition of socialist groups (including the Mensheviks) in the new government. Despite his opposition to the Bolshevik monopoly of power, Rykov nevertheless became a key figure in the early years, and in 1917 was elected to both the Bolshevik Central Committee and the Petrograd Soviet.

During the civil war he proved to be an efficient administrator, and in 1918 Lenin made him chairman of the Supreme Council of the National Economy (a post he held in 1918–1920 and 1923–1924). In 1922 he outlined his right-wing economic alternative to Trotsky and the left in his paper "The Country's Economic Situation and Conclusions as to Future work." That same year he was elected to the Politburo.

As deputy chairman of the Council of People's Commissars, Rykov deputized for Lenin in his last years of illness and appeared to be a major candidate for the leadership succession. After Lenin's death in 1924, now chairman of the council and effective head of the government, Rykov made the initial mistake (as did Tomsky, Nikolay Bukharin, and others) of underestimating Stalin and supporting him against Trotsky and the left. But as the 1920s went on he found himself increasingly clashing with Stalin over economic policy. Condemning Stalin for his lack of an understanding of economic theory and his inability to balance the interests of the workers with his management of production, Rykov alleged that his policy "[didn't] even smell of economics." Together with Bukharin and Mikhail Tomsky, Rykov opposed Stalin's policy on collectivization, but by the end of 1929 he was forced, along with them and others on the right, to publicly recant his opposition. Expelled from the Politburo in December, by early 1930 Rykov had lost all his official posts. Vyacheslav Molotov took over his position as chairman of the Council of People's Commissars.

In 1934, at the Seventeenth Party Congress, Rykov finally capitulated completely over his opposition to Stalin, acknowledging his political supremacy. Rykov's last few years saw his rapid moral disintegration into a frightened shadow of his former principled self, whose only solace was the oblivion of vodka. He had wanted to follow his friend Tomsky in preempting arrest and prosecution by committing suicide but had been dissuaded from doing so by his family, condemning himself to public humiliation at the Party Plenum in 1937, which debated whether or not to put him and Bukharin on trial.

The Plenum voted to expel Rykov as a candidate member of the Central Committee of the Communist Party, and he was subsequently arrested, charged along with Bukharin with being a member of the Trotskyist-rightist bloc and with committing various acts of terrorism, assassination, wrecking, and espionage.

Rykov had to wait a year for his trial, which came in March 1938. He was condemned to death on 13 March. Like Bukharin, he was by now prepared for death to the extent that he wearily accepted that his final admission of guilt and his call on other members of the right to "disarm" was essential to the greater good of the Party. Rykov was shot with Bukharin on 15 March. His wife was arrested and died in the Butyrki prison, and his daughter spent twenty years in the Gulag. Rykov himself was rehabilitated in 1988.

See also Bukharin, Nikolay; Collectivization; The Great Terror; Tomsky, Mikhail
Further reading: Stephen F. Cohen. *Bukharin and the Bolshevik Revolution: A Political Biography, 1888–1938.* Oxford: Oxford University Press, 1980; Robert Conquest. *The Great Terror: A Reassessment.* London: Pimlico, 1992.

Ryutin Manifesto

One of the few clearly defined acts of political defiance against Stalin's repressive rule that could be termed as a conspiracy to actually remove him from office was made in a 1932 "manifesto" written and disseminated by Martimyan Ryutin and a group of friends and Party members who had formed a small opposition group in Moscow.

The basis of this manifesto was a treatise written by Ryutin in 1930, which laid out in thirteen chapters a detailed critique of Stalin's rule, and enlarged on the alarm expressed by Nikolay Bukharin and others at the outset of the Five-Year Plans in the late 1920s that rapid industrialization and collectivization on the grand scale would bring the country to economic ruin. The whole operation should now be scaled down to avoid disaster, with the peasants being allowed to leave the collective farms if they wished. The document also described the escalating climate of fear of Stalin's regime and expressed criticism of the expulsions of Party members such as Leon Trotsky and dismay over the crushing of political and artistic freedom. It also launched an extensive attack on Stalin himself, in four of its chapters, for betraying the ideals of the revolution through his personal empire building.

Ryutin, Party secretary of the district of Krasnaya Presnya in Moscow, was a member of the Bolshevik Old Guard and had served as a Red Army commander in the civil war. When he had first voiced his disquiet about collectivization in his 1930 treatise he had been arrested and subsequently released when the authorities failed to prove criminal intent. In 1932 he renewed his campaign in another, shorter version of his original document, the "Appeal to All Members of the All-Union Communist Party," in which he courageously called upon those loyal to the spirit of Leninism to join a new Union of Marxists-Leninists and remove Stalin from power. He freely disseminated this document in the upper circles of the Communist Party. He argued unequivocally that "Stalin and his clique will not and cannot voluntarily give up their positions, so they must be removed by force." Ryutin's exhortation soon reached the attention of Stalin himself, who demanded the death penalty for Ryutin's treachery. On this occasion, a majority in the Politburo, including Sergey Kirov and Sergo Ordzhonikidze, overruled what would have been the first execution of an Old Bolshevik. The conspirators were expelled from the Party and imprisoned; Ryutin was incarcerated in a maximum security prison in the Urals for ten years.

Stalin had his revenge eventually. Most of Ryutin's supporters perished during the purges in 1937–1938. And Ryutin's manifesto became a useful tool in the hands of the prosecutors at the show trials, including Bukharin's in 1938, as a catch-all for implicating many of the defendants as supposed supporters of the "Ryutin Manifesto" in a widespread plot to organize Stalin's assassination.

In prison Ryutin remained defiant. He was brought to Moscow for interrogation; under torture by the secret police, he tried several times to commit suicide. But they did not manage to break him. His last letter, written in November 1936, survived in the KGB (formerly NKVD) archives: "I am not afraid of death, if that is what the investigative apparatus of the NKVD, in glaring contravention of the law, has in mind for me. I declare in advance that I will not plead for a pardon since I cannot confess to things which I have not done, things of which I am completely innocent." Ryutin was put through the ritual charade of a forty-minute "trial," in secret, on 10 January 1937 and shot three days later.

See also Bukharin, Nikolay; Collectivization; The Great Terror

Further reading: Robert Conquest. *The Great Terror: A Reassessment.* London: Pimlico, 1992; Robert C. Tucker. *Stalin in Power: The Revolution from Above, 1928–41.* London: Chatto and Windus, 1974.

Science

*I*t was a Bolshevik principle after the Revolution of 1917 to apply Marxist dialectics across all the sciences, which were viewed as a tool to be harnessed to the efficient exploitation of natural resources and the enhancement of technical and industrial processes. Lenin had been particularly obsessed with the need to achieve rapid electrification of the country as the foundation for a modern, socialist state. The importance of centralizing and controlling scientific effort now became paramount. In 1929–1930, under Stalin, the Academy of Sciences (which had been established in 1724 by Peter the Great and was one of the last old bastions of tsarist academia) was coerced into accepting a new charter, which would accommodate the election of Communist Party members—in other words, Stalinist monitors of scientific correctness—to the ranks of its Old Guard intellectuals.

In fact, many of Russia's leading scientists and intellectuals had already left the country at the time of the revolution, and those who remained were soon faced with the necessity of either abandoning their empirical research, which was looked upon as too purist in the new socialist society, or of adapting it to the resolution of agronomic, industrial, and economic problems. Other scientists, biologists in particular, found that Marxist dictatorship took hold within their own scientific disciplines to the extent that certain well-established scientific theories (such as Mendelian genetics) were now proscribed as being "bourgeois" or too "idealistic." In physics, the study of relativity theory, as well as quantum mechanics, was subjected to the Marxist straitjacket, a fact that might have wrecked the Soviet nuclear research program had not Stalin paid heed to warnings of the consequences. Even mathematics, that most exact of sciences, was scrutinized for the correctness of its ideological content.

Stalin was obsessed with differentiating what he saw as the productive "socialist science" of the Soviet Union from the dilettante "capitalist science" of the West. The resulting damage to research and scholarship was huge. It became difficult for many scientists to continue their crucially important work. This was the case with physicist P. L. Kapitsa, who was forced to abandon the research with Ernest Rutherford on uranium radiation at Cambridge, England, that he had begun before the revolution, because the Soviet authorities refused later to let him back out of the country. In the field of genetics, the dictatorship of the agrobiologist Trofim Lysenko and the propagation of his spurious theories on agronomic development led to the death during the Great Terror of many brilliant bio-chemists and geneticists, including Nikolay Vavilov. By the time Stalin finally put an end to the long-running controversy over this pseudoscience in 1948 and pronounced Soviet genetics as un-Marxist, most of the Soviet Union's important genetics research institutes had been closed down and many of their staff sent to the Gulag. As one Soviet professor remarked to the historian Alexander Werth in the 1960s, "If Stalin's treatment of scientists had gone on, today we would be about as backward as the Papuans or the Congolese. During Stalin's last years," he added, "we were no longer scientists, but worshippers of totem poles."

Yet Stalin was never one to allow important scientific expertise to languish. Many scientists and technicians who were sent to the Gulag during the 1930s were gathered together, especially during the war years, in *sharashi* (special scientific institutes for political prisoners) where their skills could be put to acceptable, orthodox scientific use, in particular on the atomic research program. In fact, it wasn't until the advent of atomic research during the Great Patriotic War that Soviet science finally began to recoup lost ground. Indeed, the Soviet nuclear program at this time laid the foundation for later Soviet supremacy in early space technology. A team of fine scientific minds, many of them Jews, whose usefulness to the state no doubt helped to keep them alive at a time when Stalin was becoming increasingly anti-Se-mitic, was assembled on Stalin's instructions to achieve nuclear chain reaction and de-velop the Soviet Union's first atomic bomb. This they did in record time, but not with-out covertly adopting precisely those key el-ements of Western technology and physics essential to achieving success, while in pub-lic the Soviet scientific establishment con-tinued to berate Western scientific innova-tion. In the ensuing Cold War much of Soviet scientific research was channeled into the arms race, with no expense spared. But this work, because of its secrecy, was often

carried on in such hidden locations as the secret city Arzamas–16, where the atomic bomb was developed. Scientists were iso-lated from important research going on in the West, making much of Soviet science a closed-off world, even to the Soviet people.

Throughout his rule, Stalin's insistence on promoting homegrown scientific theo-ries, however hare-brained, as long as they offered a supposed Marxist alternative to those of Western science, succeeded on nu-merous occasions in making Soviet science an international laughingstock. Stalin's gullibility for quack solutions, such as his promotion of the half-baked ideas on cell rejuvenation offered by Olga Lepeshinskaya (who, for her labors, was awarded a Stalin Prize), suggest that if cryogenics had been a viable option at the time, Stalin would cer-tainly have been the first to enlist for it.

See also Atomic Bomb; Cold War; Lysenko, Trofim; Vavilov, Nikolay

Further reading: Loren R. Graham, ed. *Science and the Soviet Social Order.* Cambridge, MA: Harvard University Press, 1990; David Holloway. *Stalin and the Bomb: The Soviet Union and Atomic Energy 1939–1956.* New Haven, CT: Yale University Press, 1994; Paul Josephson. *Physics and Politics in Revolutionary Russia.* Berkeley: University of California Press, 1991; Zhores A. Medvedev. *Soviet Science.* Oxford: Oxford University Press, 1979.

17th Congress of the CPSU
See Congress of the Victors.

Shakhty Trial

This, one of the first political trials that took place after Stalin succeeded Lenin, became the precursor and template for the very public political show trials of the Great Terror. It was initiated by Stalin on the strength of denunciations made to him by an old associate and member of the Cheka, Yefim Yevdokimov. These provided Stalin with the ideal "evidence" with which to launch a witch-hunt against supposed enemies in Soviet industry at a time when he was seeking to discredit the old Soviet intelligentsia and its links with the more moderate industrial policies of Nikolay Bukharin. The fact that the accused were engineers, three of whom were Germans, further reinforced his view that economic intervention by Western capitalists was intent upon destabilizing the Soviet state.

The town of Shakhty is a major industrial city in the Donets coal basin. In 1928 a group of fifty-three engineers and technicians who worked in the coal industry were rounded up on charges of arson, sabotaging industrial equipment, and conspiring with the Western capitalists who had originally invested in the mines to bring about the destruction of the mining industry there. The accused were paraded at the Hall of Columns in Moscow. The only evidence against them was supposed confessions made by some of them under interrogation. The resulting trial bore all the hallmarks of what would later become the routine Stalinist travesty of justice—the transformation of the legal process into a media spectacle (in the case of the Shakhty, "Death to the Wreckers" became the rallying cry). A string of confessions made prior to the trial by ten of the fifty-three accused, and which were extracted under duress, would be combined with unverified and unverifiable "evidence."

In court the accused were subjected to a barrage of abuse from Stalin's prosecutor, Nikolay Krylenko, in a trial overseen by the insidious presence of the judge, Andrey Vyshinsky. Such an intimidating atmosphere produced a trial marked by constant changes of mood. Some of the accused turned into groveling repentants (after being driven to the edge of despair, they had agreed to mouth the most absurd, scripted confessions in order to be released from continuing torture). Others remained brave and defiant to the end, after having suffered extreme intimidation and physical pain. Of the accused, sixteen capitulated and admitted their crimes (five were eventually executed), but one of them unexpectedly retracted his confession in open court after his wife had cried out from the gallery, begging him not to lie. One of the most chilling aspects of the trial was that the young son of one of the accused himself joined the chorus of those demanding the death penalty. Such were the elements of a scenario that would become all too familiar over the next ten years.

In the wake of the trial, several thousand specialists and administrators in industry lost their jobs. Stalin wanted to wipe the slate clean and enlist a new generation of engineers and technicians, whose conformity could not be called into question at a time when he was preparing to crank up the rate of industrialization to unprecedented levels. Stalin's public expression of that private objective was, as always, colored by his characteristic penchant for melodrama: "Shakhtyites are now ensconced in every branch of our industry. . . . Wrecking by the bourgeois intelligentsia is one of the most dangerous forms of opposition to developing socialism."

See also Bukharin, Nikolay; The Great Terror; Prisons; Torture

Sholokhov, Mikhail Aleksandrovich (1905–1984)

Mikhail Sholokhov's powers as one of the great exponents of socialist realist literature of the 1930s were skillfully demonstrated in his epic four-volume masterpiece *And Quiet Flows the Don* (1928–1940). As a graphic account of the turbulent years of the civil war, it was Tolstoyan in its sweep of characters and its panorama of history. But Sholokhov's huge artistic promise was later dissipated by his increasing conformity to party dogma and personal problems with alcoholism.

Sholokhov grew up in the Don country of the Cossacks, a region that had always held a romantic appeal for Russian writers. He began publishing short stories in the 1920s in collections such as *Tales of the Don* (1926). But much of his time thereafter was consumed by work on his ambitious masterpiece *And Quiet Flows the Don*. Stalin's personal endorsement of Sholokhov's novel seemed at first surprising, for it had run into considerable trouble with the censors. Its even-handed, objective view of the shortcomings of both the Reds and the Whites meant that the Bolsheviks were not always depicted in an entirely favorable manner. Stalin, however, considered the novel to be the epitome of the literary form of socialist realism and also endorsed the later operatic version of the story. *And Quiet Flows the Don*'s subsequent success was unprecedented, and as one of the most widely read books in the Soviet Union, it opened the door to privilege for Sholokhov. It also earned him considerable literary kudos outside the Soviet Union and was eventually translated into eighty-four languages.

Such was Stalin's admiration for Sholokhov's work that, during the worst period of the Great Terror in 1938, he protected him from the imminent threat of denunciation and arrest as part of a roundup of "counterrevolutionaries" in his home district of Veshenskaya. Indeed, so secure had Sholokhov felt in Stalin's admiration for him that in 1933 he had written a personal letter to Stalin complaining about the brutal methods of collecting grain quotas from the peasants used by local officials in his native Cossack country. In 1941 Sholokhov was awarded the Stalin Prize; he had become firmly entrenched as an establishment figure and a loyal party man, achieving elevation to the Supreme Soviet in 1946.

In his second major novel, begun while he was still finishing *And Quiet Flows the Don,* Sholokhov set out to tackle the subject of collectivization. The new work was equally ambitious and had an even longer gestation period than the first, being published in two volumes as *Virgin Soil Upturned* and *Harvest on the Don* between 1932 and 1960. But there were already signs in the second part of the book of a distinct falling away of Sholokhov's artistic talent, as he became increasingly constrained by the need to adhere to Party dogma and produce formulaic work.

During his later post-Stalinist career, Sholokhov (by 1962 a member of the Central Committee) became increasingly right wing, launching attacks on dissident writers such as Alexander Solzhenitsyn, Andrey Sinyavsky, and Yuli Daniel. This somewhat tarnished the international image that had earned him the Nobel Prize for literature in 1965. The awarding of the Nobel Prize had also rekindled murmurings, regularly resurfacing since 1928, about the authenticity of Sholokhov's much-lauded *And Quiet Flows the Don*. He was accused of having plagiarized the work of an obscure Cossack writer named Fedor Kryukov. While many figures in the literary world leaped to Sholokhov's defense with convincing arguments to the contrary, Sholokhov himself remained silent. In his study of Stalin, Edvard Radzinsky asserted that archival evidence now suggests that Sholokhov refused to answer the accusations because he had actually based his hero, Grigory Melikhov, on a Cossack officer, Kharlampi Yermakov, who had become a "nonperson" and was shot by the secret police in 1927—clearly an unsuitable political hero for a work personally endorsed by Stalin.

See also Socialist Realism; Stalin Prizes

Further reading: Herman Ermolaev. *Mikhail Sholokhov and His Art*. Princeton, NJ: Princeton University Press, 1982; Roy Medvedev. *Problems in the Literary Biography of Mikhail Sholokhov*. Cambridge: Cambridge University Press, 1977; Mikhail Sholokhov. *The Silent Don* (incorporating *And Quiet Flows the Don* and *The Don Flows Home to the Sea*). New York: Knopf, 1943.

Shostakovich, Dmitry Dmitrievich (1906–1975)

The story of this prolific composer's alternating phases of resistance and then capitulation to the Stalinist regime is a compelling and bitter one. The frail, bespectacled Dmitry Shostakovich would seem an unlikely survivor of the years of the Great Terror. During his life, he produced a massive body of work that included fifteen symphonies and fifteen string quartets. But it was a life that he would look back on with immense sorrow and an unbearable sense of loss.

Shostakovich studied music at the St. Petersburg Conservatoire. His first symphony, written as a graduation piece, premiered in 1926. He could have opted for a successful career as a concert pianist but chose to continue composing, embracing many of the experimental and avant-garde trends in Russian music of the 1920s. Shostakovich began running into trouble with the authorities for his radical approach to composition, after the imposition of socialist realism across the arts in the 1930s. When his opera *Lady Macbeth of Mtsensk* was first performed in 1934, it was greeted as a masterpiece. But by 1936 the climate had changed to such an extent that Shostakovich was now vilified for its decadence in a 28 January article in *Pravda* entitled "Confusion Instead of Music," which is said to have been personally initiated by Stalin. Criticizing the work for being tuneless and noisy as well as full of sex and violence, *Pravda* was vicious in its attack: "It is a leftist bedlam instead of human music. The inspiring quality of good music is sacrificed in favor of petty-bourgeois clowning. . . . He scrambles sounds to make them interesting to formalist elements who have lost all taste."

Shostakovich tried to put matters right with his next major work, his powerful and somber Fifth Symphony (1937), to which he added the epigraph "A Soviet artist's reply to just criticism." The work was soon greeted with approval by the Party, which welcomed him once more into the fold of musical orthodoxy. Many of Shostakovich's critics in the West have interpreted the writing of this symphony as a callow act of capitulation, but in retrospect it is difficult to see how Shostakovich could have done otherwise and stayed alive through the coming purges.

The symphony, however, proved to be his most enduringly popular one, and Shostakovich demonstrated, as he often would, that he could produce some of his best (and deliberately politically ambiguous music) when under extreme artistic and political pressures. The audience at the premiere in Leningrad had no doubt that this was a musical outpouring of their collective hopes and fears, although Shostakovich could not himself publicly admit that it was indeed descriptive of his own sense of despair at the horrors of life under Stalin. He later made it clear that he had deliberately hoodwinked his detractors in the symphony's "triumphant" final movement, which he claimed was in fact a deliberately hollow and forced one. As the writer Alexander Fadeev perceptively observed at the time: "The end does not sound like an outcome (and even less like a triumph or victory), but like a punishment or revenge of someone."

For a while during the late 1930s Shostakovich retreated from musical life, teaching at the Leningrad Conservatoire until called on in the motherland's hour of need to write a great, stirring, patriotic symphony after the Germans had invaded the Soviet Union. He did not disappoint with his Seventh Symphony, popularly known as the *Leningrad* (1941), which he composed in the besieged and frozen city before being evacuated. After its first public broadcast on Soviet radio in March 1942, the score, copied on microfilm, was flown out to the West, where it was a huge success and helped fuel support for the Soviet fight against German occupation. In private, however, Shostakovich had confided that the symphony was intended as a statement against the evil not only of Hitler but also Stalin, and that it was also about "the Leningrad that Stalin destroyed and that Hitler merely finished off."

Despite the huge international success of the Seventh Symphony, in the late 1940s Shostakovich was again attacked for his formalism, this time by Andrey Zhdanov, whose benchmark for good music was that it could be "whistled by any worker." Once again Shostakovich, worn down by fear, retreated in the face of harsh criticism and confined himself to writing film music and string quartets, even sitting on the committee to organize the celebrations of Stalin's seventieth birthday. Shostakovich's position improved after Stalin's death, and he continued to follow his own path musically, experimenting with twelve-tone themes and atonality, and producing another great symphony—the Tenth—which he described as being "about Stalin and the Stalin years." As late as 1963 he experienced yet another run-in with the authorities when his Thirteenth Symphony, a setting of Yevgeny Yevtushenko's grim poem *Babiy Yar,* which exposed Soviet anti-Semitism, was suppressed.

In the last years of his life, in rapidly failing health, Shostakovich dictated his memoirs, in which he revealed the deep, spiritual misery that had engulfed him during the Stalinist years. His life had undoubtedly been blighted by them: "There were no particularly happy moments in my life, no great joys. It was grey and dull and it makes me sad to think about it." His one hope, he added, was that others might learn from his painful experience so that "perhaps their lives would be free from the bitterness that has coloured my life grey."

See also Leningrad, Siege of; Prokofiev, Sergey; Socialist Realism; Stalin: Private Life of

Further reading: David Fanning. *Shostakovich*

Studies. Cambridge: Cambridge University Press, 1995; Dmitry Shostakovich. *Testimony* (as related to and edited by Solomon Volkov). London: Faber, 1979.

Show Trials
See The Great Terror.

Siberia
See Gulag.

"Socialism in One Country"

One of the primary ambitions of the Bolsheviks after seizing power in 1917 was the achievement of a chain of worker-led revolutions throughout Europe and eventually the world. Without it, many on the left of the Party, in particular Leon Trotsky and his followers, believed that a socialist state in the Soviet Union would be unsustainable. The Bolsheviks had originally hoped that the impetus of the revolution would reach Germany, where the socialist movement was also strong, and from there perhaps infect France and even Britain; all of these governments became vulnerable as World War I dragged on.

By the mid-1920s, however, Stalin realized that the possibility of international proletarian revolution was rapidly evaporating and that the Soviet Union would have to go it alone. At the end of 1924, he published an essay "October and Comrade Trotsky's Theory of Permanent Revolution," in which he challenged Trotsky's theories and argued that, although the achievement of world revolution was still far off, progress could and should be made in Russia now, despite its economic backwardness. He insisted that the foundation for this success was the "alliance of the proletariat and the toiling peasantry" and proceeded to manipulate the original ideas and writings on the subject laid down by Lenin, and by Marx and Engels before him, to make this objective now appear theoretically possible.

During his rule, Stalin found it expedient to contradict his own pronouncements on theory on several major political issues. At the beginning of 1924 in his book *The Foundations of Leninism,* he had clearly asserted that "for the final victory of socialism, . . . the efforts of one country, particularly of a peasant country like Russia, are insufficient; for that, the efforts of the proletarians of several advanced countries are required." Within months he overturned this assertion, withdrawing *Foundations* from sale and revamping his argument to fit his new theory in a reissue, entitled *Problems of Leninism,* which was aimed at silencing Trotsky and Stalin's other critics by reinventing the Leninist perspective on the subject.

The basis for Stalin's theory of "Socialism in One Country," which hinged in part on his emphasis on the exploitation of Russia's vast and as yet untapped natural resources, was, therefore, not the result of a sophisticated analysis of the actual economic situation and of what was best for the nation as a whole but rather was Stalin's personal and impatient response to a lack of economic progress. This, like all of his policy decisions, was driven by a blind, dogmatic insistence that invited neither criticism nor informed suggestion and that relentlessly drove economic change along the path that he had chosen for it, and that path only.

By the time of the Fourteenth Party Congress in 1925, the delegates had been prevailed upon to endorse Stalin's principle that "the victory of socialism (*not* in the sense of *final* victory) is unconditionally possible in one country." From then on the slogan became the cornerstone, not just of the new economic order, but of Stalin's fiercely nationalistic ambitions for Soviet political supremacy on an international scale. And here he demonstrated his characteristic skill at manipulating the emotive power of national pride by emphasizing

Soviet courage in going it alone, a convenient and much-favored method of camouflaging the shortcomings of his own theoretical argument. It was also a highly effective way of silencing his critics. To now ignore Stalin's call to arms could be perceived as a betrayal of Leninism (or rather Stalin's revised interpretation of it). The historian Isaac Deutscher has also observed that the creed of "Socialism in One Country" held out the "promise of stability" to a nation that had long endured political, economic, and social instability and that it served to pour cold water over Trotsky's theory of "permanent revolution," which now "sounded like an ominous warning to a tired generation that it should expect no Peace and Quiet in its lifetime."

With this in mind, it is understandable that the Soviets in general were galvanized by Stalin's slogan. But the price was a heavy one, for it required the large-scale industrialization of what was still an economically backward country and the collectivization at breakneck speed of its mainly reluctant peasantry. This in turn would require the institution of a tough and tightly controlled centralized government that would bring with it the oppression and repression of the Soviet people en masse.

See also Bukharin, Nikolay; Collectivization; Five-Year Plans; Trotsky, Leon

Socialist Realism

*I*n the early 1930s, with the Soviet population harnessed to the collective drive toward the Soviet Union's transformation as a major industrial and economic power, Stalin determined that the arts, too, should identify themselves more explicitly with the ideology and methods of the Communist Party and the achievement of its socialist objectives.

Since the early 1920s a variety of artistic groups in the Soviet Union had sought to dominate and dictate to each other the nature of new art forms. While a lively atmosphere of dissent and argument had prevailed for some time, it was not until the ascendancy of the dictatorial Russian Association of Proletarian Writers (RAPP) in the late 1920s that this atmosphere was deemed as having a negative effect. However, by the end of the decade Stalin had tired of the domineering stance taken by RAPP and the highly intimidating methods it had adopted in attempting to assert its hegemony over others (among them the poet Vladimir Mayakovsky, who had been browbeaten into joining its ranks shortly before his suicide in 1930). He now decided that the time had come for the government to issue its own directives on the arts. In 1932 a Communist Party decree "On the Reconstruction of Literary and Artistic Organizations" initiated the unionization of Soviet arts into several monolithic organizations under tight Party control, membership of which would become increasingly expedient for anyone who wished to ensure his artistic career. RAPP and other fringe groups were abolished and an official Writers' Union was established, closely followed by unions for artists and musicians.

For the next two years the literary establishment, led by Ivan Gronsky (editor of *Izvestiya*) and others on the Organizing Committee of the Union of Soviet Writers, mulled over the theoretical nature of the new official doctrine. Their elaboration of the doctrine of socialist realism described the kind of utilitarian and pedagogic art forms that would now be demanded and that would sound the death knell for the old rightist (bourgeois intellectual) and leftist (avant-garde) camps that had thrived in the atmosphere of creative experimentation since the revolution.

Gronsky had already made his attitude clear in a typically pragmatic statement in 1932 in which he asserted that "Socialist Realism is Rembrandt, Rubens and Repin put at the service of the working class."

Such a crude and indiscriminate generalization would typify the official attitude to the work of the artist from this point on, an attitude that would take no account whatsoever of the unique creative vision of the individual and that would encourage only the bland and the uniform.

In 1934 the Union of Soviet Writers held its First Congress under the chairmanship of the writer Maxim Gorky, who had recently returned from self-imposed exile in Italy to take on the mantle of conciliator in the Soviet arts. At the congress, he proclaimed that "life, as asserted by socialist realism, is deeds, creativeness, the aim of which is the uninterrupted development of the priceless individual qualities of man," and he went on to develop his specific thesis for Soviet literature as being a celebration of the heroic exploits of the "little man" (i.e., the proletarian) in his struggle to make his own contribution to the Soviet achievement.

The congress thus became the showcase for the formal validation of socialist realism as the benchmark for all creative work in literature as well as literary criticism, with speeches from such major figures as Andrey Zhdanov (Stalin's official spokesman on cultural matters), the economic theoretician Nikolay Bukharin, and the eminent short story writer Isaac Babel. In his keynote speech, Zhdanov provided further unequivocal assertions on the role of the writer, and by the end of the proceedings a set of statutes had been drawn up and endorsed, which finally confirmed that socialist realism "is the basic method of Soviet imaginative literature and literary criticism, [it] demands from the artist a truthful, historically concrete depiction of reality in its revolutionary development." At a stroke, experimental and avant-garde work was collectively denounced as degenerate (writer James Joyce had been singled out during the proceedings as a particularly nefarious example of Western degeneracy in literature).

The promulgation of the term *socialist realism,* however, in itself created a paradox. With the emphasis on literature holding up a mirror to life and being faithful to the true and the positive rather than the abstract, how could any writer following this formula make any realistic presentation of Soviet life in all of its highly contradictory manifestations? In order for a work to be "socialist realist" the writer in effect had to abandon objective truth and depict only what was positive, upbeat, heroic in a broadly tendentious manner. Literary protagonists had to be exemplary and any imperfections they might display had to be exorcised through dedication to the revolution or the socialist cause. Most of the settings for these new optimistic sagas of Soviet achievement would be those of civil war and revolution, or industrial production of one kind or another with the emphasis on technology, science, and engineering and away from such subjective human weaknesses as love, dejection, and despair. Any depiction of shortcomings in Soviet ideology or the negative side of socialist reality in the Soviet Union—for instance, the suffering of the peasantry in the famine, the deportation of the kulaks, or political oppression and repression of any kind—would, of course, not be countenanced.

"Party Art" (as the poet Osip Mandelstam dismissively dubbed it) must now serve the revolution, and writers were provided with a set of exemplars, drawn from the nineteenth-century academic French school of critical realism of Balzac and Stendhal, or English-language models such as Charles Dickens and Mark Twain, in preference even to Russian writers such as Tolstoy and Dostoevsky, who were considered to have been too excessively preoccupied with moral and religious issues. Authors were urged to take as their literary template earlier works of Soviet literature that reflected the spirit of socialist realism, several of which had been written under the influence of RAPP's call for a "dialecti-

cal materialist method" that reflected the struggle between the good and bad, the positive and negative in Soviet society. Novels such as Gorky's opaquely propagandist *Mother,* written as long ago as 1906 but considered a prototype of "revolutionary romanticism" for its heroine's spirited support for the revolution, would become the seminal examples. Similarly, the merits of Fedor Gladkov's *Cement* (1925), set, unsurprisingly, in a cement factory, despite being by any standards the unremarkable work of an unremarkable writer, were exaggerated to epic proportions. This novel became a favorite of Stalin's and, as a standard reading text in schools throughout the Soviet Union, was translated into many languages, selling millions of copies. Yet even Gladkov himself felt constrained to revise the novel extensively to bring it even more in line with the stylistic demands of socialist realism. In so doing he relentlessly homogenized the novel over the next thirty years, removing any last vestiges of verbal ornamentation and with them the last remnants of authorial idiosyncrasy.

Many authors, aware that they would literally starve unless they adopted socialist realism, reluctantly adapted to the exigencies of the new formula and produced variations on the prescribed theme: dedicated but slightly imperfect revolutionary activist/worker is molded by Party and people into a heroic figure and with their support achieves great works/victory over the enemy in the cause of building the Communist utopia, and so on. A long and deadening period of stagnation in Soviet writing ensued with such works as *How the Steel Was Tempered* by Nikolay Ostrovsky (1932–1934), which reaped huge successes once it was adopted as a school text in 1935, marking the literary high point. This semiautobiographical story about how a humble peasant lad espouses the revolution and transcends injury and setbacks to become a writer and teacher sold 5 million copies over ten years. Meanwhile, other and in many cases greater writers such as Mikhail Bulgakov, Isaac Babel, Boris Pasternak,and Anna Akhmatova found compromise reprehensible if not artistically impossible and fell into silence. A rare exception was Mikhail Sholokhov, who managed to bridge the demands both of socialist realism and literary creativity with his epic novel *And Quiet Flows the Don* (1928–1940), one of the few works to transcend the medium and become an enduring classic of Soviet literature.

In fine art all-out war was declared on "formalism," a collective term used with deadening regularity to condemn anything deemed remotely avant-garde. Leading painters such as Konstantin Malevich, Natan Altman, and Pavel Filonov fell victim to official disapproval and were soon banned from exhibiting their works. In art, as well as in literature, Stalin became the arbiter of socialist realist standards and an overnight expert on the subject. The artistic establishment dutifully kowtowed to his greater wisdom. According to the art magazine *Tvorchestvo* (Creative Work), "Comrade Stalin's words of genius about Soviet art as an art of socialist realism represent the peak of all the progressive strivings of the aesthetic thought of mankind."

Much of the new ideology applied to writing was transferred directly to art without much distinction made between the two genres. Again, examples were taken from the nineteenth century, in particular the Russian Itinerant school of realist painting as represented by the work of Ilya Repin, who painted great historical set pieces. In architecture an ornate mock-classical style on the grand scale was encouraged; it became nicknamed *sovnovrok* ("Soviet new rococo"). Much of socialist realist painting concentrated simplistically on instituting a "method of portraying our leaders in a way they will understand." Such an assertion opened the way for the domination of establishment artists such as Alexander Gerasimov, who developed his own virtual monopoly on the portrayal of Stalin, Klimenty Voroshilov, and other leading political figures. Increasingly, artists painted to order and were constrained to paint on certain themes only (they were allowed to "choose" from lists of subjects). Most popular were historical tableaux, scenes depicting Lenin or Stalin during the turbulent days of the revolution, muscular stevedores at the blast furnace, happy haymakers on sun-drenched collective farms. Later, as the cult of the personality gained ground, socialist realist sculptors also made a major contribution to the mythologization of Stalin as the all-seeing and mighty leader of the Soviet state, an industry that did more than any other to assuage Stalin's inferiority complex about his height (he was only 5'4") and convince the nation at large that he was a real-life colossus.

In Soviet music a particular emphasis was placed on a cornerstone of socialist realism—*narodnost'* or "national character." This was marked by the use of popular and folk melodies and a return to traditional styles of music that Stalin enjoyed. In this respect Aram Khachaturian achieved some success during the 1930s with his use of Armenian, Georgian, and Azerbaijani motifs. The work of the nineteenth-century composer Mikhail Glinka also enjoyed a huge revival with his operas *A Life for the Tsar* (revived in 1939 as *Ivan Susanin*) and *Ruslan and Lyudmilla,* particular favorites with Stalin, due to their strong patriotic content and use of folk melodies. (Indeed, a revival of interest in traditional Russian folk motifs in art and literature as well as in music was a significant factor under socialist realism.)

The official condemnation of dissonant experimentation in music put a great deal of pressure on composers such as Dmitry Shostakovich, Sergey Prokofiev, Nikolay Myaskovsky, and Georgian Vano Muradeli (all of whom were denounced for formalism in the late 1940s by Andrey Zhdanov), while inflating the work of lesser artists such as Ivan Dzerzhinsky, whose 1934 opera *Quiet Flows the Don* (from Sholokhov's novel) and whose settings of marching songs were favorites with Stalin. Similarly, other civil war operas such as *The Black Crag* (Andrey Pashchenko) and *The Breakthrough* (Sergey Potosky) both of which revived the nationalistic formula of "Great Russian Chauvinism," as historian Robert C. Tucker described it, also gained the official seal of approval. Some composers found artistic refuge in writing film music. Prokofiev, for example, wrote the score for Eisenstein's *Alexander Nevsky* (1938), and Khachaturian composed for the 1949 film *Battle of Stalingrad,* but even in this genre they were not immune from criticism.

In the cinema, too, the pattern was the same. Filmmaking was now under centralized control and paralyzed by a lack of artistic freedom, due to the attacks made on leading directors for their "ultra-leftist tendencies." These, exacerbated by the technical problems involved in making the transition to sound, resulted in the same monotonous round of propagandist, laudatory films, many of them celebrating Lenin and Stalin's participation in the 1917 Revolution (and later, Stalin's heroic leadership during the Great Patriotic War). Meanwhile, eminent directors who had pioneered Soviet filmmaking came under attack. Sergey Eisenstein was severely rebuked over *Bezhin Meadow* (1936–1937); the film's negative was destroyed. Soviet audiences, who had been extremely reluctant to forgo the escapist product of Hollywood, were now weaned on increasingly propagandist fodder such as Friedrich Ermler and Sergey Yutkevich's *Counterplan* (1933) about industrial workers striving to fulfill the Five-Year Plans. The only palliative was a series of escapist musical comedies by such directors as Grigory Aleksandrov, whose 1934 *The Jolly Fellows* (with music by Isaac Dunaevsky) hit a nerve with Stalin, who encouraged further films in the same vein. Aleksandrov duly obliged with *The Circus* (1936) and *Volga Volga* (1941);

"Song of the Motherland" was plucked from the latter to become a popular wartime anthem.

Not surprisingly, it was rare for an artist to protest against the stultifying atmosphere of creative oppression during the 1930s and 1940s. Most kept their feelings to themselves and reluctantly complied. Others lapsed into artistic inertia, while a few, such as Evgeny Zamyatin, got out of the Soviet Union in time. Those who had no qualms about lowering their artistic standards and were sanguine about the privileges to be gained from conformity and membership of their respective union adapted successfully and reaped the kudos of prizes and honors. But some artists of integrity refused to pay the new medium any attention. Nadezhda Mandelstam, in her memoirs, talked of her deliberate refusal to read any socialist realist novels, since for her "they smell of privileged rations and writers' dachas."

One of the few figures who dared to speak out openly on the emasculation of the Soviet arts was the stage director Vsevolod Meyerhold, whose innovative work in avant-garde theater had been anathematized in favor of a return to the conventional techniques of the nineteenth-century Stanislavsky school. At a conference of theater directors held in June 1939, Meyerhold had the temerity to declare that "this pitiful and sterile something that aspires to the title of socialist realism has nothing in common with art.... In your effort to eradicate formalism, you have destroyed art." Shortly afterward, Meyerhold was arrested. Earlier, at the 1934 Writers' Congress, Isaac Babel, in a pitifully self-conscious and awkwardly apologetic speech, had made oblique but pointed reference to the predicament in which all artists now found themselves: "The Party and the government have given us everything, depriving us only of one privilege— that of writing badly." Babel was of course alluding to what was considered "bad" merely in socialist realist terms. The bitter irony at the heart of this statement was that the one fundamental if mundane freedom—and the one taken for granted in any democratic society—was precisely that same freedom now denied all creative artists in the Soviet Union, the freedom to fail.

See also Akhmatova, Anna; Art and Architecture; Babel, Isaac; Bulgakov, Mikhail; Cinema; Eisenstein, Sergey; "Engineers of Human Souls"; Mayakovsky, Vladimir; Pasternak, Boris; Prokofiev, Sergey; Sholokhov, Mikhail; Shostakovich, Dmitry; Union of Soviet Writers; Zhdanov, Andrey.

Further reading: Matthew Cullerne Bown. *Art under Stalin.* Oxford: Phaidon, 1991; Katerina Clark. *The Soviet Novel: History as Ritual.* Chicago: University of Chicago Press, 1985; S. D. Krebs, *Soviet Composers and the Development of Soviet Music.* London: Allen and Unwin, 1970; R. Taylor and D. Spring, eds. *The Politics of the Soviet Cinema.* London: Routledge, 1993; Abram Tertz. *On Socialist Realism.* New York: Pantheon, 1960.

Solzhenitsyn, Alexander Isayevich (1918–)

Writer Alexander Solzhenitsyn's long and tortuous relationship with Stalin has been posthumous and one-sided. It is unlikely that Stalin ever even knew of his existence, for Solzhenitsyn was sent to the Gulag for a relatively small offense. And yet this experience would transform the rest of Solzhenitsyn's life, providing him with a mission that has become an enduring obsession, to commit his considerable intellectual powers to chronicling the abuse of human rights in Russia under Stalin and cataloging the evils of the Gulag system.

Solzhenitsyn's own bitter first-hand experience of the workings of political repression began as the result of careless remarks he made about Stalin (to whom he jokingly referred as the "ringleader of the thieves") during the Great Patriotic War of 1941–1945. Yet he had not begun his adult life as a dissident, but rather as a devout

Leninist. As a student he had shown considerable promise and studied mathematics and physics at Rostov University, where he first began writing. No sooner had he graduated, in those days still fired with Communist zeal, than Solzhenitsyn was called up for military service in 1941. He served as a crack artillery technician from 1943 and was involved in fierce fighting on the Bryansk front. Twice decorated for bravery, as well as promoted to the rank of captain, Solzhenitsyn then foolishly criticized Stalin's war strategy in letters to a friend and fellow officer from Rostov.

He was arrested in February 1945 at his battery near the Baltic coast, charged with sedition, and sentenced to eight years in a labor camp. Stalin would never know to what degree his own posthumous notoriety would later be molded by Solzhenitsyn's lone dissident voice. After initially suffering the full brunt of the system, from interrogation in the Lubyanka to the labor gangs of the Gulag, Solzhenitsyn's scientific skills in acoustics were noted and he was transferred to a *sharasha,* one of the special secure units that made use of the talents of incarcerated scientists during the war. He finished his sentence in exile in Karaganda in Kazakhstan, a city where a good half of the inhabitants were exiles like him. He worked there as a schoolteacher until June 1956. By now he had written his first major novel, *Cancer Ward,* based directly on his own brush with death when he had been diagnosed with the disease.

Settling with his wife in Ryazan, Solzhenitsyn continued to work as a schoolteacher in relative obscurity until his short novel about life in the Gulag during the Stalinist era, *One Day in the Life of Ivan Denisovich* (1962), became the first of his works to appear in print. The fact that it was published in the Soviet Union at all remains one of the great contradictions of the unpredictable rule of Nikita Khrushchev. While the novel served a purpose as a moral force in Khrushchev's program of de-Stalinization, it also precipitated Khrushchev's own fall from power two years later. But the novel shook both the Soviet Union and the West with its graphic revelations of the brutal life of prisoners in the Gulag and propelled Solzhenitsyn into the political limelight (the poet Anna Akhmatova had prophetically asked of him not long before its publication, "Can you endure fame?").

But in 1964 the literary climate changed after the fall of Khrushchev. The return of hard-line authoritarian rule under Leonid Brezhnev brought with it a creeping revival of Stalinism and made Solzhenitsyn's persecution inevitable. His works were removed from libraries and his two novels *The First Circle* and *Cancer Ward* were both first published abroad in translation, in 1968. Copies circulated on the Russian *samizdat,* the underground press that had become the lifeline for dissident writers in the Soviet Union. Years of constant surveillance, harassment, and even an assassination attempt followed. Solzhenitsyn's stubborn refusal to be cowed by the system resulted in his eventual ostracism by the literary establishment. He was expelled from the Writers' Union in 1969 and was unable to travel abroad to collect his Nobel Prize for literature in 1970, since he knew that the Soviet authorities would never allow him to return.

The last act in Solzhenitsyn's long catalog of defiance of the Soviet regime came in 1973, when he allowed his vast and detailed exposé of the origins of the purges and the workings of the Gulag system *Gulag Archipelago*—to be published in Paris. He had been compiling it in secret for more than ten years, typing it on onionskin paper. Solzhenitsyn's scientific mind (coupled with his exceptional recall of a mass of memorized material, which included 227 eyewitness accounts) enabled him to produce a monumental study of the human rights abuses of the Stalin years in the most scrupulous detail. In so doing he provided a valuable social and historical document that is still indispensable to any historian studying the period.

Wishing to be rid of their own "turbulent priest" of dissent, the Soviet authorities expelled Solzhenitsyn from Russia in February 1974, and Solzhenitsyn's arrival in the West became a major event. But now he was subjected to a different kind of harassment—by the Western media. After a period in West Germany and Switzerland he adopted a life of self-imposed isolation on a well-guarded farm in Vermont. From here Solzhenitsyn occasionally emerged as an austere figure with the long beard of an Old Testament prophet, now venerated as the ubiquitous eminence grise of the totalitarian Soviet system, to give his solemn opinion on the continuing descent into purgatory of the Soviet Union.

Solzhenitsyn's prognostications on Russia's future, however, became increasingly controversial, and his books became ever more ponderous and unreadable. People began to take exception to his retrograde view and to his insistence that a Western-style form of liberal democracy would never work in a Russia molded by centuries of despotic rule. Solzhenitsyn was now insisting that Russia's only hope lay in its readoption of what seemed to many another equally hidebound way of life, as stultifying as the old Soviet system, that of Russian Orthodoxy. Russia's only hope, he argued, lay in promoting a revival of a traditional form of Russian nationalism focused on the old historic heartland of White Russia, a Russia that by necessity excluded the great mass of its nationalities, in particular its huge Muslim population.

During the Gorbachev era Solzhenitsyn's works were at last published in Russian and his citizenship was restored. But even now he had to fight hard for the publication of *Gulag Archipelago,* which finally began publication in the literary journal *New World* (*Noviy Mir*) in 1989, but only after intercession by Gorbachev himself. Old Guard Stalinists had done all they could to subvert its publication by deliberately organizing the withholding of the supply of paper to the journal.

After the official demise of the Soviet Union in 1991, Solzhenitsyn prepared to return to his homeland. He chose to mark his return in 1994, as a latter-day prodigal son and prophet, by making a ceremonial journey that took on all the trappings of a royal progress across Russia. He was accompanied by a film crew on the Trans-Siberian express from Vladivostok to Moscow, during the course of which he took every opportunity to stop off and pontificate to anyone who would listen on Russia's terminal decline into decadent Western ways.

It soon became apparent that Solzhenitsyn's return would not be an easy one. By this time the great prophet had fallen victim, in the Tolstoyan tradition, to what the writer A. N. Wilson suggested has been the fate of several great Russian writers—he had become an "old bore." His own prime-time talk show on Russian television, *Meetings with Solzhenitsyn,* was axed when it rapidly degenerated into a one-way exercise in Solzhenitsyn's own morbid brand of moralizing. With the publication in 1998 of his latest work, bearing the gloomy title of *Russia in the Abyss,* it seemed unlikely that Russians in the prevailing economic crisis would be rushing to buy it. The publishers decided on a print run of only 5,000 copies in a country of 300 million people.

And indeed, Solzhenitsyn's return did bring with it a dimension of tragedy. For here was the great Russian writer, who had been revered throughout his long years of persecution and exile as a "voice in the wilderness" and a defender of human rights in the old Soviet Union, now faced with the reality that his own countrymen no longer wanted to listen to him. To a new generation born after the death of Stalin he seemed an oddity, a "saintly fool" in the long Russian tradition of such eccentric figures, a Dostoevskian prophet of doom who had outlived his time. His hectoring calls for a return to the traditional ways and values of Russian Orthodoxy did nothing to impress the young, and he was now deriding precisely those aspects of the modern consumer society that the average Soviet citizen had waited so long to have a taste of. And so, while Solzhenitsyn could belligerently insist that the "human soul longs for higher things" than material comforts, the bitter reality of his argument could be seen in the lines outside McDonald's.

With his audience falling away, Solzhenitsyn once more became a recluse, this time at a large new dacha built for him outside Moscow. On the occasion of his eightieth birthday in 1998 he was awarded the Order of the Apostle St. Andrew for "outstanding services to the nation." Whether he will enjoy a long-term reputation in literary terms is uncertain. His autocratic brand of self-righteousness infects all his work and diminishes its literary impact. But it is a monumental opus, which has now been set in stone as a Soviet *Book of the Dead,* and Solzhenitsyn can no doubt go to his grave certain in the belief that, as he himself once put it, "I have fulfilled my duty to those who perished."

See also De-Stalinization; The Great Terror; Gulag; Science

Further reading: Alexander Solzhenitsyn. *Cancer Ward.* London: Bodley Head, 1969; Alexander Solzhenitsyn. *The First Circle.* London: William Collins, 1968; Alexander Solzhenitsyn. *The Gulag Archipelago, 1918–1956: An Experiment in Literary Investigation,* 3 vols. London: Collins, 1974, 1978; Alexander Solzhenitsyn. *One Day in the Life of Ivan Denisovich.* Harmondsworth, UK: Penguin, 1963; D. M. Thomas. *Alexander Solzhenitsyn: A Century in His Life.* London: Little, Brown, 1998.

Spanish Civil War

At the outbreak of the Spanish Civil War in July 1936, Stalin's initial policy had been one of nonintervention. With both Hitler and Mussolini coming out in support of General Franco's fascist forces he soon felt compelled, however, to involve the Comintern in a half-hearted propaganda exercise in support of the embattled Republican government. This token gesture of Soviet support for what many saw as a "just war" in Spain fell far short of unconditional support for the government of the Spanish Republic, led by Largo Caballero. But for Stalin it served a useful purpose in diverting international attention from the political inquisition of the purges going on in the Soviet Union at the time and provided a useful opportunity, for Stalin, of ridding the world of a few more Trotskyists.

Stalin thus had his own political agenda for Soviet involvement—the infiltration by NKVD (secret police) agents of the undesirable elements fighting with the Republican forces, particularly the Trotskyist members of POUM (the Marxist party of Catalonia) in order to eliminate them. Indeed, much of the eager enthusiasm of the International Brigades who fought in Spain would soon be dissipated in factional infighting, leading to bitter disillusion for many of these committed young Communists from around the world who had volunteered through the Comintern to fight for the Republican cause.

Beginning in September 1936, at the suggestion of the French Communist leader Maurice Thorez, who remembered the non-Russian Communist sympathizers who fought in special brigades in the Russian-Polish War of 1919–1920, the Comintern recruited and sent to its main base at Albacete in La Mancha a total of about 42,000 fighters (including some women). These volunteers served in seven International Brigades, each divided into battalions by nationality under the overall command of the Spanish Republican Army, with at most 20,000 fighting at any one time.

France sent by far the greatest number, 10,000 volunteers. Many of these were already committed Communists recruited by the French trade union organization, the Confédération Générale du Travail, by way

of its principal recruiting office in Paris run by Josip Broz (the future Marshal Tito). But at the other end of the spectrum there was even a contingent of Russian émigrés and former White supporters who fought on the Republican side. Considerable support also came from volunteers from Germany, Austria, Poland, Italy, the United States, the United Kingdom, Yugoslavia, Czechoslovakia, Canada, and Hungary.

Stalin sent 407 tanks and 648 aircraft to aid the Republicans, as well as about 3,000 military specialists and "advisers," many of whom were agents of the NKVD. He made clear to the few chosen Soviet generals among them that they should keep well away from the front lines. The combined forces of the International Brigades were commanded by General Emil Kleber, an Austrian who had gone over to the Bolsheviks and had taught in the Comintern military academy.

Despite some early successes in battles at Jarama and Guadalajara in 1937, it soon became apparent to Stalin that the war in Spain was unwinnable. In any event, the political climate had changed, and he now saw it as more advantageous to seek an economic and political rapprochement with Hitler's fascist Germany. The Republicans were now outnumbered by fascist forces bolstered by an influx of supporters of Hitler and Mussolini. As Soviet support waned, recruits to the International Brigades began to dwindle, to be replaced by Spanish Communists. Meanwhile, many of the brigades now found themselves caught up in witch-hunts against non-Communist fighters within their own ranks, such as the anarchists or Marxist members of POUM in Catalonia. Fighting in Barcelona between Communists and anarchists/POUM supporters resulted in 400 deaths in 1937. Not long after, Andres Nin, the leader of POUM, was arrested and murdered by NKVD agents.

A miserable fate awaited the 6,000 or so Spaniards who fled to the Soviet Union after being defeated in Spain in the spring of 1939. Many were sent to labor camps, others deported to Central Asia. And a similar welcome awaited many Russians who had served in Spain. Soviet Consul-General in Barcelona Vladimir Antonov-Ovseenko, head of the Comintern forces General Kleber, and the eminent Soviet journalist Mikhail Koltsov were all arrested and shot on their return to the Soviet Union. Nor had Stalin's support for the Republicans been a philanthropic gesture: as payment for his supply of arms and military advisers to the Spanish Republic, he received in return the bulk of the government's gold reserves of $518 million, which were quietly dispatched from Spain to Odessa and on to Moscow.

See also; Comintern; Koltsov, Mikhail

Further reading: Gerald Howson. *Arms for Spain: The Untold Story of the Spanish Civil War.* London: John Murray, 1998; Hugh Thomas. *The Spanish Civil War,* 3d ed., revised and enlarged. Harmondsworth, UK: Penguin, 1977.

Sport

The attitude of the Bolsheviks to sport as recreation had been a negative one. After the Revolution of 1917 and in line with Lenin's own rejection of personal pursuits and pleasures, sport was condemned as a self-indulgent frivolity, as yet another manifestation of the bourgeois society that socialism was now in the process of sweeping away. The new Soviet state had more pressing economic concerns, and the only valid use for athletic prowess was in its application to physical labor on the farm, in the mines, and in the factory.

It took time for sports activity to build in popularity throughout the 1920s, at a time when the Soviet Union was excluded from the Olympic Games and not involved in international sporting competition. But by 1925 the government had recognized the value of sport in maintaining healthy bod-

ies to sustain Soviet industry and had taken control, announcing that henceforth all forms of physical culture would be incorporated into the political and cultural fabric of Soviet life. There was also another objective in this drive to create a healthy nation—the use of sport as a means of social and moral control and universal propaganda. A national fitness program was launched to promote better health among the peasants in the country and to cure them of some of the more boorish aspects of their behavior, as well as to forestall juvenile delinquency in the cities.

Under Stalin, competitive sport blossomed. Parks of culture and rest were set up in cities. Sports clubs mushroomed in factories and schools. Fitness programs, involving a daily "keep fit" routine, became a means of keeping those on the factory floor happy and, as always, collectively involved. With time, sport became thoroughly professionalized, and the Stakhanovite mentality of overachievement rubbed off even in sport. Here, as in any other field, Soviet citizens were exhorted to do better than anyone else: winning titles and competitions became as important as fulfilling production quotas. By the late 1930s, the major cities boasted several first-class football teams and, by the time war broke out, the Soviets had proved their preeminence in such sports as weight-lifting, swimming, ice hockey, and speed skating.

As sport became increasingly popular as a mass participation event, Stalin, like Hitler, also recognized the huge propaganda value of public parades of fine-looking sportsmen and women at political events and anniversaries as a means not only of arousing patriotic pride but of promoting Soviet society itself to the world outside. Showpiece parades such as the May Day celebrations would feature routines by superbly coordinated gymnasts and sportsmen, all testifying to the physical wellbeing that life under socialism offered. Images of these grand occasions filtered through to the West in the work of photographers such as Alexander Rodchenko, whose role in celebrating the prowess of Soviet athletes through the medium of photography was similar to that of Leni Riefenstahl in Nazi Germany.

Like other high-profile personalities in the arts, Soviet sportsmen enjoyed privileges and honors unknown to the average Soviet citizen and even enjoyed the rare privilege of being allowed to travel abroad to compete. Of all the countries that had adopted the English game of football, none had done so more fervently than the Soviet Union, and matches became the focal point for a public letting off of steam that was all too rare in a society that, under Stalin, was closely controlled and monitored.

Football also performed another important function—that of national integration and the defusing of ethnic rivalries in a collective pursuit of excellence that had mass appeal. The establishment of a pan-national football league in the Soviet Union in 1936 provided the major cities with their own teams, and while it subsumed national divisions, it also paved the way for serious rivalries between teams controlled by various state institutions, such as the Moscow Dynamos (supported by the NKVD [secret police]) and Spartak (the favorites of the Soviet intelligentsia and trade unionists). The latter club was the domain of the Starostins—founder and club manager Nikolay Starostin and his three player brothers. During the 1930s they built up a huge following, but when Spartak won the national championships three years in a row (1937–1939) the team had become too popular in the eyes of Lavrenty Beria, head of the NKVD. During the Great Patriotic War, all four brothers were arrested and sent to the Gulag.

See also Education; "New Soviet Man"; Stakhanovites

Further reading: Robert Edelman. *Serious Fun.* Oxford: Oxford University Press, 1993; James Riordan. *Sport in Soviet Society: Development of*

Sport and Physical Education in Russia and the U.S.S.R. Cambridge: Cambridge University Press, 1977.

Stakhanovites

The awesome achievement of the Soviet coal miner Aleksey Grigorovich Stakhanov (1906–1977) symbolized the superhuman levels of physical endurance and self-sacrifice made by a Soviet worker in the name of industrialization in the 1930s. It also inspired a frenzy of similar achievements with an obsession for "overfulfillment of the norm" gripping Soviet industry with an almost religious fervor. During the 1930s the cult of Stakhanovites dominated Soviet headlines, but latterly the inspiration behind the movement and Stakhanov's "achievement" itself have been exposed as a fraud.

The story began on the night of 30 August 1935 at the Irmino Coal Mine in the Donbass region of Ukraine, when Aleksey Stakhanov reportedly hacked out fourteen times more coal than the quota required of him during his six-hour shift, extracting 102 tons of coal in only five hours and forty-five minutes. Such an inspired piece of masochism was perfect material for the Stalinist propaganda machine, and soon others rushed to follow Stakhanov's example and earn their fifteen minutes of fame: their achievements were featured in newspapers and newsreels across the Soviet Union. Within a year it had become a mass participation, militaristic movement with "shock-workers" out to storm production quotas, and praised by Stalin as the embodiment of the "New Soviet Man." Those who could rise to the challenge and work themselves to exhaustion followed Stakhanov's example in the coming months: a milling-machine operator achieved a level of productivity 820 percent above his norm; in the massive automobile plant at Gorky, one laborer forged 966 crankshafts in a single shift; a shoemaker in Leningrad turned out 1,400 pair of shoes

The coal miner Aleksey Stakhanov (in the foreground) initiated the cult of the Stakhanovite worker in 1935 when he achieved record levels of output in a single shift. Other workers followed suit throughout industry and agriculture.

in the same period; and on a collective farm three female Stakhanovites proved they could cut sugar beet faster than was thought humanly possible. All such workers were awarded privileges of higher pay, better food, access to luxury consumer goods, and improved living accommodation. Other sectors of society—writers, filmmakers, and artists—were also exhorted to celebrate and encourage the achievements of the Stakhanovite, as in Leonid Lyukov's 1939 film *A Great Life,* about coal miners in the Donets Basin, which was given Andrey Stakhanov's personal seal of approval.

While the rises in industrial output brought about by the efforts of Stakhanovites were welcomed by Stalin and while there was undoubted enthusiasm for the movement among some workers, it also brought increased and unwanted pressures for the vast majority of the workforce. With the mentality of Stakhanovism permeating the whole of Soviet society, excessive levels of achievement were encouraged everywhere, particularly on building sites and in industry, but also in agriculture. On the collective farms, however, the movement was greeted in the main with apathy by exhausted workers with such remarks as, "We have done enough fulfilling; our horses will all be dead by spring." The already hard-pressed Soviet workforce and its bosses, many of them struggling to meet production levels on poorly maintained and often outmoded equipment, increasingly suffered the consequences of industrial accidents or production problems. Some grew to resent their Stakhanovite co-workers for pushing up the production quotas demanded of them to unreasonable levels. Resentment often boiled over into violence and acts of sabotage and machine wrecking, with some Stakhanovites even being attacked by their workmates.

Eventually the movement began to lose momentum when it became apparent that it was impossible for industry to sustain such high levels of production. Workers actually began petitioning their bosses to reduce the workload, and it was later revealed that Stakhanov's achievement was not quite as heroic as it had seemed. Apparently, he had not achieved his record single-handed but with the support of a back-up team of workers, who had maintained the momentum by shoveling away the coal as he cut it and had kept the machinery going. In addition, they had also had that rare advantage—machinery that actually worked, unlike elsewhere in the Soviet mining industry.

See also "Life Has Become Better, Life Has Become Merrier"; "New Soviet Man"

Further reading: L. H. Siegelbaum. *Stakhanovism and the Politics of Productivity in the U.S.S.R. 1935–41.* Cambridge: Cambridge University Press, 1988.

Stalin: Birth of

According to most reference sources, and indeed many standard monographs written on him, Stalin's date of birth was 21 December (9 December Old Style according to the Julian calendar then in use) 1879. However, recent examination of documents newly available in the central archive of the Communist Party by the writer Edvard Radzinsky and others has revealed that this date is fictitious.

According to baptismal records from the Cathedral of the Assumption at Gori, where Stalin was born, Iosif Dzhugashvili (Stalin's birth name) was born on 6 December (Old Style) and christened on 17 December 1878. Stalin's certificate from school also confirms this date. The alteration to Stalin's date of birth in official Soviet records seems to have first occurred in 1922. While Stalin is known to have been obsessive about suppressing the unattractive details of his pre-1917 life and particularly the circumstances of his childhood in Georgia, there appears to be no logical reason why he should choose to change the date of his birth by a year to the official date of 21 December 1879, except perhaps as a mere whim, in some way to distance himself from his less-than-memorable humble beginnings. The official Soviet date still persists in many historical texts, and the newly confirmed date is still taking time to gain widespread acceptance.

See also Dzhugashvili, Ekaterina; Dzhugashvili, Vissarion; Gori
Further reading: Edvard Radzinsky. *Stalin*. London: Hodder & Stoughton, 1996.

Stalin: Dachas of

Throughout his life Stalin, who disliked his official apartments in the Kremlin with their vast, ornate surroundings, decamped whenever possible to one of his dachas near Moscow. During his rule he had several dachas and villas built for him, but his two favorites were the dacha at Kuntsevo, nicknamed "Blizhny" ("the near one"—it was 15 miles from Moscow), and his "further" home, the dacha at Zubalovo (20 miles further south).

In her memoirs of her father, Svetlana Allilueva recalled some happy times spent at the dacha at Zubalovo before her mother's death in 1932 as well as the hot summer months of July and August, when the family spent vacations further south at government dachas in the Crimea, particularly Sochi. At Zubalovo, Svetlana and her brother Vasily enjoyed themselves in the midst of an extended family that included many of their mother's relatives and sometimes the relatives of Stalin's first wife. There were also regular visits from Party bigwigs—Sergey Kirov, Nikolay Bukharin, and Grigory Ordzhonikidze—and their wives in the days before the Great Terror engulfed all their lives.

Stalin had acquired the dacha at Zubalovo not long after his marriage to Nadezhda Allilueva. It had once been one of several grand country villas owned by a family of Caucasian oil magnates, the Zubalovs, who had made their money on the oil refineries of Stalin's old revolutionary stamping-ground of Baku and Batum. Zubalovo, like many other properties belonging to the Russian bourgeoisie, was confiscated at the time of the revolution, and many were reallocated to leading *apparatchiks*.

After Nadezhda's suicide in 1932, Stalin stopped going to Zubalovo, because the memories it evoked were too painful a reminder of the bitter circumstances of her death. In 1934 he had a dacha built for himself in the village of Kuntsevo, a short car journey from central Moscow. Since the nineteenth century, Kuntsevo had been a popular country retreat for such writers as Gogol, Turgenev, and Tolstoy. For the rest of his life Stalin spent increasing amounts of time here, constantly having parts of the

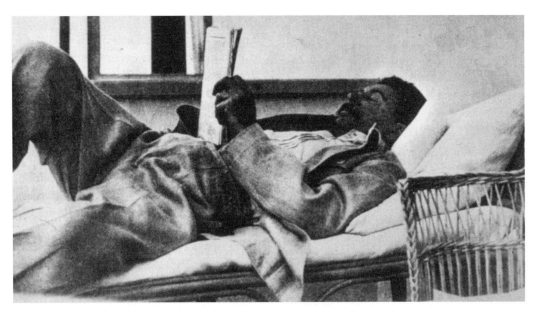

Stalin relaxing (although no doubt reading official papers), his uniform unbuttoned, at one of his dachas. He rarely took holidays but had several dachas built for himself, including his favorite at Kuntsevo just outside Moscow.

villa modified and rebuilt and eventually having a separate smaller house built within the grounds, in which he later stayed. No matter how late his work kept him in the Kremlin, he preferred to return to Kuntsevo to sleep. Secure within a double perimeter fence, and with the grounds patrolled by Russian wolfhounds, Stalin was looked after by his faithful housekeeper, Valentina Istomina (a waitress whom he had transferred from the Zubalovo dacha), his personal physician, and other servants who lived in a separate wing.

Stalin himself used few of the rooms available. The second floor, which he added in 1948, remained unoccupied. Most of his time was spent in his favorite room, the dining room with its open fire in winter and its collection of records of Russian, Georgian, and Ukrainian folk music. Ever more nocturnal in his habits, Stalin would sit up drinking and joking with his guests into the early hours of the morning. Meanwhile his Politburo toadies, who were obliged to keep awake until Stalin deemed it was time for bed, would try hard to enjoy themselves. But the atmosphere was often tense, and as the Yugoslav politician Milovan Djilas observed on a visit to Kuntsevo in the late 1940s, dinners at Kuntsevo "resembled a patriarchal family with a crotchety head whose foibles always made his kinsfolk somewhat apprehensive." Eventually Stalin would sleep, albeit fitfully, for an hour or two before dawn on a bed made up on the sofa. When alone at Kuntsevo, he ate his meals at his desk. His only relaxation was taking strolls on the terrace and tending his beloved garden, which he often did in the dead of night.

In 1949 Stalin had a dacha built in an almost inaccessible spot on the cliffs above the Black Sea at Kholodnaya Rechka ("Cold Stream"), which after his death was used as a private sanatorium for senior *apparatchiks* from the Comintern. Light and spacious, with parquet floors, its own private cinema, and billiard tables, the house enjoyed the most spectacular views, and he later had another dacha built in the grounds for his daughter Svetlana. As he aged, Stalin became increasingly obsessed about death and the possibility of assassination and would sleep here in a different room every night. Even at Kuntsevo he would order fresh sets of bed linen to be left out for him to make the bed himself, and he always insisted on checking underneath his bed before retiring. Stalin's favorite bedroom at Kholodnaya Rechka had one wall built against the rock face. He was more interested in security than the sea view and would bring with him to the dacha an entourage of as many as 700 guards.

It was at Kuntsevo, near Moscow, that Stalin had his fatal stroke on the night of 28 February–1 March 1953 after an evening in the company of Marshal Bulganin, Lavrenty Beria, Nikita Khrushchev, and Georgy Malenkov. But he did not die until five days later, still at Kuntsevo, although the official announcement told his grieving public that he had died at the Kremlin. After his death there was talk of converting the dacha to a museum of Stalin's life, but Khrushchev's denunciation of Stalin in 1956 put an end to all plans. The house was closed up and the servants' quarters turned into a sanatorium.

See also Stalin: Death of; Stalin: Private life of
Further reading: Svetlana Alliluyeva. *Twenty Letters to a Friend*. London: Hutchinson, 1967; Milovan Djilas. *Conversations with Stalin*. London: Hart Davis, 1962; Adam Hochschild. *The Unquiet Ghost: Russians Remember Stalin*. London: Serpent's Tail, 1995.

Stalin: Death of

The official communiqué of Stalin's death on 5 March 1953 informed the Soviet people in portentous tones that "the heart of Josef Vissarionovich Stalin, Lenin's comrade in arms, and the inspired continuator of his work, wise leader, and teacher of the Communist Party and the Soviet people, has stopped beating." But the true circumstances of Stalin's death, not at the Kremlin as the nation was told but at his dacha at Kuntsevo, were far from dignified. His lingering end between his first stroke

on 28 February and his final demise five days later was played out like a grotesque black comedy, heightened by the sheer, paralyzing terror of those who witnessed Stalin's final hours and were too afraid to intervene.

For the last few years of his life, Stalin had become increasingly reclusive and paranoid, spending more and more time at his dacha at Kuntsevo with grounds patrolled by guard dogs and his food and medicines closely monitored by his most trustworthy servants. On the evening of 28 February, after watching a film at the Kremlin, Stalin, as was his habit, returned to his dacha with his closest cronies from the Politburo—Lavrenty Beria, Georgy Malenkov, Marshal Bulganin, and Nikita Khrushchev—and spent the rest of the night drinking Georgian wine until 4 A.M.

The following day Stalin did not emerge from his room. The hours passed, the lights came on in his room at 6:30 P.M., but his servants were still too frightened to enter uninvited. After hovering indecisively outside Stalin's door, a bodyguard finally plucked up the courage to open it later that evening and found Stalin lying on the floor, semiconscious, soaked in his own urine. The Politburo was summoned from the Kremlin, but they were reluctant to intervene, accepting Beria's suggestion that the snoring noises Stalin was making indicated that he was "sleeping peacefully." They left without ordering medical help for Stalin, who had now been lifted onto a sofa. Doctors were finally summoned the following morning and, overcoming their terror (they were visibly shaking), examined the prostrate leader and confirmed that he had suffered a brain hemorrhage. The reluctance of anyone to rush to Stalin's aid has suggested that his end was hastened in some way. Lazar Kaganovich's biographer claimed that the Politburo had conspired to tamper with Stalin's anticoagulant medication in order to precipitate his physical decline. Whether or not this is true, Stalin's entourage ensured the inevitability of his death by not taking prompt medical action.

Eventually, the entire Moscow Academy of Medical Sciences was harnessed to try to save Stalin's life. At Kuntsevo the doctors made futile attempts at treatment with leeches and various injections. A Russian newspaper article in the 1990s relates how Dr. Galina Chesnokova, who specialized in brain surgery (as well as the more dubious science of reanimation), spent three almost sleepless days at Stalin's bedside in an attempt to revive the dying man, who seemed to her "very old." Daily radio broadcasts to an anxious nation reported every fluctuation in the leader's physical condition. Death was inevitable. As everyone gathered around to watch the death agony, Stalin, prostrate and unable to do more than make occasional incoherent sounds, never spoke again. At ten minutes to ten on the evening of 5 March he finally died "a difficult and terrible death," in the words of his daughter Svetlana. Both she and Dr. Chesnokova have described how, at the last moment, Stalin opened his eyes and gave those surrounding him a terrifying look. He then "raise[d] his left hand. It seemed as though he was coming to and wanted to say something . . . but his hand dropped and he said nothing."

Stalin's body was immediately embalmed in the special laboratory, set up in the Lenin Mausoleum to maintain Lenin's corpse, and he then lay in state in the Hall of Columns in Moscow. The nation at large was numb with shock and people wept on the streets. So many thousands of the grief-stricken people tried to get into Moscow to pay their last respects that the authorities sealed off the city. Tragedy followed when 500 people were crushed to death as the vast crowd surged to file past the corpse. On the day of Stalin's funeral, 9 March, the Soviet Union stood still. For the Russian people it was a devastating blow, the loss of the nation's father figure, the loss of the "embodiment of everything sacred." More frightening still was the thought of the future without him.

Stalin's reign as an immortal, as a latter-day pharaoh mummified alongside Lenin in the Lenin Mausoleum, was short-lived, however. After an initial wave of effusive tributes, written in the all-too-familiar hyperbole that had been transmuted into a Stalinist art form ("Death closed those eyes which had looked so far into the future"), the Stalin cult began to fade and disintegrate, and its demise was made official three years later with Khrushchev's denunciation. In 1961 Stalin's body was removed from the Kremlin and sealed under concrete in a grave near the Kremlin Wall.

See also Stalin: Private Life of
Further reading: Svetlana Alliluyeva. *Twenty Letters to a Friend*. London: Hutchinson, 1967; Amy Knight. *Beria: Stalin's First Lieutenant*. Princeton, NJ: Princeton University Press, 1983; Dmitri Volkogonov, *The Rise and Fall of the Soviet Empire: Political Leaders from Lenin to Gorbachev*. London: HarperCollins, 1998.

Stalin: Imprisonment and Exile

Between April 1902 and February 1917 Stalin experienced frequent periods of arrest, incarceration, and exile: in the nine years from March 1908 until the February Revolution he spent only one and a half years as a free man.

Since this is often a confusing period in Stalin's early history, and one that he sought to obscure rather than clarify, there are times when little is known of Stalin. A certain contradiction over dates in published sources often arises, due to the fact that the Russians were still at this time using the old-style Julian calendar (thirteen days behind the Gregorian). The truth of Stalin's activities during these years was further muddied in the 1930s, when Soviet historiography falsified the record as part of the general directive to attribute to Stalin a more prominent revolutionary role than he had in fact played. Speculation also continues on how Stalin managed to escape from exile five times with such apparent ease, and unsubstantiated rumors abounded that he operated during this period as a double agent for the tsarist authorities.

Stalin was first picked up by the police in April 1901 and shut away in the filthy prison at Batum in Georgia. Here he quickly adapted to the harsh regimen to become acknowledged leader of the inmates. After spending eighteen months in prison in Batum and Kutaisi he was moved to Nizhnaya Uda in Siberia. He attempted to escape during his first Siberian winter of 1903, but cold and frostbite held him back until the following January, when he escaped and made his way back to Tiflis, Georgia, on forged documents.

For the next four years Stalin managed to evade arrest, until the tsarist authorities caught up with him again in March 1908. He was sent to Bailovka prison, Baku, before being sentenced to two years' exile for his membership of the Baku Committee of the Russian Social Democrats. This time he was exiled within European Russia to Solvychegodsk in Vologda province, but he took sick with typhus on his way there. He escaped from Solvychegodsk in the summer of 1909 and once again headed back to Georgia, only to be recaptured in March 1910 and sent back to Bailov jail and then back to Solvychegodsk. Here in 1911 Stalin rented a room in the house of a widow, Marya Prokopievna Kusakova, where he remained until the end of his term of exile, after which he was forbidden return to the Caucasus or to live in any major cities for five years.

In June 1911, his exile ended, Stalin moved to Vologda. No sooner had he ventured again to St. Petersburg on a stolen passport two months later than he was rearrested. In mid-December he was exiled back to Vologda, but, on receiving a visit there from his fellow revolutionary Sergo Ordzhonikidze in February 1912, he answered the Bolshevik Party's call and evaded police surveillance to head for St.

Petersburg again. Stalin managed to evade arrest for a few more weeks before being caught and sent to the more remote and much harsher surroundings of Narym in northern Siberia in May 1912. But like a bad penny, he turned up yet again in St. Petersburg after only two months.

Stalin's final arrest by the authorities came in February 1913, when he was sent even further away to a settlement at Turukhansk on the river Yenisey in Siberia. When the authorities got wind of his plans to escape in 1914, Stalin was again moved further up into the Arctic Circle to a remote settlement at Kureika. For once in Stalin's long and tortuous catalog of escape and rearrest, it really was impossible to get away. Now more than ever, with money for food and fuel running out and reliant on handouts from friends, Stalin found himself pining for the balmy climate of his Georgian homelands. He wrote friends that "this accursed landscape is hideously bare, and I have fretted myself stupid longing for a landscape to look at, if only on paper." In Kureika he sat out the rest of his sentence until, after being rejected for military service during World War I, he was allowed to move to Achinsk in south-central Russia in 1916. From there he traveled to Petrograd on the eve of the revolution, in March 1917.

See also Baku; Batum; Historiography
Further reading: Edvard Radzinsky. *Stalin.* London: Sceptre, 1997; Edward Ellis Smith. *The Young Stalin. The Early Years of an Elusive Revolutionary.* New York: Farrar, Straus and Giroux, 1967; Robert C. Tucker. *Stalin as Revolutionary 1879–1929.* New York: Chatto and Windus, 1974.

Stalin: Nicknames, Aliases, and Official Titles

During the course of his early revolutionary career, through 1912, Stalin used a string of aliases. Such bogus and often deliberately parodic names were the prerequisites of any Russian revolutionary operating underground and living under constant threat of arrest by tsarist authorities. Between 1899, when he first took the revolutionary code name Koba, and January 1913, when he finally and publicly settled on the new name of Stalin, the true personality of the man who had been born Iosif Dzhugashvili remained hard to pin down. Secretive in both his revolutionary and private life, Stalin ensured that his precise movements during this period are not always clear, and the constant changing of aliases underlines his deliberate elusiveness at this time.

Later, with the inception of the cult of the personality in December 1929, the comic names concocted to subvert tsarist authority were replaced with a new genre of even more patently absurd epithets. But this time there was nothing funny about these new flights of hyperbole, for they were the product of desperate imaginations, anxious to underline their loyalty to Stalin at a time when the slightest political sin could lead straight to the Gulag. While loyal Stalinists at large strained their brains to come up with superlatives that would encapsulate the breadth of Stalin's great mind and vision, behind closed doors there were still some in the Soviet Union who had their own private and less flattering names for Stalin. There may well have been many more names than are listed here, but we shall never know; such was the nature of the Great Terror that anyone publicly uttering derogatory remarks about Stalin did so at their own peril.

Batyushka—a colloquial form of "little father." In tsarist times it was used to address priests and, in particular, used by the peasantry to refer to the tsar. This popular epithet was later revived among ordinary people to refer to Stalin, particularly in situations of request or petition, and the sentiment was extended to other Christ-like attributions, such as the *Father of the People*. Similarly, the word *dyadya* ("uncle") was used among the peasantry to refer to Stalin on occasion.

Benevolent Friend of All Children; The Wise Helmsman; The Mountain Eagle; The Leader and Teacher of the Workers of the World; The Greatest Genius of All Times/of Our Epoch; The Titan of the World Revolution; The Best Disciple of Comrade Lenin; The Most Profound Theoretician of Contemporary Times—a selection of the grandiose epithets applied to Stalin during the cult of the personality.

J. Besoshvili—a Georgian alias used by Stalin in the 1900s.

Comrade Card Index (tovarishch kartotekov)—Stalin's nickname among *apparatchiks* after he became general secretary of the Communist Party in 1922. It alludes to his phenomenal powers of recall and his ability to remember the most trivial names and facts.

Chizhikov/Chichikov—an alias used by Stalin in 1911 when he arrived in St. Petersburg; probably taken from the hero of Nikolai Gogol's 1842 novel *Dead Souls*.

The Cockroach (tarakan)—a nickname for Stalin popularized in the 1930s. The word *tarakan* already had a colloquial use, as a nickname for someone with a mustache. It also had literary allusions to banditry and tyranny. It became associated with Stalin through the unofficial popularization of two satirical images of him—in the narrative poem written in 1923 by Korney Chukovsky, *The Big Bad Cockroach,* and in the infamous poem by Osip Mandelstam in 1933 in which he referred to Stalin's "cockroach whiskers."

Generalissimo—Stalin's self-appointed rank, acquired shortly after viewing the Victory Parade through Red Square, held at the end of the Great Patriotic War on 24 June 1945, from the top of the Lenin Mausoleum. He also made himself a "Hero of the Soviet Union" at around the same time.

Gensek—the Soviet abbreviated form of "General Secretary," a title often used among party bureaucrats to refer to Stalin in his role running the Communist Party.

The God-appointed leader of our military and cultural forces—The Russian Orthodox Patriarch, Sergius, propagated this religiose title during the Great Patriotic War, at a time when Stalin had allowed a relaxation of restrictions on religious practice in order to galvanize public support for the war effort.

Ivanovich (literally, "son of Ivan")—the alias was used by Stalin when he first traveled abroad to meet Lenin at Tammerfors in Finland in 1905. In Russia, Ivanovich would be as common as "Smith" in other areas of the world, therefore ensuring anonymity. Stalin also used it at Party congresses in Stockholm and London in 1906–1907. Lenin continued to use the name in relation to Stalin until 1912, no doubt symptomatic of the fact that he had trouble remembering Stalin's real name. Ivanovich was often used in conjunction with Stalin's other favored alias, Koba, as Koba Ivanovich.

K. Kato—the by-line used by Stalin for articles published in the Baku trade union news sheet *The Siren* (*Gudok*) in 1907. This is probably derived from his wife Ekaterina's pet name, Kato.

Genghis Khan—Nikolay Bukharin's nickname for Stalin, in an allusion to Stalin's Asiatic qualities of brutality, although the attribution is incorrect since Stalin was Georgian, from Transcaucasia, not Asia.

Khozyain ("the Boss")—this was the nickname that stuck with Stalin's associates within the government and the Politburo, although he tried hard to assume the mantle of Lenin by adopting the more benign title *starik* ("the old man"), the affectionate, self-deprecating signature used by Lenin in the years before the revolution.

Koba—Stalin's chosen alias as a member of the revolutionary underground of the Mesame Dasi, the Georgian Social Democrats, throughout his activities in the Caucasus. It was taken from the name of the hero of a popular nineteenth-century novel, *The Parricide,* by Georgian writer Alexander Kazbegi (1848–1893), in which this Robin Hood-like freedom fighter battles against Russian domination and the exploitation of

his homeland. Stalin continued to use this code name during his early association with Lenin and the other leading Bolsheviks in exile. Although he adopted the name "Stalin" in about 1911, he continued to be known privately as Koba among some of his older associates and intimates, particularly Nikolay Bukharin, who in one of his last tragic notes to Stalin before his execution in 1938 invoked the name, asking, "Koba, why do you want me to die?"

The Lenin of Today—Stalin particularly liked this epithet, which was adopted as one of the most popular slogans of his rule. He created it for himself and deliberately inserted it into the draft of his official *Short Biography,* published in 1939 on the occasion of his sixtieth birthday. It went on to sell 18 million copies. The text, carefully amended by Stalin in several places, included the addition by him: "Stalin is the worthy continuer of Lenin's work, or, as it is said in our Party, 'Stalin is the Lenin of Today.'"

Zakhar Gregorian Melikyants—the name on a false passport issued to Stalin in July 1909 in Baku, which he was carrying when arrested in March 1910.

Gaioz Nizharadze—the alias used by Stalin when working underground in Baku circa 1907, as recorded in his police file at Bailovka prison, Baku.

Ryaboi ("the pock-marked one")—Stalin's nickname among the tsarist police and informers.

K. Solin/K. Stefin/Salin—pseudonyms used by Stalin for his articles in revolutionary journals up to early 1913.

Soso/Soselo—The pet name used by Stalin's mother when he was a child. A diminutive form of Iosif, it is the Georgian equivalent of "Joey" or "little Joe." In support of the argument that Stalin may have been Ossetian by origin, the pet name "Soso" could have easily been an abbreviated form of the Ossetian form of Jozef, Suslan.

Stalin—An artificial name, meaning "man of steel" (like Kamenev ["man of stone"] and Molotov ["man of the hammer"]), used by Stalin officially for the first time in a letter to the *Social Democrat* newspaper, 12 January 1913. He had, in fact, been using the name intermittently since 1911. This remained his newspaper pseudonym until after the Revolution of 1917, when he adopted it full time.

Oganess Vartanovich Totomyants—a deliberately nonsensical pseudonym with a strong ethnic ring to it, no doubt devised to deliberately mislead and confuse—the equivalent of Charles Dickens's use of hyperbole in the names of his characters.

Uncle Joe—the popular Allied nickname for Stalin used during the war years, the heyday of the Big Three. It was supposedly coined by Franklin Roosevelt, although it was not used in face-to-face situations with Stalin. No doubt Roosevelt gave his ally this pet name because it had a more reassuring timbre than the intimidating sounding "Stalin." It was certainly used by Roosevelt and Churchill to refer to Stalin away from the negotiating table and went very well with the avuncular, pipe-smoking image that Stalin projected. Eventually the name worked its way into the popular Western press (helping to endorse the image abroad of Stalin as a friendly ally), but Stalin is reported to have been incensed when he first heard about it, seeing it as an insult. It took some persuading by his allies for him to accept the element of affection intended, although it was an affection with a patronizing, if not mocking, edge to it.

Comrade Vasiliev, Comrade Ivanov—wartime code names used for Stalin in 1943. Both are equally bland and anonymous, like "Smith" or "Jones."

Ivan Vasilievich—a wartime name used by Stalin often in encoded messages. These are the Christian and patronymic names of one of Stalin's heroes—Ivan the Terrible.

Vassil—a code name used by Lenin to refer to Stalin when Stalin was exiled to Turukhansk.

Vozhd ("the leader")—a title that Stalin encouraged from circa 1933 as an equivalent to the German "Führer" or Italian "Duce." It was a catchall for Stalin in his various incarnations as political, military, and spiritual leader. The title was promoted by *Pravda* on the occasion of Stalin's fiftieth birthday celebrations in 1929 and was particularly linked with the Stalinist cult of the personality.

See also Dzhugashvili, Iosif; General Secretary of the Communist Party; Mandelstam, Osip; Russian Revolution of 1917; Stalin: Imprisonment and Exile

Further reading: Rosalind Marsh. *Images of Dictatorship: Portraits of Stalin in Literature.* London: Routledge, 1989.

Stalin: Personality of

In the spring of 1918 the British diplomat R. H. Bruce Lockhart met various members of the new Bolshevik government at a meeting of the Central Executive Committee in Petrograd. One of those he was introduced to was Stalin, but Lockhart took little notice of him, so captivated was he by the commanding presence of Trotsky. He was so convinced that Stalin "did not seem of sufficient importance," that he later wrote, "If he had been announced then to the assembled Party as the successor to Lenin, the delegates would have roared with laughter." How was it then, that Stalin, the supposedly inconspicuous "backroom boy" of the revolution, managed to transform himself from the nonentity of 1918 into the charismatic leader who would be promoted to godlike status by the Soviet cult of the personality launched in December 1929?

Stalin had a cynical attitude to life and a deep mistrust of humankind. Psychologists might consider that this originated in his deprived childhood, when he had many of his natural sensitivities beaten out of him. His early experiences of poverty and deprivation taught him, as a friend from the Tiflis seminary, Soso Iremashvili, observed, "to [see] everywhere in and everything only the negative, the bad side." Stalin, he continued, "had no faith at all in men's idealistic motives and attributes." This attitude was no doubt further ingrained during his early experiences as a revolutionary, when he had to learn to be streetwise and live on his instincts.

Indeed, Stalin placed great stock in his skills at character assessment. But such skill, which rested in the main on an innate peasant instinct for sniffing out an enemy, would turn increasingly in his later life into a morbid and compulsive suspicion, which became so extreme that he viewed every political ally as a potential rival and allowed himself to be convinced of the supposed treachery of even his oldest friends. He had a habit of suddenly turning on his closest colleagues in the Politburo for no apparent reason and without any warning. As Khrushchev would later relate, Stalin "could look at a man and say: 'Why are your eyes so shifty today?' or 'Why are you turning so much today and avoiding looking at me directly in the eyes?'" Everywhere and in everything he saw "enemies," "two-facers," and "spies." Indeed, Stalin spent all his life working hard to do what others could not. He tried to get inside people's very minds to "open windows into men's souls" (to use the words of Elizabeth I of England).

Stalin admitted as much to his German biographer Emil Ludwig (who wrote a 1940 study of Hitler, Mussolini, and Stalin) when he described his favorite technique of homing in on a person's weaknesses and penetrating his innermost thoughts in order to make him feel vulnerable and at his mercy. And it was precisely this quality that struck U.S. photographer James E. Abbe, when he was allowed to photograph Stalin in the Kremlin in 1932: "As soon as I saw the whites of his eyes I recognized that Stalin has the surgical ability to remove a man's thoughts from his head and sort them out on the table."

Some of these and other telling observations of Stalin's personality and demeanor bear the hallmarks of his close study of Machiavelli, whom he read avidly in exile. There are sections of the sixteenth-century writer's classic works on statecraft that could have been written to describe Stalin. Machiavelli's attitude toward mankind, for example, is that "one can make this generalization about men: they are ungrateful, fickle, liars, and deceivers." Stalin felt this way about people too. In his attitude toward totalitarian power, Machiavelli believed that "he who establishes a tyranny and does not kill Brutus, and he who establishes a democratic regime and does not kill the sons of Brutus, will not last long"—an obvious parallel to Stalin's hounding out of power of Trotsky and others. But most important of all, Stalin eventually made himself the prisoner of Machiavelli's classic dictum "it is much safer for a prince to be feared than loved."

This latter epigram might seem at first a contradiction in Stalin's case. After all, was he not loved and revered to excess by the population at large? It depends very much on the nature of that love. In Stalin's case it was a love built on and given out of fear. Nevertheless, this unnatural love lavished on Stalin through the cult of the personality fed his vanity and validated his belief that he had a great, historic role to play as Lenin's peer. It also convinced Soviet people, of course, that their Great Leader was much larger, much wiser, and more mysterious than any of them, and thus they felt comforted and reassured. Nadezhda Mandelstam sees this reaction as being based on a fundamental, deep-seated feeling of insecurity that had been inbred in the Russian people. They desperately needed to be told exactly where they were going and, after the experience of revolution, famine, and civil war, wanted nothing more than "for the course of history to be made smooth, all the ruts and potholes to be removed, so there should never again be any unforeseen events and everything should flow along evenly and according to plan."

Stalin as the Great Leader offered them precisely the reassurance they craved. The irony, of course, is that in this guise Stalin projected a perverse kind of charisma that disguised his own very real and fundamental sense of insecurity. For he, above all people, knew that the love and veneration offered up to him was for "Stalin," the figure of longing at the center of an artificial cult, and not to Iosif Dzhugashvili (Stalin's birth name), the short, pock-marked Georgian with a withered arm, whose native tongue was not Russian and who had no real history.

And despite rejecting all things Georgian in the course of his public image-making process, Stalin mentally nurtured a long-held personal image of himself as a latter-day Georgian Machiavelli and an obsession with being accorded the kind of unqualified respect traditionally given to a Georgian "prince." Historian Isaac Deutscher pointed out in his brief outline of Stalin's youth that Georgia was a small country overpopulated with impoverished warring princes and clans, who forever held grudges and always exacted revenge for insults. In fact, they operated much like the Sicilian blood brothers, the mafiosi. Stalin most certainly never forgave an insult and would let old grudges eat away at him until they were blown completely out of proportion. In his classic study, *Let History Judge*, Roy Medvedev related a fascinating anecdote about Stalin, dating to 1912 when he was still a virtually unknown Caucasian revolutionary on the run. He visited the home of a friend in Moscow, where he sat and talked with the friend's nine-year-old son for several hours. As he left, Stalin hit the boy hard on the cheek, saying, "Don't cry, little boy. Remember, today Stalin talked to you." The boy's parents later discovered that it was the custom "in many mountain villages of Georgia" that "if a prince came to a peasant's hut, the peasant would call in his son and hit him hard on the cheek, saying, 'Remember that today Prince so-and-so visited our house.'"

Unlike his passionate and impetuous Georgian folk heroes, however, Stalin was a master of self-control and rarely lost his temper (apart from occasional savage bouts of anger aimed at inefficient subordinates). He was supremely skillful at ensuring that the official image he projected was at all times calm, rational, and collected. James E. Abbe commented on his poise and dignity, averring that "there is nothing of the fanatic about Stalin: he is just a deliberate, persistent, calculating person whose faculties coordinate." Stalin had a gift for holding his interlocutors in his steady gaze and for making them wait for an answer through long, ponderous, deliberative silences, after which he would speak, often in monosyllables. His voice was low and he gave his answers in a slow and methodical manner with a completely blank facial expression that was betrayed only by a slight movement of the eyebrows. To say little meant one was in control. Stalin knew that this could both impress and intimidate others, depending on the objective.

Sometimes Stalin's long periods of silence would be spent pacing up and down behind people, puffing on his pipe, as he kept them waiting for a response (he himself always made a point of never ever sitting with his back to anyone!). And if there was conflict during a meeting (particularly during his wartime negotiations with his allies) Stalin always liked to make the transformation, chameleonlike, from tough negotiator to wise conciliator. His skill at gamesmanship worked to perfection. By appearing uncontroversial or unimportant, as Lockhart described him in 1918, Stalin had been able gradually to maneuver himself, unnoticed, into a position of considerable power. It was all part of his love of byzantine intrigue and subterfuge, a skill that led him to induce quarrels and mistrust among his rivals so that he could play one against the other. And when someone betrayed Stalin, and subjected himself to the official inquisition of confession and recantation, Stalin would often step in and personally reassure his victim that all would be well, only to order the person's arrest or execution soon after and even the arrest or execution of the victim's closest relatives.

It was, therefore, a combination of natural guile and intelligence, a flair for duplicity, and a disregard for human suffering that got Stalin to the top. In so doing he proved that a political leader did not necessarily have to be a great military man or a great theoretician to achieve power and stay there. He was happy to leave the intellectualizing to the likes of Lenin. Instead he offered up his own school of dogmatic Stalinist historiography that ultimately was far more politically effective, particularly as a means of social control, than any of the dazzling polemical skills of Lenin or Trotsky. Its wearisome tone pervaded and deadened every aspect of Soviet life. Stalin in his pedantry was the Mr. Gradgrind of Soviet politics. Charles Dickens created Thomas Gradgrind, the archetypal dogmatist, in his 1854 novel *Hard Times*. Gradgrind was a man who stubbornly insisted that, in all things and in all situations, he would entertain only one thing—facts. He was, as Dickens describes him—and the words could equally be applied to Stalin—"[a] man of realities. A man of fact and calculations. A man who proceeds upon the principle that two and two are four, and nothing over, and who is not to be talked into allowing for anything over . . . with a rule and a pair of scales, and the multiplication table always in his pocket, sir, ready to weigh and measure any parcel of human nature, and tell you exactly what it comes to."

It was just such a preoccupation with facts that would lead to Stalin's insistence during the Great Terror on the collection of tangible proof and the extraction of written confessions from people accused of crimes against the state. This mentality was bred in the bone at the religious seminary at Tiflis, where an emphasis on learning scripture by rote and an acceptance of the inviolable truth of written dogma were rigorously inculcated. But what makes the parallel so fascinating is the fact that Svetlana Allilueva echoes precisely Dickens's literary characterization in her own close observations of her father's behavior. Such was Stalin's lack of imagination, his propensity for seeing everything in black and white, that he resisted his wife Nadezhda's repeated requests not to invite Lavrenty Beria, his much-despised secret police chief, to their dacha, arguing, "He's my friend. He's a good Chekist . . . I trust him. *Facts, facts are what I need!* [emphasis added]" But once Stalin had those "facts" about someone, his desire for revenge was implacable, as Allilueva observed: "He was in the grip of an iron logic whereby once you've said A, then B and C have to follow." In this manner, his devoted and submissive secretary, Alexander Poskrebyshev, was dismissed from office after twenty years of voluntary enslavement. Beria had managed to convince Stalin that Poskrebyshev—the least likely of all people—had been leaking state secrets.

Stalin's tremendous powers of recall, his ability to be systematic and to pigeonhole people in his mind and never forget a face, combined to ensure that no one went unpunished. But it also ensured that Stalin spent his entire life surrounded by sycophants who had no real love for him and whose loyalty was bought by their terror that Stalin might one day blow the whistle and expose the whole grotesque charade of their phony camaraderie as a lie. It would appear that he had lost any love he might have had for humanity when his first wife, Ekaterina, died in 1907. It was she, he said, who had been the only one "to soften his stony heart." And he looked upon the suicide of his second wife, Nadezhda, in 1932 with bitter anger. It was a final betrayal that closed his mind off forever to normal human feelings. By the late 1940s it was clear to many in the Politburo and also to such foreign visitors as Milovan Djilas that Stalin's mental health was in dramatic decline. He was beginning to forget things, and by then the onset of senility had further accentuated his increasing fear of physical decline. His mistrust of everyone became so exaggerated that in 1951 Khrushchev heard him remark, "I'm finished. I trust no one, not even myself." Thus Stalin had created for himself a lonely and friendless old age and the setting for a pitiful death.

The traditional approach to Stalin as the evil genius at the center of a brutal totalitarian regime depicted him as a beast or a monster and often argued that he must have been either paranoid, or mad, or suffering from some kind of mental illness to behave as he did. Roy Medvedev related that as early as 1927 an attempt at a psychological analysis of Stalin had been made by a prominent Soviet psychiatrist Vladimir Bekhterev, who had concluded that he was indeed mentally unstable. The opportunity for a thorough clinical study, of course, never arose. It is difficult to see how Stalin could have remained in power for so long if he had indeed been mentally ill, for mental instability often brings with it a lack of emotional control, which was certainly not one of Stalin's failings.

In the late 1890s, the Russian writer Anton Chekhov began making use of the word "psychopath," which had come into popular use by way of Russian and German studies of mental illness. It was a word that rapidly became fashionable and was frequently misapplied, in precisely the same way that the word "neurotic" was after Freud published his theories on human sexual behavior early in the twentieth century. In similar manner, "paranoid" has been bandied about in the twentieth century to describe various manifestations of extreme or erratic behavior, including Stalin's. Chekhov used the word "psychopath" to describe the accumulated neuroses of his eponymous hero in the play Uncle Vanya, and the word in its original Russian sense meant something closer to "obsessive." In the absence of detailed medical diagnosis,

the use of the word "obsessive" seems to offer a clue to the unraveling of Stalin's psyche. For Stalin, like many other men of genius (and in this sense it was a perverted kind of "genius"), was a deeply and compulsively obsessive person. Although he may have been sinking into clinical dementia at the end of his life, it is impossible to determine whether there was a point at which his behavior changed from obsessive to mentally unstable. But certainly by the time of his death, having long since abandoned all those humanizing qualities that might have kept him mentally balanced, he had at long last become dangerously vulnerable.

See also Alliluyeva, Nadezhda; Alliluyeva, Svetlana; The Great Terror; Lenin, Vladimir; Stalin: Private Life of; Svanidze, Ekaterina; Trotsky, Leon
Further reading: Svetlana Alliluyeva. *Twenty Letters to a Friend*. London: Hutchinson, 1967; Svetlana Alliluyeva. *Only One Year*. London: Hutchinson, 1969; Robert Conquest. *The Great Terror: A Reassessment*. London: Pimlico, 1992; Robert Conquest. *Stalin: Breaker of Nations*. London: Weidenfeld, 1993; Roy Medvedev. *Let History Judge: The Origins and Consequences of Stalinism*. New York: Columbia University Press, 1989; Leon Trotsky. *The Revolution Betrayed*. New York: Pathfinder Press, 1973; Robert C. Tucker. *Stalin as Revolutionary 1879–1929: A Study in History and Personality*. London: Chatto and Windus, 1974; Robert C. Tucker. *Stalin in Power: The Revolution from Above, 1928–41*, London: Chatto and Windus, 1990; Dmitri Volkogonov, *Stalin: Triumph and Tragedy*. London: Weidenfeld and Nicolson, 1991.

Stalin: Physical Appearance of

*I*n 1912, on the occasion of one of his many arrests, Stalin's police file recorded the following description: "face pockmarked, eyes hazel, moustache black, nose unremarkable. Special distinguishing marks: wart over right eyebrow, left arm does not bend at elbow." For others who recorded their impressions of Stalin's physical appearance, among them Leon Trotsky, it was frequently the burning "yellow eyes," often "alive with enmity," that they usually

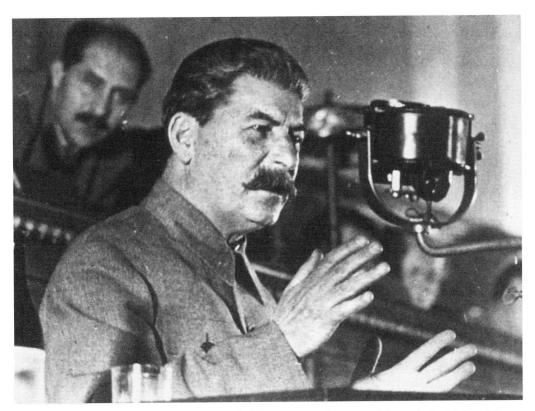

Stalin delivering a speech in 1929 during which he announced the new drive to industrialize. He made few official appearances during his years in power and disliked public speaking, remaining self-conscious about his Georgian accent.

found the most compelling and unsettling of his features.

While Stalin efficiently expunged details of his early life in Georgia in the official histories and biographies produced during his years in power, his low, guttural voice, which was often hard to make out (deliberately so), was always marked by a Georgian accent that was particularly discernible when he pronounced certain Russian words. His physical appearance, such as his shock of black hair and the thick black mustache (satirically referred to as "cockroach whiskers" in a derogatory poem about Stalin written by the poet Osip Mandelstam in 1933) always betrayed his ethnic roots. Ironically, for Stalin (who wanted above all things to be like his Russian co-revolutionaries) his looks were noted by some as "Asiatic" or "Semitic"—Nikholay Bukharin nicknamed him "Genghis Khan,"

though no doubt as much in relation to his cruelty as his looks.

Despite being deeply self-conscious all his life about his Georgian, or possibly Ossetian, origins, Stalin had an admiration for the physicality of Georgian folk heroes, and in the early days of his revolutionary career he no doubt would have given anything to cast a similarly imposing romantic figure. Unfortunately, his shortness of stature and a weak left arm prevented this, and it would need an army of image makers in the 1930s to manufacture a new, larger-than-life Stalin for mass public adoration. Stalin was, in the words of Yugoslav diplomat Milovan Djilas, small and "ungainly. . . . His torso was short and narrow, while his legs and arms were too long." Writer Boris Pasternak found Stalin's physique verging on the grotesque—"A man looking like a crab advanced on me out of the semi-darkness.

The whole of his face was yellow and it was pitted all over with pockmarks. His moustache bristled. He was dwarfish—disproportionately broad and apparently no taller than a twelve-year-old boy, but with an old-looking face."

There was much about Stalin's appearance that many found intimidating, all part of what a relative described as a demonic "sort of Mephistophelian look." The pockmarks were the result of an attack of smallpox at the age of seven. Interestingly, there were some who found these scars "strangely becoming" (one woman office cleaner was denounced during the purges for saying, as she wiped the dust off Stalin's portrait in respectful and affectionate tones, "Now, my dear little pockmarked one, I'll clean thy face"). Certainly women did find Stalin attractive; perhaps it was the lure of his unlimited power as much if not more than any raw sexuality that attracted them.

The damaged arm, which Stalin could not rotate properly at the shoulder and bend at the elbow, and which had exempted him from military conscription in 1916 (as probably had the two webbed toes on his left foot), had resulted from an accident as a child. Stalin was self-conscious about it and often wore a glove to conceal his atrophied left hand. As can be seen in official photographs (which were always cosmetically retouched to avoid betraying any of Stalin's physical inadequacies), he made a point of keeping his left hand, Napoleon-style, inside his jacket. Stalin also had a particular neurosis about his earlobes. When shown his first official portrait, drawn in 1922 when he became general secretary of the Communist Party, he scribbled on it, "this ear says that the artist is not well schooled in anatomy. . . . The ear screams and shouts against anatomy. JS." (It is also related that Hitler ordered a diplomatic envoy to Moscow to ensure that a close-up photograph was taken of Stalin during his mission, so that Hitler could check Stalin's earlobes for Semitic characteristics!)

Stalin was insistent that his public image should make him appear physically commanding and handsome. He was highly critical of official photographs and portraits, in which he was very rarely seen to smile (a case of self-consciousness about his crooked teeth, no doubt combined with the deliberate intention of appearing "enigmatic"). He gave his rare seal of approval to a portrait by the Georgian artist Dmitri Nalbandian, which contrived to disguise Stalin's physical imperfections and for which the artist was awarded a Stalin Prize in 1946. According to Dmitry Shostakovich, the portrait was much reproduced and "hung in every office and even in barber shops and Turkish baths."

Stalin also ensured that his revolutionary exploits were represented in a suitably romantic and heroic mold in the cinema. Shostakovich remarked that Stalin had a particular affection for the image of himself projected "rid[ing] by the footboard of an armored train with a sabre in his hand" in the film *The Unforgettable Year 1919,* made in 1952 by the Georgian director Mikhail Chiaureli. (Despite casting off his Georgian background, Stalin was not averse to promoting the careers of fellow Georgians in both politics and the arts.) In this film Chiaureli, Stalin's favorite director and cinematic spin doctor, gave Stalin a fictitiously strategic role in the defense of Petrograd against the Whites during the civil war. It starred actor Mikhail Gelovani, who would reprise the role of Stalin in other films with Chiaureli and whose makeup artist spent years perfecting the reproduction of Stalin's looks with uncanny accuracy.

The mass of official portraits and photographs that, with careful retouching, eliminated the pockmarks and attempted to "Russianize" Stalin's looks, carefully concealed the fact that Stalin was actually very short—five feet four inches. This lack of height was another abiding neurosis. While the doctoring of photographs could make him appear taller than he was, he could not easily disguise his shortness in public. Where possible, Stalin would resort to the old Hollywood trick of wearing boots with raised heels or standing on a raised slab. He viewed military parades from the top of the Lenin Mausoleum so that he was not towered over by lesser members of the Politburo. Perhaps one of the reasons for Stalin's avoidance of being seen in public may have been his reluctance to reveal himself to his public as anything less than a giant among men.

In his youthful days as a revolutionary Stalin had had a decidedly scruffy, unkempt appearance. Fellow revolutionaries often commented on his "dirty blouse," "unpolished shoes," his "matted hair," and "dirty moustache" and noted that he frequently slept with his boots on. His unprepossessing style of dress was in marked contrast to the dandified appearance of Trotsky, who even in prison wore wing collars and neat suits. In time Stalin became as vain about his appearance as Trotsky, although he never wore a collar and tie, but favored military-style uniforms, at first with the trousers tucked into long boots and from the war years with long trousers disguising the lifts in his shoes. Stalin's figure in uniform was seen everywhere, emblazoned with a few choice medals, especially the Order of the Hero of the Soviet Union. The whole image was topped off with that most reassuring of stage props, the Dunhill pipe, which he frequently clamped to his lips in an avuncular manner during meetings, while quietly sizing up his interlocutors. At the Potsdam Conference at the end of World War II, Stalin appeared to particularly striking effect in a dazzling white uniform that many, including Winston Churchill's daughter, remarked on, proving the old adage that there's a certain something about a man in uniform.

In 1947 the Yugoslav diplomat Milovan Djilas was for a second time one of a delegation sent to visit Stalin in Moscow. He gave a graphic account of Stalin in his declining years, describing him as having "quite a large paunch, and his hair was sparse though his scalp was not completely bald. His face was white, with ruddy cheeks. . . . His teeth were black and irregular, turned inward. Not even his moustache was thick or firm. Still the head was not a bad one . . . with those yellow eyes and a mixture of sternness and mischief." Djilas noted that Stalin's pallid complexion (shared by many in the top Soviet bureaucracy) was the result of long hours spent working at the Kremlin or watching films late into the night in his private cinema. Like Hitler and Churchill, Stalin was an insomniac and subjected his immediate entourage to a rigorously long working day.

Toward the end of his life Stalin suffered a dramatic decline in both physical and mental health and appeared weakened and short of breath. He became even more reclusive, delegating to others the hours-long keynote speeches at party conferences and congresses. The autopsy after his death revealed he had been suffering from "arteriosclerosis of the cerebral arteries," and one of his doctors later argued that the changes to his brain brought on by this condition could explain much of his later erratic and extreme behavior. The debate continues over whether or not Stalin was clinically paranoid or suffering from some form of mental illness. Djilas's observations certainly suggest the onset of senility, if not dementia. Stalin had also become a hypochondriac and was obsessive about the possibility of being poisoned. All his food was specially prepared from freshly killed meat and had to be tasted by his secretary, Alexander Poskrebyshev, Lavrenty Beria, and others. Toward the end of his life, Stalin also insisted on having his food lab-tested on a retinue of rats and mice that went everywhere with him.

See also Art and Architecture; Cinema; Stalin: Personality of; Stalin: Private Life
Further reading: Matthew Cullerne Bown. *Socialist Realist Painting.* New Haven, CT: Yale University Press, 1998; David King. *The*

Commissar Vanishes. Edinburgh: Canongate, 1997. (Svetlana Alliluyeva's memoirs of her father [*Twenty Letters to a Friend* (London: Hutchinson, 1967) and *Only One Year* (London: Hutchinson, 1969)] tend to concentrate on his personality rather than his appearance, but her books and Milovan Djilas's *Conversations with Stalin* [New York: Harvest, 1963], remain the best and most perceptive accounts of his physical appearance.)

Stalin: Private Life of

The truth about Stalin's private life is that he never really had one. As a young man, born into poverty in a mountain village in Georgia, he had endured the rigorous regime of a religious seminary in Tiflis and then spent years on the run as a revolutionary. He never had the occasion to acquire the material desires of the average person. Out of necessity, he trained himself to live an ascetic, pared-down existence of the kind also adopted by Lenin (although Stalin at least had the vices of drinking and smoking) and which both of them had plenty of time to perfect during their time in exile.

To the end of his life Stalin was not interested in the acquisition of personal wealth. One of the arguments against allegations that he may once have acted as a double agent for the tsarist police is his total disinterest in money and bribes. He left his pay envelopes to accumulate, forgotten, in his desk drawer in his Kremlin office, and nothing of any great value is described in the inventory of his possessions compiled at his death. Such a lifestyle naturally convinced many Soviet people of his inordinate modesty and abstemiousness and was promoted by the Stalinist cult as an example of Stalin's great humility.

Stalin had little time for relaxation and rarely showed any desire for it. Neither did he have the time or the patience for serious art. His tastes in everything cultural were extremely conservative. Naturally, he hated abstract art and also abhorred avant-garde music. But when Stalin did like a particular ballet, play, or film, he would return to it over and over again. Like a small child, he had his own personal comfort culture and a compulsion for endless repetition, particularly of his favorite films.

During the 1920s and early 1930s, Stalin's second wife, Nadezhda, had encouraged him to occasionally go to the ballet and the opera, but after her death in 1932 his visits became infrequent. He also liked his visits to be discreet, usually arriving at his private box at the Bolshoi Theater after the performance had started and leaving before the house lights went up. He did, however, retain a particular affection for the ballet and saw *Swan Lake* on many occasions, attending a performance on the night before his fatal collapse. His theatrical tastes were also extremely limited, although, perversely, he took a particular liking to the proscribed writer Mikhail Bulgakov's early play *Days of the Turbins* (1926). He gave it his endorsement and returned on numerous occasions, reportedly because he took particular satisfaction in the way in which it depicted the collapse of the tsarist regime.

Music had always seemed especially dangerous to Stalin, because, as Dmitry Shostakovich asserted, it could be a person's "last hope and final refuge." With his ear trained to the traditional harmonies of Russian Orthodox church liturgy, Stalin naturally loathed the modernist experimentation of Shostakovich and Sergey Prokofiev. He put his trust in popular Russian and Ukrainian folk melodies and the rousing choruses of socialist realist songs, performed by choirs such as the Red Army ensemble. Despite its highbrow associations, Stalin also liked traditional opera, particularly when it had a historical or moral tale to tell. Mikhail Glinka's long-neglected 1836 work *A Life for the Tsar* was revived as *Ivan Susanin,* with Stalin's blessing, to become one of the favorite operas in the Russian repertoire. *Susanin* shared with Mussorgsky's *Boris Godunov* a dark historical context that had a compelling hold over

Stalin. He supposedly never missed a performance of *Boris,* perhaps indicating that in some way he saw its plot full of political intrigue, betrayal, and assassination as an allegory of his own troubled life and times.

As a student at the Russian Orthodox seminary in Tiflis, Stalin had become an avid reader, spending long nights secretly absorbing classic works by Victor Hugo, William Makepeace Thackeray, and Honoré Balzac, as well as such Russian writers as Nikolay Gogol and Anton Chekhov. He also enjoyed (for more obvious reasons relating to his own background) the work of the satirist Mikhail Saltykov-Shchedrin. One of Shchedrin's most popular novels, *The Golovlev Family,* had a savage humor that particularly appealed to Stalin, for it was an excoriating attack on provincial Russian life as well as an exposé of the hypocrisy of the Orthodox clergy. With time, Stalin's reading graduated to the writings of Charles Darwin and other more sober subjects such as politics and economics, including the works of Karl Marx and his eventual mentor Vladimir Ilyich Lenin. During his political exile in Siberia, Stalin made a close study of Machiavelli's *The Prince,* a classic treatise on statecraft and the acquisition of power.

When he came to power Stalin was always self-conscious that he lacked the breadth of intellect of Lenin, Nikolay Bukharin, or even the much-maligned Trotsky. In the 1920s he took on a private tutor (Jan Sten) with whom he studied philosophy. Stalin was reputedly a prodigious reader, getting through as many as 500 pages a day. Although in later life he was obliged to spend much time absorbed in political writings and Marxist-Leninist theory (he liked to keep piles of serious tomes on his desk at the Kremlin to impress visitors), his recreational reading continued to be confined to the Russian classics and Georgian folk literature and poetry. He had a particular affection for the Georgian epic poem *The Knight of the Panther's Skin,* written in the twelfth century by Shota Rustaveli. In fact, he was something of an amateur poet himself, publishing a few of his youthful efforts such as "To the Moon" and "Old Man Nininka" in Georgian journals, signing himself by his pet family name of Soselo ("little Joe"). One of his poems even found its way into a 1907 *Georgian Chrestomathy: A Collection of the Finest Examples of Georgian Poetry.* Despite loving Georgian poetry and promoting the translation of his favorite poets Titsian Tabdize and Paolo Yashvili by writer Boris Pasternak (which may have gone some way to preserving Pasternak's own precarious position with Stalin), both these poets perished during the Great Terror.

When it came to films, in direct contradiction to all formal prognostications on political correctness in Soviet filmmaking, Stalin had an abiding love of Hollywood schmaltz. His favorite time for watching films in his private projection room at the Kremlin was late at night, when he would subject the members of the Politburo to mind-numbing reruns of his old favorites: Julien Duvivier's tale about the Strauss family in *The Great Waltz,* Charlie Chaplin's sentimental silent comedy *City Lights,* and any of the Tarzan films or Douglas Fairbanks swashbucklers. Nikita Khrushchev later recalled that the prints of these films arrived without Russian subtitles, and Stalin's Minister for Cinema Ivan Bolshakov was obliged to give Stalin an extempore translation (which he managed only by studying up on the plots of the films beforehand).

As for the homegrown cinematic product, Stalin's favorites were socialist musicals, such as Grigory Alexandrov's *Volga Volga* or Ivan Pyriev's *Cossacks of the Kuban.* His other preference was for films that promoted his own manufactured revolutionary image, such as Mikhail Romm's *Lenin in October.* In 1992 the émigré Russian film director Andrey Konchalovsky produced a chilling film about Stalin's obsession with

Stalin at his Kuntsevo dacha with his two children by Nadezhda Allilueva—Vasily and Svetlana. Vasily, a wastrel and a drunk, died in 1962; Svetlana sought asylum in the West and published a classic account of her father in 1967.

cinema, *The Inner Circle,* which conveyed the stultifying lives of those trapped inside the morgue that the Kremlin became during Stalin's years and the endless nights endured by the members of the Politburo watching the same films over and over again. It is also a penetrating re-creation of the terrible fear that gripped the lives, even of Stalin's top apparatchiks, during the Great Terror.

Stalin hated traveling. He only flew once, under duress, to the Yalta Conference in 1945 and made only one more subsequent trip abroad, to the Potsdam Conference later the same year. He did not visit the front lines during the war or make more than the occasional token visit in peacetime to a factory or a collective farm. He drove everywhere in a fleet of large armored cars, often U.S. Packards. Despite being a workaholic, he did take an annual leave in the summer months to go to one of the several dachas he had built for himself in the Crimea. When his wife was alive, they went to their own dacha at Sochi or stayed nearer home at the Zubalovo dacha twenty miles from Moscow. Stalin did not, however, take vacations on a prolonged basis until his health began to decline in the late 1940s, when he would spend most of the months between August and November at the Black Sea. Vacations, in any event, always seemed a strain, as his daughter Svetlana recalled, and Stalin never really relaxed. He naturally had little time for socializing either, except with his closest friends and family. At his dacha at Kuntsevo near Moscow he would occasionally indulge in a little gardening, but he had no interest in sports or any physical activity more strenuous than billiards, although he had learned to hunt and fish when living in exile in Siberia.

As far as his personal habits were concerned, Stalin was not a heavy drinker, and like a true Georgian preferred the light wines of Georgia, such as Kinzmarauli and Hvanchkara, to Russian vodka. He also liked syrupy sweet Russian brandies and herbal tea. The Georgian people have a great tradition of hospitality and generosity, but Stalin, while possessed of all the required social graces at official functions, behaved quite differently in the company of the closed circle of the Politburo. After working late at the Kremlin, Stalin would usually go to his dacha at Kuntsevo, no matter how late, to have his evening meal (although when matters dictated he would sometimes sleep on a small bed in his office at the Kremlin). While he ate greedily and often to excess in later life, there was nothing he liked better than to foist drink on his ministers and sit silently and soberly watching as they made fools of themselves in their drunkenness.

The late-night suppers he held at Kuntsevo were often the occasion for the only real sport Stalin indulged in—coarse language (including Georgian swearwords, which he delighted in sharing with fellow Georgian Lavrenty Beria), childish practical jokes (such as putting tomatoes on people's chairs or throwing someone, often his poor secretary Poskrebyshev, into the pond), and making cruel remarks about a person's physical inadequacies (such as Vyacheslav Molotov's stutter or Georgy Malenkov's pudgy face). Stalin's only vice, as such, was his love of strong tobacco and his pipe, a fact well noted by Churchill who sent his ally gifts of Dunhill pipes during the war. But in later life Stalin's smoking, which he did incessantly throughout his sixteen-hour working days, aggravated his angina and heart disease, and he was eventually forced to give it up.

Stalin's relationship with all three of his children was difficult. He virtually rejected his elder son Yakov (probably because he looked and sounded unmistakably Georgian), leaving his second wife, Nadezhda, to take pity on and befriend Yakov. Stalin's other son, Vasily, was a terrible disappointment to him—weak, dissolute, and alcoholic, he died an early death. Stalin's complex relationship with his daughter, Svetlana, for whom he undoubtedly had a great affection and to whom he wrote many touching letters addressed to his "Little Housekeeper," has been described in her powerful memoirs of him, published in 1967 and 1969. They were the first books to reveal anything of the private man behind the public image and had a considerable impact on people's perception of Stalin. They will probably remain the definitive account of what little there is to tell about Stalin's private life. He so rarely indulged in any personal interests that conjecture and rumor will always prevail, particularly over the contentious issue of his sexual nature and whether or not there were other women in his life after the death of his wife, Nadezhda, in 1932. This and other aspects of his private life that can never be properly substantiated are best left to works of imaginative fiction, such as Robert Harris's *Archangel*, a novel about Stalin's last days and his worrisome political legacy.

See also Allilueva, Svetlana; Cinema; Dzhugashvili, Yakov; Lenin, Vladimir; Russian Revolution of 1917; Socialist Realism; Stalin: Dachas of; Stalin: Personality of; Trotsky, Leon; Stalin, Vasily

Further reading Svetlana Alliluyeva. *Twenty Letters to a Friend.* London: Hutchinson, 1967; Svetlana Alliluyeva. *Only One Year.* London: Hutchinson, 1969; Alan Bullock. *Hitler and Stalin: Parallel Lives,* chapter 10. London: HarperCollins, 1991; Robert Harris. *Archangel.* London: Hutchinson, 1998; Edvard Radzinsky. *Stalin.* London: Hodder & Stoughton, 1996; Robert C. Tucker. *Stalin in Power: The Revolution from Above, 1928–41.* London: Chatto and Windus, 1990; Dmitri Volkogonov. *Stalin: Triumph and Tragedy,* chapter 16. London: Weidenfeld & Nicolson, 1991.

Stalin, Vasily Iosifovich (1921–1962)

Stalin had far more affection for his son by his second wife, Nadezhda Alliluyeva, than he ever showed for his other son Yakov, the son of Ekaterina Svanidze. Vasily Stalin, a coward, a bully, and a womanizer, did nothing to merit his father's preferential treatment. His military career was one of drunken incompetence, and he died a hopeless alcoholic at the age of forty-one. His short, wasted life, in the words of Dmitri Volkogonov, became "an illustration in miniature of the moral sterility of Stalinism."

Vasily spent most of his childhood at Stalin's dacha at Zubalovo in the company of a phalanx of security guards. He failed dismally at school, exasperating even his father. Stalin frankly admitted in a letter to his son's teacher that Vasily was "a spoiled youth, of average ability, a little savage (a sort of Scythian), not always truthful . . . if [he] does not succeed in ruining himself it will be because there are in our country some teachers who will not give way to a young master's caprices."

Stalin never had time to spend with his son, which, combined with the fact that Vasily had lost his mother when he was eleven years old, explains some of Vasily's bad behavior. After leaving school he was sent to the elite Kuchinsky Flying School of the Red Army in Moscow. At the outbreak of war he had already been made a colonel. His record in combat during the Great Patriotic War is dubious. He was promoted higher and higher in the space of four years, so that by 1946 he had actually become commander of the Soviet Air Force. But a catalog of violence, boorish behavior, and uncontrollable temper made him unpopular.

Stalin had Vasily grounded after the capture of his half-brother, Yakov, by the Germans in 1941. He proved inept even at desk jobs, and in 1950, when he made a shambles of organizing a military air display at Tushino, Stalin sacked him from his posts and ordered him to retrain at the Aviation Faculty of the Military Academy.

Outside the office, which he rarely bothered to attend, Vasily indulged in drunken parties and rowdy behavior at the dacha at Zubalovo and had a string of affairs, mainly with other men's wives. After Stalin's death, Vasily was finally dismissed from the air force for his bad behavior. Not long after, he was arrested for "systematic misappropriation of state property." He was using air force funds to fuel his extravagant lifestyle and, in particular, his passion for sport (he had set up his own private hunting reserve).

Imprisoned in 1953, Vasily appealed to Nikita Khrushchev and was released in 1960, only to be back in jail a year later for his involvement in a traffic accident. Ill health and chronic alcoholism brought his early release, in 1961, from an eight-year sentence. He returned to the outside world, exiled to Kazan, a lonely and pathetic figure, disowned by his children and by now unemployable. He died less than a year later. In 1999 Russia's chief military prosecutors granted him a posthumous pardon for his 1953 sentence.

See also Allilueva, Nadezhda; Allilueva, Svetlana; Dzhugashvili, Yakov

Further reading: Svetlana Alliluyeva. *Twenty Letters to a Friend*. London: Hutchinson, 1967; Edvard Radzinsky. *Stalin*. London: Sceptre, 1997; Dmitri Volkogonov. *Stalin: Triumph and Tragedy*. London: Weidenfeld and Nicolson, 1991.

Stalin Constitution, 5 December 1936

*T*he much-trumpeted declaration of democratic rights of the Stalin constitution under the Soviet form of socialism proved a particularly cynical and hollow piece of propaganda. For it was published on the eve of the worst years of the political purges, when all the basic democratic rights that it purported to endorse were systematically abused, including its own Article 127, under which the Soviet state guaranteed freedom from arbitrary arrest.

Its composition as the most "democratic" constitution in the world was primarily the work of a collective of writers headed by two leading Soviet theoreticians, Nikolay Bukharin and Karl Radek. Initiated in February 1935 by Stalin, and remaining throughout its composition under his watchful eye, it was officially launched by him on 27 November of that year. As the first socialist constitution of its kind, it was promoted across the civilized world as the defining achievement of the Soviet state. Its contents proclaimed across-the-board equality and the joint ownership of the means of production. But it did not, however, inaugurate the totally classless socialist utopia envisaged by Marx and Lenin, instead linking Soviet workers and peasants in a mutually supporting and cooperative "two-class" state.

The new constitution was published at a time when the Soviet Union was seeking credibility in the international political arena. As a propaganda tool it served to impress some Western commentators with its democratizing principles and gave Communist sympathizers abroad some cause for hope that the system had at last proved its case. Its promises were extensive. The constitution confirmed the structure of the Soviet Union as a federal state composed of eleven union republics (each with the technical right to secede). Smaller ethnic groups were granted autonomous regions within the autonomous republics, so that on paper at least, fifty-one of the Soviet Union's nationalities had their own form of local autonomy. The old system of Congresses of the Soviets was now replaced with a single legislative body—the Supreme Soviet. Within this body, the Soviet nation as a whole was represented by elected members within a union Soviet, while the elected members of the Soviet of Nationalities served the more specific interests of the various national groups.

But final executive authority continued to reside with the Council of People's Commissars, and little in reality would change. The Soviet Union would remain, as it always had, a tightly controlled state with a central government in Moscow. Indeed, official policy throughout Stalin's rule (and particularly during the Great Patriotic War) eroded the sense of ethnic identity endorsed in the constitution, through a policy of increasing Russification of the autonomous republics, driven by Stalin's assimilationist brand of messianic nationalism.

Chapter ten of the constitution looked impressive on paper as a catalog of civil rights, listed in Article 125, which included freedom of speech and the press, the right to demonstrate (but only in terms of reinforcing the "dictatorship of the working class"), respect for the privacy of the home and personal correspondence, and the guaranteed provision of employment for all. Universal suffrage, for those over eighteen years, in free elections that respected the secrecy of the ballot box was also guaranteed. But all these civil rights were subordinate to the overriding interests of the working classes and to the Communist Party as the sole arbiter of those interests. The chapter also outlined the duties of the Soviet citizen and, in a direct snipe at the persecution of the Jews in fascist Germany, emphasized their equality in the Soviet Union.

Between June and 5 December 1936 (when the constitution was officially passed), the Soviet nation was provided with the unprecedented democratic opportunity of openly discussing the draft of the new constitution at a series of public meetings. Soviets were even allowed to suggest some modest amendments. But people, grown apathetic after years of political repression, were less preoccupied with civil liberties than they were with simply staying alive. Many, like one group of workers in a tobacco factory, were more forthright in their reaction, proclaiming that "we don't need your Constitution, we need bread and cheap food." Others objected to the division made in the constitution between "peasants" and "workers," a fact that they felt would continue to encourage divisiveness. Many peasants felt that the constitution gave precedence to workers over peasants in several areas, particularly in the length of their working day, which was shorter than for those tied to the collective farms.

The constitution did, however, have one consequence that Stalin would not have wished for. By arousing people's interest in the matter, it gave a continuing impetus to the discussion of precisely those basic civil liberties that people in the Soviet Union had for so long been denied. It was even invoked by the later dissident movement of the 1960s. Stalin had long been cold in his grave when his constitution—which he called "proof that socialism and democracy are invincible"—was finally replaced in 1977.

See also Bukharin, Nikolay; Fellow Travelers; The Great Terror; Nationalities; Radek, Karl

Stalin Prizes

These awards, inaugurated in December 1939 just before Stalin's sixtieth birthday, were handed out as an affirmation of ideological correctness in the fields of science, technology, literature, music, cinema, and art. They were to be awarded annually and graded first class (awarded 100,000 rubles) or second class (50,000 rubles).

The award of the Stalin Prize was not, however, any indicator of the true artistic merit of the work concerned, the vast bulk of which was mediocre. In the category of literature, in particular, many prizes were given to conformist writers whose names have now completely disappeared and whose works are unread. The historian Adam Ulam noted that one of the most ludicrous examples of prizes given by Stalin to the more dubious Soviet fringe sciences was the one given to scientist Olga Lepeshinskaya "for her sensational discovery that bathing in soda water prolonged life."

The titles of the works awarded the first thirteen prizes for art in 1941 underlined the conformity of content and interpretation—"Stalin and Voroshilov in the Kremlin," "Worker and Collective Farm Girl," and "In an Old Urals Factory." Year in, year out, prize-winning works of art featured Stalin in one godlike form or another. In 1939 four out of the thirteen prizewinners featured Stalin. In 1949, thirteen prizewinners dutifully chose him as their subject. This is not surprising, bearing in mind the various incentives, such as dachas in the country and tax concessions, offered to potential prizewinners. The winner of a Stalin Prize, could, like the winner of an Oscar, reap the rewards of mass exposure and, in the case of writers, vast print runs. But the system was open to abuse, with the same establishment conformists repeatedly and undeservingly awarded the prize, while other, greater talents were ignored.

During the period 1941 to 1952, 220 prizes were awarded for works of literature. The greater part of these are undistinguished potboilers, but a few justified their acclaim—writers such as Mikhail Sholokhov for his epic novel *Quiet Flows the Don* (in 1941), Viktor Nekrasov for his fine World War II novel *In the Trenches of Stalingrad* (1946), and the distinguished poet Alexander Tvardovsky, whose narrative poetry was twice awarded Stalin Prizes (in 1941 and 1946).

In the postwar atmosphere of the Cold War, an international Stalin Prize was introduced, awarded by a committee of Communist sympathizers in an attempt to disseminate propaganda against Stalin's former wartime allies. After Stalin's death and the dismantling of the cult of the personality, the Stalin Prize was rechristened the State Prize of the U.S.S.R.

See also Cult of the Personality; Socialist Realism

Stalingrad

In 1925, the city of Tsaritsyn in the Volgograd region of southern Russia was renamed Stalingrad, a symbolic act that underlined the rapid rise to preeminence of Stalin only a year after Lenin's death. As Tsaritsyn, the city had seen fighting during the civil war of 1918–1920. Stalin had been sent by Lenin to organize the defense of the city against the Whites, and at the time the Bolshevik control of the city had played a significant role in keeping the White forces apart. In 1942, the city became a symbol of Soviet resistance to the Nazi aggressor, and it was the location for one of the most decisive battles of he Great Patriotic War.

The German summer offensive of 1942 had left the Soviet Union in a desperate situation. A series of defeats had allowed German troops to take large sections of the industrial heartland of the Donbass, and they were now threatening the key industrial center of Stalingrad with its armaments factories and, beyond it, the strategically crucial oil pipelines from the Caucasus. As thousands of families from the nearby collective farms took to the roads with their livestock to escape the German advance and cross the Volga into safety, Stalin's general commanding the 62nd army at Stalingrad had come to the conclusion that the city could not be held. He advised Stalin that it should be abandoned and that the 62nd Army should be withdrawn behind the Volga.

Such an act of capitulation was unconscionable for Stalin. To give up the city that bore his name would be to recognize the superiority of German military capability and would destroy public morale. Refusing to evacuate either the civilians or Stalingrad's industry, Stalin sent Political Commissar Nikita Khrushchev to the Stalingrad front in order to galvanize both the Red Army and the civilian population of some 450,000 into action. The response from the embattled Soviet people was tremendous— 50,000 civilians volunteered for defense

The bitter struggle for Stalingrad was characterized by fierce hand-to-hand fighting between German and Soviet troops in the rubble of the devastated city. In January 1943 the German Sixth Army of 91,000 men surrendered.

duties, 75,000 citizens were attached to the 62nd army, and 3,000 women volunteered as nurses and for communications duties. Even thirteen-year-olds were recruited from the Komsomol, given arms, and attached to combat units. Newly appointed General Vasily Chuikov reflected the attitude of everyone when he baldly told Krushchev, "We will hold Stalingrad or die there."

The battle began in September 1942 and rapidly developed into bitter house-to-house fighting—a vicious form of hand-to-hand combat that the Germans called *Rattenkrieg* ("rat fighting")—in the devastated city. They had effectively taken the center of the city by 27 September but encountered fierce resistance when they turned their attention to the city's huge northern industrial plants, such as the Red October iron works and the Red Barricade gun factory. Here the ruined factory buildings, destroyed by Stuka bombs and artillery, be-

came the ideal territory for fierce guerrilla resistance to the German infantry. The fighting was conducted at close quarters in the rubble by Russians whose morale was raised by fighting slogans such as "Every soldier a fortress! / There is no land for us behind the Volga! / We must fight or fall!" German losses were high. In the words of one German officer, "the street is no longer measured by meters but by corpses. It is no longer alive. By day it is an enormous cloud of burning, blinding smoke, a vast furnace lit by the reflection of the flames. At night it is a terror. Animals flee this hell. Perhaps only men can endure it."

While Field Marshal Friedrich von Paulus's Sixth Army became encircled and trapped in the center of the city, they now also had to contend with Russia's old ally, the bitter winter weather, which had defeated another legendary fighting force—Napoleon's Grande Armée—in 1812. On 19 November Soviet troops under Marshal

Georgy Zhukov launched a massive counterattack, and Paulus was soon sending messages to Hitler asking leave to break out and abandon the city. The order came back that the Volga front must be held. There was to be no German retreat. Paulus knew that his troops, running out of supplies, ammunition, and reinforcements, were now facing annihilation but held out in the faint hope of a promised relief offensive from fresh Panzer divisions.

On 8 January 1943 the Russians offered Paulus an honorable surrender, which Hitler forbade. The final act of this tragic campaign bore witness to the tremendous courage of the German Sixth Army, now frozen (they had to endure temperatures as low as −40°C), starving, plagued with chilblains, frostbite, and dysentery and with virtually no ammunition left. They suffered catastrophic losses. On 30 January Paulus finally surrendered.

As many as 300,000 Germans were killed at Stalingrad or died of wounds later. A further 91,000 soldiers surrendered, of whom over 9,000 were held as prisoners of war in the Soviet Union until 1955; only about 3,000 of them ever returned home to Germany. The rest died in the camps of the Gulag. In 1999 President Yeltsin announced that the KGB (secret police) files on over 10,000 German POWs would finally be released to the German Red Cross, in order that the fate of so many Germans who were lost at Stalingrad would at last be known.

Soviet losses at Stalingrad have remained unquantifiable, but they probably approached 1 million. No doubt the sacrifice was considered worthwhile, for it won the nation a huge and much-needed psychological victory and marked the watershed of the war in Europe. More important, from now on not only Stalin's enemies but also his allies would have to take Soviet military strength and the determination of its fighting forces very seriously.

In 1961 Stalingrad was renamed Volgograd. A study of the battle by historian Antony Beevor, published in 1998, has since revealed the darker side to the conflict. As many as 50,000 embattled Soviet troops deserted to the Germans during the fight for Stalingrad (a fact that has long lain buried in the Soviet archives). But even more chilling is the revelation that as many as 13,500 Soviet soldiers were shot by their own side (usually by special NKVD [secret police] units) for various acts of alleged cowardice, desertion, and "anti-Soviet agitation."

See also Great Patriotic War; NKVD; Rokossovsky, Marshal Konstantin; Zhukov, Marshal Georgy

Further reading: Anthony Beevor. *Stalingrad*. London: Viking, 1998; Vasily Grossman. *Life and Fate*. London: Collins Harvill, 1985 (a brilliant fictional account); Richard Overy. *Russia's War*. London: Allen Lane, 1998.

Svanidze, Ekaterina (Kato) Semenovna (d. 1907)

Stalin was introduced to his first wife by her brother, Stalin's former school friend and fellow revolutionary, Alesha (Aleksandr) Svanidze. Uncharacteristically for a confessed Marxist, but no doubt to mollify his conventional and devout Georgian in-laws, Stalin was married to Ekaterina Svanidze, known as Kato, in St. David's Church, Tiflis. The ceremony was conducted in secret by a friend of Stalin's from the Tiflis Seminary in June 1906 (although Dmitri Volkogonov asserted that they may have married in 1903 before Stalin went into exile).

Kato, who had apparently been educated at home by governesses until the age of fourteen, proved to be a docile and religiously devout wife who tried hard to scrape together some kind of life for herself and her husband in the single room in which they lived. Indeed, to some of Stalin's contemporaries, such as Soso Iremashvili, she seemed a paragon of virtue, who "with all her heart looked after her

Little is known about Stalin's first wife, Ekaterina Svanidze, except that she was pious and dutiful and produced a son, Yakov. Stalin admitted that "Kato," as he affectionately called her, had been his only real love.

destine operations on the Baku oilfields, returning briefly and in secret. In May 1907 she gave birth to their son, Yakov, and she died on 25 November that year of typhus. Stalin is said to have displayed genuine grief at her death, asserting that "this creature softened my stony heart. When she died all warm feeling for people died with her."

Such a revelatory moment of personal grief was to be unheard-of in Stalin's later life; he even ensured that Kato's funeral was Orthodox. His sentiments did not, however, extend to her family, no doubt because they knew too much about him. Several of Kato's relatives were ruthlessly exterminated during the Great Terror, including her brother, Alesha (who was held in prison for several years and finally executed in 1943 on Stalin's orders for refusing to "confess"); Alesha's wife, who was imprisoned at the same time and died serving a ten-year prison sentence; and her sister, Maria Svanidze, who also died in prison. Even Alesha's son, who at the age of eight had dutifully cursed his parents as "enemies of the people" when they had been taken away, was later arrested and sent to the Gulag.

See also Baku; Dzhugashvili, Yakov; The Great Terror; Tiflis Theological Seminary

husband's welfare. Passing countless nights in ardent prayers, she waited for her Soso while he was busy at secret conferences." But poor Kato was neglected more and more, with Stalin frequently away on clan-

𝒯

Tehran Conference
See "The Big Three."

Third International
See Comintern.

Tiflis

The ancient capital of the kingdom of Georgia, founded in 458, was for centuries a center for Georgian culture. Captured by the Russians in 1801, it became a busy commercial and industrial center of the tsarist empire. With the opening of the area to railroads and the development of mines and factories in the late nineteenth century, there was a huge influx of workers into the city. Such a rapidly industrializing environment, in particular Tiflis's railroad center, provided the ideal breeding ground for political activity. Various illegal revolutionary groups focused on achieving a Georgian national revival here. It was the Mesame Dasi ("the third group"), an underground gathering of revolutionary Social Democrats, that the young Stalin secretly joined in 1898, while still studying for the priesthood at the Tiflis Seminary.

After leaving the seminary, the one and only proper nonpolitical job Stalin ever had was a brief period of employment at the Tiflis Observatory (1899–1901), collecting and recording meteorological data. But he soon left his work to take up a full-time revolutionary career among the oil workers, composing and distributing revolutionary literature and taking part in demonstrations, such as that held in Tiflis in 1901. Stalin became quickly adept at living a life of subterfuge. After a period of imprisonment and exile in Siberia, he returned to Tiflis in 1905 to reprise his revolutionary activities. He lived here intermittently with his first wife, Ekaterina Svanidze.

See also Svanidze, Ekaterina; Georgia; Georgian Social Democrats; Tiflis Theological Seminary

Tiflis State Bank Robbery

The Tiflis State Bank robbery was one of the most notorious "expropriations" (as Russian revolutionaries preferred to call robberies) in the history of the revolutionary movement in the Caucasus. It has always been linked with Stalin, but because of the elusive way in which he operated underground in the region at this time, the precise degree of his involvement is uncertain.

On 26 June 1907 two carriages escorted by Cossack outriders and containing a large consignment of money to the State Bank in

Erevan Square, Tiflis, were attacked by Georgian revolutionaries armed with bombs. This attempt to steal funds for the Georgian Social Democrats (known as the Mesame Dasi) was made despite the fact that the party's dominant Menshevik faction had condemned such terrorist attacks and expropriations as discrediting the Party. Stalin has frequently been credited with masterminding the raid, which was led by his associate Simon Ter-Petrosian (code name "Kamo") and in which several people were killed and injured. There is strong evidence to suggest, however, that the orders of the raid came directly from Lenin himself (who certainly looked upon any means for funding the revolutionary cause as being justified). While Kamo and some of the conspirators were rounded up and arrested, and much of the money was later traced and recovered, Stalin evaded capture. The Georgian Mensheviks disassociated themselves from this attack and demanded Stalin's expulsion from the party for his supposed involvement. Meanwhile Stalin had already melted away, back to his underground activities among the workers of the Caucasian oilfields.

See also Georgia; Georgian Social Democrats; Tiflis

Tiflis Theological Seminary

Stalin entered this seminary of the Russian Orthodox Church in 1894. It was the nearest thing Tiflis had to a university. Since the 1860s Russian Orthodox seminaries had become a breeding ground for radical thought among the many disaffected young radicals who could not get their education elsewhere.

The environment of the seminary was extremely repressive. Life for the students was one of deprivation and isolation, if not virtual incarceration, under the watchful eyes of the monks. Such a regime, of course, had the reverse effect of fomenting unrest rather than inspiring unquestioning religious devotion. The 600 seminarists had to get up early for prayers, endure a daily taxing curriculum of Latin, Greek, and Old Church Slavonic, as well as stand through the interminably long church services on high days and holidays. One of the unspoken objectives of seminaries was the Russification of the ethnic population, which was reflected in the restricted access to reading matter. On their brief periods of release from study, some of the students, Stalin included, would seek out forbidden books in the public library and read them under the covers in bed at night. It was at this time that Stalin first discovered the works of revolutionary writers such as Karl Marx, Petr Tkachev, and Georgy Plekhanov. Stalin wholeheartedly espoused the Marxist concept of the defeat of capitalism by the proletariat and the creation of a new world order through violent revolutionary change. But he kept his new-found political feelings to himself and continued to study assiduously, while quietly making contact with a group of Marxist activists in Tiflis, the Mesame Dasi, who had set up an underground social democratic group.

As Stalin's involvement in underground politics increased, he lost interest in his studies and was frequently punished for reading forbidden books and distributing subversive literature. Finally, in 1899, he was expelled, not for his political activities, but for failing to sit for his exams. Stalin continued to nurse bitter memories of his difficult years at the seminary, commenting in later life, "I became a Marxist because of my social position . . . and also . . . because of the harsh intolerance and Jesuitical discipline that crushed me so mercilessly at the Seminary."

See also Stalin: Personality of; Stalin: Private Life of; Tiflis
Further reading: Edward Ellis Smith. *The Young Stalin. The Early Years of an Elusive Revolutionary.* New York: Farrar, Straus and Giroux, 1967; Leon

Trotsky. *Stalin, vol. 1: Rise of a Revolutionary.* London: MacGibbon & Kee, 1968; Robert C. Tucker. *Stalin as Revolutionary, 1879–1929: A Study in History and Personality.* New York: W. W. Norton, 1973.

Tito, Marshal (1892–1980)

Tito, the tough-minded Yugoslav leader who after World War II proved to be a thorn in Stalin's side, displayed many of the same qualities of ruthlessness and innate peasant shrewdness possessed by Stalin, ensuring a relationship between them that was built on and fueled by mutual mistrust.

Born Josip Broz into a Croatian-Slovenian peasant family of fifteen children, the young Broz earned his trade as a metalworker and soon became active in trade union politics. Conscripted into the infantry of the Austro-Hungarian army during World War I, he was wounded and captured in the Carpathian Mountains by the Russians in April 1915. In captivity, Broz was won over to the cause of communism and in 1917, after the revolution, he managed to escape his tsarist army captors and make his way to Petrograd, where he joined the Red Army and went to fight for the Bolsheviks against the Whites in the civil war.

Returning to Zagreb in 1920, Broz resumed his trade as a metalworker and became an underground Communist activist. He was arrested on several occasions and was later imprisoned in 1928 for five years. Released in 1934, he took a leaf out of Stalin's book and adopted a new name, "Tito," as one of several aliases. Tito traveled to Moscow on several occasions and was made secretary of the Yugoslav Communist Party in August 1936. Fortuitously, he had returned to Yugoslavia in 1937, thus avoiding probable arrest and death, because in 1937 Stalin initiated a purge of the membership of the Yugoslav Central Committee in Moscow.

When the Germans invaded Yugoslavia in April 1941, Tito organized Yugoslav resistance to the German army from the mountains in southern Serbia. He drew together the various and querulous ethnic minorities into a campaign of partisan resistance, on the promise of political reunification after the war. His leadership of Yugoslav partisans in the National Liberation Front is legendary. His specially trained guerrilla shock brigades wreaked such havoc among the occupying German forces that Hitler was obliged to commit more than ten German divisions to suppressing their activities. But the partisans, adept at fighting in difficult terrain from their mountain hideaways, proved superior to the Germans, despite heavy losses. By 1943 their ranks had swelled to 250,000, and they convened their own revolutionary government, with Tito now named marshal of Yugoslavia.

At the end of the war Tito became prime minister of his own Communist Federal Republic of Yugoslavia. At first he and Stalin appeared to be set on a relationship of mutual cooperation and support through the interchange of personnel and the Soviet training of the Yugoslav military. But Tito began to resist pressure from Stalin to refer his every political decision to Moscow. While Moscow indulged Yugoslav plans to set up a federation of Balkan Communist states for a while, by 1948 Stalin had become increasingly alarmed and irritated by Yugoslavia's persistence in following a separate political path. Tito's defiance was a humiliation for Stalin, and he did everything he could to undermine Tito's power and isolate Yugoslavia politically. However, his attempts at economic sanctions and the use of political subterfuge only hardened national resistance to Soviet domination.

The continuing resentment and mistrust over differences in policy led in June 1948 to Yugoslavia's expulsion from Cominform. While Stalin might briefly have entertained thoughts of taking military action to quell Tito's rebellion (he supposedly remarked to Nikita Khrushchev that "I will shake my little finger—and there will be no more Tito, he will fall"), he soon thought better of it. He had no stomach for a fight against a fiercely nationalistic partisan force that was devoted to its leader and that was still riding high on the kudos of its heroic defeat of fascist German forces. Thus, Tito became the first leader of a satellite Communist state to break away from Stalin's domination, and he was until his death a perennial annoyance to the Soviet leadership. The split with Stalin arose in particular over Tito's resistance to the institution by Stalin of centralized economic control. Tito wanted to develop his own brand of socialism, which favored the fostering of a system of decentralized profit-sharing councils run by workers in the factories.

Shortly before Stalin's death in 1953, Tito was elected Yugoslavia's first president, and in the escalating climate of the Cold War, he became the spokesman of the nonaligned Communist movement. Although he reestablished his relationship with the Soviet Union in 1955, he remained critical of Soviet domination over Eastern Europe, particularly its invasions of Hungary in 1956 and Czechoslovakia in 1968.

A mark of Tito's successful leadership was his elevation as "president for life" in 1974. But his years in power had seen him achieve a level of political control that at times matched Stalin's in its ruthlessness and that frequently stirred up old ethnic rivalries and national divisions. After Tito's death in 1980—his funeral was attended by a glittering array of heads of state—the old wounds began to reopen, resulting in bloody civil war during the 1990s.

See also Cominform; Eastern Europe
Further reading: Phyllis Auty. *Tito*, rev. ed. Harlow, UK: Longmans, 1970; Milovan Djilas. *Conversations with Stalin*. Harmondsworth, UK: Penguin, 1962.

Tomsky, Mikhail Pavlovich (1880–1936)

An ally of Nikolay Bukharin's in the face of Stalin's dictatorial economic policies during the 1930s, Mikhail Tomsky (born Mikhail Pavlovich Efremov) was a seasoned revolutionary and a tough and dedicated trade unionist whose commitment to the rights of workers led him at times to oppose his friend Lenin over policy.

Tomsky joined the Russian Social Democrats in 1904 and became a trade union activist. As a worker (he was a lithographer), his commitment to the working classes continued in his capacity as president of the Congress of Trade Unions from 1919. He fiercely defended them against increasing pressure from the Bolsheviks to accelerate rates of production. This caused him to openly confront Leon Trotsky, who looked upon workers and peasants collectively as mere "labor armies." In 1921 Tomsky also argued with Lenin, when Lenin, fearing the trades unions would balk at the imposition of his New Economic Policy, sought to tighten Party control over them. But despite his outspokenness, Tomsky was elected to the Politburo in 1922.

In 1929, after opposing the acceleration of the program of collectivization and being accused by Stalin of joining with Aleksey Rykov and Nikolay Bukharin in "factionalism," Tomsky lost his post on the Central Council of Trade Unions. A year later he lost his place in the Politburo. By the time of the Seventeenth Party Congress in 1934, Tomsky's moral resistance to Stalin, like that of so many other leading oppositionists, had crumbled. Along with Nikolay Bukharin and Aleksey Rykov, he was compelled to admit publicly to his previous political "deviation," mouthing what by now had become the obligatory platitudes on Stalin's greatness as "the brightest of Lenin's pupils," the one "best armed theoretically and practically for the struggle against the opposition."

After being implicated in the crimes of Grigory Zinoviev and Lev Kamenev at their show trial in August 1936, Tomsky should have become the third major defendant at the 1938 trial of Bukharin and Rykov, but he shot himself at his dacha at Boltsevo on 22 August 1936. The day before, he had had a visit from Stalin, possibly on a mission to preempt such an act (which would entail the loss of a star confession), offering phony reassurances, and the two had a heated argument. No doubt this was the last straw for Tomsky, a man who had been forced to abandon all the high principles that he once had as a dedicated revolutionary. The day of his death he had read a report in *Pravda* by state prosecutor Andrey Vyshinsky, stating his intentions to investigate the criminal counterrevolutionary activities of Tomsky, Rykov, and Bukharin. No doubt suicide seemed infinitely preferable to further acts of public self-abasement and eventual official annihilation. Stalin, of course, saw the suicide as a vindication of his suspicions; it was merely confirmation of Tomsky's guilt before the Party.

At the time of his suicide Tomsky begged Stalin to spare his family, but the inevitable machinery swallowed them up—two of his sons were arrested and shot, and his wife and another son were imprisoned.

See also Bukharin, Nikolay; Collectivization; The Great Terror; Rykov, Aleksey; Vyshinsky, Andrey

Further reading: Stephen F. Cohen. *Bukharin and the Bolshevik Revolution: A Political Biography, 1888–1938.* Oxford: Oxford University Press, 1980; Robert Conquest. *The Great Terror: A Reassessment.* London: Pimlico, 1992.

Torture

Physical methods of torture were technically unlawful under the Soviet regime until 1937, although in *The Gulag Archipelago,* Alexander Solzhenitsyn described how a favorite mode of physical torture, the subjection of inmates to extremes of heat and cold, was employed in the Lubyanka prison as early as the 1920s. In this case, the air heating system was used to fill a prisoner's cell first with icy-cold air and then with intolerably hot air, until he or she literally sweated blood.

Prior to 1937, however, the preferred methods had generally been those of psychological torture. In 1919 the mere presence of a revolver on the interrogator's desk had been deemed sufficient to weaken a victim's resistance, and such methods of mental and psychological intimidation were popular with the secret police. Another method that was regularly used was the planting of stool pigeon prisoners, who would regale their cellmates with the horrors awaiting them. Other prisoners would succumb to the practice of enticement— the false promises of reduced sentences on confession—only to be taken away and shot all the same. Threats of harm to prisoners' loved ones proved extremely effective and in many cases broke those who had resisted the longest. There is some evidence of more subtle methods being used, where suggestions were made, through the use of phonograph recordings of women moaning and crying, that prisoners' wives were being tortured within earshot of their own cells. It was also rumored that head of the NKVD (secret police) Genrikh Yagoda had ordered experimentation with drugs and hypnosis as ways of breaking prisoners' resistance. It was certainly noticed that many prisoners, with their listless movements and expressionless speech, exhibited all the signs of having been tranquilized in some way.

The favorite and most effective method was that of sleep deprivation, an age-old torture in use since the Spanish Inquisition of the sixteenth century. The NKVD developed a "conveyor-belt" system of repeated nighttime interrogations, conducted on the same prisoner by relays of interrogators, who continuously shone bright lights in their faces. Nothing seemed to erode a prisoner's resilience faster than the disorientation brought on by exhaustion, and from the interrogator's point of view sleep deprivation was ideal. It left no incriminating scars and could break even the most indomitable wills within a week. Another method used was that of compelling prisoners to stand for hours on end and usually at night (sometimes on one leg) waiting outside the door of an interrogator who never arrived.

Prisoners were further humiliated and disoriented by the removal of their belts, shoelaces, and spectacles. The last photograph of the short-sighted writer Isaac Babel on his file from the Lubyanka shows a puffy-faced and bewildered man who obviously cannot make out what is in front of him. Even Stalin himself inherited a mannerism born of his many periods of imprisonment, as one colleague observed, which was a habit of constantly hiking up his trousers, a reflex action resulting from being constantly deprived of his belt.

When prisoners refused to confess, they were sometimes kept in special "standing cells," so called because the person inside could maintain no other position than standing upright with his hands to his sides. In her memoirs Nadezhda Mandelstam described how a favorite method used on her husband, the poet Osip Mandelstam, when he was in the Lubyanka in the mid-1930s, was to give him salty food and nothing to drink so that he was tormented with thirst.

By 1937, with the numbers of arrests escalating and the prisons crowded to bursting point, Stalin himself initiated the use of physical torture in order to speed up the process of confession and the execution of sentence. He insisted on the extraction of confessions at any price, complaining of one particularly recalcitrant victim, "Can't this gentleman be made to tell of his dirty deeds? Where is he—in a prison or a hotel?" For the next two years the unbridled use of torture prevailed, until in 1939 indiscriminate torture was curtailed and its use specified by decree for certain categories only, such as members of underground nationalist organizations.

Methods used during the late 1930s became more versatile and brutal—tying prisoners up in agonizing, contorted positions; tearing out toe- and fingernails; beatings with rubber truncheons on the kidneys and genitals; and breaking of limbs, particularly feet and fingers. More humiliating methods, like putting out cigarettes on the skin and urinating on prisoners, also became prevalent. Those prisoners who obstinately refused to sign "confessions" were often hauled off to the Lefortovo prison, where the regime of torture was reputedly grim, although the punishment cells of the little-known Sukhanovka outside Moscow had the reputation of being the most rigorous isolation and torture unit of them all; it was apparently a place where the NKVD was allowed to do anything.

For those summarily shot or murdered in the prisons of Moscow during the Great Terror, the ultimate resting place after cremation at Lefortovo prison and in other undesignated crematoria is unknown. Some prisoners were cremated at night at the former Donskoy Monastery and consigned there to a common and unmarked grave. In 1991 a stone was erected over the grave-pit at the Donskoy Monastery, bearing these words: "Here lie buried the remains of the innocent tortured and executed victims of the political repressions. May they never be forgotten."

See also The Great Terror; Gulag; Memorial; Prisons; Stalin: Imprisonment and Exile

Further reading: Robert Conquest. *The Great Terror: A Reassessment*. London: Pimlico, 1992; Roy Medvedev. *Let History Judge: The Origins and Consequences of Stalinism*. New York: Columbia University Press, 1989; Alexander Solzhenitsyn. *The Gulag Archipelago*, vol. 1. Glasgow: William Collins and Sons, 1973.

Transcaucasia

Transcaucasia, with its 750-mile (1,200-kilometer) range of the Great Caucasus Mountains, has for centuries been considered the physical divide between Europe to the north and Asia to the south. The region includes the three former Soviet republics of Armenia, Azerbaijan, and Georgia and, with its mix of Christians and Muslims, was a stronghold of resistance to Russian nationalist domination until it finally succumbed in the late 1870s.

Stalin served an intermittent ten-year revolutionary apprenticeship (in between periods of imprisonment and exile in Siberia) in Transcaucasia. The rugged mountainous terrain provided the ideal hideout for a revolutionary on the run from the tsarist authorities, as Stalin was between 1901 and March 1908.

As an underground agitator, first for the Georgian Social Democrats (the Mesame Dasi) and after 1907 for the Bolsheviks, Stalin affiliated himself with workers and sympathizers at industrial centers such as Tiflis's railroad center, the oilfields of Baku, and the refineries at Batum. After he was arrested in Baku in March 1910, Stalin's effective activity in the region ended. He later made only flying visits as a representative of the Central Committee of the Communist Party.

Their deep-seated sense of national identity inspired these three republics to declare their independence as a short-lived Transcaucasian Federation after the Revolution of 1917. Subsequent moves by them to go it alone were quickly suppressed by the Soviets after 1918. In 1921 they were united as an administrative district, the Transcaucasian Soviet Federated Socialist Republic under Soviet rule until 1936, when they were separated again into three union republics under the newly instituted Soviet Constitution.

Throughout Stalin's rule, tight control was kept on Transcaucasia in order to keep the lid on any attempted revival of national identity among its political elite and intelligentsia. During the Great Terror a proportionally higher number of people from the region were affected, with as many as 50,000 alone suffering arrest and exile. During the Great Patriotic War, in 1943–1944, Stalin initiated a vicious campaign of ethnic cleansing against the minorities of this region, some of whom had supposedly collaborated with the Germans under occupation, by deporting people such as the Chechens and the Ingush to locations in Siberia and Central Asia.

See also Georgia; The Great Terror; "Marxism and the National Question"; Nationalities

Further reading: Ronald Grigor Suny, ed. *Transcaucasia: Nationalism and Social Change: Essays in the History of Armenia, Azerbaijan, and Georgia.* Ann Arbor: University of Michigan Press, 1983.

Trotsky, Leon 1879–1940

Leon Trotsky (born Lev Davidovich Bronstein) was everything the archetypal romantic revolutionary should be—orator, visionary, powerhouse of energy, independent thinker, and brilliant debater. He was a man of great intellect, but he had an Achilles' heel: a complete lack of control over his temperament, which not only hamstrung his career as a Bolshevik but caused him to dissipate his remaining life in exile, endlessly berating the ills of Stalinism. The refusal to let go of his impossible dream of a permanent world revolution also left Trotsky isolated in a changing political world. He vowed that he would "die a proletarian revolutionist, a Marxist, a dialectical materialist, and consequently, an irreconcilable atheist."

Latterly, Trotsky's image as a political thinker had become associated with the fringe elements of what was popularly called the "loony left," particularly during the years of student unrest and militancy of

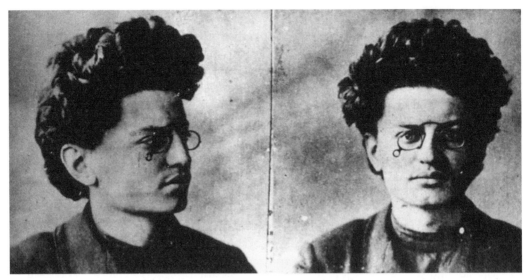

A police photograph of Leon Trotsky, taken on his first arrest for revolutionary activities in 1898. The firebrand of the Party, Trotsky was a brilliant orator who eclipsed Stalin during the days of the revolution.

the late 1960s and 1970s. His face became a commercial commodity along with that of another romantic revolutionary, Che Guevara. The images of both men were mass produced on T-shirts, badges, and posters as the icons of anarchy and protest. Such commercialization of his image did little to redress the balance of Trotsky's reputation and served only to further perpetuate his persona, particularly in the minds of the politically uninitiated, as the bogeyman of Russian revolutionary politics. Even Winston Churchill would dub Trotsky "the Ogre of Europe," while an American officer in Petrograd in 1918 more forcefully captured the inherent contradiction in Trotsky's flawed personality as "a four-kind son-of-a-bitch, but the greatest Jew since Jesus Christ."

While many of the misperceptions about Trotsky, both in the Soviet Union and in the West, were originally engineered and disseminated by Stalin's propaganda machine as part of one of the most malevolent campaigns of sustained character assassination in history, part of the blame for Trotsky's own spectacular failure as a major political player in the history of Soviet Russia after Lenin's death stems from his own in-

tellectual elitism. It was an elitism that was frequently insufferable and showed itself in a contemptuous attitude toward many of his own political colleagues, including (and in particular) Stalin. Trotsky was the lifelong victim of an unshakeable and arrogant belief in his own point of view, a view that would never accommodate the other side of the argument. Stalin, meanwhile, discovered early, in the days when he was making his own bid for political power, that the key to success was always to be seen to accommodate the other political view, a tactic embodied in his surprisingly placatory stance during 1917, when many in the revolutionary movement, Lenin included, sought to precipitate events. And so, while Stalin learned the art of patience and self-effacement, Trotsky's imperiousness prevented him from compromising on the one essential—the subordination of the individual will to that of the collective.

Born in Ukraine in 1879 as Lev Bronstein, Trotsky was the son of a relatively prosperous family of Russified Jewish farmers, who had their own land and enjoyed considerable respect in their local community of Yanovka. By coincidence, the day of his birth was to become the most auspicious one in the Soviet calendar, for thirty-eight years later, in 1917, it would mark the day the Bolsheviks seized power in the October Revolution.

As a young boy, Trotsky displayed all the characteristic Jewish passion for study and absorbed himself in books and ideas (he later became convinced that "illiteracy is spiritual lousiness"). In 1888 he was sent to school in Odessa, where he lived with family friends. Here he proved to be a star pupil and was soon making a close study of Marxism and Russian populism. But by 1897 he had abandoned his studies in favor of political activism, after becoming caught up in the strikes and political agitation of local workers, and joined the South Russian Workers Union. In January 1898 he was arrested and spent his eighteenth birthday in prison. It would be the first of many periods of imprisonment during the course of a life spent in many different countries.

After a period in solitary confinement in Odessa, Trotsky was sentenced to four years in exile and transported to Siberia in May 1900. Here, he married a fellow revolutionary, Alexandra Sokolovskaya, by whom he had two daughters. Trotsky made good use of his time, feverishly reading and writing all kinds of political tracts and pamphlets (Stalin, in comparison, wrote virtually nothing during his own long bouts in Siberia, particularly between 1913 and 1917, preferring to learn to hunt and fish). In 1902 Trotsky made his escape from exile with his wife's blessing in order to serve the revolution, leaving her and the children behind. The Lev Bronstein who escaped from Russia now became Leon Trotsky, the name given on his false passport being that of his former jailer.

Arriving in London, Trotsky sought out Lenin and his wife in their pokey accommodation in King's Cross, and together they worked on Lenin's revolutionary publication *Iskra* (The Spark) before Trotsky set off on a tour of the revolutionary bolt-holes of Europe, namely Brussels, Liège, and Paris, where he subsequently entered into a relationship with another revolutionary, Nataliya Sedova, by whom he later had two sons.

It was not long before Trotsky, refusing to compromise his own forceful views, fell out with Lenin over matters of party bureaucracy and the running of *Iskra*. In particular, Trotsky expressed his disquiet that Lenin's increasingly rigid centralization and bureaucratization of the Russian Social Democrats (the RSDWP) was far from democratic. As a result, at the time of the Second Congress of the All-Russian Social Democratic Workers Party in 1903, Trotsky sided with the more moderate Mensheviks when the party officially split into two factions. It was Trotsky's written polemical argument with Lenin during this period that Stalin would later distort in the historical record in order to demonstrate Trotsky's supposed anti-Leninist theories by quoting him out of context. It would form the main prop of Stalin's ideological campaign against him. Meanwhile, in a prophetic remark made in a pamphlet criticizing Lenin, which unknowingly forewarned of Stalin's rise to power as general secretary of the Communist Party, Trotsky observed that "the organization of the Party takes the place of the Party itself; the Central Committee takes the place of the organization; and finally the dictator takes the place of the Central Committee."

While technically affiliated with the Mensheviks, Trotsky continued to operate independently in his own inimitable way. His abrasive and dictatorial manner soon earned him enemies. In 1905 he had returned to Russia undercover to become president of the short-lived St. Petersburg Soviet of Workers, which had organized strikes and rallies in the wake of the Bloody Sunday massacre. This marked the beginning of Trotsky's political ascendancy. He became a familiar figure on the podium, and the fire and brimstone of his public speeches made him seem a natural rabble-rouser, like a latter-day Danton. And certainly it would be Trotsky's ringing, high-pitched voice and his beautiful Russian that would capture the popular imagination. Stalin, who still had a thick Georgian accent at this time and often fumbled for the right word in Russian, never made public speeches during the revolution and made few even in Party meetings. Stalin's avoidance of public speaking would be a lifelong characteristic, in stark contrast to the oratorical skills of his later wartime allies Winston Churchill and Franklin Roosevelt.

Trotsky's neatness of dress and physical demeanor also testified to a fastidiousness about image markedly different from Stalin's famously crumpled appearance at the time, or even that of an equally downtrodden-looking Lenin, who arrived in Petrograd in 1917 in threadbare clothes. With his pointed cavalier beard, his pince-nez, and his well-manicured hands, Trotsky had a preening air of refinement and self-regard. Even in prison he wore stiff wing collars and shiny boots, as a photograph taken of him in the Peter and Paul Fortress in 1906 testified. In contrast, Stalin at this time was still a long way from the all-essential image makeover; it was not until he adopted the uniform of a Red Army marshal, at the critical time of the Great Patriotic War, that he settled on his own equally pervasive image.

Trotsky soon found himself in prison again after his organization of strikes and civil unrest in St. Petersburg in 1905. But again he capitalized on his time in prison to produce his seminal political work, *Results and Prospects,* in which he described his own theory of permanent revolution, a modification of classical Marxist thinking adapted to the peculiarities of the Russian situation. In challenging existing Marxist thinking he thus set the scene for his own political vilification, initially at the hands of an equally eloquent Lenin. The classical Marxist view of revolution had been that a truly socialist upheaval could take place only in a society that had already achieved a considerable degree of technological development, in other words, as in the already developed West. This revolution would be achieved through a rising up of the bourgeoisie, who in turn would be supplanted by the truly socialist revolution of the proletariat.

Trotsky argued that in Russia at the time this situation did not prevail. The bourgeoisie was too weak and ineffectual and too tied by personal interests to the old tsarist system; revolution in Russia could only be achieved by the proletariat without the classic Marxist period of transition. Revolution in Russia would then, in turn, spark a rapid revolutionary upheaval across Europe, which would help sustain the momentum of social change in Russia. Without this, Trotsky felt that socialism in Russia would never be viable. Much scorn was poured on his vision, until the outbreak of World War I ignited hope among many activists that the war might well initiate social unrest and upheaval, particularly in Germany. Trotsky saw Germany in particular as ripe for the overthrow of imperialism, which for a short while did seem possible when the Spartacus League led an uprising in November of 1918.

On trial in June 1906 for his political activities, Trotsky produced a virtuoso display of oratory lasting several hours in a defense speech in court, but was once again exiled to Siberia in 1907, only to promptly escape and travel to Vienna. There he undertook journalistic work. At the Fifth Congress of the RSDWP, held in London in 1907, he first came across Stalin, who, also on the run from exile, was one of the 300 delegates. The two men met again in Vienna in 1913. Trotsky remained unimpressed with the gruff, unsmiling, and rather grubby-looking Stalin, whom he described as "anything but friendly" and as manifesting the "a priori hostility of grim concentration." Having summarily dismissed Stalin as a nonentity, Trotsky had already committed, in 1913, the single most costly miscalculation of his political career.

At the outbreak of World War I Trotsky was expelled by both France and Spain for antiwar activities against Russia's military involvement and went to New York, where he worked for a while with Nikolay Bukharin on the Russian newspaper *Noviy Mir* (New World). At the outbreak of the February Revolution of 1917, Trotsky made a hasty departure from his cheap lodgings in the Bronx to play a crucial role leading the Petrograd Soviet. Although Lenin had made it clear that he still considered much of Trotsky's semianarchist view on permanent revolution to be absurd, he admired his organizational skills, which were crucial at this time. Trotsky's uncharacteristic tact in his dealings with Lenin proved to be the only political concession he ever made, no doubt out of respect for Lenin's impressive intellect. As Trotsky saw it, the revolution now gathering momentum in Russia was a validation of his own infallible theories and the beginning of the permanent revolution that he had predicted.

And Lenin, too, had become increasingly impatient with the idea of the long transitional stage from bourgeois to proletarian revolution as developed by Marx. With the rapid deterioration of the political situation during 1917, he began shifting his position toward that of Trotsky, stating that Russia would have to bypass the transitional bourgeois stage of revolution and leapfrog straight into the socialist stage, with the industrial workers of the city allying themselves with the peasantry to overthrow the state. He also joined with Trotsky in hoping that the continuing war would be the catalyst, not just for revolution in Germany but also, possibly, in France and Britain. (In later years, when it was obvious that the impetus for revolution had stopped at Russia, Stalin would turn Trotsky's theories on their head, by insisting that socialism could and would be achieved in one country—the Soviet Union—without any help or support from socialists anywhere in the West.)

During the summer of 1917, therefore, Lenin made a conciliatory move toward Trotsky, who finally threw in his lot with the Bolsheviks, a pragmatic decision, based also on the realization that the other political factions of the time were in hopeless disarray. But it was an arrogant concession on Trotsky's part. He had made Lenin, the leader, come to him, and it would prompt some Old Bolsheviks to feel that Trotsky could never be trusted.

At the St. Petersburg Soviet, Trotsky took over a strategic role organizing the military side of the revolution and preparing for Lenin's return. Indeed, such was the importance of his role at the time, as the public face of the revolutionary leadership (while Lenin was in hiding and Stalin was deliberately staying in the wings), that even Stalin felt obliged to commend Trotsky in the newspaper *Pravda* in 1918. Stalin praised his contribution to "the entire work of the practical organization of the uprising," adding that "one may state without hesitation that the party was indebted first and foremost to comrade Trotsky for the garrison's prompt going over to the Soviet and for the able organization of the work of the Military Revolutionary Committee." Such a plaudit would inevitably be carefully expunged from the records during Stalin's later rewriting of Trotsky's role in Soviet history.

In the new Bolshevik government that came into being after the October Revolution, Trotsky was made commissar for foreign affairs (1917–1918) and was sent to head Russian peace negotiations with Germany at Brest-Litovsk from December 1917 to January 1918. He skillfully prolonged negotiations in the hope that the unstable civil situation and growing antipathy to the war in Germany would slide into chaos and carry the flame of revolution into the crumbling Austro-Hungarian Empire and on into Western Europe.

In 1919, Trotsky became one of the first five members of the Politburo and took on the important role of commissar for war (1918–1925), in which capacity he founded the Red Army. Dressed in long leather coat and cap, Trotsky toured Russia in a grandiose manner in his own specially equipped armored train. In the process he turned an unlikely gaggle of volunteers into a disciplined military machine that eventually defeated the Whites in the civil war. It was during the civil war that Trotsky and Stalin had their first political clash, as a result of Trotsky's creation of an officer class of military specialists based on the remnants of the old imperial army. With the Whites threatening Moscow and attempting to cut off the transportation of essential food supplies from the southwest to the northern cities, Red Army discipline at this crucial time was disrupted by regional opposition to the military specialists dispatched to them by Trotsky. This was particularly the case in and around Tsaritsyn, which was controlled by the Tenth Army under Klimenty Voroshilov, an old comrade and supporter of Stalin. Stalin had been sent to Tsaritsyn to protect the food supplies and supported this insubordination in the face of Trotsky's hysterical countercommands from the Supreme War Council. Stalin's actions were fueled by his growing resentment of Trotsky's high political profile and by their personal, irreconcilable antipathy. Lenin insisted that they abandon their personal feud, but it merely went underground.

The creation of the Red Army, while a testament to Trotsky's organizational skills, highlighted the deeply undemocratic side of his political nature and his predilection for draconian methods (such as severe punishments for desertion and insubordination and a liberal use of the death penalty). He also called, in similar fashion, for the militarization of labor and the enforced conscription of peasants and workers into disciplined work brigades. In his unpitying attitude toward the Russian people, whom he saw as a collective force for the achievement of Bolshevik objectives, he demonstrated a characteristic trait shared by most of the revolutionary leaders—an ability to

resort to what he euphemistically referred to as "the element of compulsion." His belief in coercion as an essential tool in the revolutionary process was elaborated in his *The Defence of Terrorism* (1920) after such methods were graphically demonstrated by the Bolsheviks during the period of the Red Terror of 1918. Trotsky's dictum that intimidation and ruthlessness were powerful instruments of policy was clearly seen in the workings of the first Soviet secret police, the Cheka, and often makes it hard to distinguish between Trotsky's and Stalin's views on the subject of repression. The later imposition by Stalin of a command economy during the 1930s was in many ways very close to Trotsky's own way of thinking.

After the revolution, while Trotsky might have seemed Lenin's natural successor, politically this had become unlikely, since he was unpopular within the Party and his Jewishness ultimately would have precluded him. In 1922 Lenin, recuperating from a stroke he had had in May, was anxious about his failing health and forced to seriously address the question of his successor. He was already aware of his miscalculation in agreeing to Stalin's taking on the secretaryship of the Communist Party in April, and as a counterweight he offered Trotsky the post as his deputy in the Council of People's Commissars. But Trotsky rejected the offer, never being one to play second fiddle; in addition, Lenin's proposal that they unite in a bloc against bureaucracy, in this case Stalin's growing dominance in the Orgburo of the Communist Party, never got off the ground because of Lenin's failing health.

It was during the crucial year of 1923, when Lenin was still sidelined by illness, that Trotsky missed his political moment. He vacillated, either through loss of nerve or his persisting lack of political insight with regard to Stalin, and failed to lay his claim to the leadership when Lenin suffered his second and ultimately fatal stroke. Determined always to keep the higher political and moral ground and not demean himself by indulging in political infighting, Trotsky failed to challenge Stalin's ascendancy. In a secret testament he dictated during the winter of 1923–1924, Lenin recognized this failing in Trotsky. While he did not doubt Trotsky's intellectual capabilities, he observed that Trotsky's self-confidence was too far-reaching and that he was too much attracted by the purely administrative side of affairs. The emphasis on Trotsky's administrative skills also suggested another inherent weakness—his reluctance to take direct, physical action—something about which Stalin had no qualms.

Unfortunately for Trotsky, Stalin was not deterred by his rival's sense of moral and intellectual superiority, and Trotsky's refusal to stoop to Stalin's Machiavellian style of intrigue marked the beginning of the end of his political career. From the day of Lenin's death Stalin outmaneuvered Trotsky time and time again. He even succeeded in keeping him away from the capital at the time of Lenin's death by misinforming him, when Trotsky was recuperating from illness in the Caucasus, about the date of the funeral. Trotsky was thus denied his moment of crucial, public prominence at Lenin's obsequies in Red Square. By the time of the Thirteenth Party Congress in May 1924, Trotsky and his followers were being lambasted as factionalists and political deviationists, and his political theories denounced as heretical and anti-Leninist. Stalin's objective was now no less than to bury Trotskyism as an ideology. The vilification of Trotsky was also the first move in a campaign of anti-Semitism initiated by Stalin against the leading Jewish Bolsheviks, who one by one were isolated politically as the objects of Stalin's own envy and dislike of intellectuals, particularly Jewish intellectuals.

By the time Trotsky made one last attempt to regain his position, through an alliance with Lev Kamenev and Grigory Zinoviev in 1926, his political influence had all but evaporated. He resigned his post as commissar for war before the inevitable dismissal. By the end of 1926 he had been ousted from the Politburo and expelled from the Communist Party. And now the inevitable realization sank in among Trotsky's various political opponents in the Old Guard that they had aligned themselves with the wrong man, with Stalin against Trotsky, rather than the other way round.

But it was too late. Trotsky was exiled to Alma Ata in Central Asia in January 1928 and a year later deported to Turkey, where he lived on the island of Prinkipo for four years before moving to France. But his life in Europe was unsettled, no doubt a consequence of his being considered by most governments as something of a political liability. Trotsky's last hopes of recouping his lost political forum through the establishment of a Fourth International to rival Stalin's Comintern failed due to lack of support, no doubt a result of the Soviet secret police's systematic elimination of many European Trotskyists, particularly during the Spanish Civil War.

The rise of Hitler forced Trotsky to flee again, this time to Norway in 1935. Eventually, with the help of the Marxist painter Diego Rivera, he was given political asylum in Mexico and in 1936 settled in a house at Coyoacán, Mexico City. But by now Stalin, who had long since come to regret having let Trotsky get out of the Soviet Union alive, was intent on his elimination, and in 1935 he instructed the head of the NKVD Genrikh Yagoda to speed up Trotsky's liquidation. In 1936 Trotsky was condemned to death in absentia at the first of the Moscow show trials. When Stalin heard that he was hard at work on a major exposé of Stalin's rule, under the unequivocal title *The Revolution Betrayed,* he ordered that no expense be spared in hunting Trotsky down.

Trotsky spent the final years of his life a virtual prisoner, constantly alert to assassination plots, living within a fortified compound patrolled by five Mexican policeman and guarded by an entourage of ten or so devoted Trotskyists. But this did not save him from the unlimited resources of the NKVD, and in 1940 he was assassinated by Spanish Communist Ramon Mercader, a Stalinist agent (although he never admitted to the fact), who had inveigled his way into Trotsky's inner sanctum. Mercader subsequently spent twenty years in jail, having accepted from his prison cell the award of Hero of the Soviet Union from Stalin for ridding him of Trotsky.

While Stalin's apparatchiks labored long and hard at cutting and rewriting accounts of Trotsky's career in the history books, in order to cast him in the mold of supervillain, none of them had the linguistic skill and subtlety of a Trotsky. It was he who coined the most inventive and familiar epithets about Stalin as "an outstanding mediocrity," as the "*komitetchik par excellence*" (alluding to Stalin's domination of the Soviet bureaucracy) and, most damningly, as "the grave digger of the revolution." He also chillingly referred to Stalin's alleged elimination of rivals through poisoning by describing him as the "Super-Borgia in the Kremlin" and was the first of many to allude to Stalin as an Asiatic, in reference to his byzantine penchant for slyness, intrigue, and cruelty.

Trotsky took continuous delight in indulging his brilliant verbal invective, even long distance from exile in Mexico, in his condemnation of Stalin. Yet for all of Stalin's alleged colorlessness as a personality and for all his provincial coarseness, it was he and not the blistering and brilliant Trotsky who reached the top of the political tree. Six months before his murder Trotsky was still vainly basking in what historian Robert Conquest has described as the "glamour of a lost cause." For forty-three years, Trotsky claimed, his vision had remained unsullied. He also complimented himself on the fact that his "faith in the Communist future of mankind is no less ardent, indeed it is firmer today than it was in the days of my youth." But a price had to be paid for such implacable belief, and as with so many of

the Soviet Union's lost revolutionaries, it was paid in the tragic annihilation of most of Trotsky's own family. His wife, Alexandra, died in exile in Siberia, and his two daughters by her died at a young age— Nina in the Soviet Union in 1928 of tuberculosis and Zina by suicide in Berlin in 1933. Of his two sons by his second partner, Nataliya Sedova, Leon died young under mysterious circumstances during a routine operation in Paris, and Sergey, a scientist who had remained in the Soviet Union, was arrested in 1937 and died in the Gulag. Even Trotsky's two sons-in-law died in exile in Siberia. His orphaned grandchildren disappeared, unmourned.

See also Kamenev, Lev; Lenin, Vladimir; Red Army; Russian Revolution of 1917; Spanish Civil War; Stalin: Personality of; "Socialism in One Country"; Zinoviev, Grigory

Further reading: Isaac Deutscher. *The Prophet Armed: Trotsky, 1879–1921; The Prophet Unarmed: Trotsky, 1921–1929; The Prophet Outcast: Trotsky, 1929–1940,* 3 vols. Oxford: Oxford University Press, 1954–1963; Leon Trotsky. *The Revolution Betrayed: What Is the Soviet Union and Where Is it Going?* London: Faber and Faber, 1937; Dmitri Volkogonov. *Trotsky: The Eternal Revolutionary.* London: HarperCollins, 1996; Bertram D. Wolfe. *Three Who Made a Revolution.* Harmondsworth, UK: Penguin, 1966.

Tsaritsyn, Defense of
See Civil War.

Tukhachevsky, Mikhail Nikolaevich (1893–1937)

Nicknamed the "Red Napoleon," Mikhail Tukhachevsky was one of Stalin's finest and most progressive military leaders. Yet his distinguished service record in World War I and the Russian civil war and his undisputed abilities as a forward-thinking administrator through his various reforms of the Red Army were precisely the qualities that sealed his fate as a victim of Stalin's ruthless purge of the Soviet military leadership.

Tukhachevsky was a cultured and sensitive man who spoke several languages. He also played the violin and, as a patron of the arts, was a friend and supporter of composer Dmitry Shostakovich. He was that rarity in the Red Army—an individualist who combined a powerful intellect with undoubted military charisma. Descended from the Russo-Polish minor nobility and brought up in a liberal family, he entered the Moscow Cadet Corps and trained at the Alexandrovsky Military College. During World War I he set his sights on a top-flight military career, determined that he would be a general by the time he was thirty years old. After the revolution he offered his services to Trotsky (who was in the process of setting up the Red Army) and joined the Bolsheviks in 1918. During the civil war he commanded Red Army forces against the White forces of Admiral Alexander Kolchak in Siberia and on the southern front against General Denikin, as well as fighting on the western front against the Polish forces of Marshal Josef Pilsudski.

By the age of thirty-three Tukhachevsky had become chief of staff of the Red Army, having already initiated a program of reform of its training methods at the elite Frunze Military Academy in 1921. He now began campaigning in earnest for the technical modernization of the Red Army into a major fighting force, through the acquisition of tanks and armored vehicles and an emphasis on the training of crack airborne troops. Much of this was done in the face of blinkered opposition from the old-school military diehards Klimenty Voroshilov and Semen Budenny, who still insisted on the preeminence of cavalry in military operations. At the same time, Tukhachevsky also radically reviewed Soviet military strategy, developing a deep operation theory based on offensive action, which has been seen as providing a spring-

board for the Red Army's victory over Germany in 1942–1943 at Stalingrad.

Tukhachevsky's elevation to marshal of the Soviet Union in 1935 might have seemed an endorsement of his popularity and indispensability, but by now Stalin had become mistrustful of his insistence on technical innovation. He was also jealous of the high regard in which Tukhachevsky had been held by Lenin and Trotsky after his successes in the civil war (and in comparison to Stalin's own less than distinguished military career). To Stalin, Tukhachevsky's individuality and talent smacked of an excess of independent military thinking that threatened his own position, and he began engineering Tukhachevsky's political isolation.

Tukhachevsky was dismissed from his post as head of the Red Army's technology and armament department and his influence waned, although he remained in his post as deputy defense commissar. The impetus for his arrest on 26 May 1937 came when Stalin, who had long awaited a convenient pretext for initiating the final phase of Tukhachevsky's downfall, allowed himself to believe a bogus intelligence report based on a dossier of cleverly forged documents that purported to prove that Tukhachevsky had been involved in a conspiracy with the German General Staff to usurp power. But in fact, only a year earlier at a plenary session of the Soviet High Command Tukhachevsky had actually openly warned of the growing military threat from Hitler's Germany. Such outspokenness served only to further endanger him at a time when Stalin considered it expedient to keep on good terms with Hitler. Several historians now suggest that the whole affair had originated with the Germans, as a deliberate plot orchestrated by Hitler's Gestapo second-in-command Reinhard Heydrich to undermine the Red Army leadership.

On 11 June 1937 Tukhachevsky was tried, along with seven other leading officers of the Red Army, by a military tribunal and was shot the next day. The firing squad was commanded by his friend and military comrade Marshal Vasily Blyukher, who himself became a victim of the purges in the Red Army not long after. Many members of Tukhachevsky's family also suffered arrest and imprisonment, including his wife, mother, and two brothers, who all died in prison during the Great Terror. Yet only a year after his murder, Stalin openly credited Tukhachevsky with having been the driving force behind the modernization of the Red Army. In an interview given in 1965 but not published until the time of Tukhachevsky's rehabilitation in 1988, the great Soviet war leader Marshal Georgy Zhukov was unqualified in his admiration of the man as a "giant of military thought, a star of the first magnitude in our Motherland's military constellation."

See also Blyukher, Vasily; Budenny, Semen; Rokossovsky, Konstantin; Voroshilov, Klimenty; Zhukov, Georgy

Further reading: Dimitri Shostakovich. *Testimony,* chapter 3. London: Hamish Hamilton, 1979; Harold Shukman, ed. *Stalin's Generals.* London: Weidenfeld and Nicolson, 1993; Richard Simpkin and John Erickson. *Deep Battle: The Brainchild of Marshal Tukhachevskii.* London: Brassey's Defence Publishers, 1987.

Union of Soviet Writers

In the first years of relative creative freedom after the Revolution of 1917, literary groups and factions had proliferated, stimulating an atmosphere of excitement and experimentation in writing. In 1932, when Stalin announced rigid guidelines on literature with the promulgation of the official precepts of socialist realism, the inevitable ramification of this was the establishment of a unifying body to oversee the work of writers and ensure strict political control over a new literature that was to be a "truthful, historically concrete depiction of reality in its revolutionary development."

On 23 April 1932 a Communist Party Resolution on Literature abolished all existing writers' associations, and the Union of Soviet Writers was established two years later, with Maxim Gorky as its first president. The union would become one of the most influential bureaucratic monoliths of the Stalinist system. It was given its own regulating bodies of a board, a secretariat, a president, and a first secretary, as well as provincial branches in the various Union Republics of the Soviet Union, together comprising an elite drawn in many cases from the Party and even the secret police. While membership was not obligatory, it increasingly became a necessity (as did membership of the Communist Party) for anyone wishing to make a successful career. The union's original membership of 1,500 mushroomed over the years to reach over 9,500 members in 1986. It was also set up as a model for the bringing into political line of all the major professions in the arts—architects, painters, composers—in their own respective unions.

Like many other edifices of the Stalinist bureaucratic machine, the union was far more than just a professional club. It was a controlling force in the lives of most writers, having considerable influence over the rejection and/or acceptance of their work by official publications (some of which, like the highly influential Literary Gazette (Literaturnaya Gazeta), were controlled by the union itself), as well as control over fees and print runs. The perks, as for any other functionaries within the nomenklatura, were considerable and catered to virtually all material needs. Living accommodations were available for members in an exclusive twelve-story apartment block in a pleasant suburb of Moscow, as well as in the much-sought-after dachas at the writers' colonies of Peredelkino (twenty kilometers [twelve miles] southwest of Moscow), Komarovo, and Koktebel. Also available were higher education for the children of members at the union's own Gorky Literary Institute, special clinics, medical facilities (including the exclusive Kremlin Hospital), and sanatoria, as well as access to their own exclusive restaurant, luxury goods, and chauffeur-driven cars. The greatest prize of all, undoubtedly, was the rare opportunity to travel abroad on informational trips and to conferences and seminars, such as the Anti-Fascist Congress in Defense of Peace and Culture, held in Paris in 1935 (attended by writers Isaac Babel and Boris Pasternak).

The union held its first Congress in August–September of 1934, when the dogma of socialist realism was lectured about and debated at length, and the collective membership endorsed statements by such figures as cultural affairs spokesman Andrey Zhdanov that "in the age of the class struggle a non-class, non-tendentious, apolitical literature does not and cannot exist." As political orthodoxy became ever more essential for survival during Stalin's rule, those writers who did not toe the line faced increasing recrimination and even expulsion from the union. Expulsion was a form not only of literary but also of social excommunication, and several eminent writers, most notably Anna Akhmatova and Mikhail Zoschenko in 1946, suffered this fate during the era of Zhdanovism. Both writers had to live in extreme penury as a result. When Boris Pasternak was awarded the Nobel Prize for literature for his novel *Dr. Zhivago,* which had been published in Italy in 1958, the union condemned Pasternak's book in a resolution published in the influential *Literary Gazette* as "the cry of woe of a frightened Philistine." At Nikita Khrushchev's instigation a campaign of persecution was launched against Pasternak for having betrayed "the Soviet people, the cause of socialism, peace, and progress," and he was expelled from the Union.

Having spawned its own hierarchy of bureaucrats and its own system of almost military-style disciplinary measures for those who stepped out of line, the union provided ample opportunity for the little man to rise through the ranks to a position of power. In this way, those more vocal and politically motivated members were able to compensate for their own indifferent literary talents by dominating the political machinery of the union. One such writer was Alexander Fadeev. During the 1920s he had published several undistinguished short stories before producing his popular civil war novel *The Rout* (1927). Having been a leading supporter of the creative dictatorship of the literary union RAPP (All-Russian Union of Proletarian Writers) in 1934, Fadeev became a member of the board of the Writers' Union. He rose through the ranks to become general secretary and chairman by 1946; by this time he was also a member of the Central Committee of the Communist Party.

From this position of power, and together with Maxim Gorky, Fadeev had become the leading promoter of socialist realism. After becoming general secretary, he dominated the union, making full use of his power to make or break the lives of writers. He had no compunction in inciting the vicious chorus of voices raised in condemnation of Pasternak's independent stance during the 1940s and 1950s. Indeed, he even went to considerable lengths to rework (and in so doing, emasculate) his own 1945 novel *The Young Guard* to meet criticism that this story of partisan resistance during the Great Patriotic War did not give sufficient emphasis to the role played by the Communist Party. After Stalin's death, Fadeev lost his chairmanship of the union, and his position in the new climate of the thaw became untenable. He committed suicide in 1956, many say as a result of a crisis of conscience over the literary reputations he had earlier been instrumental in destroying as head of the Writers' Union.

See also Akhmatova, Anna; Babel, Isaac; Kataev, Valentin; Mandelstam, Osip; *Nomenklatura;* Pasternak, Boris; Sholokhov, Mikhail; Socialist Realism; Zoshchenko, Mikhail

Further reading: Ronald Hingley. *Russian Writers and Soviet Society, 1917–1978.* London: Methuen, 1981; Wolfgang Kasack. *Dictionary of*

Russian Literature since 1917. New York: Columbia University Press, 1988; A. Kemp-Welch, *Stalin and the Literary Intelligentsia, 1928–39*. Basingstoke, UK: Macmillan, 1991.

United Nations

The Soviets had only briefly belonged to the United Nations' unsuccessful predecessor, the League of Nations, between 1934 and 1940, withdrawing after the German-Soviet Non-Aggression Pact, when Stalin no longer found it expedient to support a drive for collective security against the rise of Hitler. During the Great Patriotic War, talks held at Dumbarton Oaks in Washington, D.C., by the United States, United Kingdom, Soviet Union, and China resulted in a basic proposal that was further discussed by the "Big Three" (the first three of those powers) at Yalta in February 1945 and was finalized by the fifty nations that drafted the Charter for the United Nations at the San Francisco Conference later that year.

The Soviet Union took part in the first session held in London in October 1945, as one of the five permanent members of the Security Council. From then on, through the years of the Cold War, UN sittings would be subjected to the idiosyncrasies of the Soviet version of international diplomacy. In New York the Security Council would echo to the repeated cries of *"Nyet"* ("no") as Soviet representatives (led in the early years by Mr. "No" himself, Vyacheslav Molotov) demonstrated their less-than-subtle stonewalling tactics in a blatant and repeated abuse of the veto.

At the Dumbarton Oaks talks in 1944, Stalin's foreign minister Andrey Gromyko had insisted that all sixteen of the constituent republics of the Soviet Union should have a seat in the General Assembly. Stalin was anxious that his Communist state should not be isolated from the rest of the capitalist world and wanted to hedge against occasions when the Soviet Union might be outvoted on important issues. But at Yalta he changed his tune, and by offering concessions over this issue and another sticking point, the Soviet right to veto procedural questions in the Security Council, he smoothed the way for the Allied acceptance of his territorial gains over Poland and his increased sphere of influence over Eastern Europe in general. Stalin was now prepared to accept seats for the Ukrainian and Belarussian Soviet republics only, in addition to that for the Soviet Union as a whole.

Not long before his death Stalin found himself in a difficult position over UN intervention in the war in Korea. In March 1950 Stalin boycotted the Security Council's call to condemn the actions of North Korea in invading the South (which he quietly supported) rather than use his veto. But while he publicly sought to avoid an open confrontation with the majority of the UN membership, which supported intervention, his covert endorsement of the North Korean regime of Kim Il-Sung would end in an embarrassing moral defeat for the Soviet Union after his death when it was obliged to accept a compromise settlement that curtailed Sung's territorial ambitions.

See also Korean War; Molotov, Vyacheslav; Vyshinsky, Andrey

Vavilov, Nikolay Ivanovich (1887–1943)

*T*he eminent Soviet biologist and leading figure in the study of genetics, Nikolay Vavilov was one of many leading Soviet scientists persecuted during the Stalinist pseudoscientific dictatorship of Lysenkoism.

Vavilov had studied with English geneticist William Bateson at Cambridge before the revolution and at the John Innes Horticultural Institute in Surrey before returning to Russia as a professor of botany at Saratov University. After the revolution, he had traveled extensively abroad, collecting seeds and samples from botanical populations, including thousands of species of wheat and other crop plants. Vavilov took these back to the Soviet Union for further research and breeding, publishing his findings on the centers of origin of plant species in 1920.

Vavilov's theories on genetic diversity and the adaptability of species were now given a Marxist perspective. If Soviet society at large could be molded to optimum performance, so too could plant life, and Vavilov's argument for the importance of genetic engineering to "sculpt organic forms at will" was an attractive scientific proposition, promising control over plants and, concomitantly, agriculture itself. The importance of Vavilov's work was quickly recognized, ensuring the rapid promotion of genetic research in the Soviet Union.

In 1924 Vavilov became director of the All-Union Institute of Plant Breeding and went on to eventually head 400 institutions grouped under the All-Union Academy of Agricultural Sciences. By the late 1920s he had risen to a position of considerable prominence in Soviet science, as well as being recognized abroad for his work. In 1933 Vavilov set up his own Institute of Genetics at the Academy of Sciences, but by 1937 he was coming under increasing attack for his Mendelian-based theories of plant breeding by his former protégé, geneticist Trofim Lysenko.

By 1940 and with Stalin's tacit approval, Lysenko had demolished Vavilov's reputation and, after orchestrating Vavilov's removal and that of his two successors in 1935, he had taken over as director of the Academy of Agricultural Science himself. Vavilov was arrested that same year on a charge of spying for the British, as well as setting out to sabotage Soviet agricultural science with what Lysenko had called his "bourgeois biology." Vavilov was held under interrogation in Moscow for eleven months before being tried in July 1941 and sentenced to death. But first he was left to languish in Saratov prison in a basement cell without daylight and fresh air. Various people, including his brother Sergey, an eminent physicist, petitioned Lavrenty Beria for his release. Vavilov's election to the British Royal Society in 1942 helped secure the commutation of his sentence to twenty years' imprisonment, but by now his health had declined to such an extent that he was no longer able to stand up and walk. He died in January 1943 of malnutrition and dystrophy.

Many of Vavilov's scientific disciples also followed him into prison and met a miserable death in the Gulag. With Lysenko's final debunking in the 1960s, Vavilov's scientific credentials were reinstated, and he was officially rehabilitated.

See also Lysenko, Trofim; Science
Further reading: Mark Popovskii. *The Vavilov Affair*. Hamden, CT: Archon Books, 1984.

Voroshilov, Klimenty Yefremovich (1881–1969)

One of Stalin's most stalwart allies and dutiful "yes" men, Klimenty Voroshilov rode on the back of past military glories for many years until his incompetence and lack of comprehension of modern warfare were exposed at the outbreak of the Great Patriotic War.

Voroshilov was one of the prerevolutionary breed of old-style cavalrymen, who like his friend and later fellow marshal Semen Budenny long outlived his military usefulness. His career epitomized the banality of a system that rewarded the blind obedience of the colorless, talentless bureaucrat or soldier with high office, awards and titles, a dacha in the country, and a comfortable pension. In return, Voroshilov's loyalty was tested to the extreme when he was called upon to condone the mass purge of the officer corps of the Red Army in 1937–1938 and rubber-stamp the executions of many of his closest military colleagues.

Voroshilov's father was a peasant coal miner in the Donbass. During the early 1900s Voroshilov himself had had a succession of such menial jobs as miner, shepherd, laborer, and factory worker. He joined the Russian Social Democrats in 1903 and became involved in revolutionary activities in the Caucasus. It was here, while organizing a strike of oil workers in Baku, that he first became friends with Stalin.

After the revolution, Voroshilov fought with some distinction during the civil war in the Caucasus and Crimea. He was a supporter with Stalin of the use of a people's militia in preference to the Red Army being created by Trotsky under the leadership of former tsarist officers. At Tsaritsyn on the southwestern front, he connived directly with Stalin to flout Trotsky's authority by taking over control of Red Army forces in the area. The defense of the city was his one and only moment of military glory, and he would exploit it for the rest of his political career. It also brought him into Stalin's inner coterie and with it a life of preference and privilege, beginning with his election to the Central Committee of the Communist Party in 1921. From then on Voroshilov set about proving himself "an obedient and consistent executor of other people's wishes." In 1925 he supplanted Trotsky as people's commissar for war (a post he held until his ignominious removal in 1940). From this position he created his own minicult as a military leader. A heavy tank was named after him. Part of this self-promotion was achieved through Voroshilov's patronage of the arts, in particular his association with and support for the socialist realist artist Alexander Gerasimov, who returned the compliment by painting numerous flattering portraits of Stalin and his comrade-in-arms Voroshilov in the 1930s.

During this period Voroshilov was constantly at Stalin's side and a regular visitor to his dachas. But throughout he manifested no aptitude for independent, original thought as either a military man or an apparatchik. In 1935 he was made marshal of

One of the most celebrated paintings of Stalin, shown walking in the Kremlin with Klimenty Voroshilov. The artist, Alexander Gerasimov, a leading exponent of socialist realism, won a Stalin Prize for the painting in 1941.

the Soviet Union, but in the Finnish-Soviet Winter War of 1939–1940 his military incompetence was finally exposed. Stalin and Voroshilov had both seriously underestimated the tough resistance of the Finns, and the war ended in a Pyrrhic victory over them, with 70,000 Soviet soldiers dead. As a result, Stalin took Voroshilov to task in 1940 and swiftly replaced him as people's commissar for defense with Marshal Semen Timoshenko. But Stalin was still willing to give this dutiful soldier another chance, since he had need, at the outbreak of war with Germany in 1941, of popular military heroes such as Voroshilov to galvanize the masses.

Voroshilov was put in charge of the Defense Council of Leningrad and appointed commander-in-chief of the Leningrad front. But after he failed to prevent the on-

slaught of the long siege of the city and in the process attempted to launch a style of counterattack that had long since been abandoned, and that drew nothing but contempt from most of his military colleagues, Stalin relegated Voroshilov to a desk job on the General Staff. It was now patently clear that Voroshilov had neither the technical skill nor the intelligence to come to grips with the new theories of combined operations warfare, but Stalin still kept him on as an important wartime figurehead. And once again, in 1945–1947 Voroshilov responded to the call of duty by supervising the establishment of the Communist government in postwar Hungary.

The last days of Voroshilov's career under Stalin were hollow, but he survived to see his tally of Orders of Lenin rise to a record eight. He continued to be venerated as an "old warrior" of the heroic days of the civil war. Between 1953 and 1960 he was accorded the figurehead role of chairman of the Presidium of the Supreme Soviet, even surviving an attack from Nikita Khrushchev during the process of de-Stalinization of the 1950s.

See also Budenny, Marshal Semen; Civil War; Great Patriotic War; Red Army; Leningrad, Siege of; Trotsky, Leon

Further reading: Roy Medvedev. *All Stalin's Men.* Oxford: Basil Blackwell, 1983; Harold Shukman, ed. *Stalin's Generals.* London: Phoenix, 1997.

Voznesensky, Nikolay Alekseevich (1903–1950)

A leading Soviet economist and talented administrator, Nikolay Voznesensky rose quickly to a preeminent position as chairman of the State Planning Commission (Gosplan) in 1938. His position seemed secure until Georgy Malenkov and Lavrenty Beria launched a roundup of supporters of Andrey Zhdanov during the "Leningrad Affair" of 1949–1950.

After training as an economist at Moscow, Voznesensky had taught before becoming one of the team of elite party intellectuals and bureaucrats gathered together by Zhdanov as first secretary of the Communist Party in Leningrad. Here, Voznesensky took a leading role in the city's economic planning between 1935 and 1937, before winning the plum job as head of Gosplan at the age of only thirty-four. In this capacity he rebuilt Gosplan's personnel after the depredations of the purges and soon found himself given additional roles. During the war, Voznesensky was made deputy prime minister in 1941 and deputy chairman of the State Defense Committee in 1942. His handling of the Soviet economy during the crucial years of the war, which included the successful relocation of much of Soviet heavy industry

beyond the Urals, led to his being made a full member of the Politburo in 1947.

Voznesensky was an independent thinker, outspoken in his economic views. He had not been afraid to offer his own solutions, such as recommending that peasants should be able to cultivate their own plots of land during the war and sell the produce through the state. His reputation as a leading economist grew apace. In 1946, Voznesensky launched the Fourth Five-Year Plan, aimed at outstripping prewar output, particularly in heavy industry, while his mentor Andrey Zhdanov lined him up for the important role of monitoring the East German economy and organizing its payment of war reparations.

In 1943 he had been one of the few top Soviet politicians to be made a member of the Soviet Academy of Sciences. Even Stalin acknowledged Voznesensky's contribution, awarding him a Stalin Prize in 1948 for his account of his work at Gosplan, *Wartime Economy of the USSR in the Period of the Patriotic War.* By the end of the 1940s, Voznesensky ranked high in Stalin's estimation and seemed a potential successor to Stalin until Zhdanov's premature death in 1948 suddenly left him exposed to political rivals with their own sights on the succession, in particular Lavrenty Beria, head of the secret police. In March 1949 Voznesensky was summarily removed from his post at Gosplan and as deputy prime minister. Soon after Beria contrived a bogus charge against him of "losing important state documents."

Although he was acquitted, Voznesensky was now a marked man, for this bogus accusation had been sufficient to make Stalin suspicious of the growing influence in Leningrad of Voznesensky and other Party officials. Since the war, Stalin had been particularly resentful of the international respect for the achievement of the Leningraders in surviving the terrible 900-day siege by German troops. In his view, such a capacity for resistance and self-sacrifice might one day be redeployed against him.

This fear, coupled with the fact that there had been discussions to make Leningrad the capital of the Russian Soviet Federated Socialist Republic (RSFSR) and thus a potential political rival to Moscow, unnerved Stalin sufficiently to move against such an outcome. He now ordered his number two man, Georgy Malenkov, to prepare a case against Voznesensky and the Leningrad Party during July and August of 1949.

Meanwhile, Voznesensky, out of a job and under house arrest, was left alone to continue writing his book *The Political Economy of Communism*. Stalin, despite being jealous of Voznesnesky's reputation, still seemed undecided on his fate. But eventually Voznesensky was rearrested in November 1949, along with his brother Alexander (also an economist and rector of Leningrad University) and as many as 3,000 other leading Leningrad Party members, in a purge that became known as the "Leningrad Affair." Both Voznesensky brothers were tortured into confessing to crimes they had not committed (in Nikolay's case, that he had "deliberately set low output targets" during the Five-Year Plans). The death sentence, abolished at the end of the war, was reinstated for the Leningrad accused, including the Voznesenskys and M. I. Rodionov, the prime minister of the RSFSR. Voznesensky's sister, Mariya, a Leningrad Party worker, was also arrested and shot not long after. All three were rehabilitated in 1954.

See also Leningrad, Siege of
Further reading: Alec Nove. *An Economic History of the USSR, 1917–1991*. London: Penguin, 1992.

Vyshinsky, Andrey Yanuarevich (1883–1954)

Stalin's chief prosecutor and the key writer on Stalinist jurisprudence, Andrey Vyshinsky holds a place of infamy in Soviet history as the figure who held sway, like a latter-day "Witchfinder General," over the major show trials of 1936–1938.

The excesses of Vyshinsy's courtroom behavior became legendary. His penchant for screaming hysterical abuse at defendants was characterized by the use of his favorite epithets, such as "vermin" and "mad dogs." Some have seen his behavior as an act of neurotic overcompensation for his less-than-perfect political past as a Menshevik; he had joined the Mensheviks in opposition to the Bolsheviks in 1903, an act that would always haunt Vyshinsky. Before the October Revolution, as a supporter of Alexander Kerensky's provisional government, he had actively joined in the condemnation of Lenin as a traitor and spy. After the revolution and with the Bolsheviks now in the ascendant, Vyshinsky, like many others who wanted to ensure their future careers, found it expedient to change sides. In 1920 he became a member of the Communist Party. He would prove to be one of the few former Mensheviks who survived unscathed. After studying law, he became a leading legal theoretician and taught and lectured at Moscow State University before rising to prominence as a prosecutor for the Russian Soviet Federated Socialist Republic in 1931.

Vyshinsky's relationship with Stalin went back to 1907 in Baku, where they had shared a cell in Bailovka prison after Vyshinsky had been imprisoned for inciting a strike on the railroads. Stalin, aware of Vyshinsky's considerable legal skills and equally aware that his neurosis about his political past would ensure his undying sycophancy, decided to make good use of him as prosecutor at the first trials of supposed industrial "wreckers" in the late 1920s. It was at the Shakhty trial of 1928 that Vyshinsky first made his mark.

In 1935, with Vyshinsky taking advantage of every opportunity to effusively reiterate his devotion, Stalin put him to work on the judicial removal of all his political enemies by making him prosecutor of the

The tight-lipped, hunched figure of the chief prosecutor of the Moscow show trials, Andrey Vyshinsky (center front), is surrounded by the staff of 228 who helped him administer Soviet "justice" during the Great Terror.

Soviet Union. Vyshinsky acknowledged the honor in his characteristically groveling tones: "Sparing neither my strength nor my life, I am ready to serve the great cause of Lenin-Stalin to the end of my days." Despite his preeminence as a writer on jurisprudence, Vyshinsky had no scruples about tailoring the indictments of the major accused in the show trials to Stalin's own demands or about allowing Stalin to edit the speeches for the prosecution in order to comply with his carefully predesignated scenario. By now, Vyshinsky had also formulated the legal procedures for the Moscow show trials, which were to be based not on the traditional cornerstone of evidence, but on the personal confessions of guilt made by the accused (no matter under what kind of duress). It was a principle that Nikolay Bukharin was to famously shame

Vyshinsky with at the end of his trial, saying, "The confession of the accused is a medieval principle of justice."

Soon Vyshinsky's idiosyncratic line in vicious verbal abuse and bombast became a trademark that other prosecutors adopted. In 1937, on the eve of the last big show trials of Nikolay Bukharin and Aleksey Rykov, Vyshinsky wrote that "one has to remember comrade Stalin's instruction, that there are sometimes periods, moments in the life of a society and in our life in particular, when the laws prove obsolete and have to be set aside." Certainly by now all sense of justice had evaporated, as Vyshinsky once again harangued and humiliated Bukharin and his codefendants as half-crazed animals and as every conceivable form of ordure, excrement, and filth.

After the purge trials, Vyshinsky went

back to writing on jurisprudence and produced *The Theory of Legal Evidence in Soviet Law,* which became a primary text and was awarded a Stalin Prize. He now became an establishment figure with election to the Soviet Academy and, in 1939, membership to the Central Committee of the Communist Party. In 1940 he gave up his role of public prosecutor and settled into a comfortable life at his dacha (once the home of a victim of the purges) until called upon to assume another important role for Stalin as deputy commissar of foreign affairs. In this capacity he took charge of the incorporation of Latvia into the Soviet Union in 1940. Vyshinsky subsequently spent much of the war abroad, as a roving diplomat at the various wartime conferences. In a crudely propagandist wartime film (*Mission to Moscow,* 1943) made in Hollywood to promote the Russians as allies, U.S. Ambassador Joseph E. Davies, on being introduced to Vyshinsky in the Kremlin, is seen to shake his hand with a smile and say, "We've heard of your great legal work"!

Despite his seniority in the Soviet government, and even after he supplanted Vyacheslav Molotov as minister of foreign affairs in 1949, Vyshinsky continued to feel insecure. Throughout his career, he had connived with Stalin to prosecute and condemn the Bolshevik Old Guard and many of his own former comrades in the Menshevik Party. He lived in constant dread of his past catching up with him. Another U.S. ambassador to Moscow recalled a meeting in 1949 when Vyshinsky "was hopping around like a pea on a hot griddle to do his [Stalin's] slightest wish." Vyshinsky's neuroses were probably justified. His turn probably would have been next, with Lavrenty Beria on the ascendant at the NKVD (secret police) and Stalin now plotting the final removal of his former loyal servants and, in particular, a purge of the purgers.

Fortunately for Vyshinsky, Stalin died in 1953, and he was instead demoted and packed off into effective exile as chief Soviet delegate to the United Nations. Here, unable to learn new tricks, he entertained an international audience with his familiar invective and his confrontational outbursts of bad language, which this time were mostly aimed at the United States over its involvement in the war in Korea. It was in the comfort of his New York apartment on Park Avenue that Vyshinsky died of a coronary a year later, having collected his sixth Order of Lenin. As a mark of respect, his body was flown back to Moscow and buried in the Kremlin Wall.

See also Bukharin, Nikolay; The Great Terror; Rykov, Aleksey; Shakhty Trial; United Nations
Further reading: Arkady Vaksberg. *The Prosecutor and the Prey.* London: Weidenfeld and Nicolson, 1990.

White Sea–Baltic Canal

This 227-kilometer (141-mile) waterway (known to Russians as the Belomor Canal) was built from 1931 to 1933 to
link Leningrad on the Baltic Sea by way of a
system of rivers, lakes, and an artificial canal
from Ponevetsk to Belomorsk on the White
Sea. It was heralded as one of the great engineering achievements of the First Five-
Year Plan and was originally intended to
provide the Soviet Union with faster access
from the Baltic to the White Sea than by the
existing 4,000-kilometer (2,500-mile) route
around the Baltic to Archangelsk.

However, the canal's real claim to fame
and notoriety is that it was created by the
labor of thousands of male and female
Gulag prisoners, many of them the kulak
peasants who had been deported in the
wake of collectivization, and who lived and
worked in appalling conditions during the
period of its construction between November 1931 and May 1933.

For Stalin, building the canal seemed the
perfect way of achieving two objectives: the
construction of an important new strategic
waterway as a public showpiece of Soviet
industrial achievement and the harnessing
of the yet-untapped supply of free labor
filling the newly created Gulag system of
labor camps that was mushrooming across
the country.

Stalin entrusted the overseeing of the
canal's construction to his head of secret police, Genrikh Yagoda. It was very much
Stalin's pet project. As a propaganda exercise,
he sent eminent writer Maxim Gorky, along
with a group of thirty-six other writers, to
observe work on the canal. They were to
write a book about its construction, in
which the workers would be depicted as
transformers of nature, and critics, who were
unhappy about the conditions under which
prisoners toiled, would be reassured that the
workers were happy in their work.

Gorky's apologia *The White Sea–Baltic
Stalin Canal* (1934), complete with phony
photographs of happy workers lining up for
hot pies, described the canal's construction
as "a triumph for progressive penology," observing that the hard physical labor had
been a cathartic experience for many of the
workers and had reeducated them and reformed them socially. The reality, however,
was grim. One work supervisor on the
canal, D. P. Vitkovsky, later recorded how at
the end of every winter day there were
corpses abandoned on the work site, often
frozen into grotesque positions. Some were
collected, but others remained until the
summer, when "together with the shingle
they got into the concrete mixer. And in
this way they got into the concrete of the
last lock at the city of Belomorsk and will
be preserved there forever."

The Gulag prisoners who worked on the canal had originally been promised a reduction of their sentences for their efforts. As many as 100,000 prisoners may have died during its construction, although writer Alexander Solzhenitsyn claimed that this figure represented the deaths for the first three months of construction alone. This isn't surprising when one considers that the workers had the crudest means at their disposal to gouge out the canal. They used wheelbarrows and pickaxes and had virtually no mechanized assistance, just a few half-starved weary horses. When these methods failed they used their bare hands. Those who survived, physically broken by the experience, received no promised amnesty but were simply moved on to forced labor on Stalin's next project, the Moscow–Volga Canal (1933–1937). Similar conditions prevailed here, with just three mechanical excavators to serve the whole of this canal's 80-mile extent. But as with the White Sea–Baltic Canal, the rationale behind such an enterprise was irresistible to all good Soviet workers: "Drinking Water for Moscow!"

Like many other showpieces to Soviet achievement, such as the BAM (Baikal-Amur Magistral) railroad in the Far East, the White Sea Canal's construction was ill-conceived and its execution was slipshod, with inferior materials being used. There had been no time for proper surveys to be taken of the terrain before construction began, since Stalin had ordained that "the canal must be built in a short time and it must *be built cheaply!*" By the time he performed the official opening ceremony, it had already been found to be too shallow—only 16 feet deep—to carry naval vessels of the size intended to sail through it. Plans were immediately made to reconstruct the canal, but when they did not materialize due to lack of finance, the canal soon became idle and fell into disrepair.

See also Gorky, Maxim; Gulag

Further reading: Alexander Solzhenitsyn. *The Gulag Archipelago,* vol. 2. New York: Harper & Row, 1975 (especially chapter 3).

Women

After the revolution, Lenin had made clear his plans for women's liberation, stating that "the chief thing is to get women to take part in socially productive labor and to liberate them from 'domestic slavery,' to free them from their stupefying and humiliating subjugation to the eternal drudgery of the kitchen and nursery." Women's equal status with men in all spheres of life was proclaimed as a founding principle of the new socialist state.

Yet for all this high-minded idealism and despite an influx of women into the Communist bureaucracy after the revolution, there was only one prominent female member of the first Bolshevik government—Aleksandra Kollontai. Kollontai herself was a proponent of women's sexual equality with men and had once famously proclaimed that the satisfaction of sexual desires should be as free and uncomplicated as "drinking a glass of water." In 1930 Stalin announced with confidence, as he shut down the *zhenotdels* (womens' sections of the Communist Party that had encouraged women from 1919 to take a more active part in politics), that the "woman question has now been solved" and that such organizations were now superfluous. This untapped labor force was now being rapidly recruited to play its part in a program of intense industrialization. The female population was now called upon to stand shoulder to shoulder with their menfolk in the heroic enterprise of building socialism. If men could wield hammers and pitchforks, dig canals, and drive trucks, so could women. During the 1920s and 1930s about 5 million women were dragooned into work on building sites across the Soviet Union. By 1939, half a million of them

This Soviet woman, reaming out a huge industrial cog wheel in a Leningrad tractor plant in 1934, illustrates the crucial role women played in industry by undertaking every kind of heavy work.

were working on the railroads, and 160,000 women were driving tractors on state and collective farms by 1942.

While the creation of many new jobs for women in industry was welcomed by them as a liberating factor, women's status was si-multaneously undermined by Stalin's view of them as an endless source of cheap labor—"the colossal reserve of the work force," as *Pravda* put it in 1936. Soon women could be found in heavy industry (mining, metallurgy, chemical processing) and on building sites, exhausting themselves with the kind of arduous work that previously had been undertaken only by men. Because the state could get away with paying them less, women often ended up doing the jobs that men avoided. Between 1928 and 1940 the number of working women in the Soviet Union increased from 3 million to 13 million (39 percent of the work force). During the 1930s, with the birthrate falling, women were bombarded with exhortations in the press to have more children: "Women, as fully fledged citizens of the freest country in the world have received from Nature the gift of being mothers. Let them take care of this precious gift in order to bring Soviet heroes into the world!" Stalin himself made pronouncements in the press that abortion was now unacceptable. His view of a woman's role was unequivocal: "She is mother, she gives life."

By the end of the 1930s women in Stalinist Russia appeared to be enjoying economic and political rights that now placed them ahead of women in many other countries. But these rights had been won at the price of their physical enslavement. The achievements of Soviet women were lauded in socialist realist literature and cinema, where they were frequently depicted as rosy-cheeked, buxom collective farm workers and happy tractor drivers. But the image was bogus. For many women the privileges they enjoyed were hard-earned at the expense of juggling marriage, home, and children, as well as lining up for food after a long working day. In 1938 maternity leave for women was cut from sixteen to nine weeks. Meanwhile, the Soviet male's pathological dislike of sharing the housework, as well as his predilection for vodka, became endemic. The burden on women increased during the war years, so much so that by 1945 women occupied an all-time high of 56 percent of jobs.

During the Great Patriotic War thousands of Soviet women trained for service on an equal level with men and were subjected to the same strict discipline. They learned to be sharpshooters, to parachute jump, to handle rifles, and to ride in cavalry charges. They also studied military science and were admitted into every aspect of training in warfare at such institutions as the signal schools of Kiev and Leningrad, the armaments schools in Tula, and the artillery, military-topographical, and communications schools in Leningrad. They played a critical role in the defense of the motherland, helping to run key industries such as the railroads.

After the war, there was no let-up from the burden of combined work and child-rearing, for many women had now been left widows and the demographic imbalance persisted for many years—as late as 1959 there were still 20 million more women than men in the Soviet Union. But after the war Stalin exhorted women to even greater glory (in order to make up the huge deficit of male war losses) by awarding those who had more than ten children the title "Heroic Mother," while giving those who had between seven and nine offspring the Order of Maternal Glory. Such awards continued to underline the chauvinistic Stalinist attitude to women as procreators and providers rather than as prime movers in the skilled professions or in government. Indeed, very few women made it to the top of the political tree under Stalin, and it was not until after Stalin's death that a woman was finally recruited to the Politburo, in 1956.

See also Education; Family Life; Five-Year Plans; Great Patriotic War

Further reading: Mary Buckley. *Women and Ideology in the Soviet Union.* New York: Harvester Wheatsheaf, 1989; Wendy Goldman. *Women, the State and Revolution: Soviet Family Policy and Social Life, 1917–1936.* Cambridge: Cambridge University Press, 1993.

World War II
See Great Patriotic War.

Yagoda, Genrikh Grigorevich (1891–1938)

Genrikh Yagoda was born Heinrich Yehuda in Lodz, present-day Poland, then part of the Jewish Pale of Settlement of the Russian Empire. Along with Lazar Kaganovich, he was one of the few Jews to rise to political prominence during the Stalin years. During his brief ascendancy Yagoda has been credited with orchestrating the murders of Sergey Kirov, Maxim Gorky, and several other leading political figures.

Like Nikolay Ezhov, who supplanted him, Yagoda learned his trade at the Cheka (the prototype of the Soviet secret police), which he joined in 1920. During his early career he had aligned himself with the right wing and for a while had been a supporter of Nikolay Bukharin. He was to compensate for this political lapse later by organizing the show trial of his erstwhile colleague.

As deputy head of the secret police from 1924 to 1934, Yagoda organized the building of the White Sea–Baltic Canal (which was built by slave labor from the Gulag at breakneck speed between 1931 and 1933). For his distinguished contribution to the canal's construction he was later awarded the Order of Lenin. Soon after, he became a member of the Central Committee of the Communist Party. Thus, in 1934, Yagoda was well placed for the assumption of directorship of the NKVD (as the secret police was then known) and for the inauguration of years of political terror and repression that followed.

Documentary evidence that Stalin gave instructions to Yagoda to organize the assassination of Kirov has yet to be found, although several historians, Robert Conquest and Edvard Radzinsky included, asserted that Stalin gave verbal instructions to this effect. In his 1989 memoirs Nikita Khrushchev also revealed his belief that "the murder was organised by Yagoda, who could have taken this action only on secret instructions from Stalin, received face to face." While more recent archival evidence suggests that the killing may after all have been the act of a lone and crazed jealous husband (Kirov had been having an affair with the man's wife), it is more than possible that the assassin, Leonid Nikolaev, a highly neurotic and unstable figure, was being manipulated behind the scenes and that Yagoda was the one pulling his strings. Yagoda had already done his fair share of string pulling in inducing the playwright Maxim Gorky and the composer Sergey Prokofiev to return to the Soviet Union from their self-imposed exile abroad.

Yagoda had worked as a chemist before the revolution. When he was head of the

NKVD, rumors persistently circulated that his interest in chemistry had led to his setting up a secret experimental laboratory in the Lubyanka prison, where he oversaw the refinement of the use of drugs and hypnosis on prisoners and the development of subtle poisons for the elimination of political undesirables (thus the long-held rumor that Gorky had been poisoned).

For a while Yagoda held Stalin's ear. For example, Yagoda took great delight in repeating Osip Mandelstam's derogatory poem about Stalin to the Great Leader himself in 1933, which resulted in the poet's arrest. At Stalin's behest, Yagoda set up the first major purge trial, held in Moscow in August 1936, of the Old Bolsheviks Grigory Zinoviev and Lev Kamenev. But by now Stalin had become impatient with the slow rate at which the NKVD was rooting out the enemy within. He sent a famous telegram to the Politburo in which he declared that "Yagoda has definitely proved himself incapable of unmasking the Trotskyite-Zinovievite bloc. The OGPU is four years behind in this matter." Soon after, Yagoda was removed from his post and replaced by Nikolay Ezhov.

Relegated to a lesser job after his removal from the NKVD, Yagoda now languished as people's commissar for posts and telegraph until his arrest came in April 1937. Now he, too, became a major defendant at the show trial of Trotskyites held in March 1938 along with (ironically) Nikolay Bukharin, Aleksey Rykov, and Nikolay Krestinsky. Yagoda appears to have put up little resistance to the long list of crimes to which he now found himself compelled to confess. Ironically, in his case many of them were probably true, such as his complicity in the murder of Kirov as well as those of Valeriyan Kuibyshev, and eventually Gorky's son Maxim Peshkov—in the latter three cases through his involvement in the deliberate mismanagement of medical treatment given them at the time of their deaths.

According to writer Alexander Solzhenitsyn, at his trial Yagoda begged Stalin directly for mercy (possibly acknowledging the fact that Stalin is known to have watched the trials from behind a hidden screen) with the outburst, "I appeal to you! *For you* I built two great canals!" (the Moscow-Volga Canal being his second achievement). But nothing could save him, and he was shot in the Lubyanka on 15 March 1938. He has never been rehabilitated.

See also Beria, Lavrenty; Ezhov, Nikolay; NKVD; White Sea–Baltic Canal
Further reading: Boris Levytsky. *The Uses of Terror: The Soviet Secret Police, 1917–1990.* New York: Coward, McGann & Geoghegan, 1972; Vitaly Shentalinsky. *The KGB's Literary Archive: The Discovery of the Ultimate Fate of Russia's Suppressed Writers.* London: Harvill Press, 1995.

Yalta Conference (4 February 1945–11 February 1945)

By the time the "Big Three" Allied leaders Joseph Stalin, Franklin Roosevelt, and Winston Churchill (and their entourage of 700 officers and officials) met at the Livadia Palace in the Crimea to plan their strategy for the last days of the war, it was already a foregone conclusion that they would divide up postwar Germany between them, with little thought for sustaining the destitute German civilian population at large.

It was also by now apparent that with the advance of the Soviet army across Europe, Stalin would drive a hard bargain at any postwar peace settlements. During the conference the British were increasingly marginalized, as Stalin and Roosevelt dominated most of the key decision-making. Roosevelt, now terminally ill, seemed anxious to conciliate with the Russians over every issue, a fact of which Stalin took full advantage and which Churchill found deeply frustrating.

To the surprise of many observers, Stalin

proved to be a skillful negotiator at Yalta, with an instant recall of things said, despite not taking any notes of the proceedings, and an ability to turn on the avuncular charm during the sumptuous dinners of caviar, sturgeon, and Russian champagne with which his guests were feted. On such an occasion Churchill praised Stalin as the "mighty leader of a mighty country which had taken the full shock of the German war machine." Genial Uncle Joe (as Churchill liked to refer to Stalin behind his back) himself made sure his own half-drunk glasses of vodka were refilled with water, so that he could stay alert while his guests got progressively drunk.

The main bone of contention at the conference proved to be the future of the countries of Eastern Europe, Poland in particular. Stalin's insistence on supporting a Communist-dominated Polish committee of national liberation based in Lublin was part and parcel of his game plan to see most of Eastern Europe become one vast Soviet satellite as soon as the war was ended. As the negotiations continued, he went through the motions of supporting a "Declaration on Liberated Europe," promising support for free elections in Poland, Czechoslovakia, Hungary, Romania, and Bulgaria after the war. As a major incentive aimed at ensuring Stalin's support for the final onslaught against Japan (which Churchill and Roosevelt misguidedly believed could not be achieved without the Soviets), the U.S.S.R. was promised the return of territories in Manchuria and elsewhere that it had lost to Japan in the disastrous Russo-Japanese War of 1904–1905.

It was not until the release of archival documents in the 1970s that the full implications of a secret protocol to the Agreement on Prisoners of War, signed by Churchill and Stalin at Yalta, were revealed. Negotiations for the repatriations of these and other Soviet nationals, slave laborers, army deserters, and anti-Communists who had fought with the Germans, all of whom were now stranded in Allied-occupied territory, had been first conducted at a secret meeting between foreign ministers Anthony Eden and Vyacheslav Molotov in Moscow in 1944. There was nothing in the actual Yalta agreement stipulating the enforced repatriation of Soviet citizens, but Stalin stubbornly insisted on it (with much of the negotiating handled by secret police head Lavrenty Beria), despite the moral objections raised by some of the Allies. They, however, they were equally anxious about the safe return of their own prisoners of war from Soviet-occupied German territory.

Many of those whose names were on the lists drawn up for repatriation to the Soviet Union naturally had no wish to return and the process became an extremely traumatic one, not just for them but for the Allied officers obliged to enforce it. One particularly tragic aspect of the story was the return to the Soviet Union of 40,000 Cossacks and 5,000 Georgians, many of whom had fought for the Germans and who were being held in camps in the Drau Valley in Austria. Their numbers also included many women and children, as well as others who had left Russia as voluntary émigrés at the end of the civil war. Most of them were eventually handed over (although around 2,000 escaped and many others committed suicide). Stalin's secret service men dealt with them harshly. The Cossack and Georgian officers were summarily executed on their return to Odessa, and the rest were sent to the Gulag.

It is not surprising, therefore, that Roosevelt remained baffled and disturbed by the behavior of Stalin—by turns amiable, by turns ruthless. He admitted to his aides that he could not figure Stalin out and didn't know "a good Russian from a bad Russian." Not long before his death, two months after the Yalta Conference, with Soviet troops now having overrun most of Eastern Europe, Roosevelt saw only too clearly the limitations to Stalin's personal interpretation of "democracy," not only toward the people of Eastern Europe, but also toward his own countrymen. Exhausted and disillusioned, he admitted privately, "We can't do business with Stalin. He has broken every one of the promises he made at Yalta." The political honeymoon between "Uncle Joe" and his wartime allies was over.

See also Beria, Lavrenty; Great Patriotic War; Gulag; Nationalities; NKVD

Further reading: Alan Bullock. *Hitler and Stalin: Parallel Lives.* New York: Alfred A. Knopf, 1992; Richard Overy. *Russia's War.* London: Allen Lane, 1998; Alexander Solzhenitsyn, *Gulag Archipelago,* vols. 1 and 2. London: Harper & Row, 1973; John Toland. *The Last 100 Days.* London: Phoenix, 1994; Nikolay Tolstoy. *Victims of Yalta.* London: Hodder & Stoughton, 1978.

Yezhovshchina
See Ezhov, Nikolay Ivanovich.

Young Pioneers
See Komsomol.

Z

Zamyatin, Evgeny Ivanovich (1884–1937)

One of the most idiosyncratic stylists of Soviet literature in the 1920s, the satirist Evgeny Zamyatin produced a chilling novel about a totalitarian socialist state of the future, *We* (1924), which has been unjustifiably overshadowed by the better-known variations on this theme—Aldous Huxley's 1932 novel *Brave New World* and George Orwell's classic *1984* (published in 1949), both of which were in fact inspired by Zamyatin's novel.

Zamyatin trained as a naval engineer. His early satirical writings got him into trouble with the tsarist authorities, and he stopped writing for a while, spending some time in Newcastle-upon-Tyne in England overseeing the building of icebreakers for the Russian navy. During this time he wrote some penetrating satires on bourgeois English society ("Islanders" and "The Fisher of Men") before returning to the Soviet Union at the time of the revolution. He took a leading role as an editor of several literary journals, lectured on writing, and produced some fine essays, such as "On Literature, Revolution, Entropy and Other Matters" (1924). Having renounced his youthful affiliation with Bolshevism, Zamyatin kept himself apart politically and artis-

tically and took an uncompromising stand against literary oppression, warning that true literature could not be created by "diligent and trustworthy officials," but only by "madmen, heretics, dreamers, rebels, and sceptics." In the early 1920s Zamyatin achieved some success with his stage plays, notably *The Flea,* a 1926 adaptation of a story by Nikolay Leskov.

Not daring to publish his dystopian novel *We* in the Soviet Union, Zamyatin had allowed it to appear abroad but was soon made to pay the price when his works were banned in the Soviet Union and his plays taken out of the repertoire. Along with Boris Pilnyak, who later also published a novel abroad (*Mahogany*), he was demonized in the Soviet press. By the early 1930s Zamyatin's prediction, which he made in 1924, was becoming a bitter reality. Soviet literature was degenerating into exactly the kind of "newspaper literature" that he said would be "read today, and used for wrapping soap tomorrow." Unable to publish or earn a living, Zamyatin took the bold step of writing a personal letter to Stalin in 1931, saying that being condemned to literary silence was "nothing less than a death sentence." He asked to be deported from the country for at least a year, or until such time as "it becomes possible in our country to serve great ideas in literature without cringing before little men." Miraculously,

Zamyatin was allowed to leave for Paris. Perhaps writer Maxim Gorky's intercession on his behalf, in a piece he wrote for the official newspaper *Izvestiya,* had something to do with it, or perhaps Stalin admired the sheer nerve of someone taking such a gamble in confronting him. In any event, it is hard to comprehend the willful arbitrariness of a system that allowed such an outspoken critic to leave while condemning others for lesser acts. Zamyatin was to be the last literary dissident to leave the Soviet Union for many decades.

See also Gorky, Maxim; "New Soviet Man"
Further reading: D. J. Richards. *Zamyatin: A Soviet Heretic.* London: Quartet Books, 1991; Alex M. Shane. *The Life and Works of Evgenij Zamjatin.* Berkeley: University of California Press, 1968.

Zhdanov, Andrey Aleksandrovich (1896–1948)

Like many petty but malevolent dictators in history, Andrey Zhdanov was a little man with big pretensions. The Yugoslav diplomat Milovan Djilas described him as "rather short, with a brownish clipped moustache, a high forehead, pointed nose, and a sickly red face." The image is unavoidably that of a little Hitler, particularly in official photographs. In Russia his name, as Soviet spokesman on the arts, has been given to one of the most ferocious periods of ideological baiting and persecution in the Soviet arts—the *Zhdanovshchina* of 1946–1948. Zhdanov's premature death, the result of a weak heart, but its circumstances manipulated by Stalin to appear as murder, resulted in the persecution of many innocent people during the "Doctors' Plot" of 1952–1953 and led to a renewed attack on Soviet Jews by Stalin.

Zhdanov joined the Bolsheviks in 1915 and acted as a political commissar during the civil war. He might well have remained an anonymous, gray apparatchik had it not been for his elevation to oraclelike status on matters relating to the arts. This process began when he took the podium at the inaugural Congress of the Union of Soviet Writers in 1934 to give the keynote speech on socialist realism, during the course of which he issued the literary community with their new artistic battle orders as "engineers of human souls."

Indeed, Zhdanov's career was very much on the ascendant during 1934. As a local Party secretary, he was elected to the Central Committee and later stepped into dead men's shoes after being appointed by Stalin to succeed assassinated Leningrad Party Chief Sergey Kirov. By 1939 Zhdanov had become a member of the Politburo. He set his imprint upon Leningrad affairs when he was put in charge of the defense of the northwest front, in particular Leningrad itself during the 900-day siege. He was later rewarded for his efforts by Stalin with promotion to major general and a transfer to Moscow in 1944. For Stalin now had a more important role for him.

In August 1946, as a result of a decree passed by the Central Committee of the Communist Party, two leading Soviet writers, Anna Akhmatova and Mikhail Zoschenko, became the object of unprecedented personal attack initiated by Zhdanov during the course of two speeches he made in Leningrad before Party officials and members of the Leningrad intelligentsia. On these occasions Zhdanov resorted to the old familiar rhetoric reserved for perceived heretics and nonconformists (a vocabulary perfected by prosecutors such as Andrey Vyshinsky during the purge trials of the 1930s), labeling Akhamatova and Zoschenko as "slimy literary rogues" and demanding their expulsion from the Union of Writers. Both writers, as a result of this action, were treated as literary and social pariahs. Akhmatova, driven by her tremendous willpower, transcended her literary martyrdom with her own heroic brand of dignity in poverty. Zoschenko was utterly destroyed.

Not content with handing down his prognostications on literature, Zhdanov then turned his attention to philosophy, science, history, the cinema, and the visual arts, lambasting all of them for succumbing to the influences of decadent Western culture. Zhdanov personally joined Stalin in chastising film director Sergey Eisenstein when he was called to the Kremlin to answer for the ideological errors in the second part of his film *Ivan the Terrible*. Eisenstein's account of the interview bears testimony to Zhdanov's overweening sense of self-importance. In fact, for a brief time it seemed as though Zhdanov, and not Georgy Malenkov, was the man most likely to be Stalin's successor.

In 1948, Zhdanov turned his attention to music and launched a virulent attack on the "formalist, antipeople" compositions of Dmitry Shostakovich, Sergey Prokofiev, Aram Khachaturian, and Nikolay Myaskovsky, four leading composers who only weeks previously had been lauded in the Soviet press as "the supreme and world-wide glory of all contemporary music." The destruction of contemporary Soviet music then proceeded with horrifying speed. The work of leading composers was supplanted by that of hack musicians such as Tikhon Khrennikov and Vladimir Zakharov, and the ballets *Romeo and Juliet* and *Cinderella,* for which Prokofiev had written the scores, were withdrawn from the repertoire at the Bolshoi Theater. It would be ten years before the Central Committee of the Communist Party recognized the errors of Zhdanov's vilification of Shostakovich and Prokofiev and rehabilitated them artistically.

Zhdanov now also extended his influence on Communist ideology abroad when he oversaw the First Congress of Cominform in 1947. By now there were towns, institutes, streets, and factories all over the Soviet Union named after him. Indeed, Zhdanov was getting dangerously close to having his own cult in Leningrad to rival that of Stalin. This has prompted some historians to question whether Stalin's perceived jealousy of Zhdanov's high public profile and the heroic status accorded him after his leadership of Leningrad during the siege might have led to complicity in Zhdanov's premature death in 1948.

For a brief time Stalin and Zhdanov (by this time deceased) were actually linked by marriage. Stalin's daughter Svetlana, at a time when she was trying to retrieve her increasingly uncertain relationship with her father, had married Zhdanov's son Yuri in 1949, but the couple separated in 1952. And even Yuri Zhdanov, a scientist of some ability, found he was not immune from the mandatory act of ideological recantation during the heyday of the *Zhdanovshchina,* when he and other scientists were prevailed upon to publish letters of "self criticism" in *Pravda*.

Such was the pervasive power of Zhdanov's poisonous ideology that even after his sudden death on 31 August 1948, his cultural policies continued to be upheld. In late 1952 the uncertain circumstances of Zhdanov's death were used as evidence in a fabricated attack on several eminent Kremlin doctors accused of hastening the death of several Party bigwigs, Zhdanov included. It was not until Nikita Khrushchev initiated de-Stalinization in 1956 that the legacy of *Zhdanovshchina* was finally exorcised. Meanwhile, it took a surprisingly long time for Zhdanov's exaggerated local reputation in Leningrad, where for years he continued to be looked upon as a war hero, to fade away. Finally, in 1988, Zhdanov's 1946 resolution condemning Akhmatova and Zoschenko was rescinded by the Communist Party and Zhdanov's name was removed from the Zhdanov Leningrad State University.

See also Akhmatova, Anna; Malenkov, Georgy; Leningrad, Siege of; Socialist Realism; Zoschenko, Mikhail

Further reading: Sheila Fitzpatrick. *The Cultural Front: Power and Culture in Revolutionary*

Russia. Ithaca, NY: Cornell University Press, 1992; Harold Swayze. *Political Control of Literature in the USSR, 1946–1959.* Cambridge, MA: Harvard University Press, 1962; Alexander Werth, *Musical Uproar in Moscow,* London, 1949; Andrey Zhdanov. *Essays on Literature, Philosophy and Music,* New York, 1950.

Zhdanovshchina

See Zhdanov, Andrey Aleksandrovich.

Zhukov, Georgy Konstantinovich (1896–1974)

The outstanding Soviet military commander of World War II, whose grasp of mechanized warfare was manifested in the decisive tank battle at Kursk, Marshal Georgy Zhukov was sidelined politically by Stalin in 1945, when his huge popularity as a military leader had made him seem a potential rival if not successor to Stalin.

From peasant stock, Zhukov had served as a conscript in the tsarist army and as a cavalry commander during the civil war. Keen to develop theoretical as well as leadership skills, he studied as a tank specialist under German instructors at Kazan in 1921–1922 and then went on to study military science at the elite Frunze Military Academy in the 1930s. Zhukov demonstrated his abilities in his first major command in charge of five armored tank brigades in the Far Eastern campaign of 1939. At Khalkin-Gol in August, he scored a decisive victory against the Japanese along the Mongolian/Manchurian border and was accorded the top honor of Hero of the Soviet Union.

After holding a command in the 1939–1940 Winter War against Finland, Zhukov's skill and his specialist grasp of armored warfare became indispensable to Stalin as second in command during the Great Patriotic War. Zhukov also developed a reputation for his decisiveness as a tough and accomplished strategist. This toughness soon became manifest in his ruthless attitude to the expendability of the lives of his soldiers. His zeal in implementing Stalin's notorious Order No. 227, banning retreat by frontline soldiers, was such that later, at Stalingrad, he ordered officers in tanks to follow behind the attacking lines and shoot any troops whose resolve faltered. Zhukov was outspoken in his views and not afraid to oppose Stalin on certain points of military strategy. This set him apart from many of Stalin's old-school civil war generals, such as Marshal Semen Budenny, who still swore by the good old cavalry charge and had no comprehension of modern warfare. During the war Stalin delegated more and more responsibility to Zhukov.

In January 1941 Zhukov was assigned the role of chief of the General Staff of the Red Army; in this capacity he spared no Soviet sacrifice in the defense of Leningrad in September of that year. Promoted again to commander-in-chief of the western front, Zhukov oversaw the counteroffensive that saved Moscow in December 1941 from imminent capture by the Germans.

In January 1943, Zhukov was made a marshal of the Soviet Union and was now also deputy supreme commander of the Red Army, in which capacity he planned the hard-fought Soviet winter offensive of 1942–1943. It turned the tide of the war in Russia by encircling the German Fifth Army at Stalingrad and driving it out of Russia after the most decisive tank battle in history, which took place between 5 and 15 July at the 100-mile-wide Kursk salient. During the decisive engagement at Provkorovka on 12 July, Zhukov's army of 850 mainly T-34 tanks outstripped some 600 German machines. Much of the fighting was carried out at point-blank range within an area of only 3 by 4 miles; as many as 700 tanks were destroyed and the losses on both sides were extremely heavy. Kursk saw the final annihilation of the cream of the Wehrmacht, which would now be on the defensive against Russian forces for the rest of the war.

From January to April 1945 Zhukov completed the rout of the Wehrmacht, commanding the Soviet 400-mile push eastward to Berlin and committing the last resources of the Red Army at the price of heavy losses (as many, perhaps, as the United States lost in the entire war, according to historian Norman Davies). He fulfilled Stalin's wish that the Russians should get to Berlin ahead of their allies, and having witnessed the official surrender of the German High Command, Zhukov remained as commander of Soviet occupation forces in Germany, returning to the Soviet Union in 1946.

Stalin by now had become jealous of Zhukov's popularity, as he did of anyone who dared to stand in his light. He particularly resented the victor's glory Zhokov had garnered from Western observers and journalists in Berlin and recalled him to Moscow. He had now engaged secret police chief Lavrenty Beria to concoct a case against Zhukov as the central figure in a supposed "military conspiracy" against Stalin. But, as a much-decorated national war hero Zhukov was one of the few people Stalin could not touch. Zhukov was also far too popular with his own men in the Red Army, and Stalin, sensing this, left him alone, relegating him instead to the obscure command of a military district in Odessa and then posting him to the Urals. Before long, the official Soviet press and history books began effacing Zhukov's contribution to the war effort.

After Stalin's death Zhukov reappeared from political obscurity to take on a major role as deputy minister of defense, from which position he supported Nikita Khrushchev's bid for the Party leadership by providing the planes to fly in Central Committee members to support Khrushchev's challenge to the Malenkov-Molotov ticket. For a while he seemed on the political ascendant again and became the first soldier to be made a full member of the Presidium (the successor to the Politburo) in July 1957. But four months later Khrushchev had him removed from office when he exerted too much pressure for the military autonomy of the Red Army as a professional body.

Zhukov found his enforced retirement hard to deal with but spent some of the time writing his memoirs, in which he found room to praise the qualities of Stalin's wartime leadership and singled out his "native intelligence" and "unusual memory." He was generous enough to say without hesitation that Stalin "was master of the basic principles of the organization of front-line operations and the deployment of front-line forces. . . . He controlled them completely and had a good understanding of major strategic problems. He was a worthy Supreme Commander."

See also Great Patriotic War; Khrushchev, Nikita; Manchuria

Further reading: Otto Chaney. *Zhukov.* Newton Abbott, UK: David and Charles, 1971; Harold Shukman, ed. *Stalin's Generals.* London: Phoenix, 1977; Georgiy Zhukov. *Memoirs and Reflections.* London: Jonathan Cape, 1971.

Zinoviev, Grigory Evseevich (1883–1936)

From a lower-middle-class Ukrainian Jewish farming family, Grigory Zinoviev (born Ovsel Gershon Aronov Radomyslsky) joined the Russian Social Democrats in 1901. His position of preeminence in the Bolshevik leadership up to Lenin's death was not, however, earned through the exercise of his skills as a politician. Although he was a gifted and persuasive orator, Zinoviev was no theoretician, nor was he, like many Old Bolsheviks, from the ranks of the intelligentsia.

After joining the Bolshevik faction when the Social Democratic Party split in 1903, Zinoviev spent the years 1909 to 1917 in exile. It was this period that established him

The Soviet politician Grigory Zinoviev, circa 1933. Accused of being a Trotskyist, he was put on trial with his close colleague, Lev Kamenev, in Moscow in April 1936 and was shot soon after.

as a close associate and adviser of Lenin, who was also in exile at that time. Such was Zinoviev's influence that the Mensheviks described him as "Lenin's mad dog." When Lenin returned to Russia in April 1917 after the abdication of the tsar, Zinoviev was at his side.

Together with Lev Kamenev, his long-standing friend and ally, Zinoviev opposed the Bolsheviks' ruthless seizure of power by force in October of that year and protested their desire for one-party control. He had favored a period of conciliation and cooperation between the various socialist groups, and he resigned from the Central Committee of the Communist Party, asserting that the Bolsheviks were pursuing a policy "against the will of the vast majority of workers and soldiers."

Lenin had by now grown dependent on Zinoviev as his right-hand man and felt the need of his reassuring presence. He wooed

Zinoviev back, rewarding him with the leadership of the Petrograd Soviet and chairmanship of the newly formed Comintern in 1919. Zinoviev was an early candidate member of the Politburo in 1919 and a full member by 1921. He also gained considerable local influence as head of the Petrograd (later Leningrad) Soviet.

Zinoviev's name is best known in the West for the notorious case of the "Zinoviev letter," supposedly written by him as chairman of the Comintern to members of the British Communist Party telling them to begin agitating for revolution. The letter was published in the British press just before the general election of 1924 and, although new archival evidence suggests it was forged by White émigrés disgruntled at Britain's cooperation with the Bolshevik government, it provoked an anti-left backlash among voters and contributed to the downfall of Ramsay MacDonald's Labour government. It also put further strain on the Soviets' already difficult relationship with the European powers.

In the early 1920s Zinoviev, despite his innate mistrust of Stalin, had aligned himself with him and Kamenev in opposition to Leon Trotsky, whom he trusted even less, and this triumvirate had dominated the Politburo. But after Lenin's death in 1924, Zinoviev suddenly found himself compelled, in 1926, to realign with Trotsky when Stalin showed his true colors by seeking to remove his Old Bolshevik allies from the political picture. Kamenev and Trotsky united later that year with other prominent figures, such as Lenin's widow, Nadezhda Krupskaya, and Lev Kamenev in a united opposition against Stalin. While lacking a sound power base, the opposition acted as a moral voice of protest at Stalin's destruction of democracy and freedom of debate within the Party. Within months Zinoviev's position, now inextricably linked with Trotsky's, had become untenable. Tarred with the Trotskyist brush, he had now given Stalin an excuse for attack, and he was forced to resign from both the Politburo and Comintern. At the end of 1927 Stalin expelled Zinoviev from the Central Committee of the Communist Party.

A familiar pattern of official victimization of Zinoviev was initiated, which in turn sparked acts of betrayal by him. He was forced into a humbling political capitulation for his anti-Leninist activities, then turned on Trotsky, and gained his own brief readmittance into the Party in 1928 for denouncing him. Stalin, knowing Zinoviev's inherent moral weakness, played a cruel game with his particularly febrile nerves, frequently reducing him to fits of panic and hysteria and acts of craven self-degradation. Zinoviev was expelled from the Party again in 1932, reinstated in 1933 (having promised that he would be "the most devoted member of the Party"), and then expelled a third time in 1934. By now a political pariah, Zinoviev was left to wait for the inevitable, which came in 1935 when he was accused, together with Trotsky and Kamenev, of "moral complicity" in the 1934 murder of Leningrad Party leader Sergey Kirov. He was jailed for ten years.

The following year Stalin hauled Zinoviev back in front of the courts as one of the major defendants in the first of the show trials held in Moscow, to stand accused of being a Trotskyist conspirator. He gained the terrified Zinoviev's "confession" to the charges on the promise that this would guarantee his being spared the death penalty and protect his family from persecution. Zinoviev had by now become a groveling wreck, writing frequent letters to Stalin from prison, in which he promised, "I belong to you body and soul."

Zinoviev was tried along with Kamenev in August 1936 in a carefully stage-managed two-day process held in front of a hand-picked audience of foreign journalists and diplomats. Despite submitting himself to a public ritual of self-castigation, during which he admitted in his final plea to the court that "Trotskyism is a variety of Fas-cism and Zinovievism is a variety of Trotskyism," Zinoviev was sentenced to death. He was shot in the Lubyanka along with his codefendants within twenty-four hours. Nikolay Bukharin commented at the time of this execution that he was "terribly glad . . . that the dogs have been shot." But in a world gone crazy, and after being forced to levels of the same abject, groveling repentance himself, eighteen months later it would be his turn.

See also Bukharin, Nikolay; Kamenev, Lev; Krupskaya, Nadezhda; Trotsky, Leon
Further reading: Robert Conquest. *The Great Terror: A Reassessment.* London: Pimlico, 1992; Anatoly Lunacharsky. *Revolutionary Silhouettes.* London: Allen Lane, 1967.

Zoshchenko, Mikhail Mikhailovich (1895–1958)

Now much neglected, Mikhail Zoshchenko was once one of the most popular and widely read of Soviet satirists. His personality was defined by that classic contradiction so often encountered in the great comic writers and performers—he was a profoundly melancholic man who suffered all his life from acute and at times debilitating bouts of depression.

Zoschenko came to literature by a circuitous route. Born into a family of Ukrainian gentry, he studied law and served as a soldier in World War I, when his health was impaired by gassing. He later worked variously, as "accountant, shoemaker, a poultry raising instructor, a frontier guard telephonist, an agent of the criminal investigation department, a secretary of the law court, a clerk," before taking up writing full time in 1921. Zoshchenko remained determinedly uncommitted politically in his writing. In his comic tales and sketches of the 1920s, written in the vivid *skaz* style of colloquial Russian storytelling, he described the unattractive underside of Soviet life, exposing the petty quarrels brought about by communal living, the philistinism of ordinary people struggling to deal with shortages, and the dislocations of life under the Communist system. Much of his work followed in the Gogolian and Chekhovian tradition of the little man at odds with the labyrinthine workings of officialdom.

Zoschenko's collections such as *The Tales of Nazar Ilich* (1922) and *Nervous People* (1927) were hugely popular. Between 1922 and 1927 he sold more than a million copies of his stories. But his unappealing view of the banalities of Soviet society, and an increasing air of pessimism in his later work, inevitably led to criticism. In the 1930s, under increasing pressure to adapt his writing to the formulas of socialist realism, Zoshchenko attempted to broaden his range and conform by writing more topical stories. But, a pessimist by nature, his heart was not in the creation of conventional positive heroes, and the results were mediocre. During the Great Patriotic War, Zoshchenko began serializing a revealing semiautobiographical collection of writings, *Before Sunrise* (1943), in which he described his own personal search for happiness and revealed something of his darker side. It was this side that led the composer Dmitry Shostakovich to describe Zoschenko as "the greatest specialist in depression, despair, melancholy and suchlike of all the people I've met in my life."

Stalin had originally enjoyed Zoschenko's writing and had read Zoschenko's stories to his children but loathed this latest work as a piece of indulgent navel-gazing, coming at a time when a writer's duty was to encourage the war effort. The publication of *Before Sunrise* was suspended after the work was deemed "individualistic and petty bourgeois." For daring to talk of his personal psychological preoccupations, Zoschenko was condemned as a "pernicious Freudian."

Although his work still remained hugely popular—a collection of stories published in 1946 had a print run of 100,000 copies—he was soon to suffer for his lapse into "acute individualism." One of the stories in this collection, "Adventures of an Ape," depicted life for the animals in a Soviet zoo as being infinitely better than for the average Soviet citizen, who was portrayed as boorish and obtuse. Zoschenko was hauled over the coals for this "disgusting calumny on the Soviet People." When Andrey Zhdanov initiated the crackdown on Soviet literature in the wake of the ideological lapses in Soviet writing that had diluted socialist realism during the war years, Zoschenko and the poet Anna Akhmatova were singled out as scapegoats. It was precisely because of their huge popularity, both at home and increasingly in the West, as well as the esteem in which they were held among the disaffected Soviet intelligentsia, that they were now publicly ridiculed and then expelled from the Writers' Union.

This effective literary excommunication killed Zoschenko's spirit as a writer. He lived out the rest of his life in penury, scraping together a living as a translator. After Stalin's death he was reinstated in the Writers' Union, and his works began to be published again after 1956, but his years in the literary wilderness had failed to produce any work comparable to his early writings.

See also Akhamatova, Anna; Union of Soviet Writers; Zhdanov, Andrey

Further reading: Rebecca Donmar. "The Tragedy of a Soviet Satirist." In Ernest J. Simmons, ed. *Through the Glass of Soviet Literature: Views of Russian Society.* New York: Columbia University Press, 1953.

CHRONOLOGY

Note: Dates prior to 31 January 1918 are given according to the Old Style, Julian calendar that was in use in Russia. At the end of January 1918 the Soviets adopted the Western, Gregorian calendar; all subsequent dates in the chronology refer to this New Style.

1878   *6 December* Stalin born in Gori; speaks only Georgian till age 8–9.

1879   *21 December (New Style)* Official Soviet date of birth.

c. 1884–1885   An attack of smallpox leaves Stalin permanently scarred.

1888–1894   Educated at Gori church school; Stalin, known to the family as "Soso," starts using name "Koba"; leaves school with top marks.

1894   Enters Tiflis Seminary to train for priesthood.

1895   Publishes six poems in *Iveriya*, a Georgian-language journal.

c.1897   Takes up Marxism.

1898   Russian Social Democratic Workers' Party (RSDWP) founded in Minsk and holds its first congress 1–3 March; Stalin joins the Mesame Dasi (the Georgian Social Democrats based in Tiflis).

1899   *29 May* Expelled from Tiflis Seminary; formally takes revolutionary code name Koba.

1899–1909   Stalin's ten-year revolutionary apprenticeship in the Caucasus at Tiflis, Baku, and Batum.

1899   *December* Takes job as observer-calculator at the Tiflis Observatory.

1900   First publication of Lenin and Yuli Martov's journal *Iskra* [The Spark]; Stalin becomes an eager supporter of Lenin and the journal.

1901   *March* Observatory raided by police; Stalin leaves job; elected to All-Caucasian Social Democratic committee in Tiflis; goes to Batum (now a new center of oil industry with opening of pipeline from Baku).

December Writes first article for Georgian journal *Brdzola* [The Struggle]: "The Russian Social Democratic Party and Its Immediate Tasks."

1902   *March* Publication of Lenin's *What Is to Be Done?*

February Helps incite oil workers' strike in Batum.

March Helps incite a demonstration by workers.

April Arrested for first time; jailed at Batum and Kutaisi in Georgia, and then Batum again (18 months).

1902   *July* Sentenced to three years' exile.

November Arrives at Novaya Uda, Siberia.

| 1903 | *July–August* Second Congress of the All-Russian Social Democratic Workers' Party is held in Brussels and London; there is a split between Bolsheviks ("the majority"), led by Lenin and the Mensheviks ("the minority), led by Yuli Martov and Trotsky. |

1903   *July–August* Second Congress of the All-Russian Social Democratic Workers' Party is held in Brussels and London; there is a split between Bolsheviks ("the majority"), led by Lenin and the Mensheviks ("the minority), led by Yuli Martov and Trotsky.

1904   *January* Stalin escapes and makes his way back to Tiflis by February; remains on the run as an illegal till 1908, hiding out mainly at Baku.

1905– 1908   Stalin mainly operating underground in the Caucasus, addressing meetings and writing for underground press.

1905   *January* Revolution: Bloody Sunday. Government promises constitution and elections to Duma.

December Stalin meets Lenin for the first time at Bolshevik conference in Tammerfors in Finland, then part of Russian Empire.

1906   *April* Stalin's first journey abroad, to attend Fourth (unifying) Congress of the RSDWP in Stockholm; publishes anti-Menshevik article in *The Baku Proletarian,* which gains Lenin's approval.

April–July First State Duma.

ca. June Marries Ekaterina Svandize at St. David's Church, Tiflis (historian Dmitri Volkogonov contends the marriage took place in 1903 before Stalin went into exile).

1907   *April* Meets Trotsky for first time at Fifth Party Congress of RSDWP in London; meets with Lenin in Berlin.

ca. May Birth of son Yakov.

June Georgian revolutionaries stage Tiflis State Bank robbery in Erevan Square, Tiflis, to raise funds for Bolsheviks; Stalin implicated and Menshevik-run Georgian Social Democrats expel him.

Autumn Goes to Baku and with others forms a breakaway Bolshevik

committee there; takes part in elections of workers' delegates to the Duma; writes "Instruction of the Baku Workers to Their Deputy"; campaigns among oil workers for single trade union.

November Death of wife, from typhus.

Now stops speaking and writing in Georgian. Publishes articles in Russian in *The Baku Proletarian.*

1908– 1917   Years of imprisonment and exile: arrested seven times, escapes five times: spends only one and a half years at liberty out of nine.

1908   *March* Arrested again, imprisoned at Bailov prison, Baku.

September Sentenced to two years' exile.

November sent to exile at Solvychegodsk, northern Vologda.

1909   Escapes again; returns to Caucasus. In Baku July; hides out at Balakhlana oilfield; works on *The Baku Proletarian* again; writes "Letters from the Caucasus" for the *Social Democrat;* organizes strike at Baku oilfield.

1910   *March* Rearrested. Sent back to Bailov jail for six months. Deported back to Solvychegodsk; he will remain here till the end of his term of exile; end of Stalin's Caucasus period.

1911   *January* Arrives at Solvychegodsk; lodges with Maria Prokopievna Kuzakova; she has illegitimate son Constantin Stepanovich, probably fathered by Stalin.

June At end of exile moves to Vologda (forbidden to live in Caucasus or big cities for five years).

Hears of his election to the Central Committee of the RSDWP *in absentia;* at Lenin's behest, goes to St. Petersburg.

1912   *December* Arrested and sent back to Vologda.

1912   *22 April* First issue of *Pravda,* with editorial signed by Stalin as "Koba."

Ordzhonikidze visits Stalin in exile at Vologda; escapes February.

March visits St. Petersburg; rearrested May. Held at Shpalerny prison, exiled for three years to Narym in western Siberia.

Absconds again in summer; returns to Tiflis, then Petersburg, and takes charge of Party's electoral campaign for delegates to Fourth Duma.

Rearrested and sent to Narym. Escapes two months later for a fifth time.

November visits Lenin in Cracow.

1913   *January* Sends letter to the *Social Democrat* signed "Stalin"; it now becomes his official pseudonym.

January–February Spends month in Vienna to study work of Austrian Social Democrats (does not travel abroad again until 1943); meets Nikolay Bukharin and Trotsky.

Publishes first important article "Marxism and the National Question" (as K.[oba] Stalin) (this leads to his appointment after revolution as commissar for nationalities).

February Rearrested on return to St. Petersburg (betrayed by police agent Roman Malinovsky); sentenced to four years' exile; deported to Turukhansk region of Siberia, where he studies Machiavelli.

1914   Outbreak of World War I: Russia enters the war in October.

St. Petersburg changes its name to Petrograd.

1914   *March* Stalin moved to far north to Kureika on Yenisey River.

1915   *July* Goes to meet other Bolsheviks in exile at Monastyrskoe to discuss Bolshevik position on the war.

1916   Called up for military service in war, along with other deportees; taken to Krasnoyarsk but exempted in December because of his deformed arm; allowed to complete exile at Achinsk with Lev Kamenev.

1917   *27 February* Revolution.

2 March Tsar abdicates, Provisional Government installed.

March Stalin arrives back in Petrograd; joins *Pravda* as editor with Kamenev; becomes delegate to Executive Committee of the Petrograd Soviet; takes control of Bolshevik leadership pending Lenin's return from exile (3 April); negotiates with the Mensheviks.

Stays with Alliluyev family in Petrograd during revolution, where he meets his future wife, Nadezhda Allilueva.

April 7 All-Russian conference of the RSDWP: Lenin recommends Stalin for re-election to the Central Committee (comprising Lenin, Zinoviev, Kamenev, Stalin).

May–June Stalin behind the scenes negotiating with various opposition groups; organizes demonstrations against continuation of war, including major demonstration on 18 June in Petrograd.

June Stalin is a delegate to First All-Russian Congress of the Soviets; in World War I Russian Provisional Government launches military offensive on southwestern front; mass antiwar demonstrations in Petrograd, Moscow, and elsewhere in Russia.

July Helps Lenin escape to Finland when Provisional Government threatens arrest of Bolshevik leaders.

1917 cont.	Stalin in control of Bolsheviks while other leaders in hiding or prison.

1917 cont. Stalin in control of Bolsheviks while other leaders in hiding or prison.

July–August Sixth Congress of the RSDWP.

August Trotsky joins the Bolsheviks.

25 October Revolution: Government overthrown; Trotsky plays crucial role in seizure of power (Stalin later distorts facts to give himself role played by Trotsky); Bolsheviks promise "Peace, Land and Bread"; Lenin appoints Stalin as people's commissar for nationalities and Trotsky commissar of roreign affairs.

November Decree on Nationality.

December Formation of the Cheka. With the establishment of the Bolshevik government, and in order to disassociate themselves from the Social Democrats, the Bolshevik faction finally breaks with the Mensheviks in the RSDWP to form the Russian Communist Party (Bolshevik).

1918 *March* Capital transferred from Petrograd to Moscow. Treaty of Brest-Litovsk ends Russia's involvement in World War I; creation of Red Army; separation of church and state.

March Georgia, Armenia, and Azerbaijan declare their independence.

1918– 1920 Civil War period.

1918 Stalin sent to Tsaritsyn (later Stalingrad) (1918) as director general of food supplies in the south of Russia. Stalin orders first executions (of captured Whites); marries Nadezhda Allilueva at the Tsaritsyn front.

17 July Tsar Nicholas II and family murdered at Ekaterinburg, Siberia.

1919 *March* Eighth Congress of the Russian Communist Party in Moscow; creation of Politburo and Orgburo; Comintern set up at Third International in Moscow; Stalin becomes head of Rabkrin.

1919– 1920 Russo-Polish War.

1920 Poland invades Ukraine; Stalin sent to Lvov; armistice with Poland; Bolsheviks achieve one-party control after banning all other political parties.

1921 Creation of Gosplan; Red Army invades Georgia on Stalin's orders; Kronstadt Revolt; Tenth Party Congress adopts Lenin's New Economic Policy; birth of Stalin's son Vasily.

1921– 1922 Volga famine; Lenin appeals for international food aid.

1922 Cheka reorganized as GPU. Stalin becomes general secretary of the Communist Party.

May Lenin has his first major stroke; property of the Russian Orthodox Church confiscated.

December Formation of USSR; Lenin has second stroke and between 23 December and 4 January 1923 composes his "Testament," which includes a call for Stalin's removal from power.

1923 *March* Lenin has third stroke, which leaves him severely disabled.

April Twelfth Communist Party Congress; USSR Constitution published.

1924 *21 January* Death of Lenin, followed by battle for power between Bukharinists, Trotskyists, and troika of Stalin, Kamenev, and Zinoviev.

May Thirteenth Party Congress; Soviet Union recognized by Britain and other countries; Trotsky dismissed as war commissar.

December At the Fourteenth Party Congress Stalin announces concept of "socialism in one country."

1926   Zinoviev, Trotsky, and Kamenev expelled from Politburo; Bukharin replaces Zinoviev in Comintern; Family Code; birth of Stalin's daughter, Svetlana.

1927   Trotsky and Zinoviev expelled from Comintern's Executive Committee and Communist Party.

December Fifteenth Party Congress announces plans for collectivization; Kamenev expelled from Party.

1928   *January* Trotsky exiled to Alma Ata, Kazakhstan, then deported in February.

January–February Grain crisis.

May–July Shakhty trial.

October First Five-Year Plan, in draft since 1925, is introduced.

1929–   Lenin Mausoleum built.
1934

1929   *January* Trotsky deported from Soviet Union.

April First Five-Year Plan formally adopted at Sixteenth Party Conference. Bukharin expelled from Politburo; Stalin defeats the "right Opposition."

November Stalin announces the "Great Turning Point"—the end of NEP and onslaught of collectivization.

December Stalin's fiftieth birthday celebrations initiate the "cult of the personality"; Stalin initiates forced collectivization and the elimination of the kulaks.

1930   *March* Stalin's "Dizzy with Success" article calls a temporary halt to the too-rapid rate of collectivization.

April Suicide of leading Soviet dramatist Vladimir Mayakovsky.

1931   Gulag labor begins constructing the White Sea–Baltic Canal; Gorky returns to the Soviet Union from self-imposed exile in Italy; introduction of Soviet falsification of history under Stalin.

1932   *April* Central Committee announces reformation of literary-artistic organizations; establishment of Union of Writers.

June–December Ryutin manifesto and its supporters crushed by Stalin.

Opening of Dneprostroi hydroelectric plant and first blast furnace at Magnitogorsk; reintroduction of internal passports for Soviet citizens; peasants refused right to leave collective farms; first major transports of political prisoners to Kolyma in the Gulag.

December First Five-Year Plan completed in 4.5 years; suicide of Stalin's wife, Nadezhda.

1932–   Famine in Ukraine, North
1933   Caucasus, and Kazakhstan.

1933–   Second Five-Year Plan.
1937

1933   White Sea–Baltic Canal (Belomor Canal) opens; Hitler becomes chancellor in Germany.

1934   *January* Seventeenth Party Congress (of the Victors); August: First Writers' Congress; promulgation of socialist realism.

OGPU becomes NKVD; Soviet Union joins League of Nations; Prokofiev returns to the Soviet Union; Cathedral of Christ the Savior is blown up to make way for a vast new Palace of the Soviets.

December Assassination of Kirov; beginning of political purges.

1935   *August* Beginning of Stakhanovite movement; Stalin's speech "Life has become better, life has become merrier" marks an end to rationing of meat, fish, sugar, potatoes, etc.; first stage of the Moscow Metro opens.

1936   *June* Death of Gorky; new family law makes divorce difficult.

July Outbreak of the Spanish Civil War.

August Trial of Zinoviev and Kamenev; harvest failure; Ezhov succeeds Yagoda as head of NKVD; Shostakovich denounced for *Lady Macbeth of Mtsensk*.

December Stalin Constitution.

1937   *January* Trial of Radek, Pyatakov; suicide of Ordzhonikidze.

June Trial of Tukhachevsky and purge of Red Army and Navy; Bukharin and Rykov expelled from the Communist Party; worst period of Great Terror (to March 1939).

1938–   Third Five-Year Plan.
1941

1938   Stalin's *Short Course* becomes the bible of Party and Soviet history; trial of Bukharin, Rykov, Yagoda.

December Lavrenty Beria succeeds Ezhov at NKVD.

1939   *March* Eighteenth Party Congress announces end of purges; German-Soviet Non-Aggression Pact; Soviet invasion of eastern Poland; clashes with Japanese in Manchuria.

November–March 1940 Winter War with Finland; introduction of Stalin Prizes.

September: Germany invades Poland.

1940   Annexation of Baltic states: Lithuania, Latvia, and Estonia; assassination of Trotsky in Mexico;

officers' ranks reintroduced in Red Army; massacre of Polish officers at Katyn.

1941   *22 June* German invasion of Soviet Union under Hitler's "Operation Barbarossa." Stalin sets up State Defense Committee.

3 July Stalin's first radio broadcast.

July Germans approach Moscow; Kiev captured.

September Beginning of Siege of Leningrad.

1942   *July* Beginning of battle for Stalingrad; Establishment of Anglo-Soviet alliance after Churchill and Stalin meet in Moscow.

November German Sixth Army is encircled at Stalingrad.

1943   *January* German forces surrender at Stalingrad; Stalin becomes a Marshal of the Soviet Union; Stalin dissolves Comintern; reintroduction of officers' epaulettes and other militaristic trappings; Russian Orthodox Patriarchate reestablished.

July Battle of Kursk.

November Tehran conference of Allies.

1944   *January* Siege of Leningrad lifted; Eisenstein's *Ivan the Terrible;* introduction of Soviet national anthem.

June Allies open second front in Western Europe; Red Army reaches Bucharest, Sofia, Belgrade— beginning of Soviet influence in Eastern Europe.

1945   *February* Yalta conference.

May Red Army in Berlin; election of Patriarch Alexey.

July Potsdam conference.

August United States drops atomic bomb on Hiroshima, prompting

Stalin to accelerate Soviet nuclear program.

1946–1950   Fourth Five-Year Plan.

1946   Council of People's Commissars becomes Council of Ministers.

February Stalin, the sole candidate, gives a rare public speech; Andrey Zhdanov attacks Anna Akhmatova and Mikhail Zoshchenko in renewal of political orthodoxy in literature.

March Churchill makes his famous "iron curtain" speech.

1946–1947   Famine in Ukraine.

1947   Establishment of Cominform; new wave of persecution, this time of Soviet Jews, dubbed "rootless cosmopolitans" (to 1953).

1948   Communist coup in Czechoslovakia; Yugoslavia expelled from Cominform; Lysenko's theories of agrobiology dominate Soviet agricultural practices; death of Zhdanov.

1949   *June–May* Berlin blockade.

1948–1949   Collectivization of agriculture in Baltic states.

1949   Purge of the Communist Party in Leningrad ("Leningrad Affair"); closure of Jewish State Theater in Moscow.

August Soviet Union tests its first atomic bomb.

1950   Stalin's article on linguistics puts an end to the spurious school of Marrism; political show trials in Eastern Europe, including that of Czech president Rudolf Slansky.

1950–1953   Korean War.

1951–1955   Fifth Five-Year Plan.

1952   Nineteenth Party Congress; Politburo renamed the Presidium.

1953   *January* The "Doctor's Plot" sets the scene for Stalin's renewed attack on Soviet Jews.

5 March Death of Stalin; arrest and execution of Lavrenty Beria; Soviet Union tests its first hydrogen bomb.

1954   Rehabilitation Commission established to examine cases of those who were executed and imprisoned during the Great Terror.

1955   *May* Warsaw Pact establishes cooperation between Eastern European Communist states.

1956   *February* At the Twentieth Party Congress Khrushchev denounces Stalin in his "Secret Speech."

1958   Boris Pasternak is awarded the Nobel Prize for Literature for *Dr. Zhivago*; Khrushchev launches vicious campaign against him.

1961   Khrushchev intensifies de-Stalinization; Stalin's body is removed from the Lenin Mausoleum; Stalingrad is renamed Volgograd.

1962   Publication of Alexander Solzhenitsyn's *One Day in the Life of Ivan Denisovich,* one of the first works to describe life in the Stalinist Gulag, signals brief period of political thaw.

1968   Robert Conquest publishes his ground-breaking study of Stalin's rule, *The Great Terror.*

1969   Stalinist revival attempted on anniversary of Stalin's ninetieth birthday.

1988   Election of President Mikhail Gorbachev; policies of glasnost and perestroika allow publication of first studies of Stalinism based on suppressed archival material, e.g.,

| 1988 cont. | revised and enlarged version of Roy Medvedev's *Let History Judge.* | | from the Soviet Union of the majority of its national republics. |
| 1991 | *December* Soviet Union is officially dissolved after the failure of the August coup and the secession | 1999 | Stalin's grandson, Evgeny Dzhugashvili, is elected leader of a neo-Stalinist left-wing political party, the Patriotic Union. |

GLOSSARY

All-Russian Central Executive Committee. *See* **Central Executive Committee.**

All-Russian Congress of Soviets Delegates from the various city and regional soviets that came into existence in Petrograd and elsewhere during the revolutionary year of 1917 attended the first All-Russian Congress of Soviets in June 1917. A fifth congress in 1918 legally recognized the soviet as the body of local and regional elective government. While technically having control over **Sovnarkom,** the Congress of Soviets was closely monitored by the Communist Party and by 1921 had lost control to it.

apparatchik From the Russian *apparat* (apparatus), referring to someone who is a member of the **Communist Party** or who works in the administrative or Party bureaucracy.

Bolsheviks The majority group (from the Russian *bolshoy* [big]) in the **Russian Social Democratic Workers' Party (RSDWP),** which was founded in 1898. After a factional split in the party between them and the **Menshevik** group in 1903, the Bolsheviks went on to seize political power under Lenin in October 1917.

Central Committee (of the Communist Party) The policymaking body of the Communist Party, which was elected by the **Communist Party Congress,** which in turn elected the **Politburo** and the **Secretariat.** The Central Committee became the effective body of government from one congress to the next.

Central Executive Committee A body elected by the **All-Russian Congress of Soviets** that operated from 1917 to 1936 as the central policymaking organ of the Soviet government, although it had lost much of its power to **Sovnarkom** not long after the revolution. Stalin replaced this body with the **Presidium** of the **Supreme Soviet**.

Cheka Russian acronym for *chrezvychainaya kommissiya* (extraordinary commission), this organization was established by the Bolsheviks in December 1917 to fight "counter-revolution, sabotage, speculation and misconduct in office." As the precursor to the Stalinist secret police, it became the **GPU** in 1922. *See also* **OGPU; GPU; NKVD; NKGB; MGB; KGB.**

Comecon Council for Mutual Economic Assistance, established by Stalin in 1949 as a trade and economic union of Communist states. It later attempted to rival the European Common Market.

Cominform Communist Information Bureau, which succeeded the **Comintern** in 1947 to coordinate the activities of Communist parties outside the Soviet Union. It was dissolved by Nikita Khrushchev in 1956.

Comintern The Communist International, also known as the Third International, was set up in 1919 to coordinate various Communist parties in Europe under centralized Bolshevik control from Moscow. It was abolished by Stalin in 1943, during the Great Patriotic War, at the time of his alliance with the United States, France, and Britain. It was replaced after the war by the **Cominform**.

Communist Party Congress The most important gathering of Party members, expected to meet once every five years to elect a new **Central Committee.** In 1936 Stalin's new constitution introduced the **Supreme Soviet** in its place.

Communist Party of the Soviet Union (CPSU) Communist Party that originated from the **Bolshevik** faction of the **RSDWP**, which so named itself in 1912. Stalin was elected to the party's **Central Committee** in 1911 and in 1922 became its general secretary. The Party was officially established in 1918 as the All-Russian Social Democratic Workers' Party (Bolsheviks). After the Bolsheviks had established a government and changed the RSDWP's name to the All-Russian Communist Party, in 1925 it was renamed the All-Union Communist Party, with (Bolshevik) added in parentheses. In 1952 the name was changed again to the Communist Party of the Soviet Union.

Council of Ministers. *See* **Council of People's Commissars.**

Council of People's Commissars (Sovet narodnykh komissarov, or Sovnarkom) Soviet equivalent of a Western European cabinet, with its chief commissar equivalent to a prime minister. This was the original name given to the Bolshevik governing body created after the 1917 revolution. It operated under this name until the outbreak of war in 1941. Its officials were called "people's commissars" and their departments "commissariats." Stalin was appointed people's commissar for nationalities immediately after the revolution. The republics of the Soviet Union also had their own Sovnarkoms, which reported to the central one in Moscow. In 1946 the Soviets adopted the Western convention of calling their commissariats ministries and their commissars ministers; the body was renamed the Council of Ministers.

Duma Russian state parliament from 1905 to 1917.

Ezhovshchina The Russian word, meaning "the time of Ezhov," used to describe the period marked by the highest level of mass arrests and executions, initiated during 1936–1938, by **NKVD** head Nikolay Ezhov.

Five-Year Plans (*Pyatiletki*) The Soviet blueprint for economic achievement, laid down in great detail by **Gosplan**, often with unrealizably high targets. The First Plan was launched in October 1928 and finished ahead of schedule in December 1932.

GKO (Gosudar tsvennyi komitet oborony) Soviet State Defense Council, set up on 30 June 1941, after Hitler's invasion of Russia, to take charge of the country's economy and ensure that military requirements were prioritized during the **Great Patriotic War**. The members of the GKO also liaised with the **Stavka.**

Glasnost Russian for "openness" or "publicity"; it became the key word of Mikhail Gorbachev's liberalizing policies as Soviet president during the late 1980s. It was marked by a relaxation in censorship, the long-overdue opening of many Soviet archives, and a renewal of debate over Stalin's years in power.

Gosplan (Gosudartsvennaya planovaya komissiya) The Soviet State Planning Committee founded in 1921 with the primary task of drafting economic plans and policies. It worked out the schedules for the **Five-Year Plans** and provided production statistics.

GPU (Gosudartsvennoe polilcheskoe upravlenie) State Political Administration, which operated as the secret police in 1922 and 1923, to be replaced by the **OGPU.**

Great Patriotic War/Great Fatherland War The Soviet name for World War II, or, more specifically, the Soviet people's fight against Hitler's Germany, 1941–1945.

Gulag The acronym for the Chief Administration for Corrective Labor Camps from 1930 (Glavnoe upravlenie ispravitelno-trudovykh lagerey). The word has since been applied generally as a collective noun for the whole network of camps and their system of forced labor. The concept originated with the setting up of the first corrective labor camps by the Cheka in 1919.

Third International. *See* **Comintern.**

KGB (Komitet gosudafstvennoi bezopasnotsi) Committee of State Security, the secret police body that in a reorganized form replaced the **MGB** in 1954. Since the Cold War this has since become the most familiar and widely used of all the many acronyms applied to the Soviet secret police during its lifetime, thus leading to its frequent and anachronistic misattribution, in a strictly historical sense, by many Westerners.

Kolkhoz Soviet acronym for *kollektivnoe khozyaistvo* (collective farm), a cooperative agricultural unit introduced on a widespread scale under Stalin during 1929–1930. Members of the collective were obliged to fulfill specified quotas under the demands of the **Five-Year Plans,** after which they could divide the surplus and receive a share of any profits.

Komsomol   acronym for Kommunisticheskii soyuz molodezhi (Communist League of Youth), an official Soviet youth organization run by the Communist Party for those between the ages of 14 and 28. Its junior branch was the Young Pioneers, for children aged 10–15.

kulak   Disparaging term used during collectivization (although the word had been in use long before) to refer to any supposedly rich peasant who enjoyed a modest surplus in production but who was deemed self-seeking and exploitative.

Mensheviks   The more moderate wing of the **Russian Social Democratic Workers' Party,** who constituted the minority (from Russian *men'shiy* [smaller]). They opposed the Bolshevik seizure of power in October 1917 and viewed the Bolshevik centralized control of the state after the revolution as undemocratic. Their attempt to form an effective opposition group was crushed by the early 1920s.

MGB   (Ministerstvo gosudarstvennoi bezopasnotsi) Ministry of State Security, successor to the **NKGB** in 1946; in 1953 it became the **KGB.**

MVD   (Ministerstvo unutrennykh del) Ministry of Internal Affairs, which succeeded the **NKVD** in 1946; between 1953 and 1954 it combined the roles of secret police and ministry of interior affairs.

New Economic Policy (NEP)   The relaxation of the draconian Bolshevik economic policy known as "war communism" saw its replacement with the **NEP,** introduced by Lenin in March 1921 and eventually superseded by Stalin's **Five-Year Plans** in 1929.

NKGB   (Narodny Komissariat gosudarstvennoi bezopasnotsi) People's Commissariat for State Security, set up in 1941 as a complementary department to the **NKVD;** it dealt with matters relating to the everyday running of the Soviet police. In 1946 it was renamed the **MGB,** again in tandem with the **NKVD,** which later was renamed the **MVD.**

NKVD   People's Commissariat of Internal Af-

fairs (Narodniy komissariat vnutrennykh del*),* more familiarly known by its acronym, NKVD, the name given the organization of Soviet security in 1934, when the powers of the commissariat were extended to combine both state security and the running of the Stalinist secret police (from 1934 to 1943). The NKVD was responsible for many of the purges and executions during the Great Terror. During the war (1943–1946 the NKVD relinquished control of the secret police to the **NKGB.** In 1946 the **NKVD** was renamed the **MVD.**

Nomenklatura   Body of specially selected senior Soviet government and Party officials appointed by the **Secretariat,** who became the Soviet Union's political elite. They controlled the machinery of government and were selected from lists of approved candidates, who, as they rose through the ranks, enjoyed many special privileges.

Old Bolsheviks/Old Guard   Long-standing members of the Russian revolutionary movement, many of whom had joined the **Russian Social Democratic Workers' Party** at the end of the nineteenth century and had supported Lenin at the time of the Bolshevik/Menshevik split of 1903. Their continuing idealism with regard to the original precepts of the Russian version of Marxism would make them vulnerable later when both Lenin and Stalin considerably remolded original Russian socialist theories to suit their own political ends.

OGPU   (Otdelenie gosudarstvennoi politicheskoi upravi) The United State Political Administration, the reformed secret police that replaced the **GPU** in 1923 and was itself replaced in 1934 by the **NKVD.**

Orgburo   The Organization Bureau of the Central Committee of the Communist Party, this body handled the everyday organization and running of the Communist Party. Stalin was appointed head of the Orgburo in 1919.

Pale of Settlement   The twenty-five provinces in the western borders of the Russian Empire in which the Jewish population were legally obliged to live. The Jewish villages of the Pale were popularly referred to in Yiddish as the *shtetl.*

People's Commissars. *See* **Council of People's Commissars.**

People's Commissariats. *See* **Council of People's Commissars.**

Perestroika   Russian for "rebuilding," "reconstruction," used by Mikhail Gorbachev to underline the reform policies initiated by him in both the Soviet government and the Communist Party from about 1987.

Petrograd   Name given to St. Petersburg in 1914 at the outbreak of war with Germany. It was renamed Leningrad in 1924 after Lenin's death; after the break-up of the Soviet Union in 1991, it reverted to its original name.

Petrograd Soviet of Workers' and Soldiers' Deputies   Soviet originating in St. Petersburg during the unrest of 1905 and representing striking workers in the city. In March 1917, after the setting up of the Provisional Government, the Petrograd Soviet was revived in opposition to it, and many similar soviets were set up in cities and towns across Russia.

Politburo   Political Bureau of the Communist Party, the controlling body elected by the **Central Committee** at **Communist Party Congresses;** it made all major political decisions between 1919 and 1952. Although the Central Committee was the country's major governing body, much of its control was usurped by the Politburo. Each republic within the USSR had its own Politburo, which reported to the Moscow Politburo. Stalin was elected to the Politburo in 1919.

Presidium   The body of government ministers that replaced the Politburo in 1952. It was abolished in 1966.

Rabkrin   Soviet acronym for the People's Commissariat of the Workers' and Peasants' Inspectorate, a body that supervised the workings of the Soviet civil service between 1920 and 1934 and was particularly vigilant over matters of mismanagement and inefficiency. Stalin was head of Rabkrin from 1919 to 1922.

RAPP   (Rossiskaya assotsiatsiya proletarskikh pisateley) Soviet acronym for the domineering All-Russian Union of Proletarian Writers, inaugurated in 1928 but abolished by Stalin in 1932, after the introduction of Socialist Realism. Its ideological role was assumed by the Union of Soviet Writers.

Red Terror   Period of mass arrests and executions carried out by the **Cheka** in 1918, following an unsuccessful attempt on Lenin's life.

Russian Social Democratic Workers' Party (RSDWP)   (in Russian RSDRP—Russkaya sotsial-demokraticheskaya rabochaya partiya) the Russian Social Democratic Workers' Party, also known as the RSDLP (Russian Social-Democratic Labor Party); the forum for a wide-ranging mix of socialist, Marxist, and other political parties in existence in Russia before the revolution.

RSFSR   (Rossiiskaya Sovetskaya Federativnaya Sotsialisticheskaya Respublika) The Russian Soviet Federated Socialist Republic, created in 1918 after the Bolsheviks took power. In December 1922 it was incorporated as one of the four constituent republics of the USSR. It remained the Soviet Union's political heartland until the dissolution of the USSR in 1991.

Russo–Polish War   Conflict between Bolshevik Russia and the Polish government over border territories in Ukraine, 1919–1920. Polish forces under Josef Pilsudski joined with Ukrainian nationalists to overrun Ukraine and take Kiev. Pressure from Western European powers brought an armistice between them and the Red Army in October 1920, leaving most of Ukraine a Soviet republic, thus sowing the later seeds of Ukrainian national resentment of Soviet domination.

Secretariat   The key administrative body that composed the agendas for **Politburo** meetings and was elected by the **Central Committee** of the Communist Party. It was also responsible for overseeing the bureaucracy of lesser organizations within the Communist Party, as well as the subordinate secretariats of other Soviet republics. As general secretary of the Communist Party from 1922 Stalin was also chairman of the Secretariat.

Social Democrats. *See* **Russian Social Democratic Workers' Party.**

Socialist Revolutionaries (SRs)   Agrarian socialist group founded in 1902 that campaigned heavily for support among the Russian peasantry. A few joined the Bolsheviks after the revolution, but the alliance was uneasy and most of the SRs had been ejected from the party by 1920.

Soviet   Russian for "council"; the network of elected bodies in industry, trade unions, and local government that technically governed the Soviet Union as a collective entity from October 1917. By 1921, however, they had lost their power as the Bolshevik government became more centralized within the machinery of the **Communist Party** and control eventually devolved more and more to the **Politburo.**

Sovkhoz   (*sovetskoe khozyaistvo*) Government-owned collective farm, where the workers received a wage.

Sovnarkom. *See* **Council of People's Commissars.**

Stakhanovites   Named after a coal miner, Aleksey Stakhanov, who far exceeded his coal output on a shift in August 1935. The Stakhanovite movement sought to galvanize workers into raising Soviet industrial output to record-breaking levels.

Stavka (Supreme Command) The Russia *stavka,* meaning "military headquarters," was the nerve center of the Soviet Supreme Command during the **Great Patriotic War**.

State Defence Council. *See* **GKO.**

Supreme Soviet   The central body of Soviet legislation, introduced under the 1936 constitution. It acted as the highest agency of state power, which in turn elected the country's **Council of People's Commissars.**

Third International. *See* **Comintern.**

Transcaucasia   The three republics of Georgia, Armenia, and Azerbaijan, which declared themselves independent in 1918, only to be forcibly incorporated as a single unit, the Transcaucasian Soviet Federated Socialist Republic, in 1921, after which (1936) they became three separate union republics of the Soviet Union.

Trotskyist, Trotskyite   Originally a name (in its Russian form—*trotskist*) applied to any supporter of Leon Trotsky and his political faction on the extreme left and to the later United Opposition formed against Stalin by Trotsky, Grigory Zinoviev, and Lev Kamenev. The term "Trotskyist" was widely applied to many innocent people during the political purges of the late 1920s and 1930s as a convenient derogatory label (Trotskyite is its more pejorative English form) for any perceived enemy of the state or opponent of Stalin's regime.

USSR or **Soviet Union** (Soyuz sovetskikh sotsialisticheskikh respublik) From 30 December 1922 to 25 December 1991, the Union of Soviet Socialist Republics.

War Communism Lenin's draconian economic policy introduced during the civil war of 1918–1920, characterized by the forced expropriation of peasant stockpiles of grain, their produce, and their livestock.

Zhdanovshchina   Russian term to describe the hegemony of one man, **Central Committee** secretary Andrey Zhdanov, who in the postwar years of 1945–1948 launched an enforced return to political correctness across all the Soviet arts.

SELECTED BIBLIOGRAPHY

STALIN'S WORKS

The collected works of Joseph Stalin fill some sixteen volumes, although publication in the Soviet Union (which began in 1946) was suddenly terminated at the thirteenth volume, on his death in 1953. It remained for an American academic, Robert H. McNeal, to edit and supervise the publication of the remaining three volumes, which came out in 1967.

Stalin's own major political writings, or works that were either written at his behest and/or closely edited by him, are as follows (in chronological order):

Anarchism or Socialism (Georgian articles from 1906–1907)

Marxism and the National Question, 1913 (Note: The title is variously translated.)

The Road to October, 1925

Problems of Leninism, 1926

On the Draft Constitution of the USSR, 1936

Dialectical and Historical Materialism, 1941

The Great Patriotic War of the Soviet Union, 1945

History of the All-Union Communist Party: Short Course, 1939

Stalin: Short Biography, 1940

The Great Patriotic War of the Soviet Union, 1942; later revised and enlarged 1946–1952

Marxism and Linguistics, 1951

Economic Problems of Socialism in the USSR, 1952

Collected Works, 13 vols. (1946–1952 in Moscow; vols. 14–16, 1967 in the USA)

For further details of Stalin's writings, see Robert H. McNeal, *Stalin's Works: An Annotated Bibliography.* Stanford, CA: Stanford University Press, 1967. For representative collections of Stalin's political theorizing, see *The Essential Stalin: Major Theoretical Writings 1950–52,* ed. Bruce Franklin. London: Croom Helm, 1973; and *Leninism: Selected Writings,* Westport, CT: Greenwood Press, 1975.

SOVIET HISTORY, POLITICS, AND POLITICAL MEMOIRS

Bacon, E. T. *The Gulag at War: Stalin's Forced Labour System in the Light of the Archives.* Basingstoke, UK: Macmillan, 1994.

Barber, J. D., and M. Harrison. *The Soviet Home Front: A Social and Economic History of the USSR in World War II.* London: Longman, 1991.

Beevor, Anthony. *Stalingrad.* London: Viking, 1998.

Berchin, Michel, and Eliahu Ben-Horin. *The Red Army.* London: George Allen and Unwin, 1943.

Bialer, S. *Stalin and His Generals: Soviet Military Memoirs of World War II.* New York: Pegasus, 1966.

Bobrick, Benson. *East of the Sun: The Conquest and Settlement of Siberia.* London: Heinemann, 1992.

Buca, Edward. *Vorkuta.* London: Constable, 1976.

Bullock, Alan. *Hitler and Stalin: Parallel Lives.* London: Fontana Press, 1993.

Cambridge Encyclopaedia of Russia and the Former Soviet Union. Cambridge: Cambridge University Press, 1994.

Caute, David. *The Fellow Travellers: Intellectual Friends of Communism.* New Haven, CT: Yale University Press, 1988.

Carr, E. H.. *The Russian Revolution from Lenin to Stalin 1917–23.* London: Macmillan, 1950.

———. *The Twilight of Comintern, 1930–35.* London: Macmillan, 1982.

Chaney, Otto Preston. *Zhukov.* Newton Abbot, UK: David and Charles, 1972.

Claudin, Fernando. *The Communist Movement: From Comintern to Cominform.* New York: Monthly Review Press, 1996.

Cohen, Stephen F. *Bukharin and the Bolshevik Revolution: A Political Biography, 1888–1938.* Oxford: Oxford University Press, 1980.

Conquest, Robert. *The Great Terror: A Reassessment.* London: Pimlico, 1992.

———. *The Harvest of Sorrow: Soviet Collectivization and the Terror-Famine.* London: Hutchinson, 1986.

———. *Inside Stalin's Secret Police: NKVD Politics, 1936–1939.* Stanford, CA: Hoover Institution Press, 1985.

———. *Kolyma: The Arctic Death Camps.* London: Macmillan, 1978.

———. *The Nation Killers: The Soviet Deportation of Nationalities.* London: Sphere Books, 1970.

———. *Stalin and the Kirov Murder.* Oxford: Oxford University Press, 1989.

———. *Stalin: Breaker of Nations.* London: Weidenfeld, 1993.

———. *Tyrants and Typewriters: Communiqués in the Struggle for Truth.* London: Hutchinson, 1989.

Conquest, Robert, ed. *Soviet Nationalities Policy in Practice.* London: Bodley Head, 1967.

Daniels, Robert V., ed. *The Stalin Revolution: Foundations of the Totalitarian Era.* Boston and New York: Houghton Mifflin, 1997.

Davies, Norman. *Europe: A History.* London: Pimlico, 1997.

Davies, R. W. *The Industrialization of Soviet Russia,* 3 vols. Cambridge: Cambridge University Press, 1980–1991.

Davies, Sarah. *Popular Opinion in Stalin's Russia: Terror, Propaganda and Dissent, 1934–1941.* Cambridge: Cambridge University Press, 1997.

Dedijer, V. *Tito Speaks.* London: Weidenfeld and Nicolson: 1953.

De Jonge, Alex. *Stalin and the Shaping of the Soviet Union.* New York: Morrow, 1986

Deutscher, Isaac. *The Prophet Armed: Trotsky, 1879–1921.* Oxford: Oxford University Press, 1954.

———. *The Prophet Unarmed: Trotsky, 1921–1929.* Oxford: Oxford University Press, 1959.

———. *The Prophet Outcast: Trotsky, 1929–1940.* Oxford: Oxford University Press, 1963.

———. *Stalin: A Political Biography.* London: Oxford University Press, 1967.

Djilas, Milovan. *Conversations with Stalin.* London: Hart Davis, 1962.

Dunmore, T. *The Stalinist Command Economy: The Soviet State Apparatus and Economic Policy, 1945–53.* London: Macmillan, 1980.

Edelman, R. *Serious Fun: A History of Spectator Sports in the USSR.* New York: Oxford University Press, 1993.

Edmonds, Robin. *The Big Three: Churchill, Roosevelt, and Stalin in Peace and War.* New York: Norton, 1991.

d'Encausse, Hélène Carrère. *Big Brother: The Soviet Union and Soviet Europe.* New York: Holmes and Meier, 1987.

Erickson, John. *The Road to Stalingrad.* London: Weidenfeld and Nicolson, 1975.

———. *The Road to Berlin*. London: Weidenfeld and Nicolson, 1983.

Evans, Harold. *The American Century*. London: Jonathan Cape, 1998.

Fainsod, Merle. *Smolensk under Soviet Rule*. London: Macmillan, 1958.

Figes, Orlando. *A People's Tragedy: The Russian Revolution 1891–1924*. London: Jonathan Cape, 1996.

Fitzpatrick, Sheila. *Education and Social Mobility in the Soviet Union, 1921–34*. Cambridge: Cambridge University Press, 1979.

———. *The Russian Revolution*. Oxford: Oxford University Press, 1982.

Freeze, Gregory L., ed. *Russia: A History*. Oxford: Oxford University Press, 1997.

Geiger, K. *The Family in Soviet Russia*. Cambridge, MA: Harvard University Press, 1968.

Gelb, M., ed. *An American Engineer in Stalin's Russia: The Memoirs of Zara Witkin, 1932, 1934*. Berkeley: University of California Press, 1991.

Getty, J. Arch. *Origins of the Great Purges: The Soviet Communist Party Reconsidered, 1933–1938*. Cambridge: Cambridge University Press, 1985.

Getty, J. Arch, and Roberta T. Manning, eds. *Stalinist Terror: New Perspectives*. Cambridge: Cambridge University Press, 1993.

Gilbert, Martin. *Russian History Atlas*. London: Weidenfeld and Nicolson, 1972.

Gill, Graeme. *The Origins of the Stalinist Political System*. Cambridge: Cambridge University Press, 1990.

———. *Stalinism*. London: Macmillan Press, 1998.

Goldman, Wendy Z.. *Women, the State and Revolution: Soviet Family Policy and Social Life, 1917–1936*. Cambridge: Cambridge University Press, 1993.

Goncharov, S., and J. Lewis. *Uncertain Partners: Stalin, Mao, and the Korean War*. Stanford, CA: Stanford University Press, 1993.

Gorky, Maxim. *Untimely Thoughts: Essays in Revolution, Culture and the Bolsheviks, 1917–1918*. New York: Paul S. Eriksson, 1968.

Graham, Loren R.. *Science in Russia and the Soviet Union: A Short History*, Cambridge: Cambridge University Press, 1993.

Harriman, W. Averell, and Elie Abel. *Special Envoy to Churchill and Stalin, 1941–46*. New York: Random House, 1975.

Robert Harris. "The West Prefers Its Dictators Red." In *Sunday Times* [London], 11 October 1998.

Hasegawa, T. *The February Revolution: Petrograd 1917*. Seattle: University of Washington Press, 1981.

Heller, Mikhail. *Cogs in the Soviet Wheel: The Formation of Soviet Man*. London: Collins Harvill, 1988.

Hindus, Maurice. *Humanity Uprooted*. London: Jonathan Cape, 1929.

———. *Red Bread*. London: Jonathan Cape, 1931.

Hingley, Ronald. *Joseph Stalin: Man and Legend*, London: Hutchinson, 1974.

Hochschild, Adam. *The Unquiet Ghost: Russians Remember Stalin*. London: Serpent's Tail, 1995.

Hodgson, Geoffrey. *People's Century: From the Dawn of the Century to the Start of the Cold War*. London: BBC Books, 1995.

Hollander, Paul. *Political Pilgrims: Travels of Western Intellectuals to the Soviet Union, China and Cuba, 1928–1978*. New York: Oxford University Press, 1981.

Holroyd, Michael. *Bernard Shaw, vol. 3, The Lure of Fantasy, 1918–1950*. London: Chatto & Windus, 1991.

Holloway, David. *Stalin and the Bomb: The Soviet Union and Atomic Energy 1939–1956*. New Haven, CT: Yale University Press, 1994.

Hosking, Geoffrey. *A History of the Soviet Union 1917–1991*. London: Fontana Press, 1992.

Isaacs, Jeremy, and Taylor Downing. *The Cold*

War: For 45 Years the World Held Its Breath. London: Bantam, 1998.

Joravsky, David. *The Lysenko Affair.* Cambridge, MA: Harvard University Press, 1970.

Josephson, Paul. *Physics and Politics in Revolutionary Russia.* Berkeley: University of California Press, 1991.

Khlevniuk, O. *In Stalin's Shadow: The Career of "Sergo" Ordzhonikidze.* Armonk, NY: M. E. Sharpe, 1995.

Khrushchev, Nikita. *Khrushchev Remembers,* 3 vols. Boston: Little, Brown, 1970, 1974, and 1990; esp. vol. 3, *The Glasnost Tapes.*

———. *The Secret Speech* [1956 speech at the Twentieth Party Congress]. Nottingham: Spokesman Books, 1976. (Also in R. V. Daniels, ed., *The Stalin Revolution.*)

Knight, Amy. *Beria: Stalin's First Lieutenant.* Princeton, NJ: Princeton University Press, 1993.

Kochan, L. *The Jews in Soviet Russia since 1917.* Oxford: Oxford University Press, 1972.

Kolarz, W. *Religion in the Soviet Union.* London: Macmillan, 1961.

Kravchenko, Victor. *I Chose Freedom: The Personal and Political Life of a Soviet Official.* London: Robert Hale, 1947.

Laqueur, Walter. *Stalin: The Glasnost Revelations.* London: Unwin Hyman, 1990.

Laver, John. *Joseph Stalin: From Revolutionary to Despot.* London: Hodder and Stoughton, 1993.

Leggett, George. *The Cheka: Lenin's Political Police.* Oxford: Clarendon Press, 1981.

Levytsky, Boris. *The Uses of Terror: The Soviet Secret Police, 1917–1970.* New York: Coward, McGann & Geoghegan, 1972.

Lewin, Moshe. *Lenin's Last Struggle.* London: Faber and Faber, 1969.

———. *The Making of the Soviet System: Essays in the Social History of Inter-War Russia.* London: Methuen, 1985.

Lewin, Moshe, ed. *Russian Peasants and Soviet Power: A Study of Collectivization.* London: Allen and Unwin, 1968.

Lih, Lars T., Oleg V. Naumov, and Oleg V. Khlevniuk, eds. *Stalin's Letters to Molotov, 1925–1936.* New Haven, CT: Yale University Press, 1995.

Lincoln, W. Bruce. *Red Victory: The Russian Civil War.* New York: Simon and Schuster, 1989.

Lockhart, R. H. Bruce. *Memoirs of a British Agent.* London: Putnam, 1932.

Lynch, M. *Stalin and Khrushchev: The USSR 1924–1964.* London: Hodder and Stoughton, 1990.

MacLean, Fitzroy. *Eastern Approaches.* London: Jonathan Cape, 1949.

Malia, Martin. *The Soviet Tragedy: A History of Russian Socialism, 1917–1991.* New York: Free Press, 1994.

Mastney, Vojtech. *Russia's Road to the Cold War.* Columbia: Columbia University Press, 1979.

Mawdsley, Evan. *The Stalin Years: The Soviet Union 1929–1953.* Manchester: Manchester University Press, 1998.

McCauley, Martin. *Stalin and Stalinism.* London: Longman, 1983.

———. *Who's Who in Russia since 1900.* London: Routledge, 1997.

McNeal, Robert. *Stalin, Man and Ruler.* London: Macmillan, 1988.

Medvedev, Roy. *All Stalin's Men: Six Who Carried Out the Bloody Policies.* Oxford: Oxford University Press, 1983.

———. *Khrushchev.* Garden City, NY: Anchor Press/Doubleday, 1983.

———. *Let History Judge: The Origins and Consequences of Stalinism,* rev. ed. New York: Columbia University Press, 1989.

Medvedev, Zhores A. *The Rise and Fall of T. D. Lysenko.* Columbia: Columbia University Press, 1969.

———. *Soviet Science.* Oxford: Oxford University Press, 1979.

Mikoyan, Anastas. *Memoirs of Anastas Mikoyan.* Madison, CT: Sphinx Press, 1988.

Miner, Steven M. *Between Stalin and Churchill: The Soviet Union, Great Britain and the Origins of the Grand Alliance.* Chapel Hill: University of North Carolina Press, 1988.

Molotov, Vyacheslav. *Molotov Remembers: Inside Kremlin Politics.* Chicago: University of Chicago Press, 1994.

Moynahan, Brian. *The Russian Century.* London: Chatto and Windus, 1994.

Muggeridge, Malcolm. *Chronicles of Wasted Time.* London: Collins, 1972–1973.

Nadeau, Remi A. *Stalin, Churchill, and Roosevelt Divide Europe.* New York: Praeger, 1990.

Nettl, J. P. *The Soviet Achievement.* London: Thames and Hudson, 1967.

Nisbet, Robert. *Roosevelt and Stalin: The Failed Courtship.* Washington, DC: Regnery Gateway, 1988.

Nove, Alec. *An Economic History of the USSR, 1917–1991.* London: Penguin, 1992.

Nove, Alec, ed. *The Stalin Phenomenon.* London: Weidenfeld and Nicolson, 1993.

Orlov, A. *The Secret History of Stalin's Crimes.* London: Jarrolds, 1954.

Overy, Richard. *Russia's War: A History of the Soviet War Effort 1941–45.* London: Allen Lane, 1998.

———. *Why the Allies Won.* London: Jonathan Cape, 1995.

Paul, Allen. *Katyn: The Untold Story of Stalin's Polish Massacre.* New York: Scribner's, 1991.

Pipes, Richard. *Russia under the Bolshevik Regime 1919–24.* London: Harvill/HarperCollins, 1994.

———. *The Russian Revolution 1899–1919.* London: Fontana Press, 1992.

———. *Three Whys of the Russian Revolution.* London: Pimlico, 1998.

Pipes, Richard, ed. *The Unknown Lenin: From the Secret Archive.* New Haven, CT: Yale University Press, 1996.

Pitcher, Harvey. *Witnesses of the Russian Revolution.* London: John Murray, 1997.

Pitman, Lesley, ed. *Russia/U.S.S.R.* World Bibliographical Series. Oxford: Clio Press, 1994.

Ponting, Clive. *Armageddon: The Second World War.* London: Sinclair-Stevenson, 1995.

Popovskii, Mark. *The Vavilov Affair.* Hamden, CT: Archon Books, 1984.

Pospielovsky, Dmitri. *The Russian Church under the Soviet Regime 1917–1982.* Crestwood, NY: St. Vladimir's Seminary Press, 1984.

Radzinsky, Edvard. *Stalin.* London: Sceptre, 1997.

Rancour-Laffierière, Daniel. *The Mind of Stalin: A Psychoanalytic Study.* Ann Arbor, MI: Ardis, 1988.

Ransome, Arthur. *Autobiography.* London: Jonathan Cape, 1976.

Rapoport, Louis. *Stalin's War against the Jews: The Doctors' Plot and the Soviet Solution.* New York: Free Press, 1990.

Rapoport, Yakov. *The Doctors' Plot: Stalin's Last Crime.* London: Fourth Estate, 1991.

Rauch, G. von. *The Baltic States: The Years of Independence, 1917–40.* London: Hurst, 1974.

Redlich, Shimon. *Propaganda and Nationalism in Wartime Russia: The Jewish Antifascist Committee in the USSR, 1941–1948.* East European Monographs. Boulder, CO: East European Quarterly, 1982.

Reed, John. *Ten Days That Shook the World.* Harmondsworth, UK: Penguin, 1974.

Rigby, T. H. *Political Elites in the USSR: Central Leaders and Local Cadres from Lenin to Gorbachev.* Aldershot, UK.: Edward Elgar, 1990.

Sakharov, Andrey. *Memoirs.* London: Hutchinson, 1990.

Salisbury, Harrison E. *Russia in Revolution 1900–1930.* London: André Deutsch, 1978.

———. *The Siege of Leningrad.* London: Secker and Warburg, 1969.

Scott, John. *Behind the Urals: An American Worker in Russia's City of Steel.* Cambridge, MA: Harvard University Press, 1942.

Serge, Victor. *Memoirs of a Revolutionary, 1900–41.* London: Oxford University Press, 1963.

Service, Robert. *A History of Twentieth-Century Russia.* London: Allen Lane, 1997.

———. *Lenin: A Political Life,* 3 vols. Basingstoke, UK: Macmillan, 1985–1995.

Shukman, Harold, ed. *Stalin's Generals.* London: Phoenix, 1997.

Siegelbaum, L. H. *Stakhanovism and the Politics of Productivity in the USSR, 1935–41.* Cambridge: Cambridge University Press, 1988.

Slusser, Robert M. *Stalin in October: The Man Who Missed the Revolution.* Baltimore: Johns Hopkins University Press, 1987.

Smith, Edward Ellis. *The Young Stalin: The Early Years of an Elusive Revolutionary.* New York: Farrar, Straus and Giroux, 1967.

Smith, Graham, ed. *The Nationalities Question in the Soviet Union.* London: Longman, 1990.

Smith, Hedrick. *The New Russians.* London: Hutchinson, 1990.

———. *The Russians.* London: Sphere Books, 1976.

Smith, Kathleen E. *Remembering Stalin's Victims: Popular Memory at the End of the USSR.* Ithaca, NY: Cornell University Press, 1996.

Slusser, Robert M. *Stalin in October: The Man Who Missed the Revolution.* Baltimore: John Hopkins University Press, 1987.

Solzhenitsyn, Alexander. *The Gulag Archipelago, 1918–1956: An Experiment in Literary Investigation,* 3 vols. London: Collins, 1974, 1978.

Souvarine, Boris. *Stalin: A Critical Survey of Bolshevism.* London: Secker and Warburg, 1939.

Spahr, W. *Zhukov: The Rise and Fall of a Great Captain.* Novato, CA: Presidio, 1993.

Sukhanov, N. N. *The Russian Revolution 1917: A Personal Record,* ed. and abridged by Joel Carmichael. Oxford: Oxford University Press, 1955.

Suny, Ronald Grigor. *The Making of the Georgian Nation.* Stanford, CA: Hoover Institution Press, 1988.

Swayze, Harold. *Political Control of Literature in the USSR, 1946–1959.* Cambridge, MA: Harvard University Press, 1962.

Thurston, Robert W. *Life and Terror in Stalin's Russia, 1934–41.* New Haven, CT: Yale University Press, 1996.

Timasheff, N. *The Great Retreat: The Growth and Decline of Communism in Russia.* New York: Dutton, 1946.

Tolstoy, Nikolai. *Stalin's Secret War.* London: Jonathan Cape, 1981.

———. *Victims of Yalta.* London: Hodder and Stoughton, 1977.

Trotsky, Leon. *The Revolution Betrayed: What Is the Soviet Union and Where Is It Going?* New York: Pathfinder Press, 1973.

———. *Stalin: An Appraisal of the Man and His Influence.* New York: Harper, 1941.

Tucker, Robert C. *Stalin as Revolutionary 1879–1929.* London: Chatto and Windus, 1974.

———. *Stalin in Power: The Revolution from Above, 1928–41.* New York: Chatto and Windus, 1990.

Tucker, Robert C., ed. *Stalinism: Essays in Historical Interpretation.* London: Chatto and Windus, 1977.

Tumarkin, Nina. *Lenin Lives!: The Lenin Cult in Soviet Russia.* Cambridge, MA: Harvard University Press, 1983.

Ulam, Adam. *Stalin: The Man and His Era.* Boston: Beacon Press, 1989.

Urban, G. R. *Stalinism: Its Impact on Russia and the World,* London: Maurice Temple Smith, 1982.

Vaksberg, Arkady. *The Prosecutor and the Prey: Vyshinsky and the 1930s Moscow Show Trials.* London: Weidenfeld and Nicolson, 1990.

Vaksberg, Arkaday. *Stalin against the Jews.* New York: Vintage, 1995.

Viola, L. *The Best Sons of the Fatherland: Workers in the Vanguard of Soviet Collectivization.* Oxford: Oxford University Press, 1987.

Volkogonov, Dmitri. *Lenin: Life and Legacy.* London: HarperCollins, 1994.

———. *The Rise and Fall of the Soviet Empire: Political Leaders from Lenin to Gorbachev.* London: HarperCollins, 1998.

———. *Stalin: Triumph and Tragedy,* ed. and trans. Harold Shukman. London: Weidenfeld and Nicolson, 1991.

———. *Trotsky: The Eternal Revolutionary.* London: HarperCollins, 1996.

Ward, Chris. *Stalin's Russia.* London: Arnold, 1995.

Ward, Chris, ed. *The Stalinist Dictatorship.* Arnold Readers in History Series. London: Arnold, 1998.

Werth, Alexander. *Russia at War 1941–1945.* London: Pan Books, 1964.

———. *Russia: Hopes and Fears.* Harmondsworth, UK: Penguin, 1969.

Wilson, Edmund. *To the Finland Station.* London: Fontana, 1967.

Wolfe, Bertram D. *Three Who Made a Revolution.* Harmondsworth, UK: Penguin, 1964.

Zhukov, Georgi. *The Memoirs of Marshal Zhukov.* London: Jonathan Cape, 1971.

ARTS, LITERATURE, LITERARY AND CULTURAL MEMOIRS

Abbe, James E. *I Photograph Russia.* London: George G. Harrap, 1935.

Akhmatova, Anna. *The Complete Poems of Anna Akhmatova.* Edinburgh: Canongate Books, 1998.

Alliluyeva, Svetlana. *Only One Year.* London: Hutchinson, 1969.

———. *Twenty Letters to a Friend,* London: Hutchinson, 1967.

Babel, Isaac. *Red Cavalry.* Harmondsworth, UK: Penguin, 1994.

Barnes, Christopher. *Boris Pasternak: A Literary Biography, vol. 1, 1890–1928; vol. 2, 1928–1960.* Cambridge: Cambridge University Press, 1989, 1999.

Benn, Anna, and Rosamund Bartlett. *A Guide to Literary Russia.* London: Papermac, 1997.

Bergan, Ronald., *Eisenstein: A Life in Conflict.* London: Little, Brown, 1997.

Berlin, Isaiah. "Meetings with Russian Writers." In *Personal Impressions.* London: Hogarth Press, 1980.

Billington, James. *The Icon and the Axe: An Interpretative History of Russian Culture.* New York: Vintage Books, 1970.

Birkos, Alexander S. *Soviet Cinema: Directors and Films.* Hamden, CT: Archon Books, 1976.

Borras, F. B. *Maxim Gorky the Writer: An Interpretation.* Oxford: Clarendon Press, 1967.

Bown, Matthew Cullerne. *Art under Stalin.* Oxford: Phaidon Press, 1991.

———. *Socialist Realist Painting.* New Haven, CT: Yale University Press, 1998.

Braun, Edward. *The Theatre of Meyerhold: Revolution on the Modern Stage.* London: Eyre Methuen, 1995.

Briggs, Anthony. *Vladimir Mayakovsky: A Tragedy.* Oxford: William A. Meeuws, 1979.

Brown, Clarence. *Mandelstam.* Cambridge: Cambridge University Press, 1973.

Brown, Edward J. *Mayakovsky: A Poet in Revolution.* Princeton, NJ: Princeton University Press, 1973.

———. *Russian Literature since the Revolution.* London: Collier Books, 1969.

Bulgakov, Mikhail. *Days of the Turbins.* In E. Lyons, trans., *Six Soviet Plays.* Boston: Houghton Mifflin, 1934.

———. *Manuscripts Don't Burn: A Life in Letters and Diaries,* compiled by J. A. E. Curtis. London: Harvill, 1992.

———. *The Master and Margarita.* London: Collins and Harvill Press, 1967.

Charters, Samuel, and Ann Charters. *I Love: The Story of Vladimir Mayakovsky and Lili Brik.* London: André Deutsch, 1979.

Clark, K. *The Soviet Novel: History as Ritual.* Chicago: University of Chicago Press, 1985.

Cornwell, N. *Pasternak's Novel: Perspectives on "Doctor Zhivago."* Keele, UK: Keele University Press, 1986.

Dickinson, Thorold, and Catherine De La Roche. *Soviet Cinema.* London: Falcon Press, 1948.

Elliott, David. *New Worlds: Russian Art and Society 1900–1937.* London: Thames and Hudson, 1986.

Fanning, David. *Shostakovich Studies.* Cambridge: Cambridge University Press, 1995.

Sheila Fitzpatrick. *The Cultural Front: Power and Culture in Revolutionary Russia.* Ithaca, NY: Cornell University Press, 1992.

Fitzpatrick, Sheila, ed. *Cultural Revolution in Russia, 1928–1931.* Bloomington: Indiana University Press, 1978.

Ginzburg, Evgenia S. *Into the Whirlwind.* London: Collins Harvill, 1967.

———. *Within the Whirlwind.* London: Collins Harvill, 1989.

Granta no. 64. *Russia: The Wild East* (Winter 1998).

Grossman, Vassily. *Life and Fate.* London: Collins Harvill, 1985.

Günther, Hans, ed. *The Culture of the Stalin Period: Studies in Russia and East Europe.* London: Macmillan, 1990.

Gutman, David. *Prokofiev.* London: Omnibus, 1990.

Harris, Robert. *Archangel.* London: Hutchinson, 1998.

Hingley, Ronald. *The Russian Mind.* New York: Charles Scribner's, 1977.

———. *Russian Writers and Soviet Society, 1917–78.* London: Weidenfeld and Nicolson, 1979.

Ignatieff, Michael. *Isaiah Berlin: A Life.* London: Chatto and Windus, 1998.

Ivinskaya, Olga. *A Captive of Time: My Years with Pasternak.* London: Collins and Harvill Press, 1978.

Kasak, Wolfgang, ed. *Dictionary of Russian Literature since 1917.* New York: Columbia University Press, 1988.

Kataev, Valentin. *Time Forward.* Bloomington: Indiana University Press, 1976.

Kemp-Welch, A. *Stalin and the Literary Intelligentsia, 1928–1939.* London: Macmillan, 1991.

Khan-Magomedov, S. O. *Pioneers of Soviet Architecture: The Search for New Solutions in the 1920s and 1930s.* London: Thames and Hudson, 1987.

King, David. *The Commissar Vanishes: The Falsification of Photographs and Art in Stalin's Russia.* Edinburgh: Canongate Books, 1997.

Kelly, Catriona, and David Shepherd, eds. *Russian Cultural Studies: An Introduction.* Oxford: Oxford University Press, 1998.

Koestler, Arthur. *Darkness at Noon.* London: Vintage, 1994.

Krebs, S. D. *Soviet Composers and the Development of Soviet Music.* London: Allen & Unwin, 1970.

Krupskaya, Nadezhda. *Memories of Lenin.* London: Panther, 1970.

Larina, Anna. *This I Cannot Forget: The Memoirs of Nikolai Bukharin's Widow.* London: Hutchinson, 1993.

Lavrentiev, Alexander. *Alexander Rodchenko: Photography 1924–1954.* Cologne: Könemann, 1995.

Levin, Dan. *Stormy Petrel: the Life and Work of Maxim Gorky,* London: Frederick Muller, 1965.

Leyda, Jay. *Kino: A History of the Russian and Soviet Film.* London: George Allen and Unwin, 1973.

Mandelstam, Nadezhda. *Hope Abandoned.* Harmondsworth, UK: Penguin, 1976.

———. *Hope against Hope.* Harmondsworth, UK: Penguin, 1975.

Mandelstam, Osip. *Selected Poems.* Cambridge: Cambridge University Press, 1973.

Markova, G., ed. *The Great Palace of the Moscow Kremlin.* Leningrad: Aurora Art Publishers, 1990.

Marsh, Rosalind. *Images of Dictatorship: Portraits of Stalin in Literature.* London: Routledge, 1989.

Marshall, H. *Masters of Soviet Cinema: Crippled Creative Biographies.* London: Routledge & Kegan Paul, 1983.

Mayakovsky, Vladimir. *The Bedbug and Selected Poetry.* New York: Meridian Books, 1960.

Milne, Lesley. *Mikhail Bulgakov: A Critical Biography.* Cambridge: Cambridge University Press, 1991.

Norman, Geraldine. *The Hermitage: The Biography of a Great Museum.* London: Pimlico, 1999.

Nowell-Smith, Geoffrey, ed. *The Oxford History of World Cinema.* Oxford: Oxford University Press, 1996.

Pasternak, Boris. *Dr Zhivago.* London: Collins and Harvill Press, 1958.

Payne, Robert. *The Three Worlds of Boris Pasternak.* London: Robert Hale, 1962.

Pil'niak [Pilnyak], Boris. "The Tale of the Unextinguished Moon." In *Mother Earth and Other Stories.* London: Deutsch, 1968.

Pirozhkova, Antonina. *At His Side: The Last Years of Isaac Babel.* South Royalton, VT: Steerforth Press, 1996.

Prokofiev, Sergei. *Prokofiev by Prokofiev: A Composer's Memoir.* London: Madconald & Jane's, 1979.

Reeder, Roberta. *Anna Akhmatova, Poet and Prophet.* London: Alison and Busby, 1995.

Robin, R. *Socialist Realism: An Impossible Aesthetic.* Stanford, CA: Stanford University Press, 1992.

Robinson, Harlow. *Sergei Prokofiev: A Biography.* London: Robert Hale, 1987.

Roxburgh, Angus. *Pravda: Inside the Soviet New Machine.* London: Victor Gollancz, 1987.

Rybakov, Anatoly. *Children of the Arbat.* Boston: Little, Brown, 1988.

Sandrow, N. *Vagabond Star: A World History of Yiddish Theater.* New York: Limelight, 1986.

Scatton, L. H. *Michael Zoschenko: Evolution of a Writer.* Cambridge: Cambridge University Press, 1993.

Shalamov, Varlam. *Kolyma Tales.* Harmondsworth, UK: Penguin, 1994.

Shentalinsky, Vitaly. *The KGB's Literary Archive: The Discovery of the Ultimate Fate of Russia's Suppressed Writers.* London: Harvill, 1995.

Sholokhov, Mikhail. *The Silent Don* (incorporating *And Quiet Flows the Don* and *The Don Flows Home to the Sea*). New York: Knopf, 1943.

———. *Virgin Soil Upturned.* London: Putnam, 1935.

Shostakovich, Dimitri. *Testimony: The Memoirs of Dimitri Shostakovich,* as related to and edited by Solomon Volkov. London: Faber and Faber, 1981.

Shudakov, Grigory. *Pioneers of Soviet Photography.* New York: Thames and Hudson, 1983.

Simmons, Ernest J. *Through the Glass of Soviet Literature: Views of Russian Society.* New York: Columbia University Press, 1953.

Sklar, Robert. *Film: An International History of the Medium.* London: Thames and Hudson, 1993.

Slonim, Marc. *Soviet Russian Literature: Writers*

and Problems 1917–1967. New York: Oxford University Press, 1967.

Solomon, Michael. *Magadan*. Princeton, NJ: Princeton University Press, 1971.

Solzhenitsyn, Alexander. *Cancer Ward*. London: Bodley Head, 1969.

———. *The First Circle*. London: William Collins, 1968.

———. *One Day in the Life of Ivan Denisovich*. Harmondsworth, UK: Penguin, 1963.

Taylor, R. *Film Propaganda: Soviet Russia and Nazi Germany*. London: Croom Helm, 1979.

Taylor, R., and D. Spring, eds. *Stalinism and Soviet Cinema*. London: Routledge, 1993.

Terras, Victor. *Handbook of Russian Literature*. New Haven, CT: Yale University Press, 1985.

Tertz, Abram. *On Socialist Realism*. Introduction by Czeslaw Milosz; translated by George Dennis. New York: Pantheon, 1960.

Thomas, D. M. *Alexander Solzhenitsyn: A Century in His Life*. London: Little, Brown, 1998.

Vassilieva, Larissa. *Kremlin Wives*. London: Weidenfeld and Nicolson, 1994.

Volkov, Solomon. *St Petersburg*. London: Sinclair Stevenson, 1996.

Werth, Alexander. *Russia: The Post-War Years*. London: Robert Hale, 1971.

Wilson, E. *Shostakovich: A Life Remembered*. London: Faber & Faber, 1994.

Zamyatin, Yevgeny. *A Soviet Heretic*. London: Quartet Books, 1991.

Zamyatin, Yevgeny. *We*. New York: Dutton, 1959.

Zbarsky, Ilya, and Samuel Hutchinson. *Lenin's Embalmers*. London: Harvill, 1998.

Zoschenko, Mikhail. *Scenes from the Bathhouse*. Ann Arbor: University of Michigan Press, 1961.

INDEX

Khasan, Lake, 26
Khayutina, Nataliya, 83
Khazariya, 129
Kholodnaya Rechka dacha, 260
Khozyain (nickname for Stalin), 265
Khrennikov, Tikhon, 323
Khrushchev, Nikita, **145–148,** 146(photo)
  advancement of, 197
  on the arrest of Jewish doctors, 68
  atomic bomb and, 12–13
  attacks on Pasternak, 148, 204, 205, 302
  Beria and, 23
  China and, 37
  Cominform and, 54
  cult of Stalin and, 58–59
  de-Stalinization and, 65–66
  dismantling of the Gulag and, 124
  on films seen by Stalin, 275
  Kaganovich and, 140
  Katyn massacre and, 145
  on Kirov's assassination, 317
  at the Kuntsevo dacha, 34
  Malenkov and, 147, 174, 175–176
  Mikoyan and, 184
  Molotov and, 186–187
  Moscow Metro and, 188
  on Poskrebyshev, 209
  release of records on the Great Terror, 117
  "secret speech" of, 147
  siege of Stalingrad and, 281, 282
  Solzhenitsyn and, 252–253
  Soviet historiography and, 129
  at Stalin's fatal stroke, 261
  on Stalin's personality, 267
  Vasily Stalin and, 279
  Voroshilov and, 308
  Zhukov and, 325
Kim Il Sung, 153, 154, 303
King, David, 130
Kirghiziya, 190
Kirov, Sergey, 21, 149–150
  assassination of, 96, 110, 112, 317
  at the Congress of the Victors, 56, 57
  praise of Stalin, 59
  at Stalin's dachas, 259
  Yagoda and, 317

Kleber, Emil, 255
Knight, Amy, 128
Knight of the Panther's Skin, The (Rustaveli), 275
Koba (nickname for Stalin), 31, 70, 71, 96, 179, 264, 265
Koestler, Arthur, 130
Kogan, M. B., 68
Kolchak, Alexander, 299
Kolkhozy, 43–44. *See also* Collectivization
Kollontai, Aleksandra, 314
Koltsov, Mikhail, 88, **150–151,** 256
Kolyma, 122, 123, 124, 177
Kolyma Tales (Shalamov), 114
Kommunistchesiky Soyuz Molodezhi. *See* Komsomol
Komsomol, **151–153**
  during collectivization, 51
  denunciations by, 86
  Great Terror purges and, 116
  indoctrination by, 77
  laborers on the Moscow Metro from, 188
  "New Soviet Man" ideology and, 193
Komsomolsk, 151
Komsomolskaya station, 188
Konchalovsky, Andrey, 275, 277
Konev, Ivan, 221
Königsberg, 211
Korean War, 43, **153–154,** 303
Kornilov, Lavr, 235
Kosarev, Alexander, 152
Kosygin, Aleksey, 148
Kozintsev, Grigory, 40
Kremlin, **154–155**
Kremlin Wall, 168
  burial of Stalin by, 169
Kresti prison, 212
Krestinsky, Nikolay, 31
Kronstadt rebellion, 35, 41
Krupskaya, Nadezhda, 3, **155–157,** 161–162, 168
Krylenko, Nikolay, **157–158,** 243
Kryukov, Fedor, 244
Kseshinskaya Mansion, 165
Kuibyshev, Valeriyan, 318
Kulaks, 19
  construction of White Sea–Baltic Canal and, 313
  forced labor at Magnitogorsk, 173
  Lenin's Red Terror and, 167
  liquidation of, 43, 46, 47–49

Kuleshov, Lev, 37
Kun, Béla, 55
Kuntsevo dacha, 6(photo), 34, 139, 155, 259–260, 261, 276(photo), 277
  Stalin's death at, 261–262
Kuomintang, 176
Kurbsky, Andrey, 133
Kurchatov, Igor, 11–12
Kureika, 263
Kuropaty Forest, 181, 195
Kursk salient, 107, 229, 324
Kusakova, Marya, 263
Kutaisi, 263
Kvali (newspaper), 98

Labor
  child labor, 77
  First Five-Year Plan and, 93
  at Magnitogorsk, 173–174
  Stakhanovites and, 257–258
  women in industrialization, 314–316
  See also Slave labor
Labor camps, 35. *See also* Gulag; Slave labor
"Laboratory art," 7
Ladoga, Lake, 89, 170
Lady Macbeth of Mtsensk (Shostakovich), 245
Laqueur, Walter, 136, 137
Latvia, 18–20, 311. *See also* Baltic states
"Law of seven-eighths," 50
League of Nations, 89
League of the Godless, 225
Lean, David, 205
Lebensborn, 192–193
Lefortovo prison, 181, 212, 213, 290
Lend-lease aid, 107
Lenin, Vladimir Ilich, **159–167,** 162(photo), 166(photo)
  agricultural cooperatives and, 43–44
  Allilueva, Nadezhda, and, 4
  "April Theses," 165, 233
  attitude toward peasants, 50
  Bolsheviks and, 163, 164–165
  Bukharin and, 27, 28
  on the cinema, 37
  Civil War of 1918-1920 and, 41, 42
  collectivization and, 45
  Comintern and, 54
  concentration camps and, 120

Pasternak and, 204
poem on Stalin, 71, 264, 271
on socialist realism, 249
torture of, 290
Manizer, Matvei, 188
Mann, Thomas, 87
Mannerheim line, 89
Mao Zedong, 36, 37, 131, 148,
153, 154, 176
"March of the Shock-Brigades"
(Mayakovsky), 143
Markish, Peter, 137
Marr, Nikolay, **178**
Marrism, 178
Marshall Plan, 42, 54
Martov, Yuli, 162–163
Marx-Engels Institute, 159
Marxism, Lenin and, 161
"Marxism and the National
Question" (Stalin), 164,
178–179, 189
"Marxism and the Question of
Linguistics" (Stalin), 178
Mass graves
from the Great Terror, 181
in Katyn Forest, 143–144, 145
Master and Margarita, The (Bul-
gakov), 32, 33
Mayakovskaya station, 188
Mayakovsky, Vladimir, 37, 143,
179–180, 181, 182, 203, 248
Maynard, John, 50
McCarthyism, 43
Medvedev, Roy
on the Great Terror, 115–116
on Lubyanka prison, 213
Memorial and, 181
on Soviet historiography, 129
on Stalin's mental health, 270
on Stalin's personality, 268
Meetings with Solzhenitsyn (televi-
sion show), 254
Melikyants, Azkhar Gregorian
(alias of Stalin's), 265
Melnikov, Konstantin, 10
Meltzer, Yuliya, 72
Memorial organization, 66, 125,
181
Mendel, Gregor, 172
Mennonites, 227
Mensheviks
early prevalence of, 128
February Revolution and, 232
Georgians in, 97
Great Terror and, 111
Jews in, 135

split with Bolsheviks, 163, 164
Stalin's break with, 98
Tiflis State Bank Robbery and,
286
Trotsky and, 67, 293
Vyshinsky and, 309
Meori Dasi, 98
Mercader, Ramon, 298
Mesame Dasi, 98, 265, 285. *See
also* Georgian Social Democ-
rats
Meshketians, 191
Mexico, Trotsky in, 297–298
Meyerhold, Vsevolod, 78, 151,
180, **181–182,** 251
MGB, 22, 193
Michurin, Ivan, 172
Mikhoels, Solomon, 68, 137,
182–183
Mikoyan, Anastas, 57, **183–185,**
194, 208
Military academies, 220, 222
Mingrelia, 21
Mining, slave labor and, 123
Mir, 44
Missile Crisis of 1962. *See* Cuban
Missile Crisis
Mission to Moscow (film), 311
Modernism, Prokofiev and, 214
Molière (Bulgakov), 33
Molotov, Polina, 186
Molotov, Vyacheslav, **185–187**
Agreement on Prisoners of War
and, 319
atomic bomb development and,
12
Baltic states and, 19
in Cold War politics, 43, 303
at the Congress of the Victors,
57
death of Stalin and, 65
Eisenstein and, 81
exile of wife, 137
Great Terror and, 117
Khrushchev and, 147, 176
Meyerhold and, 182
Potsdam Conference and,
210–211
on the State Committee of Defense, 106
at the Tehran Conference, 25
Molotov Cocktail, 185
Monasteries
attacks on, 223
converted to concentration
camps, 223, 225

Montgomery, Bernard, 230
Morozov, Grigory, 6
Morozov, Pavlik, 80, 152
Moscow
attacks on churches in, 223
German attack on, 106
the Kremlin in, 154
Palace of the Soviets and,
201–203
prisons of, 212–213
remodeling of, 146
Stalin's rebuilding of, 10
Moscow (Feuchtwanger), 88
Moscow Arts Theater, 32, 33, 102,
182
Moscow Dynamos (football
team), 257
Moscow Jewish Theater, 137
Moscow Metro, 33, 145–146,
187–188
Moscow show trials, 112–113
condemnation of Trotsky, 297
Jewish victims, 137
Kamenev and, 142
Kirov's assassination and, 150
Vyshinsky and, 310
Yagoda and, 318
See also Great Terror; Show tri-
als
Moscow State Jewish Theater, 182
Moscow University, architecture
of, 10
Moscow-Volga Canal, 314
Mosfilm, 81
Mother (Gorky), 103, 249
Mother (Pudovkin), 38
Movy Mir (journal), 148
"Mr. No." *See* Molotov, Vyach-
eslav
Mukhina, Vera, 8(photo), 10–11
Muradeli, Vano, 250
Museums
on Lenin, 160
on Stalin, 100
during World War II, 106, 170
Music
socialist realism and, 250–251
Stalin's preferences in, 274–275
Zhdanov's attacks on, 323
See also Prokofiev, Sergey;
Shostakovich, Dmitry
Musical comedies, 39
Muslims, 190, 191, 227
Mussorgsky, Modest, 274–275
MVD, 22, 193
My Apprenticeship (Gorky), 102

Pasternak, Boris, 107, 113, **203–205**
  Anti-Fascist Congress in Defense of Peace and Culture, 302
  Dr. Zhivago, 113, 148, 204, 205, 302
  Khrushchev's attacks on, 148, 204, 205, 302
  Mandelstam and, 177
  on Mayakovsky, 179–180
  socialist realism and, 250
  on Stalin's physical appearance, 271–272
  "the inhuman power of the lie," 50
  translations of Georgian poetry, 275
  Union of Soviet Writers and, 302
Pasternak Museum, 205
Patriotic Movement for the Study of Stalin's Heritage, 70
Paulus, Friedrich von, 72, 107, 229, 282, 283
Pavlovsky Regiment, 232
Peasantry
  collectivization and, 43–45, 46–52, 67–68
  educational opportunity, 77
  famines and, 44, 50–52
  liquidation of the kulaks, 43, 46, 47–49
  Stalin's attitudes toward, 46
People's Commissar for War, 295–296, 306
People's Commissariat for Internal Affairs, 110. *See also* NKVD
People's Commissariat for Nationalities, 58, 97, 179, 189, 236
People's Commissariat of Education, 127
People's Commissariat of Justice, 157
People's Commissariat of State Security, 206
People's Commissariat of the Workers' and Peasants' Inspectorate (Rabkrin), 58, 95, 165, **205–206**
People's Commissariats, 58
People's Republic of China, 36–37
Peredelkino
  Pasternak at, 204, 205
  Pilnyak at, 206

Perin, Ilya, 7
Peshkov, Aleksey Maksimovich. *See* Gorky, Maxim
Peshkov, Maxim, 318
Peter the Great, 228
  Soviet historiography and, 129
Peter the Great (Petrov), 40
Peters, William, 6
Petrograd, 97
  Civil War of 1918-1920 and, 41
  Revolution of 1917 and, 231–236
  See also Leningrad
Petrograd Soviet, 232, 234, 235, 236, 295
Petrov, Vladimir, 40
Pevsner, Antoine, 9
Photographs
  official falsification of, 129, 142
  retouching Stalin's appearance in, 272
Photography, 9
Physical torture, 115, 290. *See also* Torture
Pilnyak, Boris, **206,** 321
Pilsudski, Józef Klemens, 27
Pipes, Richard, 45
Piriev, Ivan, 38, 275
Pirveli Dasi, 98
Place names, **206–207**
Plekhanov, Georgy, 162–163
Poetry
  derogatory of Stalin, 71, 264, 271
  about the Great Terror, 1, 3, 114
  by Stalin, 275
  Stalin's preferences in, 275
Pogroms, 135
Poland
  German-Soviet Non-Aggression Pact and, 99
  Katyn massacre and, 143–145
  Potsdam Conference and, 211
  Rokossovsky and, 230
  Soviet domination, 74
  during World War II, 73–74
  Yalta Conference and, 319
Polish Communists, Great Terror and, 55
Politburo, **207–208**
  Bukharin in, 29, 30
  Bulganin in, 33
  creation of, 200
  election of, 55
  Great Terror purges and, 116

  Kamenev in, 141
  Khrushchev in, 147
  liquidation of the kulaks and, 47, 48
  Malenkov in, 174, 175
  Mikoyan in, 183
  Molotov in, 186
  Ordzhonikidze in, 199
  Rykov in, 238
  Stalin and, 96, 165
  Trotsky in, 295
  Zinoviev in, 326
  See also Presidium
Political trials. *See* Moscow Show Trials; Show trials
Popova, Lyubov, 7
Porkkala, 90
Port Arthur, 36, 37, 176
Poskrebyshev, Alexander, **208–210,** 269
Poskrebyshev, Bronislava, 210
"Potemkin villages," 50
Poteshniy Dvorets, 155
Potosky, Sergey, 251
Potsdam Conference, 11, 53, **210–211,** 272
POUM, 255
Pravda (newspaper), **211–212**
  Bukharin and, 28, 29
  cult of Stalin and, 61, 62(photo)
  Kamenev and, 140, 141, 233
  Koltsov and, 150, 151
  Molotov and, 185
  during the Revolution of 1917, 233, 235
  Stalin as editor, 233
Preobrazhensky Regiment, 232
Presidium, 200, 208
  Bulganin in, 33
  Mikoyan in, 184, 185
  Voroshilov in, 308
  Zhukov in, 325
  See also Politburo
Prince, The (Machiavelli), 275
Prinkipo, 297
Prisoners of war
  German, 283
  Great Terror and, 116
  Order No. 270 on, 105
  "repatriation" of, 116, 195, 319
  Yalta Agreement on, 116, 319
Prisons, 115, **212–213**
  Bailov, 263
  Bailovka, 309
  Butyrki, 55, 181, 212
  Kresti, 212

*H*elen Rappaport, who holds a degree in Russian Special Studies from Leeds University, has worked as a freelance writer and editor for a number of leading reference book publishers. She also works as literal translator in the theater, mainly for the Royal Shakespeare Company.

B
STALIN   Rappaport, Helen

Josef Stalin

DUE DATE $55.00
